HUNTING NUKES

A FIFTY-YEAR PURSUIT OF
ATOMIC BOMB BUILDERS AND MISCHIEF MAKERS

Richard Phillip Lawless

FOREWORD BY JOHN BOLTON

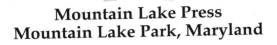

Mountain Lake Press
Mountain Lake Park, Maryland

Hunting Nukes - A Fifty-Year Pursuit of Atom Bomb Builders and Mischief Makers

By Richard Phillip Lawless

Published in the United States of America
By Mountain Lake Press

ISBN: 978-1-959307-39-6

Design by Jutta Medina

Registration Number TXu2-233-419
Effective Date of Registration: December 9, 2020

Registration Decision Date: January 12, 2021

Author's Note:
The text of this book transliterates certain words, names and places from non-Roman foreign languages. Every effort has been made to convey the precise meaning or pronunciation, in keeping with established norms. In the case of text involving the Korean language, most instances reflect the previously accepted McCune–Reischauer (MR) system, which the Korean government revised in 2000. Events pre-dating that change, to what is called the Revised Romanization of Korean (RRK) have been rendered using the former method. For example, Kimpo Airport represents the MR spelling, instead of the current RRK form, Gimpo Airport.

All redactions imposed on the text of this book, some 97 of them, involving 28 pages and the removal (blackout) of 1743 words, are those required by the U.S. Department of Defense (DOD) as of January 1, 2023. While some of the DOD redactions relate to individual words, most involve entire paragraphs or groups of paragraphs, and several involve entire pages of text. All of the DOD redactions are currently being contested in court proceedings.

Contents

Author's Extended Note
on the CIA and DoD Publications
Review Processes

This manuscript was submitted to the Publication Classification Review Board of the Central Intelligence Agency, pursuant to the author's responsibility to do so under the terms of the Secrecy Agreement which the author executed at the time of his entry on duty with the CIA in June 1972. This PCRB review process consumed nine full months and required extensive interaction with the PCRB staff. The initial PCRB review resulted in over 500 required "redactions" in the manuscript submitted. While many of these redactions were the result of long-established Agency policy practices, many were arbitrary and subjective, the norm in these cases.

A process of compromise ensued and while many exchanges produced mutually acceptable agreements on the text, several did not. Too often the required redactions resulted in entire pages being deleted or required the deletion of multiple paragraphs, resulting in the destruction of the flow of the narrative, or created a disruption that produced an unreadable account of events. In this published version the author has elected not to include the PCRB redactions. The PCRB staff was always polite, sometimes flexible and accommodating, and often adamant in its delivered verdicts on the text.

The above is by way of explaining why the reader might find certain elements difficult to read or follow portions of the narrative. My apologies for this, and I regret that this outcome was unavoidable. That said, the Agency's statement, conveyed to the author on June 16, 2021, speaks for itself.

> *The Prepublication Classification Review Board completed its review of your non-fiction manuscript received on 15 June 2021 and titled, "Hunting Nukes, A Fifty-Year Pursuit of Atom Bomb Builders and Mischief Makers." The Board determined that your submission contains no CIA-related classified information. Please be aware that this successful completion of the Agency portion of your manuscript review does not represent Agency endorsement or verification of this work. The PCRB will turn over the revised manuscript and primacy of the case to DoD for subsequent completion of ongoing review. As previously stated, you do not have permission to publish this manuscript until DoD completes its review and all DoD classification objections are addressed.*

The Agency handoff to the Department of Defense (DOD) occurred on this same date (June 15, 2021) with DOD then responsible to complete the DOD review process. As of January 2023, some 16 months after the DOD review began, and after nearly two-and-half years after DOD had access to the manuscript, DOD and the author have not reached agreement on the content of the book. Although the DOD was in the possession of the original complete manuscript from October 2020, DOD elected to take no action until the CIA's PCRB completed its review. The DOD review initially produced a demand for more than one hundred additional redactions. Notwithstanding an active exchange between the author and the DOD for over one year, with the latter supported by the DOJ, some 97 redactions remained unresolved. The author initiated legal action against the DOD in late 2021. One year later this process is still playing out in the U.S. Federal Court system. The manuscript contains and identifies as such the remaining and unresolved DOD redactions. Page 3 further references the current situation with regard to the DOD classification review process and the redactions that process has imposed on this book.

Richard Phillip Lawless
January 2023

Richard Lawless has done his fellow Americans a great service by writing *Hunting Nukes* and seeing it through the U.S. government's required prepublication-review process. His recounting of a distinguished career in the intelligence community, in a variety of vital but challenging assignments, is well worth reading by policymakers, members of Congress, scholars and general readers, not to mention the coming generations of intelligence operatives and analysts who are critical to ensuring our national security in a dangerous world. In particular, Lawless describes one of Washington's greatest counterproliferation successes, with South Korea, in which he played the central role.

The first five nuclear powers; the United States, the Soviet Union, the United Kingdom, France, and China—coincidentally or not, also the five Permanent Members of the UN Security Council—tried to address the risks of more and more countries developing nuclear weapons through the 1968 Nuclear Non-Proliferation Treaty, which legitimized the five existing nuclear-weapons states and encouraged everyone else to join the NPT as non-nuclear weapons states. Cold War tensions, perhaps more than anything else, should have motivated the U.S.S.R and America to clamp down on further proliferation, largely to avoid the perilous bipolar nuclear standoff between their respective alliances from becoming even more fraught than it already was.

The United States played it straight, as usual, making repeated efforts over the years to persuade its allies that the "extended deterrence" of America's own nuclear arsenal obviated any need for our friends to have their own nuclear-weapons capabilities. Most of Washington's treaty allies, and many other states more loosely associated with the global West, accepted the U.S. argument, some more rigorously than others. And some made clear strategic decisions to proceed with nuclear programs whether the United States approved or not.

Russia, of course, did not play it straight, and its clandestine cooperations, typically denied all around, together with publicly acknowledged cooperation on "civil nuclear power" projects with the likes of North Korea, Iran and India, empowered if not directly aided explicit weapons development. Providing Soviet ballistic-missile technology to Moscow's partners similarly demonstrated the Kremlin's malign intentions. Communist China, of course, followed suit, directly aiding the North Korean and Pakistani nuclear-weapons and ballistic-missile programs.

France also did not play it entirely straight, providing Israel with the Dimona reactor and spent-fuel reprocessing technology, which have been central to the still-unacknowledged Israeli nuclear-weapons program. Israel, however, has proven to be a rare paradigm of nonproliferation virtue, making it plain, in its neighborhood, that its unstated nuclear weapons were purely for deterrence and defense. It is no exaggeration to say that Israel has been the most determined counter-proliferator in the world, using military force on several occasions, notably bombing Saddam Hussein's Osirak reactor near Baghdad in 1981 and an Iranian reactor under construction in Syria in 2007, not to mention countless smaller raids, overt and covert, and much else still left to the imagination and history to reveal.

There were other actors as well, such as the A.Q. Khan proliferation network, emanating from Pakistan and directly utilizing stolen European technology and Chinese knowhow previously transferred to Islamabad. For the right price, Khan's nuclear bazaar aided North Korea, Iran and Libya—and perhaps others—with both uranium-enrichment technology and weapons-design information. Khan's entrepreneurial activities alone constitute a narrative that deserves far more assessment by anti-proliferation countries, and its ultimate demise should not lead to the conclusion that the threat has ended, and that other mini-Khan entrepreneurs are not busily at work aiding other would-be nuclear powers.

In fact, the struggle against the proliferation of weapons of mass destruction (chemical and biological as well as nuclear) has not gone well for America and its allies over the past three decades. India, which detonated a nuclear device as far back as 1974, conducted five underground nuclear tests during the period May 11-13, 1998, likely reflecting capabilities actually developed several years earlier. Pakistan, India's archrival on the Subcontinent, immediately responded by lighting off six underground nuclear devices just over two weeks later, from May 28 to May 30. Both countries had carefully planned their test sequences to achieve maximum results, scientifically and militarily, before the expected global outcry brought the testing to a halt. Without doubt, the biggest impact of India's testing was right next door in Pakistan, just as Islamabad's testing raised deep concern in New Delhi.

North Korea has detonated six nuclear devices as of this writing and is perfecting its ICBM delivery systems. Iran has so far escaped from the risk of having its nuclear-weapons program shut down, and an over-eager Biden administration is still desperately hoping to negotiate with a regime that has never shown the slightest evidence of a strategic decision to give up its nuclear programs. And even though Saddam's nuclear aspirations have been laid to rest (along with Saddam), the war that eliminated the Iraqi nuclear threat is now widely condemned by the *bien pensants*. Among other things, their 20-20 hindsight ignores one of the most important side-effects of Saddam's overthrow: convincing a terrified Libya's Muammar Ghaddafi, in 2003-04, to abandon his nuclear aspirations, turning them over to the United States, now stored at Oak Ridge, Tennessee.

This brief history of nuclear proliferation is far from comprehensive, but it indicates clearly how difficult and elusive success is against a determined nuclear aspirant. Some might think U.S. victories in early counterproliferation efforts came easily. But the story Richard Lawless presents here shows that it has never been easy. American counterproliferation achievements, as Lawless describes the ending of South Korea's clandestine pursuit of nuclear weapons, are

15

in many senses more difficult than trying to prevent adversaries and rogue states from achieving their objectives. When friends are trying to deceive us to achieve goals they know we oppose, especially in so serious a matter as nuclear weapons during the Cold War, almost every step U.S. intelligence, defense and diplomatic policymakers take is agonizingly complicated.

There is nothing hypothetical or academic in this memoir; not only did it all happen, hard as it might be for many not involved in national security to imagine, but a lot of it is still happening in other national capitals and terrorist base camps. Richard Lawless also describes many other examples of life in the intelligence community, outside the proliferation context, that might seem almost as unbelievable, including the obstructionism and bureaucratic infighting in our own government that so often paralyzes our efforts to protect the American people. That is precisely why his memoir is so important and deserves wide distribution.

Readers should also understand, of course, that *Hunting Nukes*, like almost all memoirs of former national security officials, tells only part of the story. The overwhelming majority of all such writers begin and end their manuscripts firmly intending not to divulge any classified material, meaning that significant aspects of their careers and duties will not see the light of day in the unclassified world until far into the future. There are, of course, notable unsavory exceptions to this generalization, namely those few who write (or act) intentionally to reveal classified information, knowing full well the inevitable harm it will cause the United States.

Richard Lawless served his country for decades, and he has capped his career with a story that few can match. He then endured, and is still litigating against, an exceptionally onerous prepublication review by his former government employers. We are all enriched that he persevered, both during his service in the intelligence community and in making so much of it available to enhance public understanding of the hard work that goes into counterproliferation and national security affairs generally. Let's hope he prevails in court.

Ambassador John Bolton
Former U.S. National Security Advisor

In mid-January 2023, international media devoted extensive coverage to the suggestion by South Korean President Yoon Suk-yeol that his nation, in the face of new provocations and threats of nuclear destruction from North Korea, might develop its own nuclear deterrent. Excited speculation by political commentators in Asia and in the United States continued despite the South Korean government backtracking on Yoon's comments a few days later. The question begged: Was not South Korea revisiting an option it had previously explored as a covert undertaking, a gambit which the U.S. had forestalled, nearly five decades before? My thoughts carried me back to those events, bringing back memories I will here attempt to reconstruct with clarity.

In late fall 1974, I hosted a man whom I will call Mr. Chang at my home on the U.S. Embassy compound in Seoul. After dinner and cordial conversation, Mr. Chang joined me in a side room for a private session. Over coffee that long evening, he provided me with critical information that would substantially advance my government's ability to confirm, define and eventually defeat South Korea's attempt to develop a clandestine nuclear weapons program.

South Korea, under the administration of autocrat President Pak Chung-hee, had signed the international Treaty on the Non-Proliferation of Nuclear Weapons six years earlier. But Seoul was still stalling on ratifying that agreement. Absent ratification, a delay which the Pak government was blaming on bureaucratic infighting, the safeguards and other non-proliferation assurances the treaty invoked were missing . In signing the treaty the Pak regime had signaled that it would forever forego developing or possessing nuclear weapons. Mr. Chang, a South Korean patriot with access to sensitive information, had learned otherwise. That evening with me, and during several more private meetings, he confirmed that the regime, unbeknownst to the U.S. government, had indeed ordered a covert strategic-weapons-development effort.

Thanks to Mr. Chang, our Seoul Station now possessed detailed plans for a military research complex in a remote location in the central part of the country. The plans specified the parts of the complex meant to house strategic-weapons activity, including technologies unmistakably related to nuclear weapons as well as ballistic missiles. Some months earlier, Seoul Station had determined that planning for the facility was underway, but we lacked details. We had now discerned what work would be undertaken there.

We could confirm, with a high degree of certainty, that South Korea's leadership was moving into strategic-weapons development. The plans in our hands involved construction of the South Korean Agency for Defense Development's new headquarters near the city of Taejon. We also had acquired building-by-building explanations of the research teams involved. From the information, Seoul Station could develop a clandestine collection program that would finetune our understanding of what was afoot, and the U.S. government could replace supposition and informed speculation with hard facts.

For me, only two years into my service with the Central Intelligence Agency, the revelation was a game-changing experience. I had labored for months building a relationship with Mr. Chang, engendering mutual respect and trust. I suspected that the regime's public declarations—including its acceptance of the NTP while delaying its ratification—might well suggest that South Korea was hedging its bets on nuclear weapons. At the CIA station level, we appreciated that Pak's decision, if allowed to proceed, would fundamentally disrupt and damage his nation's relationship with the United States. Even beyond the bilateral U.S.–South Korea alliance, what Park was planning would disrupt America's security relationships across all of Northeast Asia.

After my session with Mr. Chang, I worked through that night and into the next morning to organize and present to the Station everything I had learned. Others on our team would format the information for transmission to Agency Headquarters at Langley. From there, it would be disseminated to our analysts and later circulated as finished intelligence throughout the policy community.

Within six months, our Station's intelligence-gathering had allowed Langley to produce a comprehensive picture of the Pak regime's weapons development program. And that intelligence, presented to policymakers in the administration of President Gerald Ford, permitted them to see what was really occurring in the southern half of the Korean Peninsula. As a result, U.S. policy makers would be able to resolve this highly sensitive issue. In coordinated diplomatic efforts from Washington, involving Seoul, Paris, Quebec and Vienna, among other venues, the United States drove home its message to South Korea – and to the other parties inadvertently abetting Seoul's nuclear ambitions – that such activities would not be tolerated.

That said, the effort took time. America's nuclear weapons showdown with South Korea extended over two years and often seemed to defy resolution. But the Seoul Station's reporting continued to feed the U.S. policy process and, eventually, we decisively shut down President Pak's nuclear gambit.

My encounters with Mr. Chang were by no means unique. His dedicated efforts on behalf of his country possibly prevented a serious or even fatal disruption in the U.S–South Korea relationship—the bilateral military alliance that assured the survival of that nation. Other potential downsides of a matured South Korean nuclear weapons program included renewed military conflict with North Korea as well as decisions by other nations, namely Japan, to embark on their own nuclear weapons programs. I worked hard to develop a protected relationship with this man. He would risk his position and his career, and possibly more, to share protected information critical to thwarting Pak's nuclear ambition. Throughout this book, I will describe others who took similar risks to promote the causes of freedom and nuclear non-proliferation. As I recount interactions with them, my intention is to demonstrate that these individuals who elect to cooperate with the United States represented the finest aspects of their respective countries. These individuals are the real heroes of this saga.

INTRODUCTION:

Northeast Asia—The Nuclear Powder Keg

In late May 2020, Kim Jong-un, the young ruler of the People's Democratic Republic of Korea, reappeared in public after weeks of seclusion to validate the announcement of a major initiative. To the applause of the third-generation helmsman of the Kim family dictatorship, the Central Military Commission of the Korean Workers Party declared a new strategic policy. Rather than something original, however, the declaration was yet another threatening and indulgent diatribe from North Korea since becoming a de facto and self-proclaimed nuclear weapons state. According to Supreme Leader Kim's national security team, the nation's "nuclear war deterrence" would be fortified in the months ahead, signaling the probability of more testing and deployment of nuclear weapons and missiles.

The political dynamic of Northeast Asia has been altered utterly by a belligerent North Korea armed with a credible nuclear weapons arsenal. Complementing the weapons themselves, the North can deliver them anywhere on the peninsula as well as regionally and beyond. Civilian targets in Japan and South Korea, along with the U.S. military bases there and in Guam, are consequently held at risk. More recently, North Korean invective threatened the U.S. homeland, backed up with real capability.

Because of these developments, the regime in Pyongyang has become the poster child for the failure of U.S. and international nuclear non-proliferation policies. By mastering nuclear weapons, a strategically placed but impoverished nation overturned a regional balance that had held since the armistice halting the Korean War in 1953. In recent years, other factors have brought increased instability to Northeast Asia, most critically the rise of China as a Great Power, both economically and militarily. But North Korea is a special case. It has defied every attempt to be constrained in its march to possess a nuclear weapons capability.

A core factor driving this transition of Korea's security construct, from a tense status quo and armed peace to the nuclear powder keg that now dominates the peninsula, was intelligence. More precisely, one major facilitator of the destabilization of the Korean Peninsula and beyond delivered by North Korea was a sustained inability to collect, analyze and predict the path on which Pyongyang had embarked. Beyond the failure to access protected information, we consistently lacked the reasonable assessments we could have constructed because of limited intelligence.

Given such an information shortfall, our attempt to assess the North's capabilities resorted to best guesses. We reached conclusions that often seemed compelling, though in reality those conclusions were anything but. Perhaps out of a sense of caution—a reluctance to overstate the severity of the situation—we consistently underestimated North Korea's intent and capability. The respective intelligence communities of all three of the involved major powers made major misjudgments, leading directly to individual and collective failures in policy development and execution. Along with China, Russia and the United States, South Korea and the entire international community acted as sleepwalking enablers of the North Korean threat.

Our failures on North Korea delivered other consequences as well. The Kim regime is as close to a nation–state terrorist organization as might be possible, eclipsed only by Iran in its duplicitous activity. Worse, Pyongyang can claim a first-in-class leadership position as a nuclear proliferator. Such a characterization is important. North Korea has demonstrated its willingness and ability to export capabilities that would enable other aspirants to become nuclear weapons states. The provision to Syria of a nuclear research reactor and chemical weapons, as well as the sale of ballistic missile technology to Iran, are but two examples of North Korea's predilection to sell anything it has to anyone with the cash to pay for it.

Intelligence Failure Enables Policy Failure

Inadequate performance on the North Korean non-proliferation issue began as early as 1970 and sustained itself during the 1980s, as Pyongyang's covert weapons program picked up momentum. The decade of the 1990s was one of self-deception on the part of the United States, until the Clinton administration was forced to admit, belatedly, that something had to be done. America found itself compelled to take the initiative and negotiate directly with Pyongyang, concluding the Agreed Framework in October 1994. The bilateral initiative was hard-fought by dedicated U.S. negotiators, who probably achieved the best deal they could at the time. Unfortunately, the Framework was based on a bogus assumption; namely, Pyongyang was willing to honor, and could be trusted to deliver, the agreed conditions.

True to form, Pyongyang had no intention of honoring the Framework, and their covert nuclear march continued apace. Incomplete intelligence and less-than-aggressive analytical processes over the next decade led the United States and the rest of Asia to a precarious position in 2002, one that triggered the Six-Party talks in Beijing. I participated in those talks and watched as the United States fumbled forward and the effort failed. North Korea bobbed, weaved and gamed the international system, improving their weapons and the ability to deliver them, bringing us to where we are at the beginning of 2023.

The Nuclear Past as Prologue

The North Korean advance in nuclear weapons, while the world was committed to restraining proliferation, represents but one glaring example of a broader policy failure. Over the past decades, several nations determined to join the nuclear weapons club succeeded beyond all expectations, namely, ███████████, India and Pakistan. Others have seen their ambitions partially met, only to be frustrated or defeated. Along with South Korea, the governments of South Africa, Taiwan, Libya and, more recently, Iran have made similar attempts. In each case, intelligence served as the handmaiden of counter-proliferation policy development and action. Still other nations have toyed with proliferation, including Syria, Brazil, Argentina and Romania, among others. All have either been dissuaded or failed due to internal constraints. Even in the cases of stillborn programs, intelligence often played a critical role. The unfortunate corollary is that when aspiring proliferators succeed, as they have and will again, intelligence failure will often be the facilitator.

No doubt, in the future more nations will aspire to membership in that exclusive club of strategic weapons states. They will be motivated by heightened concerns for national security, and each will have concluded, perhaps reluctantly, that they must take themselves down the nuclear path. Whenever a nation–state enjoys the capacity to pursue such a weapons development program, but had previously elected to not do so, the possibility of dynamic change looms. Japan is a perfect example of this last-mentioned candidate category.

My book's central theme regarding nuclear proliferation is how the United States has either dealt successfully with the threat or failed to do so. I offer the majority of my narrative from the perspective of a career clandestine service officer, working in the field at the level of the attack. Each mission was straightforward: Search, discover, define, penetrate and, when directed, disable nuclear weapons development activity. Some readers, including those transfixed by the theory and practice of non-proliferation policy at elevated levels, might find my experiences too narrow or confining. To those I would say, "It is what it is. This is how it happens at the tip of the spear."

On the proliferation front, the Korean Peninsula provides a useful beginning and end for the narrative. My deep involvement in the aborted South Korean weapons development effort in the mid-1970s is a point of departure. I relate those events from the standpoint of my role as an intelligence collector who directly identified and penetrated that covert undertaking, and who occupied a front-row seat in the policy process that brought the program to an end. My military service in U.S. Army counterintelligence in that nation, prior to my Agency career, provided a solid grounding for the events I witnessed in Korea.

The South Korean Nuclear Weapons Program

As I just mentioned, the early part of my narrative delves deeply into events that occurred in the early and mid-1970s, where I describe an instance of Central Intelligence Agency success, namely, the penetration and takedown of the covert Republic of Korea strategic weapons program. I believe my extensive focus on that activity is warranted for several reasons.

First and foremost, that narrative has never been related before, not as it actually transpired or in this level of detail. Others have made respectable efforts to do so and have come close in certain aspects. But they have lacked the advantage of "being there" and cannot offer a comprehensive picture of the complex intelligence and diplomatic dances that played out in Seoul, Washington and other locations.

Second, though the events described here occurred in South Korea nearly 50 years ago, they remain relevant to where all the players involved in Northeast Asia, including the United States, find themselves in early 2023. The logic of the decision by South Korea's Pak regime, taken many decades past, might be difficult to fathom in retrospect. But today, many of the same factors remain in play or have become even more pressing. The North–South Korea dynamic on their contested peninsula is as unsettled as ever. Now, as then, Pyongyang's constitution embraces "reunification" by all means necessary, and this commitment remains the regime's *raison d'étre*. South Korea is again openly questioning the wisdom of relying on the United States and the U.S.–ROK bilateral alliance for its strategic deterrence. There is no escaping the fact that North Korea is now a self-declared and credible nuclear weapons state, and its ambition to reunite the peninsula under its terms has not waned.

Third, at present, we have before us the future of the U.S. security relationship with the Republic of Korea, a nation that until recently was led by a progressive government that gave lip service to that alliance while seeking a separate path forward. The progressive inclinations of the previous administration in Seoul emphasized the proverbial "middle way" or "balancer" concept as a useful mechanism to inject space between South Korea and the United States. The newly installed South Korean administration is much less inclined to take the alliance for granted, and its tougher approach to its northern neighbor has garnered an even more aggressive stance from the North, reinforced by expanded threats and continuing provocations.

In America, there is frustration with obligations overseas and commitments that might be too burdensome. This is particularly true because South Korea, today, is reasonably searching for greater levels of assurance that the promise of U.S. strategic deterrence (Read: the explicit use of nuclear weaponry) will be there to match North Korean aggression, be it in the form of a conventional attack backed by its nuclear arsenal or a limited nuclear strike designed to destabilize South Korea and destroy the U.S.–ROK alliance. Seoul's decision in 1974 to gamble on a covert strategic nuclear deterrent had its roots in the growing perception that the United States was no longer a credible defender. Now, South Korea is feeling its own oats and is increasingly wondering if it should no longer count on that U.S. "extended deterrent." Indeed, is the administration of President Yoon Suk-yeol asking itself whether there are other options to provide Seoul with its own sovereign capabilities—is there a better way to checkmate Pyongyang's growing ability to dominate the peninsula?

In June 1950, the United States began a brutal three-year war to rescue South Korea from the communist invasion. The all-out attack was mounted by the same North Korean regime that now possesses nuclear weapons and the capability to deliver them to all nations within the region and beyond. In 1974, South Korea was a nation into which America had recently poured considerable wealth, and into whose soil American sons had shed their lifeblood.

In 1974, there was a tangible bond between the United States and South Korea, and we Americans who were there then felt an obligation to respect our shared history. Although Korean War hostilities had halted under an Armistice Agreement in the summer of 1953, over two decades later we retained a force of more than 50,000 combat-ready troops on the ground in that country. Positioned forward and postured as a "trip-wire" deterrent, American service members would be among the first to die if North Korea repeated its aggression. Americans were then still dying on the ground and in the skies of Korea at the hands of the North Koreans, and we faced a "near-war" situation there.

Today, nearly a half-century after the events described in this book, some 20,000 American servicemembers remain on the ground in South Korea, exposed to a North Korea that remains poised to attack. But with nuclear weapons, the North might well be calculating that it has checkmated the U.S. nuclear deterrence on the peninsula and is better positioned than ever to impose its system on the South.

My point here is that a question begs: If South Korea's decision to undertake a covert nuclear weapons program in 1974 was in any way rational or even unavoidable, is not the option of a sovereign nuclear capability today even more compelling? Understanding this evolving dynamic is critical if the United States can continue managing the "politics of the vortex," as it is called, in Northeast Asia.

In 1975, in a discussion with the architect of the successful resolution of the South Korean nuclear mini-crisis—then-National Security Advisor and Secretary of State Henry Kissinger—I used an analogy. I told Kissinger, "in the nuclear reactor that is Northeast Asia, only the United States possesses the 'control rods' that are inserted to moderate that reactor's nuclear core … remove the rods and the reactor goes critical. This is a chain-reaction process that, once begun, can only be reversed with great difficulty." He nodded in agreement.

My analogy is truer today than it was in 1975; those control rods are now halfway out of the reactor core, and the United States is no longer manning the control panel. It is important to appreciate what went wrong, not so much because that knowledge provides us with a solution to the current dilemma, but because we now see more clearly what our options are going forward: accept this threat as it continues to evolve, or step up with difficult solutions.

Fourth, important lessons exist for intelligence collectors and policymakers embedded in the prospect of a South Korean nuclear weapons program. As a first-tour CIA officer suddenly immersed in a major national security issue with alliance-breaking implications, I was fortunate that Seoul Station senior leadership, in the person of Chief of Station Donald Gregg, grasped the importance of this issue. Gregg, and those managers at Agency Headquarters to whom he reported, fully appreciated the seriousness of that development, both in the context of the U.S.–South Korea political and security relationship and in the broader scheme of Northeast Asian security.

CIA leadership at the senior-most levels of the Clandestine Service; that is, the leadership of the Directorate of Operations, instinctively understood the broader policy issue the South Korean covert activity presented to the United States. Beyond its impact on the bilateral relationship with South Korea as well as U.S. alliances across Asia, a South Korean nuclear weapons program would pose a direct challenge to the international nuclear non-proliferation concerns of the United States. An unchecked South Korean nuclear weapons program, which had progressed under the very noses of U.S. alliance managers, would greatly damage our ability to restrain other nations harboring similar ambitions.

It therefore follows that the South Korean nuclear gambit, ill-considered as it was, became a priority activity of Seoul Station—if not THE intelligence collection priority of the Station—for several years. More important, the issue became a priority U.S. national policy activity. It involved a direct U.S. confrontation with South Korean leadership that was executed below the radar of public comment, media examination or overt friction between the two nations. The fact that it was accomplished in a manner that did not disrupt our basic political relationship with the Republic of Korea was no small feat.

Also notable, the effort to confront and dismantle the South Korean program was accomplished by consciously avoiding serious damage to the U.S.–ROK relationship. Discreet management of that sensitive issue at the highest diplomatic level allowed us to avoid weakening the bilateral military command structure, including the United Nations Command presence extended by the UN Security Council. During this tense period in the region, any hint to North Korea that the U.S.–ROK alliance was in trouble could have triggered an attack or an attempt to undermine the bilateral relationship that protected South Korea and its citizens.

In the end, the real credit for resolving the crisis must go to those South Koreans who understood the danger the covert nuclear program posed to their country's security and the safety of its citizens. Their willingness to discuss the issue privately with American counterparts, often at considerable risk to themselves, displayed considerable courage. Those special men were Korean patriots in the truest sense of the word.

Other Operations Along the Nuclear Way

Beyond the events in Korea, I will share my experiences in other aspects of advancing nuclear non-proliferation, much of it done in the context of the broader U.S. effort. It includes actions by the International Atomic Energy Agency in the early 1980s, as more comprehensive and aggressive U.S. policies were put into place to deal with the proliferation threat. We were fortunate that these policies and actions came together when they did to produce real results at a time other nations became attracted to the nuclear option. Each of those countries seriously examined the potential for nuclear weapons, each for its own reason but always with considerable determination. I also include an eclectic mix of experiences in other covert and overt intelligence areas that influenced U.S. policy during that period, or failed to do so, for any combination of good and bad reasons.

Going 'Off-Line' with Director Bill Casey

I also describe a brief but turbulent 18-month experience working for and with a man who brought with him, and created in his wake, no small amount of controversy: William J. Casey, the Director of Central Intelligence during the Reagan administration. He arrived at the Agency as a man with a mission and was inclined to wild rides down dark roads. Yet he also was an interesting and compelling character.

Treading the CIA path with Casey was survivable only if one knew or sensed which curves to navigate or potholes to dodge along the way. To observe that he was controversial both within and outside the Agency is an understatement. I managed to collect my share of burns during that brief period of direct association. All and all, however, the Casey experience was worth the acquired bumps and bruises and, although my seat was not always at ringside, I was close enough to feel the heat and watch some of the history Casey made.

PART ONE

The Making of a Nuke Hunter

(1946-1972)

Chapter 1. Before Korea
1946-1968

In June 1969 at the ripe old age of 22, I found myself aboard a U.S. government-chartered Boeing 707 headed for Seoul. I had traveled an uneven route leading to the aircraft, where I sat among 100-plus U.S. Army personnel slated for tours of duty in the Republic of Korea. The flight was about to deliver me to a decisive point in my life, even if the importance of that moment escaped me at the time. I had recently graduated from the U.S. Department of Defense's Defense Language Institute in Monterey, California, and after a year of intense instruction, I had attained the tenuous claim of "Korean linguist."

I previously had completed a U.S. Army counterintelligence course at Fort Holabird in Baltimore, earning me a military occupational specialty designation, or MOS, of 97-B-40. Technically, I was a Regular Army enlistee with a three-year commitment to active-duty service. Given the MOS, in which I had elected to serve, and the dynamic of the late 1960s, I assumed when I signed on in the summer of 1967 that I would be sent to Vietnam. In fact, I volunteered to serve there, to the extent the Army might see its way to make that happen. I assumed it would not be a problem, given that just about all Army enlistees and draftees at the time were either veterans of recent service in Vietnam, currently serving there or headed there as expectant combatants. Many in my generation of soon-to-be warriors headed to Southeast Asia were not eager to join the fight, but they had agreed to serve and went where they were ordered to go. I was fortunate to discover new friends who were likewise motivated to join our national undertaking in Vietnam or serve wherever they were sent—determined to do their very best. We welcomed the experiences to come and held no reservations about the call to serve. As for me, my background seemed to be driving my destiny.

Central Illinois 1946-1964

Born in Peoria, Illinois, in the first year of the "Baby Boomers," I was incredibly fortunate to have a solid family that delivered a strict but fair upbringing to me and my younger brother, all set in a small city downstate. Raised in a home that my father built, literally, with his own hands over a three-year period, our middle-middle-class position was guaranteed by the blessing of the post-war prosperity that sustained my father's career as a senior tradesman. He had returned from the war as a commissioned Navy aviator and worked in a field he loved. In my childhood, I was surrounded and embraced by my father's generation, men who had served in World War II, and it fascinated me to listen to their discussions over beers late at night as the ladies played cards in the next room. They spoke of their respective experiences as they enlisted, trained and then went to war in the European and Pacific theaters (my Uncle Bob was an artillery man in

Patton's Third Army).

My father assumed that his path had been chosen. He would join the steam-fitters as a five-year apprentice based on a nomination that came from his uncle, a fellow tradesman. By that time, my grandfather had started his own construction business, in a partnership with Peoria's mayor, so my father's plan was to earn his journeyman's credentials and become a part of the business. Then the Japanese struck Pearl Harbor, and his world was turned upside down, along with every other able-bodied man in America. On a bright spring day in 1942, Dad and three of his best friends walked into the Navy recruiting station at the local Post Office building and announced they all wanted to fly. Two made it past the first cut and were selected for Navy aviation: my father and another son of a pipefitter, a slightly older young man who was a senior in college. The other two went down the hall, one to join the Army Air Corps and another to enlist in the Army infantry.

Two of the four young men would survive the war: my father and Thomas "Bud" Salter, the Air Corps pilot, who would fly 40 combat missions over Europe in his P-47 Thunderbolt fighter. The war would claim the other two. Lieutenant Tom Galvin, the fellow Navy aviator, died when his PV-1 Ventura patrol bomber lost power in both engines and crashed into the sea off the coast of Italy, just as the Allies landed at Anzio to fight the German army there. And Francis "Bud" Downing would die in infantry combat in March 1945, when his Ninth Armored Division fought to liberate an Allied prisoner of war camp outside Limburg, Germany. **[SEE CHAPTER NOTE 1]**

My father received his commission through the V-5 Navy Aviation program. He graduated with honors at Pensacola and served as a flight instructor and as a VIP aircraft command pilot. His onward orders instructed him to report to an aircraft carrier in early August 1945 for movement to the Pacific. America's preparations were then underway to invade the Japanese home islands, scheduled to begin in early November 1945. Then his overseas movement was stood-down, in military parlance, days before his ship was to sail, after the B-29 bomber named "Enola Gay" dropped the first atomic bomb on the Japanese city of Hiroshima. Dad was discharged with a reserve-service obligation a few months later.

After the war, the men of my family returned home as veterans to pick up their lives. They married and had children, finished their educations and started businesses. They did it all with confidence and a determination they had developed because the war catapulted them out of Peoria, or wherever, into the wider world. I recall that, several years later, when I first saw the movie *The Best Years of Our Lives*, a 1946 release that claimed several Oscars—including Best Picture—it resonated completely with me. The movie captured the hopes of the men and women of my parents' generation who had lived through that tumultuous period, particularly as they returned from war and attempted to reset their lives. John F. Kennedy was one of them. To my parents, his election as President of the United States in 1960 seemed to bless and acknowledge all of this. It was particularly so with the second- and third-generation Irish–American Catholic community of my youth.

Those men constituted what came to be called "the greatest generation," and they surrounded me in the 1950s and '60s. They remain so today, six decades later. They were, almost to a man, humble and thankful, both to be alive and to be Americans. Having experienced the Great Depression and the monumental saga of World War II, they appreciated everything they accomplished and took nothing for granted. They worked hard, seldom complained and were unabashedly patriotic. In retrospect, it was not easy to measure up to the image or the reality of those men. In truth, I did not even know how best to try.

The U.S. Navy—Dreams of Annapolis

Returning to the narrative of my own life, and the events that placed me on that plane headed to Korea in 1969, I had not enlisted in the U.S. Army. Instead, I was transferred from the Navy. In 1967, I walked away from a full-scholarship Regular Navy ROTC program at the University of Missouri in Columbia after completing my junior year. In a sense, I had been in the military for four years at that point, based on my enlistment in the Navy Reserves on my 17th birthday. My enlistment had taken place in the July that bridged my junior and senior years in high school, in the summer of 1963. As others stood lifeguard duty at a local country club or worked under the sun in the hay and cornfields of central Illinois, I completed basic training at Treasure Island Naval Base in San Francisco Bay. At TI, our class had been "ridden hard and put up wet" by a pickup instructor cadre of no-nonsense Navy Seabees and Marines.

After basic training, I was transferred back across the country for a six-week shipboard tour, assigned to the USS *Ely*, a World War II-era vessel that cruised the Great Lakes. The *Ely*, designated Patrol Craft Escort 880, had been consigned to serve out its days on Lake Michigan as a training vessel for reservists. My time spent on that ship as a lowly "snipe," or engine-room apprentice, among an eclectic cast of crewmates and fellow trainees, delivered a memorable closing for my summer of '63. Aboard the *Ely*, we simulated anti-submarine exercises; namely, the skipper would toss hand grenades into the water from his command chair on the wing of the bridge. We detected no Soviet submarines on the Great Lakes that year. The ship's permanent crew pushed us hard, and we learned the arts of deck work and basic seamanship.

My brief duty was highlighted by one off-ship event: a nightlong party ashore in Sheboygan, Wisconsin. On that occasion, we had returned to the *Ely*'s homeport for a weekend to join local citizens in celebrating their annual Bratwurst Festival. In the collegial streets of Sheboygan, the cold beer flowed, the 'brats sizzled on the grill and the locals polka-danced well past midnight. We sailors ended up closing the place down. Our captain, something of a hero to the patriotic German–American folk there, outdid himself on the beer and schnapps front. Afterward, we carried him back to the ship where we lowered the *Ely*'s liberty cutter to rest just above the pier and loaded him into it. Hoisted back aboard, we secured the small craft, and our executive officer took command, letting the captain and his party companions sleep it off where they lay, and proceeding to cast off and sail away at dawn. We left Sheboygan a bit worse for wear, but no less so than our captain. **[NOTE 2]**

When I enlisted in the Navy Reserves on my 17th birthday, it was for one reason: my abiding determination to enter the U.S. Naval Academy in Annapolis. I was consumed by the desire to follow in my father's footsteps and become a naval aviator, and Annapolis was the required path to achieve that end. I thought I had a reasonable chance for an appointment by my congressman at the time, Robert Michel. But my high school grade-point average was not where it should have been to cinch the nomination. Looking for a backup plan, I discovered that the Reserves had some 200 appointment slots retained for each year's class at Annapolis, an allocation that often went unfilled. So, enlisting in the Reserve unit in Peoria in my junior–senior summer seemed a reasonable strategy.

Midshipman Years 1964-1967

My time at Missouri passed quickly, with each summer spent on active duty in the company of other NROTC and Annapolis midshipmen. My third-class summer cruise placed me aboard the USS *Hornet*, CVS-12, an aging Essex Class aircraft carrier modified for anti-submarine warfare. Flying from that ship as a midshipmen passenger on its S-2F sub hunters, and watching the deck launches of A-4 Skyhawk attack aircraft, were a dream come true. I delighted in my shore leaves in Seattle, Hawaii and Long Beach, as well as the friendships made afloat, whether in the engine room or on deck watch. All afforded special bonds between us NROTC types and our Annapolis cruise-mates.

In 1965, I was ordered aboard the attack transport USS *Montrose*, which some of us joined in San Diego. We embarked with a Marine battalion headed to Vietnam. It was my first interaction with that war. One early highlight was a cross-border morning run to the jails of Tijuana, Mexico, to bail out a dozen Marines. This "hard corps" crew had elected to celebrate their last night ashore, and their pending deployment to Vietnam, by destroying a Mexican strip joint and kidnapping a performing donkey. To prevent the jailed Marines from missing "ship's movement," the *Montrose* captain gathered the 20 midshipmen on board and took up a collection to bail out the incarcerated men.

In this exercise, we got little help from the Marines who had escaped the police and found their way back to the ship. Barely standing in the early morning hours, most of them badly needed rest and recuperation, and all were broke. The collection completed, the captain sent a handful of us south to deal with the Mexican jailers. Bail paid, all missing Marines accounted for and our mission accomplished, we sailed from San Diego. Our journey west into the broad Pacific had us pause briefly in Hawaii (no liberty opportunity there for the Marines) to allow the midshipmen to change ships. We disembarked from the *Montrose* and watched from Pearl Harbor as she sailed west to Okinawa, from where the Marines would be onward deployed to Vietnam.

Then, at the beginning of my junior year at Missouri, I learned I would never fly, at least with the U.S. Navy, because I was red–green colorblind—a disqualifying condition for naval aviation that literally appeared out of the blue. The news crushed me. I had been flying on weekends at Missouri with my NROTC instructor, taking maximum advantage of the T-28 Trojan prop trainer stationed for midshipmen at the Columbia city airport.

My instructor, Lieutenant James Brown, was a great guy and a totally unreformed Navy aviator, not to mention a dedicated bachelor who regularly exploited the singles community around the Columbia campus. A career attack pilot, he was marking time on-staff at Missouri as a ROTC instructor, waiting for a tour that would return him to his favorite "ride"—an A-4 Skyhawk attack fighter, on a carrier steaming at Yankee Station—a location in the South China Sea—flying missions into North Vietnam. His reaction when I shared my disqualification with him? "That's a tough one." He counseled me to "just swallow it and move on."

I did. I left the Navy ROTC program a year early and entered the Army's intelligence program. I was drawn to the war in Vietnam and the assurance that I would be there in less than a year. Part of the beckoning to that conflict, along with a tinge of guilt that my friends had gone, or been drafted to serve, stemmed from my sitting it out at the university. In retrospect, such a sense of obligation might seem odd, particularly because the war was portrayed so negatively in the following years as a waste of national treasure and life. The perception was reinforced by the recognition that our national leadership during the Vietnam conflict consistently failed to support the men who were fighting and dying in the jungles of Southeast Asia.

Domestic political considerations trumped any rational approach to the war: either do what was necessary to win or, failing that, just get out. Many of my generation thought they had been cast into a no-win conflict by a national political leadership that subordinated their lives to political considerations or other convoluted priorities. The soon-to-be-delivered wisdom by our national media that Vietnam was a failed enterprise, coupled with a growing belief among some in my generation that serving in Vietnam should be disdained, did not exist for me at the time. Nor does it now. But one had to be there to understand.

Chapter 2. The United States Army and Korea
1967-1969

U.S. Army Intelligence and Fort Holabird 1967-1968

By the time I began my Army stint in the summer of 1967, I was comfortable with military service. I was well-adapted to its culture, I understood its inherently unpredictable nature and frequent irrationalities, and I welcomed the opportunity to serve the nation. My three-year commitment involved entry into the Army intelligence program as a counterintelligence, or CI, agent. My initial assignment was to the Army's Intelligence School at Fort Holabird, Maryland, to be followed by transfer to a unit in Vietnam. But Dame Fate intervened.

During our final days at Fort Holabird, in May 1968, as our counterintelligence course work was winding down and graduation loomed, my class of 40-plus was called into a conference room where we received our onward assignments. The school commandant confirmed that we were headed for Vietnam. That came as no surprise. We all knew where we were destined to spend the next year or two of our lives. But then came the good news that all CI course graduates would first be assigned to a year of Vietnamese language training at Fort Hood, a huge facility in a semi-remote location near Waco, Texas. Thus, some more bad news. **[NOTE 1]**

The "Congratulations, you are all headed to Fort Hood for a year" carried a slight caveat. Four of us had instead drawn the Presidio of Monterey (not to be confused with the Presidio of San Francisco, in Golden Gate Park), where we were slated to attend the Defense Language Institute. There, we would undergo an intensive course in Korean. The working assumption was that on graduation from DLI one year later we would go to Vietnam and serve with the South Korean forces there. We knew this probably meant a year or more in Vietnam with either the ROK "White Horse" Ninth Infantry Division or the ROK "Blue Dragon" Marine Brigade.

The gist of the unexpected development was that we four had lucked out, at least temporarily, because we were headed for the beach in California rather than the badlands of West Texas. But the downside was that, on graduation, we would head straight to Vietnam to serve with the ROKs in combat there. It was delivered wisdom that South Korean infantrymen tended to welcome hard contact with the enemy, spent a lot of time in the bush and did not mess around. Our Vietnam destiny had been delayed, but we could look forward to being embedded and in the field with some of the meanest players out in the jungle, or so we assumed.

Defense Language Institute
at the Presidio of Monterey 1968-1969

The DLI was a special place, and I enjoyed my year there immensely. I found Korean to be an intriguing language, complex due to its structure and its mix of a phonetic alphabet mated to Chinese characters. But it was also straightforward and practical in its delivery, and I seemed to grasp with some ease its speech patterns and expressions. Overall, I admit, I was a below-average student, spending too much time on the beach or in weekend dashes with fellow students to Reno or San Francisco. My roommate, John, a bit of a wild man from Maryville, Tennessee, was a bad influence for sure. But others were far worse. The class attitude seemed to be "since we are all headed for Vietnam to join the crazy Koreans there, let's just enjoy the moment and go with the flow."

Everything we heard at the DLI concerning the ROK soldiers fighting in Vietnam, our soon-to-be brothers in arms, reinforced our earlier understanding of the Korean psyche. The established ROK profile was that they were professionally ruthless, totally bad actors who were always looking hard for a fight with the Viet Cong or North Vietnamese regulars and saw no problem in scorching the earth in the process. To some degree, we endured our language studies at DLI just enough to stay in the course, often grabbing beach time at Carmel when we should have been in the language lab refining our dialect.

That is not to say we did not appreciate the gravity of our pending assignment to Vietnam. In the summer and fall of 1968, we experienced from afar the destruction of that country brought by the grind of war in the wake of the Tet '68 communist offensive. Daily, we watched media reports on the pitched battles, as nearly half-a-million American soldiers, Marines, airmen and sailors fought across the length and breadth of that nation under the North Vietnamese siege.

We also could not miss the none-too-subtle shift by the media, as it pivoted from initially supporting the war, to tepidness toward our involvement in Vietnam and finally settling on its new mantra that the war was "unwinnable." America's television father figure, Walter Cronkite, intoned solemnly that we had no purpose being there.

President Lyndon B. Johnson and the national security team, comprising the "Best and Brightest" he had inherited from President John F. Kennedy, basically had reached the same conclusion, whether they admitted it or not. Procrastinating the hard decisions before them, Johnson and his advisers, abetted by a complacent military leadership unwilling or unable to stand behind their men in the field, were unable to find an honorable path out of Southeast Asia. **[NOTE 2]**

Media distortion notwithstanding, we knew Tet '68 had been a resounding defeat for the communists, a failure that could have turned the war against them. We also sensed that, to win the war, both the Johnson administration and the South Vietnamese would have to demonstrate leadership and the will to stay the course. But it was becoming apparent that the American body politic no longer possessed the necessary will. Our leaders, both civilian and military, seemed adrift, uncertain and clueless. At the same time, the South Vietnamese commitment to the fight grew more ambiguous, as its soldiers died in the field and its leaders wrangled. In Saigon, military leadership staged coup and countercoup, as competing factions vied for control of the nation.

By the time we prepared for DLI graduation in the early summer of 1969, most of us knew 1968 represented a turning point for the war in Vietnam. The groundwork for a self-inflicted strategic defeat was in the offing. We also began to realize, even as we assumed we were still headed for Vietnam, that the American public had turned its back on us. Informed by a media that likewise had turned against the war, the American elite no longer retained any stomach for the mishandled endeavor. Future Presidents Bill Clinton and Donald Trump, both of whom shared my birth year of 1946, found their ways to dodge the draft, as other young men packed their bags and ran north to Canada.

Some of us assumed we would be "fighting to leave" Vietnam sooner rather than later. But we were young, committed to going to Vietnam and almost eager to "get on with it." The attitude prevailed to the degree that several of our fellow Korean language classmates at DLI elected to drop out at midcourse in favor of an immediate ticket to Vietnam. We called the group our "early graduates," and we farewelled them as they headed north to Fort Lewis to collect jungle gear and board their aircraft to join the war.

In May 1969, in the run-up to our graduation, the DLI commander called a handful of us into the commander's office. I assumed we would be braced for our poor academic performance rather than promoted, the latter being the norm after graduation. But I stood stunned as the commander related our fate to us. "Gentlemen," he said, "turn in your Vietnam gear, your fatigues, whatever. You are not going to Vietnam. We have near-war brewing in Korea, and you are needed there." He told us to take three weeks' leave and be on a flight to Seoul in early June. Our assignment there would be determined once we arrived in-country. Fate had taken me away from Vietnam—at least initially.

Assignment: South Korea — Summer 1969

We should have seen it coming. There were rumors about Korean troops fighting in Vietnam rotating home early as the ROK reduced its presence there—perhaps the Koreans sensed our loss of conviction. We also knew the Army's military intelligence units in the ROK were short on Korean linguists with counterintelligence credentials.

In that same period, as America appeared mired and increasingly undecided about the winnability of the war, the conflict on the Korean Peninsula again heated up. North Korean armed provocations against the South and the U.S. military presence there were coming fast and plenty. On January 23, 1968, as we were finishing our seventh month at DLI, the North mounted its most serious and direct military provocation to date. The U.S. Navy intelligence-collection ship, the USS *Pueblo* (AGER-2), stuffed to its gunnels with highly classified signals-intelligence equipment, code machines, top-secret technical manuals and a crew of 83, was attacked, boarded and seized some 15 miles off the port of Wonsan by the North Korean Navy.

The *Pueblo*, on its first intelligence-collection cruise, was a tiny ship, some 170-odd feet in length and by no means capable of resisting the attack. She had been hastily converted a few months before from an aged Navy small cargo ship, or AKL, of World War II vintage, and assigned a signals-collection mission that placed her in an incredibly vulnerable situation. All involved in the Navy's chain of command should have known better.

Among the *Pueblo*'s crew were 30-plus Naval Security Group communications technicians, skilled eavesdroppers closely associated with the National Security Agency and its signals-collection programs. Part of the U.S. Navy's CLICK BEETLE operations, as they were called, the *Pueblo* cruised at a leisurely 12 knots in international waters, hugging the North Korean coast to collect and analyze their military signals. The star-crossed mission was a classic example of incomplete if not incompetent planning, incredibly so in light of other, ongoing events on the peninsula. As a result, the ship and its crew were badly exposed and had placed themselves, under orders to do so, squarely in harm's way.

Sailing independently in an exposed location, with little real-time contact with any major U.S. fleet units in the region, the tiny ship was in no position to resist the North Korean attack. With one crewman dead and several others, including Captain Lloyd M. Bucher, wounded from enemy gunboat fire, the ship was captured virtually intact, the destruction of priceless equipment and codebooks incomplete. The *Pueblo* became a North Korean prize, its attack and seizure in international waters by any definition an act of war.

As the North Koreans dragged the crew off the ship in Wonsan harbor, U.S. military planners scrambled to explain to President Johnson how it happened. In the tense days ahead, the administration planned options as carrier battle groups were massed and airstrikes prepared, with the prospect of an expanded conflict dominating our military planning. The *Pueblo* crew would sit in captivity under deprived conditions for nearly a year before the Johnson administration bartered them back with an apology that degraded our country and enraged our ally, South Korea. Once again, North Korea had paid no price for its attack on and capture of our ship.

Within the overall drama of the *Pueblo* capture, our military command's immediate reactions, or lack thereof, were notable. One exception to general paralysis in the command chain was the decision, taken on his own initiative immediately after the attack, by Lt. General Seth McKee, the Fifth Air Force's Commander. At first word of the ongoing assault on the *Pueblo*, McKee scrambled a squadron of F-105 fighter–bombers from Okinawa's Kadena Air Base and ordered them to a forward strike position at our airbase at Osan, South Korea. Refueled and up-armed with 1,000-pound bombs, the 12 Thunderchiefs sat there with pilots in their cockpits, positioned to launch in the dead of night.

From the tarmac at Osan, the F-105 strike force was 25 minutes' flight time from the *Pueblo*, by then tied fast to a pier in Wonsan Harbor by the North Koreans. Squadron leader Major John Wright had orders to sink the *Pueblo* at all costs, but he needed the "go" order to launch. He and the pilots he led remained in the chill of their cockpits and waited for hours for that signal from the Osan control tower. The signal never came. At some point, they were told to stand down, with the explanation that higher command authority had determined the destruction of the *Pueblo* was not an option.

At the same time, to the east of Osan in the Sea of Japan, our nuclear carrier *Enterprise* ran at flank speed toward the North Korean coast, preparing its air wing for a strike against the gunboats that had captured the *Pueblo* and escorted her into the harbor. The battle group commander developed a plan for an accompanying destroyer, the USS *Ozbourn*, to shoot its way into Wonsan harbor, there to lash itself to and drag the *Pueblo* back into international waters. Deemed to be impractical, the hastily assembled recapture plan was scrapped as well. Act of War, a recent book by Jack Cheevers, does a good job summarizing those stillborn retaliatory and recapture schemes, both of which were discarded in favor of a "diplomatic engagement" approach to crisis resolution. As might be imagined, in no case did any of the soft-edged responses reassure the South Korean leadership or its citizens; nor did it reassure the U.S. troops stationed in South Korea that their national leaders had the back of those on the front lines.

The *Pueblo* crisis presented President Johnson and his national security staff, not to mention his party in a presidential election year, with a frustrating political dilemma. Johnson needed to resolve the issue, and our government contorted itself in an attempt to find a compromise to bring the hostages home. After months of negotiation, and a signed "Letter of Responsibility" and apology from the United States (of course), the *Pueblo* crew was allowed to depart its prison camp with a humbling "walk of shame" procession that crossed into South Korea over the Bridge of No Return. As light snow fell, the *Pueblo* crew entered and exited the Demilitarized Zone, bringing with it the body of slain crewman Duane Hodges. With that incident, the North Koreans had brought the peninsula to the brink of all-out war. Pyongyang had also delivered the message that it would not hesitate to sustain its armed confrontation with South Korea and its ally, the United States. Worse, North Korea communicated to the rest of Asia that the United States could be intimidated and outplayed. [NOTE 3]

Asia Conflict and Near-War in Korea

The capture of the *Pueblo* was, first and foremost, an American-at-sea national humiliation. But the action did not pose an existential threat to our nation. South Korea was not so fortunate. North Korean on-the-ground aggressions against that republic on a near-daily basis suggested the increasing possibility of a renewed Korean War. On January 21st, three days before the *Pueblo* seizure, a 31-man North Korean commando unit slipped through the DMZ and penetrated the defenses of the capital city, Seoul.

The North Korean hit team moved undetected to within a few hundred meters of the Blue House, South Korea's presidential residence and administrative center. The team's path was blocked by a chance encounter with a police unit, and a shootout ensued. The commando group had one mission: Kill President Pak Chung-hee and destroy his leadership team. The plan was, by decapitating the ROK leadership, Pyongyang could create enough chaos to topple the government, potentially allowing further attacks by the North if not precipitating another all-out invasion of the South.

The commandos had infiltrated across the DMZ that served as the Armistice firebreak at the 38th parallel. They avoided detection by soldiers of the U.S. Second Infantry Division, the unit forward-positioned to guard that sector of the border. The Blue House attack, combined with the seizure of *Pueblo* and overlaid by a dozen other, full-frontal North Korean commando attacks on both ROK and U.S positions over the previous two years, had shocked South Korean leadership and brought them to the point of unilateral military retaliation.

President Pak ordered his planners to prepare for a counterstrike. Such a return attack would not be a minor probe but rather a battalion-sized assault across the DMZ, to be mounted with or without U.S. approval or participation. In that instance, Pak's inclination to retaliate quickly and heavily was forestalled by U.S. intervention—but blood was in the water. With reason and much emotion, South Korea was deeply determined to hit back, hard.

America's overall situation in Asia, and the national debate over our military commitments, had taken a further turn for the worse a week after the *Pueblo* capture and the Blue House raid. In South Vietnam, the communists' nationwide attack that became known as Tet '68, exploded with full force. The event destroyed any myth that the United States and its Vietnam allies were winning the war. As mentioned, Tet '68 suggested the best we might be able to achieve was a stalemate and cast doubts for many that the war was winnable at all.

South Korea, responding to President Johnson's request several years before, had committed more than 40,000 troops to fight in Vietnam alongside us and the Vietnamese. Two ROK divisions and a Marine brigade served there at one point. As the *Pueblo* sat hostage in Wonsan harbor, and its crew endured daily beatings in a North Korean prison camp, the Blue House licked its own wounds while more Koreans and Americans continued to die in combat in South Korea as a consequence of North Korean aggressions. The question arose whether it was time for President Pak to bring his troops home. The Johnson administration beseeched him to maintain his military's presence in Vietnam. The ROK troops stayed, at least temporarily.

It also is worth noting that, in the aftermath of the Blue House attack, the pursuit and destruction of the balance of the commando team claimed the lives of 68 South Korean soldiers and policemen, not to mention three U.S. Army infantrymen. Moreover, North Korea's belligerent acts did not begin with that January 1968 leadership-decapitation attempt. The previous year, 1967, involved

North Korean attacks against the U.S. military presence in the South, with DMZ-crossing commando teams hitting an Corps of Engineers unit, killing three and wounding 25. And a raid against a Second Division barracks killed two.

The magnitude of the North Korean provocations against South Korea—both its military and its civil society—as well as the U.S. military, is underappreciated and seldom discussed. Many historians writing about more recent events on the peninsula tend to ignore or gloss over those incidents and tend to discount the risk of war that existed on and around the peninsula during that period. In the five years relevant to my narrative, 1966-1970, North Korea perpetrated more than 500 incidents on South Korea, within either the country or its territorial waters. The attacks resulted in more than 400 South Korean soldiers and civilians killed and 700 wounded, with some 200 American soldiers likewise killed or wounded.

One example that predates both the *Pueblo* incident and the Blue House raid demonstrates North Korean determination to resort to deadly provocations to test the will of the United States. In October 1966, Premier Kim Il-sung announced in a speech to the Korean Workers Party that the status quo, which had endured on the peninsula since the Armistice, would soon change, referencing the ongoing war in Vietnam. The following month, President Johnson visited Seoul to meet with President Pak and interact with the U.S. troops serving there under the United Nations flag in the defense of South Korea.

As Johnson's plane lifted off from Suwon Airfield to head home, a North Korean commando team made its way across the DMZ to ambush and kill six U.S. infantrymen a few hours later. With that act, Pyongyang was delivering a special farewell salute to President Johnson on the occasion of his state visit to the Republic of Korea. The North Koreans pumped 50 rounds into each of the dead Americans, mutilating their bodies. A second Pyongyang commando team then went on that same night to ambush and kill other UN soldiers, this time South Koreans, a few miles away. It was but a taste of what North Korea planned for the future. Over the following 12 months, 26 more American soldiers died at the hands of infiltrators, and many more were wounded in the attacks, mostly in the DMZ frontline area.

But North Korea did not limit itself to such actions. During that period, commando teams also struck in the heartland of South Korea, with shootouts in Taegu and agent infiltrations across the southwestern coast, where ROK defenses were less robust. In January 1967, the North Koreans attacked the ROK Navy patrol ship *Tang Po* (PCE-56) in the East Sea, a sinking that killed or wounded more than 50 sailors. The *Tang Po* was the former USS *Maria* (PCE-842), coincidentally a sister ship of the USS *Ely* mentioned earlier. North Korean shore batteries sank the *Tang Po* as it attempted to herd South Korean fishing vessels back across the sea leg extension of the DMZ demarcation line.

That same year, more than 150 South Korean soldiers and civilians died on their own soil from North Korean provocations. The following year, 1968, the year of the *Pueblo*, saw the Pyongyang regime ramp up its attack program further with more than 500 separate incidents of spy team infiltrations, railroad sabotage missions that caused derailments and direct military actions, again resulting in hundreds of deaths. As I watched all of it evolve, trending into 1969, things seemed destined to get worse—and they did.

Respected sources tracking North–South hostilities over the past 50 years note that 1966 to 1970 was by far the "deadliest span of time on the Korean Peninsula in the post-Korean War period," resulting in more than 2,700 casualties. The following five-year period, 1971-1975, relevant to my narrative, saw the tempo of attacks reduced to 50 or so, with only about 50 casualties. The North Koreans, instigators of these incidents, often appeared to mix random attacks with those involving careful planning and intent. Elsewhere, I will cover several deadly provocations that occurred during my tour. [NOTE 4]

More recently, after a period of relative calm, incident-wise, in April 2010 the North Koreans executed a carefully planned near-war provocation in the ROK's West Sea. They torpedoed the South Korean Navy patrol ship *Cheonan*, killing 46 sailors and generating an international outcry. The attack challenged the ROK leadership and the U.S.–ROK alliance, and it created yet another military and political crisis. In that case, the ROK government, for whatever combinations of good reasons and excuses, allowed the deadly incident to pass without retaliation.

At the time of the *Cheonan* sinking, the position of the Korean government had been undercut by the "progressive" administration that had preceded it during 2003-2008. Compromised by a "sunshine" engagement policy—all give to North Korea and no get—the serving South Korean administration was not prepared to take serious issue with the *Cheonan* sinking. The order of the day was an international investigation that sought to determine if the North Koreans really had torpedoed the ship—a "perish-the-thought" approach that sought and found excuses to take no action. The United States, for its own reasons, felt no inclination to part company with an ally eager to compromise on such incidents, no matter how blatant.

As of this writing, the progressive administration that had managed South Korea's relationship with Pyongyang for five long years, ever hopeful it could find common ground with its long-lost brothers in the North, has been replaced by a more conservative government. The latter is more realistic and much less inclined to subordinate itself to Pyongyang's demands. Responding to the new-found firmness on the part of Seoul, and emboldened by its nuclear weapons capabilities, North Korea has doubled down on its provocations.

With its playbook expanded and even less to lose, the coming months and years will no doubt see Pyongyang continue to create mischief with another nuclear test, a missile launch, a cyberattack or another cross-border incident—any or all in the offing. As if to underline their capabilities and intent, in January 2023 the North Koreans sent a bevy of drones across the DMZ to harass and embarrass the new administration, including one that penetrated and circled menacingly over the protected no-fly area of the Blue House. The message from Pyongyang was clear: We have many options to challenge South Korea, and our nuclear forces are prepared to back-up every one of them.

Shootdown

In April 1969, as we completed our final weeks at DLI, we were hit with the news that an unarmed U.S. Navy EC-121 electronic-reconnaissance aircraft, flying a routine intelligence-collection mission in international airspace, had been blown out of the sky by a North Korean Air Force MiG-21. Again, this dramatic provocation was carefully planned and executed, occurring some 60 miles off the North Korean coast. It claimed all 31 officers and men on board and provoked another act-of-war scramble by an unprepared U.S. military and national command structure.

Several of the men on the aircraft, call sign "Deep Sea 129," were recent DLI graduates, U.S. Naval Security Group Korean language specialists, a mixed team of Navy and Marine officers and men assigned to the aircraft's squadron VQ-1 and based at Atsugi, Japan. The shootdown was no accident or misunderstanding. In fact, the event was not a miscalculation by an overly aggressive pilot. Rather, it was a carefully planned and executed provocation timed to coincide with North Korean dictator Kim Il-sung's birthday and designed to sting the United States as it attempted to deal with and our presumed overcommitment in Vietnam. Only two bodies were recovered, and the cold sea consumed the rest, while American national leadership remained preoccupied with the war and domestic unrest.

Apart from some huffing and puffing, the new administration of President Richard M. Nixon and his able realpolitik national security advisor, one Henry Kissinger, opted to let it all pass. But the North Koreans took note of the American decision, yet again, to turn the other cheek, as did our ally in Seoul. With the U.S. commitment in Vietnam deeply in doubt, Dr. Kissinger began secret negotiations in Paris with his North Vietnamese counterpart Lê Đức Thọ to seek an "honorable exit" from the war and the security commitments involved. In that uncertain environment, and in the face of repeated North Korean provocations claiming the lives of Americans and South Koreans alike, many in the South Korean government wondered just how long the U.S. commitment to their defense would endure. They were not wrong to have that concern, as future events would soon confirm. Thus, we had a significant and growing problem on our hands involving our credibility in South Korea. **[NOTE 5]**

For those of us preparing to leave the comforts of the Presidio of Monterey for Korea, the fact that we were no longer headed for Vietnam was of little relief. We assumed that once on the ground in the ROK, we would be assigned either to a frontline unit on the DMZ, supporting the U.S. Army's Second Infantry Division, or be embedded with Korean units engaged in counter-infiltrator missions elsewhere on the peninsula. We bid farewell to those in our class who were headed to Vietnam, there to liaison officer assignments with the Korean forces in combat zones. Either way, for all of us, after nearly two years of preparation, the summer of 1969 was showtime.

Chapter 3. The Land of the Morning Calm
1969-1970

Arrival in Seoul and Counterintelligence Command

When our small group of counterintelligence agents disembarked at Kimpo Airport near Seoul, we discovered we would be temporarily assigned to the nearby headquarters of our parent unit in-country, the 502nd Military Intelligence Battalion. We were screened and interviewed there for onward, permanent, length-of-tour assignments. Some of us would head north to work with U.S. combat units positioned on or near the DMZ, several would stay in the Seoul area at the battalion headquarters or at Eighth Army itself, and a couple of us would be distributed to the south. In the last-mentioned category, small CI units functioned on a provincial level and worked closely with South Korean military and civilian counterintelligence units.

One evening, during my in-process week at the battalion, I returned to my quarters to find a Western Union telegram waiting on my bunk. It conveyed that my grandfather, Patrick Lawless, had passed away several days before, apparently at the same time that I was winging my way over the North Pacific en route to Korea. "Pappy" was a friend, a large but quiet man. He was a first-generation American, born in 1896 to immigrant parents and served his country in World War I as a member of General "Back Jack" Pershing's American Expeditionary Force in France. I had the good fortune of spending almost every day with him in the weeks before my departure for Korea back home on leave. I sat with him on my last day of leave and, for the first time I could recall, we discussed his early life. I was headed overseas, and he wanted to talk, so I listened. For hours. I would miss him dearly. **[NOTE 1]**

Early on, as I gained the lay of the land in Seoul, I discovered that, although we intel guys were known to our own military in Korea as "502 MI" counterintelligence agents, to the world outside the U.S. military structure we remained, at least in Korea, "the CIC." This cryptic form, for Counterintelligence Command, was a legacy identity from the Korean War, but it carried a very special meaning to all Koreans. The CIC was widely respected, if not often feared, as the strongarm enforcer responsible for rooting out and eliminating North Korean agents. The latter typically comprised small, stay-behind forces stranded after the North Korean army had been expelled from the south in 1953, as well as numerous teams inserted by Pyongyang during the ensuing years of quasi-war conflict.

In the years since the war, the CIC also had been closely identified with two companion South Korean organizations, the ROK Army Security Command (ASC) and the ROK Central Intelligence Agency (KCIA). Both entities maintained a formidable presence throughout the South, and both conducted themselves with a confidence that sometimes bordered on arrogance. They were widely viewed by Koreans of every stripe as closely aligned with the CIC. There was also a longstanding relationship between the CIC and the Korean National Police (KNP), a tough public service organization that brooked no backtalk.

The perceived alliance between our CIC and the ASC, and to a lesser extent with the ROK's version of the CIA and the KNP, was deeply rooted in the events in the decade or so after the war. During that period—roughly the entirety of the 1950s and well into the '60s—combat with the North Korean agent teams was a routine occurrence, and strident and vigilant anticommunism was the order of the day. That was the case both in the northern portion of South Korea, where U.S. Army units were positioned just south of the DMZ to deter a repeat of the invasion of 1950; as well as in the southern provinces, where the CIC worked with the ASC and KCIA. Each provincial capital had an ASC and KCIA local office, and counterterrorism units were further deployed in areas where the North Koreans had been active in the past. All paid special attention to the landing sites along Korea's western coast that availed themselves to shipborne insertions of one- and two-man teams from the North.

In the southern provinces, essentially everywhere below Seoul, in addition to the ASC and KCIA counterparts, the CIC also worked with the KNP, mainly its counterespionage division. At the province, county and city levels, the KNP was tasked to monitor domestic political developments and investigate criminal activity. Its units directed particular vigilance against any resurgence of communist affiliations suggesting North Korean agent activity. The KNP was then more than a nationwide gendarme. They were respected—though often resented—as street-level enforcers of the peace. After all, it had been a KNP team that, the year before my arrival, stood their ground and defeated the Blue House raid mounted by the North Korean commando team.

As I prepared to close out my brief stay at battalion headquarters in Seoul, all that background understanding of what the 502nd—or rather the CIC—constituted was beginning to come together. I had not appreciated, back at Fort Holabird or at DLI, the political dynamics at work in the ROK, or the real sense of what was ongoing in that sustained, low-order conflict. In Korea, the potential for the return to war was continually real, and the reality permeated daily life.

Stonestown Bound—June 1969

On assignment day, the 502nd's executive officer called me to his office. He handed me orders that would take me to the Taejon Field Office of the battalion. The CIC team was located on a small post in the city, some 100 miles south of Seoul. The battalion XO explained that I would be joining a rather isolated small group of CI career officers and men there, led by one Robert Beamer, the team chief. The Taejon Field Office, or TFO, handled all U.S. military intelligence activity in the two middle provinces of the country, North and South Chung Chong, which together constituted about one-third the land area of South Korea.

The XO further explained that there was a lot of territory to cover from the TFO, supporting liaison relationships with the KCIA, ASC and KNP. The TFO also was responsible for security coverage of several small U.S. units scattered over a dozen west-facing mountaintops. The message he conveyed was the assignment presented a different intelligence world from that of Seoul or the American military positioned on the DMZ, and I should be prepared to adapt. He finished by asking me to turn in any military clothing and handing me $200 cash to "go out and buy three or four suits."

Last, the XO told me to my surprise that I was no longer 22 years old but 28. He add that, to the world outside the U.S. intelligence team, in my interactions with both American military and Korean counterparts, I was now a CIC civilian intelligence agent. I came to learn that age was all-important in Korea, and normally I could not interact on a near-peer footing with more senior Korean military officers and civilian security types unless I was at least 30. Even elevated to age 28, I would still be pushing it. The XO handed me new U.S. military identity cards showing my advance in age along with proof of my freshly minted GS-7 civilian status.

As I walked out the door, we had one final exchange.

"Have you read Heart of Darkness?" he asked. Before I could answer, he added, "I've been here in Korea for more than a year, but I have been down to visit the TFO in Stonestown just once. And once was enough."

"Sir, if you mean Joseph Conrad's Heart of Darkness, yes, I've read it. I think I understand what you're suggesting."

"You may not. Colonel Kurtz is already there in the TFO. He's waiting for you. Maybe you can be his Marlow. And it WILL be an interesting tour for you. Have some fun."

The Taejon Field Office

I boarded a train at the Seoul Main Railway Station, an impressive relic from the Japanese colonial presence, on a humid Saturday in late June for the three-hour ride south to Taejon. Back at home, NASA was preparing to launch the Apollo 11 mission to the Moon, and Senator Edward Kennedy had just driven off a bridge in Chappaquiddick, on the island of Martha's Vineyard, and left a young woman to drown in his car. The Apollo mission was to realize a national goal set by President John F. Kennedy in May 1961, when he promised that, within a decade, we would go to the Moon, perform a crewed landing there and return home. Apollos 8 and 10 had preceded Apollo 11 with flights to and around the Moon, testing various programs and procedures, and paving the way for the ultimate mission. Back in May, as we prepared to graduate from DLI, Apollo 10 had reached and orbited the moon to accomplish a full-scale dress rehearsal, even descending its Lunar Lander to within a few miles of the surface.

On July 20, as Apollo 11 astronauts Neil Armstrong and Buzz Aldrin walked on the lunar surface, I and thousands of Koreans in Taejon City were glued to publicly screened television broadcasts that left us speechless, in awe of America's technology and our nation's pioneering spirit. A few days later, when the Apollo 11 spacecraft splashed down in the Pacific Ocean, returning its crew safely, waiting at the landing site to recover the space travelers and their capsule was the USS *Hornet*. When the astronauts stepped out of the helicopter and walked across her flight deck, I recognized the exact spot from my U.S. Navy service on that proud ship four summers before. The old *Hornet* seemed a long way from my new post in Taejon. **[NOTE 2]**

When my train from Seoul arrived early afternoon at Taejon Station, not an American was in sight, either on the train or among the bustle of the crowd in the station proper. On that trip, I received my sink-or-swim introduction to the Korean language, and I quickly accepted that a reasonable command of Korean would be a necessity and not a luxury. After a wait on the station platform, I spotted my ride, approaching from across the fields, bouncing over the train tracks. A U.S. Army 3/4-ton vehicle jerked to a stop at the rear end of the train, its entire body shaking as the engine chugged dead. The truck was unmarked and somewhat beat up, so I assumed it was my TFO welcome committee.

A beefy blond man in a Hawaiian shirt slid out, flicked away a cigarette and approached. "Lawless, is it? I'm A. B. Hitt, the commo guy." I started to reply but got a, "Well, you really fucked up my Saturday. But it's okay." The gist of A.B.'s take during the ride to Stonestown was that the TFO needed some "new blood," Saturday afternoons were a drag and it was still too early for a beer, at least for him. And, anyway, "Beamer wants to see you right away."

In that summer of 1969, the tiny military facility of Stonestown was something of an Army encampment lost in time. Think not so much of the desert fort in *Beau Geste* but a nondescript mini-base ringed by a light blue stone wall enclosing a dozen or so Korean War-dated structures. Over the past decade or so, Stonestown had been degraded and downsized from its heyday when it hosted a larger U.S. military operation. Nestled in the southwestern corner of this bustling city of about 200,000, our little post at Stonestown was out of place, out of time and off the grid. In fact, you could not even find Stonestown on most maps of U.S. facilities in Korea.

Our military had established a large training team at Stonestown soon after the Korean war to work with Korean Army and Air Force technical schools established by the U.S. Military Assistance Command in the area. As the Korean military developed the ability to train its own soldiers, the camp's mission had been mostly phased out by the late-1960s. The locally based U.S. training team was reduced to just four individuals: three Air Force officers and a single Army civilian. Our small CIC team in the TFO completed the presence there, in company with a U.S. Army signals unit. The latter supported the military backbone communications network running the length of the Korean Peninsula.

As A.B. and I rolled into Stonestown, the civilian gate guards either were sleeping it off or had drifted away somewhere for coffee. We headed straight to the Officers' Club. At midafternoon, we entered a small building that was dark as night inside; all curtains drawn tight. In the far corner, next to a row of slot machines, a green lamp hung low over a table. Four men engaged in a poker game that looked as if it had been running for hours. (In fact, as was the Saturday norm, the game had been in session since the previous evening).

I could barely make out a man positioned in the corner, his back to the wall, sitting hunched over the poker table contemplating his hand. An attentive lady, easily 30 years his junior, sat tight at his side. The obvious boss of the game, he looked up from his hand and waved me over to join him. Our TFO leader, Robert Beamer, sat before me. He was mustached, his face weatherbeaten to the point that I could not tell if he was 50 or 70. He motioned "Miss Kim" out of her chair and seated me next to him. Too close, I thought. Without turning away from his cards, he extended his formal welcome—no handshake, it was a 20-second, one-way conversation.

"Glad you joined us. (a long pause) I run this place. Get some lunch from the bar and grab a beer. I'm buying you your first beer, right here in the club. Then you're on your own. Have a great Sunday. (another long pause) See you Monday at oh-seven-hundred in my office. Don't be late."

I departed the club with A.B. to find my residence and meet the rest of the team—not an easy matter because three of the four of them lived off-compound, comfortably "shacked up," in the local vernacular, with their Korean girlfriends. The intros would have to wait until Monday morning, when I would meet Tom Carmody, a Rhode Island tough guy and our office manager, as well as my fellow TFO field agents. We also had Bernie, a Cornell bred-and-graduated intellectual from upstate New York; Jim, from a Midwest J-school; and Ken, origin unknown, our office lost soul. With the exception of Bernie, all were either Army CIC lifers or candidates for the same destiny. Beamer might not have been their idol, but he was their model. And all had extended their tour of duty in Taejon at least once.

Carmody was a Tae Kwon Do black belt, polishing his snap-kick form with daily routines in the local *dojo*. He ran the office administratively with one hand tied behind his back. Think of Radar O'Reilly of "M*A*S*H" fame on speed: intense, hardwired, a serious drinker, always ready for a fight but usually not looking for one. A.B., our communications technician, was a kindhearted bear of a man, deeply in love with his girlfriend of two years. His dilemma was to marry or not, and if so, how best to bring her home with him. His solution? He was planning to get married right there in Taejon and stay at the TFO as long as possible.

We would be joined shortly by the oddest and least-adapted member of our small group, an Army Lieutenant fresh from Fort Holabird. Tom, the lawyer, really did not want to be in Taejon and might not have wanted to be in the U.S. Army. He was a Boston boy who had not really grown up, admitting to us over an initial beer in the Officers' Club that his first night away from home had been his virgin day in Baltimore at the Holabird intel school. Incredibly naïve, he was soon dubbed "Skippy" by the lifers, and he would serve with us well short of a full tour. He was technically Beamer's second in command, or the TFO Executive Officer.

It turned out that Beamer had served in combat in both World War II—the "Big Deuce" to him—and Korea, apparently with distinction. He was by any measure a true military intel lifer. The Taejon office was his fiefdom, and he ruled it as a mini-kingdom, both operationally during the day and in the off hours at the Officers' Club. At the latter, he was the de facto imperial potentiate of the camp, presiding there from dusk forward. His ladyfriend owned half the property near the post and might have been the best-known coffee-house proprietor in the city. Beamer was her man, and though he was usually irritable with others, he was always pleased to have her at his beck and call.

Low-Visibility Stonestown

Stonestown was the base camp and headquarters for the U.S. Army's STRAT-COM Long-Lines Battalion South, servicing the VHF/microwave communications network that supported the American military presence in Korea. A major facility on a nearby mountaintop, Site Richmond, also caused Stonestown to be referenced as the Richmond Relay Base Camp by those in the Army signals community. Although it comprised mostly aging Quonset huts and temporary structures, the base included a hilltop collection of half-a-dozen large homes that had been constructed for the more senior military who occupied the base in its halcyon days.

The base's permanent party comprised, all told, roughly 40 officers and men, our TFO CIC team included, with about 100 local employees providing a career cadre of support and technical types. Although the post at Stonestown was technically a U.S. Eighth Army installation, to this day it continues to maintain a low-to-nonexistent profile. Some 50 years after my assignment there, Wikipedia's list of "Current and former U.S. Army installations in South Korea" fails to mention Stonestown.

At the time of my service there, I assumed Stonestown was intentionally left off most Army and public maps because of its association or proximity to a highly sensitive nearby base, Camp Ames. I have since concluded that our facility was simply too marginal to mention, and the Army's attitude was something along the lines of, "If you need to get there, you will somehow be able to find it."

The TFO, by dint of its extended presence at the base, had acquired ownership of several residences, with the result that each of the six agents assigned to the field office enjoyed his own room—with room to spare. Our TFO leader and his deputy each had his own residence, and our office space was more than adequate. In a sense, the TFO crew was living large in that compound. Our Officers' Club boasted nine members, a great bar and grill and three massive slot machines lined up for business in the center of the room. The slots were kept busy by local employees and Korean businessmen, and ladies deemed by the O Club to be trusted associates who enjoyed base privileges. The one-armed bandits were set at a high payout rate and were busy at all hours of the day. If the club was open, the quarters were dropping, and slots were humming. A cadre of replacement players huddled, drinks in hand nearby, ready to glide into place when a visitor had exhausted his or her nightly spend.

The revenues from the three slots not only supported the O Club but also underwrote the operations of four smaller clubs at the mountaintop radar and missile-defense facilities located in our area of responsibility. The latter could not support themselves and were not allowed to host outside visitors. In that regard, the tiny Stonestown O Club paid its own way and supported the operation of its remote counterparts. As a consequence, we TFO CIC agents were always welcome guests when we had business at the isolated hill sites occupied by our Hawk and Nike Hercules antiaircraft missile friends.

In our small Stonestown community, the CIC team—that is, our TFO—had long been a core presence, in part because so many members elected to extend their stay in Korea over multiple tours. Most of them had not only decided to make military intelligence a career but also sought to remain in Taejon as long as possible. Often, a lady or multiple ladies were involved in the personal decisions to remain at the TFO, and marriages were commonplace.

Irrespective of personal relationship considerations, the TFO was a comfortable assignment, and the city and its people were seemingly pleased to have Stonestown nestled quietly in their midst. Our team's extended tours contrasted with most of our military serving in Korea, which typically involved one-year unaccompanied (by family) tours. Most military personnel simply sought to do their year of duty there and depart for a better posting, either back home or in Europe.

Assignment: North Chung Chong Province

So began my year as a member of the Taejon CIC. Beamer assigned me responsibility for the entire province of North Chung Chong, in part because the province was landlocked and therefore no coastline had to be protected against North Korean shipborne intruders. The remaining three CIC field agents would cover the sister providence of South Chung Chong, of which Taejon was the capital city. In that province, they would work from Stonestown to interact with KCIA, ASC and KNP officers in Taejon and in the coastal towns to the west.

In North Chung Chong, with the run of the entire province and no other U.S. units of any variety in the area, I quickly established relationships with my counterparts from the three ROK intel organizations. On a weekly if not daily basis, I spent more time with the ASC and KNP peers than the KCIA officers. In part, it was because the KCIA was then heavily focused on domestic politics, exercising a heavy hand with the local populace, the mass media and the politicians. The KCIA was President Pak's main instrument of domestic political control. As an organization, it was dedicated to dominating—and reshaping as necessary—local politics and the media while coercively mitigating any random political thoughts. The KCIA's overriding objective was to ensure that Pak's rule was not challenged.

My local TFO employee, or agent assistant, usually accompanied me on my weekly field trips into my assigned province. He was on hand to arrange meetings, to help me with translations when I was at a loss—as was too often the case—and generally to keep me out of trouble. Mr. Yo Han-ku became a best friend and confidant. The fact that I somehow got through my year at the TFO, and my near-constant time out in North Chung Chong, mostly unscathed was due in no small part to Mr. Yo. We traveled the main and back roads of the province in a small staff car or civilian jeep and overnighted in traditional open-bay hotels or *ryo-guans*. I adapted to sleeping on straw-mat floors with a mosquito net draped over me and adjusted my diet, which featured *kimchee* three meals a day.

In our routine, we managed to spend time with local businessmen and industry owners, attempting to judge the political and economic progress at the county and township levels. Mr. Yo was a great teacher of all things Korean, big and small, and he worked hard with me to improve my Korean language. I jammed my notebooks with trivia, history and some culture.

Important to his background, Mr. Yo had grown up during the Japanese colonial occupation of Korea. He imparted a strong sense of the humiliation and frustrations he experienced from that unique relationship, a complex formula of mutual bitterness, suspicion and borderline hostility that endures to this day.

At the Taejon CIC Field office, my counterintelligence command responsibilities fell into three discreet categories; two exclusively related to Chung Chong Province with the third having a broader context.

First, most of my time was devoted to straightforward liaison with the three mentioned South Korean intel organizations, spending four days a week in the provincial capital Chungju City. I would meet during the day with various officers to review their ongoing operations and arrange any assistance we at the CIC level could provide. At night—every night without exception—I met with one of the groups for an extended dinner and drinking session that invariably ran well past midnight. The ASC officers were absolutely the hardest drinkers, preferring rotgut whiskey and the locally distilled liquor *soju* to beer, better to get drunk as soon as possible to best enjoy the evening.

On a good night in a Chungju second-class eatery or hostess club, the ASC officers would mix their *soju* with beer, at a one-to-three ratio, to create a cold brew dubbed *so-meck* and down the concoction in one gulp. They were quick to pass the glass or switch their attack to drop shots of the crude White Horse Special whisky into tall beakers of cold beer. The latter drink was appropriately designated "the Korean nuclear depth charge." Somehow, at nine the next morning, they were always waiting for me with a smile, seated at their desks, ready to engage over coffee and talk the North Korean provocations of the day.

Second, as we interacted with the South Korean intel organizations, we conducted discreet unilateral intelligence collection operations to report on government actions geared to influence the political process in the ROK. At that early stage in Korea's political development, true representative democracy based on free and fair elections was an aspirational goal but far from any reality. In 1960, the 12-year, ostensibly democratic administration of President Syngman Rhee had ended in an agony of mismanagement and corruption, when the clique around the aging Rhee attempted to manipulate the political process to extend its rule. The revolt that ejected Rhee and his cronies occasioned a period of national uncertainty, dysfunction and drift. A semblance of order, direction and control was restored only by the military coup led by President Pak in 1961.

When my service in Korea began, Pak had been in power for eight years, some of them politically tenuous on the domestic front. During my tenure, Pak's overriding goal, beyond preserving national security, was implementing an ambitious national economic development program. He was determined to move Korea from a relatively poor, mainly agrarian country hugely dependent on U.S. foreign aid into the ranks of a true middle power. He built his economic development strategy around an export economy, evolving from light industry to medium and heavy industry as its centerpiece.

Pak's economic planning team crafted a series of five-year plans that embraced all elements of industrial production, from integrated steel mills to state-of-the-art petrochemical facilities, automobile production, electricity generation and a viable defense industry. Pak managed that dynamic process with a passion for detail. He often handpicked the leadership of each critical company, with many in leadership lifted from the ranks of his military contemporaries. His strategy was near-genius, and it worked for the nation.

Toward that end, Pak maneuvered to maintain absolute political power. Yet he had allowed, at least for a time after his coup, a measure of democratic process. His approach was a function of Korea's evolving political consciousness and steady pressure from its lead foreign benefactor, the United States. Pak tolerated some political dissent, but only to a level that permitted him to claim he was a democratically elected chief executive. He rose to power via heavily managed elections in 1963 and again in 1967, and by 1970 he was teeing up for another run at the presidency. A few months after my departure from the TFO, Pak won that 1971 election, but only narrowly. He then shifted gears in 1972 to abolish direct elections, installing a new governance construct that would allow him to rule unchallenged until his death—by assassination in 1979.

Back in the countryside and cities of Korea, where I functioned in my CIC role, the KCIA, KNP and even the ASC assisted in the process of domestic political control and direction. In Korea, as the ally committed to that nation's defense, CIC was tasked by its leadership in Seoul, and in Washington, to track political developments, all to predict the stability and sustainability of the Pak regime. We did it with a stream of clandestinely sourced reporting that detailed the control and influence mechanisms the Pak government brought to bear. Our reporting attempted to judge, at the local level, the degree to which Pak's program was succeeding. By any yardstick, and to the extent our limited reporting contributed to a broader understanding, it appeared that Pak and his team had things well in hand.

Third, our TFO activities involved support to the U.S. military units scattered throughout the two-province area, for which our small detachment was responsible. Several of them were missile-defense and radar units positioned on the west coast, there best oriented to detect and defend against incoming air threats—be they from North Korea, China or the Soviet Union. The missile units were either Hawk or Nike Hercules surface-to-air batteries █████████ ████████████████████████ as conventional. Because of their critical mission, the American camps needed to be highly secure facilities. But they were also deemed vulnerable to commando-style land attack given their isolated locations.

North Korean agent teams regularly penetrated the western coastal areas, typically to establish networks further inland and infiltrate the larger cities. With incursions such as the Blue House raid of 1968, larger commando teams were always a threat, and it was apparent the North Koreans saw real vulnerabilities on the west coast. And our air-defense missile and radar sites presented themselves as prime targets, exposed and isolated as they were. I was always surprised that none had been attacked.

We ran regular security inspections on the air-defense units, supplemented by irregular security challenges to determine if they were maintaining required physical security procedures. In the challenge inspections, we would attempt to maneuver our way onto a facility, typically by misrepresenting our identity, bluffing our way through the front gate or using a ruse to avoid detection. Almost all of those penetration-and-compromise exercises failed, due either to the alertness of the gate defenders or simply ineptitude on our part.

I was not routinely involved in any of the efforts and was pleased not to be assigned to execute them. Our second-in-command, Lieutenant Skippy, delighted in his roleplaying for the operations and frequently donned the garb of a missionary priest in making his attempted penetrations of the bases, mainly by bluffing his way through the main-gate guards. The positive aspect was that within the TFO they presented a distraction for Skippy and kept him away from the real CIC business at hand. In fairness, however, the CI ops, as we called them, were necessary, and they kept the gate guards and physical security operators on their toes. I do not know if those guards ever shot a priest trying to talk his way onto a protected missile base, but if they did, the Skippy operation was the reason.

Best of Friends—The Army Security Command

As I describe in more detail elsewhere, the ASC was in many ways the political elite of the ROK Army, and as such it enjoyed a special relationship with the military leadership. Throughout its ranks, the ASC, or the Po-An-Sa-Ryung Bu in Korean, gave its total loyalty to the president, to the degree that the ASC was widely perceived to be a Pak-controlled counterweight to the domestic power exercised by the KCIA. After all, the ASC was a vital organ of the ROK Army, the

ASC leadership was one with Pak, and Pak was first and foremost a creature of that military.

On another level entirely, the ASC provided Pak with a direct view into the dynamics of the Korean military and served as his watchdog over that organization. As a result, the ASC was often more focused on internal Army politics, personalities and factions than on the North Korean threat. Pak selected his ASC commanders carefully, kept them close and demanded and received pledges of personal loyalty.

Pak also expected ASC leadership to ferret out any dissidents or malcontents within all three of the services, with the goal of identifying any disgruntled or overly ambitious officer who could pose a threat to his regime. Once identified by the ASC, a challenged officer would be denied advancement, redirected away from his next command or forced out of service. The ASC had the mandate to provide that control capability over the rank-and-file military and routinely did so. In sum, the ASC was a quiet and effective instrument of oversight and intimidation, and it worked efficiently to keep the peace within the ROK military.

Those men, then, would be my associates and friends for the next 13 months of my life. The ASC thought of themselves as my first point of responsibility and interaction. They extended themselves to me, from the level of the unit commander to the lowest private, and we bonded firmly. The KCIA types were somewhat aloof and sometimes difficult to work with. They recognized me as too close to their rival organization, the ASC. The KCIA types knew we were working with our own local agents to collect information on regime stability. But they were fine with our level of contact, probably because the KCIA had compromised all of them. The KNP counterintelligence division group also was great, in part because my CIC predecessors had ignored them by not seeking them out. The KNP folks were always my first and last points of call when I visited Chungju City, and they were the first to call me when an incident arose in the province. All great people.

███████████████████████████

Some useful background information is in order about America's nuclear deterrent posture in South Korea in the 1970s; how it came about and why that ███████████████████ was sustained over so many years on the peninsula. In truth, the U.S. military had long regarded South Korea as a potential destination for nuclear weapons. In the first months of the Korean War, the Defense Department had urged President Harry S. Truman to consider scenarios for using nuclear weapons against the communist forces fighting UN troops. In response, Truman approved their forward deployment. The catalyst for the request, by the combat commanders in Korea, involved a deepening concern that Chinese and Soviet forces, located across the Yalu River in Manchuria, would soon expand their presence. Likewise, the build-up of enemy MiG-15 jet fighters seeking to dominate the air over the combat area was a real concern. Consequently, the administration considered a nuclear strike to destroy those airfields. **[NOTE 1]**

The White House authorized the transfer of ██████████████████ ████████████████████████ to Guam, marking the first time since the twin bombings of Japan in August 1945, that nuclear weapons were positioned outside the continental United States. ████████████████ was a five-ton beast, with a variable nuclear yield ███████████████████████████████████████ was a first-generation weapon, an improved version of the Fat Man device that took out Nagasaki. It was ████████████████████████████████████ ████████████████████████████████ mated for airborne delivery to the B-29 Super Fortress—the same type of aircraft that had bombed Hiroshima. Tactical planning suggested that, to vaporize the Chinese and Soviet airfields in Manchuria, ████████████ aircraft would have to be launched from ███████████ █████████████████████████████████████Okinawa.

In the aftermath of the Korean War, America's decision ████████████ ██ ███████████████████████████ was not taken lightly. Rather it became the subject of debate at the highest levels of the Eisenhower administration, a debate that pitted officials within the Department of State against one another, and State's senior managers against the Department of Defense. The context of that decision, taken in 1957 after months of discussion, involved a general inclination by U.S. national security leadership to deploy tactical nuclear weapons broadly. It included extensive deployments in Europe in support of NATO, typically as a hedge to bolster conventional forces considered to be overmatched by the Soviets.

The same time such tactical deployments became the norm for U.S. ground forces, America's strategic nuclear component, under control of the Strategic Air

Command and optimized to wreak atomic destruction on the Soviet Union and its Warsaw Pact allies, also was forward-positioned in many of those same allied countries. ██

██

██ The U.S. forces in the ROK were present under UN Command authority, and that presence was governed—or at least informed—by the terms of the July 1953 Armistice Agreement that halted the Korean War. The agreement stipulated that neither side would introduce new weapons into Korea, other than "piece-for-piece" replacement of systems already on the ground at the time of the Armistice. As in all agreements undertaken by the North Koreans and their Soviet and Chinese sponsors, Pyongyang began expanding its forces even before the ink was dry on the Armistice.

By 1957, the U.S. government faced a dilemma. In a budget-constrained environment, where the Department of Defense was faced with reducing expenditures for its conventional forces, our conventional position in the ROK was fast eroding, and our deterrence was judged to be inadequate to the mission. The military balance on the peninsula was negative and trending badly, suggesting that by 1960, the North Koreans might well consider reprising their June 1950 invasion of the South. ███

██
██
██
██
██
██
██

███████████████████████████ [NOTE 2]

██
██
██
██
██
██
██
██
██

████████████████████████████ Curious, but at that time in the Cold War, the United States often sought the advice of its allies and was constrained in its decision-making by concerns about reactions from other nations in Asia, not to mention a presumed negative reaction in the United Nations.

██
██

Of much greater relevance, however, was the concern that, in introducing those weapons systems into the U.S. arsenal in the ROK, we would face a demand by the ROK government to similarly equip South Korean forces. One document, an internal State memo in May 1957, ████████████████████████████████ ██ cautioned that America could expect a "serious political problem" with the ROK. The memo opined that providing such weapons to U.S. forces "would almost certainly lead to continued and stronger demands by President Syngman Rhee, and the ROK government and military, to equip ROK forces with weapons ████████████████████ ██████████.

Interesting, but the State memo also suggested that such an option—to equip "token" Korean units ████████████████████████████████ ████████—already had been studied in a policy paper. After all these years, that paper has yet to surface, but the fact that such options even were considered, if only by U.S. military planners, reflected growing concern over ROK sensitivities and the intimidating influence of President Rhee. Such determination on his part to possess, if only in a shared relationship, a nuclear capability at that early stage in the alliance might have presaged a later development (to be discussed in Chapter 11) reflecting Rhee's continuing ambitions.

One apparent concern on the American side was, if we explained how the introduction of ████████████████████████████████████ would enable us to reduce our own, as well as the ROK's, conventional strength, it was likely the ever-irascible president Rhee would insist that his forces be equipped with the same ██████████████ capability. At the time, U.S. Army leadership was being pressed by Pentagon leadership—there were budgetary pressures across the U.S. government—to reduce both our troop presence in South Korea as well as our underwriting of ROK divisions.

Complicated issues all, and many factors played into the debate, including the existence of the UN Command, the North–South Armistice Agreement and the ongoing standoff of the forward-deployed conventional forces on both sides of the DMZ. ███

Camp Ames and ██████████

The CIC's Taejon Field Office—where I experienced considerable interaction—also commanded Camp Ames, one of our most critical military installations on the peninsula. Ames was tucked away deep in a mountain valley just 20 miles north of Taejon City ██
██
██
██
██
████████

U.S. nuclear-capable artillery, short-range rockets and landmine systems with nuclear cores were assigned to support our forces as well as ROK units at the DMZ. As mentioned, ████████████████████████████ were a central component of the U.S. military presence in Korea, particularly given the numeric superiority of the North Korean army. More menacing, Pyongyang's troops were forward-positioned at the DMZ in an attack-tomorrow profile, and the unpredictable nature of its leadership suggested we would have little advance warning if an all-out attack began. Our nuclear deterrent served a second, no less important, function. It reassured ROK leadership and the nation's body politic that the United States was a capable and dependable ally. ██████████
██
██
██
██
██
████████████████████
██
██
██
██
██
██
██
██
██
██
██
██
██

The camp was situated in an isolated mountain valley near the village of Chang Dong Ri, a hamlet of 30 or so homes, small businesses and bars. The community hosted a diverse collection of camp-following personages, all dependent on the facility for livelihood. ████████████████████████████████

██

██

██

██

██

██████████████ existed the larger camp itself with sustaining support facilities, including barracks, mess halls, motor pools and the headquarters building.

Ames could be reached by air, typically with CH-47 Chinook heavy-lift helicopters ███ into and out of the facility, or alternatively by a twisting, single-lane road. In the latter case, heavily guarded Army truck convoys would find their way off the main north-south highway to wind into the countryside, track a narrow road that ran across the rice patties, and then climb the steep hills that led into and protected the installation.

An interesting incident occurred in the late 1960s when an Army truck, apparently separated from its military escort, showed up at the front gate of Stonestown at three in the morning to ask for directions to Ames. At the gate, the two confused and tired drivers were at a loss to explain where their escort had disappeared, noting that they had been part of a 10-truck convoy ████████████ ███ ██████████████████████.

The driver thought somewhere along the way they had taken a wrong turn and, since no one had found them, offered that they and their ███████████ cargo might not even have been missed. The Stonestown MPs made arrangements to bed down the truck, with its tarp-covered ███████████ under guard until the next day. At first light, the Ames folks arrived from the mountain to collect the missing vehicle ████████████████████████. No one the wiser, there had been no "incident" to report to higher authorities.

We were able, informally, to confirm later that ███████████ on the truck did not contain its ██ ████████ and already had arrived safely and resided ███████████ ██████████████████████████. Thus, the "Taejon ███████████ incident" as we called it, would not have technically presented a genuine ███████████ ████████ misstep. That said, it seems someone might have learned a lesson there, maybe along the lines of, "I have an idea; let's stop the convoy and count the trucks every hour or so … just to make sure we don't lose ███████████."

Perimeter Security and a Demoralized U.S. Army

A U.S. Army infantry company, typically based at Ames on a rotational assignment from its parent Seventh Division up on the DMZ, was assigned to guard the outer perimeter of the camp. That outer perimeter was defined by high barriers, minefields, watchtowers and guard posts, all knitted together to provide the first line of defense against North Korean commando attacks. Reasonable planning assumed Ames ███████████████████████████████████ would be a priority target in any North Korean contingency, whether a single-strike attack or a dedicated and sustained assault in the case of all-out war.

But the U.S. Army of 1969—at least as it was able to deploy itself forward in East Asia—was hurting. America's strategic drift and our pending withdrawal from Vietnam were now facts. President Nixon's 1968 campaign pronouncement, in which he claimed that, if elected, he had a plan to end the war, governed our strategy. His commitment to exit Vietnam and forgo victory—implying that the South Vietnamese would be left to their fate—was followed by his April 1969 hyped announcement to begin delivering on his promise immediately. He did so by reducing our Vietnam troops by 150,000. It was a clear signal that "ending the war" would probably mean we would be settling for something less than a win, if not eventual defeat. Many in Korea, as elsewhere, correctly perceived the Nixon–Kissinger program to "Vietnamese" the war, as we drew our troops down, was nothing more than a disguised and calculated process to abandon the South to the communist North.

Among many U.S. units on the ground and in the fight in Vietnam, morale was bad and trending worse. Nobody wanted to be last to die in a war our leadership had decided to lose. Widespread drug use became a curse among units deployed in-country in 'Nam, a curse that destroyed cohesion and promoted racial conflict. Added to that internal disconcert was the impatience by an increasingly hostile U.S. public, abetted by a mass media that had concluded the war was not being won and was unwinnable. All of it was shaped and emphasized by violent protests led by antiwar activists. In that environment of national-level leadership drift and indecision, it was not unreasonable that the average troop in the field, particularly if he was a draftee, could wonder what he was doing knee-deep in a marsh in Vietnam, waiting for the next onslaught of North Vietnamese regulars.

As a result, unit-level discipline within the Army grew loose, and insubordination was rampant. In our disorganized drawdown from Vietnam, some Army units were unavoidably rotated out before completing a full 13-month tour. Likewise, individual soldiers were serving there who had not completed their full overseas assignment and had months, or years, before completing their active-duty service. South Korea became a destination for some of those units and soldiers, and our Army in South Korea found itself much the worse for it.

U.S. Army leadership in the ROK attempted to cope with the Vietnam-castoffs situation. But the problem was simply too complex and worsened with time. Our combat units at the DMZ, where any massed North Korean attack would strike first, were an obvious priority and received the best of the new arrivals in-country. But even in those forward areas, many units were demoralized, depleted and dysfunctional.

In late 1969, about six months into my tour with the TFO, the problem hit Camp Ames in spades. Prescription drugs (mostly "uppers") were widely available in the Korean economy. Likewise chemicals that allowed soldiers who had become addicted in Vietnam to concoct their own injectables anew. It all created an environment in which men used drugs indiscriminately, often overdosed and too often died. Stoned troopers fell from guard towers or drove trucks off mountain roads, killing or injuring themselves or fellow GI's. With discipline relaxed, drugs and liquor combined to cause hallucinations and erratic behavior.

At Ames, at the midpoint of my tour in Taejon, a young and overdosed infantryman, armed with his M-16 rifle, dragged his girlfriend through the camp's front gate and took over the infirmary. With the young lady at gunpoint, the wide-eyed soldier demanded an X-ray to confirm that she had, as she claimed, swallowed a 20-dollar bill and not spent it. On that occasion, the camp got lucky and no one was injured, but the luck did not last. The trembling X-ray technician attempted to reason with the soldier, explaining that the image probably would not show the chewed-up bill in her stomach.

After several hours, with no shots fired, the matter was resolved by allowing the X-ray to proceed, with the technician fabricating a shadow on the developed film. A feigned careful assessment of the image showed, sure enough, there was the missing bill. Satisfied, the soldier decided he would not have to shoot his girlfriend after all (the X-ray had proven her loyalty), nor anyone else, and he gave up his weapon. He was shipped out to Seoul for processing and a quick trip home, his star-crossed relationship not fated to endure. In dealing with such situations, Ames leadership was not always so lucky.

In a related case, we discovered that an entire squad, having rotated down from duty on the DMZ, during its brief period of frontline deployment in the bunkered DMZ had injected into their veins a concoction that included melted peanut butter. From this, they had apparently suffered massive collective hallucinations of naked girls bathing in the DMZ proper. Consequently, they claimed to have entered the DMZ, wandering there among the minefields, to join the ladies bathing in the spring. In more ways than one, the young men were lucky to be alive. But even after interrogation and some counseling, they remained detached and self-destructive.

That group of disoriented and disaffected young GI's was sent back to the States for dishonorable discharge. I did not know if they simply had invented the entire episode to secure an early trip home, or they had actually done all they claimed. To a large degree, it did not matter. At Ames, such young men were liabilities and a threat to the camp's security. Elsewhere in Korea, they would be a burden to any other unit, particularly on the front lines. They had to go, and they went, laughing as they jumped onto the truck that took them, under guard, back to Seoul.

My saddest experience was an emergency call from the camp commander on an otherwise quiet Saturday afternoon. An emotionally distressed GI, high on pills, had snapped and barricaded himself in a camp building. Emotionally strung out, he threatened to use hand grenades to attack the camp's petrol oil and lubricant storage area. The POL facility sat uncomfortably close to a gate for the inner camp ██ ██████████████████████████—a dash distance from where the soldier had positioned himself.

Racing to Ames in a borrowed Jeep, I arrived and passed through the main gate shortly after the incident ended in tragedy. The man had charged from the building in a wild dash toward the POL area, grenade clasped in his hand with the pin pulled. A squad of six MPs barred the way. They were ordered to stop the man and did so. He went down, shot in the knee, and released the grenade that exploded near him. He died instantly.

One Ames MP told me that the infantry company there had more men killed and seriously injured in its first three months in Korea than the unit had lost during its last three months in Vietnam. I believed it. A week later, I participated in a meeting where we discussed solutions to the unraveling state of affairs. Some of the actions mulled were radical. One proposal was to replace the infantry company with a similar-sized perimeter security contingent made up of ROK Special Forces, thereby removing U.S. troops from maintaining the security of the camp's outer perimeter. The MP commander agreed, as did the camp commander—as did I, for what my opinion was worth in that politically charged discussion. In the end, a cleaned-up and well-disciplined U.S. unit was brought in to replace the hard-luck company. Most of the latter were rotated out of Korea, sent back to the States and quietly discharged.

██
████████████████████████████ at least from the standpoint of local threats. The MP unit that guarded the inner area was highly competent, and the most sensitive area was always secure. ████████████████████████████████
██

████ and support from U.S. forces elsewhere in Korea was always available. But my greatest concern was not an internal vulnerability or a compromise of the facility by its security force. Rather, Ames always seemed to me to be an incredibly vulnerable and attractive target for a North Korean commando attack.

One could easily envision a light-of-moon assault, with the camp overrun and occupied ██
████████████████. The North Korean special-attack units were an elite force, well-equipped with a fleet of Antonov An-2 aircraft for low-level approaches and assault-team delivery. It was impossible that Pyongyang did not know what was present at Ames, and how much damage a commando-style attack could have done there. In a full-war scenario, if the North Koreans mounted a frontal attack across the DMZ, we expected their special-operations forces to be out in front and in force, attacking a dozen high-value targets throughout the South. U.S.

and South Korean airfields and headquarters would be high on the hit list, but facilities such as Ames had to be at the very top.

We were fortunate we did not have that war, that Ames served its purpose and went away ███████████████████████████████████ ███████████████. Gone and almost forgotten. For all of us based at Stonestown, Ames was a world unto itself; isolated and remote despite the helicopters that shuttled in and out and the occasional resupply convoy of trucks accessing the facility. Camp Ames, and indeed the entire history ████████████████████ ████████████████████████████████, is a *story* unto itself, and that story remains to be told.

No Heart of Darkness

Back at Stonestown, Beamer continued to manage the day-to-day activity of our Taejon CIC Field Office. He crafted agent assignments, oversaw the report-writing and interacted by secure phone line with the 502nd headquarters in Seoul. No one from that higher authority bothered us at our outpost, nor did anyone "up at the flagpole" seem to care. As long as we completed our field-reporting assignments and maintained close liaison with our Korean counterparts, we were considered solid gold all the way up the line. And Special Agent Beamer was in charge.

The delivered wisdom at battalion headquarters in Seoul was that Beamer and the TFO were the 502nd's own "Heart of Darkness" post. But that allusion really was not valid. Beamer was not Conrad's demented and obsessed Colonel Kurtz, even as much as he might have wanted to style himself as such. And while "the Old Man" kept a tight hand on his office staff—namely, his orderly Carmody, the XO Lieutenant Skippy and A.B., the communicator—he let the rest of us run with our assignments.

Once Beamer and I found common ground, Beamer gave me a relaxed hand in North Chung Chong Province. As a result, I would be "out there" in the province and out of touch with the TFO for a week or more at a time. I was with my Korean intelligence counterparts almost constantly, and I enjoyed their camaraderie immensely.

During that one year-plus in Korea, I developed a deep respect for each of my Korean security associates, be they ASC or KNP or KCIA. With the familiarity came a reasonable appreciation—if only a lay understanding—of the Korean personality and character. As my tour came to a close, I declined an offer from the 502nd headquarters to extend my stay, as well as a companion offer to attend Officer Candidate School for a career in Army Intelligence. Instead, I was processed for a return home. I was discharged on July 4, 1970, and went back to school. I had some things to accomplish and some catching up to do.

Recruitment by the CIA

After returning from Korea, I completed my undergraduate year back in my hometown of Peoria at Bradley University's Institute for International Studies. I stayed three semesters and secured a B.S. in International Finance. The founder and dean of the school was a character of some note, a larger-than-life personality, Dr. Miklós Nyárádi. A member of the resistance who fought the Nazi occupation of his nation in World War II, he had been Free Hungary's first Minister of Finance when the country aspired to democracy in 1948. He soon fled when he realized the Soviet Union was not about to tolerate a "free and democratic Hungary." An energetic and enterprising man, "Nicky" as he was called by his friends, found his way to New York City and later was invited to found an international studies program at Bradley.

I mention Dr. Nyárádi because he took a strong interest in me when I entered his school. It later became obvious he was acting as the channel through which the Agency found me and inducted me into its ranks.

One afternoon as graduation approached, Dr. Nyárádi pulled me aside in class and asked if I could join him for dinner that evening. He had "an old friend visiting from Washington" whom he would like me to meet. The old friend was a senior Agency clandestine service case officer who was capping his career as a scout and recruiter for its career-training program. I later discovered that this gentleman—I will refer to him as Mr. Johnson—was a published historian and an expert on Japanese samurai regalia and weaponry. An established Asia hand, he was a near-perfect match to assess me as a potential recruit. It was no surprise that, given his own history, the good Dr. Nyárádi was a longtime Agency contact and spotter. He had dutifully placed me on their watchlist over a year before my introductory dinner. The Agency also had done its homework over that period. Now, a gentleman had "come knocking" to see what they might have in me.

Mr. Johnson's approach was mildly encouraging but not overdone. He wanted to know in detail about my military service, why I had failed to enroll in Annapolis, why I had walked away from the Navy ROTC program in my third year, and what I had done in Korea during my CIC assignment. He also probed my Korean language abilities and my willingness to serve my country.

Fairly standard, but he made me understand he was not offering employment. Rather, he was suggesting a possible career path—if I could cross a high bar. If I elected to apply, I should understand it would be for overseas service in the Directorate of Operations. I would be accepted as a clandestine services trainee, but if the Agency ever deemed me unsuited for a career in the DO, I either would have to accept an assignment in the Directorate of Intelligence, the analytical side of the Agency, or resign. Mr. Johnson noted that each year the Agency enrolled one or two CT classes, each with about 30 candidates, and of those no more than half would be accepted into the DO. He also emphasized that the selection process would be rigorous. Each year, 2,000-plus candidates applied, and some 200 would be down-selected for further testing and interviews in Washington. Only from that group would the Agency select a final CT class. Thus, I began the process with little certainty about the outcome.

As my Bradley graduation approached, with no word from the Agency, I assumed the radio silence was a bad omen, so I sought employment in the investment banking community. Then the Agency offered a ray of hope when they summoned me for five days of testing in March 1972. But those evaluations scorched me—multiple polygraphs overlaid with psychological evaluations, more testing and interviews. In a departure session I learned that I might be a candidate for the December CT class, or perhaps an opening the following year. In other words, the Agency was in no hurry, and I was considered no real catch. **[NOTE 1]**

Months of quiet followed the March message, so I accepted a position with a Chicago-based international bank, starting that summer. Meanwhile, as winter moved into spring, I worked—like my father did before World War II—as a steamfitter on a pipeline crew, welding sections of a new line running to a tank farm alongside the Illinois River. I needed to stay employed, having taken on the responsibility of a young family at that point. But I knew I had options after graduation, and I was inclined to wait out those options, hoping for the best but not really sure what the "best" might be. Frankly, I lost track of the Agency possibility, though I was eager to leave the pipeline work behind me—notwithstanding the great salary the 6/10 schedule provided me (six days a week, 10 hours a day, double-time pay for all hours worked over 40 a week).

Then, in late May, when I returned to Peoria after a trip to Chicago to complete my investment-banking employment paperwork, I found a Western Union telegram stuck sideways in my front door. It basically said, "You are to report to Washington, D.C., to begin your in-processing for your GS-7 position as an area analyst for the Central Intelligence Agency. Your employment will begin June 19, 1972." It seemed I was headed to Langley, Virginia, to join the incoming CT class. I scrambled to pack my worse-for-wear VW Beetle, drove 14 hours straight, and walked in the CIA doors on June 19th. As it happened, it was a great class, and the invitation to join it would provide me with a fine start to a 15-year Agency career.

The Career Trainee Class – June 1972

I was among 30-or-so new hires when we reported for duty as first-day CTs. I quickly realized that, at age 25, my friend Mike and I were the youngest in the class. Many were in their early 30s, and most were three-to-four years older than we were. Also, most had obtained advanced degrees, including a couple with Ph.Ds. A half-dozen were females, and it turned out we had several legacy CTs with us; that is, second-generation, would-be intelligence operatives. Some of the legacies might have assumed, at least at the outset, that they would be accorded special treatment. If so, they would be deeply disappointed.

Mike was a Vietnam veteran, serving there as a U.S. Army artillery forward observer. A first-generation Ukrainian–American, Mike spoke fluent Russian as well as Ukrainian. At the end of the first month, Mike and I compared pay slips and confirmed we were the lowest-paid in the class, both on-boarding as GS-7s Step 1, with an annual salary of $10,060. Our older, better-educated classmates were entering as GS-8s or GS-9s, or higher. But to us, compensation was not an issue. We were just happy to be there, at any wage level.

Our class featured a real cast of characters. Likewise, the "Farm class," with whom some of us would mix within a year. On the one hand, we had Peace Corps veterans who brought great area knowledge and language skills. On the other, we had hard-core—by their own definition—gung-ho Marines who had led platoons in Vietnam. The latter typically had no foreign language credentials or area knowledge, but they were super enthusiastic, a couple of whom spent their post-Vietnam tours delivering in-person notifications of death to spouses or parents. They were extreme examples of men we wanted in the Agency in the years ahead, perhaps in the Deputy Directorate of Operations in the field, but whom we knew in our hearts were too emotionally explosive to handle the craft. Eventually, our early readings became all too prescient.

Suffice it to say, the core CT group was destined to flow into the DO as clandestine service operations officers. The rest were destined for careers in the Directorate of Intelligence, the DI, the analytical side of the Agency. The group was impressive, having specialized in their education or field experiences in specific regions of the world or in selected technical disciplines. In addition to the DO case-officer candidates who spoke a variety of Asian languages, we had Turkish and Farsi linguists, fluent or native speakers of German and Soviet Bloc languages, plus Baltic states language-capable officers. Most were military veterans, and many had seen combat.

Our first few weeks involved an introduction to the Agency; basically a force-fed indoctrination featuring the normal in-processing, lectures by senior officers and security briefings. Among the lectures, the one I found most entertaining was a steely speech by a senior clandestine service officer. Before us stood a man with a reputation that proceeded him: Theodore "Ted" Shackley. He spoke to the class as if each and every one of us would be selected for the Operations Directorate when clearly some were not destined to end up there, and others had no desire even to claim that role. Shackley scared the living hell out of those who had any doubts about being a case officer. His rhetoric began with something like, "There are only three kinds of officers in today's DO: those who are in Vietnam, those who have served in Vietnam and are going back, and those of you who are all—make no doubt about it—headed there real soon!" I glanced around and saw a lot of my classmates swallowing hard. **[NOTE 2]**

Two Great Interim Assignments

My intro-to-the-Agency period was followed by the first of two, four-month-duration interim assignments. These mini-postings were a routine feature of the CT program, where all CTs were given a chance to work on a DO desk or branch. This first stint would be complemented by a subsequent dispatch to work in an analytical branch on the DI side of the house. I was extremely fortunate, drawing the Indonesia Branch as my DO assignment. The chief there was one of the most impressive middle-grade officers I would encounter in my entire career at the Agency.

Vince had been a U.S. Navy officer, had joined the DO through the CT program and had worked his first Agency tour in the hills of Laos. As a case officer assisting Laotian General Vang Pao and Pao's Montagnard tribesmen, Vince was among the handful of officers who advised and supported those troops as they fought to defend their own land. The mountain warriors tied down thousands of North Vietnamese troops that otherwise would have been fighting American and South Vietnamese soldiers in Vietnam. When I checked in to begin my assignment, Vince was managing the Indonesia Branch in preparation for his pending dispatch to Jakarta Station as the deputy chief there.

On the Indonesia desk, I was able to work on active cases, support the station and its branch units, review reporting and participate in operational planning sessions. Vince accorded me full access and encouraged me to invest as much time as possible in researching agent operations. I focused on the agents themselves, on the reports they provided, and on the tasking the station received for the case officers to pass along to their agents. I learned a lot and watched as Vince assembled a hand-picked team at Headquarters that he would send to Jakarta over the next two years.

Near the end of my assignment, Vince told me he had "bid" for me to be assigned to Jakarta the following year, after I had completed the operational program at our clandestine training facility, called the Farm. After a stint back on the desk, I would arrive in Jakarta in the summer of 1974. I accepted his proposal on the spot and expressed that it would be an honor to serve with him. I began studying Bahasa that same evening, an after-hours program I would continue for the next several months. Now, all I needed to do was complete my second interim assignment and be selected for the Farm training program by DO leadership—only CT officers selected for a DO career would be awarded that training. Once nominated, the goal would be not to mess up at the Farm or get thrown out for poor performance.

My follow-on interim assignment, in the DI, proved interesting and a real challenge, given that I essentially had "DO BOUND" stamped on my forehead. The fact that I did not aspire to become one of "them"—that is, a career DI analyst—gave me some leeway to roam within the division. That is, because no division of the directorate was interested in having a DO-bound CT officer working in an interim assignment, I could interview with several, and each judged me based on what they could extract from me during my four-month stay. In that situation, I had to sell myself to different components of the DI. I was most interested in the weapons side and found some traction there because I could talk their talk, at least up to a point.

Eventually, I was posted to the Office of Weapons Analysis, Asia Branch. Most of my effort there focused on Chinese military systems, particularly missile improvements and deployments, with a side interest in North Korean activities. My group comprised mostly "missilemen," individuals who had cut their teeth on Soviet weapons programs and were now tracking Chinese developments. Although I was an obvious outlier, the weapons folks did their best to accommodate me. They included me in their working groups and in the drafting of their research memos. In sum, they tolerated me as a temporary presence, but I found the experience fascinating.

I was tasked to research a particular weapons system and given two months, with near-total access to all-source intelligence, to draft a report. The subject was the Soviet ground-to-air data link—NATO code name MARKHAM—used by their air force in managing ground-controlled-intercept, or GCI, fighter missions. In this case, I would examine MARKHAM's use by North Korea's air force in the shootdown of the U.S. Navy EC-121 intelligence collection aircraft some four years before, on April 15, 1969. I was all too familiar with the shootdown, having been exposed to the event during my days at DLI and my subsequent tour in South Korea.

The mission, called BEGGAR SHADOW, had gone down in the Sea of Japan about 60 miles from the North Korean shore, well into international waters. The attack had killed the 31-member Navy and Marine aircrew. Several of the men had been in Korean or Russian language classes the cycle before mine at the Defense Language Institute. Coming fast on the heels of the USS *Pueblo* incident a year before, wherein the North Koreans sought out a U.S. military ship and staged an armed and deadly provocation, it was clear North Korea was willing to risk war to maintain its pressure on South Korea and the American military presence there.

The two North Korean provocations, plus a dozen more mounted on the ground in the South in the 1967-1970 period, prodded the United States toward a retaliatory strike. Those flagrant life-taking actions, particularly in the case of the EC-121—where the North Korean attack was so deliberate, the loss of life high and with no Americans held captive—induced detailed U.S. military planning for retaliation, either in kind or worse. In the case of the EC-121 incident, there had been strong consideration at the highest levels of our government for counteractions, including the option for a limited nuclear strike against North Korea. This was obviously serious stuff, and I was pleased to be able to examine the record of what had transpired before and after the MiG-21 Fishbed-F interceptors carrying out the attack had ranged out of Hoemun Airfield. The interception was managed via MARKHAM, and once the MiGs homed in on our aircraft, the ground controller instructed the North Korean pilots to blow the EC-121 out of the sky.

My research also examined three related issues. First, how the North Koreans employed MARKHAM to direct the two MiG-21s to the location of the EC-121 and command its shootdown. Second, how the North Koreans prepared for the incident; that is, how they staged the interception and what signals or indicators we had missed in the weeks and days before the shootdown. It was an assessment of the North Korean decision-making process as much as an operational understanding of their planning for the event. Third, whatever lessons could be learned, from an intelligence perspective, that hopefully could improve our ability to predict and plan for such orchestrated provocations in the future.

Unmentioned and not addressed in my research: As in the case of the USS *Pueblo*, as with the series of deadly commando attacks on the ground in South Korea, why did the United States consistently and predictably elected to not respond other than to shout protests of North Korean perfidy and turn the other cheek? The North Koreans learned their lesson well: Their deadly provocations worked, they commanded attention, and there was no retribution. Those of us who would be involved with the challenge of North Korea for the balance of our careers took note of this painful question. As a result, we expected to see more of the same from North Korea. We would not be pleasantly disappointed. [NOTE 3]

Lunch with Director Helms

An incident worth mentioning occurred during our roughly eight-month period of interim assignments: a CT lunch with Agency Director Richard Helms. It happened that one of our CTs, an exuberant self-promoter—code name Denny—encountered and cornered the good Director in the Agency gym one day. Denny introduced himself as the latest-edition CT phenom and, never doubting his own value, urged the Director to "reach out and bond" with the current CT class. Denny proposed a personal discussion, perhaps with the Director hosting our classmates over lunch. For whatever reason, Helms agreed, and Denny's proposal evolved into five separate lunches, each an intimate discussion with six of our colleagues. In the sessions, showing obvious pain and discomfort, Director Helms shared his appreciation of the world then solicited and listened to the concerns and goals exposed by the freshly minted CTs.

I drew the last session of the five and was placed in charge of that group. As such, I was responsible for herding the CTs as they engaged the Director and for writing a report for our CT mentors after the event. In short, the lunch was pointless, particularly for Helms, who struggled to maintain his good humor and patience as one trainee after another shared "impressions" of the Agency and its mission. I watched him endure the encounters, thinking he would probably feel more at ease in a dentist's chair enduring a root canal.

I felt embarrassed by the lack of common sense and self-control exhibited by my CT contemporaries, posturing and opining as if they actually had anything of value to communicate. My after-action memo reflected the uselessness of the one-hour, rope-a-dope experience, and I called the event for what it was: a waste of time. I recommended that it never be repeated. Denny, who was proud that he had organized the dreadful event, soon discovered my betrayal of his initiative. He declined to speak to me for three weeks, but that was itself a blessing. [NOTE 4]

Down on the Farm

In mid-spring, with interim assignments behind us, those who had secured sponsorship by the Operations Directorate moved on to the Farm training program. I recollect that about half, perhaps 14 or so in our class, had been nominated by the various divisions of the clandestine service to move on to the Farm. A nomination meant that, should a CT graduate from the Farm program, the individual would probably join his or her DO area division as a career employee.

At the Farm, our class group was mated to an equal number of career Agency officers, all DO field operations types. Recently returned from tours in Southeast Asia, these men were either being retrained or, more accurately, reprogrammed from paramilitary roles. Other Farm classmates were being promoted from a lower grade of clandestine service. They were junior-grade professionals who had proven their mettle in the field and been nominated by their parent area divisions to move up through the ranks. They were employees who had not entered through the CT program but who excelled in their service to date. I thought it was one of the most creative Agency—or, more properly, clandestine service—initiatives I experienced in my government tenure. It reflected the Agency's no-nonsense, merit-based approach.

This Farm class, in spring/summer 1973, was a remarkable combination of 30-odd characters and personalities, with three-tour paramilitary officers straight out of the hills of Laos and Vietnam spliced into the more elitist CT crowd. For those among us who had military service, albeit well short of the layers of combat experience possessed by our paramilitary classmates, it was an easy mix, and the bonding went (mostly) well. For other CTs, the rougher edges of the field officers being reprogrammed to be case officers presented a challenge. But within a month or so it mostly sorted itself out.

Getting down to business on the Farm, we entered on the first day a make-believe never-world of a country that did not exist, encountering residents of a fictional city. We would remain embedded in the made-up metropolis throughout the training program, a situation that allowed the Farm staff to manipulate and challenge each trainee, all to sort out the intelligence-officer wheat from the chaff. The problems were relentless, throwing a wild variety of situations at each individual, each event crafted to jam up the trainees, forcing them to succeed or fail. In the latter case, when failure repeated itself, the staff did all they could to encourage the man or woman to leave the program.

We had our share of resignations and failures; trainees who did not realize or could not accept they were judged unacceptable by the DO. There were a few surprises in the success and failure categories, but most individuals played out as expected. We lost most of the big-talkers, individuals who did not know when to shut up and listen, and we kept as winners those who learned how to elicit information successfully from the role-playing instructors, who were eager to comply if properly engaged. But the Farm trainees had to "earn it" every time, and our trainers cooperated only if a trainee had established the right level of dialog and trust.

My final test at the Farm involved capacity for leadership. Our capstone exercise, which took place over a week in a city far from the Farm, involved me and five other classmates. Our instructors had already designated two of them as dysfunctional, if not downright dangerous. But they had to be tolerated and managed through the end of the program to mitigate damage, given their abilities and assumed longer-term value to the Agency. Two other team members were exceptional as intuitive operators, and the fifth was a loner—think Steve Canyon, Aeroplane Commander, who nevertheless served some utility. The first two were considered lost in space and should have never been allowed anywhere near the Farm.

Our team was a mix of gender and ages, with some serious hormonal aspects running unchecked as well. All of it had to be handled, both within the group and accommodating any random outsider drifting into play. The going-in assumption, by the all-knowing Farm management group, was that this combination of personalities would self-destruct on the operational front. It was particularly relevant because one of my teammates had managed to establish special personal relationships with not one but two of the instructors, both of whom would interact with us over a week-plus period in the remote location. We all knew this complication existed. Nevertheless, it would not buy any of us special consideration as we worked the intel-collection problem we were tasked to master.

In the final remote-location exercise, our Farm managers, who had organized our mission and intel problem, decided with indiscernible logic to insert my team into the middle of a retirement colony. Here, wheelchairs and walkers prevailed, and the streets rolled themselves up at 9 p.m. The environment was predictably hostile, with watchers everywhere. Our every move was scanned by a dozen retirees who called one another to report our movements. We imagined ourselves operating in a suburb of Moscow or Berlin. We did survive, however, almost unscathed, and got the job done. But by the time we wrapped it up, I had not slept for a week. In the post-mortem assessment back at the training facility, our mentors pronounced mine as one of the best-performing teams, "in spite of what we gave you to work with." They smiled as they said this.

A Proposal from Donald Gregg

My big break came in the final weeks of the course when a senior officer from Headquarters who addressed our class pulled me aside with a proposition. His name was Donald Gregg, and he would have the single greatest influence on my Agency career—and on much of my life. Don was an experienced field officer, part of an acknowledged elite group destined to lead the clandestine service and Agency over the next two decades. He had been nominated for posting to Seoul as the Chief of Station but had come to the Farm to speak about the leadership and challenges facing the DO in the aftermath of the Vietnam War.

Like all of his peers, Don had diverted from his operational career path—in his case, Northeast Asia—to serve one or more tours in Vietnam. But he realized that Vietnam would be behind us at some point, either as a lost cause or a half-victory. Post-Vietnam, our focus would have to return to the more traditional intelligence challenges we would face in other nations, in Asia and elsewhere in the world. We needed to prepare for this redirection.

Don approached me after his presentation, and we sat at a back table in the Farm bar. He was direct, proposing something he did not expect me to decline and asking for an answer within a week. "As you know," he told me, "I am headed to Seoul as the new COS there, and I have a position for you. I need you there tomorrow, but I am prepared to wait until January—that's five months from now. But you need to decide immediately so I can get this done." Although a slot or designated position for me did not exist at that point, Gregg promised to borrow one from another station in the division. He again pressed me to decide quickly.

His offer surprised me, and I explained that I had already accepted an offer to go back to the Indonesian desk after the Farm, expecting to go to Jakarta sometime the following year. Don waved that aside, noting he had already pulled rank on my patron Vince and had obtained all the approvals required with the East Asia Division to lay a "first claim" on me. He noted that if I accepted his offer, I would be in the field in an operational role at least a full year ahead of my CT classmates.

I thought about it for no more than three minutes and told Don I was all in. From there, it was back to East Asia Division, the Japan–Korea Branch for a few months, followed by processing for overseas assignment. It had been that direct, and that simple, and Don Gregg delivered in spades on his commitment to me. The new challenge would be for me to reciprocate trust and confidence with the highest level of performance I could deliver to him, to Seoul Station and to the Agency.

Chapters 1-5 Notes

Chapter 1

- **NOTE 1 - See page 28**

   Bud Downing was my father's next-door neighbor on Peoria's Millman Street. Bud had helped my then-14-year-old father load the family posses-sions onto a borrowed, horse-drawn dairy cart in 1934 when the bank evicted the Lawless family from its home. Bud was a star athlete, married right out of high school and had two daughters and an infant son in December 1941. With a three-child family, he could have avoided the war but elected to serve. An infantryman, he died in one of the last battles in the European Theater. Bud's son, Wayne Downing, would attend the U.S. Military Academy at West Point, fight in four of America's wars, and become a leading light in the cre-ation of special operations. As a retired four-star general, Wayne Downing would be recalled to active service in 2002 in the White House as President George W. Bush's National Security Advisor for Combating Terrorism.

   General Wayne Downing died suddenly in July 2007. A few days after his death, I was honored to attend his funeral mass at St. Mark's Church in Peoria. I was then serving in the office of the Under Secretary of Defense for Policy with responsibility for the Asia–Pacific region. As Wayne's casket was borne out of the church, a formation of C-130 four-engine transports over-flew the procession, banking away in a low-level salute. The Air Force was honoring an Army leader with whom they had served and partnered in the Special Operations Command. In 2009, the Greater Peoria Airport was re-named General Wayne A. Downing Peoria International Airport in his honor. My brother Bob, son of a man who went to war with General Wayne Dowl-ing's father, Lieutenant Bud Downing, in early 1942, was standing tall as an airport commissioner the day its name was changed to honor Wayne. Bud would have been proud of his son's accomplishments. My father, who had passed two years earlier, would have been no less proud that Bob had been part of this special event.

- **NOTE 2 - page 30**

   The USS *Ely* of my summer training cruise days of 1963 was nearing the end of useful life. The *Ely* had been built as the PCE-880 by the Albina Engine Works in Portland, Oregon, in a wartime near-record period of two months in mid-1943. She was commissioned for operations in April 1944 and served out the conflict, to be transferred to duty on the Great Lakes as part of the Navy Reserve training fleet. After 23 years of faithful service, mostly cruis-ing Lake Michigan to train naval reservists such as myself, she was retired and decommissioned in July 1970. Some 40 years later, in January 2010, she was purposely sunk off Indian River Inlet, Delaware, to serve for time eternal as part of an artificial reef.

PCE-880's namesake is Eugene Burton Ely, one of America's pioneer aviators. Ely made history as the first man to fly from and land on a ship. In November 1910, he flew his Curtiss Pusher biplane from the deck of the USS *Birmingham* to land ashore two miles away. The Smithsonian's National Air and Space Museum website (airandspace.si.edu) features a succinct account of Ely's life and times.

Chapter 2

- ## NOTE 1 - page 32

The U.S. Army had long maintained its intelligence school at Fort Holabird, a compact, academic-looking complex nestled in the old Dundalk section of Baltimore. At Holabird, my course in counterintelligence delivered, to its mixed class of Army and Marine attendees, the basics of intelligence collection, interrogation and reporting. At midcourse, our studies were interrupted by the political and social events of spring 1968. In April, the Martin Luther King, Jr., assassination brought rioting and looting to Baltimore's streets. Our class was mobilized and up-armed for service among the National Guard units deployed into the city to restore order, martial law having been declared by then-Maryland Governor Spiro Agnew.

Looting and criminal activity quickly transformed the city into a virtual war zone, and local and state law enforcement were overwhelmed. On those battered streets, I had my first encounter with violent death when we turned a corner to establish a perimeter by a warehouse that was still being looted. Laid out over a shattered doorframe, a man lay sprawled bleeding out in front of us, a smashed case of whiskey close at hand. He had been shot several times in the chest and head by fellow looters, who had raced down the street into an alley when we arrived. He was dead before our medics got to him.

A few years later, the U.S. Army closed "the Bird" and handed its patch of land back to Baltimore City. Its mission was then transferred to the U.S. Army Intelligence Center at Fort Huachuca. The latter, a former Indian Wars outpost near Sierra Vista, Arizona, today hosts the above-mentioned army intelligence school as well as the Army's Network Enterprise Technology Command.

- ## NOTE 2 - page 33

No better accounting of the Johnson indecisiveness regarding America's struggle in Vietnam, nor objective accounting of his subordination of hard decisions to his ambition for reelection and the advancement of his domestic political agenda, can be found in current literature than Brian VanDeMark's Road to Disaster: A New History of America's Descent Into Vietnam (2018). It complements the earlier work of H.R. McMaster's Dereliction of Duty: Lyndon Johnson, Robert McNamara, the Joint Chiefs of Staff and the Lies That Led to Vietnam (1997). From the perspective of 2023, it is reasonable to conclude that Johnson, along with those who enabled his decision-making related to Vietnam, behaved abominably. In terms of the men who were sent to wage war in Vietnam, America was ill-served by the near-criminal conduct of his leadership, as well as the enabling indecision and indifference of the men with whom Johnson surrounded himself.

• NOTE 3 - page 36

The story of the *Pueblo* capture, the circumstances of that taking, the travails of the crew during its captivity and their fate after their release have been well-chronicled, most recently by Jack Cheevers in his excellent book, Act of War: Lyndon Johnson, North Korea, and the Capture of the Spy Ship Pueblo (2013). Mitchell B. Lerner's The Pueblo Incident: A Spy Ship and The Failure of American Foreign Policy (2002) provides a different perspective but highlights the failures at all levels of U.S. military command involved in the loss of the ship. The USS *Pueblo*, still on the active registry of U.S. Navy vessels, sits today on the river that bisects the North Korean capital Pyongyang. It is maintained there by the third generation of Kim family leadership, nearly 50 years after its capture. Until it is liberated, the *Pueblo* is destined to serve that totalitarian state as a tourist attraction, a moored museum offering visitors tangible proof positive of a North Korean victory over the United States.

• NOTE 4 - page 39

A comprehensive accounting of North Korean attacks on the ROK, and its ally the United States, during the period 1955-2010 can be found in a monograph developed by Stephen Whittles of the Center for Preventive Action, in which he credits as his main sources, "The Quiet War: Combat Operations Along the Demilitarized Zone," an article in The Journal of Military History (2000) by N.E. Sanantakes, in company with the U.S. Congressional Research Service publication "North Korean Provocative Actions, 1950-2007," by Hannah Fischer.

• NOTE 5 - page 40

The shootdown of the EC-121 was a calculated, carefully rehearsed and well-executed plan that took advantage of established international law and norms of conduct. The shootdown took place some 60 miles off the coast of North Korea in international airspace, and as mentioned it was timed to coincide with the birthday of the then North Korean leader Kim Il-sung. As coincidence would have it, some three years later, during my first year in the agency, I was assigned to research and write an assessment of the Soviet ground-controlled intercept system employed in that provocation (NATO code name "MARKAM"). The unprovoked attack was vintage North Korean, and again we had failed to anticipate the obvious opportunity we presented to the perpetuators with our mission planning. Based on their experience with the USS *Pueblo*, the North Koreans then could well have assumed—as they would continue to assume—that they would not be held accountable for their blatant hostile actions. On that day in 1969, 31 American servicemen paid the ultimate price. American leadership would learn no lesson from the incident, and the pattern of high-risk North Korean behavior would be further defined.

As mentioned in the previous chapter, on the 50th anniversary of the event in mid-April 2019, I took note of this unprovoked attack in a posting carried by the American Enterprise Institute's website "Shootdown Over the Sea of Japan."

I thought it reasonable to remind the current generation of this sacrifice and the abject failure of our national leadership, which did little more than wring its hands in response. I also wished to underline that the same regime perpetrating this aggression was still in place in Pyongyang, poised there for future provocations, with lessons for us untaught and therefore unlearned.

Chapter 3

• NOTE 1 - page 41

My grandfather, Patrick, had returned home from the "War to End All Wars" in 1919. He married, began a construction business, dabbled in politics and had three children, my father the first among them. Patrick eventually became a city alderman, representing Peoria's Fifth Ward. The latter was the home base of the Irish–Italian–Lebanese political clique that ran the city and managed its patronage for over 30 years. My grandmother, Elizabeth, also first-born of immigrant parents, was a political powerhouse in her own right and chaired the Illinois Women's Democratic Organization.

Pappy's father and mother, Richard and Elizabeth, both came to America in the early 1890s from County Louth in the "Pale of Ireland." Richard, my namesake, had followed his Elizabeth, enduring a steerage steamship passage, to catch up with the girl he had fallen for in elementary school. Elizabeth had come with her sisters as an indentured servant, working off her passage in a Peoria drug store run by a German immigrant family. With few skills other than a solid Benedictine eleventh-grade education, Richard became a Peoria city policeman. Standing six feet six inches, weighing 260 pounds and sporting size 18 boots, he was a hard man to miss as he walked his beat on the streets at the turn of the century. Peoria was then a rough river city town with an uneven reputation. Situated on the Illinois River midway between Chicago and St. Louis, it sported no less than 20 breweries, five whiskey distilleries and claimed one of the largest red-light districts in the Midwest. Richard's son, and my grandfather, Patrick, was a product of his Irish heritage and of the city into which he was born and raised. I would miss Pappy dearly.

The Lawless name boasts an interesting history, and I owe my mother's deep plunge into our family's genealogy for this explanation. The name is Anglo–Irish with strong Norman origins, the Norman–French having themselves Scandinavian roots. Sir Hugh de Laighleis, a descendant of William, Duke of Normandy, who conquered England in 1066, was one of the 400 knights who participated in the 1172 conquest of Ireland. Called the Strongbow invasion, it was ordered by King Henry II of England and most of the Anglo–Norman knights who comprised the leadership of Henry's invasion force elected to remain in Ireland as landed gentry. Sir Hugh claimed the Manor of Shanganagh near Dublin and erected there a castle, and its remains were still visible into the 19th century.

Over the ensuing centuries, branches of the family spread over Ireland, and the name continued to evolve, first to Langhles, then to Lawles and finally, by the 18th century, to Lawless. Much of the family remained in the Dublin area, just to the north in the "Pale of Ireland," close on the Irish Sea where the soil was rich and the land productive. In 1312, Richard Laghles, the Provost of Dublin, gained some fame when he averted a famine in that city by unmasking the guild of bakers who were apparently using rigged scales in the sale of their bread to the masses. Richard ordered the bread distributed and the bakers tied to the tails of horses to be dragged through the streets of the city.

In 1989, using my mother's research and ably assisted by my good friend Judge William Clark, I journeyed to County Louth, Ireland's smallest county, just north of Dublin. With Judge Clark, recently retired from the Reagan administration as its National Security Advisor behind the wheel of his Toyota, we located the Lawless family farm, a 40-odd-acre plot in sight of the Irish Sea, near the Clogher's Head. The farm buildings still stood, dilapidated but showing themselves mostly as they were when five of the seven sons of Nicholas Lawless left home in the early 1890s. Three sons came to America, and two immigrated to Australia. My great-grandfather, Richard, was among the former. As mentioned, he had followed the girl who lived down the road, Elizabeth Gallagher, with whom he had grown up. When she and her sister relocated to Peoria, Richard caught up with Liz, married her, bought her out of her indenture and had four sons. The rest is history, at least in Peoria.

Walking down the road in the dew of an Irish morning, Judge Clark and I discovered the Gallagher cottage, standing on Gallagher Cross (Where else?), all 300 square feet of it, boarded-up but intact. In this humble one-room structure, 14 siblings were born into the world, and 10 survived to adulthood. The year following the discovery journey of Judge Clark and me, I took my parents to Ireland to visit the homestead. The stories of the Lawless clan poured out as we sat for hours with long-lost relatives who had remained there over the generations, clinging to the land of our forefathers and mothers.

- **NOTE 2 - page 44**

  A great book chronicling the history of the USS *Hornet* and the important role she played in the Apollo 11 event is <u>Moon Men Return: USS Hornet and the Recovery of the Apollo 11 Astronauts</u> by Scott W. Carmichael. In my memory, the *Hornet* was a happy ship that served her nation long and well, from her commissioning in November 1943 as the CV-12, through her decommissioning some 37 years later in 1970. As a World War II Essex-class attack carrier, she fought her way across the Central Pacific with storied Task Forces 38 and 58, and by mid-1945, operated 103 fighter and attack aircraft from her deck.

  The *Hornet* was modernized and converted to an anti-submarine carrier in 1959, her designation changing to CVS-12 when the U.S. Navy pivoted its Cold War capabilities to confront the growing submarine menace posed by the Soviet Union. She operated as such when I was fortunate to be assigned to her as a Midshipman in the summer of 1967 and finished her active service in that role. *Hornet* today serves as a museum ship at the USS *Hornet* Museum in Almeda, California.

  In October 2019, the Smithsonian's Air and Space Museum acknowledged the role of the *Hornet* in the Apollo 11 mission with a special event: "The USS *Hornet*: Stories of the Apollo 11 Recovery." The panelists' webcast on 22 October focused on the command module Columbia's splashdown and recovery operation, referencing historian Robert Fish's book <u>Hornet Plus Three: The Story of the Apollo 11 Recovery</u>. The Air and Space Museum's event is profiled by http://airandspace.si.edu/events/uss-hornet-stories-apollo-11-recovery.

Chapter 4

- **NOTE 1 - page 52**

  Stanley Weintraub's <u>MacArthur's War: Korea and the Undoing of an American Hero</u>, mentions the high-level deliberations over the use of nuclear weapons, both within and outside the boundaries of the peninsula, as occurring in April 1951. He sees this contingency planning as "an ironic counterpoint to the agonizing debate over relieving MacArthur." President Truman replaced the general and brought him home that same month, but U.S. leaders

would continue to weigh the pros and cons of nuclear use through the full
duration of that war. ███
███
███
███
██████████████████████████

• **NOTE 2 - page 53**

A compilation of relevant declassified documents, an incredibly informa-
tive package of State, Defense, and National Security Council memoranda and decision papers, was published by the National Security Archive
███
██ I
commend this excellent work, edited by NSA's William Burr, to any and all
interested in this important period in Korean security history, not to mention the development and evolution of U.S. nuclear decision-making.

• **NOTE 3 - page 56**

███
███
███
███
███
███
███
███
███
███
███
███
███
███
███
███
███████████████.

Chapter 5

• **NOTE 1 - page 62**

Several years later, I found myself back at Headquarters on TDY to serve on a GS-12 clandestine service promotion panel. Four of us, as GS-14s deemed eligible to evaluate lower-grade officers for possible promotion, had been brought back from field assignments for a two-week run. We spent days poring through the personnel files of a hundred or more officers being screened for promotion to GS-13. Among the batches delivered to our conference room by the Office of Personnel wizards, there appeared an out-of-place stack of GS-14 files, mine among them. As an intel collector, I could not resist a quick look at my own file, and I focused on the section containing the assessment memos drafted by the CT screeners years before.

It was an interesting read. Several assessments were negative, based on my background, education or military service. One grumbled that I was obviously of "middle-middle-class background, therefore lacking in sophistication," while several others complained that I lacked a "solid East Coast quality university pedigree," or some such damning comment. My relatively young age—then 25—was also cited as a negative, suggesting a "lack of experience and maturity." The negative or ambivalent assessments were more than balanced by other senior review officers noting my personality was even-tempered, and that I knew how to listen and elicit and gain the confidence of others. The fact was that, despite my age, I was experienced and had compiled a solid record of achievement as an Army CIC agent/ officer in the field in Korea, and this carried some weight.

The back-and-forth assessments among the panel that selected my CT class seemed to reflect classic Agency personalities—the East Coast arrogance of the Ivy Leaguers pitting themselves against the more hardscrabble crowd, the latter having gained a deserved reputation for disdaining those who thought themselves to be a better breed. But the more I matched the names on the memos to the words recorded, I realized the reverse was true—my champions were the high-end boys who were willing to give me a chance, and the negative crew tended to be those with whom I shared middle-class status. Perhaps they felt threatened by me, and others like me. In any event, the bottom line evaluation of me seemed to be "looks interesting, let's give him a chance!"

One more point of interest was noted by one of my fellow GS-14 evaluators as we paged through our respective files: I might have benefited from the fact (or suspicion) that there was an "Irish Mafia" that had established itself within the leadership of the DO, an imagined cadre of Irishmen who advanced and protected one another. That assertion was a new one for me. But, if it were the case, I would take it—I had not seen too many instances where being a third-generation Irish–American paid dividends upfront. As I watched our senior management in action in later years, I concluded that there might indeed be an Irish Mafia within the Operations Directorate, but it was hardly impressive. In fact, the longer I stayed, and the closer to the senior levels I moved, the more it seemed that the "made men" of that Irish mafia spent more time outmaneuvering their County Mayo brethren than supporting one another.

• NOTE 2 - page 63

Two books of note are devoted to Theodore G. "Ted" Shackley. One is an autobiography, <u>Spymaster: My Life in the CIA</u>, which presented itself a few years after Shackley's forced retirement in 1979 by then-Director Stansfield Turner. A second, which seemed to be balanced against the man rather than in his favor, provides a more critical career overview. Authored by David Corn, <u>Blond Ghost: Ted Shackley and the CIA's Crusades</u>, was published in 1994. It is as much about the deeds and misdeeds of the Agency since its inception than it is about Shackley. In many ways, Shackley was the consummate intelligence collector, covert operations planner and actor. Corn's book is inherently biased; his agenda is clearly to weave Shackley into a tale of systemic Agency malfeasance over the decades.

I only stood before "the Blond Ghost" for an extended discussion once, in spring 1976. He had by then assumed the position of Associate Deputy Director for Operations, placed there by then-Director George H.W. Bush. I was back in the Headquarters building on TDY in the midst of our ongoing penetration and takedown of the South Korean strategic weapons program in Seoul. Shackley was 50 and on a trajectory that could have made him DCI—that is, Director of Central Intelligence—and I was only 29 and in the second year of my first overseas tour.

In our brief meeting, Shackley made it known he was pleased with our work but suggested he did not have much affection for the man who had replaced Don Gregg as my Chief of Station in Seoul. I avoided any characterizations or comments of concurrence that he seemed to solicit. By happenstance, the ever-watchful Don Gregg was now back at Headquarters serving as an assistant to Director William Colby, working with the Senate Select Committee to Study Governmental Operations with Respect to Intelligence Activities—aka the Church Committee—and other congressional bodies investigating the Agency. Don stood alongside me, explained some of the Seoul Station issues to Shackley, and blunted some of the jabbing that Shackley often deployed to intimidate younger officers. The Ghost pronounced himself mostly satisfied, we were dismissed, and out the door we went.

• NOTE 3 - page 66

The North Korean shootdown of the U.S. Navy EC-121 in April 1969 resonated with me then and still does today. In April 2019, to note the 50th anniversary of that loss, and the learned and unlearned lessons of that incident, I wrote a piece for the American Enterprise Institute website, which can be found at http://www.aei.org/publication/shootdown-over-the-sea-of-japan/. This same brief article was carried by Japan's Yomiuri Shimbun, that nation's largest mass-circulation daily, and in its companion English language weekly.

• NOTE 4 - page 67

In retrospect, it is possible Director Helms accepted the suggestion for the series of CT luncheons for the simple reason that his time at the Agency had run out. President Nixon, in a fit of anger over Helms's unwillingness to do his bidding, had demanded that he be forced out in the fall of 1972. This backroom drama was playing out at about the time we were sitting down to lunch with him.

It was later revealed that Helms had asked the Nixon team to be allowed to stay on until his mandatory retirement age. With 30 years in service to his country, he walked away in March 1973 when he reached age 60. Nixon then appointed him as U.S. Ambassador to Iran, where he served with distinction. President Jimmy Carter arrived at the White House in 1977 determined to put the Shah in his place, and he got busy undermining that government and its leadership. Carter's ineptitude led to an abandonment of Tehran, a ham-handed change in regime there. This in turn resulted in Carter and his team presiding over the attack on our Embassy and the hostage-taking of our diplomats. Carter would be rewarded for his unique combination of naivety, arrogance and incompetence on the Iran issue in the 1980 election when Ronald Reagan sent him packing back to Georgia.

Watching these sad events play out in Tehran from back in Washington, Helms retired from government service and went on to write his own book, A Look Over My Shoulder: A Life in the Central Intelligence Agency. It was published in 2003, shortly after his death. It was preceded in 1979 by a biography by Thomas Powers, The Man Who Kept the Secrets. Neither book, in my opinion, does reasonable justice to the man, his career, his service to the Agency and to the United States, nor does either do justice to the quality of his character.

PART TWO

Back to Korea for the CIA

(1974-1978)

Welcome to Seoul Station
and the U.S. Embassy Seoul

In January 1974, I flew Northwest Airlines across the broad Pacific to the South Korean capital, with an overnight stop in Tokyo, all of it uneventful and with our runway touchdown smooth and easy. Kimpo Airport was as bleak and unwelcoming as ever, just as I recalled it some three years before when I departed, dressed in U.S. Army livery. Our arrival was greeted by the dreary overcast skies of Korea's deep winter. If we needed to be reminded where we were, an ice-cold wind blasted through the 747's cabin as soon as the door was popped open.

Greeting me planeside was the personification of Korean winter gloom: Carl, an elderly American assigned as my "sponsor." He had been nominated to handhold and walk me through the first few days on the ground. Carl was not a bad guy, just grumpy and rumpled. But he disliked Seoul, the Koreans and pretty much every other person with whom he worked. I realized Carl and I would get along just fine because it quickly became obvious he would have little interest in my Agency activity and no inclination to interfere.

That evening, my immediate boss—I will call him Paul—chief of the Operations Branch, stopped by my temporary quarters to say hello. He was eager to provide me with the proverbial "30,000-foot view," the big-picture briefing delivered to all incoming first-tour officers. He told me Seoul Station was a relatively small operation despite Korea's geopolitical importance, not to mention the 50,000 troops we had stationed in-country. In contrast, our Embassy represented a rather large mission. The number of diplomats and contractors assigned to the overall U.S. government presence totaled in the hundreds. Consequently, Paul explained, as a newcomer I would have to ease gingerly into the overall mix.

As I got to know him, I enjoyed working with Paul. He had a laidback personality. A former career Navy officer about 20 years older than I, he had seen a lot over his several tours in Asia, particularly during his Agency stint in Vietnam. He was looking forward to his upcoming retirement, yet he was engaged, interested and encouraging. When he needed to be critical, he was always constructive. Best of all, he was a "guy's guy" in attitude and approach. He pushed his officers "to get outside the building and on the street" as much as possible. He expected them to roam the city and learn its byways while making new contacts.

That would prove especially useful as daylight turned to dusk, and we Station officers fanned out for our operational meetings. We were working our relationships at least four nights a week; more if possible. Paul's approach basically was hands-off, roughly translating as, "You know what you have to do, so just get your ass out there, work the street and do it!"

In my callowness, I assumed Paul represented the kind of leadership I would encounter during my Agency career. That expectation was alternatively satisfied and deeply disappointed. In any event, Paul was a stalwart supporter during my first two years in Seoul, and I owe him a great debt of gratitude.

My first day, I made the early morning rounds to meet the Station crew in their varied offices and then attended a routine staff meeting in the chief's conference room. I quickly discovered I would have almost no opportunity to leverage my assigned tasks to secure access to the individuals with whom I would need to establish a relationship. That is, my official responsibilities involved few of the contacts I would need to gain access to the individuals and organizations of highest interest to the Station and the Agency.

Ambassador Phil Habib — A Man's Man

My next stop that first day was a courtesy call on our Ambassador, a remarkable character both in personality and career accomplishments, the redoubtable Philip C. Habib. His reputation as a no-nonsense tough guy and a skilled manager of men and women preceded him. When I inquired about him in Washington before deploying to Seoul, an associate cautioned me, "Don't mistake him for a typical State career guy. He is the antithesis of that. He's from Brooklyn but could be straight off the streets of Hell's Kitchen." That was followed by the admonition, "Don't get on his bad side. He does not suffer fools gladly. And he doesn't forget anything." Forewarned, I was prepared but somewhat apprehensive to meet the man, even if it was only a 15-minute drop-in to introduce myself and then duck for cover. **[NOTE 1]**

It turned out that first brief meeting with Phil Habib was one of the most important encounters of my life, impacting, as it later did, my professional future. Habib's initial decisions influenced the years immediately ahead for me in Seoul, and it subsequently factored heavily in determining my career path in the Agency. For the meeting, I was accompanied by my rumpled colleague Carl, the well-worn careerist who had greeted me at planeside.

Habib began with a quick question, almost as a half-courtesy, to Carl. It went something like, "Well, Carl, I understand we have offered you that nice Japanese-style house on the main Embassy compound. Guess you will be joining us there soon?"

Carl grimaced and mumbled a response. "Well, you see, Dolores, my wife, hasn't decided yet, Mr. Ambassador. She says she thinks she really doesn't like that house all that much." It was clear Habib considered the house to be a real catch, in part because it was located near his own official residence. It definitely would be an uptick in status for Carl, relocating from the less-prestigious Embassy Compound Two. It also seemed clear Habib himself had decided to offer the residence to Carl and his wife, perhaps as a bonus of sorts.

Carl's clumsy response clearly agitated Habib. "So, who makes these decisions in your house Carl, you or your wife?" Carl apparently missed the drift and came right back with, "Well, Dolores, my wife, she makes most of those kinds of decisions, and on this house she just can't decide."

Silence in the room. Habib held back a bit. "Carl, I know Dolores is your wife! Now, men are supposed to make these decisions. And it affects your job, because that house, that nice big traditional Japanese house and garden, that's a house you can entertain in. Where you get those Koreans in for dinner ... you know, do your thing with them. And, it's on Compound One."

Again, Carl gave the wrong answer. "Well, Dolores doesn't like to entertain, and she says we don't have to do that."

I could see Habib starting to react, but he contained himself—barely. In an even voice he dismissed my escort with, "Carl, why don't you go on down to the Econ Section and let Richard and I talk a bit."

When he closed the door behind him, Habib focused on me. "So, what do you think of that?" I said I was not really in a position to make a comment. Habib countered, "Forget it. I already read your bio. You're real middle class, aren't you, and a veteran. You know Korea, and Don Gregg (my Chief) thinks you will do just fine here."

We then talked about upbringing, what my father had done in the war, respective Irish and Lebanese pedigrees or lack thereof, and his impressions of the challenges we faced in Korea. He closed the conversation with, "So what can I do for you?" I told him I was pleased to be in Seoul and would do my best to serve him, my organization and my country. He followed with a handshake and a "welcome aboard," and a sincere and all-important comment of encouragement as I walked out the door of his office. "Have a great tour here. There is plenty for you to do."

Habib Goes Ballistic

My next experience with Habib occurred a week or so later. In the company of a handful of other recently arrived, first-tour officers, he summoned us to a Saturday morning Ambassador's roundtable. We had been told to report to the Habib's conference room at 9 a.m. sharp, where we would have an off-the-record exchange with him—just the new officers and the Old Man. A great idea, but it did not unfold well. In fact, that inaugural gathering also turned out to be the last.

Nevertheless, the narrative of that brief meeting is worth retelling because it provides an insight into Habib the man. It reinforced my initial impression that he was a totally dedicated professional who cherished his country and its values, and who would not hesitate to give voice to them. He began the session by explaining that every month he would place a topic in front of us to challenge our professionalism, and each officer would respond by relating an incident faced in the course of that officer's routine. It was a closed-door discussion, so any subject was considered fair game.

In that first session, we would discuss compromising situations, issues of judgment and decisions that had to be made on the fly. Ron, an eager-beaver officer, who claimed a Peace Corps tour in the south of Korea prior to entering career Foreign Service, volunteered his story first. As a typical young State career type, he had been assigned to the consular section, where his responsibility was issuing visas for travel or residence in the United States. Ron had been working in that section for several weeks and was soon to relocate to the political section, his designated career "cone" within the State bureaucracy.

At the time, during the mid-1970s, a U.S. visa issued in Korea—which would allow immigrating to and residing in America, followed by a Green Card as the path to U.S. citizenship—was highly prized and carried great value. Tens of thousands of Koreans awaited the chance to emigrate, and more thousands applied each year for student or business visas. It was a busy part of the Embassy, one that had accumulated a deserved reputation for corruption, or what was called influenced decision-making, on the part of the employees who controlled the flow of applicants and completed the screening process.

Our Embassy career local employees were overwhelmingly honest, though a few bad apples had settled into positions of authority. Regarding those who would receive those priceless visas, and those who would not, that group made the up-or-down recommendations. During my five years in Seoul, I would be impressed by their professionalism. But I also recognized that, within the system, they, and not we Americans, constituted the permanent party. It was doubly true in the consular section, where the all-important immigration, business and tourist visas were meted out, often with too much subjectivity.

Ron related that, a few days before, he found himself in a compromising situation when he was invited to a teahouse near the Embassy by one of his trusted local employees. In the course of their tea break from the daily grind of visa decision-making, a second Korean joined them at the table. It seemed a chance encounter, but soon the visa advisor took his leave, noting the pressure to return to work.

After a few minutes, Ron's new acquaintance referenced a specific visa applicant whose file Ron would be reviewing. The application had been denied twice before, but somehow the visa-selection process had delivered it to Ron's desk with a recommendation for reconsideration, an uncommon but not unreasonable occurrence.

At that point, Habib interjected himself. "Ron," he said, "excuse me, but didn't you smell a rat when that local employee got up and walked away from the table?"

Ron replied in the negative and said the entire thing had come out of the blue. He explained that his new friend had just been talking about "hometown things" when an envelope slid discreetly across the table. The envelope contained more than a thousand U.S. dollars.

Habib again interjected. "What happened then? What did you do? Did you punch that sonofabitch? Well, did you? He was trying to bribe a U.S. government official!"

Ron calmly related that he had handled the situation well, he thought, by sliding the envelope back across the table and then carefully explaining to his would-be briber there was "obviously a cultural gap" between the two men. That is, an action that was standard or normal in that person's lifestyle was not normal in Ron's. He could not accept the money. His tea partner understood. They talked a bit more, Ron paid the tab and they parted company.

By then, Habib was livid. "Okay, when you got back to the Embassy you did report this to the security officer, right? You wrote this up? Made a report on the guy, nailed the local employee who set you up?"

Ron said he considered it a genuine misunderstanding, a "cross-cultural thing," and there had been no reason to report it.

Habib, turned red-faced, rose from his seat at the table and yelled out a blistering lecture, directed first at Ron and then to the other three 27-year-olds in the room. "That bastard tried to bribe you, cash on the table? Damn!" Habib's eyes scanned all of us. "You gutless, clueless guys call yourself men? You are the kind of men who would stand by and watch an old lady get mugged on the street in New York and look the other way. When I was your age, and right now, I would beat the hell out of that bastard, even if he kicked the shit out of me. Left with you, the old lady is lying there on the curb."

Silence. Ron began to speak, but Habib cut him off with a final blast: "Get the hell out of here, all of you, this meeting is over! You're all gutless!"

We filed out, a couple of us exchanging bewildered glances that communicated, "What a dumbass! Old Ron is in permanent deep shit, and there is no way Habib will not remember this Saturday morning."

The following Monday I received a call from the Ambassador's secretary, a career State employee who guarded his door and managed his schedule like a pit bull. She asked if I could come see her. Habib was out of the Embassy for an appointment, and she needed to talk with me. We sat down in a side room, and she asked me to relate what had happened in the Saturday morning session. I explained the sequence of events and his outburst.

She replied that the Ambassador suffered from a heart condition that was worse than he admitted to others. She said his blood pressure had soared Saturday morning to dangerous levels, and that could not be allowed to happen again. He apparently had suffered a previous heart incident and normally had things under control, but that was a bad incident. She added that the Embassy doctor and the Ambassador's wife were involved and asked if I understood how serious the situation was.

I suggested that we forgo any future Saturday morning roundtables because there would be a high potential for a replay. She said she already had canceled the next session. Ron remained oblivious. Some 20 years later, at another Embassy where he was serving as a senior diplomat, I reminded him of the exchange. Incredibly, he claimed he had no recollection. Really?

Knowing what I now know of heart conditions, and recalling Habib's bulging neck veins and stammering anger, I think we were fortunate, as he was that day, he did not die at the conference table. And I do believe, had Phil Habib been the one to whom the bribe was offered in the Korean tea house, he would have punched out the "sonofabitch" without the slightest hesitation.

Congressional Delegations—Habib the Enforcer

I think Phil Habib would have enjoyed this story if he were still among us. He passed away in 1992 at the age of 72, having served as Special Envoy to the Middle East under President George H.W. Bush. The State Department memorialized his service by naming the conference room in the East Asia Affairs Bureau in his honor. In the early 2000s, when I served as Deputy Under Secretary of Defense for East Asia and Pacific Affairs, I would often find myself in that room in Foggy Bottom, discussing North Korea and other pressing issues.

But there is a better vignette that recalls Habib in Seoul in the early 1970s. It underlines one of the problems we had to handle on a recurring basis during the five years I spent in Seoul, namely, influence-peddling from the U.S. side and influence-meddling by the South Koreans active among the lobbyists in Washington.

Back then, corruption was a standard feature of the domestic Korean scene, often occurring at the highest levels of government. Businessmen traded cash-back payments for regulatory favors. President Pak himself was clean, but his trusted associates frequently abused his confidence by receiving kickbacks and special favors. Pak appeared oblivious to his close associates' skimming or soliciting kickbacks on major projects. As long as his orders were executed and the country was developing its industries apace, he seemed content to ignore the rest.

In that vein, we faced sequences like: (a) The Republic of Korea was still recovering from the Korean War and, although it was developing economically at an incredible pace, its agricultural sector lagged badly. (b) As a result, the nation was still a net importer of grain. (c) Much of that grain, mainly rice, arrived in Korea via U.S. grants or concessional loans tied to U.S.-origin rice. (d) Almost all of the rice was exported from our Deep South rice-producing states. (e) The rice export trade to Korea was important economically to four or so states. (f) The entire rice-export chain carried considerable political value in the Old Boy politics deeply rooted in those states.

One byproduct of that construct was the annual pilgrimage to Korea by top-level politicians, other officeholders and their cronies, American and Korean alike. All were linked to rice-sale transactions. The state government-related groups, usually arriving one at a time, descended on Korea two or three times a year. They ostensibly attempted to confirm that the rice sales were in order and, as they would declare, to "boost our rice exports." In reality, those so-called trade missions displayed an unbridled debauchery not seen since the days of Bacchanalian Rome.

To someone with the sensibilities of Ambassador Habib, the entire cycle of rice sales funded by the U.S. government, connected to kickbacks to American politicians and enabling Korean officials and businessmen to benefit from the sales, was an abomination. Worse, that the boys traveled to Korea to sow wild oats and spread the wealth, usually as official state excursions—apparently blessed by his own State Department—drove Habib crazy. The Embassy was required to support those official delegations while they were in Korea, usually by making hotel and local travel arrangements. During Habib's tenure, however, along with designating a "control officer" for the group, depending on how wild a bunch they seemed to be, Habib also would deploy an unofficial team of officers to track their behavior—to the degree it was possible.

It came to pass that I was one member of the junior officer team responsible for monitoring those activities, but I quickly discovered that controlling them was not part of the bargain. As expected, the boys, ably encouraged by their Korean contacts, were out of control within hours of getting off the plane. In a working session in Habib's office the day before one group's arrival, we reviewed the rice delegation's formal schedule, confined to daylight hours. We also tried to anticipate what the nightlife component might produce, both for the American community and for the population of Seoul.

We checked our walkie-talkie call signs (Habib was always "Control One") and promised to stay in regular contact with one another. The real concern was the boys would get themselves either compromised or arrested, or both. Because they were determined to accomplish the former and probably didn't care about the latter, we knew we had a real challenge on our hands.

The first couple of nights went well enough. Daytime courtesy calls on Korean government agencies involved in the rice trade were perfunctory at best. They were followed by blowout dinners where vast quantities of liquor were consumed, dance bands featuring karaoke were the norm, and relays of Korean hostesses were subjected to all manner of craziness. The boys typically crawled into their beds, or somebody's bed, by 2 a.m. The ad hoc surveillance team would then contact Control One who, once reassured the rice gang was down for the night, would breathe a sigh of relief and turn in himself.

On the next-to-last day, the delegation made the mandatory courtesy call on President Pak. Someone among their Korean support team apparently thought it would be wise for one of the state representatives to present President Pak with a token of gratitude. He did: a diamond-studded Rolex watch, resplendent in its presentation box and giftwrapped to the nines. When the state rep handed it to Pak, he apparently passed it off, unopened, to an aide. Hours later, when the President's staff examined the box, they discovered they had a problem on their hands.

President Pak was an austere individual who disdained luxuries. He had no interest in a jewel-encrusted, three-pound Rolex. As such, he would have been furious if told by his staff what had been presented to him. It was a stupid move that could have backfired badly. Fortunately, we learned about it in time to squash what could have been an embarrassing incident. The chief of the Presidential Security Service used his private channel to our Chief to request an emergency get-together—an off-the-record, quick and confidential meeting. A PSS senior officer handed the Rolex to our Deputy Chief and explained that Pak's team wanted nothing to do with the gift. Basically, they saw it as a mutual embarrassment and wanted us to know that the extravagant timepiece would be our problem and not theirs.

Our Chief then reported the situation to Habib, and the watch found its way quickly to a middleman. He converted the timepiece into cash, pocketed a commission, and placed the balance into the account of a local orphanage. We verified that the donation had reached the orphans.

That night, the rice sellers' delegation saw its final bacchanalia launched early. By midnight, when I took over on my shift, as always from a safe distance, the group split up, reconnecting around 1 a.m. in the lobby restaurant of the Chosun Hotel, where they were lodged. Now, all we had to do was get them through the morning hours, checked out of the hotel, out to the airport and poured onto the plane.

At the early hour, I signed in with Control One as "Tracker Three" on our walkie-talkie link. The crackling, high-static dialog went something like this:

CONTROL ONE, I HAVE THE BOYS IN SIGHT ... MOST OF THEM ANYWAY.

TRACKER THREE, WHAT'S THEIR 10-4 NOW? (Habib liked to use real police lingo on the radio.)

IN THE CHOSUN HOTEL LOBBY RESTAURANT. THEY ARE ALL PRETTY DRUNK, SINGING AND YELLING. A COUPLE OF THE CREW ARE DANCING.

(Habib, upset) DANCING, WITH WHO, WHERE, WHAT THE HELL?

WELL, THEY ARE SORT OF DANCING BY THEMSELVES, MOSTLY AROUND THE TABLE. BUT 'GATOR' IS UP ON THE TABLE, DANCING. HE ALMOST FELL OFF JUST NOW!

DAMN! YOU GOTTA GET THEM OUT OF THERE. IS HE STILL ON THE TABLE? GATOR IS THE LIEUTENANT GOVERNOR, RIGHT?

I had made the mistake of giving the Ambassador far too much information, but then I stepped in it a bit deeper. I added that "Gator" was dancing in his undershirt and boxer shorts, and he was still up on the table.

Habib became more upset. He said he was going to get dressed and head over to the hotel, which was about 15 minutes away. The Station officers knew that Habib, against all security rules, had access to a beat-up Ford Falcon he occasionally sneaked into during the dark of night and drove around town.

The problem was Seoul's permanent, military-enforced national curfew that locked down the city from midnight to 6 a.m. The lockdown was a serious undertaking, with soldiers and policemen stationed behind barricades at all major intersections, armed and authorized to shoot to kill. At a minimum, if Phil Habib had tried to drive to the hotel at two in the morning, the President's office would know about it within 10 minutes of the Falcon's first encounter with a military checkpoint.

"Sir," I assured him, "I think things are calming down. No need to make the trip. I think they are burned out and will hit the rack soon. I will call back only if they try to leave the hotel." Habib really had no intention of jumping into that Falcon and driving himself to the scene, but he had to threaten to do so. It made him feel a lot better.

Daylight came quickly, the severely hungover boys were bundled into the Embassy bus, and the delegation departed for the airport and the flight home, their mission to secure more rice exports for the state accomplished. The Embassy made no official report on their hijinks, and the tale of the returned gem-encrusted Rolex was quickly forgotten, probably not recorded or mentioned again until now. [NOTE 2]

Back to Business — And a Life-Changing Moment

Returning to 1974, I resume the narrative a few months into my tour. In my adjusted position, I was able to devote several hours a day to Station meetings, and I read extensively the operational case files. I assumed I would be in Seoul for a double tour, meaning four years, and my reading seemed a great way to accumulate institutional knowledge and gain momentum for the long run.

Along with my Operations Branch Chief, I went to the Station Chief to explain that I needed a position providing better access to the Korean community, namely, government and defense officials as well as the business sector. I had a solution in mind, and the Chief bought it. It allowed me to improve my access substantially to individuals of interest. Later that day, Habib called me into his office. I found him in a great mood, in part because he had been notified he was to be reassigned from Seoul.

We briefly discussed our respective families and his life experiences. He recalled from our earlier meeting he was the same age as my father (born in 1920) and repeated that he served in active duty in World War II as an Army captain. Things began to jell between us, and I realized that my Chief had greased all the skids.

Habib asked if I had any ideas how I could best position myself in the overall U.S. official community to improve my ability to collect intelligence on behalf of the Agency. I replied with my own impressions. He pushed me to explain what I optimally would like to see in work assignments to achieve that end, and I did. Habib responded enthusiastically and said he would see that my request would be met.

Then he asked if I knew anything about nuclear energy.

I replied I did not, noting only that, during my high school and college days, I worked as a welder in three powerplants. I also said I knew what steam turbines and steam generators were, and how an electric powerplant was laid out and operated. All true, but I was not sure where the conversation was headed. In typical Habib fashion, however, it was clear he had a plan.

Habib explained that he needed an Embassy "Nuclear Energy Officer" because Korea's first nuclear powerplant had just been contracted, and construction was slated to begin that year. Some months earlier, he had asked the State Department to assign him a qualified nuclear officer, but the department's personnel management system stalled the matter. More recently, they told him it would take two years to find the right man, prepare him for overseas duty, and provide the Embassy with the State position, or "slot," required. Habib added that he had posed the opportunity with three other Foreign Service officers at the Embassy, and all three had turned him down.

I jumped at the chance, noting that covering nuclear power writ large would mean monitoring both the powerplants themselves and the Korean firms and government institutions involved. It would be particularly true if the South Koreans pursued an ambitious nuclear power program.

I went further, getting a bit ahead of myself, and said if he would give me the responsibility, I would petition the Agency to bring me home on Temporary Duty and educate me on all aspects of nuclear energy.

Habib reached out to shake my hand and said, "You have the job. It's done. So, tell Don Gregg that he has to send you back to Langley for a decent education."

Within a matter of weeks, I had increased my nuclear knowledge base and portfolio, to the point where I could access every Korean company worth its salt, all of whom were seeking U.S. Export–Import Bank financing for everything from new Boeing 747 airliners to nuclear powerplants, steel mills and shipyards. Equally important, I had acquired the prospective Nuclear Energy Officer designation.

Down Hard But Not Out

My ease-in routine, along with the great news of my newly installed superior position, hit a sudden and unexpected brick wall in mid-May when I managed to injure myself badly in a Sunday baseball game. The Embassy Marine Guard contingent had challenged the Station's younger officers, to be followed by a beer fest. We had cut the grass away from the base's helicopter pad to create a primitive diamond. The game was on.

Somewhere in the upper innings, with the Marines slightly leading the Station pick-up team, a gunnery sergeant hammered a drive to deep centerfield. I was playing that position too close in, out of place for such a deep-lofting hit. I ran hard to intercept, jumped and caught the ball, hitting the knee-high grass in the deep outfield at full speed. Unseen in that higher grass, a narrow-diameter, three-foot-deep hole was in my path, and my left leg slammed into it. I went down hard and passed out briefly from the pain. I vaguely recall being loaded into someone's station wagon for a dash to the base hospital, the infamous U.S. Army 121st General Hospital that had evolved from the Korean War-era "MASH" of movie fame.

It was a compound fracture. My left tibia was protruding from the side of my leg. The entire knee and top half of my lower leg were shattered. The first set of X-rays showed a dozen bone shards where the bones and knee of my left lower leg had been at the start of the game. The emergency room doctors ran a heavy volume of pain killer through the IV to knock me out, and before I drifted off, they told me they would operate the next morning.

Sometime after 2 a.m., I was awakened by a hand squeezing my shoulder. The doctor, whom I could not make out in the dim light and haze of drugs, explained himself.

"Look, I am Doctor James, orthopedic specialist here," he told me. "Do you know they are planning to stabilize you and ship you out on a special flight first thing tomorrow? All they are waiting for is the okay from a special doctor they are flying in from another Asian location who has to give his approval. The senior orthopedic surgeon here agrees with this plan. He considers the surgery you need to be too complex. He doesn't want to do it here."

From this, I realized that the Agency was moving quickly to organize the end of my tour in Seoul and get me home to a specialist. The doctor coming from another country was our Agency's regional medical officer who had to sign off on all the medevac arrangements and probably fly home with me. The Agency took very good care of its people.

I appreciated it all, but I did not want to go home if at all possible. The young doctor at my bedside offered a solution.

"Listen to me carefully. I am 28 years old. I specialize in hand reconstructive surgery. I just spent two years in Geneva studying this type of work under a world-class specialist. If you let me take your case, I will rebuild your leg and reconstruct your knee, and you WILL walk again. If you go back to go Georgetown (University Hospital in Washington), they will take good care of you, but you will definitely walk with a limp—that is, when you walk again."

I asked what I had to do.

"Sign this document. I will be standing here tomorrow when the group gathers—the doctors from this hospital, the guy flying in from Tokyo and some senior guy from the Embassy. In that meeting you must insist—demand—that I operate on you here and that I control your case. You got it?"

I signed, fell back asleep, and awoke to find a collection of folks around my bed in the late morning. My Chief spoke first. "Rick, we have decided to send you home today. Doctor Brown is here, in from Tokyo, and has spoken with the other doctors at 121. All agree that you need to go home immediately."

I scanned the faces surrounding the bed, found the youngest-looking one there, and made my statement as I had been scripted. I told them I did not want to go home, that I had signed a document (or maybe I was dreaming that) in the middle of the night, and that I trusted the young doctor to reconstruct my leg. The reaction among the others was confusion and dismay. The document was produced, and they all took the argument down the hall. Ten minutes later they were back. Don Gregg put his hand on my shoulder and said, "Rick, it's a close call here. Doctor Brown will support me, and you. If you want to stay, you stay. This young doctor says he can do it, but it will require multiple operations. Your decision."

I elected to stay, and it was absolutely the right decision. A five-hour operation followed, with two more thrown in to touch up the surgeon's handiwork, and I had a handful of infections. But I was out of the hospital in mid-August, wearing a massive hip-to-foot, custom-made, leather-and-chrome-steel leg brace. The latter allowed me to hobble back into the Station's morning staff meetings by early September, grimacing but there. I was fulltime by October, but my abilities to move about town, walk the streets at night and conduct my operations were made all but impossible by the injury. [NOTE 3]

My rehabilitation regime focused on the Embassy swimming pool, where I spent at least two hours a day just walking on the bottom. I started in the deeper water where the pool carried most of my weight then migrated to the shallow end. As the days and weeks passed, my leg found its strength returning. I unstrapped the leg brace and walked the first time without it on Christmas Eve. The young doctor who had roused me in the middle of the night saved my leg, my career and in many ways allowed the course of my life to proceed.

Chapter 7. Full Speed Ahead in Seoul
Fall 1974

First Operations

By early September, I was back at work with fulltime responsibilities. Often well into the evening and always on Saturday, I read case files and the reporting compiled by my colleagues. Still walking with a full brace and cane but gaining strength in my leg by the day, I resumed moving about the streets of the city, both during daylight on official Embassy business and at night doing my Station's bidding. I was beginning to hit my full stride again, and the movement felt good. I owed the Agency a debt for having stuck with me, and I was eager to repay it.

My Korean language was likewise improving. My training at DLI some years before had given me the foundation of the language's structure, pronunciation and vocabulary—within limits. Spending a year in the field with the CIC Taejon Field Office, where I had essentially been embedded several days a week with ROK Army Security Command, the ROK's CIA and the Korean National Police counterintelligence officers, also provided great, real-world, man-to-man language exposure. All that plus a six-month language-refresher course at Yonsei University—a tutoring program that brought my teachers to my bedside at the 121st Hospital while I recovered—gave me enough confidence to wade back into Korean language territory.

Equally important was the fact that I had not learned syntax from female teachers, the fate of most State Department employees, none of whom seemed to realize the distinction. They would deploy with great language abilities—on paper—but the female constructs did not travel well among male Korean counterparts. More bluntly, female Korean syntax sparked turnoff with Korean military types. They brooked little time for Americans eager to parley in a dialog that featured effeminate terminology.

In the evenings, I met agents whom I had inherited, or individuals I was assessing as I developed new contacts. Too often I found myself crawling home just before midnight to beat the nationwide curfew.

My first clandestine sources included lower-level contacts designed to facilitate what was called potential agent development; that is, gaining access to higher-value potential targets. The contacts focused mostly on ROK domestic politics and their military. The latter area was all-important, and my colleagues and I worked overtime to establish and sustain personal relationships with mid-level officers in all three military services.

In Vietnam, the End Nears

At that time in my career, the security situation on the Korean Peninsula was relatively stable—notwithstanding the constant state of near-war with the North. Incidents regularly occurred, including life-taking North Korean provocations. Beyond the peninsula, however, in the balance of Asia, the situation was bad and trending worse. Cold War tensions involved both China, then as now striving to be the main player in Asia by expanding its nuclear and conventional arsenals; and the Soviet Union, the dominant strategic contender. The latter, America's penultimate global competitor, had renewed its emphasis on a strong strategic presence in Northeast Asia. It included expanding submarine operations and ballistic missile deployments, complementing a hostile posture challenging the United States and attempting to erode our security guarantees in the region.

In Vietnam, autumn 1974 saw the American body politic, encouraged by an increasingly negative mass media, determined to extract the country from involvement in, and responsibility for, the survival of the Republic of Vietnam; that is, the South. Under the rubric of what Washington called Vietnamization, our military mostly had disengaged from combat there and completed the Henry Kissinger-engineered, "decent interval" deployment out of the country. Driving the final nail in the coffin of that hapless nation, our Congress cut off funding to the Vietnamese military, thereby severing the military supply lifeline, without which the war-ravaged country could not survive. For their part, the Vietnamese did themselves no favors, fielding a series of governments hobbled by military leaders incapable of coping with the inevitability of American abandonment.

The North Vietnamese, emboldened by the duplicitous Paris Peace Accords negotiated by Kissinger, relentlessly pressed their frontal attacks, flaunting any pretext of agreed national boundaries or international law. Hanoi blatantly upped the ante by sending tanks rolling south across the DMZ to spearhead its main-force units. The South Koreans had seen that movie before; on June 25, 1950, when North Korean T-34s led the invasion of the ROK. They broadly recognized the similar scenario about to unfold in Vietnam.

The writing was on the wall for anyone remotely possessed by common sense and even a minimal understanding of South Vietnamese inadequacies. Absent American military support, the Saigon government was overmatched by North Vietnamese capabilities and intentions, and was doomed to fall.

One of my operational relationships back then was with a mid-level Vietnamese officer stationed in Seoul. Trang and I regularly met to discuss the situation and the steady deterioration of South Vietnam's position. He was loyal to his country and was motivated by his Catholic faith to resist Hanoi's determined imposition of a communist system on the South. But he was also realistic. He realized that the end for his nation as a separate entity would come sooner than later. Feeling his pain and recognizing his years of cooperation with us, the Agency provided for him and his extended family to resettle in the United States.

In one of our meetings, Trang presented a difficult issue. Apparently, when a major South Korean military unit, stationed several years in Vietnam, packed up and headed home, the Vietnamese Air Force inherited the base. The Korean unit's sprawling complex covered several acres and accommodated a division-size presence of 10,000-plus soldiers. It had provided a support hub for the overall ROK presence in Vietnam and included a massive warehouse complex. The Korean departure, in keeping with the broader American decision to slide out Vietnam's back door en masse under the cover of Vietnamization, had been accomplished in haste. The Korean warehouses had been emptied; all weapons, ammunition and supplies loaded on Korean ships, and the keys to the ostensibly empty facility literally tossed to the Vietnamese.

A few days after the new tenants took over the base, they noticed a strange phenomenon. The entire base seemed to float as they drove its streets or walked on its metal pathways. Vietnamese combat engineers were called in and began to peel back the plates that pinned much of the complex together. They were amazed by what they uncovered: literally, a subterranean base beneath the base, which the Korean military had constructed and operated over the years. The subterranean complex held a massive stash of illicitly acquired U.S. military supplies.

The material ran the gamut from new, off-the-boat M-113 armored personnel carriers to Sheridan tanks, trucks, jeeps, diesel generators and massive refrigeration units, as well as hundreds of tons of sheet aluminum and other high-value construction materials. Plumbing fixtures including, literally, kitchen sinks as well as gleaming toilets were found as well. If anything had value to Korea, and resale there into the gray or black market, the Korean military requisitioned it from Uncle Sam and stashed it away for shipment back home. More likely, the Koreans had just boosted it from U.S. supply centers in the middle of the night, or they forged acquisition paperwork.

The South Vietnamese had discovered, beneath the former Korean base camp, one of the biggest illicit snatch-and-grab stashes of the war. And Trang had been given an unenviable task by his government. He was ordered to approach the Korean military to explain what had been discovered at the base camp and ask how they wished to handle the matter. The list was incomplete because the Vietnamese engineers were still uncovering the stash.

I told him to take the issue, inventory included, to the Korean military as he had been instructed—otherwise, his intent would have been suspect—but not to press for a response. Meanwhile, we relayed the information to Langley in the form of a backchannel cable, along the lines of, "We have some information here and really don't know what to do with it."

We both saw the potential for a lose–lose scenario with a disseminated Agency report.

First, once spread around the intelligence community, someone in our military would order a formal investigation of the Korean military's five-year program of organized theft of our stockpiles in Vietnam. Such an investigation then would take on a life of its own, creating an uncertain impact on the U.S.–ROK military relationship, and therefore the alliance, and resulting in a problem for the United States that, given the already-dreadful Vietnam situation, we could well live without.

Second, because we had obtained the information from a covert source, any attempt to use it to confront the Koreans, or the Vietnamese, stood a good chance of compromising our source, namely, Trang.

Headquarters fortunately saw things the same way. We figured out how to ignore the information, and we knew we could count on the Koreans to deny everything. True to form, our Korean friends delivered a somber response to the Vietnamese. "Tanks and trucks buried under our former base!" they asserted. "How could that have happened? Really, we are shocked to learn this!" I doubt Captain Renault in *Casablanca* could have bested their staged reaction.

One thing we did do was inject an admonition to the Koreans. The RVN government, having now informed the Koreans what they had found, would not look favorably on any Korean attempt to recover the goods. Such a move was not beyond possibility and, had the Koreans done so, we would have a serious policy issue on our hands in Seoul. It was not beyond possibility that both the Defense and State departments, plus some watchdog agency of the federal government—and, even worse, our ever-ready-to-pounce-and-avowedly anti-Vietnam-engagement Congress—would investigate the matter, with fingers pointing at the ROK military. It was indeed a lose–lose proposition that called for quick burial in the desert.

In any event, the entire incident went away, the Vietnamese did what they did with the discovered materials—probably absorbing the military items into their army and selling the balance, from steel plates to toilets, into their own black market—and the good Trang continued his work for his government and, as he was able, for us. When South Vietnam fell some months later, the Agency saw to it that he and his family received expeditious treatment as they headed to their new life in America.

In the final weeks of that battered nation's existence, we watched from Seoul as the tank-led North Vietnamese military conquered all before it. Along with the rest of the world, we witnessed the Fall of Saigon and the humiliation of the rooftop U.S. helicopter evacuation from our Embassy there. Not surprising, others in Asia, including the people and leadership of Korea, watched it play out as well. Reasonable men drew their own conclusions about the dependability of American security guarantees.

Understanding the ROK Military

During those early months in the Station, I was indoctrinated into the intricacies of the South Korean military; namely, its organization, factions and cliques, and key personalities. The ROK military had been the galvanizing force for the nation as the country, devastated by the Korean War but determined to survive, pulled itself together under a U.S.-inspired constitution and an embryonic form of democracy. The Korean military, including all services, attracted and maintained members the elite of Korean post-World War II society as its core leadership. Most of those young leaders were products of the Japanese military establishment, many having trained at Japanese academies and technical schools. Several had even served in active Japanese units during World War II, including President Pak, who had trained at the Japanese-managed Central Police Academy in Manchukuo, Manchuria, and served briefly with the colonial police force.

That cadre of Japanese-schooled military leaders moved to the fore during the Korean War, when many returned to active service from nondescript civilian positions. The young officers, rallying to defend their nation, rose in rank to assume command positions as the ROK Army rebuilt itself. One such example was a man who would later become President Pak's KCIA chief. Hailing from Pak's home area, and bonding with him during the Korean War, Kim Jae-kyu would ascend to three-star Army rank and become one of the President's most trusted advisors. Kim entered active duty at the outset of war from a middle-school teaching position in a rural township. He led in combat for two-plus years and, in company with Pak, would exemplify the absolute hold on Korea by the ROK Army for over three decades. Yet, Kim would assassinate Pak in October 1979, as they sat and argued at a dinner table.

During the decade that spanned the war and its aftermath, roughly 1950-1960, South Korea's young military leaders maintained an arms-length relationship with the civilian government. To their credit, though not necessarily embracing democracy, they did give the nation's constitutional government a fair chance. The democratically elected President Syngman Rhee brought legitimacy based on his nationalist credentials, and he saw the nation through the devastation of three years of war. But Rhee and his cronies then squandered the opportunity they had been given by steadily drifting into an isolated, if not paranoid, mentality. Thus, the political class proved itself unworthy to lead the nation by becoming, by late-decade, increasingly authoritarian and more than a little corrupt.

When that government's time ran out, the citizens of South Korea revolted in the streets in 1960 and threw out the Rhee administration. The military was then compelled to watch as the nascent democracy went wild, with coalitions flourishing and half-baked governments failing. Then, in April 1961, the military moved decisively to end it all with a *coup d'état* that gave Pak and his Army group absolute control.

In the years that followed, the U.S. government adjusted to the new reality of Pak and his interim military establishment. The Agency, somewhat belatedly but with vigor, focused on the military cliques and loyalty relationships predicted to determine the future of the nation. Reflecting 3,000 years of Korean history and culture, the key ROK Army groups aligned to sustain the Pak's rule. The ruling clique reflected regional affiliations, mostly at the provincial level.

Those bonds were overlaid by class loyalties associated with the Korean Military Academy, the equivalent of our West Point. Each Army clique identified with the war experience of its individual members, often on a regimental or division level, and reinforced by the all-important, regional-based relationships. Those in turn were overlaid by KMA class affiliation, with each clique strengthening its respective position as the years passed, and organized to secure the best promotions and key commands. For the United States, the ROK military connections were critical to understanding and assessing the stability of the government.

Facing the reality that the Pak-led administration was in power to stay for some time, a critical element of the Agency's mission was to engage and understand his military from every angle possible. With tens of thousands of U.S. troops ███████████████████████████ present on the peninsula to defend that nation, and a U.S.–ROK bilateral military alliance in place to formalize their presence, it was the Agency's responsibility to study, penetrate and report in as much detail as possible the military's inner workings. To do less would have been irresponsible. My prior service down-country in the Taejon CIC Field Office had given me a solid base to work that aspect of my assignment.

Pak was strongly in control in 1974, but Washington had its doubts about his staying power. On February 1, 1974, a CIA-drafted Intelligence Memorandum—declassified for release in January 2003 and titled "South Korea: Can Pak Hold On?"—detailed internal unrest and widespread dissatisfaction with Pak and his authoritarian controls. Examining student-led political opposition groups, the memorandum speculated that Pak was out of touch with his base and risked losing control of the forces at work against him.

The theme of the CIA assessment was advanced in a discussion paragraph that included this passage:

> Pak continues to firmly believe that a combination of strong
> leadership and economic prosperity is what South Korea needs and
> what the people really want. His authoritarian constitutional system
> is based on the thesis that continue d economic growth requires a
> type of stability only possible in Korea under a rigidly controlled
> political system in which real popular participation has no place.
> The crux of the present impasse is that a growing number of South
> Koreans are no longer willing to accept this premise.

Irrespective of the early 1974 assessment, Pak would continue to rule the ROK firmly until his death at the hand of his best friend years later, delivered by a handgun from across the dinner table. This is not to gainsay the CIA's assessment. Pak was in political trouble in that critical year when he decided to undertake a covert strategic weapons program he deemed necessary to secure his nation's future. On the domestic political side, however, he was managing things quite well, the judgments conveyed·by the CIA memo notwithstanding. **[NOTE 1]**

Sell your books at
World of Books!
Go to sell.worldofbooks.com
and get an instant price
quote. We even pay the
shipping - see what your old
books are worth today!

Inspected By: Carmen_Vasquez

000911772979

Commercial Section Responsibilities and Opportunities

I sought out specific assignments in areas where I thought I could make a real contribution to the work. I also wanted to secure a role in projects that could provide access to Korean government officials and businessmen involved in activities where the Station could collect protected information. Leveraging the political stability provided by its military, the Pak government at the time was executing a highly ambitious industrial development program.

The United States held great hope that Pak would deliver economic prosperity and create an expanded middle class and a political climate for a transition to true democratic rule. Although Pak was a heavy-handed autocrat, it was clear his intentions for his people and the nation were good. His economic programs were well-designed and had begun to deliver real results.

Washington was similarly determined to foster the growth of South Korea's economy and reduce that nation's dependence on foreign assistance. As a related goal, we assisted the ROK's ability to defend itself, to stand tall against North Korea and provide a positive model for the other emerging economies in East Asia. We perceived by the mid-1970s that selected nations in Asia, following Japan's export-driven model, were true "Baby Tigers," as they were called, and we wanted South Korea at the forefront of that wave of prosperity. Pak's Blue House team of technocrats was first-rate. They drew top-quality managers who knew how to accomplish things. With Pak's approval, those men carefully targeted key industries for financial support. They made sure the management of each new heavy industry was closely coached and monitored.

Selected family-owned business groups were designated to own and expand key sectors. In aviation, it was the Hanjin Group with Korean Airlines; in electronics, Samsung and Lucky Goldstar. Where new business lines were identified as critical to the success of the economy, such as Pohang Steel or, for shipbuilding, Hyundai Heavy Industries, the Blue House chose champions, directed funding, and empowered their growth. Entering that dynamic economic environment, I focused my attention on heavy-industry development with defense applications, including shipbuilding, machinery manufacturing, the airline industry and the energy and power sector.

Defense Industry Officer

Following up on my conversation with Ambassador Habib, the same week he offered me the Nuclear Energy Officer position, I sought out and secured an appointment that turned out to be equally important, access-wise. It was a position that had not previously existed but whose time had come, and it was tailormade for my interests and responsibilities—I became the Defense Industry Officer. In that capacity, I could reach into the growing sector where a range of manufacturing facilities were being established, all coordinated by Blue House managers. The new companies were established, often under the corporate umbrella of the larger, family-owned business groups, or *chaebols*, dedicated to the manufacture of selected weapons systems. Such firms were tasked to induce foreign technology and knowhow, often by licensing weapons and component designs from overseas manufacturers.

Pak and his team considered the creation of an indigenous weapons-manufacturing capacity a national strategic priority. As such, the effort benefited from virtually unlimited funding. The program was guided by a master plan that identified key technologies, including missile systems, armored vehicles and tanks, assault rifles and ammunition plants—basically anything and everything deemed essential to South Korea's defense. One motivation was national self-sufficiency; the other, a desire to weave arms-production capabilities into Seoul's overall export program to create a place for Korea in the international arms arena.

My new staff position satisfied the Station's desire to gain access to the epicenter of the new Agency for Defense Development. The organization had been created roughly in 1972 as a quasi-independent arm of the ROK Ministry of National Defense. Its mandate was twofold.

First, the ADD was to build an all-Korean indigenous military research and development establishment able to induce foreign weapons technology and, based on what it induced, create its own designs.

Second, the ADD was to act as a clearinghouse to transfer induced technology to the Korean private-sector manufacturers being established by the Blue House as part of the overall industrial plan.

In 1974, the agency remained in its infancy, still developing programs as it captured increasingly larger slices of the nation's defense budget. It also was maintaining a low profile and, in fact, presented itself not as the ADD but rather as the Hong Nung Machinery Company—Korean name, Hong Nung Ki-Kae Ju-Shik Hwe-Sa—derived from the district in Seoul where it was located. Its original headquarters were nondescript, a loose collection of light industrial buildings in a small compound. But within that group lay great ambitions. As far as we knew, the ADD focused on conventional weapons development but with an eye for foreign technology inducement. It had undertaken the aggressive recruitment of Korean-born foreign engineers to manage its expanding force of locally hired technicians. But to what end? Their plan was not well defined, and the situation had to be remedied.

Within the American presence in South Korea, responsibility for supporting the ADD and monitoring its activities fell squarely and solely on our military—United States Forces Korea, Eighth Army; and its subordinate organization, the Joint U.S. Military Assistance Group-Korea. JUSMAG-K was a force of its own in South Korea, dating from the time the United States began to help the ROK create its own armed forces in 1947. The Korean War found the South Korean military deeply deficient in all manner of weapons, supplies, leadership and organization. Rightly or wrongly, as the war played out, KMAG, as JUSMAG-K was then named, received much of the blame for the poor performance of the underequipped ROK forces that were scattered by the June 1950 North Korean offensive. [NOTE 2]

In retrospect, there was little doubt the Korea Military Advisory Group had not been allowed to do its job in the run-up to the first North Korean attack. But our military more than made up for it after the war. KMAG doubled down from 1953 forward and became a major presence, training all ROK forces and managing the equipment flow that built a conventional military force to deter another North Korean invasion of the South. As the ROK military structure grew and incorporated air force and navy elements, KMAG became a "joint" activity, with U.S. Air Force and Navy assistance folded into the mix. Hence, the name JUSMAG-K by the time of my work in Seoul in the 1970s.

By 1975, however, the organization had become a shadow of its former self, having completed its mission, decreasing to a few hundred officers and men in its compound on Yongsan Base in Seoul. Commanded by a series of U.S. Army major generals, JUSMAG-K maintained an active role in advising the ROK Ministry of National Defense on weapons procurement, military logistics planning and selected training programs. Its relationship with the newly created ADD was somewhat ambiguous. Its mission was simply to monitor the ADD's progress and provide its researchers with the information needed to do their mission.

JUSMAG-K's assistance typically took the form of U.S. military-controlled technical data packages that conveyed specifications of individual weapons systems and components. Such information was sensitive but had been deemed releasable to the ROK for its indigenous weapons programs. The JUSMAG-K relationship with the ADD was low-key, relegated to the responsibility of a middle-grade officer, who in turn relied on a senior noncommissioned officer to manage the routine interaction of advisory assistance and TDP handling.

I did not realize it at the time, but when I adopted the Defense Industry Officer mantle, the access I secured to the ADD turned out to be golden from the aspects of contact and collection. I soon discovered their operations were a near mystery to the Station, in part because the agency was only a few years old and still staffing out its core team. Also, the group organizing the ADD had done a lot of work beneath the radar to keep the agency's profile low and its mission vague.

Nuclear Energy Officer and Other Tasks

As mentioned, my responsibilities included the ROK nuclear energy program, both the commercial side of power generation and nuclear research activity, along with a companion task called "major project reporting." In that period of Korea's rapid and expansive industrial development, organized and managed by the top-down command authority of Pak's Blue House, the country's critical industries were experiencing dynamic growth.

101

My interest in the defense sector initially focused on a huge new industrial park at Changwon in the far south. There, factories to manufacture tanks and military vehicles, artillery and small arms were being built. I also spent time visiting several new shipyards, an industry that would make South Korea, within a decade, the world's leader in new-build tonnage. The county's first nuclear powerplant was being built in the far southeast at Kori, as was the new integrated complex of Pohang Iron and Steel, near the shipyards to which Pohang would soon supply world-class product.

My position allowed me to travel widely, engage at project sites during the day and continue with personal engagements in long evening dinner sessions, often with the leaders of the new industries. It was a heady time for all Koreans involved, and I was fortunate to occupy a small part of that dynamic activity. I soon found that access begat more access, to companies, facilities and industry leadership. Within the industrial development sector, there was overlap between defense and non-defense, and good work in one reinforced access to another. Though nuclear projects were my primary focus, all of the industries seemed to offer useful relationships.

About a year into my assignment, a foreign diplomat approached me at a social event. The man, from the local Philippine Embassy, had a special request for assistance. For some reason, which he never explained, he was convinced I might have influence over the disposition of retired U.S. Navy ships, which were routinely released to foreign navies. The ships lay in mothballed storage in various locations back in the States. I had no responsibility for such matters. But my suitor refused to be disabused of his notion about my influence and continued to outline his scheme. He needed me to transfer, "at a very low cost," two World War II destroyers of the Gearing class. He even had their names, hull numbers and storage locations.

His plan was simple and had the advantage of being secretly backed by none other than the Philippine First Lady. They hailed from the same region, and she was one of his silent partners, or so he claimed. He wanted me to transfer the two destroyers, not to the Philippine Navy but to a commercial entity, maybe a Manila scrapyard, where the ships would be repurposed as deluxe, high-speed gambling casinos. The "casino-stroyers" would run nightly at flank speed, about 35 knots, between Manila and Davao City in the south. They would charge exorbitant cover fees for the passage and allow gambling during the entire voyage. Back then, there were no casinos in the country, and all gambling on those two ships would occur in international waters. He pitched it as a "cash-cow proposition" from day one and, of course, he planned to cut me in on the action. He had not yet put together all the fine points but was working on it.

I carefully explained to him that, though this seemed like a great plan, it had certain shortcomings. First of all, I did not have the authority in Seoul to decide which ships could be sold or transferred. I was responsible for monitoring and certifying the scrapping of former U.S. Navy vessels in Korea; it was only an after-sale activity. (I had by chance the previous week spent the day at the nearby port of Inchon, watching the scrapping of two former U.S. Navy cargo ships, in company with an Australian Navy carrier.)

Second, operating a destroyer, or any ship for that matter, at full or flank speed for an extended period consumed massive quantities of fuel oil, something like three times the amount on a per-mile-steamed basis. If they intended to run at full speed on both legs of their casino operation, the fuel cost would be prohibitive. Moreover, such a tempo would burn out the steam plant and turbines of the two 30-year-old, worn-down vessels. That would be highly inefficient from a business standpoint.

In a classic case of listening to me but not hearing what I was attempting to convey, he noted only that those were small details that could be worked out. He just needed me to get the two destroyers. Besides, even if the casino operation was a bust, we could either sell the entire operation to somebody else—After all, who would not want to own a couple of destroyers?—or scrap them and pocket the money. I sent him away and told him I would be in touch. Whenever he called, I would always be "out of town."

Such experiences did not phase me, and I enjoyed all such interactions. By late 1974, I had hit full stride in my work. The timing could not have been better. Likewise, the potential for access to my collection targets, as they came into focus when things began to heat up on the nuclear front.

The First Tell

Seoul Station's Liaison Branch played an absolutely critical role in the success of the Agency's mission in Korea. That close-knit group included Agency officers who were broadly respected for their individual accomplishments and knowledge. The men, mostly middle-aged Korean–Americans, had cut their teeth in the Korean War period, some even serving with the OSS in World War II. They typically interacted with or, in Agency parlance, "liaiz'd"—conducted liaison—with their KCIA counterparts on a daily basis. Maintaining close personal relationships over many years, they shared information and acted as ground-level conduits between our Agency and Korea's national security services.

Beyond the intelligence and law enforcement communities, the Liaison Branch team also maintained lifelong relationships, often originating back in middle school and high school classrooms, with selected Korean public and private officials, media personalities and businessmen. It was a fact of life in a country where childhood friendships, and family or same-surname clan connections typically forged in a regional city, were paramount.

The trust those older Agency officers enjoyed in their personal relationships was overlaid with street smarts and an intuitive understanding of the motivations of the Korean national players, from President Pak on down. In the relatively new and turbulent nation then the Republic of Korea, those individuals would determine the future of their nation. Because we were tasked to understand and track that evolution of South Korea as a nation, fully comprehending the motivations of the men surrounding President Pak, even at degrees of separation, was a reasonable Agency mission.

The older Liaison Branch officers possessed a wealth of knowledge, at least for me as a first-tour case officer. I did not realize it then, but their presence in the Station, and their willingness to share their insights, presented a freshman officer with the opportunity of a career. No story told any number of times by those men, whether sober across the table in the Station or in a cubbyhole eating stall in a Seoul alleyway, moving toward intoxication as the evening deepened, failed to deliver value. Without exception, they were eager to share their war stories, insights and concerns, always recognizing that the next generation of case officers needed that knowledge to succeed.

Several of them had reached retirement age years before, but they continued to serve the Agency out of a sense of duty. They also held the conviction that things in South Korea were moving too fast for the nation's own good. It was all too fragile, they thought, and wanted to continue to be there as events unfolded. In a few years, all the old hands would be gone from Seoul Station, and the

Agency would be the worse for it. Realizing that, my superiors were scrambling to address the problem. But for my five-year run at Seoul Station, we had those aging gentlemen with us, and they were great colleagues.

I mention all this because one of the old hands delivered a subtle but critical bit of information in a morning staff meeting in early September 1974. It changed everything, and I almost missed it.

As my colleagues made their five-minute-or-so reports, each summarizing his operational work over the past day or two, John, the senior Liaison Branch officer, related an unusual President Pak private conversation, the gist of which had been passed on to John by a longtime contact in the Korean press. It concerned a late-night dinner and drinking session the previous week at the presidential retreat on the island of Jeo, near the Chinhae naval base on the southern coast. Since occupying the Blue House in a military coup in 1961, Pak had made it his habit to vacation for 10 days every August. He typically invited along a select group of longtime trusted friends, often relaxing with them in extended drinking parties where they reviewed the previous half-year and pondered the months to come. [NOTE 1]

John mentioned Pak's week of retreat in the south and the fact that Pak, refreshed and refocused, had returned with his core Blue House team working at full speed. John recounted what we knew of the various planning meetings during Pak's vacation and, noting the nightly drinking sessions, he ticked off the subjects Pak had covered. Apparently, much of the discussion involved events in Asia, the deteriorating Vietnam position, uncertainties about the attitude and staying power of the United States in Asia, North Korean moves and general economic concerns.

Closing his update, John said, as I recall the moment, "Oh, and also, Pak told his intimates that he had decided to build an atomic bomb."

There was little reaction to the comment, presented as it was in the context of Pak's drinking session. But I did notice that our Chief leaned into the statement with an "Oh, really?"

The meeting proceeded apace with other presentations, concluding on schedule with each of us reviewing our upcoming agent meetings. We then disbanded to shuffle off to our various offices and duties.

Later that day, I sought out John for a one-on-one, sensing he had failed to convey fully what he wanted to say earlier. We met that night in a pitched-tent, *bulgogi* grilled beef house over beer. I asked him to expand on what he had related at the staff meeting. I needed to hear the context for Pak's remark; specifically, I wanted to know if Pak was serious or merely blurting out an alcohol-enabled midnight boast.

John was patient and precise. He explained that those drinking sessions at Pak's summer retreat were serious affairs among trusted friends, with lots of good food and substantial quantities of traditional *soju*, a distilled liquor similar to Japanese *sake*. It was the drink of the common man, one step up from the farmer's rice wine called *makgeolli*. In Pak's drinking session, his *soju* was often mixed with cold beer (*maekju*) to create *somaek* for the smooth flow of a strong cold drink. The sessions involved no women servers or entertainers as distractions. In short, they were all-male extended events with plain talk among trusted friends.

I asked if there was any scripting of conversation in those sessions. John's reply was slow in coming but unequivocal. "I know these conversations, these relationships, and these people. This is not where Pak would make an idle boast. Do you want me to follow up with my source?"

I told him we had no choice. I asked him to go back to his contact, spend as much time as he needed and capture every word and nuance of Pak's statement. Three days later, John and I met again, his mission accomplished. He made a few points.

First, the dinner party group had not yet become that intoxicated when Pak made his statement. Rather, there was a serious exchange among a small group of well-informed friends, including three journalists with whom Pak enjoyed a bond based on hometown mutual trust and affection. The discussion centered on Korea's security and Pak's responsibility to ensure it, no matter what the Americans chose to do.

Second, Pak was not considered by his close friends to be a braggart. If he said something, he meant it. There was no idle talk.

Third, the source considered Pak's comment to have conveyed a decision made, not a pondering on a possible decision or a random thought. If Pak said that, it meant had decided to do what he said and perhaps had even begun to act on his decision.

John and I went to the Chief, where we were joined by the Deputy and my Branch Chief. The Chief listened as we reconstructed that shard of uncertain and speculative information. He put the hard question to John. "Given that this is all we have now, can this source get us more?" John explained he had drained the source fully, that the source was essentially tapped out, and the man had no avenue to go back to Pak to solicit anything more.

John shook his head and explained, "It was a once-in-a-year session, among six people. My guy will not raise this subject with Pak, nor with anyone else present at that dinner party again. He has nothing further to give us and, if I ask him to do more, force the issue and probe deeper, we may lose him as a source." The Chief raised his hand, cutting off the discussion. Enough said.

We decided to treat the information as an "interesting but unverifiable, possible first indication." As such, it would be useful as a pointer to future events. Nevertheless, it was certainly worthy of our operational attention.

In the formal sense of the Station's mandate to, covertly, collect and submit verified and reasonably finished information, our reconstruction of Pak's comments failed to reach the bar of well-sourced intelligence. We elected to investigate further, but we also decided to do so on a "close-hold" basis within the Station. Further, we knew it had to be accomplished based on a collection plan drawn broadly enough to capture any related activity that could add clarity to Pak's comment. [NOTE 2]

An ROK Strategic Weapons Program—
Critical Assumptions

Unspoken in that Station meeting where the subject of Pak's comment was first mentioned was the fact that any program to acquire a strategic weapons capability of any kind, be it nuclear, chemical or biological, would violate the letter and spirit of our entire bilateral military alliance with the Republic of Korea. We therefore had to assume that an ROK program in any of those politically toxic areas would be undeclared and covert in nature. That is, President Pak and his team would be undertaking such an effort knowing full well they would be violating all aspects of our relationship. In other words, Pak would be placing at risk America's treaty commitments to the ROK.

By 1974, the United States had stationed nearly 60,000 troops in the ROK to ensure defense of that country. It was a troops-on-the-ground, front-line conventional deterrent against a repeat of North Korea's June 1950 invasion of the South. Often referred to as a trip-wire presence, the U.S. forces at the DMZ guaranteed that Americans would be among the first to die if the North Koreans attacked again, thereby committing us to the fight from minute one.

Overlaying the bilateral commitment was a United Nations mandate dating from the Korean War, defined by the Armistice Agreement that had brought active combat to a close in July 1953. That mandate included a forward-based U.S. military structure, serving under the flag of the UNC—the United Nations Command. A UN Security Council resolution, passed in June 1950, directed that command to defend the ROK until a war-concluding peace treaty was signed and declared effective. The UN mandate was also important because it allowed the United States to mobilize its warfighting capacity in the entire Far East to defend South Korea, including critical UN-authorized bases in Japan.

If that were not enough, added to the impressive U.S. conventional deterrence posture, ██████████████████████████████████ ██████████ on South Korean soil for immediate use in the face of any North Korean, Chinese or Soviet attack. Had President Pak even considered developing an independent nuclear capability, deciding that our conventional and nuclear-based security structure in Korea was inadequate, we needed to understand what provoked his decision. Still, the attitude within the Station was it was not logical for Pak to take such a course. The odds were 10-to-1 against it.

Still, the risks of our not focusing on such a possibility were too high. Our Chief, with a mature perspective on the entire matter and a deep background in Far East security considerations, and buttressed by tours in other Asian nations, was adamant. He put it to us quite succinctly: Make no doubt, any attempt by the ROK to develop its own nuclear capability would trigger consequences for the United States far beyond our relationship with the ROK. Should South Korea even contemplate such a program, Japan and the rest of Asia would react accordingly, damaging all of our security relationships.

Common sense also dictated that, at some point early on, any such effort by the Koreans would no longer be a secret program. It was simply too dramatic a development to stay under wraps for very long. And once detected, the U.S. security policy community would spin itself senseless, including bureaucratic finger-pointing, accompanied by the inevitable leaks to the news media. Confidential discussions with our allies would not remain protected for long, and as knowledge of the Korean efforts surfaced, speculation and facts would tumble out in ways we could never control or contain.

Obviously, the first casualty of such a program would be the U.S.–ROK relationship itself. It would change immediately and probably dramatically. A reasonable assumption—and we would later game it out—would be a semi-public confrontation, threats to restructure our alliance agreement and the probable departure of the UN security guarantee on the peninsula. Beyond Korea itself, any South Korean breakout on the nuclear front had the potential to damage severely America's strategic credibility in the region as a nuclear manager and strategic overseer of multiple alliances.

Among those alliances, and of great concern to policymakers, would be Japan. Never far from such a capability itself, Japan historically viewed Korea as a dagger poised at its belly. Japan would draw its own conclusions about Korean intentions, make its own assessment, and certainly give thought to developing a civilian nuclear program to widen its options. Indeed, we assumed many Japanese would view a Korean nuclear program as forcing a Japanese counterpart. The decision would be deemed necessary from Japan's national security perspective, rather than a mere option to be pondered. U.S.-dictated "peace constitution" or not, Japan would be off to the nuclear races.

China, as Korea's traditional overlord and North Korea's sworn treaty ally, and itself having sacrificed more than a million troops during the Korean War, would adjust its own posture accordingly. Although the armistice had been declared 20 years earlier, the war remained unsettled with no peace treaty in place. Serious North Korean provocations were ongoing and systemic, based on Pyongyang's declared national priority to unite the peninsula by any means necessary. The Democratic People's Republic of Korea's conventional arms buildup, war-footing rhetoric and forward-positioned posture on the DMZ made broad and open conflict constantly possible. Furthermore, the UN-brokered armistice, governing the so-called temporary truce among the warring parties, was no guarantee war would not erupt again.

China was deeply entangled in it all. Its proxy Korean War entity, the Chinese People's Volunteer Army, was a signatory to the Armistice. In reality, China had little real control over the actions of the North Koreans. Consequently, a South Korean nuclear capability would present the Chinese with increased uncertainty, rattling a leadership increasingly at odds with the Soviet Union and slowly building ties with the United States, following President Richard M. Nixon's visit with Premier Zhou Enlai in February 1972.

The Soviet Union, at that time, was very much a force to be reckoned with in the Far East. Its Cold War strategic buildup in the region, its Pacific fleet deploying the latest and best capabilities in surface and subsurface combatants, the Soviet air force upping the ante by fielding increased levels of the latest-generation fighter and bomber units, and its Far East ground forces, all were well-postured to threaten China and strike another traditional regional rival, its declared or presumed adversary—Japan.

Meanwhile, the United States, Japan's alliance partner, maintained its own active posture vis-à-vis the Soviets in the Far East, both in regional security and strategic defense of the homeland. It had to be done. A new generation of a more capable Soviet Navy ballistic missile submarines patrolled the Pacific Ocean from Siberian ports and ranged to the U.S. West Coast, Hawaii and our bases throughout Asia.

In sum, tensions were high on all sides, with no real improvements in prospect. By then, Korea had been well-defined as the vortex of Asia, the locale over which China, Japan and Russia had feuded politically and contested in war for centuries. At that point, in summer 1974, nothing was trending well in the region inhabited by the two Koreas, either between them or among the larger players, and the strong drift was toward the negative. The Korean War was the fourth major land conflict fought between 1890 and 1950 on, around and over the control of the peninsula. That reality was not lost on any of the contenders and defenders actively involved.

The North Korean Aspect

North Korea, in the form of the primitive authoritarian regime of Kim Il-sung, probably would view a South Korean initiative to create its own nuclear force as a hugely aggressive and destabilizing factor. Such a perception would add a new and unneeded explosive element in the overall hair-trigger situation. In an important sense, the North–South dynamic had the potential to ignite into war independent of any restraints available to the major players, including the United States and China. Thus, it was reasonable to assume that if either side of the DMZ moved toward an independent nuclear capability, the action likely would provide a catalyst for war.

Not that the North Koreans weren't massively armed conventionally. They were increasingly well-postured, with their best forces forward deployed in an attack-tomorrow mode. Since the 1953 Armistice, North Korea had devoted its entire economy to a sustained military buildup—they wanted an independent capacity, apart from their Chinese sponsors, to wage war. And they accepted as the price of that ambition the deprivation and starvation of a large cohort of their population. The quantity and quality of men under arms in the North, with massed artillery and tank forces posing an immediate threat to the South, was impressive and hugely destabilizing.

Concurrently, we—the U.S. intelligence agencies—routinely underestimated certain North Korean military capabilities. Such underestimations contrasted with the regular accusation that our intelligence community frequently overestimated our adversaries' strengths. North Korea's ability to amass forces, including its special operations troops for first-strike deployment, made Pyongyang's threat legitimate, if not existential. Such posturing allowed the DPRK leadership to hold onto the dream of repeating the June 1950 invasion; the surprise attack on the ROK that nearly succeeded in overrunning the entire peninsula.

Within such an environment, a South Korean capacity to wage a nuclear war, or even threaten to wage one, would negate much of North Korea's conventional military power. That in turn would erode much of the effort and national sacrifice Pyongyang's leadership had devoted to its massive conventional arms buildup. At the ultimate level, with South Korea holding the nuclear card, Pyongyang would see its entire *raison d'étre* as a nation–state—the unification of the peninsula by arms or political intrigue—effectively checkmated. Bottom line: If North Korea judged that the ROK had initiated a nuclear weapons program, they would quickly conclude the ROK had the capability of a preemptive nuclear attack, independent of any U.S. ability to restrain such action. At a minimum, the North would adopt a use-it-or-lose-it posture, most likely leading to a conventional attack. Those were our Station-level assumptions, and we did not consider them farfetched.

As the line of logic continued, with any firm indication to North Korea that the Pak regime had initiated a nuclear weapons program, we could expect Kim Il-sung to throw his country into its own nuclear effort. We assumed, based on recent experiences, there would be little or no ability by Pyongyang's Chinese or Soviet sponsors to monitor, restrain or constrain the endeavor. Neither Moscow nor Beijing exercised any real control over North Korea, nor had they any substantial influence on Pyongyang's decision-making. Repeated North Korean provocations against the ROK and the United States, any one of which could have easily escalated into a full-blown shooting war, saw the Russians and the Chinese either oblivious or uncaring. We also assessed that the North Koreans had an active chemical weapons program and had forward-deployed that capability in a ready-for-battle-today mode. The companion assumption was that a parallel biological warfare program existed. We subsequently would confirm both assessments with hard intelligence.

At the same time, we had no assessment of an active North Korean nuclear weapons program. In truth, we had almost no ability to detect such a program even if there had been one. The standing opinion among the technically schooled was such an effort was beyond Pyongyang's technological or industrial capability. Nuclear research reactors supplied by the Soviets, and monitored by the IAEA, were judged to be the extent of the DPRK's nuclear activity—or so we thought. As usual, we underestimated the ambition and determination of the North Koreans, and we were wrong.

Much later, we would learn that the North Koreans had been dreaming the nuclear weapons dream for several years and had taken initiatives to develop a range of capabilities predating the South Korean decision. Because so little was known about the North's nuclear intentions or their efforts, the issue did not factor in our budding concerns over what their cousins in the South were considering on the same topic.

Station and Embassy Cooperation from Day One

All of this was mulled in a series of conversations among the Chief and a select few officers in the autumn of 1974. Because we shared the most sensitive reporting with our Ambassador, our work received his input as well. And in September, Richard L. Sneider replaced Philip Habib. Sneider, with whom our Chief enjoyed a great personal relationship, was a true East Asia professional and a respected Japan hand. When briefed on Station reporting, he immediately gleaned the importance of the potential negative trend in the bilateral relationship. As with our initial reaction, Sneider was doubtful. He considered a strategic nuclear program to be self-defeating for the Pak team. But he was willing to be convinced. His request to our Chief was simple. "Bring me everything your Station sends to D.C. I need to see that reporting first!"

Managing the Station-to-Embassy information flow on such a highly sensitive matter, and creating policy responses to those developments, became a major challenge. When intelligence collection, reporting and analysis transitioned to the policy side of our government, the policymakers needed to formulate and deploy diplomatic actions. The Embassy and the Ambassador would be at the tip of that spear as we took up the issue with the Pak administration. There also would be issues of intelligence-sharing back in Washington as well as interactions with other nations as we discovered their respective roles in the Korean program. At that early stage, however, none of those issues had yet come to the fore.

As we began focusing on all this, our Chief recalled a discussion that had taken place back in the summer of 1973, during his parting meeting at Headquarters with his immediate superior, the East Asia Division Chief—the infamous Theodore "Ted" Shackley.

Closing off their meeting, Shackley stood to shake hands. He wished his newly minted Seoul Chief "good hunting" then fixed him with the "Blond Ghost's" trademark stabbing stare. Shackley intoned, "Don, one more thing. I am sending you out to Seoul Station, so rule number one is no goddamn surprises!" Recounting that exchange, Don mulled aloud, "Gentlemen, I think that this is one of those 'no goddamn surprises' situations that Shackley is worried about."

Things were becoming a lot more interesting, in ways we could have never imagined. The way it all transpired caused me to consider, over the next several years, if somehow Phil Habib in early 1974 did not have a sixth sense about it. Perhaps he just saw the broader sweep of events coursing through the Far East and witnessed a growing sense of uncertainty among the Koreans and others in Asia about America and its role there. He might even have inferred the possibility of negative outcomes in Korea and wanted us to cover all the bases.

Habib's determination to have a nuclear energy referent was stimulated by the Korean decision to embrace nuclear power and build plants quickly. But he likely expected that Korea's nuclear ambitions would grow to include other options. If so, there was a Habib prescience at work. In a cable he sent a few days before departing Seoul, he lamented the overall trend of U.S. disengagement from Asia. His frustration was compounded by the perception that we were looking for options to back away from our commitments there. As his concern with Korea grew, and he saw as failed his attempts to mitigate the growing distrust on the part of the Koreans, he referenced a Chinese proverb, something along the lines of, "The best we may be able to do is 'burn the rice fields and poison the shrimp' as we walk away."

In Seoul, we were all pleased that Phil Habib had gone home to assume the position of Assistant Secretary of State for East Asian Affairs. Over the ensuing months and years, we would need all the help we could get, and Habib was in just the right spot to deliver for those of us out there on point in Seoul. And, as Ambassador Sneider settled in for what would become a four-year run in Seoul, we found that we had in him a most receptive State Department partner.

Defining the Target

The intelligence-collection plan evolved by Seoul Station to tackle South Korea's presumedly covert nuclear weapons program was straightforward. We would figure out where the locus of any related activity could take place or was already underway. Once we identified that activity, we would have to penetrate the targets. In our parlance, it meant we would attempt to acquire and maintain clandestine sources within the entities harboring protected information and have those sources reliably convey the information to us. Those sources, in turn, would allow us either to confirm the existence of a covert program or, alternatively, conclude that President Pak had ordered no such effort and that no program existed.

Straightforward in principle, yes, but it turned out to be anything but.

We also would have to assume that, if such a program existed, it only could have resulted from a top-down, well-considered decision. The ROK leadership enjoyed near-total control over every aspect of national decision-making, decision-execution and process. It was therefore inconceivable any mavericks were working on serious but unauthorized activities. The Pak administration employed a strict and responsive command structure, in both its military and non-military iterations. Although technically a functioning democracy (Pak had been reelected in 1971 by an overwhelming majority, albeit via highly suspect numbers), the instruments of near-authoritarian power and control had long been in place. That power and control had been uninterrupted and continuously refined since the day Pak seized power in a *coup d'état* in 1961.

On the military side, Pak's personal authority over the national defense structure was absolute, both constitutionally and on an individual loyalty basis. Beyond the Ministry of National Defense and its subordination to Pak as President, the elite Capital Defense Command, a full division of select troops plus ancillary air defense and armored formations, manned the checkpoints around the city. The CDC literally controlled everything military in greater Seoul, from barricades enforcing the midnight-to-dawn curfew to the Vulcan anti-aircraft batteries positioned atop buildings downtown.

The omnipresence of the CDC within central Seoul, and its mandate to shoot first and ask questions later, was brought home to me one night in December 1974. As I worked in my office to finish a report, a 20-millimeter Vulcan air-defense gun suddenly opened fire from a rooftop a few hundred feet across

113

the street, its six barrels spitting a stream of tracer rounds into the skies above. The target was a lone Northwest Airlines 747 passenger aircraft inbound to Kimpo Airport. The aircraft somehow had drifted off its designated line-of-approach and, in attempting to correct the error, crossed into the no-fly area above the presidential Blue House and was flying above Seoul's main avenue. Realizing a bit too late what was happening, I sought cover under a nearby desk.

The aircraft was not hit, but the pilots and 300 passengers were shaken by the stream of anti-aircraft fire directed at them. The Vulcan's projectiles spent themselves in the night sky and returned to earth in a deadly rain. The spent shells fell into a crowded bus a half-mile away and tore it apart, killing several civilians. It would not be the only air-defense incident during my tour. The U.S. Army lost a helicopter to those same Vulcan gunners a couple of years later, the shot-up chopper spinning into a riverbed, wounding several airmen. The Koreans did not take chances in the airspace above Seoul, and no one was ever disciplined for shooting at a target that might have been another North Korean attack. In fact, no one could blame them for firing first, and no one did.

The CDC held exclusive responsibility for the defense of the entire metropolitan area, including all government facilities and the inner defense circle around the Blue House. Its commander reported directly to the President. In its own way, the CDC was Pak's insurance policy against an ROK military coup, one that conceivably could displace him by rolling tanks into Seoul, just as he and his group had done a decade before. Such action by disaffected military commanders had become much less of a threat by 1974, but powerful ROK Army factions still existed, and Pak's strategic direction was not uniformly embraced. Nevertheless, the regime and its elite forces enjoyed total control of the streets and skies of Seoul, full stop.

In addition, that elite, handpicked, quasi-military force guarding the final perimeter of the Blue House and its occupants, the Presidential Security Service, was in place, serving Pak as his Praetorian Guard. The PSS was equivalent to the U.S. Secret Service, but on steroids, its troops kitted out in combat gear, all with *de rigueur* blood oaths sworn to protect the President.

Nationwide, an outer security perimeter for the President and his government was provided by two organizations, one military and one ostensibly civilian. The former, the previously referenced Army Security Command, provided the Ministry of National Defense and the Blue House with a nationwide network of military counterintelligence agents. Established as a stepchild of Pak's coup to enforce loyalty within the ranks, the ASC was chartered to defend against communist infiltration and North Korean espionage, both legitimate and constant threats. That said, the ASC was then something of an untouchable, and its leadership often operated well beyond its military mandate.

The ASC was tasked to probe all sectors of the national political structure for any signs of disloyalty or discontent that might threaten the Pak administration. But it was more than matched in its investigative, enforcement and intimidation capacities by its civilian counterpart and sometime rival, the Korean Central Intelligence Agency. The organization, with all senior officials hand-picked by

Pak, included many career ASC officers who had fleeted over to the KCIA from the sister agency. It held responsibility for both foreign intelligence (read: North Korea) and domestic counterespionage—imagine a combination of the CIA and FBI.

Birthed by and patterned on its U.S. namesake, the KCIA collected information, analyzed that information and presented its analysis to Pak and his lieutenants. The KCIA's mandate was loosely defined as the defender of the ROK body politic against all forms of malevolence, making it a ready instrument of intimidation for arbitrary use against any political opposition. Our Agency and the Station were compelled to work with the KCIA on several levels, first and foremost in our respective assessments of North Korean capabilities and intent. In that area, we found them eager and capable counterparts.

On the domestic scene, however, where suppression of dissent was the order of the day, the United States was less influential on the KCIA. Our counterparts typically declined to defer when we sought to moderate their actions. I recall vividly our Chief of Station, returning from a meeting with the KCIA Director and his staff, shaking his head in disbelief and wondering how he should report the results to the Ambassador and to Headquarters.

We commonly understood that, within the Blue House, President Pak managed his governance and decisions through his trusted team of senior secretaries, a half-dozen experienced technocrats with political and bureaucratic savvy. Pak entrusted each of those men with developing and enforcing his policies within a specific sector of the government or economy. In most cases, his senior secretaries demonstrated repeated success in formulating and executing the multi-year industry development and investment plans that had orchestrated the ROK's dramatic growth. Each of them sat above and dictated to the various ministries nominally responsible for a given sector. **[NOTE 1]**

Each senior secretary buttressed his respective position with a further echelon of special aides—junior secretaries—often engineers in their mid-40s with technical expertise in selected trade, economic or industrial areas. Working from the Blue House, those low-profile technocrats were able to interact, coordinate and enforce policies at the sub-ministerial level. Pak's organization, though far from perfect, was effective and provided certainty of execution once a decision was made.

The combination of the intelligence organizations, the military and the Blue House senior-secretary cadre provided Pak with close control over all elements of his regime. Taken together, they functioned in a well-coordinated manner that assured the President a level of privacy and protection then unequaled anywhere in the Free World.

As we evaluated our own collection program, we understood that any covert weapons development project the Pak government desired to hide from us would be wrapped in a comprehensive, multi-layered security blanket. If a non-declared weapons program did exist, it would be jealously guarded and its security enforced. Moreover, it certainly would be organized to allow Pak some degree of plausible denial if any hint of it surfaced.

Crafting an Intelligence Collection Plan

Recognizing all of the above, my assignment was to formulate a comprehensive plan of covert collection and then execute that plan in collaboration with my colleagues. I felt relatively well-positioned, both to develop the plan from a knowledge-of-target perspective and adjust it as we teased out the covert program's details. Meanwhile, I soon would supplement my layman's understanding of the topic by taking a stateside TDY for a cram course in the nuclear fuel cycle. The assignment allowed me to operate openly, in keeping with our plan. That is, under my cover I could seek direct access to certain Korean entities and organizations and, once I secured that access, sustain it in an attempt to acquire protected information.

Our first assumption about an ROK undeclared strategic weapons program was it would contain both overt and covert aspects. We knew the components would have to be carefully coordinated to complement one another—with some aspects hiding in plain sight as reasonable parts of nuclear research activities. We also knew a visible and declared program could harbor covert elements—if that was the intention. After all, declared nuclear facilities, functioning in a legitimate manner, would have to conform to sanctioned international practices covering the "peaceful uses" of atomic energy.

Likewise, internationally sanctioned nuclear energy activities could be both commercial and research-related, the latter involving reactor fuels and medical applications. On the commercial side, there had been dramatic progress in efficient electric power production based on the second-generation nuclear reactors deployed in many nations. At the same time, there was broad adoption of smaller, research-related nuclear facilities, often to produce isotopes for medical use, not to mention operational training for the much larger commercial reactors.

The sensitive areas of research encompassed fabrication of reactor fuel, observance of that fuel's performance in a nuclear reactor and examination of spent or irradiated material. All could be undertaken within the context of learning how to manage and master the nuclear fuel cycle, and managing the nuclear fuel cycle represented a natural extension of the normal operation of commercial nuclear facilities. Therefore, such activities normally would not be challenged by either the international community or the United States.

The ROK government had embraced nuclear energy for all the right reasons and had established appropriate relationships with the leading nuclear nations, including the United States. The ROK was a vigorous supporter of the UN-affiliated International Atomic Energy Agency and was a candidate to join the recently concluded Treaty on the Non-Proliferation of Nuclear Weapons. The IAEA's charter was established to promote nuclear power adoption and safety as well as to enforce safeguards designed to thwart proliferation. Further, by its own national law, the ROK had created a Nuclear Energy Commission, modeled on our Atomic Energy Commission (later the Nuclear Regulatory Commission), to oversee all nuclear activity, be it civil or government, commercial power

116

generation or research-related.

The ROK, in keeping with its industrial development strategy, had every reason to embrace peaceful nuclear energy and companion research programs. In 1971, encouraged by the United States, South Korea decided to accept commercial nuclear power to ensure efficient baseload generation for its expanding electrical grid. That decision was the initial step along a path that would see South Korea launch an expansive commercial program. Over the ensuing decades, the ROK's commitment to nuclear energy would create one of the world's most aggressive and successful programs.

In 1974, Korea Electric Power Company, or KEPCO, the national electrical utility, was one year into constructing its first commercial reactor. Supplied by an international consortium led by Westinghouse Corporation, Kori 1, located at the site of a small fishing village on the southeastern coast, was a 600-megawatt, pressurized-water reactor, a design that represented the latest evolution in PWR design technology. The reactor was something of a poster nuclear export project for the United States and for Westinghouse. Kori 1 enjoyed the full support of the U.S. Export–Import Bank and had received substantial political endorsements from both governments. All parties were able to highlight Kori 1 as a success story in the context of America's broader support for Korea's accelerating economic development. [NOTE 2]

The Blue House Mandate to the Korea Atomic Energy Research Institute

As noted earlier, starting from the mid-1960s forward, the ROK wholeheartedly had embraced nuclear energy, and it gradually made the effort a national priority. That strong commitment to a nuclear future was encouraged and complemented by the promise of technology-sharing, originally offered to the world under President Eisenhower's Atoms for Peace initiative. The peaceful-uses concept was sustained politically and accompanied by active programs of technical assistance through the Kennedy, Nixon and Ford administrations. Along with dozens of developing nations, the ROK had taken up the offer by the United States and like-minded nuclear allies to foster nuclear energy development, both in the research areas related to technology mentoring and on the power reactor side for electrical generation.

The designated recipient in South Korea was the Korea Atomic Energy Research Institute, operating under the supervision of the nominally independent Nuclear Energy Commission. KAERI was bureaucratically administered by, and derived its annual national government budget allocation from, the Ministry of Science and Technology. The latter reported to the Blue House directly, although the MOST Minister, as a member of Pak's cabinet, technically reported to the cabinet secretariat and therefore to the Prime Minister. The quasi-independent Economic Planning Board maintained overall national authority, budget-building and budget-execution responsibility, with spending parameters and priorities set by the Blue House. Within the latter, the Senior Secretary for Economic

Affairs, and his sectorial deputies and their staff, answered directly to the President.

The senior secretaries—in effect, Pak's inner circle—exercised hands-on direction over the EPB, the Ministry of Finance, all industry-specific ministries and, by extension, KAERI. For our purposes of understanding the funding dynamics of the ROK's strategic weapons development program, both its covert and overt components, the key ministries were the Ministry of National Defense, the Ministry of Science and Technology and, to a lesser extent, the Ministry of Energy. Above them all sat the Blue House senior staff.

I need to backtrack briefly about KAERI. By the yardstick of any developing nation's nuclear program, the institute was a success, particularly given its limited funding in the early years of the Pak regime. Established as a corporate entity in 1973, in parallel with the establishment of MOST's Bureau of Atomic Energy, when three existing nuclear-related institutes were consolidated, KAERI had established an attractive campus in the suburbs of Seoul, recruiting a small cadre of researchers and administrators. Along the way, it managed to acquire two research reactors from the United States: a General Atomics TRIGA Mark II (250 kilowatts) and the much-larger TRIGA Mark III (2 megawatts). Both were supplemented by basic nuclear fuel research facilities. KAERI's modest research and training programs received a mini-boost when the ROK decided to embrace nuclear power in 1970, and KEPCO was directed to negotiate the purchase of Korea's first nuclear reactor, the aforementioned Kori 1.

The advent of that commercial program, undertaken by KEPCO (under the control of the Ministry of Energy), allowed KAERI and its overseers, the BAE and MOST, to press the Blue House for a dramatic increase in the scope of its work along with substantial increases in KAERI's budget. All of this would be an expected component of a growing nuclear power program, particularly if KAERI was charged, as it would be in due course, with creating a reactor-operator training program.

By our observations, KAERI's leadership was seized with the possibility of creating and managing all aspects of the entire nuclear fuel cycle, meaning the ROK eventually would be able to produce its own reactor fuel and reprocess the irradiated material into plutonium when it was extracted from the reactor. Such an achievement eventually would guarantee Korea's nuclear independence from foreign suppliers and place it in the running to be a sovereign nuclear state.

KAERI's and the ROK's ambition required mastering the front end of the fuel cycle, in which Korea would mine and process natural uranium, enrich it to a grade capable of fueling a nuclear reactor and then fabricate the enriched uranium into fuel assemblies. To complete the cycle, the spent nuclear fuel that would have been irradiated by, and emerged from, the reactors then would be chemically reprocessed. In the so-called back end, the reprocessing or separation program would permit the extraction of plutonium. The latter, once refined, would emerge as a highly toxic heavy metal and be available for blending into a more sophisticated nuclear fuel. Such would be KAERI's challenge, and Pak's inner circle wholeheartedly supported that lofty goal.

We could understand how the ROK, in designing its nuclear fuel cycle program, might have kept a weather eye on Japan, not to mention other developing nations with nuclear power ambitions. In Japan's case, an expansive reactor program, involving multiple technologies, system vendors and utilities as operators, was underway. Its nuclear push was complemented by a well-advanced, national-level nuclear fuel cycle, including pilot-scale uranium enrichment and reprocessing research. All of that activity was a matter of public record and subject to U.S. as well as international inspection and monitoring. But the South Koreans were watching every Japanese move and were determined to come abreast of those programs as quickly as possible.

By any metric, the fuel cycle mandate given to KAERI by Blue House planners was wildly ambitious in scope with an aggressive timeline. The mandate was accompanied by an instruction to conceal, for as long as possible, as much from public knowledge as practical. That meant some of the planning would be shared early on with the U.S. side, but much would not be disclosed. The information came to us only incrementally as we managed to tease it out. Beyond KAERI and the activities for which it was responsible, there existed a broader plan, conceived at the highest level. The plan was designed to equip the ROK with a solid path to a substantial and possibly unsupervised (and undetectable) supply of plutonium, a path that would deliver nuclear fissionable material required for weapons.

Not surprising, the ROK's civilian nuclear leadership, top-down from the corridors of the Blue House to the NEC commissioners through the MOST bureaucracy and into the management of KAERI, perceived that a window of opportunity had opened to secure increasingly larger budget allocations. MOST's vision to expand KAERI's facilities by entering new areas of nuclear research, and substantially increasing its staffing, was fast becoming reality. President Pak and his top advisors promoted and endorsed the broader nuclear program as a strategic national priority. They could make the reasonable case that South Korea's expanding economy and emphasis on heavy industry demanded no less. As with all ROK decisions, they examined in great detail, and even admired, Japan's similar emphasis on the broad adoption of all things nuclear. Replicating Japan's all-in approach to mastering the nuclear fuel cycle was deemed not an option but an absolute necessity.

One glaring need in that broad ambition by the Blue House, the NEC and KAERI involved a dramatic increase in experienced staff. Consequently, they began seeking out, recruiting and bringing home—ideally on a permanent basis—key Korean-national nuclear researchers, engineers and managers working abroad. Those individuals typically held advanced degrees and had been trained and employed overseas. The expanded ROK national budget allocations to support the nuclear sector as a strategic priority would pay for this talent with offers of higher salaries and relocation bonuses, not to mention impressive levels of responsibility and status. Sustained recruitment from foreign talent pools of

Korean scientists and engineers of every persuasion had begun in 1972, focusing mainly on the United States and Germany, and first among the sought-after talent were those in the nuclear field.

With the envisioned programs and efforts falling into place, Pak would depend on KAERI to deliver the fissile material required for a credible nuclear weapons capability. And the institute indeed would come close to acquiring all of the necessary components. Had we not disrupted those efforts when we did, the ROK would have possessed, certainly by 1978, everything it required to realize Pak's nuclear objective.

The Overt Nuclear Program as a Collection Target

As we observed the ROK nuclear effort unfold, some key questions emerged. For example, to what extent and in what ways (including new facilities, staffing and capabilities) would KAERI move forward? Also, as KAERI expanded its activities, what role could existing facilities and added capabilities play in facilitating a discrete nuclear weapons program, if such a broader covert program existed or was about to be commissioned?

We judged that, on the overt side, there simply was no way the ROK could build and operate the facilities required to produce fissionable materials. A nuclear fuel cycle producing the materials required for a device must involve a capability sophisticated enough to yield highly enriched uranium or, alternatively, a reprocessing program that generated high-quality plutonium from spent reactor fuel. The former path—the enrichment of processed natural uranium—would allow the creation of the "Little Boy," a device similar to the one employed at Hiroshima on August 6, 1945. The alternative approach would create the "Fat Man," a plutonium-fueled bomb such as the weapon dropped on Nagasaki three days later.

In the former case, at least in the timeframe of those events, creating and running a uranium enrichment facility would have involved a complicated, expensive and no doubt high-profile industrial undertaking—a World War II-style Manhattan Project. Pursuing such an option would unavoidably result in a declared and therefore IAEA-safeguarded facility. Moreover, there would be no economic justification for such a massive operation. Then, too, the Kori 1 plant, and the pressurized-water reactors slated to follow, required nuclear fuel supply contracts. The contracts, at least for the initial load of fuel and several subsequent reloads, would be guaranteed by the reactor vendor and sourced to an American or third-country provider. As such, the uranium would arrive with full safeguards covering the fuel bundles and secure-forever control over the irradiated byproduct.

Given all of the above, we reasoned that the ROK would not develop its own enrichment capacity, not to produce the type of mildly enriched nuclear fuel required by Kori-type PWRs. In addition, the Koreans apparently were attempting to court, or were being courted by, other commercial reactor suppliers, some of which had no requirement for enriched fuels. We had yet to piece that together, but the Canadians, with their own natural-uranium-based CANDU reactors, had sensed an opportunity and been invited by KEPCO and the NEC to present their wares. If the ROK intended to adopt the natural-uranium-fueled CANDU as a parallel technology to the light-water-moderated PWRs, there would be even less justification for an enrichment program.

In the plutonium approach, the fissile material used to create an explosive device could be chemically separated or reprocessed from irradiated fuel elements. The latter would occur either in a commercial-scale reactor or a smaller research reactor. And such a reactor could generate the maximum amount of optimally irradiated plutonium. Using irradiated fuel elements from a commercial reactor to secure fissionable material constituted an illegal diversion. Nevertheless, it seemed the more likely approach.

If that was the ROK's chosen path to acquiring fissionable material—producing plutonium at the purity level needed for explosive purposes—it would be even more problematic. Plutonium is the byproduct of nuclear fission, typically created in either a commercial reactor or a smaller reactor specifically configured to yield high-quality product. Thus, any attempt to create a capability to produce and separate plutonium would suggest only one purpose, at least as the nuclear fuel cycle was then understood.

There was, in the early 1970s, a desire by the advanced nuclear countries to recycle spent nuclear fuel to recover plutonium for use in other experimental reactor types. But any such ambition by the ROK seemed impractical. The above-described two paths to secure the fissionable material necessary for a successful nuclear detonation—the enriched uranium and plutonium options— were widely appreciated, both technically and from the lay perspective of policymakers. In fact, the United States had pursued both paths with the Manhattan Project. Other nations, such as the United Kingdom, France, Russia, China and, more recently, India, had traveled those same routes to design, fabricate and explode nuclear devices. In doing so, they had demonstrated that, with a determined approach, necessary funding, an adequate amount of time and the nuclear feedstock material needed, building a nuclear device was achievable.

The mechanics of the two approaches were well understood. Because we assumed the ROK would pursue one or perhaps both of those paths, we knew what to look for. We also assumed that some or all of the activity would be overt, at least at some point. Therefore, any such activity could be anticipated, observed and tracked. We did not have far to look or long to wait.

The Blue House-managed, overt nuclear research community already had obtained its roadmap and marching orders and was moving ahead with its mandate by mid-1974. It took us a couple of months to pull the information together and, with our appreciation of what was required, match the overt side with its covert counterpart. Once we identified the dots and connected them, the ROK plan became fairly clear. As we expected, the Koreans had selected the plutonium route to acquire fissile material, and that part of the effort was well underway at KAERI as part of its multi-faceted, overt program.

Accessing KAERI with a Direct Approach

Focusing on the overt aspect of the Korean nuclear equation, and putting aside for the time being KEPCO's two parallel commercial reactor programs, the U.S. government sought clarity from their ROK counterparts about the KAERI projects. I sat squarely in the middle of it all in my role as the Nuclear Energy Officer. It was a position I was not interested in handing over to another officer, even if one was nominated to take my place. I had fallen comfortably into my role, and the management, up to and including the recently arrived Ambassador Sneider, accepted that I was well-suited for the task—at least until a true nuclear expert could join the staff. That expert, Dr. Jerry Helfrich, would arrive in the summer of 1975. Helfrich would come to play a critical role in our effort to turn the South Koreans away from their objective. But his arrival was a half-year away, and the ROK was moving with dispatch.

Regarding our ability to establish intelligence collection, it helped that I had, by that point in the overall nuclear narrative, become involved in KEPCO's Kori 1 project as the construction of the powerplant advanced. My access was based on a personal friendship and professional dialog with the Westinghouse representative, as well as interaction with some mid-level KEPCO managers involved in nuclear power planning. At the time, the ROK and KEPCO were petitioning my government hard to finance the second unit at Kori, and we were managing that dialog.

I was able to develop a personal and protected relationship with two KAERI senior researchers, each of whom was directly involved in the fuel cycle planning effort. One was responsible for executing the institution's relocation to the new and greatly expanded KAERI facility near Taejon, which later became its main research campus within Taeduk Science City. The man, an engineer, would play a role in the program's construction and operation, including the desired reprocessing plant and fuel fabrication. The second was involved in research and training, focusing on the role provided by an anticipated natural-uranium-fueled research reactor. I will explain the importance of the two facilities in a later chapter. But for now, suffice it to say that KAERI was abuzz with activity in late 1974, when I secured access there.

Motivation to Share Protected Information

After a standard period of personal acquaintance development, I had cultivated semi-covert relationships with the two individuals. Both were motivated to demonstrate or confirm that all aspects of their work would be aboveboard and consistent with the non-proliferation commitments accepted by the ROK. They knew the nuclear fuel cycle was subject to misuse; that the diversion of nuclear fuel—not to mention the production of plutonium outside a safeguards regime—would mean someone in the ROK government wanted a covert weapons program. Both men had heard such rumors, and both wished to demonstrate that, if there were such a program, they and their new facilities would not be a part of it. Yet both knew it was a commitment to maintain clean hands they personally could not keep. They understood if higher authority ordered KAERI's fuel cycle to produce unsafeguarded fuel, divert fuel or undertake unsafeguarded reprocessing, those same KAERI managers might protest but nevertheless would have to find a way to comply.

From my two contacts, I learned the details of an overt but veiled fuel cycle program, including the contracting status of the reprocessing plant, the fuel fabrication component and the research reactor. More important, I learned the identities of non-KAERI nuclear researchers with whom the staff was familiar and who were then serving with or being recruited by the ADD for work there.

The loyalty of the two men who agreed to cooperate with us was to their own nation as well as to their institution. At the same time, they knew exactly with whom they were sharing protected information, and they wished to define in detail what KAERI was and was not doing with its new facilities. I prefaced every discussion I had by acknowledging their commitment to protect the ROK from imprudent decision-making and self-defeating activity in the nuclear arena. Both hoped KAERI would find a way to avoid violating their own moral principles and prevent the rupturing of the U.S.–ROK alliance, in particular the security guarantee provided to South Korea and its citizens. We discussed those issues and dangers often and openly, and it was clear the subtext was the growing realization that the Pak regime planned to use KAERI as a component of a strategic weapons program.

From the outset, the process of discovering and clarifying the overt nuclear fuel cycle program also involved my direct interaction with senior Ministry of Science and Technology nuclear bureaucrats, as well as the three atomic energy commissioners. Establishing several professional relationships at senior levels permitted us to tease out more of the MOST and KAERI fuel cycle game plan. Whenever I met with my counterparts, I almost always knew the answers to the questions I was asking, often from our clandestine or cooperating sources. We needed our ROK counterparts to confirm the facts directly, mainly so the information could be placed on the record and reported back to Washington, to the benefit of both the analysts and the policymakers. Getting as much as possible into open channels allowed us to lay the basis for an official bilateral dialog.

Covert Elements of a Strategic Weapons Development Program

The darker side of a weapons program was another matter entirely. The covert components of the equation would include elements that complemented the visible activity. They included design of an actual explosive device and the testing and perfection of systems critical to the workings of an effective weapon. Likewise, the effort would need to refine the arming and fusing components while building a structure to contain the device. Beyond those engineering disciplines, some protected mechanism would have to exist to coordinate such a complex effort.

In sum, all explosive-specific elements of any nuclear weapons program, plus complementary efforts to design, test and build a delivery system, necessarily would have to be covert. And by "covert," I mean a program organized and managed in a manner that would hide the sensitive activities from any party capable of detecting, disrupting or defeating them. The overriding priority would be to conceal the program from outside parties, including both the United States as the ROK alliance partner and the ROK body politic. A parallel priority would deeply compartmentalize those secrets within the military and government, making the project secure from any party not possessing an absolute need to know.

Obviously, such sensitive activities would need to be concealed from the ROK's declared enemies: North Korea, China and the Soviet Union. But the ROK parties involved, seeking the success of the program, also needed to conceal their effort from the party best positioned to discover and challenge their clandestine strategic weapons program: the United States. If the ROK indeed initiated such a program, we assumed their immediate concern would be that we would gain knowledge of it and, with that knowledge, attempt to disrupt such a politically sensitive activity. Knowing the thoroughness of the Koreans, respecting their growing technical abilities, and assuming such a toxic program would be protected as a national strategic priority, we realized our ability to detect, penetrate and define such activity would be a challenge.

Learning How to Spell 'Nuclear'

As our understanding of that challenge grew, I headed back to Washington, and Headquarters, in the fall of 1974. The operations folks there, namely the Directorate of Operations reports officers, had scrambled to organize a deep-immersion nuclear technology education program for me. It was a catch-as-catch-can agenda. I worked initially with the Directorate of Intelligence's analysts at Langley, whose daily obsession was to study and assess the inner workings of the Soviet and Chinese weapons programs. There, I was made to understand what they did in the fields of weapons development and deployment analysis, and how they reached their conclusions for our senior policymakers.

My time there also involved a lay tutorial on the nuclear fuel cycle, as preparation for the time I would spend with engineers and weaponeers at Los Alamos National Laboratory in the coming two weeks, and later at Sandia Laboratories, both in New Mexico. I should note that, at that relatively early period, nuclear non-proliferation was not a well-defined policy priority at the Agency or even in the U.S. government. Our government had shifted from the full-blown nuclear advocacy of the Atoms for Peace vision that defined the 1950s and 1960s to more cautious support for nuclear energy adoption and nuclear reactor export promotion. But the evolution still constituted a work-in-progress.

At many levels within both the Executive and Legislative branches, as well as the broader nuclear community—including academics, researchers and would-be exporters—concerns over the inherent dangers of non-nuclear states building their own bombs mostly remained unheard of. In 1973, through the point of the first detonation by India in 1974, nuclear weapons analysis by the intelligence and policy communities focused, for reasonable reasons, only on the fellow superpowers; namely, the Soviet Union and China. Each of the established, self-declared-and-proud-of-it weapons states was busy building its respective arsenal with more sophisticated bomb designs and more capable delivery systems.

Because proliferation per se was not a topic of the hour, and within the Agency's Directorate of Operations there literally was not one officer trained or directed to collect intelligence on non-nuclear-weapons state targets, it was new territory for the DO. We were starting behind the power curve to educate ourselves in order to develop an intelligence-collection program in the field. In many ways, driven only by the special circumstances we encountered in South Korea, and to a lesser extent in Taiwan, I would be the first of my type to ascend that learning curve.

Struggling to understand all of the information to which I had been exposed, I hurried back to Seoul within the month and rejoined the active pursuit of the target. I probably knew just enough "nuclear" to be dangerous. But I did know something, and I worked hard to become the best possible field operator active on the nuclear target. To quote an old adage, "In the land of the blind, the one-eyed man is king." I was pretty sure I was now that anointed one-eyed, nuclear energy royal. The State Department would get around to sending a real expert to the Embassy, the aforementioned Dr. Jerry Helfrich. But that did not occur until mid-1975. Until then, I did my level best to pursue my various nuclear duties.

Chapter 10. Chasing Atomic Dragons
Fall-Winter 1974

The Covert Strategic Weapons Program Assessed

In autumn 1974, when we learned of President Pak's comments, the Station began to identify the overt and covert elements of the Korean nuclear program. After several months of hard work, assisted by some overconfidence on the Korean side, we were able to convince ourselves we had identified the beginnings of a dedicated covert program. How those pieces came together is worth a careful telling, both to demonstrate the sophistication of the Korean effort and provide a case study on how to detect and confirm a government-sponsored, covert strategic weapons development effort.

Our first solid opening came from targeting the most likely candidate for signs of non-declared—to the United States as the ROK's ally—research and development activities: the Agency for Defense Development. As explained, the ADD had been established several years earlier to develop military technology. Its mission was to introduce advanced U.S. weapons systems into the Korean military and develop Korea's own defense products and systems.

The ADD was directly subordinate to the Ministry of National Defense and drew its annual budget from that institution. The ADD's full Korean name— Hankuk Kukbang Kwahak Youngku So—was seldom used outside military channels. Up to that point, the Station really had not focused on the agency as a collection target, deferring instead to our military colleagues to cover their counterpart entity. We did assume the ADD maintained a direct link to the Blue House, and we suspected it reported either to the Blue House Secretary General or his direct subordinate, the Senior Chief Secretary for Industrial Development, both of whom sat in the office of President Pak.

As far as the ADD's contact with our military, it occurred through the Joint U.S. Military Assistance Group-Korea, the longstanding military office subordinate to our 8th Army's in-country presence. In the years after the war, JUSMAG-K's staff had shrunk to a couple of hundred officers and enlisted men. The reason was simple. The ROK military by 1974 was reaching the point that JUSMAG-K had little left to teach their armed forces. Nevertheless, JUSMAG-K retained some status in the overall military alliance. It operated out of our Army's Yongsan headquarters compound in Seoul, with a two-star general in command. Further checking suggested that our military intelligence organizations active in the ROK did not consider the ADD an active target.

The ADD had begun life as a low-key organization assisting Korean industry to produce components locally for selected conventional weapons and ammunition. The agency typically accomplished that by introducing technical data packages, or TDPs; essentially, engineering drawings for conventional weapons provided by JUSMAG-K on a component- or weapon-specific basis. The ADD's research and development efforts on its own weapons systems were initially limited, and the agency was sparsely staffed by a mixture of active duty officers and enlisted men. The former mostly were locally trained engineers, and the latter were military weapons technicians plus some Korean civilian engineers.

As mentioned earlier, at some point in the 1972-1973 period, a decision was made at the highest level—we assumed by President Pak—to expand the organization dramatically, with generous, multi-year budget allocations. That top-down support permitted increased staffing levels, recruiting more civilian engineers from abroad and underwriting a host of new weapons development programs. Those programs ran the gamut: new types of ammunition and artillery shells, locally developed military rifles, artillery and air defense systems, tactical communications equipment and military vehicles, including tanks.

The Agency for Defense Development in the Gunsight

The ADD in 1974 maintained a relatively low profile. In fact, it was ostensibly a classified organization within the ROK government that was not listed on public documents. As mentioned earlier, the ADD functioned under a cover organization, the Hong Nung Machinery Company, or Hong Nung Ki-Kae in Korean. At the Station, we knew the ADD existed and that JUSMAG-K was technically its U.S. equivalent, but little else. Our discussions with JUSMAG-K at the senior-officer level were not very productive, the attitude being a combination of, "Why do you, the Station, need to know about the ADD?" and, "The ADD is a U.S. military responsibility and we have it well covered." They provided us with a dated ADD organization chart, but it seemed no one at JUSMAG-K could provide the details we were looking to secure.

In keeping with our operational plan to secure as much access as possible to all targeted entities, I decided to establish a direct relationship with ADD senior management. Through my Defense Industry Officer self-designation, I cold-called the agency to introduce myself and arrange for a tour of the complex. I explained that my mandate was to promote cooperation between the U.S. private-industry defense sector and its counterparts in the ROK. The ADD folks were taken a bit off-guard, but after a few weeks of stalling they invited me over to meet with them.

My priorities in visiting Hong Nung Kikae were threefold. First, we badly needed to understand the organization as it then existed and as it planned to evolve in the near term, particularly because JUSMAG-K was not inclined to cooperate with us on that front.

Second, we needed to lay groundwork for sustainable relationships we could use to access the facility, as well as the local companies and tech centers working with the ADD on selected projects.

Third, I wanted to meet as many ADD staffers as possible to identify key individuals as potential contacts, ideally outside the protected compound and hopefully on a one-to-one basis. That was my overriding objective, mainly because no one could tell us who the critical players were and which of them managed the ADD's diverse programs.

My first meeting at the ADD was productive. I received a reasonably comprehensive—up to a point—management briefing, and the organization made sense as explained. The programs, some of which we knew and some new ones, all seem to fit into the ambitious-but-plausible mode. I met about 15 managers that first time, along with about half the senior staff and a few project engineers. I assumed I had received what we called a 90-percent brief—the ADD kimono remained semi-closed and still hiding a lot, at least in the planned expansion-of-ADD department. In many areas, however, I did not understand the programs briefed to me. But it was a good start. Still, the more we looked at the ADD and built our file on it, the more we realized we needed help.

When JUSMAG-K found out, soon after the fact, about my visit, their reaction was negative. In the following months, my attention to the ADD became a minor turf issue. The complaint, delivered at a fairly high level to our Station, was that "a certain party" was inappropriately and unnecessarily inserting itself into U.S. military business. My Chief batted away the complaint with a simple, "He's just doing his job." But the matter of turf would not go away. It would present us with problems over the next few years and beyond, as the Station honed in on the activities at the ADD and its surrogate institutions.

Mac Walks In

A week after my visit to the ADD, a heaven-sent "guiding light" appeared at my office door, an individual who would help our collection activity immensely. And I would come to regard him as a true friend and colleague. He introduced himself as Master Sergeant Hugh MacElvoy, assigned to JUSMAG-K with lead responsibility for technical data package interaction with the ADD. It probably was one of the most significant meetings of our entire effort to penetrate the ROK's covert strategic weapons program.

"Mac," as he asked me to call him, got right to the point. "So, are you really serious about ADD? Are you really committed to knowing what they do there and what they are planning to do there?" With that opening, Mac and I talked ADD deeply. Then came his follow-on query. "Also, if I were to work with you, can I trust you?" We got past the trust issue with a full discussion of our respective backgrounds, my commitment to the long haul in Seoul, my previous military experience in Korea and his explanation of his strong identity with everything Korean.

It was clear that we were discussing, literally from hour one, a discreet relationship of full information-sharing outside JUSMAG-K channels, at least up to a point. He wanted to work with us—the Station—directly, until he and we could find a way to channel our association with him through his JUSMAG-K chain of command. We both knew continuing such a discreet arrangement would not be easy. He explained he had concluded that the situation, "as it is playing out now at ADD," was so important he was willing to risk censure from his command by reaching out to us. He explained his access at the ADD, his relationships and interactions there, and then his own difficult situation within JUSMAG-K. [NOTE 1]

A few days later, in a subsequent conversation with Mac's direct supervisor at JUSMAG-K, an Army lieutenant colonel from the Artillery Branch, I satisfied myself that Mac's assessment was accurate. His own leadership was indifferent and dismissive on the subject of any sensitive activity at the ADD. I discerned that his superiors regarded Mac as "a tech sergeant with responsibilities to transfer documents," the guy who handled day-to-day contact with the ADD. The colonel, the lead officer interacting with the ADD, had other, non-ADD duties. He had not visited the ADD in several months and seemingly harbored little interest in the activity there. JUSMAG-K's focus was on equipping and training the ROK military, particularly procuring weapons systems by that military and training personnel in systems required to improve ROK capabilities. Fair enough, as far as that went. JUSMAG-K was not an intelligence-collection organization, and thus we decided that Mac would operate with the Station outside the parameters of his defined duties.

During our initial meeting, Mac and I discussed my recent visit to the ADD and my broad range of interests in research activity there. He told me that information he had gleaned in the halls of ADD, and fortified in the course of extended beer-hall evenings in the aftermath of my visit, conveyed concern about my intentions. Middle-level ADD staff had informed Mac they were instructed to "exercise caution" with the visiting officer. The new ADD internal ground rules limited contacts and did not permit discussion of ADD programs with any outsiders unless cleared by senior management.

Mac also learned that, from the perspective of the old-timers at Hong Nung Kikae, there were new faces at the ADD, mostly civilian researchers, some apparently imported at considerable cost from the United States and Europe. All were Korean-born nationals recruited from high-quality American and European firms, the latter typically returning home from extended stays in the States, Germany or the United Kingdom. Just as important, there was that growing security clamp-down within the ADD along with more physical compartmentation and tighter controls on information flow.

On the positive side, in that changing environment, Mac surprisingly retained access to his established contacts there. He thought it mostly was because he had become "one of them," based on carefully constructed personal relationships built up over six-plus years. He interacted with ADD researchers daily to support their programs. He dealt with them almost exclusively in Korean. And he ate and drank with them after hours in the byways of Seoul. The mid-level exchanges allowed us, via Mac's contacts, to confirm that something was indeed afoot within the ADD.

Soon, we were soon able to confirm that, along with its expanded mandate of conventional research and development programs, the ADD was adding new research elements that required a different set of engineering specialists, with all of the expanded activity overlaid by increased security. There also appeared to be areas of activity that either were fenced off from discussion or reluctantly acknowledged by senior management. And their various descriptions simply did not add up. At that stage of our evolving understanding of the target facility, Mac proved invaluable. He corrected, expanded and validated the organization chart the ADD had provided. Over several meetings, he and I compiled a directory of every employee by name, title, department and area of expertise.

Another plus: Mac's area of specialization, beyond his understanding and mastery of the technical data package flow—which provided us access to a wide range of the ADD's departments—was ordnance, namely, ammunition design and production and the related field of high explosives. His familiarity with explosives was fortuitous. Any nuclear work would involve certain complex issues where the ADD could not easily recruit civilians to replace military experts. In the Korean private sector, the sole relevant player was Korean Explosives Group, a significant business conglomerate that enjoyed close ties to the government leadership. Its founder and chairman, still active in the mid-1970s, was none other than Kim Chong-hi, better known as "Dynamite Kim," a man who literally had built a business empire on explosives manufacturing. Dynamite Kim was then something of a legend, a man who enjoyed a personal relationship with President Pak and kept a firm hand on his various commercial programs.

KEC, as it was generally known, was then and remains a core enterprise of the Korea Explosives Group. Founded in 1952 at the height of the Korean War, the business group, or *chaebol*, changed its name to Hanhwa Group in 1992 and is today one of Korea's most diversified business conglomerates. Group founder Dynamite Kim was a freewheeling character in the Korean business community, and his firm had established a reputation of a tightly bound collection of tough men—explosives makers and handlers all—who were not beyond taking a reasonable risk here and there.

Mac provided a window into that otherwise closed world. **[NOTE 2]**

Building the Clandestine Asset Team

Beyond what Mac could provide with his access to the ADD and KEC, my Station's task was to identify individuals who might be willing to discuss responsibilities, both within the ADD and those of their compatriots. We had gained a fairly good idea what we were looking for, in terms of individual disciplines required for the military side of a nuclear weapons development program. But we had no idea of the scope—or level of immediate ambition—of such a program. The more we learned, however, the greater our confidence grew that, if such a covert activity existed, the ADD was, or was close to, its center.

Within weeks of my visit to the ADD, a new concern surfaced. We discovered the agency was accelerating its plan to relocate outside Seoul to a remote location some 100 miles to the south, near the city of Taejon in central South Korea.

The relocation represented the core element of a wholesale expansion of ADD as *the* national defense research institution. The expansion involved not only a new central research facility but also a separate subordinated installation for naval weapons research, and another site dedicated to missile testing. The Taejon location, organized in a distributed campus-like configuration, would make it much easier to compartmentalize activity and isolate the most sensitive ADD projects.

It became obvious that when the ADD's relocation moved forward, our access to activity would be severely circumscribed. Beyond physical access to the facility itself, we would experience a de facto denial of access to personnel who worked there. Therefore, the Station's ability to establish and sustain contacts with ADD personnel, for the purposes of recruitment and clandestine reporting, would be heavily and permanently degraded.

Regarding the Taejon location, here again we caught a break, or at least a head start. As it happened, I knew the area quite well, having been stationed near Camp Ames during my military intelligence days four years before. ███████ ██ ██████████████████████████████████████ The terrain and the villages, valleys and mountains were familiar to me. Equally useful, because the Taejon area for several years had been considered the logical location for Korea's "new capital" city, maps and concept plans existed for the area. All valuable input as we tried to understand where the "new and improved ADD" would be located.

The timeframe proved almost providential. Had we failed to realize what was happening when we did—by taking Pak's August 1974 comments seriously—and organizing ourselves quickly to engage ADD as a primary and priority intelligence target, the agency would have completed its expansion, improved its security practices and slipped away to the new location over the next year. Therefore, any penetration of the target facility and its people would have grown exponentially more difficult.

Underestimating a Man

Two early recruitments at the ADD were critical. One was a relationship I initiated within the hour of my first visit there. It involved an official, whom I described in the Preface as Mr. Chang. We assessed him as having only marginal access to sensitive issues because he was not an engineer or scientist and did not participate in any research group. In short, we were dead wrong. Our relationship quickly moved outside the ADD, developed on a social basis and, over a period of months, blossomed into a high level of trust between us.

Mr. Chang was a true Korean patriot. He strongly believed in the U.S.–ROK alliance and had experienced the sight of "dead American Marines, their blood pooling around them, lying in the streets of Seoul." Those young Americans had fallen as they liberated the city, and his home, from the communist North Koreans. His family, as upper-class Christians, had fled North Korea before the war and restarted their lives in the South. Family members left behind in Pyongyang had been stripped of their homes, imprisoned and killed.

Mr. Chang was committed to doing everything possible to ensure the safety of his family. He did not trust the North Korean regime not to invade the South again in the absence of an American military presence. Just as important, he did not wish to be part of any activity that would jeopardize the U.S. pledge to defend Korea and, by extension, his family. His commitment to the U.S.–ROK relationship was based on the logic of the partnership, but it was also emotional and deeply rooted. Bottom line, he was willing to act on this conviction, understanding it would be at his own risk.

Men such as Mr. Chang also embraced Korea's evolution to democratic rule, using the United States as their model. I was able to bring the fact that other patriotic Koreans had identified Mr. Chang as a next-generation patriot into our personal discussions to great effect. Our honest dialog essentially reinforced my impression that Mr. Chang's devotion to Korean democracy was an established element of his persona, and it had been for over 20 years.

Over private dinners in small restaurants, Mr. Chang and I bonded. We discussed scenarios in which the bilateral relationship might be put at risk, including a range of unilateral actions by the Pak government. In our discussions, we imagined how the alliance would be impacted by ROK military planning or actions destabilizing the tense situation on the peninsula and committing U.S. forces to combat. It was a real problem at the time and an issue about which he, as a former ROK Army officer, had some knowledge. We also discussed, hypothetically, the potential for Korean unilateral actions against a third nation, such as a Korean lash-out strike at Japan in one scenario. Such worse-case-but-still-realistic scenarios would damage America's ability to defend the South against North Korean or Chinese aggression. Chang was adamant about the dangers and found many of his contemporaries and colleagues at the ADD naïve on the U.S. willingness to accept actions that would compromise or jeopardize the alliance.

In reality, we were beating around the bush in what we both knew was a probing effort on my part, with my challenging him to think hard about certain activities that might be underway at the ADD. I progressed the dialog to share with him our thoughts about what might be going on within the ADD, based on decisions made at a much higher level, even in the ROK presidential office. I did not expect he enjoyed broad access, but I thought he might know something or could point us to one of his ADD colleagues who did possess direct knowledge.

In the meeting in my home, recounted in the Preface, Mr. Chang confided that "I have something very important to discuss, but can we meet somewhere secretly?" A few days later we met over drinks in a discreet room salon, reserved by a Station support officer in alias, to continue our dialog. Mr. Chang arrived that evening with his decision made. He would cooperate clandestinely with us, albeit on his own terms. He began by noting that the previous week the president of ADD had assembled a small group to review planning for the new agency compound near Taejon. He produced a detailed map he had traced from the displayed planning document and staked it out on our table with beer glasses.

132

Before identifying the various structures and so-called research zones, Mr. Chang offered his own assessment. "I am afraid you are right. They have made a decision to move forward with a strategic weapons program, actually four parallel programs, and they are in a big hurry to do this." Before we got into details, I asked him to explain what "this" was. He looked down and simply said, "Whatever the logic, they want to be able to claim that they have these programs underway, to show that they can deliver these strategic capabilities to the Blue House. This is not a hypothetical or paper exercise. ADD leadership has been authorized and funded to engineer, develop and build these systems." He added, "And, they think they can do it!"

The trace map, with referenced valley and mountain points, showed a central command and administrative area, a housing-and-apartment area, security control points and three distinct research areas, with selected sub-areas for "testing" and storage. The structures were fairly distinct: a chemical warfare development center, a biological warfare research center and a nuclear weapons development center, with a related explosives test area, complete with bunkers for storing high explosives.

In addition to the main ADD facility, which would house the ongoing conventional military systems research and development programs, a separate area—a fourth "sensitive project building"—would focus on missile development. Activity there would include the guidance system, rocket motor and other missile research activities in an effort to deliver the design of an advanced surface-to-surface missile. Such a system would be capable of carrying the various conventional and, as needed, unconventional warheads deep into North Korea. From a strategic weapons development program, the ADD's new campus near Taejon would have it all—or almost all.

First Reporting on the ADD

I worked from Mr. Chang's hard confirmation of the ROK's covert nuclear program to create a comprehensive description of the projected new ADD facility and its various functional elements. I was able to describe a complex that had yet to be built based on ADD's own senior-level planning briefing. My Station colleagues and I supplemented the narrative with the trace map, matching the terrain of the area. We believed we had the location nailed down—if not to the meter then at least to the valley enclosing the site.

Additional clandestine meetings with Mr. Chang, using maps and reference points, allowed us to compile follow-up reports. Each of our field disseminations was sent to Headquarters for review, revision and subsequent transmission as final "dissems" to our raw intelligence customers. The analysts at Langley, within the various divisions of the Directorate of Intelligence, drew their own conclusions and provided feedback. The first Station report, repackaged pretty much as I had written it, elicited a heavy amount of Headquarters attention and comment. It also generated more than a little doubt. Bottom line at that point: Our report, based on my and other protected and open source information, seemed compelling. Nevertheless, we were asking our Langley counterparts to accept a lot.

The reason for the skepticism? Mr. Chang was new and untested. In our parlance, he was yet to be independently validated and could well be a provocateur. Our description of him acknowledged those facts, but the specifics of the reporting soon demonstrated his credibility. The beauty of that early critical intelligence was we knew details of the new ADD complex even before ground was broken and within weeks of approval of the complex's design. We also had obtained some good indicators of the purpose and function of the various structures there. Satellites tasked, we could watch from the sky as the land was cleared, the utilities run in, the foundations of structures poured and the buildings roofed over and occupied.

Within the DO, the Reports cadre, an inbred institution that passed judgment on all incoming intelligence, gave the initial Chang report a passing, medium-quality grade. As expected, they asked for more and in greater detail. They did not have long to wait. Within a fortnight, Mr. Chang, previously instructed and practiced to probe for selected critical information, produced much more reporting. Meeting me at a protected location, he revealed he had gained access to the ADD relocation budget's numbered, line-item amounts for all major programs, including the four sensitive activities. From the information, we worked backward from other reporting—as I will explain elsewhere—to understand how those sensitive projects were being funded. Later, we duplicated everything using other sources, further validating our ADD-related reporting.

Simultaneously, we carefully tasked Mac to work his contacts, both at ADD and within the Korean private sector firms supporting that agency's activities. We wanted him to ferret out details that would collaborate our initial reporting. Mac did not disappoint. He was able to determine which elements of ADD were slated to relocate to the Taejon complex as priority moves, which components were taking on new employees and which private-sector firms would win research contracts. Much of it was hearsay within the ADD camp, but most of it subsequently was proven to be accurate, often amazingly so.

Just as important, Mac elicited unverified information that allowed the Station to task other sources more precisely. The details of specific programs began to flow in and reinforce one another. An example was the ADD's requirement to perfect the manufacture and assembly of high explosives to be used in a complex "lens" configuration to implode a plutonium core. The RDX-based explosives were new to the ADD researchers, and the concept of creating an electrical firing mechanism and wiring harness to deliver the charge to the individual lenses to achieve precise detonation presented a real challenge. The conceptual work on the new explosives might begin in Seoul, but the Taejon facility was designed from the outset to provide protected space to roll out the actual testing program. Thus, the explosives team would be one of the first to pack up for the move to the south, including ADD contractors working with Korea Explosives Group experts.

Funding the Beast: The Yulgok Plan

Other Station sources reported that President Pak had approved a multi-year defense buildup effort, code-named the Yulgok Plan. Yulgok was a prominent 16th-century Confucian court scholar and reformer, a man whom many Koreans acknowledge to be the most revered philosopher of the Chosun dynasty. For President Pak and his ambitious defense buildup program, with military research as a core element, the ancient scholar was a ready reference to all Koreans familiar with their nation's history.

It seemed fitting that Pak looked to Yulgok as his model. Pak conceived a broad, overarching program to expand his nation's defense capabilities by upgrading its equipment and creating a viable domestic defense industry to provide that equipment. The program included, as one of its many objectives, the ultimate goal of acquiring independent nuclear capability. And Yulgok, a man who saw great threats ever-looming in Korea's future, had pressed for self-reliance to meet those threats. **[NOTE 1]**

Initially, the South Koreans did not share or discuss the Yulgok Plan with the U.S. government, and it was not included in U.S.–ROK military planning. The reason was simple. President Pak and his inner circle did not see such dialog as necessary or useful. Also, Yulgok essentially was a work in progress, subject to modification as the government worked out program specifics. But our clandestine reporting—verified intelligence gleaned from multiple sources—allowed our military to probe deeply for details and force issues into the open within the military alliance.

In the case of the Yulgok Plan—in Korean, the Yulkok Kaewik—our early penetration of strategic weapons development activity at the ADD, and the fact that its funding components were included as numbered line-items in the agency's budget, provided the impetus for us to unpack and understand the funding systematically. By late 1974, we were able to pinpoint the strategic weapons component to line item 890, and future reporting often referenced "Yulgok 890" as the weapons program itself; at least, the elements that were covert and the ADD's responsibility.

The importance of our capabilities at the time cannot be overstated. We were able to tie Yulkok Kaewik, and the specifics of its line-item budget allocations, to respective ADD projects, be they conventional weapons efforts or the four areas of strategic work. If we wanted to understand the Blue House directive to the ADD thoroughly, and be able to prove it back in Washington, we needed to make the connection by the numbers.

A Missile Program Is Identified

A second, early stage recruitment provided direct, sustained and detailed access to the ADD's covert program to develop a ballistic-missile delivery system. That effort contained two overlapping elements. As a top priority, the ADD was rushing to use an existing missile system—in this case the U.S. Nike Hercules air-defense missile—as the base on which to produce a weapons-delivery capability. The system would allow the ADD to claim to the Blue House that its personnel had created a rapid, though temporary, solution for weapons delivery. Moreover, that critical element of the overall strategic program would underlie a first-generation ballistic missile that could range into North Korea.

Another, equal ADD priority was to provide, within four to five years, an all-new, totally indigenous missile-delivery system. The Nike Hercules program would inform it, particularly perfection of a missile guidance system. Though we also tracked the ADD longer-term program, our immediate focus was on the Nike Hercules effort. It was clear that the ADD had sold the adapted missile program to President Pak as a warhead-delivery capability the ADD could perfect and operationalize within a few years, thereby meeting his desired system capability goal of 1980, if not earlier.

The Nike Hercules: A Delivery System in Waiting

Two interesting parts of the picture at the ADD came into focus during the early months of 1975 that improved our confidence. First, as mentioned, after a lengthy development and cultivation period, we were able to add a source, a high-quality technical specialist with direct knowledge of the Yulgok Plan's missile development program. The individual was motivated mainly by a personal determination to protect the U.S.–ROK military alliance. Once brought into the ADD program from the private sector, he concluded that the covert program in which he was involved, when detected, probably would damage the bilateral defense partnership. From that new relationship, which another Station officer and I initiated, we were able to confirm the Yulgok Plan provided for a redesign of the Nike Hercules missile to serve as a ballistic weapons-delivery system for various warheads.

The ADD redesign of "Nike Herk," an air-defense system then deployed by both U.S. and ROK forces to defend against strategic attacks from Russian, Chinese and North Korean bomber forces, was straightforward. The existing missile body would be adapted to extend its range and alter its guidance system. A proven surface-to-air missile would be converted to a surface-to-surface weapon capable of carrying a 500-pound payload to targets as deep into North Korea as possible.

In air-defense service, the Nike Hercules system, officially designated the MIMI-14, was a mainstay weapon. It had served the United States, NATO and other allied nations, including Japan and Korea, for nearly 20 years. Nike Herk was essentially a first-generation, command-guided, long-range air-defense missile that utilized vacuum tube technology. It was typically deployed and operated by the U.S. Army from fixed sites. It was initially deployed in the States in 1958 to defend against and defeat what was then considered the main threat to the American homeland, namely, fleets of Soviet bombers attacking from high altitudes.

███
███████████████████████████████████████ The missile eventually was deployed by the thousands among some 130 bases in the United States alone. In the hands of overseas allied nations, it carried a conventional high-explosive warhead, the 1,100-pound T-45. ██████████████████
███
███
███
████████████████████ I had visited some of those same NH batteries deployed in Korea during my CIC days in 1969-1970 and thus had limited familiarity with the system.

In selecting NH for covert, reverse engineering as a weapons-delivery system, the ADD planners were taking a safe path to a less-than-optimal solution. The standard-issue NH did indeed have ground-to-ground capability, but as an air-defense missile it could only be commanded by its tracking radar. In surface-to-surface mode, the NH had to be tracked and relayed to flight-control instructions based on a line-of-sight link between the missile and its radar system.

That arrangement allowed the NH to be guided to a predesignated location and then commanded to dive into the target. The relatively short range of the missile—somewhere between 120 and 150 miles, plus the line-of-sight guidance requirement—limited its utility as a surface-to-surface weapon. It would have to be substantially upgraded to satisfy the Yulgok Plan's requirement to deliver a strategic strike.

The ADD's challenge was to adapt the existing NH airframe, propulsion and payload to a longer range, inertially guided, payload-improved missile. The ADD's intent to design a prototype and improve the system would have to include an all-new missile-guidance component, propulsion enhancement and expanded payload capacity, including fusing, depending on the warhead to be carried.

Given the combination of inherent limitations of the NHK-1—or "NH Korea," as the ADD's people came to call it—was considered no more than a gap-filler, in that role serving only to allow ADD officials to claim they had fielded a viable strategic weapons delivery capability. The ADD's parallel program for a range of next-generation missile technologies, such as its quest for an indigenous, solid-fuel rocket motor production capability, meanwhile was proceeding apace. In the missile-propulsion area, our government had blocked an American defense firm from supplying required technology—but the French were eager partners. They quickly sold technical cooperation to the ADD and its private-sector associates. In future years, the successful ROK missile program advanced from that humble beginning, with Yulgok 890 as the unregistered godfather.

Our missile expert confirmed the parameters of the NH research and development effort, along with the configuration and performance changes being undertaken, and the timeline to which the ADD was committed. Work already underway soon would to shift to the new Taejon complex. It involved the design, guidance and fusing areas, with actual testing of rocket motors and eventually the complete system to take place at another new ADD facility on South Korea's upper east coast.

It would be difficult for the ROK and the ADD to conceal such a program from us for any length of time. But their plan was to design and develop its key elements quickly—perhaps in no more than two years—then reveal an overt effort to deploy a conventional, surface-to-surface counterstrike weapon. After the eventual forced shutdown of the strategic weapons component, the program surfaced in the U.S.–ROK bilateral context, with modifications to placate U.S. concerns. The program survived the U.S.–ROK confrontation over strategic weapons, and the ADD was allowed to continue developing a de-tuned, restricted-range, conventionally armed strike missile. Its evolution would produce the Nike Hercules Korea, or Nike Herk-Korea.

The system's evolution as an overt program obscured the basic fact that, at the point the program was detected—in roughly early 1975—it had progressed covertly for well over a year. That is, there was and remains no doubt whatsoever that the ADD and Blue House undertook the missile element of the Yulgok Plan with the sole goal of mating a variety of strategic warheads, including nuclear, to the redesigned Nike Hercules missile. If successful, by 1978 the ROK would have perfected and possessed the delivery component of a complete, credible and politically independent strategic weapons system. [NOTE 2]

Reporting on the Missile Program

As we continued our reporting on the missile aspect of the Yulgok Plan, we again encountered resistance at Headquarters. Reports cadre remained dubious, mainly because their analysts, schooled and wedded to deep-diving technical critiques of Soviet or Chinese missile systems, declared the "NH secret project" a less-than-optimal, if not flawed, delivery-system design. By the analysts' reckoning, it was a poorly crafted effort doomed to fail or underperform.

The failure, however, was with the analysts. They failed to appreciate that the Koreans understood the inherent limitations of such an adaptive effort but, in acknowledging it, were simply working with what they had. Their plan was to take a missile with which they were familiar and create a first-generation, strategic or conventional weapons-delivery capability.

To us in the field, and eventually to policymakers who understood the implications-the necessity of an independent delivery system was self-evident. The ROK was undertaking that particular risk as part of its covert and well-integrated plan to achieve, on an expedited schedule, national strategic capability. As our early reporting had explained and attempted to convey, the NH project was only the first stage, or rather an expedient fast-track component, of a longer-term commitment. The ADD and the ROK were hellbent on developing missile subsystems, including more advanced rocket motors and guidance hardware. The goal was an all-Korean, solid-fuel-propelled, inertially guided ballistic missile of much longer range and more accuracy, capable of targeting all of North Korea.

The ADD's initial missile effort, including a subordinate launch and command facility on the ROK's northwestern coast, was detected and defined by Station reporting in early 1975. It was not an end in itself. Rather, it was a first-step gambit in a generational push to develop and refine an indigenous missile capability. [NOTE 3]

Pak Reveals His Requirement for an Independent Missile Capability

Some months later, probably compelled by continued probes by the U.S. military and growing concern that we had collected intelligence on the ballistic missile component of the Yulgok Plan, President Pak discussed the issue with Ambassador Sneider. The exchange occurred in a direct and somewhat confrontational manner, but there is an interesting story behind the event.

In a reporting cable tagged Seoul 3061 (SECRET/EXDIS) of April 1, 1975, Sneider described a conversation with Pak in which the president "set forth his determination to develop a Korean missile production capability ... for counterattacks on North Korean airfields and major population centers ... premised on the possibility of U.S. forces withdrawal from Korea."

In the conversation, Pak was frank, determined and demanding in noting that, in the face of a recent U.S. "failure to agree" to the sale of a missile-propellant plant, the ROK would look elsewhere. Pak noted he had "instructed ADD President Shim to develop an in-country missile capability within the next three to five years while U.S. forces were still in Korea."

Throughout the discussion, in which Pak asserted he had no plans to develop nuclear weapons, Pak emphasized his expectation, if not his assumption, that a U.S. departure from the peninsula was probable and should be planned for by his country. He also brushed aside Sneider's attempts to redirect his decision to a high-level U.S.–ROK military dialog. Instead, Pak emphasized his personal commitment to ROK self-reliance in military production capability and insisted that the United States had an obligation to support the effort.

In closing his reporting cable, Sneider made this comment:

> IN THIS AND PREVIOUS CONVERSATION, PRESIDENT PAK HAS UNVEILED MORE EXPLICITLY HIS PROGRAM FOR DEVELOPING KOREAN SELF-RELIANCE ON THE CONTINGENCY OF U.S. WITHDRAWAL. ONCE MORE HE HAD MADE CLEAR HIS EXPECTATION OF PROBABLE WITHDRAWAL ALONG WITH PLANS FOR URGENT DEVELOPMENT OF SELF-RELIANT DEFENSE INDUSTRY DURING THE REMAINING YEARS OF U.S. DEPLOYMENT IN KOREA.

The Ambassador went on to urge that Pak's planning be given urgent attention in the context of an overall Korea policy review, an initiative he had advocated but senior policymakers failed to take up.

The cable contained one of the clearest views into Pak's logic, detailing his rationale for the strategic programs he had initiated. It established for us that Pak had placed his firm hand on every detail of the Yulgok Plan. What interested the Station, and the Embassy, was Pak feeling compelled at that point to open a discussion with the Ambassador on the missile program. Pak was careful to avoid providing any details about a project then underway. Nor did he hint at the full extent of the mandate for the range of weapons he had given to the ADD.

An interesting point related to the Sneider–Pak discussion and the Ambassador's reporting cable relating the conversation: In my recollection, that was not exactly how the information surfaced. Prior to his meeting with Pak, Sneider asked me to explain exactly what the ADD was doing with its missile program, and we sat together to review the clandestine reporting we had filed on the ADD's covert Nike Herk-Korea project. Sneider met with Pak determined to "smoke him out" on that single component of the overall strategic weapons program. He was attempting to show that Pak had decided to share sensitive information with him, and through Sneider, with the U.S. government. Sneider also wanted to use the forced missile discussion to pry open the door for a confidential dialog on the more sensitive nuclear issue. That goal was not realized.

My point is it was Sneider, not Pak, who raised the missile issue. In pressing Pak to confirm the existence of the project, and pushing him for details, the Ambassador used Agency intelligence to do so, albeit in a carefully nuanced manner. Sneider achieved his first goal, up to a point, as the text of the reporting cable reveals. But Pak deflected and dodged the larger issue. Sneider was pleased that he now had the missile program and Pak's ambitions "on the record," along with Pak's ostensible justification for that activity. Sneider assumed the admission by Pak would allow future discussion in formal U.S.–ROK channels. In other words, a future dialog would begin in State and Embassy channels. If so, the discussions would bring the subject out of CIA intelligence reporting channels, where it had been residing exclusively. Such was Sneider's prerogative, and the Station elected to ignore his "sources and methods" transgression.

ADD Explosives Work and Another Surprise

Around that time, a new development emerged that could have been Mac's most important contribution to our clandestine reporting effort. The opening occurred as his effort to teach me about explosives progressed, and as our understanding of the ADD's advanced explosives-testing program picked up momentum. Tracking the explosives-related research at the ADD had narrowed to construction of the new test facilities at Taejon, the identity of the outside explosives contractors involved, and the team working the related electrical and fusing issues.

Our successes notwithstanding, we still lacked one critical element of the nuclear weapons program: the ADD's effort to create a viable design. Several years before, Mac had established a close and mentoring relationship—Mac being the mentored party—with an ADD scientist whom he knew had worked extensively on the dynamics of explosive events, apparently related to conventional weapons development. We assumed that the researcher—I will call him Dr. Kang—would know about any clandestine weapons program, given his reputation at the ADD and his involvement in explosives research. We also thought he would be willing to share his knowledge if we properly elicited the information. So, we crafted an approach to him. Mac followed a scripted dialog to engage Dr. Kang in a wide-ranging, "What if?" discussion about nuclear weapons design.

Once engaged, Dr. Kang proved eager to share his impressions of what he called the "recently renewed" research into nuclear weapons at the ADD. He said he had shared his own designs with the new team. He was not part of that group, however, which comprised mostly outside engineers coming home to Korea. He likewise did not enjoy routine access to the budding effort. Dr. Kang also noted he did not hold much confidence in the group's ability to complete a good design, at least not in their allotted timeframe.

Dr. Kang shared with Mac the reference weapon design he had passed along to the ADD team, both the scale model of the multiple-lens system and his working drawings. Mac dutifully copied the latter. The information did not provide a complete or updated understanding of the ADD's weapons design-in-progress. But it did contain two indicators. First, a plutonium-based design effort was underway, with Dr. Kang's input. It soon would be expanded with the arrival of more researchers, and we knew the effort had the benefit of the good physicist's earlier work. Second, we learned the device-design work was being coordinated with ongoing, and soon-to-be-expanded, high-explosives research and development.

Tangentially, we were intrigued by Dr. Kang's offhandedly terming the new ADD design activity a "restart" of work previously done by someone else, and that he had firsthand knowledge about the effort. That last bit would have to wait for a future discussion, but when we investigated it would prove a marker for both Korean ingenuity and that old saying, "Where there is a will, there is a way."

We carefully drafted our field report profiling Dr. Kang's information. Likewise, we properly qualified the nature of the design, including diagrams of the device and lens. Within a week, we sent everything to Headquarters. We should have expected the response it received. Incredibly, the Reports masterminds awarded it a "One," a grade usually assigned to something of mild interest. Such a grade communicated none-too-subtly that no further reporting on the subject would be welcomed. The Reports weekly wrap-up sent to Seoul noted something along the lines of,

> THE NUCLEAR WEAPONS DESIGNERS AT SANDIA
> LABS HAVE FURTHER COMMENTED THAT THIS IS
> A VERY POOR DESIGN [AND] PROBABLY WOULD
> NOT FUNCTION.

The implication of the feedback was the information probably was a fabrication, a misreading or misreported. Worse, the comments suggested that the people back home totally missed the critical point: Korea in 1975 had previously designed, and was attempting to improve its design of, a nuclear weapon. What did it matter how good the reported design was or how well it would function? One can imagine the reaction of those of us on the collection end of that bizarre exchange. Undaunted, we pressed on.

Although it rarely happens, Station management elected to appeal the grade given our report, not to mention question the logic that went into assigning such a grade. After a front-and-back-channel exchange of views with Headquarters, the report received a more reasonable "V," or "Five." Eventually, they upgraded it to an "X," meaning a "superior field intelligence report," requiring priority, follow-on collection. That happened when more senior levels joined the dialog and connected the policy-implications dots.

We continued to collect pieces related to the design team until the overall nuclear program was shut down a year or so later. We could not flesh out the precise weapons-design organization within the ADD, but we did come close.

For example, we were able to confirm the arrival of selected researchers recruited from abroad by name, even in cases where the ADD attempted to conceal their identities. In sum, we knew those individuals were coming. We watched them arrive and settle into ADD-provided apartments, and we confirmed that the ADD's master program to, quietly but efficiently, recruit and repatriate the researchers was progressing on schedule.

Earlier South Korean Nuclear Weapons Efforts Revealed

From Dr. Kang, we soon learned to our surprise there actually had been two former nuclear weapons research projects in recent ROK history. The most relevant had been tasked to him a few years earlier in the life of the Pak Chung-hee government, roughly in the 1971-1972 period, wherein Kang and a small ad hoc team were directed to report on the possibility of creating a nuclear device. The group was instructed to create a weapon design to explain the nuclear basics to Pak and his inner circle.

That briefing to Pak and his team reviewed the existing weapons programs of various nations, the technologies involved and the requirements of a real program, which then was judged to be beyond the ROK's means. The briefing included a design and mockup for a Nagasaki-type, plutonium-fueled implosion bomb. The design, and the model incorporating the explosive lenses and detonation system, was the one Kang shared with Mac, with some improvements. It happened that Kang's same design package had been offered to the new ADD team in 1974 as a point of departure for their work.

We also learned from Dr. Kang that Pak personally had been intrigued by early discussions of a neutron bomb, deeming it ideal for use on North Korean troops and tanks. The concept of a weapon that would irradiate and kill humans, while only mildly damaging the land or the weapons themselves, was attractive. Pak apparently mused to Dr. Kang and others that ███████████ deployment of such tactical nuclear weapons would checkmate the North Korean conventional advantage ███ ███.

Dr. Kang also noted, again in an offhanded manner, there had been a serious earlier effort, albeit with some comedic overtones, to acquire a nuclear capability. The initiative was instigated by Syngman Rhee, the elected first-president-turned-autocrat of the ROK. Rhee was one of Korea's great modern patriots who had crusaded for the independence of his country from Japanese colonial rule, only to see the nation divided in 1945 during the process of liberation. He had weathered the devastation of the Korean War and begun the slow rebuilding process that would lead eventually to the country's economic recovery.

Unfortunately, as Rhee and his regime aged through the mid-1950s and into the end of the decade, he became detached from reality. Rhee and his team manhandled, abused and undercut the budding democratic process in South Korea.

The oppressiveness caused his government to lose popular support, eventually resulting in riots in the streets and anarchy. He was deposed by a popular insurrection, followed by a period of political upheaval overlaid by a series of ineffectual coalition governments. Further anarchy resulted in the successful military coup organized by President Pak in 1961.

Unknown to most, and certainly not detected by the United States as Korea's security guarantor, Rhee had attempted to take things down the nuclear road. Or, at least, he attempted to travel in that direction and probably thought he had done so. In Dr. Kang's explanation, which rang true with all we knew of Rhee's attitude and declining mental state, Rhee had concluded, sometime around 1958, that South Korea needed its own atomic bomb. He was driven by a determination to reunite Korea on his own terms, with or without American help and reinforced by his deep suspicions of Japan, not to mention the threats posed by China and the Soviet Union.

According to Dr. Kang, Rhee apparently had initiated his "exploratory atom bomb project" by enlisting a man whom he believed could deliver. The instigator was a childhood friend who approached him with the claim that he could build the bomb if Rhee gave him the funding. The engineer/entrepreneur apparently explained that the critical element of any atomic bomb, in addition to the nuclear material, was the high-voltage electric system required to detonate the explosives surrounding the bomb's core. And the key to the bomb's electrical system, so the explanation went, was massive battery power. Thus, it followed that Korea needed to have its own modern battery factory. The essential pitch was, "no batteries, no bomb," and the approach worked. Rhee gave the businessman his special funding, and he quickly established Korea's first commercial-scale, automobile battery factory by licensing the manufacturing process from Japan.

South Korea's first-ever attempt to create its own nuclear deterrence did not produce Rhee's atomic bomb. But the country did get its first battery factory. It began commercial production around the time the demonstrators in Seoul were running Rhee and his dysfunctional and discredited inner circle out of town. From that humble beginning, the smooth-talking businessman created, in 1960, what became South Korea's leading car battery corporation. The factory coincidentally arrived just in time to complement the national strategic push into automobile manufacturing and exporting.

A reader might ask, given the unreconstructed condition of the economy back then, the post-war condition of North Korea and the presence of 60,000 U.S. combat troops (tactical nuclear arms included) under a UN mandate to defend the South, what was Rhee's logic in undertaking such an inept effort to acquire an atomic bomb?

I am convinced that, in Rhee's assessment, the Republic of Korea faced a number of strategic enemies, each and all worthy of being threatened and targeted by such a weapon. That was particularly true when Rhee viewed the sustainability of U.S. and UN security guarantees as highly suspect. Threats to his vulnerable nation included a rearming and unrepentant communist North Korea, overlain by the aggressive Cold War postures of China and Russia. Rhee

144

probably also imagined that there loomed, in the future, Korea's perennial foe, a Japan armed with nuclear weapons eager to impose itself again. For the increasingly isolated and paranoid Rhee, building an atomic bomb of his own seemed a reasonable ambition.

I assert all this because Dr. Kang's recounting of Rhee's attempt to develop a nuclear weapon for use against South Korea's perceived enemies rang true to me, on several fronts. For example, Rhee's mentality and extreme behavior were matters of record. He was the source of great frustration for a host of American officials who dealt with him over the 15-year period that spanned from Korea's independence in 1945 through the course of his presidency. I likewise received a personal, though second-hand, introduction to his state of mind that seemed to cap it all.

During the months we were tracking Pak's nuclear weapons program, I coincidentally was exploring other interests that would feed into our understanding of the Korean psyche. As a lay aviation historian and as a personal initiative, I sought out former ROK Air Force officers who had served with the Japanese Air Force during World War II. I was chronicling the experiences of that interesting collection of men. In August 1946, they had gathered in a tent at Seoul's Kimpo Airport to create an association that would evolve into the ROK Air Force. The meeting was organized by former Japanese Army Air Force Captain Kim Chung-yul. Kim's invitees included pilots who had been trained by and flown for the Japanese Army and Navy in combat against China, the United States and other Allied nations.

From 1947 onward, Kim would lead the formation of that embryonic air capability. He would command its fighter–bomber contingent during the Korean War and preside over the growth of the ROK Air Force in the war's aftermath. Kim would become South Korea's first Air Force Chief of Staff and rise to the position of Minister of Defense during Rhee's presidency. He also served as Seoul's ambassador in Washington. In later years, Kim became Prime Minister during the presidency of Chun Doo-hwan in the late 1980s.

In one of our private sessions, as we moved the discussion from his Japanese Army service to his post-Korean War dealings with President Rhee as his Minister of Defense, from 1957 to 1960, General Kim shared some of his experiences in dealing with the irascible Rhee. Kim explained that his most frustrating exchange—one in a seemingly nonstop series of talking Rhee down from bad decisions—involved Rhee's determination to invade a Japanese island.

The incident had occurred in early 1960 when then-Defense Minister Kim was summoned to the Blue House for an emergency planning session. There, he was greeted by an irate Rhee, who was obsessed with the Japanese government's decision to allow Korean residents in Japan to be repatriated to North Korea. The Japanese decision had been facilitated by the International Red Cross in an agreement reached in 1959. The ongoing repatriation program was made worse by the fact that the General Association of North Korean Residents in Japan, the "Chongryon," was managing the process. They collected donations to ensure the maximum number of Korean residents could move to North Korea for permanent resettlement. The repatriated included Koreans who had relocated to Japan during World War II, mostly to work in war facilities. But the program also included Koreans who had originated from the South.

The Japanese decision to allow the repatriation, a political gesture long advocated by North Korea and the Chongryon, had been perceived by many South Koreans to be a betrayal of the ROK and a slap in face to their government. Rhee considered it yet another insult by Korea's former colonial masters and perceived it a calculated act designed to undermine South Korea's claim on the entire peninsula. Rhee formally protested the repatriation program and used Korean Residents Union in Japan, or the Mindan, a pro-South Korean organization in Japan, to agitate politically against it. But he was unable to block the shipborne transfers. The departures for North Korea began on December 14, 1959, and over the next year more than 50,000 Koreans made the transit, in ships chartered from and flying the flag of the Soviet Union.

Amid considerable fanfare and much propaganda from Pyongyang, the repatriation program drove Rhee to extremes. He was irate and wanted a response that punished Japan, ideally an intercession to disrupt or block the ferry service. He demanded that Kim and the Ministry of National Defense prepare a plan for immediate execution. It would have South Korean forces invade and occupy the Japanese island of Tsushima. The island was positioned in the Korea Strait at a strategic midpoint between Korea's city of Pusan and Japan's Fukuoka. As such, Tsushima was the closest Japanese territory to the peninsula. The island's ownership had been disputed over the centuries, but by 1960 there was no doubt Tsushima was legally and administratively Japanese sovereign territory.

In demanding that Minister Kim plan an invasion, it was clear Rhee was prepared to wage war on Japan and, in the mix, present the United States with a major political and military crisis. America would have been forced to inject itself into an active military situation to deconflict the two sides, with Japan and the ROK both looking to their bilateral security arrangements with the United States. Kim and his staff officers were taken aback by Rhee's demand. They returned to their headquarters to ponder a response.

The following day, Kim carefully detailed to Rhee why such an action would be difficult to execute. He explained the challenges in mounting the landing itself and noted that, even if the island was successfully occupied by ROK forces, they would be hard put to defend the island against a Japanese counterattack. Kim argued the entire operation would be problematic. It would be particularly true given the ROK military's heavy dependence on the U.S. forces in Korea, not to mention the existence of the UN Command that normally would exercise control over any deployment of Korean forces. He cited a host of challenges that made such an action ill-advised if not impossible. Rhee was unmoved. He demanded an invasion plan. Attacking those chartered, Soviet-flagged ships was out of the question, a concept that Rhee appeared to grasp. Still, he rejected the assessment and insisted that Kim come up with something new.

A week later, after discussing and colluding with other military leaders—

along with Blue House officials normally involved in restraining Rhee's worse impulses—Kim again briefed Rhee and took a different tack. He vowed to plan for a more comprehensive "retaliation" directed against both Japan and North Korea, a plan that would create the crisis with Japan, the United States and North Korea that Rhee wanted. Rhee accepted, but Kim allowed the planning to drift slowly for several months.

A few months after that conversation, in May 1960, Rhee would be deposed by civil unrest. Crisis delayed and crisis averted, Minister Kim resigned. That October, the voluntary repatriation program was extended by Tokyo and Pyongyang for another year to permit 50,000 more Koreans to emigrate from Japan. In the near-anarchy that prevailed in the South during that period, few would notice the Koreans from Japan steaming northwest to land in North Korea for their new life there.

When General Kim related this and other Rhee incidents to me, I asked about Rhee's possible inclinations to develop a nuclear deterrent. I already knew about the battery-factory excursion of the late 1950s, when Kim was serving as Rhee's Minister of Defense. But Kim waved his hand at me and laughed. "Rhee was more than a little crazy by that time," he said. "He did not like or really trust me because I was a former Japanese Army Air Force officer. And remember, I was a member of the Japanese-educated 'colonial occupier elite' that he hated. So, he would not have told me if he had such a scheme. But he probably did!"
[NOTE 3]

Mitigating Conflicts with the U.S. Military

During our Station's effort to penetrate and report on the covert South Korean strategic weapons program, we had to dodge some internal bullets. They were all-too-avoidable misfires that endangered our ability to report, and they episodically complicated our attempts to sustain clandestine coverage of the ADD's advancing efforts.

The source of the difficulty was pressure by the U.S. military on their South Korean counterparts incited by Station reporting. The pressure often consisted of ham-handed, aggressive approaches to senior-level Ministry of Defense staff as well as ADD leadership. The problem for us was such approaches too-often suggested our clandestine reporting. True, the none-too-subtle, steady probing by senior U.S. military personnel did compel the Ministry of National Defense to share the Yulgok Plan, or most elements of it. But, all too often. the U.S. military people were drawing directly from sensitive Station reporting. They disclosed, for example, the manner in which ADD activity was funded, intending to elicit information the Korean side was previously unwilling to share. But the practice, driven more by embarrassment and curiosity than any real need to know (we already knew), was always counterproductive and consistently endangered our sources and methods.

We at the Station and the Agency had seen this movie before. There was an established pattern of semi-confrontational use of clandestine reporting by our U.S. military colleagues to compel truth-telling by the Koreans. The problem would resurface in various ways—both with our resident military and to a much lesser degree with the State Department—as our knowledge of Seoul's nuclear program and other sensitive activity grew.

Assessing the Quality of Our Intelligence Coverage

As more months passed, we worked our collection efforts to acquire additional sources capable of providing information on other, protected aspects of the strategic weapons program, as well as confirming those aspects already uncovered. In many cases, we worked with single-source access; that is, one source of information on a given aspect of a complex program. Not an ideal situation for Headquarters analysts or the policy community alike. We needed to verify, ideally with multiple sources, what the individual assets had told us. Nevertheless, all of the pieces were coming together by early spring 1975, and we had no indications any of the information conflicted with the bigger picture being assembled back home. Nor did we suspect what we were detecting involved a ruse by the Pak government, or was a random collection of unauthorized activity, either by the ADD establishment or government nuclear policymakers.

Assessing all of the covert and overt reporting we had collected by early 1975, we concluded that our coverage of the military side of the strategic weapons effort, almost exclusively residing in the ADD complex, was solid and growing stronger. Still, the intelligence remained incomplete and admittedly could be better.

From Mr. Chang, we held a top-down view of the covert budget process and overall multi-program organization, including its physical layout at the new ADD facility near Taejon. To that source, we could add the information provided by our missile expert. Then there was Mac's interaction with the explosives group and the design-related comments of Dr. Kang, the senior nuclear scientist. We also worked with two additional candidate sources, both of whom had direct access to components of the program. We hoped to bring them into our vetted reporting within a matter of weeks.

My own interaction with senior ADD managers, limited as it was, allowed us to identify and track some of the new arrivals, particularly those scientists whose ostensible programs at the ADD had conventional explanations. Those higher-profile researchers, confident their covert programs were well-disguised, interacted with the U.S. diplomatic or business community, thereby allowing us to access them within that social mix. Other returning scientists and engineers, some of whom had arrived with aliases, were shielded from foreign contact. We needed considerable work to identify them. Moreover, the sensitive researchers were slated to relocate to Taejon in the months ahead, making direct contact almost impossible.

Our picture of the ADD's role was not complete, but it was becoming clearer, and the comprehensive nature of our intelligence allowed predictability in the reporting process. That is, because we knew what the ADD expected to accomplish, and on what timeline and with whom, we could target the project milestones and individuals as they arrived on the scene. That, in turn, fostered credibility with the analysts back home. But understanding the ADD component of the overall effort was not enough. We needed to know how Pak's regime planned to mate the covert military effort with the overt civil nuclear side, namely, how the government-managed nuclear research would be structured—how the ROK would justify its push into the nuclear fuel cycle. Concurrently, we needed a better appreciation of what Pak was attempting to achieve with his high-risk program, and why he and his inner circle judged that a strategic weapons development gambit was worth risking the U.S.–ROK alliance.

Melding those two additional components—the overt nuclear fuel cycle effort and the rationale for the overall strategic weapons program—and then combining them with what we were learning about the ADD's mandate and its effort, provide the balance of the story.

Chapter 12. U.S. Government Policy Development Late 1974-Early 1975

Initial Washington Reactions to Intelligence Reporting

Seoul Station's reporting on ROK strategic weapons development garnered senior-level U.S. policy attention almost from day one, to the degree that the Agency's Reports cadre began demanding more and more field disseminations. They also directed us to expand our asset base to verify our initial indications. Likewise, the analytical side at Langley, both the Intelligence and the Science & Technology branches, which had been initially skeptical, quickly joined in on the collection-tasking process. It was a mixed blessing. They often leveled reporting requirements that were difficult to accommodate, at least during the first months.

We were fortunate, however, in that mid-to-late 1974 timeframe. Two parallel nuclear issues involving the ROK already had seized the attention of our policymakers: the ROK's refusal to accede to the Treaty on the Non-Proliferation of Nuclear Weapons and, almost coincidentally, the ROK's quiet negotiations with the French to purchase a spent-fuel reprocessing plant. Both issues generated State Department initiatives that were directed and monitored by the National Security Council. And both are worth mentioning in more detail. Together, they overlaid the more dramatic developments our Station's efforts had unearthed.

On the NPT issue, the U.S. government had been dialoging with the ROK since at least early 1974, urging them to complete accession to the treaty. In doing so, they formally would renounce the development of nuclear weapons. Consequently, the ROK government would have to submit itself to comprehensive safeguards regarding nuclear facilities and arrangements for assistance, both of which would involve interaction with the UN's International Atomic Energy Agency. When our Embassy pushed in July about NPT ratification, the ROK demurred, claiming their leaders shared no consensus to join the treaty. Apparently, both the Ministry of National Defense and the KCIA were opposed. As a Seoul Embassy cable at the time commented:

> ROK INTENDS TO KEEP ITS OPTIONS OPEN. [further hinting that] WE HAVE A VISCERAL FEELING, BASED ONLY ON GROWING INDEPENDENCE OF ROK ATTITUDES TOWARD DEFENSE MATTERS, AND INCREASING DOUBTS ABOUT

THE DURABILITY OF U.S. COMMITMENTS, THAT MOST SE-
NIOR ROK DEFENSE PLANNERS DESIRE TO OBTAIN CAPA-
BILITY EVENTUALLY TO PRODUCE NUCLEAR WEAPONS.
[NOTE 1]

Within the same timeframe, responding to the Embassy cable, the U.S. mission
to the IAEA in Vienna expressed its increasing concern about the ROK's refusal
to join the NPT. Our people there noted South Korea's interest in reprocessing
technology. They emphasized that the U.S.–ROK bilateral nuclear agreement
contained major deficiencies and stressed that:

THE QUESTION OF ROK RATIFICATION OF NPT
WARRANTS VERY HIGH PRIORITY (U.S. POLICY)
ATTENTION.

As of late 1974 and well into 1975, the two governments remained at odds over
the issue. U.S. concerns grew that South Korean "fence-sitting" on the NPT
would continue, as the ROK expanded its commercial nuclear program. From
an NPT perspective, the ROK stall underlined the conclusion that South Korea
would indeed strive to "keep its options open." [NOTE 2]

Regarding the French reprocessing plant, our nuclear policy planners had
been caught wrongfooted. The ROK had made rapid progress in negotiating a
pilot-scale, spent-fuel reprocessing facility and associated technologies from the
French firm Saint-Gobain Techniques Nouvelles. Stated simply, the two parties
had outpaced development of a coherent U.S. response. The sale was encouraged by the French government as part of its own promotion of nuclear systems
abroad. The French stance reflected an aggressive attitude to sell all elements of
the nuclear fuel cycle wherever and to whomever possible—a similar reprocessing plant sale to Pakistan by France also was under discussion at the time. And
secret talks with Taiwan for another such facility had been ongoing since 1973.

The August 1974 cable from the U.S. Mission to the IAEA noted the ROK's
acquisition of a reprocessing plant could allow production of large quantities of
plutonium. It urged haste in coming up to speed on the issue. Although our government was actively discussing the matter with the French, that government
was strongly disinclined to reverse the sale. Instead, the French claimed bilateral
or multilateral safeguards would be sufficient. With a similar defensive mindset,
they also perceived the United States might be attempting to undermine French
commercial efforts to sell reactors and fuel solutions to third countries, such as
the ROK.

French coolness to a dedicated dialog with the United States on the Korean
sale was one element of a bigger problem, namely, their unwillingness create a
common policy platform to, more carefully, manage nuclear exports. As of late
1974, the French were not willing to join a "conference of nuclear exporters."
Rather, they suggested that attempts to limit exports of sensitive technology,

such as reprocessing, were problematic because such technology already existed in the public domain. At that point in our dialog with the French, we failed to judge the degree to which both they and the ROK were determined to continue with the reprocessing plant contract. The diplomatic battle on that critical element of the overall U.S.–ROK nuclear confrontation would drag on for another year or more.

We continued our clandestine source reporting on ROK intentions, beginning in early fall 1974 and well into 1975. The resulting analyses soon found a policy audience in Washington. Senior State Department officials, led by our former Ambassador to Korea, Phil Habib—then Assistant Secretary of State for East Asia—immediately elevated the matter to the attention of Secretary of State Henry Kissinger. With Kissinger involved, all elements of the U.S. policy community began to coalesce by late 1974 to understand and manage the Korean nuclear problem more fully. Almost everyone appreciated the matter for what it was: an issue harboring a high potential to inflict serious damage on US–ROK alliance as well as a frontal challenge to our then-nascent international nuclear non-proliferation strategy.

An 'Alert Report' Briefing to Kissinger

In their November 20, 1974, "Briefing Memorandum–Second Alert Report," for Secretary Kissinger, the State Department memo-drafters highlighted concerns under a section titled, "Korea Advanced Weapons Developments—Secret/NO-FORN." The text drew directly from our early clandestine source reporting, leading with the sentence, "Apparent South Korean interest in developing a nuclear and missile capability by the end of this decade poses this issue—the implications for our interests of further Korean efforts and what we can or should do about it over the coming six to eight months." The memo then cited (somewhat incorrectly) our Station's first dissemination of President Pak's private conversation in his summer home the previous August.

The message to Kissinger included this admonition:

> IF, OVER THE NEXT SIX TO NINE MONTHS, THE ROK
> MOVES FURTHER TO DEVELOP A NUCLEAR CAPABILITY,
> THIS COULD HAVE A DEEPLY UNSETTLING EFFECT ON
> REGIONAL STABILITY AND ON OUR NON-PROLIFERA-
> TION STRATEGY, AS IT BECAME KNOWN
> TO OTHER POWERS.

Setting the stage for the crafting of a major foreign policy initiative, the cable concluded with:

WE MAY NEED TO PUT DECISIONS TO YOU IN THE NEAR
TERM DEPENDING ON HOW OUR NON-PROLIFERATION
DEVELOPS AND AS WE GET A CLEARER PICTURE OF KO-
REAN INTENTIONS AND ACTIONS.

The last portion of the message clearly conveyed that the drafters were not fully
convinced President Pak was out of the nuclear box. Even so, the onus remained
on the Station and the intelligence community to track the South Korean program and validate the existence and pace of such a program.

Early Policy Deliberations: Embassy and State Exchanges

As the information moved into U.S. policy hands from intelligence channels, it
was important to create a complementary avenue of communications from the
Embassy and State Department perspective. That is, we needed to get what we
knew of the ROK strategic weapons development into State hands to accelerate
the policy process. We also needed to confirm that intelligence from our Station
and Langley was synced up with U.S. decision-making and execution on the
policy side, at least from the State Department's perspective.

In fact, by late 1974 when it all was coming together, the U.S. side was playing catchup. The ROK program had raced ahead and was picking up momentum. We judged the Korean side might assume that, if their policymakers moved
fast enough to develop all elements of their program, and the various teams assembling the physical components moved rapidly as well, the U.S. government
might not be able to inhibit or halt their fast-moving strategic weapons development train.

A series of State Department messages initiated in late 1974 is instructive.
The exchanges were possible once the South Korean trajectory had been fairly
well confirmed, by both our Station reporting and the expanding Embassy dialog with ROK nuclear managers. The dialog was designed to ferret out specifics
of their declared (if reluctantly shared) nuclear research program.

■ *Seoul 8023 of December 2, 1974, Secret/NODIS, subject "ROK Plans
to Develop Nuclear Weapons and Missiles."*

The Embassy cable overviewed the activities contributing to an Embassy assessment that a decision had been made, and a program had begun:

EVIDENCE ACCUMULATED IN RECENT MONTHS JUSTIFIES
STRONG PRESUMPTION THAT THE KOREAN GOVT HAS DE-
CIDED TO PROCEED WITH THE INITIAL PHASES OF A NUCLEAR
WEAPONS DEVELOPMENT PROGRAM. [But the cable hedged by
adding] EVIDENCE IS STILL NOT CONCLUSIVE.

In the heavily redacted document, references are made to the ROK's continuing stall on the NPT accession, its determination to control its own nuclear fuel cycle, including spent fuel reprocessing, the ongoing program to acquire from any and all sources additive technical expertise and the ROK effort to develop an independent missile capability. The December 2, 1974, cable also included a section that stated:

> WE CONCLUDE THAT DECISION HAS PROBABLY BEEN MADE TO LAUNCH INITIAL STAGES OF NUCLEAR WEAPONS DEVELOPMENT PROGRAM.

That same cable also noted certain critical items, which would appear to be required for such an effort, remained unsourced or perhaps undetected. Last, in a "Recommended Actions" section, the authors suggested a set of immediate measures, including a strong push toward NPT ratification.

The cable, including a companion alert more widely referenced over the years as the "SOMETHING IS CLEARLY AFOOT" cable, was meant to bring the dialog into formal State–Embassy channels. The objective was accomplished by year-end 1974. The extensive redactions contained in the publicly available texts reflect the extensive input provided by our Station's efforts.

- *National Security Council Memorandum, SECRET, attention to Henry Kissinger, of February 28, 1975, titled, "Development of U.S. Policy Toward South Korean Development of Nuclear weapons."*

The document was prepared to allow Kissinger to bless a draft State Department cable to Seoul, informing the Embassy about the approach our government intended to employ to respond to developments in the ROK. A draft State cable responded to the Seoul 8023 cable. The NSC memo summarized the pending State cable and recommended that Kissinger approve it, which he did.

- *State 48573 of March 4, 1975, Secret/NODIS, titled "ROK Plans to Develop Nuclear Weapons and Missiles." The State cable notified U.S. Embassy Seoul that:*

> WASHINGTON AGENCIES CONCUR FULLY THAT ROKG IS PROCEEDING WITH INITIAL PHASES OF A NUCLEAR WEAPONS DEVELOPMENT PROGRAM. SUBSEQUENT INTELLIGENCE REPORTING ON THIS HAS ADDED FURTHER CONFIRMATION TO EMBASSY'S EXCELLENT SUMMARY OF EVIDENCE CONTAINED INREF CABLE SEOUL 8023.

That important State cable is now declassified and available in its complete five-page, fully unredacted version. An essential read, it indicates that the State Department sought and achieved, in drafting the message, broad policy and intelligence community consensus on all aspects of the South Korean gambit.

The guidance cable casts a broad net on all bilateral, regional and international policy concerns that would surface if such a program proceeded, let alone achieved its goal. It noted that U.S. government policy was still being formulated to deal with the issue and emphasized that:

> [The U.S. Government's] BASIC OBJECTIVE IS TO DISCOURAGE ROK EFFORT IN THIS AREA AND TO INHIBIT TO THE FULLEST POSSIBLE EXTENT ANY ROK DEVELOPMENT OF A NUCLEAR EXPLOSIVE CAPABILITY
> OR DELIVERY SYSTEM.

The State guidance cable went on to identify a range of policy courses then under consideration, and it noted the ongoing, close coordination with the Canadian government on the evolving ROK–Canadian nuclear relationship. The cable included a proposal to "defer" the supply by Canada of the research reactor added to the pending nuclear deal. Also mentioned was the U.S. determination to compel the ROK to ratify the NPT, stating the overriding concern that all issues undertaken with the South Koreans had to be consistent with broader U.S. international non-proliferation goals.

The March 1975 State cable is important because it established firm U.S. resolve to take an active role in all aspects of the ROK nuclear program, both overt (subject to strengthened bilateral and international safeguards) and covert, plus the determination to address the issue in direct dialog with the ROK government.

■   *Seoul 1637 of March 12,1975, Secret/NODIS referenced the State guidance cable, using the same subject line. It pushed back firmly on the State message by noting, in its opening line:*

> WHILE EMBASSY IN BASIC AGREEMENT WITH DEPARTMENT'S SUMMARY ANALYSIS OF SIGNIFICANCE OF ROK PLANS TO DEVELOP NUCLEAR WEAPONS AND MISSILES AND WITH THE PROPOSALS OUTLINED...WE BELIEVE A MORE EXPLICIT COURSE VIS-À-VIS ROKS WILL
> EVENTUALLY BE CALLED FOR.

Seoul Embassy's response challenged Washington's assessment that the ROK nuclear program might need a decade to complete and noted the ROK's goal was achieving capability by the "early eighties," a seven-year time frame at best. Important, in shoving back, Seoul Embassy warned Washington policymakers that:

WE SHOULD NOT UNDERESTIMATE ROK ABILITY TO OB-
TAIN EQUIPMENT AND TECHNOLOGIES REQUIREMENTS
FOR WEAPONS DEVELOPMENT FROM THIRD COUNTRIES,
IN THE EVENT WE TURN THEM DOWN.

So that U.S. policymakers did not miss the assessment made from the ground in Seoul, the Embassy cable offered:

WE BELIEVE THAT IN WORKING OUT DETAILS OF OUR
APPROACH TO THE ROK'S THERE IS NO NEED TO PUSSY-
FOOT. ROKS ARE SERIOUS TOUGH CUSTOMERS BENT IN
THIS CASE ON A POTENTIALLY HARMFUL CAUSE.

The cable also noted that recent ROK-proffered compromises on the NPT issue, and safeguards on the Canadian and French sales, suggested it was possible that:

THEY ALREADY HAVE WORD WE ARE ON TO THEM, BUT
IT IS NO INDICATION THAT THEY ARE GIVING UP.

The Seoul Embassy cable closes by recommending:

GIVEN IMPLICATIONS OF THEIR PLANS, THEIR TOUGH
MENTALITY... DIRECT, EARLY AND FIRM APPROACH
[would be required to give the U.S. the best chance of success].

Ambassador Sneider, at that point some eight months into his tour in Seoul, was fully engaged on all aspects of the nuclear and strategic weapons issue. He recently had admonished his Political Section folks to "drop the denial and get with the program." He was working closely with our Station Chief Don Gregg to appreciate every element of the Korean plan and attitude. He coordinated informally but usefully on many of our reports as they were dispatched to Langley.

In drafting the Embassy response, a small working group discussed the situation with Sneider and concluded that Washington still did not "get it." It seemed to us in Seoul that Washington, in allowing we had a tough road ahead with the ROK, assumed we still had sufficient time to derail their nuclear ambitions by exploring various "compromises." We disagreed and judged time was against us. It would serve no purpose to discuss alternatives to a complete shutdown of both the declared-but-dangerous aspects of the overt ROK program (the fuel cycle plans), as well as the covert components.

Part of the assessment underpinning the Embassy cable of mid-March 1975 was based on expanded, real-time intelligence reporting. But much of it was instinctive. At the Embassy level, from the office of the Ambassador on down and from Station sources, a certainty prevailed. We knew, once President Pak decided something had to be done, it would get done. Be it another shipyard, a steel mill or a nuclear powerplant, all hands would work day and night to accomplish the

156

goal. That Korean mindset, often referred to as *han*, basically reflected a mentality that no goal was impossible if one just threw oneself relentlessly at the objective. Pak clearly had decided to proceed with the program as a national priority, for whatever combination of reasons, and unless he took his foot off the accelerator, it would get done one way or the other.

A Mandate to Push Ahead on the Intelligence Front

Such were the policy deliberations in early 1975 at the National Security Council and senior State Department levels, as well as within the Embassy. The decision then taken to develop a comprehensive response to the ROK's overall strategic weapons development program, and address directly its various elements as they were being confirmed, required more knowledge about ROK intent and capabilities. The longer-standing and still-ongoing disagreements remained, including the ROK's stubborn determination to delay accession of the NPT, and the reluctance of both the ROK and France to reconsider the reprocessing facility contract.

As events progressed that year, it became obvious the nuclear policy frustrations were being made doubly urgent by the ROK's overarching determination to pursue its strategic weapons program. There was a realization at the highest levels of our government that we had a far larger and more complex issue on our hands, and we needed to deal aggressively with it. We had a Canadian nuclear reactor sale pending, a French reprocessing plant sale well advanced and a leadership in Seoul determined to forge ahead on its overt and covert nuclear fronts. The order of the day was to acquire a more complete picture of what was happening with the programs themselves and, as the diplomatic approaches played out, determine how the ROK leadership was reacting to America's growing knowledge about their actions and intentions. **[NOTE 3]**

Enter the Canadians

Paralleling the contentious U.S.–ROK faceoff over the French nuclear reprocessing plant, early 1975 brought a new element into the South Korean nuclear equation: Canada. In late 1974, we confirmed the ROK had decided to introduce the Canadian heavy-water reactor, or CANDU, as a second nuclear power technology. The new fuel cycle component made resolution of the reprocessing plant issue all the more urgent. And though Canada's involvement eventually would assist our government in resolving the issue, it initially complicated matters.

ROK Embraces the Canadian CANDU Power Reactor

At first, the ROK had selected the U.S. power reactor technology offered by Westinghouse, namely, its pressurized-water reactor. In 1974, contractors were busy constructing the first of that type, the Kori Unit 1, on South Korea's southeast coast. Also in 1974, KEPCO, the ROK's state electric utility, was negotiating with Westinghouse and the U.S. Export–Import Bank to finance the sale of a second PWR, the companion Kori Unit 2. But Seoul's ambitions were such that one reactor type was not enough. After some deliberations, their nuclear planners selected Canada's CANDU as a second technology for KEPCO's fleet of commercial powerplants. Discussion had begun with Atomic Energy of Canada Limited some years before and, by 1974, the two parties had reached a preliminary agreement for the first AECL reactor.

The CANDU system, also known generically as a pressurized heavy-water reactor, differed markedly from the American PWR. CANDU was a heavy-water-moderated, natural-uranium-fueled reactor. The PHWR involved fuel bundles cycled through the reactor as it operated. In contrast, the U.S. PWR involved fuel assemblies remaining in place for several years, with the reactor shut down periodically to remove the irradiated assemblies and insert replacement fuel. To many proliferation specialists, CANDU presented significant safeguard challenges because of its design and the manner in which fuel was irradiated.

Naturally, the Canadians—both AECL as the reactor provider and the government itself—did not see CANDU as a safeguards challenge. They were quick to reassure all parties, including the United States, that their bilateral safeguards imposed on CANDU exports to the ROK would meet a high standard. The CANDU reactors also would be subject to International Atomic Energy Agency standards. In any event, the natural uranium used in fabricating the fuel bundles would be safeguarded before, during and after irradiation. Moreover, though

Canada and AECL technically would not own the fuel bundles, any reprocessing of plutonium-bearing material would require Canadian government permission. Or so it was asserted.

The problem was the plutonium. It rendered fuel-bundle accountability something of a crapshoot, particularly if a sophisticated operator was determined to violate the safeguards. Also, the ROK's stated desire was to control all aspects of the "front end" of the fuel cycle, including provision of the uranium feedstock and fabrication of the fuel bundles. South Korea made known its intent to mine and process uranium, and the hunt had begun for those domestic sources. The CANDU fuel bundles would be manufactured in a KAERI-owned and operated facility; the latter prospectively induced as part of the first CANDU transaction.

As the issue of Canadian safeguards applicable to the CANDU reactors gained attention in Washington, the focus fell on the deficiencies of those safeguards, including political loopholes, allowed by the existing U.S.–ROK nuclear cooperation agreement. That dated agreement on the "peaceful uses of atomic energy" committed the ROK to subject itself to IAEA safeguards, even in the absence of ratification of the NPT. But it indeed contained a loophole through which many believed a truck could be driven. The shortcoming, also known as the PNE Loophole, came about because the bilateral agreement specifically prohibited diverting plutonium for nuclear weapons—but made no provision for nuclear explosives work or other actions involving "peaceful nuclear explosives."

A declassified State Department TOP SECRET memorandum prepared for then-National Security Advisor Brent Scowcroft, dated November 18, 1974, and titled "Sale of Canadian Nuclear Reactor to South Korea," expressed growing U.S. concern about the so-called PNE Loophole in the context of the impending Canadian sale. Although heavily redacted even in its declassified version, the memo explained that the United States needed to resolve the PNE issue via an improved agreement with the ROK. The text added there seemed to be no urgency in resolution because the South Koreans "have no chemical reprocessing plant for extracting plutonium from spent fuel, and they are very unlikely to have such technology for some time." It is instructive that the State memo was written just as the ROK negotiators were putting the final touches on their contract with the French for delivery of their much-anticipated reprocessing facility. Little did we know there was no time to lose.

The NRX Research Reactor Gambit

There was another problem with the ROK's decision to embrace a CANDU reactor—a big problem, one that almost escaped our notice. It seemed, in negotiating the purchase of the first CANDU, with a strong ROK hint that KEPCO would purchase at least one more reactor, the Koreans tabled a companion request to AECL and Canada. They had determined KAERI eventually would require a larger research reactor, a 40-watt, thermal, NRX-type design, something, something of a standard offering by the Canadians.

The NRX desired by the ROK was almost identical to the reactor AECL had supplied to India some years before. It became the reactor into which the Indians fed natural uranium bundles to maximize production of plutonium. That NRX-irradiated and covertly reprocessed plutonium, further refined into metal, provided the core for the first Indian nuclear test—a 12-kiloton blast at the Pokhran test site conducted on May 18, 1974.

Although Prime Minister Indira Gandhi declared that the "Smiling Buddha" detonation was a "peaceful test," the world saw it differently. Concerned nations included, most prominently, Pakistan and China, for obvious reasons, as well as some of the countries that had served as handmaidens for the Indian detonation. Prominent among them was Canada, and it became immediately obvious the plutonium fueling the Indian bomb had come from the NRX. The Canadian government was embarrassed, and the Indian use of the Canadian-supplied technology soon became a significant domestic political issue. [NOTE 1]

During the same period, we were dealing with a sister of the Indian NRX, the Taiwan Research Reactor, up and operating in a country where we were trying to head off a potential proliferation issue. If the TRR were not enough, we had indications other nations were seeking to buy or replicate the special qualities of the natural uranium-fueled NRX. Taiwan and its TRR is a story in itself, as told from the perspective of potential East Asia proliferation challenges. Taiwanese nuclear development played indirectly into the Korean equation at precisely the time we were attempting to head off KAERI's desire for its own NRX. Well-founded U.S. concerns over Taiwan's nuclear ambitions reinforced our determination to deal aggressively with the ROK over that type of reactor. [NOTE 2]

The ROK's desire to include the NRX as an adjunct to the CANDU deal with Canada could not have come at a worse time. Their insistence that an NRX be included in the reactor package arrived fast on the heels of India's Smiling Buddha test and the continuing political fallout from that detonation. The leadership at the Ministry of Science and Technology and at KAERI, and the national-level financial planners at the Economic Planning Board all thought they had struck a deal for the NRX, namely, a combination of a grant and soft loan from the Canadian government.

Assumptions aside, the NRX project was in trouble almost from the outset. What had seemed a reasonable inducement, if not a straightforward quid pro quo, wherein the purchase of the power reactor delivered the NRX was too late by a matter of months. The NRX soon became a contaminating element in Canada's attempt to establish the CANDU in Korea as a direct competitor to the Westinghouse PWR. As one Canadian diplomat put it to me in Seoul, for Canada and its ambition to sell the CANDU power reactor to the ROK, the NRX quickly became the proverbial "whore at the church picnic."

On the intelligence-collection side, once we caught the scent of the NRX deal, we were able to verify it with good clandestine reporting. We immediately recognized that this low-profile gambit on the ROK's part to secure a first-class plutonium producer was politically vulnerable. Station intelligence turned to identifying the various players, both Korean and Canadian, involved in the NRX transaction. We also were able to track a third-country national who had long been active in the ROK as a middleman working on behalf of the Canadian supplier. [NOTE 3]

The bottom line? When paired with the ROK's determination to develop its own sources of natural uranium, and the knowhow to process uranium into fuel bundles, the NRX would have provided a complete front-end program capable of generating plutonium for use in a weapon. The NRX-produced plutonium would be recovered in the French-supplied reprocessing plant, then already contracted. Fuel laboratories from other suppliers, mostly Belgian, would complete KAERI's ability to generate fissile material.

Our appreciation of that approach on the part of the ROK nuclear planners, as well as solid intelligence, confirmed their plan. The reporting permitted our government to shift the dialog to a more formal Embassy discussion with MOST leadership, as well as surface the issue more forcefully with counterparts in the Ministry of Foreign Affairs. It also allowed a direct engagement with the Canadian Embassy and, from the Washington side, encouraged a sustained dialog with Ottawa. Not coincidentally, at the same time there were rumblings in Canada's Parliament over the pending CANDU sale from the standpoint of safeguards. Aggressive questioning by opposition politicians there about the strength and credibility of the safeguards agreement being negotiated placed additional and useful pressure on Canadian decisionmakers.

U.S.–Canadian Cooperation Shifts into High Gear

By spring 1975, as the Canadians sharpened their push to complete the initial CANDU sale and restructured their safeguards to ensure the politics of that sale, the NRX component went quietly away. In Seoul, the Pak government was not happy with that development. We knew the KAERI team and its MOST overlords placed the blame on the United States. But if the ROK wanted the CANDU program, for whatever combination of reasons, it was a development they would have to live with.

The importance of the NRX cancellation, or rather its quiet removal from the CANDU sale, should be fully appreciated—it often is not. What we had achieved was substantial. We managed to delete a critical resource that would have allowed KAERI to install and operate a standalone, major plutonium-generating reactor that could be used to manufacture material for a nuclear weapon. To be employed for that purpose, the NRX needed to be operated in a way that violated both Canadian and IAEA safeguards. With an NRX in place at KAERI's new facility in Taejon, such a potential would have existed. Because the NRX essentially was a tried-and-true bombmaker-in-waiting, the safeguards, and their enforcement, would have to be ironclad. We considered such a prospect doubtful, given the inherent skill of the Korean researchers, the operating parameters

161

of the reactor and the deficiencies at the time in the IAEA safeguards.

Even with the NRX departed, we had to deal with the prospect of the CANDU reactor as a secondary source of fissile material. The fact remained that the technologies, equipment and knowhow included in the CANDU package could provide substantial proliferation capability based on the natural uranium fuel cycle. If the NRX served as a small-scale nuclear bombmaker, the 680-megawatt CANDU powerplant could be a mega-producer of high-quality plutonium. Because CANDU's design and operating parameters offered the opportunity to divert fuel bundles within a sophisticated covert plan, the Canadians, encouraged by our government and the IAEA, wrapped the reactor deal in an expanded safeguards program designed to forestall such misuse.

Senior U.S. policymakers decided to share our intelligence information. They related what we knew of President Pak's nuclear ambitions to the Canadian government. The heads-up was done on a close-hold basis, with much of the assessment sanitized to protect sources and methods, but with enough detail to force the strong attention of the Canadians. It also was done to elevate the issue to the level of the Prime Minister's inner circle. Our government had to persuade the Canadians we were absolutely certain about the ROK's strategic weapons development plan, particularly regarding what Seoul was planning for its completed nuclear fuel cycle.

At the same time, we needed to address and remove any Canadian concerns that our approach to them was an attempt to gain commercial advantage for American reactor suppliers. Fortunately, the approach was well-received in Ottawa, and thus began a period of deep cooperation between our countries to coordinate approaches to the ROK on safeguards and reactor sales. We and the Canadians also teamed to deal with other suppliers, namely, the French, employing a common position that demanded their cooperation.

As I mentioned in the previous chapter, by mid-year 1975, as the United States sought to block ROK acquisition of the French reprocessing plant, the White House, under President and former House Minority Leader Gerald R. Ford, cooperated with Congress to bring additional pressure to bear on Seoul. The policy included credible and hardnosed threats to deny Export–Import Bank funding for any American-origin reactor beyond the Kori 1, then under construction. Reinforcing the U.S. campaign, and acting fully in concert with our government, the Canadians separately demanded that the ROK ratify the NPT as a condition to sell the first CANDU reactor. They also insisted on an expanded safeguards agreement tied to the pending sale. Because of the unique ability of the CANDU system to accept natural uranium fuel bundles as the reactor operated, it was critical the Canadian safeguards acknowledged the potential risk and be organized to detect any attempted misuse. The Canadian agreement handled the accountability issue directly and in a manner that, hypothetically, would prohibit any reprocessing of fuel irradiated in the CANDU system.

By summer 1975, with the CANDU sale still pending, and the related bilateral safeguards agreement under negotiation, Canada's pressure on the ROK increased significantly. The stiffened position complemented American mounting assertiveness, including an *aide-mémoire* presented to the ROK in an effort to discourage the French plant.

I can cite two instances of Canadian proactiveness. One was an early July cable from our Seoul Embassy describing a briefing on a recent meeting by Canadian Foreign Minister Allan MacEachen with President Pak and his Foreign Minister, Kim Dong-jo. In the meeting, MacEachen confronted the South Koreans over suggestions they had embarked on a nuclear weapons program, apparently referencing a Newsweek magazine story suggesting such activity was underway at the ADD. Pak and Kim vehemently denied the report. They asserted that such a program made no military or strategic sense. Nevertheless, the probing by MacEachen, in direct dialog with President Pak, unambiguously demonstrated the Canadians had focused on the issue.

A related instance involved the Canadians reporting they had experienced a "long battle" with the ROK Foreign Ministry in crafting a bilateral communique following the MacEachen visit to Seoul. The ROK side acquiesced to the Canadian language, even though they had strongly resisted the inclusion of a statement committing the ROK to the "non-manufacture or acquisition of nuclear weapons or a device."

Canada Stands Firm on Safeguards

The ROK finally accepted giving Canada effective control over the spent fuel generated by their CANDU reactor, as well as veto rights over any reprocessing of the CANDU-specific spent fuel. In that case, the Canadian message was clear: Oversight of the fuel was to be comprehensive, operational loopholes would be locked down, and the ROK's ability to divert reactor fuel to any undeclared activity would be severely constrained.

Within a week, the Canadian Embassy in Seoul, acting on instructions from Ottawa, took a complementary action. Apparently motivated by "very hard" opposition pressure in Parliament, Ambassador John Stiles informed us he had sought "clarification from the ROK government on the reasons for the purchase" of the French facility. The ROK had done a tap dance and suggested, at the senior bureaucratic level, that the plant was required to reprocess the American-origin fuel used in the U.S.-provided reactors. We clarified to our Canadian counterparts we had no intention of allowing U.S.-origin fuel to be reprocessed in any ROK facility.

Ambassador Stiles added that, back in Ottawa, the French facility issue had elevated political concerns to such a degree that the ROK's failure to explain itself risked cancellation of the CANDU sale. Needless to say, the firming up of the Canadian position encouraged our Ambassador Sneider to push Washington to adopt a more aggressive approach. He judged the time was right to do so, and that it was appropriate to press the Pak administration hard on all aspects of its nuclear program.

The American detection of ROK intentions and our policy reaction had come at the right inflection point to drive home to the Canadians the absolute necessity of their improved safeguards approach. The ROK side eventually accepted the Canadian safeguards. The contracts were signed, and the first CANDU sale became a reality, KEPCO's soon-to-be Wolsung 1 powerplant. Canada and AECL eventually would add three additional CANDU 6-type reactors—Wolsung Units 2, 3 and 4—to the ROK power grid over the 1997-1999 period. Commercial operation of Wolsung 1, the original CANDU reactor that had generated so much concern back in 1975, would be extended in 2014, allowing it to operate until 2022. The Canadians went on to sell several CANDU reactors to other nations in the coming years. All of the transactions benefitted from the enhanced safeguards developed by Canada as a consequence and useful byproduct of the U.S.–ROK nuclear showdown of 1975. **[NOTE 4]**

A Lesson in Corruption

One additional aspect of Canada's sale of the CANDU system to the ROK is worth mentioning. With the KEPCO Wolsung 1 transaction, South Korea experienced perhaps the most egregious example, in terms of financial gain to the instigator, of blatant corruption involving a project of strategic importance to the nation.

In the mid-1970s, sales and commissions from major ROK purchases of foreign facilities typically were instigated by well-connected middlemen, both Korean and foreign, with the illicit benefits of consummated sales distributed generously among those making the decisions. Management-level graft in the form of cash distributions was the norm in a given sale, to the degree that briefing documents weighing competing proposals and presented to company officials often contained hundred-dollar bills stuffed between their pages.

Several of the highest-level managers in the state-controlled firms were close to President Pak. All were critical to deciding which facilities would be purchased and what price would be paid. Though Pak was never involved, directly or indirectly, with any of those arrangements, and he maintained an austere lifestyle, he often turned a blind eye to the graft or outright corruption among his close subordinates. He probably reasoned that allowing such gratuities would help ensure their personal loyalty to him and his regime. In sum, he accepted the corruption as an evil necessity to getting projects done.

In the case of the initial CANDU sale, we tracked the involvement of a "sales agent" who had long been active in the ROK. The foreign tradesman carried no fewer than five passports and had managed to establish his firm in South Korea to represent various European equipment vendors. For nearly two decades, he promoted sales to ROK government-owned companies and enterprises dependent on foreign-government-backed lending for their major system purchases. The sales agent worked on a commission basis. He often sold second-tier or used facilities dismantled in Europe, claiming they were new or "rehabilitated" systems. The sales involved large profit margins for the sellers and provided substantial commissions for all the silent partners.

164

I happened to be familiar with the earlier sales activity of that middleman, based on reporting from protected sources within KEPCO and the ROK government. My information included a hushed-up investigation into an explosion in a chemical plant handled by the man's firm, a facility sold into Korea as "nearly new and refurbished." It turned out the equipment that exploded, with fatal consequences to a number of employees, dated back to 1925. I would encounter that dynamic entrepreneur again during a tour of duty in another country.

In the case of KEPCO's Wolsung 1 CANDU powerplant, a commission in the range of $15 million-$20 million apparently was required by the middleman to secure the deal. Some combination of the reactor manufacturer, Canada's AECL and a supplier in the United Kingdom stepped up to the fee to complete the sale. The commission was so egregious that a Canadian Parliament investigation was mounted soon afterward. Much to the embarrassment of Ottawa and AECL, the actions of the sales agent and the company were exposed to the public. The benefit to South Korea was that the magnitude of the corruption, in that case, brought the schemes to light and invited public scrutiny. As the country matured to become an economic powerhouse, such practices went by the boards and became a sin of the past.

Chapter 14. The Reprocessing Showdown 1975-1976

The Nuclear Fuel Cycle as a National Obsession

As mentioned earlier, the Station's intelligence collection on the Korean nuclear program focused from the beginning on the Korea Atomic Energy Research Institute and its fuel cycle activity. The effort was complemented by the Embassy's direct engagement with that organization and feedback between the Station and Embassy, occurring on a near-daily basis. It was clear by late 1974, as the Embassy engaged directly with KAERI and its bureaucratic masters at the Ministry of Science and Technology, that both were working with a strong Blue House mandate.

Our realization dawned slowly there were two components of a broader ROK nuclear policy and technology-acquisition plan, much of which was being organized below our radar. Once we did understand the comprehensive nature of the ROK program, however, we drew an obvious conclusion: KAERI's overt and quasi-declared fuel cycle activity was designed to deliver the capability of producing fissile material for a nuclear device. That capability was perfectly complemented by the Agency for Defense Development's covert weapons program. Put more directly, KAERI's ambition to fast-track the acquisition of a complete nuclear fuel cycle would create the potential to extract high-quality plutonium from spent reactor fuel. KAERI facilities would chemically process irradiated fuel to reclaim plutonium, and then work the material into plutonium metal to meet weapons specifications.

KAERI's capability would arrive as the ADD's effort to design a weapon and its delivery system matured. The latter would require a warhead with a plutonium metal core. We judged the point of planned convergence between the overt and the covert efforts, KAERI's and ADD's respectively, would be no later than 1980—in five years, if not before. Some reporting even suggested President Pak had been promised all elements required to guarantee his covert nuclear weapons program would be "secured" by 1978. If accurate, it meant Pak was hoping the country's sovereign strategic capability would become irreversible by that year; standing tall, immune to any U.S. or international interference or reversal.

In retrospect, given the speed with which KAERI was moving, and its determination to complete a nuclear fuel cycle, if the Pak administration had not initiated the covert weapons program at the ADD, and had we not confirmed its existence, the United States likely would have faced a *fait accompli*. That is, by 1976, all of the induced elements of the fuel cycle either would have arrived or been under contract and on the way to KAERI's new Taejon campus. At that point, even if the U.S. policy team organized itself and determined the ROK nuclear fuel cycle effort had to be restrained or highly modified, it would have faced a much more difficult challenge. By late 1974, KAERI already had signed some contracts, and several more were being negotiated. The following year would see all elements of the comprehensive ROK program well under way.

Although the ROK's eventual ratification of the NPT would have given us greater influence, had we not forcefully intervened in 1975, by mid-1976 KAERI would have completed an advanced fuel cycle program contract and begun construction, and the ADD would have had a year-plus of weapons-design work under its belt. The result: We would have had to address the ROK strategic weapons problem equipped with much-reduced leverage. Put another way, the ADD covert effort, and our ability to detect and define that effort, doomed their attempt. That was an outcome which, to this day, nearly 50 years later, causes great resentment within the ROK nuclear community—a community which in many ways in 2023 still is attempting to recover its fuel cycle options. [NOTE 1]

Reprocessing Unleashed and Gone Wrong

The U.S.–ROK dispute over KAERI's attempt to purchase the reprocessing facility from the French, and the eventual cancellation of that contract at our behest, has been fairly well told. Yet the reprocessing plant represented only a part of the overall fuel cycle showdown. Other aspects of the encounter remain unclear or have been misreported, so it is worth an abbreviated retelling.

From the first years of the South Korean nuclear experience, and that nation's preoccupation with completing the fuel cycle, the reprocessing component was seen as essential and achievable. That attitude was widely shared among other developing nations, likewise determined to master all aspects of nuclear technology offered by the major nuclear powers. As such, access was perceived more as a "right" to acquire technology than a privilege to be granted by the nuclear haves.

At the time, it was natural the ROK would closely eye its historical rival and recent colonial master, postured just across the Sea of Japan. The Koreans were determined to possess a complete and comprehensive nuclear fuel cycle, and they saw their rival was well along in the process of inducing that capability as a strategic national asset. Tokyo's ambition included not only reprocessing technology, albeit on a pilot-plant-scale basis, but also enrichment capability—everything designed to support one of the most aggressive electric power reactor programs in the world.

The ROK assessed correctly that the Japanese had jumped out of the gate by 1970 and enjoyed full U.S. support for their comprehensive approach. The commitment of Japan's government and private sector to build and operate both types of enriched uranium-fueled, light-water-moderated reactors; that is, systems using boiling water or pressurized water—respectively, BWRs and PWRs—

was impressive. The French firm Saint-Gobain Techniques Novelle provided the reprocessing technology. Therefore, the ROK would turn to that company and the French government to purchase the reprocessing facility.

Initial Korean overtures had been made to the U.S. private sector in 1974 to determine its willingness to supply such technology. They met a cool reception. The Koreans then pivoted quickly to the ever-eager French to purchase the plant and the knowhow required to run it. For their part, the French at every level—government, research community and industry—were eager to promote all aspects of their nuclear technology. It was in part a French national effort to secure peer status as a first-tier nuclear player, and partly designed to improve the chances for a French sale of its own PWR power reactors to foreign client states. By the early 1970s, France had bet big on nuclear power to feed its own electrical grid, a wager that would pay substantial economic benefits over the next half-century.

The French communicated broadly within the international community its official attitude toward export of nuclear technology, and specifically to the sale of reprocessing knowhow. Specifically, there should be no prohibitions on such technology, so long as adequate safeguards, mostly bilateral in nature, accompanied any sales and assistance. Besides, it was good business, and other first-tier nuclear nations, the United States included, were active in that same commercial space. It followed that France should not be denied the same opportunities to promote its nuclear wares. A final French rationale was that the basics of chemical reprocessing of spent nuclear fuel were broadly known. Thus, there was little proprietary or secret knowhow to protect or control.

At the time, reprocessing capability was being sought by a number of would-be nuclear states, including Pakistan, Argentina, Brazil and Taiwan, among others. SGN, with active French government support, was willing to discuss commercial arrangements with all of them. We had approached the French regarding several of those prospective sales to express concerns, but the reality was the international nuclear community, including the IAEA bureaucracy, remained of two minds on the transfer of the technology. There was no formal, or even ad hoc, "nuclear suppliers group" arrangement available to coordinate concerns on the export of nuclear fuel cycle expertise. Consequently, France was not inclined to be convinced that the sale of reprocessing technology was inherently dangerous—particularly in an environment that had yet to define nuclear non-proliferation as an accepted goal.

In a similar vein, other countries active in the early development of their own nuclear expertise, such as Germany and Belgium, likewise were willing to sell nuclear technology and facilities. Several nations were eager to vendor commercial power reactors of their own designs as well as the supporting fuel-fabrication plants. Prominent among them were Canada and Germany, each with the ability to offer power reactor technologies. The point was, consistent with the wide range of nuclear exports then being promoted by several competing nations, the ROK's ongoing exploration of reprocessing possibilities was not recognized for the serious non-proliferation issue it shortly would become. That, of course, would change once the full scope of the ROK program was identified, in both its cloaked and overt manifestations.

India obviously had exploited several foreign-supplied systems to, covertly, produce and detonate its first nuclear explosive device earlier in 1974. But the Indian event was downplayed and mostly consigned to the "anomaly" category by those nations eager to promote nuclear technology and reactor sales aggressively. But Pakistan and China did not share that somewhat relaxed attitude toward the initial Indian detonation. China had its nuclear weapons program well in hand, but Pakistan was caught napping. Yet, that government responded quickly, inspired by the Indian test, to accelerate its own effort to acquire a nuclear weapon. And Pakistan's must-have list included a reprocessing plant, with equal priority assigned to a large power reactor capable of generating irradiated fuel to feed that plant.

Eventually, the Indian test was perceived by a slowly awakening nuclear proliferation community as the proverbial "canary in the coal mine." But the magnitude of the growing international proliferation tide was not well appreciated by the South Koreans, among others. That soon would change. The not-so-benign ambitions of the ROK, Taiwan, Pakistan and other candidate proliferators arrived at stage front for U.S. policymakers in the 1974-1975 timeframe. Even in an environment of heightened concern, however, on the reprocessing side, France remained eager to sell sensitive fuel cycle facilities and found customers lined up at its door. [NOTE 2]

KAERI Buys Its Repro Plant

Sometime in mid-1974, in discreet negotiations not declared to the U.S. government, KAERI and MOST senior officials drafted an agreement with SGN to acquire a reprocessing facility. While commonly identified as a "pilot scale facility," the scale of the plant was similar to that of Japan's Tokai–Mura facility. It also appeared to be, at least at the time of the negotiations, similar in capacity to plants being sought by Pakistan, Taiwan and others. Coincidentally, as the SGN–KAERI contract reached its final stage of negotiation, Seoul Station reporting on the decision by President Pak to pursue a strategic weapons program began to arrive to the hands of our intelligence analysts. They in turn encouraged the attention of our policymakers, who were beginning to focus on the inherent danger posed by the impending proliferation of reprocessing technology. As a direct result, they honed in on South Korea and Taiwan, with Pakistan thrown into the mix.

In late November 1974, the French reluctantly revealed to us that a reprocessing plant sale to South Korea was pending. They noted "acceptable" bilateral agreements with the ROK and Pakistan on safeguards were included, a development that would allow the ROK purchase to proceed. Simultaneously, the French government pushed back on U.S. efforts to create a multilateral approach to nuclear exports, an uncooperative position Paris would sustain through the following summer. With the France–ROK deal, the United States had a problem.

Examining those events, we realized things had gotten by us. The comprehensive Embassy Seoul 8023 SECRET/NODIS cable of December 2, 1974, noted *inter alia* that the ROK seemed determined specifically to acquire reprocessing capability. Although the cable in its declassified version is heavily redacted, it makes clear the Embassy was struggling to come abreast of the reprocessing plant sale.

As 1974 moved into spring 1975, and our policymakers slowly but deliberately built their response, the possibility of the ROK purchasing a reprocessing plant became a reality. The SGN contract was completed and ready for signature, France internally approved the accompanying bilateral safeguards package and a French government loan was organized to support the SGN sale. On the U.S. side, our knowledge of the deal was incomplete, not helped by the French unwillingness even to confirm a sale was in the works.

French resistance to U.S. intervention in the sale was deliberate and sustained. They would not yield to a consensus approach, involving our growing concern over the transfer of fuel cycle technology and with specific regard to the ROK–SGN contract. At some point, it appeared the French had begun to get the message, in part because we shared our intelligence detailing what we knew of the ROK covert weapons development program. It was obvious the French plant, when mated to the Canadian reactors, would be part and parcel of such an ROK ambition.

Despite our discussions with Paris, however, the French resisted imposing safeguards beyond their own bilateral arrangements. They remained reluctant to abandon the sale at their own initiative. In the end, with U.S. and Canadian pressure building, the French allowed that, should the ROK elect to cancel the contract, and compensate SGN for the damages incurred at the point of cancellation, the French would raise no objections to a U.S.-compelled ROK cancellation. With that major concession, we were now better positioned to increase pressure on the Pak government to consider cancellation.

Notwithstanding the French willingness—albeit with reluctance and displeasure—to step back from the deal, at that stage the ROK stood firm and indicated it would not consider canceling the contract. The South Koreans understood the French were not inclined to renege on the deal, and the contract for the reprocessing plant would go forward unless the Pak government elected to cancel it. We had expected that reaction and were not disappointed. As the standoff continued into summer 1975, we brought other levers to bear on the ROK reprocessing plant decision.

As the French and Koreans moved forward based on their signed contract, the U.S. policy community developed a consensus position and finally responded in March 1975 with its own assessment, contained in SECRET/NODIS State 048573. The assessment conveyed a U.S. government draft plan of action designed to discourage certain actions on Seoul's part. The State cable was obviously the product of an interagency assessment and reflected a two-month, multi-layered drafting and approval process. It conveyed serious concerns but lacked a sense of urgency. It suggested that our government adopt a sequenced, steady-as-we-go approach. In Seoul, however, we had expected much more and, to say the least, we were not impressed by the cable's tone and substance.

Reflecting this disappointment, as noted elsewhere, Embassy Seoul responded a week later with Seoul 01637 SECRET/NODIS. It politely but firmly took issue with State's guidance and its preferred plan of action. Seoul essentially demanded a more aggressive approach:

> THE FACT THAT THEY (ROK) HAVE MOVED AS QUICKLY AS THEY HAVE RECENTLY TOWARD RATIFICATION OF THE NPT AND TO ACCOMMODATE THE CANADIANS AND THE FRENCH RE SAFEGUARDS IS VERY PROBABLY BECAUSE THEY ALREADY HAVE WORD THAT WE ARE ON TO THEM, BUT THIS IS NO INDICATION THAT
> THEY ARE GIVING UP.

The above language reflected Ambassador Sneider's recrafting of our draft cable in sharper tones to emphasize his growing frustration. Sneider discerned a lack of appreciation in Washington policy circles regarding the gravity of the situation on the ground in Seoul. In fact, Sneider and his predecessor, Philip Habib— then moved on to be the State Department's Assistant Secretary for East Asian and Pacific Affairs—were in lockstep, a process facilitated by their back-channel exchanges and phone calls. Sneider was pushing against an open door with Habib. In Washington, in interagency meetings and with Secretary Kissinger directly, Habib sounded the alarm at State and the National Security Council for a sterner approach to the ROK. Station clandestine reporting continued to fuel the initiative for action back home, while in Seoul that same reporting allowed Embassy officers to probe ROK government contacts carefully for confirmation of activities we knew were underway.

Washington Wrestles with Reprocessing Policy Options

Over the next several months, roughly April through June 1975, the Washington policy community seemed asleep at the wheel. That characterization might seem harsh, mainly because various policy planners and intelligence analysts were beavering away with their own assessments of ROK capabilities and intentions. Station and Embassy reporting fed into that mix and the pondering of policy options, but the wait in Seoul for decisions seemed interminable.

Ambassador Sneider returned to Washington in July for an extended leave and consultations, and he made it a point to urge policy development, decisions and direction for his follow-on action in Seoul. By then, we knew President Pak was at least one year down the road with his nuclear program. Some hurdles were being put into place by U.S. and Canadian officials, but the fact was that KAERI still had its fuel cycle program in place. Likewise, the ADD was humping away with its work, and both were in the process of moving to their respective new facilities near Taejon. We had not appreciably slowed the overall ROK program, and we were drifting into an "out of sight, out of mind" situation with the new facilities.

In July, policy deliberations in Washington generated a series of State and National Security Council memoranda drafts based on policy and intelligence community coordination. The memos eventually made their way to Secretary Kissinger for deliberation and decision. A careful review of the policy documents is warranted, if only to demonstrate how advocates for strong actions too often are watered down to a least-common-denominator position as a selected policy option. In assembling the memos, the National Security Archive has provided the narrative and East Asia history a great service. From the NSA effort, a combination of three draft memos can be found in their original format—as declassified—combined in an NSC decision document presented to the Secretary on July 24, 1975, by his staff, with the imprimatur of National Security Advisor Brent Scowcroft.

The memos reflect a policy process that attempted to gain Kissinger's agreement among three options for approaching the ROK on the reprocessing facility. As the NSC Action Memo of July 24, 1975, titled, "Approach to South Korea on Reprocessing SECRET," noted in its opening:

> As a result of growing concerns over South Korea's nuclear weapons
> intentions and specifically over their intention to purchase a pilot
> reprocessing plant from France, there is a bureaucratic concurrence
> at the staff level that would authorize the Embassy in Seoul to approach
> the Koreans directly ... (to explain) that Korean reprocessing plans
> could jeopardize US peaceful nuclear assistance including the pending
> US Export–Import Bank loan for Kori-II ... (and) ask them not to
> proceed with their planned reprocessing plant ... (and) offer support
> for ROK participation in an eventual multinational regional reprocess
> ing plant in East Asia.

Interesting that the memos raise two related issues. First, at that point, we had active congressional attention to the pending Export–Import Bank loan that would support the Kori 2 reactor sale. The chairman of the House Banking Committee stated that unless the ROK would forgo the reprocessing plant purchase, "we will likely find it most inadvisable to proceed with the ($249 million) in financing" for the second Kori 2 reactor.

Mention also is made in the memos that the French more or less agreed not to protest a ROK cancellation of the reprocessing plant contract—as long as the involved French firm was fully compensated. But absent an ROK decision to cancel, the sale would proceed. To underline the French determination to move the sale forward, France planned to bring its safeguards package to the IAEA shortly, for approval in early September.

The memos teed up a Kissinger-level decision for the next steps in dealing with the ROK on the reprocessing plant issue. They proposed and defined three options, citing the pros and cons of each, and recommending an option supported by the State Department. A July 2 memo apparently had not impressed Kissinger, in that it acknowledged it was a "relatively limited one." It proposed that the U.S. approach the ROK government to:

(1) state our concern about Korean national reprocessing plans and point out that such a development could jeopardize U.S. nuclear assistance, particularly the pending Exim loan for the Kori II reactor;
(2) ask the ROK not to proceed with its planned reprocessing plant; but
(3) offer support for the idea of ROK participation in a multinational regional reprocessing plant for East Asia.

On the latter point, the memo emphasized such an "idea" would assume, but defer for later explanation, perhaps, that such a regional plant could not be located in the ROK.

The follow-on July 24 decision memorandum explained that a possible, "more stronger" course could be considered at some point, but it should be ruled out in the near term, given that, "we believe (such measures) are unnecessary now and could prove counterproductive."

The memo also noted the United States had received recent reassurances from the ROK that "its civil nuclear program is for peaceful purposes" and they finally have acceded to the NPT, albeit based in part on Canadian insistence the ROK do so as a precondition to receiving the Canadian reactors. The State memo also offered that the ROK had accepted, "our tortured interpretation of our bilateral nuclear agreement," which gave the United States veto rights on reprocessing of spent fuel from American reactors. The memo closed by cautioning, "The Koreans undoubtedly have their limits, though, and the request from the US for them to forego the reprocessing plant may approach that limit."

The July 24 memo, and its attendant precedents, are works of bureaucratic art. As such, they are comprehensive and, at some level, seemed persuasive with their easy-as-you-go attitude. But the recommended "course of action" was, at least to us in Seoul, too little and way too late, as reflected in the instruction cable received from State more than two weeks later.

Ambassador Sneider had returned to Seoul by that point and, in advance of the receipt of the State guidance cable. The "relatively limited" course of action, decided at the senior policy level, landed like a dead fish on our Seoul doorstep. Sneider confided to me that the Washington policy elite simply failed to understand how their instructions would not get the job done with the ROK. He added that Habib aggressively agreed with his position.

Ambassador Sneider Leans In

The operative instruction cable was dispatched to Seoul as State 195214 SE-CRET/EXDIS on August 16, 1975, titled, "ROK Nuclear Reprocessing Plans." The Ambassador approached the ROK directly on August 23, in company with the newly arrived Science Counselor, the de facto Embassy nuclear referent, dispatched there about a year and a half after Habib had requested such an expert.

Sneider took up the discussion with Science and Technology Minister Choe Hyung-sup, taking as much of a positive approach as possible. He stressed U.S.–ROK nuclear cooperation and future opportunities. He was polite but blunt, stating, "the ROK had no real requirement for a reprocessing plant and that costs and technical risk factors argued against ROK acquisition of this capability." Sneider strongly urged cancellation of the deal and raised the possibility that future U.S.–ROK nuclear cooperation otherwise likely would be impaired. It was agreed a more technical meeting would take place where the ROK people would explain the rationale for and the status of the project. The discussion was reported in detail in Embassy Seoul 6495 SECRET/EXDIS of that same date.

We expected the ROK response. Their leadership did not take long to convey displeasure. On August 26, our Embassy nuclear referent met with KAERI President Yun to receive, with "some resentment" evident, the rationale and justification for the purchase of the reprocessing plant. KAERI's leadership made it clear they were determined to acquire the facility and all related fuel handling technology. For the first time, they provided a detailed explanation of which facilities would be included and what processes would be undertaken once the capabilities were in place. Layered atop the technical explanation were other considerations, including the fact that the reprocessing facility was critical to the ROK assumption that "nuclear power was the only solution to its future energy requirements," and KAERI's fuel cycle program was an essential component to that strategic assumption. KAERI leadership pointed out any cancellation of the contract would involve a great loss of face among all involved.

The more formal response arrived two weeks later on September 8, 1975, in a meeting between Sneider and Foreign Minister Lho Shin-yong. As reported in Embassy Seoul 6989 SECRET/EXDIS sent to State that same day, the Summary paragraph captures the essence of the ROK considered response:

> ROKG HAS REJECTED OUR REQUEST TO CANCEL THE FRENCH REPROCESSING PLANT AND PROPOSED US IN-SPECTION OF REPROCESSING PLANT OPERATIONS AS A COMPROMISE SOLUTION TO CURRENT IMPASSE.

In the meeting, Minister Lho had MOST Bureau of Atomic Energy Director Yi Pyong-hui at his side to explain the purchase as well as the rationale. Yi conveyed a more nuanced description than the earlier KAERI overview. After his description of previously unproductive interactions with us on reprocessing, he took the meeting into a discussion of the French contract, the costs incurred to date and other costs anticipated. Lho picked up on the policy side and asserted it would be "impossible to cancel the contract and still maintain ROK credibility with the French." He asserted he had no knowledge the French were prepared to accept a ROK cancellation.

Completing his formulated response, Lho suggested the United States basically should resolve the issue by accepting the reality of the contract and committing to suitable U.S. inspections of the operating facility. When Sneider pushed back on U.S. concerns and the inherent dangers to U.S.–ROK nuclear cooperation should the plant go forward, Lho did not give ground and stated the contract and the facility should be considered a *fait accompli*. The Ambassador said he would convey the ROK position to Washington and asked Lho and the ROK leadership to reconsider all the points he had raised.

A Key Question: Who Knows What

It is noteworthy that the reporting cable mentions certain "high-level consultations with Prime Minister Kim Jong-pil and Deputy Prime Minister Nam Duck-woo."

Our Station reporting was important because we could confirm the danger posed to the entire U.S.–ROK bilateral relationship—economic, political and security—by the festering reprocessing plant issue. The matter had migrated to higher-level ROK officials and was under active discussion. Moreover, the reporting allowed our government to structure formal and informal engagements with each of the key individuals involved with arguments supporting our position that the ROK must consider canceling the project. And such conversations over the French plant allowed Ambassador Sneider, in company with other Embassy officers, to suggest the U.S. demand to cancel the French contract constituted but one aspect of our determination to terminate the closely held strategic weapons development effort.

At that point, our government had frontally surfaced the reprocessing plant issue with much of the ROK leadership, essentially demanding they cancel the contract. The implication was we suspected they had a covert plan to develop nuclear weapons. Thus, the question begged: Who among the key policy players within the government and the Blue House knew of Pak's plan to create a strategic capability? Or, more directly, whom had Pak trusted with knowledge of his plan?

A reasonable assumption was that Pak's righthand man for all seasons, Presidential Secretary General Kim Chong-yom, was aware of every detail and therefore understood exactly where the KAERI fuel cycle initiative fit into the overall scheme. Kim was the master cylinder of the Blue House operation. He supervised all of the Chief Cabinet Secretaries, and he was Pak's controlling hand in the management of the government. His responsibilities did not extend to the military or security services, but he did have access to all budget decisions and confidential matters of national significance.

175

We assumed Prime Minister Kim did have, or should have, firsthand knowl-edge based on his deep personal relationship with President Pak. Kim had been Pak's confidant and partner in every political move he ever made from the time of their jointly mounted 1961 military *coup d'état* through the present day. More-over, Kim was intimately involved in the security of the regime. He founded the KCIA and remained well-informed on all military planning. Our betting was that Economic Planning Minister Nam did not enjoy access to any protected mil-itary program, for the simple reason that, his position notwithstanding, he had no reason to know. True, Nam was an ardent supporter of the ROK's embrace of nuclear power and oversaw all budget allocations for the development of heavy industry. But his commitment to nuclear energy merely was a consequence of his responsibilities for economic policy and industrial growth.

We also assumed Acting Foreign Minister Lho, although a respected senior official, had no knowledge of the protected weapons program—for the same rea-son that Nam probably was in the dark. In the case of MOST Minister Choe and BAE Director Yi, we assumed both were so completely committed to the KAERI fuel cycle program that it made little difference how much they knew or did not know about weapons development. They might well have imagined what was behind the MND and ADD curtain, but the two technocrats were fully engaged in their own fuel cycle ambitions and could easily convince themselves the objec-tives were reasonable unless shown to be otherwise. [NOTE 3]

In the face of the ROK's formal rejection of America's initial request to con-sider canceling the reprocessing plant, Embassy Seoul pressed the issue with its ROK contacts, with mixed results. In late September, Ambassador Sneider met again with the cabinet-level players, separately and privately. His reporting ca-ble, sent September 30, 1975, as Embassy Seoul 7642 SECRET/EXDIS, was brief and to the point. The Summary paragraph said it all:

I HAVE NOW COMPLETED A SECOND ROUND OF AP-PROACHES TO ROKG ON FRENCH NUCLEAR FUEL REPRO-CESSING LABORATORY. OVER THE PAST FEW DAYS, I HAVE PRESENTED BOTH POSITIVE AND NEGATIVE ASPECTS OF THE US POSITION TO DEPUTY PRIME MINISTER, ACTING FOREIGN MINISTER, MINISTER OF SCIENCE AND TECHNOL-OGY. INITIAL RESPONSES WERE UNEQUIVOCALLY NEGA-TIVE, INDICATING UNIFORM AND FIRM DETERMINATION TO GO AHEAD WITH PURCHASE OF FRENCH REPROCESS-ING PLANT AND DISAPPOINTMENT OF (U.S.) UNWILLING-NESS TO ACCEPT PREVIOUSLY OFFERED RATIONALE FOR ROK POSITION.

At that point, the Embassy backed off official discussions with the ROK to await a formal response to a second round of approaches.

A week after the Sneider cable, the ROK sent MOST's Atomic Energy

Director Yi to Washington to make the case for the reprocessing plant. But Yi's presentations fell on deaf ears. Meeting with a range of U.S. officials, he provided more details on the KAERI contracts with the French. Yi acknowledged two signed KAERI contracts, one with SGN for the plant, with completion and operation due for 1979, including some irradiated fuel for testing the reprocessing activity. The second contract with another firm provided a fuel fabrication facility slated for completion in 1977.

Yi characterized the prospects for canceling the plant as "impossible or almost impossible." He noted the facility would be subject to IAEA safeguards and open to U.S. inspection. Our side took the position that the issue was not one of facility safeguards per se; rather, it was the unacceptability of a plutonium facility physically present and active in the ROK. Yi and his team departed Washington, having made no progress, and they headed for Vienna to attend the annual IAEA general meeting.

Direct State Department Engagement in Washington

Consistent with the dialog in Seoul, our State Department went directly to the man we considered one of the most intelligent and influential officials on Pak's team, Ambassador Hahm Pyong-choon. On October 7th, Deputy Secretary Robert Ingersoll, with Assistant Secretary Habib at his side, met with Hahm to convey a message that carried a polite but "just in case the word is not getting through to President Pak in Seoul" tone. The U.S. side was unambiguous, insisting the ROK had failed to appreciate the seriousness of its request that the ROK cancel the project. State's approach was timed to impact the decision then being taken in Seoul by the Pak government about how it would respond to Ambassador Sneider's late-September *démarche*.

As the U.S. team made its points, Hahm delivered a carefully crafted response, insisting the ROK position rested on a sound technical, economic and political base. He presented a detailed exchange on the Korea–Japan reprocessing inconsistency and the ROK's requirement to match Japan's capabilities. Our side was insistent, however, coming to the point that the United States could not accept a facility that "could produce weapons-grade plutonium." Hahm noted the argument about the production of explosive material was "devastating." In a follow-up private session, Phil Habib drove home the real point of the meeting: It was time that Hahm, who was not invested professionally in the reprocessing plant, "make a forthright recommendation to President Pak, who has also remained personally disengaged, to decide in favor of cancellation." Conversations between treaty allies at this level do not get much more direct than that.
[NOTE 4]

The ROK Rejects Sneider's Late-September Re-Approach

On October 23rd, the ROK's formal response was conveyed by Acting Foreign Minister Lho—an unequivocal "no," stressing it would be impossible to cancel the contract at that point. The stance initiated yet another State-led decision cycle, captured in an extensive document submitted to Secretary Kissinger on November 18, 1975, titled, "Korean Reprocessing—The Next Step," SECRET/NODIS. The paper, drafted by Habib and Winston Lord, State's Policy Planning Director, redefined "the problem" in terms of the reprocessing plant's "capacity to produce enough weapons-grade plutonium for several nuclear bombs per year, in advent the ROK abrogated its NPT and other safeguards commitments." It urged Kissinger to select the option of a direct approach to Prime Minister Kim and, if unsuccessful, a direct approach to President Pak. **[NOTE 5]**

Back in Washington, after various approaches mulled at the senior-most policy levels, Kissinger made his decision. He accepted the strongly advocated Option 3 of a direct approach to Kim and, as necessary, to Pak, essentially conveying a U.S. demand for the immediate cancellation of the French plant. State 283167 SECRET/NODIS of December 2, 1975, notified Embassy Seoul the decision had been taken, and further instructions would be forthcoming.

Approaches to the ROK were to take place in both Seoul and Washington, but Ambassador Sneider would take the message into the Blue House. The political magnitude of the "request" to be put to the ROK leadership cannot be overstated. Sneider was authorized to:

- Request the ROK reconsideration of its position, pointing out that (refusal to cancel) would seriously impair America's ability to continue to cooperate with ROK in the nuclear energy area.
- Clearly convey that Korean plutonium production, lacking any commercial justification, would raise grave doubts about the ROK's peaceful nuclear intentions. It inevitably would affect our ability to sustain an overall bilateral relationship and stability in the region.
- Forewarn the ROK government that a refusal to alter its decision to proceed would lead to withdrawal of its request to Congress for Kori 2 nuclear reactor credits. In addition, we would confirm our intention not to authorize ROK national reprocessing of U.S.-derived nuclear fuel and would inform Congress that going ahead could seriously affect future assistance to the ROK.
- Reiterate formal U.S. support for safer and more economic regional alternatives to meeting long-term reprocessing needs.

Ambassador Sneider's insistence on such guidance for his use was driven by his personal conviction that nothing short of a direct approach to President Pak would resolve the issue. He also was convinced, as were many in the Embassy decision circle, that in confronting Pak on the French plant the ROK nuclear weapons program would have to be raised. As the U.S.–ROK confrontation progressed, and their resistance to cancellation hardened, it became clear the reprocessing plant issue had become a proxy for the entire nuclear weapons program—unstated but tangible.

The ROK appeared to realize, absent a reprocessing capability, that the entire covert program would be in jeopardy, if not effectively checkmated. It became painfully obvious to ROK leadership that we were determined to cut the heart out of the overall project by killing its key component. In effect, the United States was now engaging frontally on the covert program without disclosing the extent of our knowledge.

Sneider was reluctant to confront Pak directly on the weapons program. But by implying he was prepared to do so, he hoped to force the issue by taking it first to members of the President's most-trusted inner circle. We assumed the inner-circle group would include Blue House Secretary General Kim and Prime Minister Kim. We also assumed the forced cancellation of the reprocessing plant, while a priority U.S. objective, would compel a closed-door discussion by Pak with his top aides on the broader issue. That is, he would be forced to address, frontally, the advisability or practicality of continuing the covert nuclear program. It also was clear Pak was calling all the shots personally and was determined to proceed with the program.

We knew Pak's determination to stay the course was solidly based on his long-held concerns about U.S. staying power in the ROK. It included his reasonable assumption that domestic U.S. politics, sooner or later, would see an American decision to leave South Korea to its own fate. It had been a constant Pak theme over several years, both within his inner circle where it was expressed as a conviction, and in discussions with U.S. counterparts, all of whom witnessed it in his April discussion with Sneider over the ROK missile program.

Pak's fundamental distrust of U.S. credibility as a dependable ally drove his determination to build an indigenous military capability to guarantee the ROK's security if and when America walked away. He had watched America abandon South Vietnam. He had listened to President Nixon's 1969 Guam speech—also known as the Nixon Doctrine, in which the President had outlined the limitations of U.S. defense policy relating to our allies—and read the writing on the wall. Pak's determination to plan for the worst included securing a sovereign strategic weapons capability. It was the only explanation for the ROK's obsession with the reprocessing plant.

Pak's willingness to risk a breach with the ROK's principal security partner in the context of the reprocessing plant showdown demonstrated that he considered the French plant to be an absolutely critical element of the strategic hedge he was determined to create. The balance of the hedge, beyond the reprocessing plant and the other elements of the fuel cycle, was of course the strategic weapons program.

The Showdown Sharpens

A number of actions came together to force the ROK decision on the French facility. In Seoul, Ambassador Sneider, working from the above-described guidance and talking points, met with Prime Minister Kim on December 8th, with uneven results. Kim pushed back hard, frontally challenging any concern the United States might have regarding ROK nuclear weapons development. He argued that the U.S. threat to withhold the Kori 2 EXIM Bank loan contrasted U.S. policy toward the ROK with the pass we had given Japan on reprocessing. He added that President Pak would make the final decision on the U.S. demand.

Sneider emphasized he needed a "positive answer within a week" and, in the absence of such, he would ask to meet with President Pak directly. Concurrently, Sneider asked Washington to make a strong approach to ROK Ambassador Hahm to reinforce his discussion with Prime Minister Kim, the hope being that Hahm would communicate the separate approach in Washington directly to President Pak.

The day after Ambassador Sneider met with Kim, Assistant Secretary Habib, who had flown into Seoul to add his personal weight to the confrontation, met with President Pak. Habib's mission was to brief Pak on the results of President Gerald Ford's just-completed visit to East Asia, including meetings in Beijing with Chinese leadership. That essentially was a "reassurance" session in the name of President Ford, emphasizing to Pak and the ROK that, in our discussions with Chinese leadership, we had taken ROK security concerns into account. Habib used a follow-up Blue House meeting with Presidential Secretary General Kim to reinforce the Sneider–Prime Minister Kim discussion on reprocessing, repeating the U.S. demand that the ROK cancel the French contract.

Consistent with our all-fronts, steady pressure program and Sneider's request, Acting (at the time) Secretary of State Joseph Sisco met with Ambassador Hahm a few days later to press the U.S. demand. Hahm was well-prepared and pushed back, offering various compromises but remaining "intransigent" on the possibility of any cancellation. The U.S. side again made clear its concern that an ROK reprocessing capability would have "far-reaching consequences and adversely impact our mutual interests." To avoid missing the main political issue at hand, Sisco stated, "Our request to the ROK is to avoid an action that would be widely interpreted as a step toward nuclear weapons development."

Seoul responded with a formal demand for further U.S clarifications. Seoul asked what America was prepared to offer in return for a possible cancellation of the French plant, noting any decision would be deferred until we had satisfied their request for clarification. Most interpreted this as either a stall tactic or a legitimate search for a face-saving compromise. Sneider, now working in side meetings with Secretary General Kim and Foreign Minister Kim Dong-jo, thought he was making progress. His Korean counterparts conveyed to Sneider he would not be able to meet with President Pak unless and until the ROK side was satisfied with the U.S. responses.

Back in Washington, reaction to the ROK response was negative, to the degree that Sneider's inclination to formulate a considered counterresponse was received with disappointment. The suspicion was it merely was Korean gamesmanship, a stall for time or just a negotiating tactic to see what they might be able to tease out of us as a consolation prize. State came right back to emphasize it, "did not wish to get bogged down in technical discussions in the absence of ROK assurances of their intention to abandon this facility." Sneider was told to proceed with his meeting with Pak, while at home senior policymakers studied what it would take to respond to the ROK demand.

At that point came the beginnings of a rift between the course Sneider wanted to take and the standard impatience and distrust in Washington. We would comply with the ROK request for discussions, along the lines they had requested and as best we could. Also, we would send a high-level technical team to Seoul for those discussions. But we would in parallel proceed with the original plan to approach Pak directly and demand he forgo the plant and the capability it would provide. Sneider pushed back on State's instructions, convinced if he insisted on meeting Pak the request would be refused, as had already been suggested to him.

Sneider had a deeper concern. If his request to meet Pak was accepted, and he sat with Pak to convey the talking points and the demand directly, Pak likely would react negatively. Sneider judged that Pak would perceive the demand as an assault on his authority and an insult to the ROK. That was a real possibility, but within the Embassy there was a growing consensus we were being played by the ROK side. So, State insisted that Sneider get on with the Pak meeting.

Pak Confronted with a Decision

The high-level game ran its course through the balance of December and into January 1976. As instructed, Sneider requested the appointment with Pak and instead was received the day after Christmas by Secretary General Kim, who had in hand the ROK counterproposal. South Korea would "withhold action on the French contract for about six months" as U.S.–ROK discussions on nuclear cooperation progressed, with the strong suggestion that the plant would not be purchased if a "mutually satisfactory (U.S.–ROK) agreement" was reached. Kim made sure we understood he was speaking with the voice of President Pak. Sneider emphasized the bilateral political and national security aspects outweighed all technical considerations. He made clear to Kim—and by extension to Pak—that America required him to cancel the project in advance of the proposed discussions, not after those discussions were completed.

Kim called Sneider later in the day to say he had briefed Pak on the exchange. It reconfirmed Pak had been engaged directly on the issue and the decision was his to make. In Embassy discussions, all agreed Pak's direct involvement in the exchange meant he now clearly understood his decision was not just about the reprocessing plant. Rather, Pak understood that the United States was coming after his nuclear weapons program, determined to deny him the ability to produce the plutonium required to build a device, when and if he might order the ADD to build such a device.

It was clear to Pak that the Americans and he shared the same appreciation of the situation: The ADD was progressing with its weapon design activity, perfecting the non-nuclear components required and a delivery system to make a weapon credible. Meanwhile, canceling the reprocessing facility would mean KAERI would not have what it needed to generate the required fissile material. Although the reprocessing plant was the issue at hand, to Pak the message was clear: The United States actually was attempting to kill his entire covert program by preemptively eliminating a critical component.

All of it played out with no need, at least at that point, for a direct confrontation with Pak over his strategic weapons ambitions. In making the approach essentially a demand, America was doing so in a manner designed to protect Pak and offer him maximum flexibility. The path also allowed us to protect the underlying U.S.–ROK alliance, if not the entire bilateral relationship.

In the early days of 1976, the back-and-forth disagreement between Ambassador Sneider and his leadership at State Department continued. Sneider wanted maneuvering room. He wanted to respond to the ROK demand for technical discussions first and not insist on a plant cancellation as a precondition. Washington saw it differently, and the two sides argued it out. But Sneider carried the day. He was convinced, whatever the ROK game plan might include, that pressure was building on Pak, and the struggle was moving our way.

The U.S. technical team arrived in late January, meeting with the MOST team and generating aspirational themes for possible future nuclear cooperation. The talks had been, as expected, mostly inconclusive, but they had served their purpose. The ROK side did share that it was considering canceling the French plant, but they also signaled that all decisions were dependent on the outcome of talks with the U.S. delegation.

In that same timeframe, we had forced developments with the two other nations most deeply involved: France and Canada. In Paris, Dr. Paul Levy, the Foreign Ministry's Scientific Affairs Director, compared notes by sharing his belief that, "the ROK was committed to developing a nuclear weapons capability" and confirmed that the supplier firm, SGN, would not proceed with the plant contract until authorized to do so by the French government. They would wait until the ongoing U.S.–ROK discussions played out to make their decision, but in keeping with the established French attitude, none of the discussion "constituted a firm decision … to not proceed with the plant." France much preferred the ROK act to cancel rather than they be required to take that step, thereby maintaining the onus on the U.S. side to compel cancellation.

Canada, meanwhile, was now operating in lockstep with us at the level of the Prime Minister's office. Ottawa was determined to resolve the reprocessing plant matter so it could approve the CANDU sale before the supporting loan agreement timed out. Their first move was to postpone a scheduled contract-signing event, explaining to ROK that it needed to study the reprocessing plant issue further. It was another warning shot across Seoul's bow that Canada now had serious concerns about the facility, and the ROK's determination to proceed could risk the entire cooperative nuclear program with Canada.

Concurrently, Canada conveyed to the ROK, referencing their own bilateral safeguards agreement—which required Canadian approval of reprocessing fuel irradiated in the CANDU reactor—that no such approval would be forthcoming. To the Koreans, it should have registered that Canada had turned its critical attention to the French plant itself.

Secretary Kissinger met with Canadian Foreign Secretary MacEachen in Paris to reconfirm the U.S. position on the reprocessing plant and probe the Canadian side. The discussions were inconclusive, but the message to Canada was clear: both countries had a problem in the ROK. As events played out in Seoul in January, and the must-sign date for the ROK purchase of the CANDU reactor approached, the Canadians made their own, decisive contribution.

On January 20th, the Canadian Embassy in Washington informed our State Department that their Ambassador in Seoul had been instructed by Ottawa to deliver a hard message to the ROK Foreign Minister:

> For reasons we have already discussed with you and share in common with the U.S., we are prepared to sign the bilateral agreement as soon as you give us assurance that the ROK will not pursue acquisition of the project reprocessing plant from France.

With that formal statement, the Canadians officially conveyed to the ROK, in essence, "You can have the CANDU power reactor, or you can have your French plant, but you cannot have both." As anticipated, the ROK responded with the standard line, "We are hanging tough." It indicated they were not prepared to cancel the plant. They explained the ROK was delaying a decision until the technical-cooperation talks with the United States were successfully concluded. It demonstrated that Pak seemingly was prepared to risk cancellation of the CANDU acquisition, at least temporarily, in order to protect the French plant.

But the Canadians performed their own hang-tough routine, in part because Parliament was now fully aware of the danger signs coming out of Seoul on the CANDU reactor deal. In Brussels, Dr. Kissinger met again with Foreign Secretary MacEachen to compare notes on the ROK, the Canadian CANDU agreement and the French plant. MacEachen indicated that Ottawa planned to proceed with execution of the bilateral agreements covering the CANDU sale but would do so in a manner that would fully support the U.S. position.

In a companion statement issued with the actual January 26, Canada–ROK bilateral agreement on the reactor sale, the language was clear, as was the Canadian intent. The document, plus a parallel statement that the government of

Prime Minister Pierre Trudeau shared with Parliament, did not demand immediate ROK cancellation of the reprocessing facility contract. It went a long way, however, to assert that the U.S. position on Kori 2 financing, and the Canadian position on the initial CANDU reactor, were now hostage to near-term or eventual ROK cancellation of the project. It also was obvious that France was complicit in the understanding, and there was consensus among the three nations that the ROK would not be allowed a reprocessing capability. [NOTE 6]

End Game for the Reprocessing Plant

In the weeks following the January 1976 showdown, it became apparent that Seoul had decided, painfully, to cancel the French reprocessing facility contract. More bluntly, what would have been the centerpiece of a larger nuclear research facility, not to mention the most critical component of a weapons program, had been terminated. In reaching the decision, it appeared Seoul had elected to defer the reprocessing plant indefinitely while pushing ahead with the balance of the nuclear fuel research center, perhaps with the goal of revisiting the reprocessing component in future years. Proceeding with the new research center, KAERI would induce a spent-fuel examination laboratory, with the lab's work limited to PWR fuel assemblies and configured not to accept or process CANDU fuel bundles.

In the following months, Seoul agreed, in protected discussions with the French main contractor SGN, to pay a negotiated termination fee that covered work done to date on the planning, engineering and equipment lead purchases. Technically, the ROK could claim the sale had not been formally concluded, given that the French government's final approval was still pending. It allowed the ROK to internalize the step-back as a deferral on the project, versus admitting they had agreed to a "cancellation."

The loss of the reprocessing facility was a bitter defeat for KAERI, MOST, the Blue House and for President Pak personally. But within the Station, we never assumed Pak accepted the setback as a termination of his nuclear weapons development ambition. We continued to track KAERI and MOST but elected to focus on the ADD and the Blue House. We needed to improve our understanding of how those elements were evolving and how we might best support policy actions to mitigate and eventually forestall Pak's strategic weapons ambitions.
[NOTE 7]

Chapter 15. Game Over: Killing the Covert Nuclear Program Mid-1976

Blue House Outreach

Beyond our penetrating the covert nuclear, chemical and other weapons efforts underway at South Korea's Agency for Defense Development, and our concurrent peeling back of the overt Korean Atomic Energy Research Institute fuel cycle programs, the Station needed to secure intelligence access in one more area: decision-making at the Blue House. Acquiring that single relationship would be one of our most important accomplishments, in terms of ability to overturn the covert weapons program. A direct but discreet engagement at the highest decision-making level of the Pak government would complement the formal State-directed approach managed from Washington and implemented in Seoul by the Embassy.

Our National Security Council had developed a broad approach to take down the Korean program, and the State Department was tasked to deliver *démarches* in Seoul, Paris, Ottawa and Washington at the steps of the ROK Embassies there. All of those efforts were designed to block individual elements of the Korean effort, and by early 1976 the U.S. attempt to kill the ROK covert program was beginning to come together. But we still needed to track the impact the official, diplomatic-channel approaches were having on the man who had to decide how to respond to the U.S. offensive designed to kill his covert program. That man resided in the Blue House, and his name was Pak Chung-hee.

From the outset, it was clear President Pak had given instructions to initiate the program and directed that resources be made available, but the ongoing execution of the individual parts was in the hands of others. Implementation was well-organized and well-coordinated among the civilian and military players and, clearly, there was method in the process. No doubt the Blue House-authorized covert strategic weapons development program involved a careful division of responsibilities, and someone had been tagged by Pak to coordinate and oversee the execution.

We in Seoul Station assumed that the Blue House "someone" had to be Senior Secretary for Economic Affairs, Oh Won-chol. An engineer and technocrat who had led the planning and execution of much of Pak's industrial development program, Senior Secretary Oh deserved much of the credit for ensuring the nation's allocation of funding delivered real results in terms of ever more sophisticated and broader industrial capacity. His oversight and guiding hand seemed everywhere at once—be it added capacity at the world-class integrated steel mill at Pohang, a state-of-the-art mega-shipyard at Okpo or a machinery industrial zone at Changwon.

Senior Secretary Oh was assisted by a first-rate team of hand-picked deputies, all experienced in the real world of building and managing, and all beyond corruption. The deputies and assistants had the power to reach out directly to ministries, industrial firms and financial institutions to deliver Oh's word. He was the unsung and underappreciated master cylinder in the ROK industrial development program and lead contributor to South Korea's economic success story. He served Pak to drive and direct a multi-sector industrialization program that most foreign observers considered beyond South Korea's capacity.

An important point, which we did not miss, was Oh also directly oversaw the ROK's energy development. He involved himself in reforming KEPCO's notoriously corrupt management team. In that important case, Oh and his group cleaned house at KEPCO, the nation's government-owned power company, to eliminate the endemic corruption that had handicapped the purchase of power-plants. His management reform was to the eventual benefit of KEPCO's nuclear reactor program. Because Oh enjoyed the confidence and full support of President Pak, and because he was not a self-promoter, most foreign observers failed to appreciate his day-to-day influence on various industries. That influence promoted the emphasis Pak placed on the dramatic buildup of the ROK's domestic defense industry.

We did misunderstand Oh's role in one important aspect, however. Although he was uniquely positioned to manage the coordinated covert and overt halves of Pak's strategic weapons program, in fact, he had not been doing so. We were able to confirm it by establishing a protected relationship with an Oh associate, a special individual who would make a critical contribution to dismantling Pak's nuclear gambit. I identified the man as a potential player in that program, and I was able to develop a trusted friendship with him over several months.

My contact in Oh's circle, the man who quickly became a friend—I will call him Mr. Nam—understood almost immediately he was engaging in protected dialog with a Station officer. Equally important, he realized the issue at hand was his government's covert strategic weapons program. Mr. Nam quickly became a confidential source of information on the workings of the Blue House and the Oh–Pak interaction. Early on, as we shared information under a pledge of mutual confidence, I satisfied myself and others that Mr. Nam could secure access to highly protected information at the highest levels. In our gradually expanding discussions, my friend quickly recognized how such a covert weapons program could greatly damage the U.S.–ROK alliance. Mr. Nam was a special man—often hard-drinking, always engineer-precise and, as our personal relationship evolved, completely trustworthy.

Mr. Nam had educated himself on the KAERI projects. He carefully probed government officials about the logic and details of the semi-overt nuclear fuel cycle program and prepared his own assessment. He then sought out Senior Secretary Oh for explanations about the ADD's parallel and classified activities, encouraging Oh to probe within the Blue House for details on selected military programs. We provided Mr. Nam with some of those specific details, such as the defense budget line-item numbers under the Yulgok defense initiative that funded selected covert ADD activities. Mr. Nam then verified the information we provided to him and repackaged it for passage to Oh. The latter used his special authorities within the Blue House to peer into the individual programs, leveraging his budget-management authorities to demand briefings from various military and civilian nuclear officials.

Senior Secretary Oh Enters the Equation

As Oh built his own knowledge base, he came to two realizations. First, President Pak had indeed chartered a covert weapons program in mid-year 1974. Second, the United States knew exactly what was going on—or at least had learned enough to connect the fuel cycle dots involving the ADD's work. His conclusion was we had pulled it all together, and the entire scheme had been compromised.

We coached Mr. Nam on one theme, which he deployed to good effect with Secretary Oh. It was the discussion of the concept of a national command authority for strategic weapons. That is, once those weapons existed and the capability they provided were in place, how would those weapons be controlled? Specifically, if the ROK was going to have strategic weapons, what lines of authority would exist to control their release or use? More critically, what circumstances would govern the assignment or the delegation, from President Pak on down through the military chain of command, of weapons-release authority? Likewise, even if we accepted that Pak himself was the "national command authority," in the event of Pak's death or displacement by a deposing group, how would control over those weapons pass to a successor? For practical people, they were reasonable questions to ponder.

Senior Secretary Oh confided to Mr. Nam that he found those questions relevant and disturbing, from both a technical standpoint and his personal perspective as a patriotic Korean. Oh admitted he personally doubted that anyone, Pak included, had given the aspect much thought. If there was a covert program, those were hardly hypothetical questions.

With Oh tentatively on board, the obvious but unstated understanding was that he was indirectly being asked to intervene. That critical back-channel-to-Pak element played out as our government shifted into an even more aggressive diplomatic stance. Ambassador Sneider, working from policy decisions in Washington and directives sent to the Embassy in Seoul, *démarch*ed the ROK government at senior ministry levels, gently at first and then more directly, seeking explanations. By that point, the combination of demands to the ROK, in our coordinated effort to kill the reprocessing deal, built to an irresistible level. It included U.S. requirements for an improved U.S.–ROK bilateral safeguards agreement and the demand for ratification of the nuclear non-proliferation treaty with expanded IAEA intrusiveness.

Added to those components was the thinly veiled threat of U.S. EXIM Bank loan denials for critical projects, including any and all pending nuclear reactor purchases, and the Canadian requirements for expanded safeguards on its own reactors. The hardline approach was highlighted by the quiet evaporation of the NRX research reactor project and French indications they would not resist the cancellation of the reprocessing plant sale.

The polite-but-growing flow of in-your-face demands that any strategic weapons program be stood down was attracting an expanding circle of ROK officials who understood the intensity of the storm that had gathered and the details that attended it.

When Seoul pushed back, denying such activities or offering alternative explanations, we deployed our finished intelligence in discussions with their senior leaders. Our clandestine source reporting was backstopped and overlaid with satellite images and detailed assessments. In questioning the KAERI fuel cycle program, including the various agreements, negotiated or proposed, companion accusations surfaced of highly suspicious ADD activities, personnel and budgeting. The ADD itself fell into sharp focus as our diplomatic approaches extended to the ROK Foreign Minister, the Prime Minister, selected members of the Blue House staff and the ROK Ambassador in Washington.

Through a confidential, separate-channel dialog, Senior Secretary Oh was made aware of U.S. official approaches as they unfolded. In most cases, the details were conveyed to Oh via a protected channel handled by Mr. Nam, often on a same-day or next-day basis. That special arrangement gained credibility when the formal approaches to various ministries played out as we said they would. Though several of the official *démarches* and discussions with senior ROK officials were confrontational and involved their attempts to deflect explanations and demands, by late summer 1975, senior-level ROK officials were beginning to discuss "the nuclear problem and ADD" among themselves.

Persuading President Pak to Let It Go

In an environment of increased pressure, Senior Secretary Oh sought out others within the Blue House to express his concerns. He informed President Pak that defense funds were being misspent. He also proposed a special investigation of ADD management, focused on the agency's new facility in Taejon. Pak understood both the implication of Oh's probing and that the Americans were pressing his government across many fronts about his covert program. Pak authorized Oh to probe ADD execution of its entire research and development program, covert activities included. Oh returned with a highly critical assessment of the ADD, involving administrative incompetence, wasted funds and real estate transactions that benefited selected parties. Oh also highlighted to Pak the exaggerated claims by ADD leadership about what they could deliver in most of the ongoing programs. His bottom line might have suggested, "I really don't know fully what you have asked these (ADD) people to do, but it is highly unlikely they can deliver."

Oh's assessment compelled Pak and other senior members of his staff to face the critical question or, rather, confront Pak with a reality check: Was the risk of real damage to the ROK–U.S. alliance worth a covert weapons program that probably could not deliver the weapons systems the ADD had promised? The companion question: Given that U.S. intelligence had uncovered the program, would Washington tolerate Seoul's denials beyond a point? Oh saw his mission as persuading Pak that America knew about his covert programs and was prepared to confront his government about them. Would Pak's and the ROK's best interests be better served by his finding a way to abandon the projects he had started?

Oh's greatest concern was Pak's initiative risked America abandoning the ROK from both a national security and an economic development standpoint. Bottom line: As Pak's designated master planner for all industrial development, Oh was warning Pak that Pak's actions were a direct threat to Oh's entire heavy-industry development program.

The connection arrived at the very point the Embassy was doubling down on its *démarches*.

I accompanied Ambassador Sneider to several of these *démarche* meetings, in company with senior Embassy political officers. On several occasions, I either drafted or co-wrote the reporting cables chronicling the results, sending them back to Washington via State Department channels. As a given *démarche* was made, and the exchanges played out—with the approval of my Chief of Station—I was able to, selectively, discuss them with Mr. Nam in our confidential channel of exchange. Mr. Nam in turn took the information to Senior Secretary Oh, who continued to suggest to Pak that he needed to accept the facts. The United States was well informed and was playing hardball in its demand to cancel the projects, those of both KAERI and the ADD, both of which had been the subject of the U.S. *démarches*.

At some point, Pak ordered his team to begin dismantling the individual programs or, as was the case in certain projects, converting them to conventional activities that could be declared to and shared with the United States. All was done with the intention of securing U.S. acceptance and support for the development of defense capabilities that would provide the ROK with something less than the strategic capabilities Pak had sought. In the case of outright cancellation, the KAERI contract with SGN was terminated. KAERI paid the penalty demanded by the French to go away quietly. Other fuel cycle projects likewise were modified, and their contracts restructured to remove or modify the nuclear fuel cell capabilities sought by KAERI to work the anticipated output from the reprocessing facility.

In the case of project modification, though the ADD's nuclear team was disbanded and its key researchers reassigned to other government or private sector positions, the projects that could be repurposed, such as the Nike Hercules missile refitting, were restructured. Nike Herk was declared to the United States in a reborn form as a tactical ballistic missile armed with a conventional warhead for counterstrike missions The new system's payload and range were limited by a separate U.S.–ROK agreement. But the overall result of Pak's stepdown was that, within the space of six months or so—and certainly by year-end 1976—all of the research and development programs of greatest concern to us had been folded or contained. At the Station, we tracked each high-interest group within the ADD and KAERI and were able to report that all sensitive activity at both organizations had been wound down, and all remaining ongoing activity was fully declared, either by KAERI to Embassy officials or by the ADD to their U.S. military counterparts.

A Quiet Resolution and An Intelligence Success

In the fall of 1976, when President Pak accepted that he had no choice but to terminate his strategic weapons program and order his team to stand it down, we lacked complete confidence the decision had been made. Not too long afterward, however, we did receive a strong hint the decision to do so had taken place. Consequently, we concluded it indeed was over. We realized we had been through a high-intensity, bilateral confrontation that both sides had somehow managed to resolve quietly, with little damage done to the U.S.–ROK alliance.

As we rolled into 1977, our relationship with the ROK showed every sign of returning to its pre-nuclear-crisis stage of intense cooperation, dramatic economic development (for the ROK), and an improved alliance structure. All were based on expanding ROK's conventional capabilities, complemented by a robust U.S. military presence ██ ██.

That "quiet with damage minimized" resolution had been enabled by our Agency's early detection, penetration and validation of the entire strategic weapons development program. The Station's ability to track and report on the progress of the U.S. diplomatic offensive was critical to our government's ability to shape and execute its approach and, eventually, to shut the program down in the manner described.

On the ground in Seoul, the Station's interaction with our Embassy leadership, most prominently with Ambassador Sneider, had been intense, allowing the official approaches to be well-timed and detailed, thereby assuring success. Our ability to identify key ROK players and each man's level of knowledge and influence likewise was critical. As all roads led to one individual, our appreciation of his mindset and willingness to compromise for the sake of the U.S.–ROK relationship, all for the best future of South Korea and its citizens, was vital to the outcome.

In subsequent years, I was taken aback by some of the accounts of the ROK strategic weapons program that surfaced in various publications, including the manner in which it was detected and the U.S. government's approach to resolving the problem. Some authors speculated that the entire ROK effort was nothing more than a grand ruse on the part of President Pak and his team. They imagined

190

a scheme concocted to drive home to U.S. policymakers and defense planners the possibility of a ROK strategic weapons effort should we withdraw our forces, and therefore their deterrent, from South Korea.

I can state, categorically, that line of discussion never held water.

A Close Run Thing

There was absolutely no doubt among any U.S. official involved in the issue during the 1974-1978 period that concern by the ROK leadership about America abandoning the ROK, for whatever combination of reasons—be it logical or whimsical—was real and ever-present. Yes, we had lived through U.S. withdrawal and disengagement from the Republic of Vietnam, with our own Congress effectively cutting off military assistance to that nation as the North Vietnamese rolled across the border, in direct violation of the Paris Accords signed by Henry Kissinger two years before.

As if to drive home such concern and bring it to the fore in the ROK, the United States elected Jimmy Carter as its president in late 1976. Within weeks of Carter taking office, he and his administration would stun U.S. policymakers and shake the U.S.–ROK alliance to its foundation. President Pak and his inner circle would soon come to regret the decision to abandon their strategic weapons program, as the Carter presidency asserted itself less than a year after the U.S. forced the shutdown of that covert program.

My point is that, had the U.S. failed to detect and dismantle the ROK strategic weapons program when it did, and had that program existed in early 1977 when Carter arrived on the scene, the eventual outcome could have been quite different. It is probable that different calculations would have driven different decisions in the Blue House by mid-1977, and it was quite possible the ROK strategic weapons program would have been sustained, if not accelerated. In the final accounting, both nations were fortunate the entire issue was resolved when it was, and minimal damage was delivered to the relationship and the alliance.

Chapter 16. Nuclear Showdown
Aftermath in South Korea
1977-1980

Some Continuing Nuclear Concerns

In the months and years following our successful shutdown of the ROK's strategic weapons program in mid-1976, a reasonable question was often put to those most deeply involved: Given the factors that drove Pak's original decision, was it possible the Koreans had not really foresworn development of such a capability? Was it not more likely that, in quietly agreeing to terminate and walk away from critical elements on both the overt and covert sides of the weapons development effort, they had created a plan to conceal the core elements, to be reactivated at a future point? That concern soon would be reinforced by the advent of the Carter administration and its policies related to the ROK. I will treat the Carter element more fully later in this chapter, but that additive factor alone gave reasonable cause for concern, compelling Seoul Station to double down on its reporting.

In spring 1978, responding in part to the policy and political overhang left by the ROK's strategic weapons encounter, the CIA was tasked by the National Security Council to complete a comprehensive reassessment of South Korea's nuclear ambitions. The report reflected much broader policy concerns by U.S. leadership, including a proactive Congress then suddenly seizing on the nuclear proliferation issue. That all-source assessment, published by the Agency's National Foreign Intelligence Center in June, was titled, "South Korea: Nuclear Developments and Strategic Decision-Making." It is an impressive document and a first-rate analytical product, and it was put to good use by the policy community. The study drew heavily on our clandestine reporting, both during the nuclear standoff (roughly mid-1974 thru mid-1976) as well as our subsequent reporting in 1977-1978, while we prepared the report. **[NOTE 1]**

The Key Judgments section included the following:

- It reconfirmed that President Pak had authorized, in late 1974 (sic), a pro gram to develop nuclear weapons technology but suggests that Pak, at least at the time, did not yet decide to build a bomb,
- It judged that Pak "probably did not expect to confront the need or opportunity to make a decision on the production of either warheads or a delivery system for at least several years." Here, the drafters reference the fact that we were not in a position to "prove" Pak would construct a deliverable weapon; only that he desired to possess the capability.

Thus, Pak had decided to "hedge" and to place the key elements of that hedge in place as quickly as possible. Of course, the core issue was that, in hedging, Pak was risking it all.

■ The concerns that inspired Seoul's interest in nuclear weapons still existed as of the date of the report. Though North Korea's "unabated hostility toward Seoul" remained as Pyongyang strengthened its conventional capability, South Korea's "confidence in the U.S. security commitment and … Washington's willingness to defend it with nuclear weapons has declined." In that situation, many Korean officials believed "certain activities can and should be undertaken to keep Seoul's nuclear options open."

■ The ADD's missile program continued to have momentum and support, in part because "the [Pak] government is obsessed with acquiring a weapons system with which it can threaten Pyongyang—in the political more than the military sense…" It was an accurate appreciation of North Korea's ability to threaten Seoul with conventional artillery and short-range missiles.

■ A careful search of all available information determined, in sequence: no evidence that any nuclear design work was underway; no evidence the ROK was trying to acquire a uranium enrichment capability; no evidence the ROK was attempting to acquire a reprocessing capability; no evidence of any stockpiling of fissile material and no evidence of any weapons fabrication work.

■ South Korean officials who saw military utility in possessing nuclear weapons believed that decisions on the nuclear weapons question probably would not be made before the early to mid-1980s.

■ The most important factor in South Korea's future nuclear decisions would be " its perception of the reliability of the U.S. security commitment and, conversely, the emergence of the North Korean threat." Of note, "waning confidence in the U.S. would strengthen the hand of those who want to pursue a nuclear weapons option."

The NFIC document, in describing the genesis of the South Korean decision to embark upon the strategic weapons development program, related the progress achieved, or not achieved, by the ROK in each of the weapons areas. It spotlighted the KAERI fuel cycle initiative and the ADD's classified elements, and described the fate of each activity or research group in the wake of the December 1976 decision by President Pak to terminate Project 890 activity.

The report gave considerable attention to the surviving elements of the former program, such as the ongoing—as of the date of publication—improvements in the Nike Hercules surface-to-surface missile. One could assume it was because, at that point, the improved Nike Herk program remained an open issue between the United States and the ROK, albeit a manageable one.

The CIA analysis attempted to examine the South Korean policy planning behind the suspended program. It noted that leadership planning was erratic, if not haphazard, and it judged the decision to proceed with the covert project was Pak's alone, with no known study or decision document. Moreover, there appeared to be no ROK examination of the pros and cons of such an important decision, and no single coordinating body or even program oversight. Therefore, the attempt was fatally flawed from the outset. The analysis correctly related the role played by Blue House Senior Secretary Oh Won-chol in inserting himself, at a critical decision point, to influence and manage the dismemberment of the project.

Interesting, but the analysis does not give the U.S. government a clean bill. It notes that:

> *What patchwork attempts were made to assess the political implications of the nuclear weapons program in 1974-1975 (presumably by the Korean side) led Pak and some of his senior advisors to conclude that Washington would tolerate this work. Blue House staffers at that time drew analogy between the cases of South Korea*

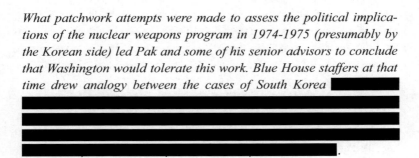

The CIA analysis also observed that the Koreans concluded the United States would "eventually recognize and tolerate [South] Korea's need to have an independent nuclear capability." Implicit was the United States failed to appreciate the Korean mindset. We failed to communicate strongly enough, and early enough, our objections to certain aspects of the overall project, namely, the French reprocessing facility. The analysis further noted that U.S. inability to force the issue of that acquisition until late 1976 delayed its injection into the overall standoff and, once injected, the issue became a forcing function compelling the Pak government to reassess its stance.

Last, an "Options and Decisions" section assessed the longer-term ROK strategic deterrence mindset and the possibility that Seoul would revisit its decision to terminate the weapons program. The document concluded:

> *[T]he most important factors in Korea's calculations regarding nuclear weapons will not be questions of technical feasibility ... rather they will be successive reassessments of the US security commitment, the threat posed by North Korea, and Seoul's success in building its conventional arms strength.*

The section specifically referenced U.S. contingency planning to complete a ground troop withdrawal in the early 1980s. It suggested that if the withdrawal proceeded, the real question in Seoul would become U.S. willingness to employ nuclear weapons in the defense of the ROK in the absence of an on-the-ground presence. The question became particularly relevant when, in the years following Pak's decision to stand down the strategic weapons program, South Korea's relationship with the United States deteriorated, and U.S. security guarantee became less credible.

Carter Elected and the Alliance Disrupted

The administration of President Jimmy Carter rolled into Washington in early 1977 and, referencing his election campaign pledge to remove U.S. forces from South Korea, Carter ordered expedited studies to make U.S. ground forces withdrawal a reality. Carter had taken the position early in his campaign and made it a recurring theme. To many, both in the U.S. policy establishment and, certainly, to all of us stationed in the ROK, it appeared to have become Carter's personal obsession. Facing that issue in our daily dealings with our Korean counterparts was not a pretty experience. When it became clear Carter could well win the election, the concern in Seoul was palpable, and with his victory in November our worst concerns were realized.

Carter's obsessive pursuit of the troop withdrawal from the ROK, in the face of active resistance from his entire national security team, remains a mystery. There is no doubt, however, his personal interest in human rights played a role, and he basically regarded the ROK as a dictatorship, in which its jails overflowed with Pak's political prisoners, and torture was the order of the day. It has been pointed out that Carter was almost entirely ignorant of East Asia security issues, and he seemingly elected to avoid all opportunities to inform himself. He declined, for example, an offer by the Agency to brief him on Korea during his transition period in fall 1976. He also routinely avoided attending National Security Council meetings that included Korea as a topic. But Carter persisted in his determination to withdraw, and his singlemindedness made rough sledding for all of us attempting to manage the alliance on the ground in Seoul.

In trying to understanding that difficult period, a time which saw our Korean counterparts distressed and the alliance tested, we are fortunate to have at hand an excellent account of the controversy. The book, The Two Koreas: A Contemporary History, by the noted journalist and East Asia expert Don Oberdorfer, is a great reference. Oberdorfer was near the center of events as they evolved. Over the ensuing years, he researched the details in an unsuccessful attempt to understand the logic of Carter's campaign to leave the ROK to its own devices. To cite one passage in the book, in which Oberdorfer devotes an entire chapter to the Carter initiative, aptly titled "The Carter Chill," he notes:

> *Two weeks before Inauguration Day, when the first informal meeting of the Carter administration's National Security Council team took place, policy toward Korea was one of fifteen items Carter selected for priority review and decision making. Presidential Review Memorandum/*

NSC-13 (PRM-13) issued January 26, 1977, six days after Carter's inauguration, and sent to the heads of key national security departments and agencies, ordered "a broad review of our policies toward the Korean Peninsula," including "reductions in U.S. conventional force levels." Despite the neutral-sounding words, officials of the new administration were shocked to discover that the basic decision had already been cast in concrete. The new Secretary of State, Cyrus Vance, returned from the White House that day with instructions that the review should not consider whether to withdraw American ground troops from Korea, but only how to withdraw them.

The Carter administration, with great reluctance at every level below the President himself, and with active and often visible resistance from the U.S. military, pressed forward in the coming months with the plan to begin disengagement from the ROK. In February 1977, Carter wrote directly to President Pak to set the stage for detailed discussions on Carter's decision. The letter was accompanied by rumors emanating from both Washington and Seoul that some form of drawdown, or even complete withdrawal, was on the table. Oberdorfer correctly related that when ROK Foreign Minister Park Tong-chin traveled to Washington to begin consultations, he discovered Carter was standing fast by his decision. Carter directed, in a memo to Secretary of State Cyrus Vance and National Security Advisor Zbigniew Brzezinski, that they were to explain to Park:

- American forces would be withdrawn but air cover would be continued.
- U.S.–Korean relations as determined by Congress and the American people were at an all-time low.
- Present military aid and (Carter's) reticence on human rights issue would be temporary unless Park voluntarily adopted open change regarding political prisoners.

[NOTE 2]

196

A Nuclear Reaction to Carter's Initiative

It was reasonable, therefore, that South Korean policymakers, both the nation's military leadership and the public in Seoul, suddenly felt less secure. Many saw their worst security concerns about to be realized. In that same period, the North Korean conventional threat became more pronounced. Unease over the viability of the American commitment to South Korea was exacerbated by the Vietnam fatigue that hung over the U.S. public, along with an accompanying reluctance to become involved militarily anywhere overseas for any cause. There also was a growing impression that Carter's decision-making, tending toward micromanagement of every issue, was erratic and unpredictable.

During that period in Korea, the U.S. military resisted Carter's inclinations almost to the point of openly challenging his withdrawal decision. The recall from Korea of U.S. Forces Korea Chief of Staff General John Singlaub in 1977, and his forced retirement the following year for publicly criticizing the administration's national security policies, underlined the standoff between Carter and the Pentagon on South Korea. In such a deteriorating political environment, it was an ongoing challenge to reassure the Korean people, not to mention their government, that the alliance remained alive and well, and would continue to function. By June 1977, a discussion of "what if they leave" had surfaced in the Korean body politic. The topic was openly debated within Blue House circles, was featured in National Assembly debate and thoroughly treated by media commentators.

Although such a connection was obvious, the certainty that the U.S. nuclear deterrent would depart with the conventional force drawdown was a reality check for Korea. Perhaps for the first time in any form of public discussion, the distinction was made between the U.S. tactical weapons, positioned to reinforce the U.S. ground force presence, and the independent presence of U.S. strategic weapons stationed in the ROK. Those weapons had been positioned there for more than two decades as a component of the Strategic Integrated Operational Plan. The SIOP long had featured U.S. Air Force aircraft assigned to strike Soviet and Chinese targets in the event of all-out war. [NOTE 3]

In the discussion of a possible ROK requirement to activate its own nuclear deterrent ██████████████████████████████████████

████████████, the Korean press speculated (accurately) about a recent visit to Seoul by Assistant Secretary of State Philip Habib and the Joint Chiefs Chairman, General George Brown. They had journeyed to the ROK to discuss the possibility of a pending drawdown of U.S. forces. In question was a U.S. pledge that ██ the U.S. would maintain its "nuclear umbrella" commitment to defend the ROK. That said, several scenarios were floated by Korean political commentators. Though U.S. assurances were welcome, they speculated, the implied trust in that commitment was suspect. Such a vague commitment left the ROK little choice but to consider its own nuclear options.

That expanded line of public commentary provided the first open discussions of the paths presumably available to the ROK to initiate and accelerate a weapons development program. The exchanges included details of the plutonium option, wherein existing Korean power reactors would be tapped for a reprocessing program to secure the necessary fissile material. Several reporters cited local or American "experts" who concluded if the ROK initiated a nuclear weapons program, then a functioning strategic deterrent might be available to the ROK as early as 1981.

As the public discussion progressed in summer 1977, it seemed every U.S. media outlet contributed its own version of what a ROK nuclear weapons program would look like. The New York Times, The Washington Post and The Christian Science Monitor all featured such speculation in their respective June 15 editions. The Monitor was all over the nuclear safeguards issue, including the U.S. and Canadian ability to block the use of plutonium extracted from their power reactors provided to the ROK.

Meanwhile, President Carter himself was hardly a reassuring presence. In a late May interview with U.S. News & World Report, Carter noted that, "he would not rule out the possibility of using nuclear weapons in Korea in case war broke out on the peninsula." In several reports, the role of the Brookings Institution, the influential Washington thinktank charged to craft foreign policy for the Carter administration ██. For a period of time, it seemed as if every breathing U.S. official, politician-turned-official or diplomat wanted to get into the Korean drawdown act.

In Tokyo, former U.S Senate majority leader Mike Mansfield, Democrat of Montana, taking up his station as the new Ambassador to Japan, pronounced that, "the proposed U.S. ground troop phasedown in Korea will be implemented over a four to five-year period, but about 8,000 U.S. Air Force personnel will remain…" But, he reassured, "the U.S. Seventh Fleet will contribute to filling the gap" in military power in Asia occasioned by the U.S. withdrawal from Korea.

Back in Seoul in that heady summer of 1977, Ambassador Sneider and General John W. Vessey, Jr., his U.S. Forces Korea military counterpart, began consultations with the Pak Blue House and ROK military on the proposed withdrawal plan.

Those discreet talks would proceed unevenly over the months ahead and fail to make much progress. In June, the U.S. Congress had become more directly involved in the controversy, with the Senate debating the pros and cons of the new Carter policy on the ROK. An exchange on the pending Fiscal Year 1978 Foreign Aid Bill witnessed a bipartisan compromise amendment that offered only lukewarm support to Carter's withdrawal initiative. The final text stated:

> *Congress declares that U.S. policy toward Korea should be formulated*
> *in accordance with joint decisions by Congress and the President.*

With that statement, advocated by Senator Howard Baker, Jr., of Tennessee, the minority leader, and his defense-hawk colleague from Arizona, Barry Goldwater, the Republican leadership had laid down a marker that Carter's plan was not a done deal and would face real resistance in Congress. ████████████

For those of us who had experienced firsthand the shutdown of the ROK nuclear weapons program less than a year before, that burst of public discussion and extended media attention was unwelcome. We were doubly thankful the resolution had been accomplished with little public attention and hoped it would remain so. We expected the Korean politicians and media to connect the dots and begin to focus on what had almost been in 1976. But it did not occur in any meaningful way. **[NOTE 4]**

Carter Checkmated

The public discussions linking a pending U.S. conventional forces drawdown ████████████████████████████████ with a requirement for a ROK strategic deterrent, continued into late 1977. The conversation took place both publicly in the media and in quiet discussions among ROK government leaders, but the Station detected no serious consideration by that leadership to revisit the nuclear showdown. A contributing factor was the reality that strong resistance existed within the U.S. national security establishment to Carter's plan, and the resistance was growing and consolidating itself. From the standpoint of the Blue House, it probably was better to talk and leak selectively. The implication was the ROK would maintain other options, essentially presenting a tough exterior while waiting out the showdown in Washington between Carter and the folks who knew better.

By mid-1978, when I was packing to depart Seoul for a new assignment, Carter's determination to compel a U.S. drawdown from Korea essentially had been deflected by the national security establishment. The struggle was resolved a year later in favor of the resistance, and by the end of that administration in 1981, America's presence in Korea remained mostly intact. Our ground-force presence continued, with steady improvement in their conventional weapons mix, and settled in for an extended stay. ████████████████████

██

██ [NOTE 5]

It is interesting to speculate that, had the covert strategic weapons program initiated by Pak in 1974 remained in place in the first months of 1977, within the timeframe the Carter presidency was pressing for a U.S. withdrawal, Pak could have assessed that his own program was far enough along for the ROK ████

██

████████████████████. That is to say, if we had failed to eliminate Pak's nuclear program when we did, by 1977 he could have perceived it as giving his nation the ability to establish its own sovereign capability. In such an outcome, at the likely expense of the U.S.–ROK alliance ██████████████████████

██

████████████████████████████████████.

Beyond Pak

In October 19, 1979, in the third year of Carter's single term, President Pak was assassinated. The event took place less than a year after I departed Seoul at the conclusion of my tour. Following a period of some political uncertainty, a military-led transition restored stability and delivered a new national leadership team. The critical link facilitating that rough but ultimately successful political transition was the bilateral U.S.–ROK political and military relationship. Absent that strong partnership, the ROK could well have drifted off-center to become an aspiring, nuclear-armed middle power. At a minimum, the ROK had the potential, once decoupled from the U.S.–ROK alliance, to emerge as a regional actor capable of disrupting all of East Asia. The knock-on effect certainly would have seen Japan initiate its own nuclear weapons program, or at least secure such a capability.

Thus, the nuclear stalemate we had managed to a quiet and successful conclusion three years earlier in Korea had preserved the overarching U.S.–ROK bilateral, political–military relationship and laid the necessary groundwork to keep Japan in a tight non-proliferation box. That accomplishment allowed the United States to sustain and expand its bilateral political and security relationship with Tokyo, further ensuring stability in Northeast Asia.

In South Korea, during the decade following Pak's departure from the scene, the inherent stability offered by the bilateral relationship permitted a combination of second-generation technocrats and enlightened ROK military officers to advance the affairs of state. The continuing stability on the peninsula witnessed those leaders slowly but surely guiding the nation into a functioning representative democracy. Political stability, and the predictability that accompanied it, allowed the South Korean economy to prosper, with the ROK joining the inter-governmental Organisation for Economic Co-operation and Development in 1996. By any yardstick, it was an impressive accomplishment, an "up from the ashes of the Korean War" success story. South Korea's prosperity had many fathers, but due credit must be given to the alliance that allowed it to occur.

During that period of sustained economic and political development, stretching well into the 1990s, the U.S. intelligence community continued to focus on the nuclear target in Korea, maintaining a quiet vigilance. Having learned the hard lesson taught by our close encounter with South Korea's covert strategic weapons program in the mid-1970s, America was doubly determined to stay well ahead of Seoul's nuclear program. The Koreans by then had been incredibly successful in the commercial nuclear field by expanding domestic nuclear power generation dramatically. In the process, the ROK created a domestic nuclear reactor and services industry that became world-class by 2000.

From the perspective of 2023, exactly 45 years after the 1978 CIA/NFIC assessment was completed and presented to U.S. policymakers, it is interesting to speculate whether the center will continue to hold in Seoul. North Korea is now a declared nuclear weapons state with a functional delivery capability. The ROK is now in the hands of a conservative government no longer eager to accommodate the North while reducing the outside role of the United States. Facing this situation, North Korea has stepped up its provocations as Seoul seeks more definition in the form of U.S. pledges of "strategic deterrence."

Now, as the ROK demands more certainty from its security relationship with the United States, and its government attempts to reframe the Alliance to make the U.S.–ROK security relationship more relevant to the increased threat posed by North Korea, the South Korean nuclear genie might again be stirring in its bottle. With its leverage reduced, the United States might not be in a position to restrain Seoul's ambitions. In such a case, we well could find ourselves proximate to where we almost were in 1975, when we struggled to understand the dynamics behind Pak's decision to attempt to take his nation to a nuclear weapons destination.

Chapter 17. Protecting the Alliance: Other Clandestine Reporting
1977-1978

Regime Stability—Constant Attention and Concern

Throughout the period of the showdown over the ROK's covert weapons program, and for well into the years beyond, the Station was compelled to double down on its other reporting responsibilities. Those coverage requirements included, but were not limited to, clandestine source assessments of the stability of the Pak government, as well as information on ROK military planning that was unilateral in nature. The latter involved South Korean military contingency war-planning not shared with ROK alliance partner entities, namely U.S. Forces Korea and the U.S.-led United Nations Command.

The Station's monitoring of the stability of the Pak administration concerned itself with both the overall political condition of the nation as well as the personal relationships among those within and external to the Blue House. The core concern was the individuals who constituted Pak's trusted circle of associates. Because the Pak government essentially was a one-man, autocratic regime, it was important to track Pak's ability to maintain the allegiance of his key lieutenants, including his praetorian guard, the Presidential Security Service. Even more critical, we needed to monitor Pak's relationship with the top military leaders who commanded the ROK Army units stationed in and around Seoul. An in-depth understanding of the various military cliques, the evolving loyalties among senior military leaders, and how Pak ensured the loyalty of the men on whom he had to rely to sustain his position, all were critical for our analysts at home.

Pak's personal vulnerability to North Korean terrorist attacks and assassination attempts, and the North's willingness to risk a lot to kill him, was an established fact. In 1969, a North Korean commando team penetrated the DMZ, fought its way into Seoul and was defeated in front of the National Police barriers of the Blue House. On August 15, 1976, Pak's vulnerability to regime stability was again driven home when he was attacked at a formal event celebrating Korea's National Liberation Day. The date, often referred to informally by Koreans as the "lifting of darkness day," honored the Korean Peninsula's release from Japan's colonial rule when the latter surrendered to the United States and allied forces in 1945.

We watched the assassination attempt, on that ROK national holiday, as it occurred literally in front of us during the dedication of the National Theater, an impressive structure. Pak had involved himself in the design of the building, rightly perceiving the Theater as a rebirth of Korea's cultural heritage. As the ceremony began, a young Japanese–Korean stepped out of the audience, approached the stage where President Pak and his wife sat during the ceremony, and emptied his handgun into the First Family. In the ensuing blaze of return fire from Pak's bodyguards, Pak's wife, Madame Yuk Young-su, was hit and killed. Others in the audience died, and several were wounded.

The attack on President Pak and the death of the First Lady Yuk, including the actions of the others on the stage and the reactions of the Pak security team, occasioned considerable turmoil within the Blue House and the national leadership. The immediate reaction was to lash out and respond to the attack, but the fact was the attempt had been made by a lone assassin from Japan, albeit a North Korean sympathizer. Pak's would-be killer and slayer of Pak's wife was a member of the pro-North Korean community in Japan, a member of the Chosun Soren political organization there. He claimed to have acted on his own initiative. [NOTE 1]

The natural inclination by many Koreans was to blame Japan and sidestep the North Korean connection. The response from the street in Seoul to the attack was immediate and sincere. In the government's attempt to channel the response, anti-Japanese demonstrations were organized and managed, at least initially, by ROK national security and police forces. At a critical point, however, emotions took over, and the managers lost control of the demonstrators. Swarming through the city's streets, the enraged protesters surrounded and threatened to attack and burn the Japanese Embassy. In a wave of anti-Japanese national passion, demonstrators in headbands lined up at the doors of that besieged Embassy to hack off their little fingers and write patriotic slogans in their own blood as a sign of protest.

I was actively involved during that tense period in planning for the evacuation of that Embassy. As we watched it all play out from a safe distance (the Embassy of Japan was just down the street from the U.S. Embassy and our Embassy housing compound was across the street from the well-fortified structure), we realized that the National Police no longer had control of the crowd and that the Blue House was adrift and confused with its response to the demonstrations, which had run amok.

The emotion of the street was spent after a few days. The Blue House made some changes, but the real damage was to Pak personally. In Yuk's death, he had lost his best friend and lifelong companion. Madame Yuk had brought an element of class to Pak's rule and was broadly acknowledged to have restrained him throughout his career. In the coming months, Pak would become more isolated, insular and inclined to depression. Inwardly, Pak became less inclined to compromise, more suspicious of his colleagues and more determined to tamp down opposition to his rule and his plans for the nation. The elevation of Park Geun-hye, his older daughter, to fill the role of Madame Yuk as a substitute first lady did little to assuage Pak's more base inclinations, and his closest friends found themselves making extra efforts to console and manage Pak to accept compromises.

Alliance Tensions

The second type of sensitive-source reporting involved ROK unilateral military planning. Such planning was done at Pak's discretion and direction, and it provided the Pak government with military options outside the U.S.–ROK joint command structure. We came to appreciate this as a result of Pak's frustration with America's unwillingness to retaliate against North Korean provocations. Likewise, in the case of U.S. and ROK joint planning for a North Korean regime collapse, detailed bilateral understandings at both the government and military levels needed to be established to allow ROK troops to move north in the event of a North Korean collapse, either in company with or absent U.S. forces.

Such bilateral contingency planning did exist, but the ROK was legitimately concerned that, in the face of a serious North Korean armed provocation or regime collapse, the United States would equivocate, defer on agreed joint plans or attempt to constrain unilateral ROK actions. In such a situation, Pak was dissatisfied with the U.S. military constraints imposed on his forces. As Pak's confidence in American security commitments waned, he and his military leadership became convinced they needed conventional military options independent of U.S. cooperation or assurances.

If Pak and his leadership needed an incentive to undertake unilateral military planning, Vietnam's recent death spiral reinforced their concerns. Pak had dispatched his soldiers to fight alongside the United States in Vietnam, and our defeat there was an all-too-real illustration of an America capable of abandoning a dependent security ally when the going got tough on the U.S. home front. Underlining and reinforcing the deteriorating credibility of U.S. security guarantees was the sustained inability or unwillingness of Washington to respond forcefully—unless bluster counts—to repeated North Korean provocations directed at American military forces in the ROK. [NOTE 2]

The summer of 1976 was a hot one on the Korean Peninsula, and no location was hotter than the Joint Security Area at Panmunjom. That village and the special zone created by the Armistice Agreement was the established meeting venue on the DMZ. Here, UN Command officers met with their North Korean counterparts to manage the ceasefire agreement. In and around that neutral location, a series of North Korean-initiated incidents would occur over several months. All involved scripted North Korean provocations, including physical attacks directed at U.S. and ROK personnel.

All came to a tragic head on August 18th. The incident, later referred to as the "Panmunjom Ax Murders," witnessed an unprovoked but carefully staged attack by a gang of North Korean Army officers and men wielding pickax handles, crowbars and metal pipes, delivered with intent on a workgroup engaged in tree pruning within the neutral zone. The Korean People's Army attack killed U.S. Army Captain Arthur Bonifas and 1st Lieutenant Mark Barrett, and injured three additional American soldiers plus five ROK officers, soldiers and workers.

The U.S. response to that vicious preplanned and deadly provocation was

204

restrained, contorted and tepid, if not mealymouthed. The incident had occurred, after all, in a presidential election year in Washington and, with the collapse in Vietnam so close in the rearview mirror, no one in the U.S. government was interested in responding with force. After days of deliberation, Washington elected to proceed with a carefully orchestrated tree-cutting action. Operation Paul Bunyan, as it was called—after the fabled American lumberjack—toppled and removed the popular tree that was the reference point of the North Korean attack, while U.S. and ROK forces stood at alert level DEFCON-3. The UN–ROK response was designed, in the words of one semi-official accounting of the event, to "demonstrate American and South Korean resolve and forcefully reassert UNC rights in the DMZ by a massive show of force." We knew President Pak and his inner circle took little solace and found renewed concern in the quality of the Alliance and American staying power with this pitiful display of U.S. resolve. **[NOTE 3]**

Watching the incident as it evolved over the next week in Seoul, we tracked the exchanges with our policymakers as they pondered various courses of action. With the U.S.–ROK alliance response, the tree-cutting executed on August 21st, I was not one bit reassured. In fact, we assumed that ROK unilateral contingency-planning would continue apace, and President Pak and his inner circle would look to expand their own range of options for responding to future North Korean provocations. Such planning would have to be tracked and dealt with carefully to maintain the quality and functionality of the Alliance.

ROK Unilateral Military Planning and Alliance Sensitivities

The Station reporting that I and other officers had assembled, on the internal workings of South Korean military planning that was not shared with the U.S. military, was doubly challenging. For one thing, ROK senior leadership had to be quietly confronted with the fact that the U.S. knew of their unilateral planning and that the United States could not accept it, from either a military command standpoint or a political perspective.

For another, such reporting by the Station tended to embarrass our own senior military leadership, and we had to manage what can best be described as their overreaction to such information. Taken the wrong way, Station reporting that confirmed unilateral ROK war and contingency plans suggested that our military, namely USFK, was not on top of its own relationships with their ROK military counterparts.

In fact, the U.S.–ROK security alliance, including the respective military leadership of the two nations, was highly integrated. Both sides shared contingency planning for war and maintained a high level of mutual respect and trust. Nevertheless, South Korea engaged in military planning and activity not shared with the U.S. side, for a variety of reasons, including senior-most national leadership instructions not to reveal such efforts. When the Station ferreted out the details, and deemed them important enough to report, the U.S. military regarded it as a direct affront, and reasonably so.

Certainly, the most sensitive category of ROK unilateral activity involved highly compartmented contingency plans for counterstrike operations against North Korea. Such planning was directed from the level of President Pak and ran the gamut. On the low-conflict part of the menu, we had commando team in-and-out raids into North Korea, scaled as retaliatory actions designed to counterpunch for the frequent provocations in the form of DMZ crossings. More ambitious ROK plans were designed as tit-for-tat responses to North Korean coastal insertions of agent teams that ambushed ROK or U.S. military forces. We also had obtained detailed ROK planning involving much-larger-scale operations designed to penetrate North Korea to some depth. In such cases, ROK military planners assumed a battalion or multi-battalion force would cross the DMZ and establish a bridgehead in North Korea. They would fight and hold there for a period and then retreat back into the ROK—message delivered.

Maintaining such plans within the Ministry of National Defense, without U.S. military or government knowledge or coordination, was a serious problem. An ROK unilateral contingency plan for a major military action, be it an attack across the DMZ or a coastal insertion into North Korea, suggested an independent capability and willingness to respond to a North Korean provocation. In the case of an internal leadership disruption in Pyongyang, or the ROK's perception of the collapse of that regime, contingency planning for a "go North without the U.S. military" scenario obviously had been sanctioned by the Blue House at President Pak's initiative. The Station, through its clandestine source reporting, was frequently able to detect and detail such unilateral planning. For obvious reasons, our policymakers assigned a priority to such reporting.

Unfortunately, our clandestine source reporting often triggered denial on the part of our military and sometimes, as mentioned, was met with hostility. In many ways, our military leadership considered themselves to be kings of the peninsula, a fully informed and dominating presence. Such an attitude disregarded the idea that ROK unilateral military planning existed. When the Station was compelled to share detailed information on such planning, including numbers, code names and details of the plans themselves, our senior military too often used the information to confront their ROK counterparts. It would occur in a manner designed to compel the Koreans to admit and discuss such planning. The problem was such confrontations placed our clandestine sources at great personal risk. Some of those sources were mine, and we Station officers were not averse to taking our concerns to the Chief of Station.

The Agency/Station disconnect with our own military occurred more than once, and our Ambassador elected to step into the conflict to add his concern, albeit quietly, to pour oil on the waters in Seoul. The intervention did not solve the problem entirely, however. Too often, the ROK side initiated counterintelligence investigations to determine the sources of our covert reporting, and we had no choice but to confront our military people with that revelation. We suggested no longer sharing sensitive reporting with them, at least in the ROK. The message was received. The Station established new procedures for intelligence-sharing, and the problem was eventually managed. But our military colleagues remained resentful.

Amateur Hour at the Apollo

We endured a similar problem with our local military leadership when we reported on sensitive ROK conventional weapons programs. It was natural that our clandestine source reporting on concealed ROK military plans or actions embarrassed our colleagues. But that resentment on the part of senior officers sometimes triggered counterproductive and ill-advised actions.

In one noteworthy case, we shared reporting on a highly classified (by the ROK side) South Korean Navy project to acquire an offensive mini-submarine capability. A senior U.S. Navy officer reacted to our clandestine source reporting by commandeering a USFK helicopter to make his own investigation and file his own report. Working from the information in our classified reporting, he had his helicopter hover 300 feet over the ROK mini-sub mothership as it sat partially complete in the South Korean shipyard. The hover allowed him to hang halfway out of the chopper door so he could snap away with his trusty 35-millimeter Canon SLR.

That U.S. Navy officer judged the details of our reporting to be inadequate. Working from what we had shared, his photo run over the shipyard allowed him to file his own report. He then confronted his ROK Navy counterparts on his initiative and without coordinating with either the Station or the Embassy, and he demanded a briefing on the program.

As the unfortunate situation progressed, we were able to monitor, with our clandestine sources, an ROK military internal counterintelligence investigation triggered by the overflight and confrontation. Their Army Security Command was handed the task and pursued its leads, determined to track down our Station source. The ROK counterintelligence team was determined to uncover who within their military had revealed a classified program to the U.S. side. All ROK personnel with access to the project were hauled in by the ASC and confronted. As a result, the secret mini-sub program was further compartmented, making our future access to the project more difficult.

Given those events, and the portent of more to come, the Station made sure our follow-on reporting on the subject to Washington included the ASC's reconstruction of the helicopter daredevil flights. Our hope was that further cowboy collector antics would be reined in. Needless to say, we shared no future reporting on the matter with those who had shown themselves oblivious to our source-protection concerns.

The ROK Army Military Clique Factor
in Regime Stability

During late 1977 thru mid-1978, I had inherited, or caused myself to inherit, an established source within the ROK military. The gentleman, whom I will reference as retired General Chung, possessed a unique perspective on the ROK Army command structure; more specifically, the makeup and priorities of the factions within that structure.

Before I relate the Chung case further, I need to provide a profile of the Pak regime's delicate power structure, along with a brief overview of the elements of the military cadre, personalities, and organizations that underpinned and sustained the regime.

President Pak himself was a product of a powerful faction within the ROK Army, the so-called Hanahwae-Ho, a semi-secret organization involving a like-minded group of young-Turk officers, many of whom, like Pak, had begun their military careers in the service of the Japanese military or police. Decorated Korean War veterans all, the men identified themselves with a shared experience and a shared regional affiliation. As I noted earlier, Pak was a product of the Kyongsan–Do region of the ROK's southeastern area, as were many of his faction members. Army clique loyalty was the leitmotif of Hanahwae-Ho and, though members of this group were dedicated to protecting and promoting one another's interests, the critical factor uniting them was their shared attitude toward Korea's leadership. Their consensus provided the security power structure required to promote and protect their nation's future.

General Chung, a senior officer of President Pak's generation, had mentored many younger officers who rose through the ranks to ROK Army regimental- and division-level command positions. Coming into their own in the mid-1970s, the officers included almost exclusively graduates of the Korea Military Academy classes 11 through 16. While the KMA was the direct counterpart of our West Point, and graduated the Army's elite, it was in fact much more, at least during the period I am describing here. The KMA, when those younger officers entered, actually was West Point, MIT and Harvard all rolled into one. Competition for a place in the entering classes was intense, equaling if not exceeding that for the nation's highest-level institution, Seoul National University. Each cadet who graduated from the KMA was accorded respect and recognition within Korean society.

Our Station fixated on the factions and cliques within the ROK Army for the simple reason that President Pak was a creature of their closed and calculating culture. Given the fragility of his one-man rule, we had to consider the possibility he could be displaced via factional rivalries, be that a highly unlikely event, or that he would pass from the scene—or pass from this life—with no real successor in sight. A related issue was much of Pak's leadership entourage comprised retired officers from his own age group, some of whom were fellow Hanahwae-Ho clique members. It was conceivable one or more of those men might harbor ambitions of national leadership. Others were more junior officers, aligned in their own cliques, who had sworn personal loyalty to Pak.

Among the elder group was Korean Central Intelligence Agency Director Kim Jae-kyu, a man whom Pak not only trusted implicitly to run his intelligence service but who also was a colleague. Pak confided his most private plans and concerns with Kim. The KCIA was then at the height of its power and could be characterized as a steroids-enhanced combination of our CIA and FBI. Kim and his KCIA operated with a blank-check mandate to protect the regime from all enemies, foreign and domestic. Kim was almost a brother to Pak, a confidant with whom he socialized as a close advisor and regaled him with stories as a frequent drinking partner.

Others in that group of close Pak associates included Prime Minister Kim Chong-pil who, although not a native of the Kyongsan region, had been with Pak since day one. Pak relied on "J.P. Kim" to manage his cabinet and oversee from a distance all domestic intelligence programs. He also handled all foreign relations, including the administration's ongoing and highly delicate political rapprochement with Japan. Kim had been Pak's right hand in planning and executing the military coup that placed Pak and his group in power in 1961, and he had founded the KCIA and built that powerful organization. Unlike KCIA Kim, Prime Minister J.P. Kim was regarded by many on our side as the single most indispensable member of Pak's inner circle.

A more junior officer likewise critical to the regime was Brigadier General Cha Chee-chol, commanding officer of the Presidential Security Service. He was considered the active-duty officer selected to replace "Pistol Pak," Pak Jon-gyu, of Korea National Theater fame. Pak, serving as the head of that protective force, had been the sole individual on the stage the day the Korean–Japanese assassin made his attempt on Pak's life, instead killing the First Lady, in the event I described earlier. Although chief bodyguard Pistol Pak had reacted with alacrity and courage to step in front of the President, his weapon blazing to cut down the would-be assassin, he accidentally killed others in the audience, and he had failed to protect Madame Yuk from death. He had to take personal responsibility for the tragic incident.

Not unlike bodyguard Pak, Cha demonstrated total allegiance to President Pak, in company with his handpicked junior PSS officers and bodyguards. Those men were the ever-constant presence in the Blue House itself. They remained at Pak's side whenever and wherever he traveled, and they had sworn a blood oath among themselves to protect Pak and the regime. Considerations of personal loyalty to Pak the leader and to his regime were everywhere in the national-defense system. Those same considerations of trustworthiness dominated the promotion and selection of key military and intelligence commands at every turn.

Two examples illustrate my point. One, the commander of the Capital Defense Command, probably was the second-most important active-duty officer in South Korea, given the CDC's role to protect the greater Seoul area. The commander reported directly to the Minister of National Defense, operating alongside the military chain of command. In practice, the CDC Commander actually reported to, and interacted with, the Blue House security team, the PSS, the KCIA and Pak himself. Its tanks, air defense systems and troops were on constant-alert status, prepared to engage in the streets of Seoul any force that threatened the Blue House and the President, be it a North Korean commando team bent on assassination or a rogue Army battalion attempting to displace Pak.

Two, the Army Security Command was all-powerful, both within Korean military ranks and frequently outside them. They were a high-status, much-storied and elite counterintelligence unit that had earned its spurs in the immediate post-Korean War years by tracking down, arresting and eliminating North Korean infiltrators and stay-behind agents. The ASC mandate was to monitor all branches of the Korean military. In reality, the ASC had authority to insert itself into any aspect of Korean politics and society, to the degree that it often rivaled its civilian counterpart, the KCIA. In October 1977, the ASC absorbed its ROK Navy and Air Force sister organizations to become the Defense Security Command. With an expanded mandate, the DSC reported directly to the Minister of National Defense. The move placed the new and improved DSC outside the nominal control of the ROK Army and made it even more responsible to the Blue House, if not to President Pak directly.

The DSC and its predecessors normally operated with a low profile in the Korea of 1974-1978, but we always understood it was out there, available to Pak and his team as part of the ROK defense establishment. The primary mission assuring its status was responsibility to ferret out any dissent within the military ranks while enforcing confidentiality inside the military establishment. That security mandate included the projects at the ADD and classified operational planning within the Ministry of National Defense. When appropriate, the DSC also was charged to validate the loyalty and effectiveness of the KCIA. As I noted, the commander of the DSC was responsible to Pak and was in his own right a potentially critical player in assuring the stability and survivability of the Pak government.

Last and perhaps most important, the Station identified as a priority the tracking of the next-generation KMA officer cliques and the leading personalities of those closely associated groups. namely, the leaders and fast-track officers from the KMA 15-21 classes. In 1978, those men typically were battalion or regimental commanders destined to move up to division command within a few years. They were typically able and highly confident, and all had established their loyalty to the system, if not to President Pak personally. In most cases, they had held or were slated to hold command of units in either the major and forward-deployed ROK First or Second Army, the CDC entrenched around and in Seoul, or the ascendant DSC. Many of those younger officers were protégées of KMA classmates of President Pak and full-fledged, next-generation informal members of the original master clique of KMA leaders, known as the Taegu Seven Stars.

Among that exclusive cadre, particularly the half-dozen next-generation leaders deemed possible successors to President Pak, the Station identified one man as the most important player we had to track. He was Lieutenant General Chun Doo-hwan. He had held a number of key command positions and was busy organizing his own group of loyal officers. It was rumored among the knowledgeable that Chun would be selected by Pak as the next commander of the DSC, a position he would assume in February 1979. A fellow officer in the Chun group was KMA graduate Roh Tae-woo, but in 1978 we did not yet appreciate his importance.

It was essential for U.S. policy overall, and for our government's interactions in South Korea, both military and civilian, to understand and appreciate how all players in the ROK power structure functioned. Whether institutions acting to defend their respective turf, or individuals maneuvering to secure their relationships with Pak and the Blue House, our mandate was to monitor and define them, based on well-sourced clandestine reporting. They were all tough calls to make. We accomplished our part of the effort by matching semi-overt information collected by our military colleagues and supplementing and clarifying it with reports from our covert sources.

The "customers" for that category of intelligence were a varied lot, from our own military leadership in the ROK to our military planners back at the Pentagon, along with the analysts at Langley—who were responsible for condensing our reporting into analyses for the policymakers. Some in the intelligence community were appreciative of our protected source information, namely, our military. Others, however, were not, particularly if the information conveyed was judged to be "routine" or lacked a dynamic flair or a hint of controversy, or failed to suggest a coming change in key relationships. All of it came home to me as I shifted gears in late 1977 going into 1978, and I found more time on my hands as the nuclear issue settled into policy channels.

Recovering a Critical Reporting Asset

Returning to my account of retired General Chung, in the fall of 1977 a situation developed where a more senior case officer in the Station allowed our long-standing covert relationship with Chung to deteriorate and die. I learned of the matter only coincidentally when another ROK military source told me how he held great admiration for General Chung, and it was widely known among that source's colleagues how the senior officers surrounding President Pak uniformly held Chung in high regard. They respected Chung as an apolitical, non-clique-affiliated, retired senior officer who, when asked, was willing to speak his mind to the President.

In the following days at the Station, I traced General Chung and confirmed that, as I had suspected, he was a trusted and fully vetted asset. His record of accurate and incisive reporting was impressive, and his motivations clear and consistent. He viewed a strong U.S.–ROK security relationship as the bedrock of his nation's survival, and he was willing to risk his career—if not his life—to protect that relationship.

Unfortunately, over the previous year or so, the Station's relationship with General Chung had fallen into a "taken-for-granted" mode, and our uneven management had reached the point where the General was self-tasked and his steady cooperation presumed. Beyond neglect, something more profound occurred. For some reason, our Station had not filed a report sourced to him for almost a year. Even more alarming, no one in the Station seemingly even noticed the change or made a formal record of his departure from the reporting team.

My deep dive into the case file, which occupied almost a foot of space in a safe drawer, involved a careful reading of the meeting-specific contact reports over the previous year. It became obvious that General Chung basically had been left out in the cold by the senior case officer who inherited his account. The officer was an Ivy League-educated fast-talker, a self-promoter and established wheeler-dealer who often spent his evenings with his poker buddies. He disdained the "street work" that most of us embraced as essential. Bottom line, the officer was lazy and had an established reputation as what we called a Headquarters politician. For certain politically correct reasons, he had been given a pass by Agency management, who were unwilling to confront his poor performance.

The contact reports the officer had filed on the Chung account were elusive and misleading. The implication was General Chung had walked away from us. Contact reports indicated that the General, who had not missed a single clandestine meeting for 15 years, repeatedly failed to show at the appointed time and place. None of it made any sense.

Moreover, with General Chung apparently gone from our reporting entourage, we were missing coverage of a key issue, namely, updated assessments of targeted military personalities and commands potentially critical to the survival of the regime. I took my reading to the Chief of Station to review the file, and he expressed the same reaction. He tasked me to take the case in hand and, at a minimum, get an independent reading, ideally from the General himself, as to what had gone wrong. The Chief fully supported the value of this type of contingency reporting. He agreed that, should we confirm General Chung as permanently lost to us, we needed to focus on replacing him by expanding our stable of reporting assets. He also removed the poker player from the case.

It took me several weeks to work up a plan to contact General Chung properly and establish a new relationship with him. Mainly, I activated a recontact plan and signaled that he no longer would be dealing with his now-displaced case officer. When we met and moved to a secure location for a sit-down over his favored Johnny Walker Red, we established a minimum level of common interest and respect. I apologized to him for whatever had gone wrong. General Chung explained that he had felt deeply insulted by the treatment he received from my predecessor, noting he had been left literally "standing in the rain" on several occasions when the case officer was a no-show. When they had met, the sessions were perfunctory and brief. Per General Chung, "that man does not know anything about the Korean military and isn't interested in learning anything." The comment was not a surprise.

Once we got past the collective anger, all was well. We waded into an intense discussion of military matters; the evolving national security command structure, which generals were slated for promotion and to which units of importance, and instances where new lines of loyalty to Pak were coming into play.

General Chung was fascinated by South Korea's next generation of military leaders, mostly Army, represented by KMA class 15 and earlier, and their impressive levels of education. He also remarked on the up-and-coming generation's comfort, or discomfort—depending on the individual—with the evolving Korean political environment. He saw South Korea trending slowly toward the acceptance of democracy, a trend which someday, he thought, actually might result in civilian control of the military. But he also was concerned that the established pattern of personal loyalties, and the nature of the Pak regime, mitigated against such evolution, at least in the near term. He agreed that the key military figures inhabiting the regime had to be known and their individual motivations charted.

The relationship with General Chung restored, and with the support of Station management for the reporting the General allowed me to draft, we resumed sending the information to Headquarters. Other sources working with other Station officers contributed exceptional reporting, but General Chung was at a level all his own. Working from several other sources, we could crosscheck, further confirm and validate the his specifics. In the process, we developed at the Station level a comprehensive reading of the men who would ascend to the next generation of Korean military leadership.

Every gain has its loss, however. As in the case of the initial nuclear reporting, I was discouraged by the reception Headquarters gave my communications. After several feedback assessments of their value to the analysts, we in Seoul recognized that somebody back home, or perhaps no one back home, had expressed more than minimal interest in our reporting.

Grades in the "I" zone for General Chung's detailed reporting were typical, with an occasional "0" for a "non-disseminated" field report by the Reports cadre, with the sought after "V" grade a rarity. (For clarification, the DO Reports staff had the option of awarding the following, in terms of value to the intelligence customers: non-dissemination or "0," progressively "I" indicating only mild interest or don't bother us again with this, "V" for good quality, we need more, "X" for significant information or excellent stuff here, please give more as soon as possible, and "XX" for incredibly valuable information of interest to senior decisionmakers or it's a bases-loaded home run.)

The assessments from home signaled that our reporting was almost a waste of time, and the disinterested commentary accompanying the grading indirectly told the Station to look elsewhere. Undeterred, with support from Station management, we continued to submit the reports. We filed draft disseminations accompanied by operational cables expressing Station judgment that it was important to track the ROK military personalities, if for no other reason than no one else was doing so, or had the ability to do so. Our reporting continued to be reduced and compressed, and less frequent, but we kept the channel alive.

After Pak, What Then and Who?

Some months later, in the fall of 1978, I made the post-Seoul-tour rounds back at Langley to meet with various Directorate of Intelligence analytical elements concerned with the ROK. In the course of one of the discussions, about analytical judgments on Station reporting, I had a mini-confrontation with a senior manager for intelligence analysis and production for East Asia. I explained the Station's perception of the importance of the reporting of ROK military cliques and asked for an explanation why she and other DI colleagues apparently had turned up their collective noses.

Her response was jarringly simple. "Why is this information so important?" Followed by, "And, we haven't asked for it!" I explained the power structure surrounding President Pak, the fragility of the military-backed regime itself, the absence of any clearly defined plan of succession, and the complex web of military factions that could come into play in a post-Pak scenario. Her response was predictable. "Yes, we understand most of these things, but what makes you think Pak will walk away or die tomorrow? He is in great health, and your reporting suggests his power base is firm."

I took a deep breath and argued that Pak was one man, and he often flew in a helicopter to meetings throughout the country. He was not reckless, but he was a chance-taker. His helicopter could go down tomorrow, and we would have a "game on" scenario to deal with. Or, he could fall down the stairs at the Blue House or be pushed. It really did not matter how Pak might die. The fact was there was no guarantee whatsoever about what could happen, irrespective of the constitutional provisions that might be in place. It was Korea, and it would be a crapshoot. To her credit, she got it. We then talked KMA classes, and the PPS, the DSC, the CDC and the KCIA, and the more we talked, the more she began to construct alternative and competing scenarios.

In the course of several follow-up meetings with her and her Korean analysts, I requested that she go back to the DO's Reports staff and engage them. I wanted her, with her "DI is your customer" hat in place, to take a position with the Reports officers who arbitrarily had decided what grades were awarded to field disseminations coming into Headquarters. She, not me, needed to "frontally take on" the DO people who routinely interacted with DI analysts to "evaluate" their individual field reports.

It was the combination of Operations Directorate types and Intelligence Directorate analysts that determined, for better or worse, what we reported from Seoul Station. To continue with a line of field reporting, it was not enough for the Station to deem it important. Rather, we needed our customers at home to advocate actively for this type of protected information. I emphasized that the perception of value delivered by Agency analysts for this category of reporting had to change, and the reporting feedback dynamic had to improve. Failing a positive attitude, there would be no more such reporting from the Station.

The attitude of "why bother" would prevail. It was a reminder that, unfortunately, the Reports officers were the "master cylinders" of the entire process of intelligence dissemination. They were the professionals who decided the value of field reporting. They were fine people, hardworking, and generally they did an excellent job. But the grades they awarded were sometimes arbitrary.

To a receptive audience, I explained the DO process to that senior DI manager and her colleagues. I described the chokehold the Reports staff held and exercised over the Stations, and the influence their judgments held over field disseminations arriving from the Station. Neither the DI manager, nor any of her younger analysis team, understood the subjectivity with which the Reports cadre managed what they received, the indiscretion with which field reporting was often evaluated, and the net impact the long-established-but-imperfect process had on individual officers within a Station who ran sources and determined what information those sources were tasked to collect.

Understanding my explanation, and satisfying herself that she now knew the way the reporting game was played in the DO, she agreed to move out smartly. I must say, she delivered in spades, at least in my case. In a follow-up with a Seoul Station officer home on a TDY a few months later, I was told that the Reports team had done a 180 in its interaction with the Station. Headquarters positively evaluated the reports from General Chung and others on the next-generation military cliques. They asked for more of the same, and in better detail. They got the requirement right, the Station responded, and the DI analysts got the information they needed.

Fast-Forward Nine Months—Pak Dies

As I described in the previous chapter, in October 1979, a little more than a year after I had bid farewell to Seoul Station, President Pak was terminated by a copper-clad handgun bullet, delivered at close range during a drinking session in a restaurant near the Blue House. The kill shot was provided by his "most loyal lifelong friend," KCIA Director Kim Jae-kyu. With that single shot, the "Pak dies, then what?" event was on, the succession game in South Korea was afoot for real, and all of the imagined control and succession scenarios were no longer hypothetical. In Seoul, a period of uncertainty and confusion ensued, and the game progressed over several weeks with predictable results. DSC Commander Chun Doo-hwan, in his position for nine months, stepped into the breach. Chun launched his investigations, shoved others out of the way and, by December, had established complete control.

In the not-too-distant future, in the immediate wake of the Pak assassination at the hands of KCIA Director Kim, DCS Commander Chun would take charge of the national security establishment, in part by launching an investigation of the assassination itself. In that process, he and his DSC team would identify and arrest other presumed contenders and displace the ROK military and civilian leadership, allowing Chun to secure control via virtual military coup on December 12, 1979. The assumption of control, often referred to as the "12-12 incident," would not have been possible had Chun not commanded the DSC and staffed that organization with his loyal cadre of like-minded officers. Chun's DSC, with

215

the support of others aligned with his group in the ROK Army, was able to claim, with some credibility, that it had inherited the Pak mantle and the Pak model of national development. A key planner and enforcer in that 12-12 ROK Army take-over was General Roh Tae-woo. Chun would be elected President in 1980 and would turn over that position to Roh some eight years later.

An interesting twist on the KCIA Kim shot-to-the-forehead murder of President Pak occurred a few months before I departed Seoul. On that day, an Embassy employee shared a story with me about Kim from the employee's childhood. The employee, a heavy-industry reporting specialist, had become a good friend of mine over several years, and somehow our discussion had turned that day to Kim, probably because I was then preoccupied with military-clique reporting. The employee offered that, in his home village in 1949, Kim had been his grade school teacher. Kim was known there for his explosive temper, including his inclination to strike students and his physical confrontations with other teachers.

When I suggested that Kim had been a career ROK military man since the Army was formed in 1946, and a second-year Korea Military Academy classmate of President Pak, my friend countered that Kim also had been court-martialed and cashiered in 1948 for killing his first wife, supposedly the "accidental outcome" of a domestic dispute. Kim had been able only to find work in his home county grade school because the school manager was a Kim relative. When North Korea attacked in June 1950, Kim seized the opportunity to regain his commission and performed in combat with distinction, winning promotions and a return to his military career. Kim managed to re-embrace and support his childhood friend, President Pak, and had been a key officer among the colonels whom Pak gathered to plan and execute his coup to seize control of the government in 1961.

When I pushed my friend on his story, he was adamant: Only those students in that school knew the real story, and all records of Kim's pre-Korean War situation had been purged. The school, destroyed in the war, had been rebuilt, but the records were gone, and Kim's identity as a fifth-grade teacher had been purged. He finished with, "and if I were to relate this true story to any Korean, I would be reported to the KCIA, and I would be gone tomorrow by Kim's hand. He is a very violent person!"

Less than a year later, we would find out just how violent Kim could be when, as they dined casually, Kim pulled out his trusty sidearm to settle a grievance with his best friend, President Pak Chung-hee.

A month or so after Pak's violent removal from the scene, while I was hard at work at Langley in the Swiss–Austria Branch in the DO's European Division, I received a call from that DI senior manager—now my friend. She said only, "I want you to know that, for the policymakers on the subject of "what comes next after Pak," we nailed it. We have the contending parties identified, Chun's in charge, and we have managed to call every change of control in advance. Thank you so much." She added, "If you don't mind, over here in the DI, we are taking all the credit." My only reply was, "So what else is new? And, if it matters, you are most welcome!"

216

Departing Seoul — August 1978

It was time to move on. I had served almost five years on the ground in Seoul. I experienced a great run there, with incredible personal satisfaction. I received three promotions and a couple of commendations, and I had operated under three of the most interesting Chiefs of Station I would encounter in my career. I watched the Station team turn over twice, with a third turnover pending. Our overall reporting program and clandestine source base was strong. All things considered, it was a good time to walk away and let others pick up the work. My new parent, the East Asia Division, agreed, and I was offered several field assignments in Asia.

They strongly encouraged me to enter the Japanese-language program. If I took the option, I would spend two years in language study, one of which would be in Japan. Then I would be expected to serve two, back-to-back, two-year tours in another East Asian city, for a total commitment to Japan of six years. That path was a natural transition for Korean-language case officers. It was correctly surmised that a strong level in one language would transition well into another. Also, officers who specialized in Japan and Korea were judged to be above-the-cut for senior positions in East Asia Division, rivaled only by the clique of "China hands." Most of us regarded the latter to be prima donnas, a group who judged themselves the Agency's elite among officers in the greater Asia clandestine service mix.

I realized that, referencing my work in Korea, I was headed full-bore into the Japan/Korea compartment of the Division. I accepted it as a reasonable near-term career path, although even at that early point, barely seven years with the Agency, I did not really see myself as a "career guy." That said, I wanted to leverage my strong Seoul Station tour to secure an out-of-division assignment, so I asked for either France or Austria. I understood the choice would mean a one- or two-year tour at Headquarters in the Directorate's European Division and some level of language training. Also, I wanted to continue my nuclear proliferation work to the degree possible, and I wanted exposure to the "hard target" community of the Soviets, Eastern Europeans, Chinese and maybe even a North Korean or two who might reside in their embassies in Western Europe.

To my pleasant surprise, my April 1978 "request for assignment" cable to Headquarters was answered within the month. I would depart Seoul in August and, after two weeks home leave, report to Langley to work in the Swiss–Austria Branch. I would study German part-time and then head to a posting in Western Europe in two years, arriving there in summer 1980. Or such was the offered plan. I accepted, sold my beatdown Datsun to a local Korean for $300 less than I paid for it five years earlier, packed up and headed home.

It had been a great five years on the Korean front, and I lasted through three chiefs of Station, three branch chiefs and three ambassadors. My current Chief was one of the directorate's Irish Mafia old-timers, and he departed Seoul the same day I did to head for a new assignment. He later would become the DO's

East Asia Division Chief, where I would find him in circumstances neither of us could have imagined in 1978. Ambassador Richard Sneider likewise departed a few days later at the end of his three-year tour. His success in managing a number of alliance issues, including our nuclear standoff, was fully recognized. He headed back to the State Department and a well-deserved promotion. For all of us, it was a good time to go.

Chapter 6

- **NOTE 1 - See page 82**

    Philip Habib, in career State Department parlance, was known as an Asian hand. After his ambassadorship in Seoul, he was appointed Assistant Secretary of State for East Asian and Pacific Affairs. Then he was promoted to Under Secretary for Political Affairs—the highest of all career positions, serving until that looming heart attack struck in 1978, forcing Phil to retire. Three years later, President Reagan summoned him back to serve in what became his best-known role, as Special Envoy to the Middle East during the turbulent 1981-1983 period. In that capacity, he received well-deserved acclaim—including the Presidential Medal of Freedom—for his handling of the Israeli–Syrian near-war over Lebanon and the related Israel–PLO war in 1981. His New York Times' obituary praised his career and noted his extensive service in Asia, including his two tours in Korea, his involvement in Vietnam and his delicate but firm handling of the political crisis engineered by Ferdinand Marcos in the Philippines.

    As mentioned, Habib was Brooklyn–Bensonhurst-born, of immigrant Lebanese Maronite Catholic parents. He served in the Army during World War II and afterward went to school under the G.I. Bill, in company with tens of thousands of fellow veterans. Numerous references to his life and 30-year Foreign Service career exist, the Wikipedia entry among them. Beyond the Korea-specific narratives otherwise cited here, two books are instructive: One Brief Miracle: The Diplomat, the Zealot and the Wild Blundering Siege by Josh Boykin, tells the tale of Habib's involvement in the Syria–Lebanon–Israel crises of the early 1980s. Capturing that moment, TIME Magazine ran a profile of Habib in its August 9, 1982, issue, titled "Habib's Grueling Shuttle" and with the description, "Reagan's peacemaker clears away some key obstacles, but each success seems to bring new frustrations."

    Another interesting profile of the man is offered in Stanley Karnow's In Our Image: America's Empire in the Philippines. This readable narrative of the U.S. relationship with the important island nation focuses on its internal political dynamic and takes the reader through the abrupt end of the Marcos dynasty. It recounts Habib's no-nonsense, no-compromise approach to dealing with Marcos when America considered forcing his ouster. Marcos had blatantly rigged the recent election there in a desperate attempt to retain power, and the country was descending into chaos.

    In mid-crisis, Secretary of State George Shultz pulled the retired Habib off a Florida golf course to dispatch him to Manila to deal with Marcos. When Defense Secretary Weinberger and others in Reagan's policy inner circle met to weigh various compromise scenarios, Habib explained that the time for compromise with Marcos had passed, injecting, "Forget reconciliation! Marcos has to go!" And go Marcos did, three days later, on February 25, 1987, when five U.S. Air Force H-3 Jolly Green Giant helicopters landed at the Presidential Palace to evacuate him and his wife Imelda, the latter minus her 3,000 pairs of shoes, to nearby Clark Air Force Base. Marcos had begun his flight to permanent exile in Hawaii.

• NOTE 2 - page 89

My experiences with the "Codels" would come back to bite me back at Headquarters soon after my return from my five-year Agency tour in Seoul. In the 1977-1978 period, Congress had been busy with its investigation of Koreagate, as it had come to be known, with the central figures being one Pak Tongsun and a number of U.S. congressmen caught up in his schemes, or accusations of same. I address this tangent in Chapter 18.

• NOTE 3 - page 92

A few days after my second surgery at the 121 Hospital in June 1974, a delegation comprising members of both baseball teams playing the day I went down hard, visited with me at my bedside. With some ceremony, and a few cold beers in hand, they presented me with a trophy. A small, bronzed baseball player with his bat cocked back for a hard swing stood atop, with the inscription "He Hung Onto The Ball" etched at the base.

Apparently when I went down, my glove closed on the ball, someone found that glove with the mitt-trapped ball nearby, and an "out" was called on the batter soon after they carted me away to the hospital and resumed the game. I have that trophy to this day, minus the batter's bat, which was snapped off somewhere between foreign assignments three and four.

Chapter 7

• NOTE 1 - page 98

The complete text of this Agency assessment, published on January 13, 2003, by the CIA FOIA organization, is lightly redacted but appears to be, in my opinion, highly biased toward Embassy reporting and comments. It makes a great deal of the student and Christian dissatisfaction with Pak and his regime, but those conclusions are far from the reality encountered on a daily basis on the streets of Seoul. Pak and his government had solid backing from his military, the business community and the populace at large, all of whom were willing to prioritize, at that point in time, stability and security over freedom of expression. The entire assessment can be found at http://www.cia.gov/library/readingroom/docs.

The degree to which the United States failed to train and equip the ROK's military forces during 1947-1950 is well-documented, in company with the abject U.S. failure to appreciate the North Korean threat. At bottom, we left the South Koreans woefully unprepared and incapable of defending themselves and their nation when the Soviets armed their North Korean ally. A number of books capture the opening days of the Korean War and the hopelessness of the South Korean response, not to mention the sad fate of the U.S. forces rushed to the peninsula from Japan in a failed attempt to mitigate the disaster unfolding there.

First and foremost, Richard K. Feuerbach's <u>This Kind of War</u> (1960) has stood the test of time and provides a classic account of the debacle. Once Soviet Premier Joseph Stalin decided to attack South Korea in the spring of 1950, the Russians managed to orchestrate a rapid buildup that U.S. intelligence—not to mention General Douglas MacArthur's Far East Command in Tokyo—either totally failed to detect or, when warned, ignored the compelling signs of a pending North Korean offensive.

A more detailed characterization of this laxity on the part of MacArthur's command in Tokyo in the months leading up to the war, from the perspective of American officers on the ground in Korea, can be found in Blaine Hardin's <u>King Of Spies: The Dark Reign of America's Spymaster in Korea</u>, published in 2017. Though the book stretches the truth quite a bit to make the protagonist, U.S. Air Force Major Donald Nichols, the epicenter of events leading up to the conflict and for years beyond, the value of the Hardin book resides in the description of the incredible denial of the obvious by the entire MacArthur team from across the Sea of Japan in Tokyo.

As the North Koreans prepared to wage all-out war, with Soviet military planners embedded in Pyongyang to manage the upcoming offensive, MacArthur's intelligence chief and confidant, General Charles Willoughby, summarily dismissed concerns. His combination of arrogance and willful ignorance represented the norm throughout the U.S. military and civilian intelligence community at the time. It became one of America's worst intelligence failures since Pearl Harbor. As a result, the North Korean preparations for the ensuing war went unremarked, and millions died as the North Korean tanks rolled south to begin a full-scale war that would last three bloody years.

Chapter 8

- ## NOTE 1 - page 105

President Pak's summer retreat near Chinhae is more of an islet than an island and is located near the larger island of Koejae (Geojedo). This isolated presidential retreat islet, Jeo Island, had been occupied by the Japanese military during that country's 35-year colonial occupation of Korea. It was reclaimed by the ROK Navy in 1954 as a military property. In 1972 it was designated a presidential retreat, informally referenced as Cheongnamdae and configured as a highly restricted area. Cheongnamdae can be translated as "Blue Ocean Structure," thereby linking its identity to the presidential residence in Seoul, Cheong Wa Dae. The latter, as a direct translation from Korean, is the "blue-tiled roof structure" and is more commonly referred to, in its better-known, English-version identity, as the Blue House.

After Pak's death, his successors continued to use Cheongnamdae as their summer retreat, until the arrival of the progressive government of President No Moon-hyun in 2013. In part, because of the venue's close association with former President Pak and his immediate military-clique successors, the progressive or leftist political class in South Korea made irregular use of this facility. In July 2019, during his visit to the retreat, the then-current ROK President Moon Jae-in declared that the island retreat would be opened to the public. On September 17th of the same year, based on local government approval, a program of twice-daily tourist visits to the island began with a daily limit of 600 visitors imposed. For many Koreans, particularly those who retain a deep respect for President Pak, this venue has become a domestic tourism attraction.

- ## NOTE 2 - page 106

The sourcing of this initial report would later cause the Agency some issues within the policy community and generate confusion about the August 1974 private discussion, in which Pak conveyed his decision to his friends. The field intelligence report contained a source byline or descriptive entry that had been in place with this particular reporting asset for some time. The descriptor did not, for reasons of source protection, convey the depth of the source's personal relationship with President Pak.

Some in the policy community, working their way backward through the analysis of the later reporting on the strategic weapons program, were inclined to focus on the original field report. From this, some elected to conclude that Pak was simply "leaking" or "planting" a story designed to secure U.S. attention, with the goal of stressing his concern over the credibility of the American commitment to South Korea. The operational reporting which had accompanied the draft field report, that is, the companion cable to Headquarters, provided context on the debriefing of the reporting agent and explained the special relationship the source enjoyed with Pak. But our analysts failed to grasp or were not privy to this important nuance. Eventually, the policy folks got it right, but the delicate problem of sourcing clandestinely acquired intelligence in enough detail while, at the same time protecting the identity of the source, remained a constant challenge.

Chapter 9

- ## NOTE 1 - page 115

President Pak's successors maintained this tried-and-true governing construct of political control and economic planning and management, to the continuing success of his national economic development program. Pak's Blue House-managed heavy hand on national planning and execution, matched by the hard work and innovation of the citizens of South Korea, created what came to be called the "Miracle on the Han (River)." Great planning and oversight at the senior levels of government, an international trade system imposed and protected by the United States, and pure hard work and ingenuity on the part of everyday Koreans would combine to elevate the ROK to the status of an OECD nation within a few years.

The same core Blue House team of Pak's immediate successor, Chun Doo-hwan, was devasted by a North Korean terrorist attack in Rangoon, Burma, in October 1983. In the course of a state visit, Chun's entire entourage was wiped out when a commando team detonated a bomb at the Martyr's Mausoleum, killing 21 officials and wounding 46.

On that day, the assassination team misjudged Chun's arrival, and he survived the attack, but South Korea was robbed of many second-generation technocrats who were only then coming into their own. Among the dead was Deputy Prime Minister Suh Soek-jun, the most senior fatality.

A good friend, Suh and his young family had often been dinner guests in our home when he was the Economic Planning Board minister a few years before. His death, and that of Chief Presidential Secretary Ham Byeong-chun and Senior Presidential Secretary for Economic Affairs Kim Jae-ik, represented yet another attempt by North Korea to destroy the leadership of South Korea and derail its economic and political development. Make no mistake, the real target of the attack was the President himself, and so the North Korean deadly provocations continued.

- ## NOTE 2 - page 117

I enjoyed an intimate relationship with the first nuclear power reactor project, the Kori 1 facility, erected at that namesake village on Korea's southeast coast. I assumed some level of involvement when I took up my position and I visited the Kori construction site several times, met with project engineers there, and worked regularly back in Seoul with the Westinghouse representatives. The latter had their hands full trying to sell additional reactors to

KEPCO while keeping the Canadians and French out of that high-stakes game.

One Kori-related highlight of my tour was to spend time with then-U.S. Export–Import Bank President Willian J. Casey, who was a one-man promoter of U.S. major project exports with a keen eye for the competition. When we discussed Kori 1 project and the pending Kori 2 loan, he expressed concern to me about the opportunities for corruption in the process of these sales and warned me that "foul and tricky individuals" had become a standard feature of such sales. While his concern was mainly directed at foreign reactor vendors, he was also focused on both the American and Korean sides of the project equation. He was wary of one Korean "fixer" and asked me to make sure that individual stayed out of the game.

I thought Casey's concern was overblown at the time, but within months I realized he was spot on with his admonition, right down to the man whom Casey sensed was out there maneuvering. In this regard, he and former Ambassador Phil Habib were of one mind, as was Habib's replacement Richard Sneider, who had arrived in the late summer of 1974. This would-be nuclear plant actor would come back to haunt us all, and when his broader scandal emerged in 1976 to U.S. Congressional attention, we would be thankful that he had been kept out of the nuclear game.

Chapter 10

• **NOTE 1 - page 129**

Mac would remain a "protected U.S. source" throughout the period of the ROK strategic weapons program, with his role revealed to his own service a year or so later, and then only to the commanding general of JUSMAG-K. The approach turned out to be well worth the effort. When the agency bestowed its own Letter of Appreciation on Mac in late 1975 in the offices of our Chief of Station, we included his commanding officer in that ceremony and asked that his service record reflect this "special service" to the U.S. Government. It is not certain that this happened, but, in any event, Mac was not motivated by recognition. He was a soldier and a patriot.

• **NOTE 2 - page 130**

In November 1977, as our nuclear issue was still playing out, I awoke one snowy morning to learn that a KEC dynamite train had exploded in the center of the town of Iri in the southwest of Korea. In an accident that was attributed to an inebriated guard who had apparently built a fire in one of the dynamite-stuffed boxcars to warm up, some 40 tons of explosives took out the center of that 100,000-plus community, leaving 59 dead, 1,300 injured, and 10,000 good citizens displaced. The town and its train station were rebuilt and renamed Iksan, but the memory endures of the Iri that had been, and that a KEC dynamite train took out the center of the city.

Chapter 11

- ## NOTE 1 - page 135

Yulgok was the pen name of a historically significant Korean scholar active at court, a nobleman who voiced strong interpretations of Korea's weakness when it was defeated by Jurchen invaders in 1582. For the purposes of President Pak and his ambitious defense capabilities buildup program, with military research and weapons development as that plan's core elements, the ancient scholar was a ready reference and rally point for all Koreans familiar with Korea's history. Among his other accomplishments, Yulgok was known to have unsuccessfully lobbied the Chosun Dynasty king and his court to reform, adopt modern ways, and expand Korea's military capability, this to better equip the "Hermit Kingdom" to resist encroachments by China and Japan. In the event, Yulgok's advice was rejected out of hand by a rival faction which then dominated at the Korean court. Soon thereafter, Korea experienced waves of invasion from Japan in the 1592-1598 period, and to Pak and his team, therein lay the message.

- ## NOTE 2 - page 139

A year or so later, after the broader strategic weapons development program was put to bed, the Nike Hercules program managed to survive, and it surfaced in the U.S.–ROK bilateral context. ADD was allowed to continue development of a de-tuned, restricted-range, conventionally armed strike missile. This evolution would produce the Nike Hercules-Korea, or "Nike Herk-K" missile, a reasonably successful activity that came to be referred to as the "NH-K project." As earlier envisioned by the ADD management, a parallel missile technology project was promoted and managed to induce a French solid-fuel rocket motor production capability. This plus other enhancements allowed the ADD and the ROK to progress a quality missile development and deployment program.

As this book was being written, the ROK ballistic missile program continued to be a contentious issue between the ROK and U.S. Governments. As mentioned above, in the aftermath of the 1976 cancellation of the ROK strategic weapons development program, the two sides negotiated a "ballistic missile guideline" agreement. The initial 1979 understanding was that the evolving NH-Korea system would be limited to a range of 180 kilometers, with a payload or warhead limit of 250 kilograms. In 2001, the two sides agreed to increase the ballistic range limit to 300 km, with the ROK side pressing for an extension to 500 km or more.

The 300 km range limit held for a decade, but in the face of sustained ROK requests to extend the range to 1,000 km, the U.S. agreed in 2012 to a new range limit of 800 km. With the advent of the progressive and more nationalistic administration of President Moon Jae—in 2018, the ROK side pushed the Trump Administration to increase both the range and payload limitations. In early 2020, the two sides reached a new compromise on both limitations, ostensibly keyed to ROK ambitions to expand their space program with the launching of larger satellites. This bilateral ballistic missile issue was in many ways a legacy of the 1974-1976 covert weapons program. An excellent summary of the ROK missile program can be found on Wikipedia at http://wikipedia.org/wiki/Hyunmoo that describes the evolution of the Nike Hercules Korea program or "Hyunmoo-1" from its operational inception in 1982 with the first test launch of that ADD-developed missile, through the Hyunmoo-4 of 2020. The latter has a claimed payload of 1,000 kilograms and a range of somewhere between 800 and 1,000 kilometers. The Wikipedia entry does not describe the NH-K-related events of 1976-1986 but does highlight the U.S. struggle to keep the ROK within the Missile Technology Control Regime. The summary does correctly note that in 2009, with the introduction of the 550-kilometer-range Hyunmoo-2B variant, the ROK managed to achieve its long-sought objective of being able to strike all of North Korea from launch sites in central South Korea. The Hyunmoo-4 was tested successfully in March 2020, launched from the ADD's Anheung test center, suggesting that this program is on schedule.

This issue of the South Korean indigenous ballistic missile program continued to encumber the U.S.–ROK political relationship into the Biden Administration. In their May 2021 meeting in Washington, it was agreed by President Biden and ROK President Moon that the United States would drop all restrictions on South Korea's development and deployment of ballistic missiles. This decision opens the path for the ROK to deploy, at its sole discretion, a retaliatory capability in the East Asia region that is not constrained by range or warhead size. Although the ostensible logic of this strategic capability is that all of North Korea will be in range of South Korean ballistic missile force, the same holds true for both China and Japan. All parties have taken note and will be watching the South Korean program with deeper interest, if not concern.

• NOTE 3 - page 139

General Kim served as the ROK's Ambassador to the United States in 1962-1963, during the period when Pak Chung-hee was successfully moving from military rule to consolidate his claim on the South Korean presidency. As mentioned, Kim would serve later as South Korea's Prime Minister under the Chun Doo-hwan government in 1988 where I would briefly renew my friendship with him when I struggled with a hostage rescue attempt. I describe the effort further in Chapter 32.

Kim Chung-yul, the former ROK Air Force four-star general, Air Force Chief of Staff, Minister of Defense, Ambassador to the United States and Prime Minister was a fascinating individual. I enjoyed the hours I spent with him immensely. The scion of a prominent Korean family, he was very much a product of Japan's colonial rule of his homeland. A graduate of Japan's Military Academy, he flew the Ki-61 "Hien" fighter of the Japanese Army Air

Force against U.S. B-24 bombers over Sumatra in 1945, and led in the creation of the embryonic Republic of Korea Air Force in 1947.

Building South Korea's air force from scratch, Kim and his ROK Air Force "first team" fought against the North Korean and Chinese armies in the Korean War in the woefully underpowered and under-armed T-6 "Texan" trainers they had been given by the U.S. and Canadian air forces. Having demonstrated their mettle in combat, Kim and his men later were allowed to adopt the P-51 Mustang and pressed the fight against the Communists through the July 1953 Armistice Agreement. He survived to an old age to laugh about it all. He passed away in 1992 at age 70. By any yardstick, he was quite a man, and I was privileged to know him as well as I did.

Chapter 12

- ## NOTE 1 - page 150
  While several declassified Seoul Embassy, State and U.S. Mission to IAEA (Vienna) cables from this 1974-1976 period are now available, Seoul 4957 of July 30, 1974, accurately captures the Embassy frustration over its attempts to persuade the ROK government to proceed with the NPT accession process. During 1974 and well into mid-1975, the ROK was essentially avoiding the issue by blaming internal bureaucratic strife and indecision at the highest levels. In so doing, the Blue House, abetted by the Ministry of Foreign Affairs (which was probably not aware of the covert program) employed its diplomatic talent to buy time. This protracted stall allowed other ROK elements to move forward quietly with the overt and covert components.

- ## NOTE 2 - page 151
  From Vienna on the IAEA side, the U.S. Mission there remained proactive throughout the showdown with the Pak government over its nuclear ambitions. Initially focused on the need to compel the ROK to accede to the NPT, IAEA Vienna 7090 cable of August 13, 1974, to Washington/State and U.S. Embassy Seoul noted the urgency of this issue, including the concurrent issues involving IAEA member safeguards with parties such as Argentina. The cable pushed for our government to make this a priority policy concern. So that the addressees did not miss its message, the cable referenced various indications that the ROK wished to acquire nuclear fuel cycle capabilities while stalling on the NPT:

    THUS, POTENTIAL FOR ACQUISITION BY KOREA OF LARGE QUANTITIES OF PLUTONIUM IS SIGNIFICANT, AND WE BELIEVE AS RESULT QUESTION OF ROK RATIFICATION OF NPT WARRANTS VERY HIGH PRIORITY ATTENTION.

  It is instructive that this same cable, acknowledging IAEA's companion mandate to advocate for broad adoption of nuclear as an energy source, noted a recent IAEA report updating a global power market survey. The IAEA study indicated it would be economical for the ROK to add increasing nuclear reactor capacity through the year 2000 and indicated the ROK could well commission increasingly larger reactors and be able to reach an installed capacity of 18,900 MW by then. In any event, the ROK did embrace nuclear power with a passion not matched in any other developing country. It managed to surpass the IAEA projection in the out years, suggesting that the IAEA planners were prescient and, in raising the alarm over the failure of the ROK to ratify the NPT, they displayed a deep appreciation of the dangers posed by the Korean nuclear fuel cycle game plan.

• NOTE 3 - page 157

As mentioned elsewhere, the various Embassy Seoul cables, State Department cables and internal State deliberation and decision documents, as well as the related cables originating from other involved embassies **(see Appendix on page 476)** all have been made available due to the excellent work done by the declassification experts at the National Security Archive Nuclear Documentation Project. The program, hosted by The George Washington University, is supported by private donations, with the NSA NDP publishing its work under the broader program of The Nuclear Vault's "Key Documents of the Nuclear Weapons Policy, 1945-1990."

Over the last few years, the NSA NDP experts have accessed a range of material on the ROK nuclear program and completed, as of early 2020, three document summaries or Electronic Briefing Books ("EBB"), collectively titled "Stopping Korea from Going Nuclear." NSA/NDP EBB Number 582 (posted on March 22, 2017), EBB Number 584 (posted on April 12, 2017) and EBB Number 668 (posted on April 1, 2018). These three NSA EBB's collectively comprise more than 75 documents, amazingly with relatively few redactions. Notably, the declassification program has acquired and collated an incredible collection of formerly classified U.S. government documents related to the ROK nuclear program referencing the 1974-1978 period. The obvious exception is that the NSA NDP has been unable to access either finished or raw Agency (field) intelligence reporting from the various resources brought to bear on these events, including the clandestine reporting originating from Seoul Station.

Credit for this splendid document accession and declassification effort, and the work product, derived goes to the NSA activity management team and the allocation of resources made by that leadership to focus on the ROK nuclear program. Full credit must be accorded to the lead researcher and writer of the three EBBs, Mr. William Burr. My personal interaction with the NSA expert team and with Mr. Burr has been rewarding and, one would hope, mutually beneficial to the overall effort to better understand this period and those events. It is here emphasized that NSA's publication of these formerly classified documents has allowed additional certainty to the narrative in this book.

Chapter 13

• **NOTE 1 - page 160**

Over the years since the first Indian nuclear test in May 1974, and with the advent of a second event involving multiple devices in May 1998, some confusion has developed over the naming assigned to the Indian nuclear tests and the test site. The initial Smiling Buddha device was detonated at the Pokhran test site in Rajasthan State and hence was dubbed "Pokhran 1" by the international community. It was detonated below ground and produced a yield later calculated in the 12 kiloton range, a bit smaller than the 20 kiloton, plutonium-based "Fat Man" device that leveled the Japanese city of Nagasaki in August 1945.

When the Indians returned to Pokhran in May 1998 with two new series of tests, they did so with devices that demonstrated their nuclear weaponeers had been busy boys over the ensuing two-plus decades. ██████ ██ in a design optimized for India's ballistic missile delivery system. Shakti-2 and Skakti-3 in same-day tests demonstrated more sophisticated design features, as did three additional blasts staged three days later, all confirming India's progress in weapons design. The NRX had given the Indian program its start, and as that program went from fusion to fusion designs and manufacturing, they did not look back. As of this writing (2023), India is judged to have no fewer ███████████████████████████████.

Back at Headquarters in 1976, in a chance discussion with one of our senior DI nuclear weapons specialists, I posed a reasonable, if delicate, question: "How was it that we (the Agency and the entire U.S. intelligence community) totally missed any anticipation of the Indian event two years before?" His response was defensive. "First of all, you collection officers in the DO failed to give us any warning or even decent intelligence before or after the fact. Second, we didn't think the Indians would do it, or could do it even if they tried. And third, they dug the damn shaft by hand, and, they may have transported the device to the shaft on a cart pulled by a water buffalo!" The above vignette provides further commentary on the U.S. intelligence community's poor ability to assess intent and capability on the part of would-be proliferators, at least as I observed firsthand during my active Agency career. With nuclear proliferators, where there is a will, there will always be a way. These lessons were hard to learn, and I found that, even after the Indian event, our nuclear analysts still focused on Soviet and Chinese nuclear designs, procedures and signatures. This attitude would only incrementally improve over the next decade or so.

More recently, this inclination endures on the part of both intelligence community and independent analysts of declining to give the nuclear proliferator devil his due for ingenuity and dedication to a goal. The systemic denial by all analysts, over a 30-year period, of North Korea's sustained progress with its nuclear weapons program, is a case in point.

• NOTE 2 - page 160

During the 1974-1975 period, I was dispatched to another East Asian location from Seoul Station for TDY discussions with my counterpart Agency officer in that Asian country. There we compared notes and operational approaches to our respective strategic weapons target organizations. This Agency officer was an accomplished case officer who would later serve in a senior position in the staff of the intelligence committees of the U.S. Congress and he would later become a U.S. congressman. Although he had a different combination of issues in this capital city, involving a more concentrated target set with higher inherent levels of security, he worked his target well. In much the same situation as I found myself, he served as a clandestine services case officer and as an officer who interacted with his local nuclear counterparts.

The tale of the two Taiwanese nuclear weapons research programs has been well told by a number of researchers, perhaps most concisely by David Albright and Corey Gay's in their article "Taiwan: Nuclear Nightmare Averted," subtitled "A nuclear-armed Taiwan facing off against a nuclear-armed China? It could have happened." This appeared in the January/February 1998 edition of The Bulletin of Atomic Scientists. A more comprehensive account can be found in the book Taiwan's Former Nuclear Weapons Program: Nuclear Weapons On-Demand by David Albright and Andrea Strickler published in 2018.

In these accounts, the authors track Taiwan's flirtation with programs to develop nuclear weapons during the 1960s, which came to naught, and detail the more determined research program that had picked up speed by the mid-1970s. By 1973, Taiwan's INER facility was operating a Canadian-supplied, 40-megawatt, thermal, natural uranium-fueled, heavy-water moderated research reactor capable of producing 10 kilograms of weapons-grade plutonium a year. The TRR was a near-identical twin to India's NRX and the very reactor for which KAERI pined. In addition, INER, located on a military research compound, had an active hot cell program capable of separating small amounts of plutonium from spent fuel and was attempting to expand into larger-scale reprocessing with the purchase of a reprocessing plant to be supplied by Saint Gobain Techniques Novelle.

By 1975, the Agency and the IC concluded that Taiwan had a full-blown covert nuclear weapons development program in the works and the U.S. stepped in to shut it all down. The IAEA began to detect and (remarkably) report safeguards "anomalies" and by 1976, pressure sufficient to block that program came into force. The hot labs cells were not expanded, the reprocessing plant did not materialize and the U.S. forced the temporary shutdown of the TRR. Modified and constrained by 1977, the Taiwan program remained harnessed until 1987 when, as the Albright/Gay article notes, "INER began building a multiple hot cell facility in violation of its commitments (to the U.S. and IAEA)." The U.S. again stepped in with a heavy hand to shut down this facility and a further tightening occurred which prevails to this day.

Not unlike the previous accounts of the covert ROK nuclear program, both the Albright/Gay and the Albright/Strickler treatments of the Taiwan experience reflect the evolution of successful U.S. efforts to shut down nascent nuclear efforts. In some cases, with advanced warning provided by quality intelligence, the U.S. Government policy initiatives were able to interdict and block potential bad actions on the part of certain third countries. Unfortunately, those accounts do not relate the successful clandestine intelligence collection efforts that allowed the U.S. to act preemptively. The Agency worked hard to penetrate the initial Taiwan program during the 1974-1976 period and managed to establish coverage of that covert effort fairly early on, though not perhaps as early in the game as was the case in the ROK.

• NOTE 3 - page 161

The two most relevant declassified cables on the subject of Canadian direct engagement with the ROK on the nuclear weapons issue, CANDU safeguards and Ottawa's growing unease with the French reprocessing plant are Embassy Seoul 4902 (CONFIDENTIAL) of July 3, 1975, titled "Canadian/ROK Talks on Nuclear Energy"; and Embassy Seoul 5016 (SECRET) of July 8, 1975, titled "ROKG/Canadian Negotiations on Nuclear Energy" respectively. Improved Canadian support for the U.S. position on nuclear cooperation with Seoul, to include Canadian encouragement of France to accept the U.S. position on improved multilateral safeguards and procedures, are evident in Embassy London cables 9224 and 9295 (both SECRET EXDIS) of June 18, 1975, that detail U.S. efforts with France and Canada to adopt a consensus approach to improve the export policies of the nuclear supplier nations.

• NOTE 4 - page 164

During the period covered by this narrative, roughly 1974-1978, and for a decade or so thereafter, some confusion existed over the designation of the component power reactors of the Korean nuclear program. The initial unit, Kori 1, and its sister Westinghouse PWR unit, Kori 2, were sometimes referenced by their owner, KEPCO, as Korean Nuclear Units 1 and 2 (KNU 1 and 2). Korean Nuclear Unit 3 was the initial Canadian CANDU PHWR located at the village of Wolsung, hence the unit designator Wolsung 1, or KNU 3. Anticipating the later build of the second CANDU unit at the Wolsung site, that reactor was allocated the KEPCO designator KNU 4. Kori units 3 and 4 (KNU 5 and 6 respectively) were Westinghouse PWRs of a larger and more advanced PWR design, while KNU 7 and 8, as similar Westinghouse PWRs, were assigned the place name designation of Yeoung–Gwang 7 and 8. French patience on the nuclear reactor front was rewarded with a KEPCO award for twin Framatome PWRs, place named Uljin 1 and 2 units, also then designated KNU 9 and 10.

In more recent years, the evolved South Korean nuclear reactor owner/operator, Korea Hydro and Nuclear Power Company (KHNP), an offshoot of KEPCO, has redesignated the various nuclear units, but in most cases, the original nomenclature remains in use. An excellent resource on all aspects of the current ROK nuclear program is provided by the World Nuclear Association in its ROK-specific country profile, most recently updated in December 2019, at http://www.world-nuclear.org/information-library/country-profiles.

Chapter 14

- **NOTE 1 - page 167**

During the four-plus decades since the forced termination of the KAERI's reprocessing program, the ROK struggled to develop technical competence indigenously, in the so-called "back-end" of the nuclear fuel cycle. The consistent ambition was to secure a capability to reprocess fuel comparable what would have been in operation by 1980 had the original fuel cycle program remained in place. The determined ROK effort paralleled a political ambition to secure U.S. and international acceptance of its ability to work, with as much freedom as possible, in those sensitive areas. The ROK's amended 1978 bilateral nuclear cooperation agreement with the United States, a modification on which we had insisted as a precondition to allow the continued flow of U.S.-origin nuclear power plant designs and the supply of U.S.-origin nuclear fuel that would sustain the operation of those reactors, placed extremely tight controls on the backside of the ROK nuclear cycle.

During the 1980s, the KAERI research program pushed the limits in the reprocessing and spent fuel handling areas and crossed the line, with safeguards transgressions that were not admitted to the IAEA until 2004. Fuel research programs in the 1990s involved discussions with various Canadian and U.S. laboratories as KAERI struggled to find a technology that would allow it an acceptable process to recover plutonium from spent fuel. These efforts were explained in the context of its determination to produce recycled fuel for its power program and parallel concerns over nuclear waste management.

These failures aside, in the 1990s KAERI turned to embrace an unproven technology known as "pyro-processing" and insisted that the U.S. allow the ROK to work with this approach experimentally on a laboratory scale.

This activity was allowed but qualified by U.S. imposed conditions, where it remains today in a peer-challenged research limbo. The current U.S.–ROK agreement, renewed in 2008, involved a high level of contentiousness over this very issue. The ROK remains a dissatisfied fuel cycle partner, quietly stewing that it continues to be treated as a second-class nuclear citizen, its impressive nuclear accomplishments notwithstanding.

A recent research paper, titled "South Korea's Nuclear Dilemmas," authored by Eunjung Lim, appears in the April 2019 edition of The Journal for Peace and Nuclear Disarmament (Volume 2 Number 1). Lim's presentation provides a comprehensive summary of the ROK nuclear fuel cycle frustrations and policy challenges since 1970. The only shortcoming in this work is a misunderstanding that the ROK's nuclear weapons development program was terminated as a consequence of the assassination of President Pak in 1979, when in fact that program was stood down by the Pak administration more than two years earlier.

This minor issue aside, the entirety of this paper brings together a host of issues and contradictions faced by the ROK with its nuclear energy programs at the present time. It places all of these developments in a historical context and in so doing, is an excellent reference document.

• NOTE 2 - page 169

The degree to which the French, by as early as 1960, were active in the proliferation of nuclear technology that enabled weapons development has only been appreciated in recent years. ███████████████████████████████████

There is a suggestion that this lapse on the part of the Agency and the U.S. intelligence community was a conscious or directed failure. The implication being that this was an instruction to ignore the obvious, directed by the highest level of U.S. executive authority, be that Presidents Kennedy, Johnson, Carter, Reagan, Bush or all of the above. As mentioned elsewhere in this book, it is also probable that the CIA's Counterintelligence czar, James Angleton, played a decisive role in protecting, if not facilitating, the ███████████████████████ program from the date of its inception. No matter, as of 2023, the full truth on this aspect ██████████████ ██ is yet to be revealed.

• NOTE 3 - page 176

BAE Director Yi became a personal friend by that summer of 1975 and talked privately about the KAERI program and U.S. concerns over the reprocessing plant and other facilities. He had previously explained to me how the Canadian NRX had been allowed to go away as a ROK concession related to the CANDU power reactor purchase, mainly as a consequence of the Indian use and abuse of this same reactor to fuel its own device. He had taken under advisement my point that the U.S. and the ROK were facing a near-term showdown over the fuel cycle issue and that, sooner or later, the reprocessing plant would have to go.

This said, I failed to detect any knowledge on his part of the parallel the ADD weapons development effort. He was a nuclear scientist and was motivated by the acquisition of the technology and value it could bring to the ROK's civil nuclear ambitions. This drove home our conclusions that knowledge of the overall program combining overt nuclear fuel activity and covert design work was highly compartmented at the Pak and Blue House level, within the ADD, and possibly known only to a very select group of officials at MOST.

- **NOTE 4 - page 177**

  The reporting cable describing this Ingersoll/Habib–Hahm meeting, STATE 240692 SECRET/EXDIS of October 9, 1975, is worth a careful read in that it presents a comprehensive summary of the evolved U.S. position on the reprocessing plant, to include the technical and policy arguments deployed by the U.S. side. It also relates the revised and expanded ROK arguments, as presented by Ambassador Hahm, in defense of the plant, placing that facility in the ROK's regional and historical context, with an emphasis on the Japan nuclear issue and the ROK's keen sense of competition with that nation.

- **NOTE 5 - page 178**

  The reference State assessment and decision document, some 34 pages of background, policy options, and assessments by various State entities, reflects the growing frustration of its drafters. State leadership was incredulous in the face of the ROK's determination to continue with this project, even as the U.S. Government continued to lay out the threat posed by the project to the overall bilateral relationship. The document assesses that the October 23rd formal ROK response had the direct involvement of President Pak, and with such, implies that Pak is personally committed to see this facility and the capability it would provide to ROK in place and operating.

  On the Embassy end, one watched the Washington policymakers deliberate and twist themselves into layered compromises and options, trying to find a solution that would resonate with the ROK leadership. To me and others familiar with the ROK personality, and knowing Pak's temperament, there was a simple reality that there was no space for compromise—the plant was either killed or remained, and in the latter case, the U.S. had to be prepared to take actions that would severely damage the alliance.

  Of note, contained in this range-of-options composition is one that demonstrates the lengths to which some U.S. policymakers were willing to compromise to find a solution, including Option 2A. This proposed to "Approach President Pak to seek a two- or three-year moratorium on the construction of the plant, indicating to the ROKG that we understand ROK interest in eventual pursuit of a nuclear weapons option." The pros and cons associated with this were nearly as bizarre as the stated option itself, but at least it would have had the value of confirming to Pak that we knew what he really wanted.

  When we read the advocacy for this option in Seoul, we nearly fell off the chair. And when we got to the line, "Ambassador Sneider would at least implicitly acknowledge that such a moratorium would not foreclose a nuclear weapons option in the future," some of the cognizant Embassy staff, as expected, did collapse in disbelief.

  Another interesting aspect of this option assessment document is the focus on the French, the growing U.S. frustrations in gaining their cooperation, and U.S. concerns over French willingness to play all parties off against one another. This concern included recently detected French moves to advance the sale of their power reactors to the ROK in the same period that we were all attempting to resolve the reprocessing plant issue. In any event, this paper, closing out the lack of U.S. progress in finding a policy solution at year-end 1975, some eighteen months after we had first detected the ROK decision to embark on a weapons development program, is an instructive read.

• NOTE 6 - page 184

The January 26, 1976, Canadian–ROK agreement on the provision of the initial CANDU reactor, defining as it did the entire Canadian–ROK nuclear relationship going forward, contained the following language:

THE CANADIAN CABINET DECIDED ON 22 JANUARY 1976 THAT THE CANADIAN SECRETARY OF STATE FOR EXTERNAL AFFAIRS SHOULD AUTHORIZE SIGNATURE OF BILATERAL NUCLEAR COOPERATION AGREEMENT WITH THE REPUBLIC OF KOREA BEFORE JANUARY 26, PROVIDED THAT THE GOVERNMENT OF THE REPUBLIC OF KOREA CONCURS WITH THE GOVERNMENT OF CANADA STATING PUBLICALLY THAT IT HAS THE ASSURANCE OF THE GOVERNMENT OF THE REPUBLIC OF KOREA THAT 1) IT IS NOT PURSUING ACQUISITION OF THE REPROCESSING FACILITY AND 2) THE PROJECTED REPROCESSING PLANT HAS BEEN SHELVED INDEFINITELY, WHICH IS UNDERSTOOD TO MEAN FOR A LENGTHY PERIOD OF TIME, AT LEAST UNTIL AFTER THE REPUBLIC OF KOREA'S NEGOTIATIONS WITH THE UNITED STATES ON FUTURE NUCLEAR COOPERATION ARE RESOLVED.

That statement, plus a companion statement that the Canadian government shared with its parliament, did not demand immediate ROK cancellation of the reprocessing facility contract, but it went a long way. It was clear that, beyond the U.S. cancellation demand referencing the bilateral security relationship, the U.S. position on Kori 2 EXIM Bank financing and the involvement of the U.S. Congress, the Canadian position on the initial CANDU reactor, both the safeguards provisions and the threat to defer the entire project, had come together to force the issue. The fact that France was complicit in the understanding, and that there was a consensus among the three nations most involved in South Korea's nuclear energy, had finally resonated and was forcing Pak to deal with it as an up-or-down decision.

Neither the Station nor the Embassy, as the nuclear cooperation dialog with the ROK progressed in the early months of 1976, assumed the ROK had foregone reprocessing. In July, the U.S. was contacted by the French Government with information on a probable South Korean attempt to covertly procure select critical equipment for a reprocessing facility. An approach had been made to French companies by a Taiwanese middleman and the equipment sought was consistent with that involved in the now-canceled SGN plant in the ROK. The French considered this a serious approach, to the degree that they had denied the French firm an application to develop the contract. Within the Station, beyond being able to confirm that this was not a KAERI initiative, we were unable to determine if our prime suspect in this initiative—namely, the ADD—had taken it upon itself or some third party, sensing an opening and eager to earn a commission, had appointed itself to secure the facility.

Interestingly, the French had been able to confirm that the Taiwan firm had also approached a French fuel fabrication firm (CIRCA) to discuss the purchase of a fabrication plant that could produce CANDU fuel bundles, for which the government preemptively denied a license. Other approaches by the middleman had been made to the Belgian firm Eurochemique and to German firms for the purchase of sensitive nuclear fuel technology, all ostensibly for installation in the ROK. In Seoul, the U.S. Embassy did not discount the validity of this French information and welcomed the fact that the French were willing to share this with the U.S., albeit only after sharing the details with their Canadian colleagues.

Within the Station, we did not determine with any certainty whether this "Taiwan middleman" approach to the Europeans was an authorized initiative from the ROK side, but we did confirm that no such equipment arrived in South Korea. With knowledge of what was then taking place in Taiwan at this time and the nuclear ambitions stirring there, it was my opinion that the Taiwanese middleman could well have been working to deliver this equipment to INER in Taipei for the use of that program. Recall that Taiwan's INER then possessed the TRR, an NRX-class heavy water research reactor and that INER had been itself shopping for a reprocessing plant. Citing the ROK as the ostensible destination of the sale could well have been a too-clever-by-half ruse on the part of the Taiwanese businessman.

The Embassy cable reporting this development, PARIS 20831 (SECRET/ STADIS) is worthwhile, if only to appreciate that this report encouraged the Seoul Station nuclear team, fixated as it was then on the ADD and the Blue House, to double down on its coverage of KAERI and MOST.

Chapter 15

• [NO NOTES]

Chapter 16

- **NOTE 1 - page 192**

  The 20-page document, classified Secret, was declassified in October 2005. As is the case with most CIA/NFAC products of this generation, its key judgments are supported by a comprehensive assessment of all the related factors, including in this case an overview of the terminated covert strategic weapons program. As such, this analysis provides a useful narrative that describes the factors judged to have motivated the decision to pursue the program, the miscalculations of the main actors and an assessment as to where that defunct effort had arrived as of June 1978. In examining the events of 1974-1976 in retrospect, with a quantity of information at hand that postdates the events, the authors crafted an accurate picture for use by the policymakers who commissioned the study.

- **NOTE 2 - page 197**

  The Don Oberdorfer book, originally published in 1997 and revised and updated in 2001, provides an excellent, often firsthand account, written as an "and I was there" narrative of the post-liberation history of the entire peninsula. He does mention the ROK nuclear weapons program of 1974-1976 and gets much of the story right, to the degree that he was able to assemble a retrospective account based on interviews with several of the main Korean players. His ability to address and explain the ROK–U.S. military and national security dynamic is solid. As such, the book is a must-read primer for any U.S. military or national security official seeking to understand how our current military and national security relationship evolved over a 70-year period.

- **NOTE 3 - page 198**

  The testimony of Phil Habib and General George Brown took place in Seoul on June 10, 1977, and was intended, we firmly believed, to shake all parties to the realization that Carter's determination to withdraw U.S. conventional forces would have serious second and third-order consequences.

- **NOTE 4 - page 199**

  Among the articles and commentary that inform the retelling of the events of the Carter initiative and the summer of 1977 are the following:

  (a)

  (b)

  (c)

  (d)

(e) ██

██
██
██
██
██
██

• NOTE 5 - page 199

██
██
██
██
██
██
██
███████████████████████

The Koreans were able to confirm their judgment of Carter's *naïveté* in future years when he discovered the charms and an opportunity for peace-making with North Korean dictator Kim Il-sung. In those heady weeks, Carter journeyed to Pyongyang to meet with the Great Leader to negotiate his own peace-in-our-time deal for the Korean Peninsula. In this adventure, he brought his Atlanta hometown-based CNN along for the ride to provide exclusive coverage of Carter's bonding experience with the North Korean leader.

Back in Seoul, our folks were able to track those events, including a mishap on the river cruise that saw Kim tossed from his chair to tumble to the deck. The boat driver who had gunned his engine to pick up some speed was, we were told and certainly believed, promptly shot for his malfeasance. A few months later, Kim died in his sleep and was mourned by millions of his loyal followers. At the working level, we thought it might be useful if we could dispatch Carter to a few other dictatorships where leadership removal was, or should be, under active consideration. I don't think this suggestion, as compelling as it was then, made it to the senior policy level.

Chapter 17

- ## NOTE 1 - page 203

The August 15, 1976, attack on President Pak, and the death of the First Lady Yuk, reinforced concern by Pak and his inner circle at the Blue House as to the loyalty, if not the competence, of the personal security team and the composition of his key advisors. The Chief Bodyguard, retired General Pak Jong-kyu, his reputation as a hard-ass defender of the President reinforced by his nickname "Pistol Pak," responded with courage. As the would-be assassin fired at the stage, Pak advanced across the stage, shielding President Pak to confront the shooter, firing as he advanced. Others seated on the National Theater dais, on chairs which flanked the First Lady, dove for cover, and she was left seated alone, if only for a few moments. In that brief period, she was mortally wounded. There was no way to avoid the impression that she had been left alone to die, Pistol Pak being the only one attempting to shield her. This scene was captured by many media cameras and versions soon found their way to the international press.

Although the Pak team sought to censure these depictions—Blue House embarrassment was palpable—public criticism of the actions of those on the stage grew. We at the Station watched the replay that same day with a feeling of dread. We were actually concerned that an enraged President Pak, witnessing the scramble on stage and the replay of the mortal wounding of his wife, would imprison or do worse to the scramblers. Cooler heads prevailed, several were ostracized by Pak, and the President drew the reasonable conclusion that only one man that day stood the true test of total loyalty: Pistol Pak. Pak would soon resign from his position, but continue to serve his nation in various roles, including the Chairmanship of the Korean Olympic Committee.

Pak's replacement as the Presidential Chief Bodyguard, Cha Ji-chul, would meet a violent end three years later when KCIA Chief Kim executed him alongside President Pak when Cha and Kim argued over dinner. Cha was a hardliner, opposed making any concessions to demonstrators or the opposition political party, and criticized Kim and his management of the political environment that obtained in Seoul. Kim and his KCIA team resolved the dispute by shooting President Pak, Cha and other Pak bodyguards present, not even sparing Pak's chauffeur.

- ## NOTE 2 - page 204

To many of us who lived through the death throes of the Republic of Vietnam, the sham of the Paris Peace Accords, and the North Vietnamese tank-led conventional invasion that finished that war in 1975, these memories are vivid. But there is one often-ignored aspect of the U.S. abandonment of Vietnam that ROK leadership watched with deep concern. That was the proactive move by the U.S. Congress to tie the hands of the Nixon Administration by imposing legislation that blocked any U.S. assistance to Vietnam in its hour of greatest need. In 1973, the U.S. Congress handcuffed the Executive Branch with Section 307 of Public Law 93-50, ostensibly as part of the rush to "end the war in Vietnam." A more honest interpretation of this act was that the denial of any U.S. support to our beleaguered former ally and dependent was a calculated green light to the North Vietnamese to invade and conquer.

The law set a deadline of August 15, 1973 (coincidentally the same date that Korea celebrated its independence), after which "None of the funds herein appropriated under this act may be expended to support directly or indirectly combat activities in or over Cambodia, Laos, North Vietnam and South Vietnam by United States forces…no other funds heretofore appropriated under any other act may be expended for such purpose." From the date of this funding cutoff, the Republic of Vietnam, by U.S. Congressional mandate, was cut loose and essentially told to fend for itself.

In Seoul, in formal or informal contacts with my Korean counterparts, and in meetings with our clandestine sources, most of whom were motivated to work with us based on their commitment to sustain the alliance, referenced this law. They asked, often in disbelief, if it was really the case that U.S. Congress could compel the abandonment of an ally. My answer was unequivocal: this was indeed the case and with Vietnam, this is what had happened. For this very reason, we all had to work hard to make sure neither our Executive Branch nor our Legislative Branch lost confidence in the U.S.–ROK alliance.

• NOTE 3 - page 205

Although much has been written about the Ax Murder incident, a good summary can be found in Dangerous Games: Faces, Incidents and Casualties of the Cold War by James Wise and Scott Baron. Chapter Seventeen, "The Panmunjom Ax Murders and Operation Paul Bunyan," provides a brief and factual account of the events over the one-week period in the summer of 1976. No judgments on the quality of the U.S. response are present in this recounting but the frustration of the U.S. military on the ground is clear.

Interestingly, this book also relates a lesser-known incident that occurred eight years later at this same DMZ Joint Security Area location, again involving a North Korean provocation. In Chapter Eighteen, "The Firefight at Panmunjom 1984—Captain Bert Mizusawa," we see the North Koreans at their standard worst. This incident was triggered by the defection of a young Soviet diplomatic trainee assigned to the Soviet Embassy in Pyongyang. In the act of defecting by bolting away from his colleagues to seek asylum in the United States by entering the United Nations side of the JSA, the American military presence there found itself under attack by North Korean soldiers attempting to stop or at least kill the defector.

The firefight within the JSA saw the North Koreans enter the UN zone and for nearly one hour, exchange small-arms fire with U.S. forces. The latter, in the form of a Quick Reaction Force stationed nearby to respond to this very type of incident, was led by the Joint Security Force commander, Captain Bert

Mizusawa. There were causalities on both sides and, on this occasion, the North Koreans got the short end of the stick. The story of this incident is told well by Wise and Baron and the book is worth a good read.

Then-Captain Mizusawa would go forward from Korea to experience a great career, would achieve the rank of Brigadier General in 2006, and retire soon thereafter. In July 2000, some sixteen years after what later became known as the "Soviet Defector Incident at Panmunjom," Mizusawa would be awarded the Silver Star for his actions that day, in the good company of three of his fellow infantrymen who fought that firefight with him.

Of note, immediately after the incident, probably because the North Korean guards posted in the JSA had failed to prevent the escape to freedom of the Russian defector, two senior officers were summarily executed by their fellow North Koreans. One of those executed appears to have been the notoriously vicious Captain Chul "Bulldog" Pak, the man who had led the ax murder attack eight years before. If so, in addition to the rescue of the young Russian, the pushback delivered by the U.S. fireteam managed to inflict a measure of revenge on the North Koreans for the deaths of Captain Arthur Bonifas and Lieutenant Mark Barrett.

An interesting antidote to this incident was that when the young Russian was debriefed, his explanation was that, among his motivations to flee to the United States was the fact that he had been treated horribly by his North Korean hosts in Pyongyang. In an "I just could not take it anymore" outburst, he explained that he was spat upon, cursed at and broadly disrespected on in the streets in that fine capital city. When the debriefers suggested that perhaps the North Korean citizens mistook him for an American, he rejected this and noted that they had routinely yelled the time-tested Korean expletive *Russ isekiya*; basically, "Russian sonofabitch," although that translation fails to convey the inherent vibrancy of the curse.

PART THREE

Headquarters and Western Europe

(1978-1982)

The Swiss–Austria Branch

Reporting for duty at Langley that late summer of 1978 delivered a real transition in many ways. I really had not served in a dedicated country desk or branch assignment before my departure for Seoul four years earlier. Back in 1974, I served only three months in the Directorate of Operation's Japan-Korea Branch and two months elsewhere, all part-time and focused on processing for the field station assignment. My four-month career trainee tenure on the East Asia Division's Indonesia Branch really did not qualify, so returning to Headquarters to ride a country desk—in this case the Swiss–Austria Branch—in the big building was a new experience. I never signed for and "owned," as an operations desk officer, files or records related to a specific covert project or an individual agent, nor had I been responsible for the Langley end of the Station-to-Headquarters exchanges that represented operational communications with a field station or base.

In Langley, I was now "at the flagpole," a location often deprecated by operations officers in the field. For the first time, I would be at the sending end I had seen generate many of the ill-informed "guidance" messages or far-removed decisions that typically harassed or complicated the progress of our operations in the Seoul Station. Nothing good seemed to emanate from Langley, and that was where I found myself sitting. I promised myself I would be responsive and light-handed in any exchanges with the stations and bases for which my branch was responsible.

The general attitude in the field, even when station officers knew differently, was Headquarters desks and branch officers kept bankers' hours and too often were stay-at-home careerists who avoided field assignments for a variety of reasons, some self-serving and some unavoidable. True, no officer in the DO could expect a promotion if he or she actively avoided an overseas assignment. But the fact was many of the people occupying desk positions willingly accepted the consequences of that situation. Indeed, many Headquarters officers excelled at their positions. They were dedicated men and women who often represented the critical institutional knowledge necessary for a given station or project to function.

A second set of desk and branch officers were career losers, often individuals simply not cut out for fieldwork. Many were would-be field operatives routinely refused assignment to a given station by chiefs who knew them or had read their personnel files. Therein lay a critical vulnerability for the Agency, writ large and involving the DO in particular, a vulnerability that would exact pain all too often over the next 30 years. The problem was most of the low-performing career types had nowhere to go, either inside Headquarters or outside, with the result that they often drifted in the hallways of the building, reposed non-performing in their cubicles, or burdened the desks to which they were assigned.

The situation existed because the Directorate was institutionally inclined to avoid discharging any officer. In part, it occurred because the mid-levels assigned to Headquarters in desk- or branch-management positions were in place for two years or less and were reluctant to initiate terminations. Complementing this was the fact that the DO wished to avoid admitting it had accepted certain individuals into its ranks, and it was continuing to retain those who had proved unwilling or unable to perform to the Directorate's demanding standards. The core concern among leadership was that a discharged employee probably would leave disgruntled, creating a potential security risk once he or she was outside the control of the Agency's security apparatus.

I discovered in the Swiss–Austria Branch, as the incoming Swiss desk chief and the deputy branch chief, that we had on staff a collection of both types of semi-permanent players. It took me about two weeks to figure out which officer occupied which category. In our branch, as with others throughout the Directorate, there also was a dearth of experienced field officers who might be returning to Headquarters from completed tours in Western Europe. The bottom line was we had a few solid career players in the branch who were first-rate, legitimate professionals who knew the agent files, knew the cases and who acknowledged what they did not know or could not appreciate from their flagpole vantage points. At the opposite end of the performance spectrum, the deadwood identified themselves with their attitudes. We marginalized them, assigning them to lesser tasks or farming them out to various self-improvement courses. On the Austria Desk within the branch, I was extremely fortunate to have one individual as my main resource, someone ever enthusiastic and possessed with incredible institutional knowledge. I endeavored to see him promoted, both to make up for lost career advancement and properly recognize his value to the Agency and the Europe Division.

The routine activity in the branch allowed me to learn a lot just by studying the exchanges of operational cables, reviewing the intelligence-reporting cables (which were few and far between, to my surprise) and delving into the individual project and agent files. I also found it interesting to participate in the Headquarters decision-making process. For example, I watched the senior management of the European Division fine-tune the priorities of its various stations and evaluate their progress, including assessments of the individual chiefs. On the personnel side, I participated in the day-to-day monitoring of assignments of individual officers slated for overseas deployment. There, the goal was to match each outbound officer to the slot a given station was considering for that individual and make sure the nominated officer spent time in the branch reviewing case files.

One institutional development that struck me was the degree to which, in the wake of the Senate hearings chaired by Frank Church, Democrat of Idaho, almost every operational initiative or change in direction now had to run the gauntlet of Directorate and Agency lawyers. It became a challenge for me and for others who had not been present at Headquarters when that particular evolution occurred. As one old hand observed to me, the ops managers used to dial up the DO's legal team only after an operation got into trouble, "dropping the proverbial dime" to extract us from the situation we had managed to get ourselves into. The new normal first required us to run anything dramatic by the inhouse lawyers, seeking their permission, resulting in an almost mother-may-we approval to mount an activity.

This "go see the lawyers first to get their 'chop' on the operation" attitude had taken root, at least as I saw it, mostly as an ass-covering exercise. It was welcomed by the permanent-party Headquarters managers, who often were more concerned about career advancement than getting the job done. The now-standing requirement to consult with and secure approval from the legal team created an intimidating effect throughout the Directorate and discouraged the risk-taking that had been a core component of operational success. As I would discover in future years, beginning with my upcoming assignment, the legal overlay even to routine decision-making carried into the field stations. The inevitable result was, too often, station leadership opted to veto or curtail operational initiatives that previously were commonsense decisions to "go for it," particularly if the risk/reward calculation looked reasonable.

Beyond those general impressions, three encounters during my first year back in Langley stood out for me, each providing its own message or lesson. They included my participation in the Agency's Mid-Career Course, an MCC-related disconcerting encounter with then-Director (Admiral, retired) Stansfield Turner and a resurfacing of a couple of distressing legacy issues from my time in Seoul.

A Mid-Career Course Diversion

Regarding the MCC, my selection at the time as a DO participant came as a pleasant surprise, mainly because I did not really consider myself, at age 32, to be in my mid-career. I had completed only one field tour, and I had not sought entry into that coveted two-month experience. The MCC was viewed, at least by the DO types, as a unique opportunity for a select few to mix with fast-track, mid-career officers from the other directorates. Those types included analysts from the Directorate of Intelligence, the technical specialists from the Directorate of Science and Technology and officers from a variety of disciplines in the Directorate of Administration, including the Office of Security.

The MCC was held three or four times a year and typically involved about 25 officers, of whom the DO normally sent five or six. It happened that in this running of the MCC, I was the youngest attendant by several years. As a result, I felt a bit intimidated when I realized most of my classmates were more experienced and often far more articulate.

The MCC was a once-in-a-career chance for all participants to be exposed to briefings and discussions with Agency senior management and to meet outside presenters from other U.S. government intelligence organizations, including the National Security Agency and the FBI. A good deal of our course time was spent offsite, and our day course allowed discussions among ourselves that carried into the evening hours, typically around the bar at the secure facility. During the daylight program, each participant was required to make a presentation on his or her respective experiences, and all were encouraged to be prescriptively critical—that is, feel free to criticize any aspect of Agency activity or policy. We also were instructed that when we did so, any discussion of a shortcoming had to offer a balanced narrative that included an honest assessment of what had gone right and what had gone wrong—and why.

Exposure to Project Azorian

One of my Office of Security coursemates had been assigned to the recently terminated Project Azorian, the Agency's star-crossed, six-year, covert effort to raise a Soviet missile submarine, the *K-129*, from the depths of the Pacific Ocean. The missile boat had suffered an engineering failure in March 1968 near Hawaii. It had burned out internally and then fallen to its imploding death to rest on the seabed 16,000 feet below the surface. The *K-129* took with it a crew of 91, along with three nuclear-tipped missiles, a handful of nuclear-armed torpedoes and its top-secret communications and command-link systems. To the Soviets, the ship simply had disappeared in mid-patrol. Their navy, unable to reconstruct events and without a clue about what had transpired, nor any idea where their submarine had sunk, suspected foul play by the United States. The possibility that the *K-129* had collided with an American nuclear attack submarine, a casualty of the high-risk undersea game of cat-and-mouse both sides played at that stage of the Cold War, was never far from their minds and concerns.

By 1972, the Soviets had given up their own hunt, but we assumed they suspected we knew what happened, and they were watching for any signs we might attempt to exploit the wreck. Although we did not know what had happened to the missile boat, our Navy did discover where the vessel reposed. Based on that knowledge, and believing the remains of the *K-129* presented a valuable intelligence-collection target, the Agency conceived an elaborate covert program to exploit the lost submarine. Project Azorian, developed and executed by the Agency and blessed at the highest levels of the U.S. government, was crafted to retrieve the vessel from great depths, ideally without the Soviets knowing about the operation. A massive ship was constructed, the Hughes *Glomar Explorer*, ostensibly to hunt for and mine rare metals, called manganese nodules, from the ocean floor. The ship came complete with a "moon pool" to house the recovered Soviet craft.

The potential intelligence value in securing and analyzing the nuclear components in the flooded vessel, not to mention the cryptographic systems, was deemed more than worth the cost and risk of the covert operation. In the end, our people pinpointed the vessel's location, and partially raised the smashed submarine. But the hull broke apart as *Explorer's* giant claws attempted to raise it to the surface, and the recovery ship returned to port to offload the portions it did capture. The *Glomar Explorer* was provisioning for a return attempt when the entire enterprise was aborted. That occurred when the project was compromised by a disloyal and opportunistic U.S. media, namely, a deadly combination of the Los Angeles Times, the New York Times and syndicated columnist Jack Anderson. With the project's purpose exposed and its cover story stripped away, the project was terminated short of its goal. In the ensuing years, the Agency maintained a tight grip on all aspects of the project and did not release any information until 2010. Even then, the Agency managed to redact a full third of the contents of the report's unclassified version.

Sharing his experiences with us in 1980, one of my MCC classmates avoided most of the specifics of the operation but did relate a good deal about the security cloaking the program involved. Of the most interest was the incredible level of planning and execution, including the multi-layered cover story that successfully shielded the project from the Soviets and the public—at least, until the destructive media leaks of February 1975. Needless to say, I was impressed by the Agency's ability to conceptualize, plan, build, deploy and operate the recovery ship in the middle of the Pacific Ocean free of any Soviet knowledge. **[NOTE 1]**

As one might imagine, the MCC was a special opportunity for our non-DO classmates. For most of those professionals, it was a first-and-only chance to socialize in a classified environment and exchange experiences with clandestine-service officers back from overseas tours. My colleagues were a mixed lot. A couple hailed from Africa Division, one was from Latin America Division and another was from the Office of Technical Services. A grizzled Soviet—Eastern Europe Division veteran who dreamed of recruiting Soviets completed our component.

I was the only East Asia Division officer in the mix, and EA consequently was underrepresented from the standpoint of experiences to share and tall tales to tell. My presentations necessarily focused on Korea, nuclear proliferation and such. The class as a whole bonded well, and by its end we gained a much better appreciation of the challenges faced by each of our sister directorates. It was an experience that would stand me in good stead in two future field assignments and in the final run at Headquarters that would cap my Agency career.

Exploding Autos—The Good Admiral Turner's Tantrum

For our final evening, the course organizers had promised that a senior Agency official would join us after dinner and deliver an off-the-record, stand-up talk. They also enjoined us to engage him in a lively discussion. The guest speaker arrived at our remote facility an hour or so late, identity still not revealed. Unfortunately, the bar had been open since after dinner, and libations had been flowing for some time, to the extent that several of the class members were a bit lit up and more than ready for the promised "open discussion."

We did know the gentleman being sent to us was one of Director Stansfield Turner's hand-picked and newly installed-from-the-outside senior managers. Turner had been parachuting those types into the Agency to enforce his "improved discipline" program directed at the career employees with mixed success. Turner was not well-liked and had made known his disdain for many of the established ways of Langley. He had singled out the Directorate of Operations for special attention and discipline. His decision to dispatch a "survey team" led by a retired U.S. Navy captain to interrogate officers and wives at several field stations, in a transparent effort to unearth and chronicle negative information, was well-known and highly resented. On that particular evening, the Director's nominated speaker, identity finally disclosed with a cursory introduction, wasted no time in conveying Turner's attitude and approach to the unwashed MCC officers assembled before him.

The Turner nominee made a rambling presentation, in which he managed to denigrate the professionalism and performance of several elements of the Agency. He then proceeded to explain how he and other Turner transplants were planning to put things right, along the lines of "changes are coming." Some of his comments demonstrated how he had no idea what he was talking about, particularly on the Operations side. He then invited an exchange, and as the dialog progressed the situation deteriorated.

When one of the course members explained that neither the speaker nor Admiral Turner seemed to appreciate the *esprit de corps* that existed within the Agency, our guest shot back with great indignation. "So, you people think you have conviction? Well, let me tell you, I just came from a 'real service.' Those people have far greater dedication than you people have ever demonstrated!"

A long silence followed. One DI officer asked quietly, "And sir, exactly what 'service' would that be?" The reply came with a snap of arrogance "Why, the Internal Revenue Service, of course." Guffaws of laughter rocked the room, along with a few not-so-*sotto-voce* mumblings along the lines of, "are you shitting me?" Turner's senior manager grabbed his coat and stormed out the door, launching himself into the misting rain and chilly night.

The next day, our course completed, we were all back at Headquarters. I was at my desk in the Swiss–Austria Branch, catching up on events in Geneva and Vienna and reinserting myself into the Europe Division staff workflow. My secretary approached me cautiously. "Richard, it's *the* Deputy Director of Operations on the phone. He says he wants you in his office in five minutes."

It seemed a bit odd, but I considered John McMahon a true leader and friend. We had not had much contact in the past, but on the few occasions when I was privileged to interact with him, he had been open, positive, supportive and, above all, knowledgeable. I knew he had played a leading role in the OXCART project, intended to supersede the U-2 spy plane program, and most DO officers considered him to be one of us. As I hustled down the hall, I did not connect his summons with the event of the night before.

John had two other Operations officers seated in front of his desk, both fellow Mid-Career Course members and career DO. The center chair was reserved for me. McMahon clearly was pained. "So, exactly what did you say or do to your guest speaker last night?" I explained, with support from my colleagues, that the fellow had been an absolute ass and that, while most had tried to respect him up to a point, his comment on the IRS had blown up the evening. Shaking his head, McMahon asked what had happened after our guest left the building. I explained that we had no idea, he left abruptly, slammed the door behind him, and no one there gave a damn where he had gone. I added that some of our classmates suggested where he might want to go.

John was angry, but not necessarily with us. "Well, we have a problem. Seems our boy drove away, and he claims that his car 'sort of exploded' 20 miles down the road, in the middle of nowhere, out in the cornfields or whatever. He was stranded, wandered through some fields, and ended up banging on the door of a farmhouse at two in the morning. He was probably lucky he didn't get shot. Security went out and retrieved him. He was waiting for Turner this morning and claims you all insulted him. He actually thinks someone sabotaged his car, and he blames you—the Operations types—for everything."

We explained to the Deputy Director how that was a wild assertion, that no one gave a damn about him or his car. McMahon shook his head and countered, "Our problem is Director Turner bought into all of this. It reinforced all his negative assumptions. He just ordered an 'attitudinal survey' of the DO—actually two surveys—to be contracted to some outside management consultants. Now we have to figure out how to do that, get these people some security clearances and all that stuff. Dammit, why did you have to do this?"

He knew we had nothing to do with any exploding car. Still, we apologized and left his office. As we departed, he cautioned, "And you all know that the Director always has the MCC members into a debriefing session for a so-called 'frank discussion' of the course. That will happen within the next two weeks." In the hall outside his office, we three paused briefly, collectively shrugged our shoulders and wandered off to our respective branches and duties. I don't recall if someone said, "Who gives a shit?" but it certainly was on our minds. We were concerned that John McMahon now had yet another stone in his Turner rucksack to carry.

A couple of weeks later, a selected group from our MCC filed into Turner's conference room and took our seats. The class monitors had met with us beforehand and coached us to attempt to script our comments, their goal being to make sure we did not rile the Director. There were moments of tension, but the dialog with Turner was mostly one-way, with him lecturing to us and explaining his reorganization concepts, laced with grumblings about the Directorate and other such challenges. At meeting's end, he asked if any of us had final comments or observations on the course. I waited until a couple of my colleagues delivered their softballs to him and said, politely, "Sir, I sit on the DO's Austria–Swiss branch, and that morning I told my staff I was coming to this meeting with you today. I asked them if they had any comments to pass along to you."

Turner eyed me with mild disdain and asked me to continue. "Well, recently you invited Jack Anderson to speak to the Agency employees in our auditorium, and he did, emphasizing the right, in a democracy such as ours, for a journalist to publish classified or sensitive information." I explained that I had not attended the presentation, but several of my staff had. In his presentation, Anderson directly solicited those in the audience to present him with any and all sensitive material and went so far as to provide his contact information. I went on to say that, unfortunately, the solicitation coincided with increased concerns among many foreigners who have collaborated with us. Several of those intelligence assets were concerned that, in sharing sensitive information with their Agency contacts, they were placing themselves at risk in working with an organization they increasingly perceived was unwilling or unable to protect its sources. The Anderson presentation at the Agency reinforced such an impression within Headquarters, correct or not.

Unmentioned, but running through my mind, was the reality that, in the Swiss–Austria Branch, we had many collaborators among the national and regional security forces who shared a great deal of information with us. They did so because they thought the information was critical to protect their own countries as well as ours. Also, it was difficult to ignore the fact that Anderson was reasonably considered by many at all levels in the Agency, including me, to be a traitor to our nation of the first order. Some four years before, in March 1975, Anderson had brushed aside pleading requests from then-CIA Director William Colby. He parted ranks with other journalists who agreed to "keep the secret" and broke the Project Azorian story. In detailed radio broadcasts, he self-righteously reported his version of the episode, including the fact that the CIA had requested him to maintain his silence in the interests of national security. **[NOTE 2]**

The good Admiral did not like the comment at all. He did not have a response, and we really did not expect one. Our out-brief monitors squirmed in their seats, some smalltalk ensued and then, to everyone's relief, it was over. As we stood to leave, Turner, relaxing in his signature maroon cardigan, remained seated. He appeared to be entirely satisfied with himself. We had just confirmed to him his presumption that the DO was arrogant and out of control; at least, out of his control. But this was the man who had ordered the "attitudinal survey" of the Directorate of Operations, so it really did not matter. We excused ourselves and returned to our respective burrows.

A few weeks later, I had a coincidental hallway encounter with DDO McMahon, who stopped me with an outstretched arm. "Regarding that MCC outbrief session with the Director, thanks a million. Our attitude surveys continue. The DO is still in his crosshairs. I think I'll send them your way for a nice interview. Or maybe not." He smiled a wry smile, signaling, "It's Turner, it's life, and what can we do about it?" **[NOTE 3]**

Back in the branch, I told the staff about the exchange with McMahon, my comments to Turner having been advocated and endorsed in advance by several fellow officers. Coincidentally, that same week the Director's staff informed us that we had no choice but to comply with a personal request from our United Nations Ambassador, Andrew Young, the former Mayor of Atlanta and a good friend of President Carter. Young, a novice in the world of international diplomacy and a "stranger in a strange land" at the United Nations, apparently wanted a list of all UN employees, and all delegates to the UN family of agencies, with whom the Agency maintained an ongoing relationship. There were to be no "hold-backs" or exceptions, and we were to prepare true-name lists—meaning no aliases—with explanations about the mechanics of each relationship. Our branch was caught up in that bizarre request because we had relationships with multiple UN agencies in Geneva and in Vienna, particularly at the International Atomic Energy Agency, headquartered in the Austrian capital.

I could not believe this insanity, and not because someone in the senior ranks of the Carter Administration had asked for it. We really could not blame Young or his staff for requesting the information. They clearly were naive or just incompetent. Such a request probably seemed like a "good idea" to someone, so they asked for the list. Rather, I was outraged that someone in Turner's office, or Turner himself, had seconded the request for our compliance. Also, DO management had not even challenged the logic of the request, at least beyond a certain point. Instead, they had passed it down the line to the DO and its branches. Needless to say, in the end, Young got the list. But we made damned sure that what came out of the DO was "sanitized." Not a single name on it in any way compromised a sensitive Agency source or relationship.

For many of us, the real issue was not Young's demand for a list of Agency "assets and contacts" within the UN structure, however preposterous such a demand might be. It was that our own Agency management, from Turner on down, seriously considered, let alone accepted, the request. It was mind-boggling. The farce demonstrated that the Turner team had no concept of an inherent requirement for an intelligence service to protect the identities of its clandestine relationships—because such assets reasonably assumed that their identities, if not their very lives, depended on our pledge to protect them. The attitude within the Directorate was to swallow hard and placate our national leadership while waiting out the Carter–Turner crowd. And while we waited, we would protect our own, meaning our assets and those who trusted us to protect them.

Korea Redux One (Falsely Accused)

Proving that, once there, no one can ever escape the "Korea pull," two Seoul Station flashback incidents occurred during my time at the Swiss–Austria Branch. The first demonstrated the degree to which, post the Church Committee and with the Carter–Turner deadly duo sitting atop us, political correctness was beginning to creep into the body of the Agency. The result was eroded authority, management drift and a steady undermining of morale.

Recalling the first instance, about three months after I left Korea, the new Chief in Seoul was back at Langley and walked into my office unannounced.

His brow was furrowed in concern. The new Chief was a fine man, careful and deliberate, and I had heard he was off to a solid start. His opening remark was cautious. "We have a problem out in Seoul, both you and I. I have been trying to manage it from out there, but now I'm back in the building dealing with it this week. I need your help."

He explained that in the process of disciplining my former Seoul branch chief, and arranging for him to leave short-of-tour, the individual had made some serious assertions. Specifically, he claimed that his predecessor, the man whom he had replaced the very day I departed Korea, had colluded with me to "fabricate the sourcing of certain highly sensitive reporting." His clear reference was to our Station reporting on the ROK clandestine nuclear program. He then took me through the allegation, and we both recognized the individual being disciplined was attempting to create an offsetting drama. The man was negotiating down or away the charges of misconduct the previous Chief had leveled at him. Those well-documented charges had been accepted by the incoming Chief and, when a new set of misdeeds surfaced, he accelerated the individual's departure.

In short, my former branch chief claimed that a year or so before, selected intelligence reporting had come from "JUSMAG-Korea asset Mac," based on my former colleague Hugh MacElvoy's discussions with his Korean sources. The implication was we had mislabeled or mischaracterized the source by assigning a false identity to Mac, thereby contaminating the intelligence. It was partly true. Regarding Mac's identity, only the Chief of Station and I knew of the action. We had done so to protect Mac from his own JUSMAG management and to protect him as a source on covert Agency for Defense Development activity.

The senior officer of JUSMAG-K, a U.S. Army major general, had demanded the identities of our protected sources at the ADD and how we were contacting our agents there. The officer had read our reporting and ham-handedly deployed selected pieces of clandestine intelligence to probe senior people at the ADD. His intention was to confirm covert ADD activities firsthand and demonstrate to his own higher command, namely, to the four-star commander of U.S. Army Korea, that JUSMAG and he were on top of ADD activities.

Korean officers were taken aback by those approaches and were quick to realize important ADD information somehow had been compromised. As a result, the ADD upped its security program, and several of our sources, including some who had no contact with Mac, feared they had been compromised. Facing an untenable situation, the Station subsequently removed the fine general from our in-country classified-reporting list. Ambassador Richard Sneider approved the action. And when the two-star realized he was being denied access to sensitive reporting, he fumed.

Facing the situation with Mac, we also worried about the emotional stability of our own Station branch chief—the man who would later accuse us of fabricating our sourcing. His behavior had become increasingly erratic, something which was overlaid by his notoriously sloppy security practices. Incredibly, he had managed to accumulate five security violations in a three-month period, a

Station record. His penultimate violation involved his leaving a file with all of his previous compromises on his desk. At that point, the Station Chief ordered his trusted support officer to reverse all the drawers in the fellow's desk and nail them shut—a security procedure probably unique in the history of the entire DO.

I explained to the new Seoul Station Chief why we had elected to disguise Mac as a source, that headquarters was fully informed about it and had approved every aspect. I also noted there was a solid paper trail, albeit in protected back-channel messages, to support all aspects of the operational decisions. He felt relieved and went off to access those messages, now able to explain all to Turner's ever-eager inhouse investigators. So armed, he could set straight the record. He also then needed to confront his antagonist back in Seoul so he could get the guy shipped home.

He wrote me a few weeks later to say he had "managed our problem," and the individual departed Seoul with all allegations of misconduct and ineptitude intact. I found out later that DDO McMahon had personally de-badged and terminated the individual, with Office of Security officers frog-marching him out the front door. The real problem was the individual had attempted to use the system against itself and almost succeeded in avoiding the consequences of his self-destructive actions. In initially accepting the allegations of the disgruntled employee, the new enlightened management of Director Turner somehow thought it had discovered another Directorate of Operations "misdeed." At least in that case, Turner's special inspector crew was turned away and went off to probe other lame allegations of DO malfeasance.

Korea Redux Two (Koreagate)

The second Seoul legacy incident during my early months at Swiss–Austria Branch, related to my tangential involvement in the so-called "Koreagate" scandal of 1977-1980. It was a national-level imbroglio, centering on a series of corruption allegations against various U.S. congressmen and staffers ostensibly influenced by one Park Tong-sun. He was a prominent Korean businessman–fixer who had moved smoothly within the Washington lobbying scene to arrange relationships between selected congressmen and Korean government officials, the latter abetted by Korean business leaders aligned with that government. Because Koreagate has its own history and is extensively documented elsewhere, there is no need for further details here.

My problem arose when I sat down for a chat with a team comprising congressional staff investigators and our own General Counsel staff. The question was, "Did you have any direct knowledge of, or dealings with, Tongsun Park (as he was more popularly known) during your five years in Seoul?" The answer was, "No, he was poison, and anybody with a half a brain stayed the hell away from him."

The second question was more difficult to manage. "Do you have any direct knowledge of any attempts to bribe U.S. government officials during this same period in Seoul?" I had no choice but to answer "Yes, but it was complicated, delicate, and I am not sure you want to get into this."

My response provided red meat to the investigators, but I had no choice. I had to explain it all, mainly because I was not sure what they knew. I was concerned they might otherwise discover what I was about to tell them as their investigation plowed its own way forward, through the Park Tong-sun fertile field of corrupt players and activity. They seemed to be piecing it all together fairly well, but they had no idea how many transgressions were involved during the years Park operated his schemes.

After sharing what I knew about Park, I shifted gears to explain that my only other brush with corruption had occurred with a different individual. In my capacity as the Station's Nuclear Energy Officer, in the course of a social event, I had been directly approached by the American owner of a major supplier of nuclear reactor components. The Texas big-hat gent laid out his corporate credentials, explained his close relationship with a certain three-initialed former U.S. President (not FDR and not JFK), and explained that the nuclear reactor supplier people "told me you are the man I have to deal with to get this deal done." Not sure what his formulation of the "deal" included, or just who had told him what, I asked for clarification. He took me into the details of a procurement package with which I was familiar—not for the reactor vessel itself but for a major portion of the so-called balance of plant equipment, as well as the heavy-gauge piping to be fabricated at his facility to connect the reactor pressure vessel to the balance of the plant.

I explained to the Texas gentleman it was my understanding that the entirety of the Kori 1 nuclear plant, including all components and construction work, involved an ongoing tender-and-bid process. The reactor builder, Westinghouse, was under close scrutiny, including audits by the loan provider, namely the U.S. Export–Import Bank. The bidding-and-contracting process was organized to be transparent and tamper-proof. The piping fabricator in front of me intimated, however, that this was not necessarily how things were done on nuclear power projects in the States. He said he had won several contracts, and he planned to do whatever was necessary to win the Kori 1 award. I told him the plant's contractor certainly would add him to the list of potential suppliers and provide information as the project progressed, just as the contractor was doing with all interested bidders.

My new friend was not satisfied. He produced a white envelope from his blazer pocket and extended it to me. "I have some other information here. Take a look." I opened the envelope to see a fat stack of hundred-dollar bills. I guessed his tender was about $3,000, offered as a "consideration." I handed it back and said, "You know, this may be the wrong envelope, so do you have other information?" He rose, shook my hand, slid the envelope back into his pocket and walked away.

About an hour later, as I was exiting the office, a local secretary stopped me with, "Mr. Lawless, the Texas gentleman handed me this envelope with your name on it. He said you needed this information." Without accepting the envelope, I asked her if it was true that the local employees had a benefit fund for scholarships for their children, and that she was the treasurer. She replied in the affirmative, so I told her the Texas gentleman had wanted to donate to the local employees. The scholarship fund seemed the best beneficiary of his generosity. Away she went, envelope in hand. I never heard another mention of that "gift," not from the would-be supplier back home or the local donation recipients.

The congressional investigators wanted to know why I had not reported the bribe attempt and wanted all manner of information on the individual. I responded that I had turned away his approach, that there was no way to prove his intent, and that his firm had not gone on to participate in the Kori 1 project. In any event, he had since passed into that great pipe-fabrication facility in the sky, or so I was told.

All of the individuals present at the interview table knew full well that, in the Koreagate mess, there were a dozen other deals consummated, most of which involved congressmen and lobbyists, where contracts were completed and side payments made. I suggested a few areas where they needed to look if not already there. I was pleased never to hear another word about the matter. I did watch from a distance as the Koreagate scandal unfolded over many ensuing months, and the various prosecutions went forward, with indictments aplenty and jail time awarded.

The Nuclear Proliferation Issue

While at the Swiss–Austria Branch, I devoted a good deal of time to nuclear non-proliferation. I enjoyed working on the subject and had come to know it reasonably well. Plus, Washington hosted the very United Nations agency established to enforce provisions of the Treaty on the Non-Proliferation of Nuclear Weapons of 1970—the NPT. The International Atomic Energy Agency already was on our radar as a troubled organization. As an independent UN entity, the IAEA still was in its formative years, and though it was well-financed through the generosity of the UN budget, and seemingly well-structured to deliver on its various missions, the IAEA remained a work in progress.

One of the agency's missions was the international promotion of nuclear energy for power generation—that is, planning and developing nuclear powerplants to generate electricity. In parallel, the agency was to promote nuclear research for educational and medical purposes, namely, through its assistance to institutions supporting national nuclear programs. The tasking included support of the construction and operation of nuclear research reactors and associated fuel-fabrication activities. A related mission involved technical assistance designed to share the experiences held by the more developed and mature nuclear nations with IAEA member countries. The United States and the Soviet Union, in company with other full-fledged nuclear states, such as the United Kingdom, France and Germany, were eager to communicate their knowledge to nations just coming into their own with nuclear programs. All of the aspiring nuclear nations were attempting to develop their own capabilities, and the IAEA promoted the process, typically by dispatching experienced researchers and engineers for hands-on assistance in selected facilities.

Last and perhaps most important, the IAEA was chartered as the safeguarding mechanism for international nuclear activity. It was responsible for organizing, staffing and maintaining a comprehensive program allowing it to track and report the degree to which each member state, as participants in the NPT, maintained full compliance with the safeguards regimes designed to curtail nuclear proliferation.

The IAEA's Safeguards Division was organized to conduct country- and facility-specific inspections on a regional basis and was staffed by career IAEA employees, including specialists and technicians.

The nuclear safeguards inspectors were a mixed lot, and various IAEA member nations maneuvered within the agency's layered bureaucracy to place as many of their nationals as possible in positions of responsibility. This related both to management positions as well as individual inspectors assigned to safeguard particular nuclear facilities of interest to a given sponsoring member. The Soviet Union and its Eastern European client states were active on that front, while the U.S. side typically did not treat inspection positions as a priority.

Each IAEA member possessing nuclear facilities, be it a developed nation such as the United States, the United Kingdom or the Soviet Union, or a developing nation hosting a single low-power research reactor, had entered into a safeguards regime or agreement. As mentioned, the IAEA was responsible for designing and executing country-specific inspection programs, including site visits, records reviews, sampling of nuclear products and other procedures. All were designed to provide comprehensive and complete profiles of ongoing activity. Within the IAEA bureaucracy, there was great pressure to demonstrate delivery on its mandate. That pressure to deliver quality performance emanated from both the United Nations—given that the IAEA was a subordinate entity—and the IAEA's own Board of Governors. The latter was responsible for certifying the IAEA was performing its duties. And nowhere within the IAEA was there higher pressure to demonstrate performance than in the Safeguards Division.

From an intelligence-collection standpoint, we had to view the IAEA organization from the outside because we had no authority to place anyone on the inside. Yet even from a distance, we could identify the safeguarded nations and facilities of greatest interest; those that posed a nuclear proliferation risk. In the years leading up to 1980, the CIA had taken a fairly loose attitude toward clandestine collection directed at the IAEA, to the extent that its workings were not seen as an intelligence target. That was due mainly to our main preoccupation with Soviet and Eastern European targets, wherever they could be found. Any attention directed at the IAEA was vectored at selected, high-priority Eastern European nationals embedded there. The fact that the Soviet intelligence organizations, both the KGB and GRU, made extensive use of IAEA career positions, with their intel officers often occupying long-term career positions within the bureaucracy, made the IAEA all the more a target activity.

The situation did not bode well for a determined collection program designed to address the proliferation issue. If a third-country prospective asset at the IAEA; that is, if a national from a non-Eastern European nation was encountered, we judged the potential value of that contact mainly on the basis of their ability to access one of our many national targets within the nuclear agency. Access to proliferation issues was a secondary consideration at best, and actual clandestine source reporting on nuclear concerns a rare occurrence.

All that said, for whatever combination of reasons, we did have vetted assets in place within the IAEA who, in addition to their Eastern European contacts, enjoyed direct access to proliferation-related reporting targets. When a once-in-a-blue-moon reporting cable arrived at our Headquarters branch that addressed a proliferation target, we valued it and made sure it was disseminated to the CIA's analytical customers. From that, at the Headquarters end, we also realized such episodic reporting was only the tip of a potential iceberg of possible nuclear-related intelligence. I and others were convinced much more of that useful intelligence could be had.

When a jewel of a nuclear-related report did come in, once it was properly disseminated, it certainly got attention. In one important instance, an asset reported on poor safeguards procedures involving the Pakistani nuclear reactor near Karachi. The facility was of high interest because we reasonably assumed Pakistan was, back in 1979, pulling out all the stops to create its own nuclear weapons capability. India's "Smiling Buddha" nuclear test had taken place five years before, in May 1974, and the two nations had fought two wars and were warming up to fight another. The report indicated that IAEA safeguards inspectors responsible for ensuring the KANUPP 1 power reactor had cut some corners. Apparently, they failed to challenge the reactor's managers when safeguards equipment appeared to have been disabled or failed, compromising the monitoring regime. More important, those same inspectors and their immediate managers failed to record the incidents. Instead, they declared the inspections flawless.

In that case, the CIA shared its clandestinely reported information with the State Department, whose senior leadership then passed along the information to our U.S. Mission at the IAEA in Vienna. Within a fortnight, our Mission discretely shared the findings with IAEA officials in an attempt to compel them to "smoke out the facts." The IAEA's response was completely predictable: There was no problem. They claimed it simply had been a misunderstanding in the process, and all errors in internal IAEA reporting were corrected. Everyone on the IAEA side of the equation, including our Mission, pronounced themselves satisfied with the inspections.

We watched the event as it developed, we read what operational reporting existed that clarified our asset's access, and matched the reporting with State channel cables flowing back and forth with the Mission. One arrived at the overriding realization that the IAEA safeguards system was deeply flawed at its core level of practice—that is, at the level of onsite inspections and the upward reporting of same. Further, the CIA's intelligence had been used by the U.S. policy side to force a particular safeguards activity to function as it was supposed to function, or at least appear to function. In reality, absent the reporting and the U.S. initiative the reporting generated, the IAEA's safeguards system did not appear capable of functioning. In that case, the IAEA system had not been corrected, and it appeared the agency would resist outside challenges to the validity of its inspection procedures, as well as its reporting and its certifications.

The incident did produce one positive result. It indicated that our access to IAEA-based sources would yield unique clandestine source reporting about selected nuclear proliferation targets. At the same time, the reporting created opportunities for our policy officials to understand the inherent deficiencies in the IAEA safeguards structure and modus operandi. Although we had succeeded in reporting clandestinely on important Pakistani nuclear facilities, we did face resistance from our own policymakers, as well as studied indifference from IAEA bureaucrats and fellow travelers, all of whom were devoted to the concept of IAEA safeguards but were unwilling to do the hard work to make them work.

From the standpoint of the DO and the CIA's responsibility, our mandate was to acquire well-sourced clandestine reporting. Beyond that, others needed to assess the performance of the IAEA and inform the policy process. Unfortunately, our mandate did not include efforts to correct the system. The issue at hand was a policy issue, and the CIA was not a policy shop.

On to a European Assignment

I originally was scheduled to relocate to my new field assignment in summer 1980, the plan being that I would begin part-time language study in January, stay active at the branch part-time, and take some additional Soviet–Eastern Europe operational courses. In early January, after exactly two days of language instruction, I was called into the Europe Division front office and greeted with "You're going to your new posting yesterday. How fast can you pack out and be out there? We have a staffing issue." Translation: Somebody just got fired. I had a good idea who it was and asked, "one or two?" The reply was "two," and it all fell into place.

The Headquarters branch responsibility included only limited oversight of the Station's organization and personnel, and though we at the branch level had no say in whom was dispatched to the Station, or to which branch within the Station they were assigned, we had a good idea which officer was performing and which was not. The Station had experienced several "curtailments of tour" over the past few years, so it was not unusual that an officer was being sent home short of tour. It would not be my last experience with the trials and tribulations of the so-called tandem-couple assignment process. But the less said about that ill-starred initiative on the part of the Agency the better, at least here. As it turned out, I accepted the early dispatch to the new posting—in any event I had no choice. I departed Washington a full six months early. But my early arrival was fortuitous, creating a parachute-in situation not unlike my early dispatch to Seoul some seven years earlier.

A Cold Welcome to a New Posting

I arrived in the city of my posting—which, for security and other reasons, I am not permitted to identify—a few days into the New Year. I was met planeside by an overcast sky and a deep-damp chill in the air. Having arrived a good six months earlier than originally planned, without benefit of the language training I had been promised, I was on the ground to stay for a multiple-year tour. It was a Friday, and I was told to be at the Station's staff meeting Monday morning without fail.

The city was still in its post-war phase, meaning it was ever-so-slowly recovering from World War II. Its economy had not been helped by the socialist government that had dominated the nation's political dynamic. That mentality remained front-and-center in the capital city, with local politics and governance focused on welfare rights, social justice and regulations that discouraged enterprise and initiative. In that economically dispiriting environment, young citizens with any strain of ambition tended to flee both city and country in search of opportunity elsewhere, be their destination other European nations, or Canada and the United States, or even South Africa. The country was experiencing negative population growth and a mean age approaching 60. The outlying provinces and the secondary cities and towns sought a balance, and that often produced right-of-center political movements. But the country as a whole essentially was stuck in its past, and the city remained a gray hostage to the Cold War.

Adding to that challenging social dynamic, the city harbored a generally depressing physical climate. The weather seemed perpetually overcast, as though we would not see the sun for months. Blending in with the general disposition of the population, our Embassy was hardly an uplifting place. Staffed by locals who rarely smiled and typically were elderly and grouchy, not to mention unproductive, many seemed to resent the Americans who rotated into and out of the Embassy in three-year tours. I also learned the hard way that Embassy working hours were less than taxing. It all presented a sharp contrast with the normal routine at Seoul Station.

As a final touch to ease my transition, the administrative section informed me that, since I had arrived "out of schedule," they had no currently contracted housing available, at least until the following summer. They placed us—my wife, two children and me—in a rundown apartment used as transient or TDY quarters. Tossing us the keys, they provided some pots and pans, and sheets and blankets, to tide us over until our household effects arrived on a slow boat from Virginia. The personal-effects shipment would show up a month later to be jammed into that beat-up, one-and-a-half-bedroom, damp and dreary dump.

Motivated by the situation, I struck up a personal relationship with a senior Embassy employee, one Karl of Czech lineage, who held no love for the locals. From Karl, I learned that the State Department paperwork helpfully had classified me two levels below my current rank, showing me as a first-tour officer with a family. The Embassy admin types judged that I should be happy with what they had given me. I could handle the Spartan accommodations, but my wife and young children could not. They felt cold, wet and cramped. With Karl's assistance, however, I found a local real estate agent and engaged her to work behind the scenes with him. We found a grand home on a classic street in an upscale district of the city. The negotiated rent was within State's financial parameters, but the Embassy stalled, offering the lame excuse that the house was unusual. The elderly owners lived in a bungalow behind the main structure, and their daughter and her family lived above the main residence. The lease, therefore, reflected the residence as "shared facilities."

We initialed the lease, and I walked into the Embassy and demanded acceptance, signature and advance payment to the landlord. I threatened to move from the apartment into a hotel if they continued to play games. They caved but then complained that the district of the city was too exclusive a location for my lowly position. We forced the deal and moved in before the bureaucrats could change their minds. I invited Karl to dinner at the restaurant directly adjacent to my new residence for an evening of cold beer, wurst and good cheer. Karl became a best buddy and my go-to guy for the remainder of the tour.

On the issue of the relaxed Embassy routine, one example will suffice. On a Monday morning a couple of weeks after my arrival, I was surprised to be summoned by the Deputy Chief of Mission for a welcome session. A career State type, he evidently was pleased to be administering the Embassy, assuming at that time his elevated appointment as Charge d'Affaires. His enhanced responsibilities had been created by the absence of our Carter-appointed Ambassador. The latter, as often the norm, was back visiting family and overseeing his California auto dealerships. The DCM delivered his wisdom, wished me a good tour and referenced my Agency sponsorship.

In a subsequent welcome briefing to a group of new arrivals, the DCM made it clear the workweek began on Monday mid-morning, would conclude on Friday at midday—or whenever the day we elected to head out of the city—and certainly did not require us to work on either Saturday or Sunday. I listened but did not believe the directives until I sat down with my Agency colleagues. They explained it was the drill at the Embassy and were quick to point out, "This is not like your last field tour. And, on the weekends, stay the hell out away from the Embassy!" It would be quite an adjustment.

Beyond the relaxed pace of activity, Embassy management also was a bit of a challenge. David Forden, our Chief of Station, was a Soviet–Eastern Europe

Division star. At that point, in 1980, he had played a leading role in sustaining one of the most productive clandestine operations ever mounted against the Soviet Union. Though still deeply compartmented at the time of my tour, the operation later would be revealed to have generated more volume and more detail on Soviet and Warsaw Pact strategic and tactical war planning than any other single project. The downside of that leadership was our posture would be all SE operations all the time. There was only token interest in other hard targets, such as North Korea and China, or nuclear proliferation operations. [NOTE 1]

The Deputy Chief was another matter. In company with other officers, I found "Marvin" very difficult to work with. It was not just because he laser-focused on the SE targets, but rather because he was by instinct incredibly cautious. To a fault, he continually expressed deep concern and discouraged any operational activity he considered "risky." The Station operations officers had tagged Marvin with the *nom de guerre* " Three-to-five Marv," based on his oft-repeated assessment and rejection when a new operation was proposed for his consideration. His standard comment was, "That's way too risky, that will get us all three-to-five years if this thing goes wrong!" Tired of bringing the same operational concept to him three or four times, with new offramps or plausible denial scenarios added for Marv's review, most officers simply gave up in frustration. The combination of the COS's detachment from the day-to-day, and the take-no-chances, extreme vetting process applied by Marv, meant we risked far too little and missed opportunities. The good news was the Station had no operational "flaps" of consequence, at least while I was there.

My unit within the Station consisted of several career SE division officers. Those men and women were skilled linguists, and all had served in denied areas. They sustained themselves in intensely hostile operating environments dominated by the Soviet KGB and GRU operatives, not to mention local intel counterparts. I had sought a position in this branch and was the only non-SE division "outsider" in the unit. The fact that my career home base was the East Asia Division probably did not help my profile.

My SE Branch Chief at the time of my arrival was a strong-charging manager eager for us operations officers to seek out and build relationships with hard-target counterparts. I found his dedication and ambition admirable, and I am sure that, during his tenure, his team left no hard-target stone unturned. He was not, however, the least bit interested in my attraction to the nuclear issue, and he discouraged intelligence reporting on the topic. But it was his call, and that of the Station, and not mine.

His replacement at my one-year point was another matter, and I felt fortunate the man arrived when he did to manage our branch. Larry was aggressive, thoughtful and much more balanced in his approach to clandestine reporting targets. He understood the value we were able to bring to our reporting on the strategic aspects of nuclear non-proliferation through the use of clandestinely managed, tasked and debriefed assets and semi-overt contacts. In sum, he "got" our intelligence reporting and the dissemination of that intelligence, and he created the space we needed to do things right.

Larry became a friend and partner but, best of all, he was a lean-in advocate for his operators. He made room for a broad range of operational activity that delivered quality intelligence reporting. That change in attitude would deliver our Station to the point where it would become, based on his leadership at the second level of management, a known and recognized intelligence production location for Europe Division. Larry pushed reluctant Station senior management, including our incoming Chief and his Deputy Chief, to accept the intelligence reporting opportunities my supervisor helped others to discover and exploit. When I departed in the summer of 1982, the only relationship I missed was the one offered by my boss and friend.

Good Socialists All

One of my first assignments was to attend a Socialist Party rally, in which the leader of the U.S. counterpart socialist party was slated to speak. And speak he did, to a good-size crowd of old-line hardcore socialists. The loyal progressives, with a few local communists thrown in, were eager to learn how their fellow travelers were doing in the unapologetically capitalist empire of America. The event was hosted by none other than the imperial potentate of all Democratic Socialists in that country.

The American's presentation impressed me as an eloquent and reasoned speech, delivered in a compelling voice, evoking sincerity for the socialist cause and the Socialist International cause. When he finished, the event's host invited questions from the audience. Rising to the occasion, an elderly citizen rose and made his own mini-speech, trashing America by name and capitalism in general. He finished by posing a question along the lines of, "Great poverty and inequality exist in America? Yet your Socialist Party there has failed completely? You have only a few thousand members. You are disorganized. There does not seem to be any future for the socialist cause there! Not even the oppressed black people support you."

The American was quick with his response. To the best of my recollection, he offered an explanation along the following lines: "I have asked myself that question many times, and I have no good answer. But I will give you an example. A few weeks ago, I was on a speaking tour in Appalachia, where there is deep poverty among both blacks and whites, but especially with the blacks. I made a speech to a mainly black crowd, mostly women. I explained how we socialists would expand taxes on the wealthy, and I used as one example the inheritance tax we would use to extract money from the rich."

The American socialist continued, "The first question came from a large black woman who stood in the front row and put a question to me. She said, 'Do you mean that if I have a million dollars, and I die, you are going to take ninety percent of that in taxes, and only leave my son with ten percent?'"

Our American speaker maintained his pace. "I responded affirmatively, but explained politely that this was not the point, as it was very unlikely that she

265

would have a million dollars, and even if she did, she would be in an absolute minority. She should think about the collective good of such a tax. The lady was very angry and told me, 'But that is MY point. In America I can make a million dollars, that is my right, that is my opportunity, and no one has the right to take that away from me. And you don't have any right to take that money away from my son if I die.'"

The American continued with his explanation to the local audience of dedicated socialists. "So you see, this is the problem we have in America with socialism. Even the most impoverished continue to believe they have the possibility to acquire wealth. They have no concept of sharing the wealth for the common good. Until this attitude changes, until these people understand that they will not be able to become wealthy, we socialists will not have a basis for success in America."

It was an interesting introduction for me into the mind of the "Red City." It also provided a great lesson about the grip democratic socialism held on the older generation of the good people of that nation and that city.

A Commendation for Agent Victor

Our support agent team was diverse and talented, with an interesting subset of Cold War widows and ladies who had retired. In some cases, the city of my posting was their hometown, but most often the ladies had fled communist-occupied Eastern Europe with their husbands. Many of those Agency cold warriors had been either lost on operations back in the occupied areas or simply had passed from this life, but the Agency judged it had an obligation to them.

It happened that several of the women, all in their 70s or 80s but active and spry, were managed by an elderly case officer who met with each of them monthly, collecting whatever documents (translations, dead-drop letters or whatever) that needed to be passed securely to the Station. In checking in on those support assets, the case officer paid each of them the monthly stipend and reviewed any changes in her tasking.

That officer, Agent Victor, had long served in the Station. In reviewing his personnel file, I found his life story something out of an action novel. He had joined the anti-Nazi resistance in 1943 at age 14 and served with a partisan unit on the Eastern Front. In that guerrilla group, he had ambushed Nazi units in the forests of his home area and often was directed to execute captured SS members. His claim to fame in the group, which apparently prized Nazi gray coats (overcoats), was his ability to shoot a man in the back of the head without leaving any residue on the collar. Doing so benefited that coat's next owner, usually another partisan fighter. By 1945 when the war concluded, Agent Victor was a made man among his peer partisans, but he opted to leave Yugoslavia when Tito's affection for communism and dictatorship became clear.

Agent Victor's unit had been supplied its weapons by the Office of Strategic Services, the CIA's World War II forerunner. The OSS remembered the young man when the war ended and sought to track him over the following hectic years. In the turbulence of post-war Central Europe, the OSS transformed itself into the Agency in 1947. When Agent Victor fled Yugoslavia, he was contacted and brought into the new organization. He relocated and began a career that delivered solid service to the Station.

Agent Victor was tough. He spoke a number of languages and could pass for multiple nationalities. He often was deployed on missions throughout Europe in many sensitive operations, always operating under an alias. He was not a legend per se, but he definitely was a talent, if always a bit independent of authority. When it came time for him to retire, he was ready to move on and had his program all arranged. A cottage and small boat awaited him and his girlfriend on a little island to the south.

Agent Victor had elected to retire on my watch back at Headquarters in 1979, a few months before I relocated to Europe. My staff processed the paperwork, including a citation for many years of great service to the Agency and the United States. As his retirement date approached, a replacement officer was assigned to take his place to manage the mostly female support team. Agent Victor went through the turnover process with the new officer, taking him to each meeting, introducing him, and bidding a tearful farewell to each lady. He typically met the ladies in their apartments, and in each case, as the young officer discovered, Agent Victor's visit was welcomed with a hardy meal, no little drinking and a bit of piano-playing with a song or two thrown in.

Agent Victor's visits were obviously welcome, as much for the *freundschaft* (deep friendship) aspect as the monthly payments. It was obvious that Agent Victor had, over the years, made many female friends among his elderly assets— eight, to be exact. The problem arose when the new officer, with Agent Victor preparing to depart for retirement in another country, began making his own monthly calls for the first time, that is, in solo sessions with the agents.

In each of the first three lunches, the lady in question was eager to get down to business as soon as the meal was finished. The lady would retire to her bedroom to emerge minutes later in her negligée, well-perfumed and ready for action. When the young officer declined the offer for intimacy, disappointment filled the air. In fact, several of the ladies told the newcomer that Agent Victor had always provided a "bonus" when he visited. The extra service apparently had long been an important component of Agent Victor's asset-management package.

That delicate situation should have been managed with discretion at the Station level by the Deputy Chief, but it was not. Instead, Three-to-five Marv decided it was a serious "disciplinary matter." As such, Agent Victor's improper conduct would require a formal report for the files, plus Headquarters attention and adjudication. The back-channel (sensitive personnel issue) cable from Marv arrived on a Saturday morning when I was in the branch office at Headquarters reviewing traffic. I had to read the cable twice to believe it. The Station decided to report all of Agent Victor's misdeeds and recommend disciplinary action, to be approved by the head office.

I walked over to sit with Deputy Division Chief Dewey Clarridge, later of Iran–Contra fame, who was studying the same cable and shaking his head in disbelief. He looked up at me with a, "Can you believe this shit?" expression. I explained that Agent Victor was slated to retire the following week and laid his eight-inch-thick personnel file on the desk. I recall saying something like, "He's been with us for many years, has nine commendations, and here we have the Station jacking him up as he retires." I asked if we could just kill the matter with a back-channel to the Station, saying, "Forget it." Dewey noted it was impossible. The cable also had been sent to the Headquarters personnel office as well as the Agency legal counsel. Agent Victor's indiscretions in the service of the Agency were now a matter of record in the building. **[NOTE 1]**

We elected to respond that weekend by agreeing with the Station that disciplinary action apparently was necessary. Our return cable suggested that the Deputy Chief personally meet with Agent Victor to deliver the formal admonition, in company with his retirement citations, and report back same in formal channels. What happened next was pure Agent Victor. After Three-to-Five Marv delivered his reprimand, Agent Victor only smiled. According to those present, he responded, "Okay, I think I understand. You want me to state that, on behalf of this fine Agency and the United States of America, you are officially recognizing that I was actively servicing the sexual requirements of six ladies at the same time. So, in addition, you are commending me for my service on the occasion of my retirement after many years of service. Fine. I agree!"

The next line, as properly recorded in Agent Victor's file from an incoming Station cable, was Agent Victor's closing admonition. "Also, and note this for the record. I ask that you do not call me to come back for duty unless you really need me for something special." I ran into Dewey a few days after Agent Victor's response arrived. He just smiled.

Operation Eagle Claw

Agent Victor's story did not end there, however. It resumed in the spring of 1980, and the infamous and star-crossed operation undertaken by the United States to rescue our diplomats held hostage in the U.S. Embassy in Tehran. After many months of diplomatic game-playing and inconclusive approaches to the mullahs, it became clear the Tehran regime would not release its American hostages, held there since early November 1979. At that point, the U.S. national security team prevailed upon President Jimmy Carter to plan a covert military operation to free our diplomats there.

Operation Eagle Claw, mulled for months as a mission planned and re-planned, was developed in great detail. The plan evolved as a combined-forces effort to land a Delta Force team in the Iranian desert and then be covertly inserted by helicopter into Tehran. The team would rescue the hostages from their captors and move by vehicle back to the desert location for airlift out of Iran and a fast ride home.

Eagle Claw turned out to be an overly complex plan. Even in concept, it was a challenge to execute. Our military side was not well-prepared to organize such an undertaking, and the assembled multi-service team was less than optimal. Beyond the intricacy of the operation itself, President Carter was conflicted and, as was his want, took a personal role in reviewing and fine-tuning the details of the mission. Carter's retuning was based in part on his demand that the planners commit to the goal that no Iranian civilians would be harmed in the operation.

Carter's intrusiveness, and the compromises he required, contributed to doom the effort from the outset. Beyond Carter and his fractured decision-making national security team (Secretary of State Cyrus Vance vehemently opposed any effort to forcibly recover the hostages, and he resigned in protest in the immediate aftermath of the failed operation), the plan itself reflected a convoluted command structure and a less-than-optimal mix of aircraft and crews.

In any event, Operation Eagle Claw required an operational presence on the ground in Tehran to prepare for the arrival of the combat unit that would infiltrate after landing at a remote desert location. The advance team inserted into the heart of Tehran would have to be Agency-led, and the Agency responded to the call by deploying its best covert officers. We needed top-quality operatives who could pass for anything but Americans, true risk-takers to operate independently on the streets of Tehran, for weeks if necessary.

The co-leader of our advance team was Agent Victor, whom we called away from his retirement. I was in my posted city when we put the plan together. From there, I communicated to those planning the operation and assembling the covert advance team. In a cable, I related how Agent Victor's career had ended and that in reactivating contact with him we told him, in essence, "You told us to only call you if we really needed you for a big one. Well, this is the call and it's a big one." We added to the team another officer whom I happened to be co-managing, and I integrated Agent Victor with him. It was a solid combination. In preparing them for their mission, we emphasized the high risk both men were taking by going in black, as we termed it, with deep-cover identities to organize the on-the-ground element of the rescue plan.

The senior operations officer in charge deserved full credit for organizing the Agency component of the rescue mission and managing our covert insertion team. In my brief interaction with him, I recognized the frustration he felt in his dealings with the Carter national security team as well as the military. The former was divided among themselves and the latter scrambled to assemble a multi-service force that had never worked together before. When we met with Agent Victor to explain the mission, he did not blink. He was ready to ride.

Our Agent Victor-led team went in, all with false identities. They established themselves on the ground and executed their mission with precision. They played their parts, including warming up the buses in the garage and staking out the hostage sites. They were ready to go when the rescue force touched down at the Desert One site to refuel the helicopters. The helicopter-borne force was to move farther forward to land at a location closer to Tehran, there to transfer to surface transportation for the final run into the city.

As the operation began, all went horribly wrong on the way to Desert One. The eight U.S. Navy RH-53 helicopters, launched from the deck of the aircraft carrier USS *Nimitz* in the Persian Gulf, ran into a sandstorm en route to the rendezvous site. With engines and navigation systems failing, two of the RH-53s turned back. The C-130 Air Force transports that landed a Delta Team for a transition into the helicopters at Desert One were on time to meet the helicopter group, but a violent sandstorm confused the team on the ground. Another RH-53 aborted, and the mission was then down to its absolute minimum of five aircraft for the last leg of the run to the advance landing site near Tehran.

As events unfolded, Carter attempted to manage the drama from the White House Situation Room, his concern reinforced by an increasingly uncertain military command chain and a wavering Delta commander. The latter made an on-the-ground decision to abort the mission. In aborting and maneuvering on the ground to retire from the area and lift off from the landing zone, a Navy helicopter collided with an Air Force C-130, resulting in a tragic explosion and the destruction of both aircraft. The burned-out wreckage was left smoldering at the site with dead U.S. crewmen lying charred next to the aircraft hulks. [NOTE 2]

The entire operation was abandoned, and the surviving aircraft, aircrews and operatives returned to their respective bases. The White House was left to deal with a disaster-in-the-desert result, for which Carter bore a good part of the responsibility, at least in the eyes of many of the men who planned it and lived through it. With no regard for our people still in Tehran, the White House Press Office implied, with complementing leaks to the media over the following days, that America still had its operatives on the ground in Iran. Rest assured, the public was told, Carter and company were working to get them out. To those of us in the field, by then well-exposed to the systemic ineptitude of that administration, the security breach and basic transgression was no surprise.

On the evening of the White House suggestion that we still had people active on the ground in Tehran, I found myself at the home of one of our operatives, reassuring his wife that we would be able to extricate her husband. He had not told her where he was going when he departed their home on a circuitous route that carried him into Tehran, but she instinctively knew from the preparations he had made. I felt strongly, with no little bitterness, that the Carter team was attempting to salvage some credit for the failed hostage-rescue effort on the backs of our dead American servicemen, then lying cold on the desert floor. And we still had at risk the Agency operatives we had sent into Tehran. At that moment, they were attempting to work their way out of Iran.

Fortunately, our men made it out a week or so later. They shrugged off the additional risk that the White House leak had injected into their exfiltration. On the Operations Directorate side, there was agreement we should not go back to those men and ask for a similar commitment until and unless we had national-level leadership willing to go the edge with them, and a plan that had a better chance of success than the one we had just watched collapse.

Thankfully, such a leader was then warming up in the bullpen. His name was Ronald Wilson Reagan. The day he took office, some 10 months after the Eagle Claw failure, and after 444 days in captivity for our people held in Tehran, the Iranians released the U.S. diplomatic hostages. The next week's cover of the German weekly Der Spiegel magazine featured a *High Noon*-themed cartoon with a lawman-and-gunslinger drawdown on the street, noting there was a "new sheriff in town." For Agency officers operating in the field, that change provided an incredible lift in morale. In the coming weeks and months, we were not disappointed in the new leadership team in Washington.

Damning Newsweek

I was somewhat emotionally, if only tangentially, involved in the events of Eagle Claw and its immediate aftermath. That said, I took strong exception to U.S. media coverage of our national failure, including the print media's exploitation of the bodies of the dead servicemen at Desert One. The U.S. edition of Newsweek of May 5, 1980, gave us a cover story titled "Special Report: A Mission Comes to Grief in Iran." It gratuitously presented photos of the charred American bodies sprawled on the desert floor. It was done in company with an amazingly complete and mostly accurate account of the mission.

That material appeared in print within days of the events described. We assumed the Carter White House was talking details to demonstrate how Carter was an "action" president while deflecting responsibility for mission failure to the Pentagon. The Newsweek reporting themed the event, however, as the major U.S. military failure that it was and predicted heavy political damage for Carter and his team. The failed mission was portrayed as a fiasco, for which Carter rightly or wrongly would be blamed. The account noted that the eight American bodies had been displayed for TV coverage at the deserted U.S. Embassy in Tehran. In an event staged for the international media, the bodies were further mutilated by Iranians, knives jammed into blackened American skulls to shatter them.

Photos of the violation of the bodies were there in Newsweek to shock and promote attention to the publication. An opening line in the story caught my eye. "Eight American servicemen died ... the rest fled to safety, leaving the bodies of their dead comrades behind." It was Newsweek's own way of jabbing another knife into the humbled body of the U.S. military.

Then the international edition of Newsweek, on May 12, 1980, outdid its domestic sister publication by placing the bodies of our dead American servicemen on its cover lying in front of a burned-out RH-53, headlined, "Rescue Mission in Washington." The reporting focused on the political aftermath, including Secretary Cyrus Vance's resignation to protest the mission, which was described as a "shattering blow" to Carter. Once again, we had many gratuitous photos of the bodies of our servicemen, including the Iranian president presiding over the knife-to-skull, body-defiling incident as the Iranians celebrated their self-described victory.

I felt compelled to write to Newsweek at some length, with no little emotion, to express my concern over the manner in which the photos and graphic descriptions of the charred bodies were extensively used in their stories. Given the nature of the publication, I did not expect any response. To my surprise, I received a reply on June 5th from associate editor David Gates, writing to explain that Newsweek regretted that its photos offended certain readers, but the decision by the magazine editors to make extensive use of the photos "was dictated by our standards of truthful and responsible reporting." Sure it was. Grotesque photos of charcoal-dead Americans sold more magazines worldwide, including Iran, where subscriptions doubled.

Then and there I promised myself that I would never buy or read another copy of Newsweek. Those types of journalists at that magazine were, then and remain today, truly disgusting individuals. I have kept that promise for nearly four decades and will never soil my hands with its newsprint, except when I remove it from someone's desk or a magazine rack to drop it into the nearest trashcan, where it belongs.

In a Tide Of Displacement, a Gem of a Man

One of the Station's single most important finds in the city of my posting during my tour there led to a lifelong friendship. The "find" also taught us a lesson we had to relearn time and again: Every strand and source of information must be accessed and filtered and mined for value. The episode involved a displaced, disoriented and desperate man who deserved to be found by the Agency. His life and future along with his young family's we were able to change dramatically for the better.

Our friendship came about early in my tour and was one part pure luck and two parts persistence and planning, much of the latter by others. In the city, we paid special attention to the flow of refugees who passed through the international processing system there—actually, a refugee center on the outskirts of the city. Through those gates passed a broad assortment of humanity; nationals from Eastern Europe who had been able to penetrate and exit the still-firm Iron Curtain of communism, as well as political refugees from various Middle Eastern nations threatened by constant turmoil. They were joined by economic refugees who had entered from Africa or elsewhere, all looking to move on to new lives in Europe or America.

A long-established local citizen, one of our friendly contacts, alerted us to an individual of "possible intelligence interest," and that asset's note to the Station found its way to me. The asset who passed along the alert was another of our assorted, second-tier support agents with whom the Station had worked for several decades, a man whose instincts we trusted. He enjoyed direct access to the refugee flow, or at least the paperwork that accompanied those individuals as they were processed, given temporary quarters and then moved on along the official pipeline to other transitional destinations in Europe.

Soon after I arrived at the Station, I registered my interest in any refugee from Iran or other Middle Eastern nations, and whose background was nuclear or with a military or high-technology connection. Refugees often claimed such experience or access, but when we examined their claims, they often proved to be exaggerations, attempts to secure expedited treatment. In this one case, our access agent spotted a man whom he thought was the real item. It turned out our asset was right.

Cyrus, as I will call him, claimed to be an Iranian nuclear engineer, but he was a refugee of unknown quality and credibility. His registration card noted only that he was "exhausted, depressed and had no plans for the future." He requested political asylum in the United States. My goal was to secure unfettered access to him as soon as possible. We acted that same day to have him paroled from the refugee holding center. We had a note slipped to him stating that an "old American friend from Tehran" wished to meet him at a downtown location immediately after his release. Once outside the facility, he was to call a number to confirm the time of the meeting, to be held at a coffeehouse.

When I entered the establishment, which was in the direction of my home in the city, I saw no sign of my intended contact. As my eyes adjusted to the dim lighting of the early evening, I checked my watch to be sure I was not early. Then I focused on a huddled shape at a corner table. I approached him and introduced myself. The man recoiled, rose quickly and, half-standing, stammered, "You, you are not Michael. Where is Michael? He promised me…"

I had no idea of the meaning of his challenge and his plea. Trying to quiet him in a café inhabited by octogenarians and their dogs, I placed my hand on his shoulder and guided him back into his seat. He resisted then half-collapsed, putting his elbows on the table, his head falling into his hands. He began to choke quietly with emotion.

I waited a bit, explained carefully that Michael (whoever he was) simply could not get to the city soon enough and had asked me to stand in for him. Over a two-hour discussion, Cyrus's story spilled out. It was tough for me to stay with the narrative, and anticipate the dialog while working to keep him calm and on story.

Cyrus had escaped from Tehran, leaving his family behind. He then traveled three weeks by car, foot and bus to cross the Iran–Turkey border, finally bribing his way to the country where we had found one another. He essentially was a fugitive from the Iranian regime of the mullahs. Having lost his position with the departure of the Shah, he had been harassed by VEVAK, the Iranian security service, and had at one time been declared to be an enemy of the Revolution. Based on his nuclear career with the former government of the Shah, he inhabited a netherworld of uncertainty and fear. Apprehensive that he could become a candidate for rehabilitation as a critical national asset of the new Islamic state, as the regime organized its own nuclear program, he fled when he realized he had a choice.

Physically and mentally, Cyrus was in a bad state. He had been taking antidepressants for over a year, waiting for the knock on the door of his apartment in Tehran. That knock had not come, but it did for others on his former nuclear team. He lived in fear while trying to support his family. In the good times, they had been among the Shah's outer circle, enjoying a prosperous life and great careers. Perhaps most important, he had been at the center of an elite management group within the budding Iranian nuclear energy program. He was both a hands-on nuclear research reactor manager, operator and instructor, and he did double service as a senior executive, advising the leading figures of the Shah's nuclear program.

That night, I made sure Cyrus was settled in a local business hotel and well-fed. I passed him some walking-around cash before confirming a plan for us to meet in a few days. I returned to my office to communicate with Headquarters about him. Obviously, there was more to his story.

My initial exchanges with home base were not encouraging. The folks back in Langley did a shallow dive into the records and managed to provide me only superficial information. Apparently, Cyrus was a "one-time established contact" but not a recruited agent. Thus, we had no recent record of him.

It turned out, however, that the initial review of our Headquarters database was incomplete, and the results returned to me were more than a little misleading. It was not an unusual situation, particularly where Iran was concerned. Many of the working files in Tehran Station had been destroyed in November 1979 when our Embassy was attacked and occupied. Further attempts to sort out what our relationship with Cyrus had been were complicated by the Iran Desk's inability to "secure access to this asset's former case officer to confirm certain details."

The sputtering from home base did not allow me much room to work with Cyrus. He needed immediate help, and we needed to assist him to find a path forward. We also had to determine what we could do for him, including financial support. And we had to understand what we could reasonably expect him to do for us.

At the Station's initiative, I advanced additional funds, got him into an apartment and met with him every few days to continue my debriefing. I attempted to elicit from him as much as possible. It was clear Cyrus had never been an agent per se. Rather, he had been a long-established contact of Tehran Station. He had helped us understand the details and ambitions of Iran's nuclear program. He also had been critical to our Agency's ability to prove to our policymakers that no covert nuclear program existed under the Shah and that all International Atomic Energy Agency safeguards were being followed.

As a nuclear official, he had worked openly over a dozen years with U.S. nuclear energy agencies to advance the Iranian program, cooperating on technical matters and managing bilateral nuclear research exchanges. Again, it all contributed to the Agency's ability to verify, comprehensively, that Iran was on the straight and narrow with its nuclear energy projects.

Cyrus would close our every meeting with profuse gratitude for the financial assistance and friendship I was extending him. He was certain about one thing, however. If the Agency really valued him and wanted him to work on its behalf, it was only right that his former case officer Michael would come to the city and assure him that all was right. Cyrus simply did not trust anyone but Michael. In his mind, only Michael, who knew Cyrus's family, would help him secure their freedom. "So, where is Michael?"

That was a good question, to which I could not get an acceptable answer. So, I figured out on my own who Michael was. I confirmed he had a great reputation within the Agency, was a Farsi linguist and had a solid technical background. But Michael seemed to have disappeared. I assumed he had moved on to another assignment and that others were determined to not resurface him to me—and certainly not to Cyrus.

After a couple of weeks, I received a back-channel note from a close friend and Agency classmate then stationed in another European country. He asked that I call him on a secure line as soon as possible. My colleague provided a direct explanation: Headquarters had a problem conveying to me the real story behind the Michael for whom Cyrus pined. Michael was dead, a delayed casualty of our expulsion from Tehran by the Khomeini regime and the capture of the Embassy there. Deepening the issue was the likely compromise of certain highly confidential records not adequately destroyed when the Embassy was overrun.

Michael might have blamed himself for the compromise of some records—and the rumored arrest, jailing and, in some cases, executions of certain Tehran Station assets and quasi-covert contacts. It appeared that Michael might have managed some of those assets as the responsible case officer. He had not been onsite when the Embassy was overrun, and he had not been responsible for the compromise of any Agency records, but he was one of a group of officers who took to heart the Khomeini regime roll-up of trusted Iranian friends and assets. I guessed Michael could well have concluded that Cyrus was among those who were compromised or even executed.

Cyrus Moves on to a Better Life

I decided to explain Michael's death to Cyrus, and I broke the news gently. I told him that Michael and his family had recently been in an auto accident. Michael had been killed, but his wife and children were safe. The Agency was caring for them as they transitioned. As I expected, Cyrus took the news very hard. He temporarily slipped back into depression but soon came out of it. His decision to work with us again became a closely held matter.

In the end, it all worked out. Independent of his decision to go forward with us, Cyrus deserved our assistance. We were in a position to make a payment from the escrow fund Michael had established for him many years back. Cyrus had no knowledge the account existed, and I secured a doubled-down amount that, when presented to Cyrus, brought him to tears. It was sufficient to pay for the eventual passage of his family to safety by buying their way out of Iran, plus resettlement in a comfortable apartment in the city of my posting.

Cyrus quickly found employment at the IAEA in its technical services division. There, he enjoyed good access to priority targets, including Soviets. I worked with him for the next two years. He was a valued and trusted member of our team, performing diligently within the UN agency to compel technical advances in safeguards equipment and systems, and in improved management practices. The program the Station mounted at the IAEA focused much of its intelligence collection on understanding its inner workings, good and bad. From that knowledge, the goal was to report prescriptively and do so in a manner that allowed our policy people to make the IAEA work as it was intended. Doing so often involved our mission defining IAEA's shortcomings to its senior management, who then intervened to compel corrective measures. Cyrus was part of the "make IAEA work as advertised" approach.

Cyrus also was of great value in helping us—the Station and the Agency—understand the complexities of the nuclear fuel cycle. Those complexities included the processes by which the IAEA attempted to monitor, with varying degrees of success, the progress of selected nuclear projects in suspect nations. Likewise the methodology by which the IAEA defined and refined its various safeguards. I believe that, had he chosen to do so, Cyrus could have remained right where he had landed and built a career within the IAEA, eventually elevating himself to a division leadership role there. He was that talented, determined and motivated to do all the right things.

Throughout that same period of active reporting, I worked with Cyrus to help him secure a professional engineering position with a U.S. firm in the States. He immigrated the year after I departed my assignment to reside for the balance of his and his family's life in their chosen home. In America, he established himself as a successful and highly respected nuclear professional, a faithful husband and father, and my lifelong friend.

By any measure, our meeting that cold evening in the darkened coffee house was fortuitous. The professional and personal relationship originated by that encounter gave me one of the most satisfying memories of my Agency service. Cyrus might agree with my assessment, but he is a humble man. He was satisfied he could bring his family to a new life, provide for them and pursue a successful career that gained him the recognition he deserved.

KGB Line KR — Dancing with the Bear

The posting in that unnamed city was my only tour where the opportunity to meet and mix it up with the Russians and an assortment of Eastern Bloc intelligence officers was front and center. In fact, the Russians—then the Soviets—regarded the city as their home field. At the time I interacted with that cast of characters, it still was their territory in the sense of an espionage playground. The Russians had occupied the city for 10 long years after the end of World War II, finally bowing out under international pressure. But the Soviets and their Eastern Bloc allies retained deep roots in the city and in that country, bolstered by a host of controlled agents and a local support structure second to none. There still was a tangible Cold War dark overhang in the air when I arrived in early 1980, not that too far removed from the greyness of the movie *The Third Man*.

As mentioned earlier, by Station directive and mission, our main function was to track the activities of the Soviets, mainly their two premier intelligence components, the *Komitet Gosudarstvennoy Bezopasnosti* and *Glavnoye Razvedyvatelnoye Upravlenie*, better known as the KGB and GRU. The objective was to interact with them to assess them as individuals and, if given the chance, pursue and recruit them to work for the Agency. A secondary mission was to track, pursue and recruit members of the Eastern European services, mainly the most aggressive officers among those Warsaw Pact allies of the Soviets, namely, the East Germans, the Czechs and the Poles. Since the Soviets and the East Bloc intelligence officers were tasked along those same lines, active counterintelligence or the disruption of nefarious spy activity likewise was a necessary priority for us.

From an espionage perspective, it was a wide-open city. The presence of professional and career employees from all the major nations at the international UN-related agencies headquartered there allowed ample opportunities for daily and sustained interactions. The Soviets were blatant in their placement of KGB and GRU operatives as well as career intel officers in all the international organizations, first among those being the IAEA.

The U.S. side was self-constrained by its own longstanding policies that all UN-related organizations were off-limits for placement of Agency officers. We did manage to access the professional staff at those organizations, including Soviet and East Bloc nationals employed there. We worked hard to establish and maintain contact with our targets based on a vetting process that identified the bad actors. We pursued nonintelligence career professionals of perceived or possible intelligence value—for example, nuclear specialists—as well as KGB and GRU officers dispatched as employees to those international organizations.

The Soviet and the East Bloc embassies also maintained large numbers of intel officers on their respective campuses, both to serve their own intelligence-collection programs in the city proper and maintain convenient bases of operations for activity elsewhere in Western Europe. Within the KGB *Rezidentura*—their word for Station—there was an interesting cohort, a compartmented special group; the counterintelligence element. Known as Line KR, the elite career group—at least in its own mind—had the mission of monitoring Soviet professionals, including fellow KGB and GRU officers, for any signs of disaffection.

The Line KR types were tasked to ensure each individual dispatched by the Soviet Union was loyal to the regime and behaved in a manner that suggested no vulnerability to recruitment by hostile organizations, essentially, the Americans or the British. Line KR also was alert to any inclination by fellow Soviets to defect outright or, in an even-worse-case scenario, take the initiative to work in place against the Soviet system. Such risks to the Soviet state of defection or offers to remain in place and oppose the system were real and growing. Line KR had its hands full in that city in the early 1980s, as the Cold War heated up and the failings of the Soviet system became manifest.

In such an environment, the KGB pretty much knew which American diplomats were Agency officers, some more prominently than others. In truth, the Soviets basically considered every U.S. official to be an intelligence operative. It was particularly true if a U.S. diplomat spoke passable Russian, Ukrainian, Polish, Hungarian or whatever. In my case, given the overt information about where I had served, the fact that I had some language skills and was working the IAEA circuit, persuaded the KGB types I was someone to whom they needed to pay close attention. Many of my Station colleagues had made careers out of their contacts with Soviet or East Bloc diplomats, often cultivating a dozen or more at a time. But such was not my main interest. Nevertheless, my existence and actions drew their attention, and they therefore sought me out.

Yuri Explains the Facts of Life

About a year into my posting, for whatever combination of motives, Yuri singled me out for attention, assessment and sustained engagement. His goal, I believe, was not so much recruitment but to jam me up and run interference against me as I attempted to engage other Soviets, thereby neutralizing whatever danger I might pose to the KGB or the greater communist presence in the city.

Yuri, my Line KR friendly contact, was persistent, sophisticated and more than a little arrogant. We met infrequently over the course of many months, and I am certain our extended dinner and drinking sessions were cataloged by him in some detail, as were his other, similar contacts with American and Western officials. Beyond the obvious, Yuri did not press for information about my personal life. He seemed to have no real knowledge or interest in affairs nuclear, and he generally seemed to relish explaining the historical context of Mother Russia. He was genuinely determined to convey with certainty that the Soviet Union would prevail in the ongoing Cold War with America and its allies.

Yuri was consistently adamant on two points, and he was ever frustrated that I seemed to not appreciate his take. First, the United States was not then and could never really be "Russia's true enemy," as Russia had only two "real threats," that is, existential threats to Russia's survival. Those would be Germany and China. Both nations were traditional enemies of Russia, with the Germans always warlike and inclined over the range of history to seek to dominate all lands to its east. Germany was now contained by the country's post-war division into its West and East components. While Russia (the word "Soviet" was hardly ever mentioned in our conversations) maintained iron control over the East Germans, while the Americans via NATO controlled and constrained West Germany. The message was that we needed to work together to keep things the way they were.

China shared a common border with Russia, along with a deep historical mistrust and a recent military conflict over an island in the river dividing the two nations. National boundaries technically had been settled. But in reality, there was much still in dispute and, deep in its body, China was not satisfied with the status quo. Yuri acknowledged there was a growing Russian weakness, demographically and economically, in the Siberian Far East that invited Chinese aggression and occupation. He also agreed that a day of reckoning would occur, if not soon then eventually, and China eventually would make its move to reset the borders, if not the entire relationship. Therefore, Russia had two natural enemies that, by virtue of its geopolitical location, would never go away. However it might be accomplished, Russia had to find common ground with America for its own benefit.

I must admit, Yuri's line of discussion contained a certain logic, and he had practiced it well. He seemed a genuine student of Russia's historical dilemma, even citing the Sino–Soviet war of 1929 that contested Manchuria. While he admitted the Soviet system, given its embrace of communism and its state direction, was dysfunctional and inefficient, he emphasized it was his system and he had accepted his place within it. It had given him a career, security and predictability. He had no real problems with the morality of any of it. Per Yuri, his responsibility was to find common cause with smart people like me who understood historic realities and appreciated the Soviet Union's (excuse me, Russia's) special situation. If that led to "something more" between us, so much the better. I appreciated that Yuri had to try that line with me, almost as his throwaway. Still, the discussion was interesting.

One particular evening was difficult to forget. Yuri arrived late to our dinner, fresh from a vodka-laced reception at an Eastern Bloc Embassy, well-juiced and ready to talk. We spent about four hours together, and I let him ramble on as he discussed his career and life, his plans, even his sponsors within the Soviet and KGB systems. He seemed to be trying to make the point that he had "arrived" as a member of the *nomenklatura*—the one-half-of-one percent constituting the real Russian elite. He planned to stay there through retirement and would of course do anything possible to sustain that same system. More vodka, some food and still more vodka got us deeper into the *nomenklatura* structure. I pushed him by asking how this multi-generational, essentially inherited status could be squared with any aspect of communism's championing the rights and equality of the Soviet everyman. He was dismissive and more than a little frustrated with me. The conversation continued along these lines:

> "Richard, you just don't understand. Think of it this way. Russia is a giant tree. The core of the tree, growing stronger year after year, is the *nomenklatura*. The tree only exists because of us, and it exists for us."

> "So, Yuri, we have a tree. And you and other members of this exclusive minority, the *nomenklatura*, is what, one percent of the mass of the tree? The rest of the tree is the 'underclass,' right?"

> "No, they are the bark of the tree. They only form the bark of the tree, thick or thin, and without the tree itself, they are nothing. Just the bark, Richard. And they are happy to be the bark."

I pushed back but met only determined resistance, with the vodka and beer combination taking near full control. I mentioned that the United States now had Ronald Reagan as its president, and he and his administration were determined to take on the Soviet Union in every sphere of competition, including military spending. That awakening by America under Reagan was just starting, I argued, and it would not stop until we had prevailed or the Soviet Union backed down.

Yuri did not skip a beat. "Listen to me. Our Russian, our Soviet system works, and you can see that. You do not understand. We need to work together to block both Germany and China, they will come at both of us!"

The owners closed down the bar, and we both went home, respective missions accomplished. Yuri was the worse for wear but seemed used to it. It took me a couple of days to fully recover, as I had not yet developed a fondness for complex history lessons delivered over quantities of vodka.

Thus it went with Yuri. He was an occasional distraction. I assumed he would arrive the following midmorning at his *rezidentura* Line KR Section office, his head pounding, to write a report on our extended evening session. Who knows what he wrote, what successes he claimed in our exchanges, and how he "assessed" me as a potential recruitment subject. And since I had always considered myself a charter member of the bark crowd, I really did not see any hope of migrating into the core of that Soviet tree.

A Life-Saving Shout-Out

Notwithstanding my encounters with Yuri and his Line KR friends, I am fairly certain the Russians, or at least one of the KGB's local hire citizens, saved my life. It happened as I was heading for a meeting with an IAEA contact on a winter day in wet snow. I was working my countersurveillance route to clean my trail by shaking off any of the Soviet trackers we knew were everywhere. It was not so easy. The Soviets had a string of first-rate surveillance teams deployed on the streets of the city, most of them multi-decade veterans operating in a variety of guises, deployed as mobile units in cars and on bicycles, and as streetwalkers.

On a bitterly cold day, as I entered the midpoint in a one-hour countersurveillance exercise, I had the neck of my coat buttoned against the wind. I assumed I still had coverage by one or more of their teams, although I could not discern who was there. I turned to cross a side street that my mind told me was one-way, I looked ahead to slip between the traffic flow, and stepped off the curb. A booming voice from across the street cut through the cold air with an "*Achtung! Achtung!*" that halted me midstride.

Off-balance, I spun myself back to the curb just as a massive Mercedes truck brushed past me at speed, its oversize side door mirror grazing my cheek. The man who had yelled the warning now had his head down, reversed course and scooted off down the street. I thought I detected a slight smile on his face. I had no doubt a KGB surveillance team veteran had just saved me from that truck knocking me off my feet. I had a few months left in my tour, and I had allowed myself on that snowy afternoon to relax a bit too much. That man had just assured me the remainder of my stay.

The Good Citizens of the City

For their part, the local citizens were apolitical, apathetic and mostly agnostic, at least when they were not spouting socialist solutions or lecturing Americans on all of the faults of our capitalist system. The rightwing fringe of broader political life was mostly confined to the provinces, mainly because the balance of the country tended to disrespect the residents of the capital city as disgruntled geezers.

Among the many benefits of a socialist government with open borders to the West was the ability of young people to leave, which they had been doing in droves, to seek better lives elsewhere. In the socialist economy the country's premier and his company had delivered, there were no significant employment opportunities for the generation of citizens graduating high school, and no paths for a merit-based career and prosperity in a free-enterprise environment. The result of that exodus of the young was an aging and increasingly grumpy population, mostly centered in the capital. The city elders too frequently disrespected the younger generation and had no use for children. Local restaurants often welcomed patrons' dogs to occupy floor space while banning children altogether.

In governing the country, the premier and his cabinet seemed content to allow the international players active in their capital city to do pretty much as they wished in the spy business, as long as the early-to-bed sensitivities of the populace were not disrupted too much or too often.

A great example was the Spy-vs.-Spy game then being played out in the city by the warring Iraqi and Iranian diplomatic teams ensconced in their respective embassies. There, we had ham-handed intel types accredited to those competing embassies engaged in Keystone Kop-quality excesses in and about town. As repressive and brutal as both security services were on their home turfs, they were only getting a running start in the city with their dastardly exploits. The city offered a testbed for both.

One such event occurred in late 1981 when a senior Iraqi diplomat summoned an Iraqi student enrolled in a local university to his Embassy office. A post-event reconstruction described how the student had been handed a large package with instructions to deliver said package to the front door of the Iranian Embassy at precisely noon. The Iraqi student apparently had no second thoughts in accepting the task. Notwithstanding that the two nations were at war, with tens of thousands already dead on the battlefield, the Iraqi student arrived at the Iranian Embassy a bit ahead of time and dutifully rang the bell, only to discover that the Iranians had closed their visa section early for lunch.

Showing great initiative, the Iraqi student lugged his parcel down the street to the nearest public phone booth and dialed in to tell his embassy mentor that they had a problem. Unfortunately, that phone booth was located in front of the Chinese Embassy. When the bomb detonated precisely at noon, it obliterated the phone booth and dismembered the courier in midsentence, the blast took out the front of the Chinese structure. Since the Chinese were at lunch at the time, apart from a shattered façade and much broken glass, the only real casualty was the hapless student.

In a typical sweep-it-under-the rug response, the investigation was soft-peddled, the press stories minimized and a certain Iraqi diplomat departed soon thereafter for home. Needless to say, the Chinese demanded that the phone booth be rebuilt elsewhere, and the locals accommodated the request. [NOTE 1]

The City and the Russians

To be fair to the locals, at the time I resided there in the early 1980s, the local population was still suffering from a bad case of Soviet occupation overhang, or perhaps a Russian hangover. The Russians still acted as if they ran the show, or at least posed as a first-among-equals in the foreign power presence in the city. The local inhabitants were expected to toe the line and remain respectful to the Soviet Union. It seemed that the Soviets always found a way to punish the locals when they strayed from the script handed to them by their onetime occupiers.

As an example, in 1982, the national government decided it needed to upgrade its air force by exchanging its 1950s-vintage, first-generation jet fighters for more modern aircraft. Someone leaked to the press—no doubt a Soviet asset hard at work in the government—that the Ministry of Defense was looking at four possible candidate aircraft, among them U.S. F-16 fighters. In company with the other candidate aircraft, perforce, was a Russian offering and one from the Swedish, the government previously having purchased an earlier-generation Swedish aircraft as their mainstay fighter. Rumor had it that the government was favoring either the Swede aircraft or, horror of horrors, at least for the Russians, the American F-16. The latter was then being widely adopted and deployed by NATO.

The Russians protested, loud and often, officially and unofficially. They leaned hard on the locals to make "the correct decision." They suggested that any number of bad things might happen if the Russian aircraft were not the choice. Beyond attempting to impose the aircraft on the local government, and all the political baggage attending that acquisition, the real issue was the prospect of selecting the American F-16. Needless to say, any decision by to buy those American fighters could be perceived as suggesting a pro-NATO drift on the part of that now-democratic country. Such a drift toward the West and NATO, real or perceived, implied a movement away from the Soviet Union toward neutrality, or worse. Thus, any choice other than the Soviet MiG option was anathema to the Russians.

To make sure the local political establishment got the message, on one crisp late fall morning, housewives in the city turned on their gas ranges (natural gas being the energy of choice) and got a nice blast of stinking sulfur as a wakeup call. The pungency was tangible and unavoidable. The irritated housewives held their breaths when they needed to flow the gas and complained to the city government. The situation continued for several days, with the Russian gas suppliers somehow unable to locate the entry point of the sulfur. Needless to say, the gas was Russian and the Russians controlled the pipeline into the country, as they continue to do to this day.

With the warning message sent and received—at least by the city's housewives—the problem was quickly solved. The Defense Ministry made it known the decision would be delayed. Two years later, the locals screwed up their courage and selected the Swedish Saab J35 Draken fighter–interceptor, placing an order for 24 of the refurbished aircraft from a non-NATO country, thereby accomplishing a balancing act between East and West. I watched the drama play out and wanted to report it through Agency channels. But it was all too obvious, and everything that needed to be understood about that humbled nation and Soviets was right there for the asking.

Similar dramas continued for a decade or so. The socialists eventually were deposed as demographics and attitudes changed. The nation's development would lag but later began to prosper, buoyed by the balance of Western Europe and the eventual collapse of the Soviet Union. I would not be there to witness the transition, but I knew change was coming and, slowly but surely, the rumpled and grumpy old town of my posting was about to change for the better.

Chapter 22. Nuclear Proliferation
As a Main Target
1980-1982

The Nuclear Target in the New Assignment

During the 18 months I spent at Headquarters before accepting the assignment in that unnamed European capital, I witnessed the strategic weapons-proliferation concerns evolve dramatically in Asia—including South Korea, Taiwan, China, North Korea, India and Pakistan—as well as ███████████ and Iraq in the Middle East. Nuclear-related activity had surged, and the Washington policy community finally had become alert to the proliferation challenge. By the time I arrived at the posting in January 1980, it was obvious that the nuclear target, as we loosely referred to it, likely would be the focus of my work. The situation was both a product of my experiences in Seoul, working against the Korean covert weapons development program, and the coincident reality that the performance of the International Atomic Energy Agency, headquartered in Vienna, was under increased scrutiny by our government.

My tenure in the Swiss–Austria Branch allowed me to follow many of those nuclear-related developments, both in the field, as selected nations strived to advance their respective programs, and in Washington, where our nuclear policy-makers attempted to make up for lost time. In the latter case, our intelligence and policy communities were scrambling to create the detection and enforcement mechanisms needed to restrain and redirect the ambitions of selected nations of concern. By then, however, the unbridled nuclear racehorses were out of the gate and running. For the policy folks, surprises were the norm rather than the exception, and successes were hard to come by.

Among the nuclear "have" nations, competition to export technology and systems was the rule, not proliferation management, with several countries striving to promote their respective reactor designs. Such competition, particularly among the United States, France, the United Kingdom and Canada, along with West Germany, the Soviet Union and latecomer China, was the rule. Each nation prepared to advocate its own favored nuclear powerplant and research facility solutions. Although the policy-cooperation corner was about to turn by the time I arrived in that dismal city, such a course change would be that of a plodding battleship, not a dashing frigate. There still was a lot to be done.

Following the takedown of the South Korean covert program, and the restraints imposed on the Taiwanese, it was clear the gambits of both nations had been inspired by the "Smiling Buddha" Indian nuclear weapon test in 1974. The reality was India had leveraged cooperation with eager suppliers to create, covertly, a successful program. U.S. policymakers, awakening slowly to the issue, held concerns that several other countries were harboring similar, questionable aspirations for their own nuclear efforts.

Certain reactor designs lent themselves to the production of fissile material. When coupled with the widespread dissemination of technical information related to nuclear research, and the active international promotion of atomic energy as an electricity-generation solution, the issue presented policymakers with a momentum that was hard to rein in. Finally, the realization began to sink in that nuclear weapons aspirants were satisfied with rudimentary paths to bomb capability, and they did not necessarily need to replicate the Manhattan Project as a means to their ends.

By 1980, our policymakers realized that the IAEA was destined to play an increasingly important role in managing the ambitions of the non-nuclear weapons states. But the agency was internally conflicted under its UN charter, reinforced by the provisions of the Treaty on the Non-Proliferation of Nuclear Weapons of 1970. On the one hand, the IAEA was responsible for both promoting and facilitating the adoption of nuclear energy. On the other, the agency maintained monitoring responsibility for holding individual states to compliance with their non-proliferation agreements, specifically those related to facility safeguards. Depending on an individual's position within the IAEA—and it was, to be sure, a UN bureaucracy with a life of its own—that person either was a promoter of the deployment and use of nuclear energy or, alternatively, an enforcer of limitations. In their enforcer role, IAEA managers, up to the level of the Deputy Director General, had to verify the responsible use of nuclear facilities by the member nations.

The NPT, negotiated between 1965 and 1968 through the efforts of a UN-sponsored organization, was opened for signature in 1968 and entered into force in 1970. As of this writing, 191 nations have acceded to the treaty, with only one departure: North Korea. Always a suspect participant, the DPRK had acceded in 1985, never complied by establishing a comprehensive inspection regime, and withdrew in 2013 after exploding its first nuclear device. ████████████

██

██

When crafted, the NPT defined the five existing nuclear weapons states as those countries that had built and detonated a nuclear device before 1967, namely, the United States, Russia, the United Kingdom, France and China.

Though the NPT and the IAEA are linked—the agency established in part to verify compliance with the Treaty—the IAEA is under no direct requirement to force any nation to accept inspections. Instead, the agency can verify safeguards compliance at any given facility—Treaty signatory or not—if a bilateral agreement exists between the relevant nation and a nuclear supplier such as the United States. In those cases, the IAEA can employ the bilateral nuclear agreement between itself and the supplier, with the agreement typically being facility- or activity-specific. For example, IAEA inspectors can certify the safeguards compliance at American-supplied nuclear power reactors in India under the U.S.–India nuclear agreement.

Overlaying the IAEA's bipolar mission of promoting and policing nuclear energy, there were the normal internal tensions and maneuverings characterizing all UN organizations. The interactions generated a range of controversies and compromises. For example, the self-inflicted wounds involved dramas surrounding which UN-member countries controlled which IAEA departments, divisions and laboratories. American, Russian, and European nationals all made careers of grabbing and claiming the best management positions. Apart from the dominant nuclear nations, even the nuclear aspirant nations—be they advanced with their own programs (Japan, for example) or countries just beginning to emplace programs—sought high-value positions for their nationals. Many slots were claimed by engineers and professionals determined to make the IAEA a career. The aspirants advocated their abilities to climb the agency's internal bureaucratic ladder, seeking more responsibility and the associated elevated pay and benefits.

In some cases, particularly among nationals inserted at IAEA in decision-making roles by the dominant weapons states, the goal was to secure a given position for that country. The subsequent objective was to establish extended if not permanent influence over IAEA policies. America was interested in all aspects of the IAEA mandate and sought to place its people in every component. Our government focused priority attention on two areas: the Safeguards Division and, as a parallel priority, the Technical Services Division, where power development and sustainment responsibilities resided.

Regarding safeguards, there was a creeping realization that the existence of an IAEA agreement with a given nation did not guarantee the nation would honor all of its aspects. Accession to the NPT and membership in IAEA implied a commitment to honor non-proliferation obligations, but actual compliance was voluntary, particularly where safeguards protocols were vague or still evolving. The situation was true especially whenever new facilities were being added to a nation's nuclear inventory, and the facility-specific protocols were still being negotiated. In too many instances, a safeguards agreement became only a means to an end, that end being expanded access to sensitive technology.

All too frequently, a nation eager to acquire nuclear technology considered an IAEA safeguards program a necessary evil, a compromise required to attain nuclear knowhow. Back at Langley, I had seen one example firsthand of how the pattern of reduced or limited safeguards functionality was evolving at the IAEA.

I discussed the genesis of the incident in the previous chapter from a Headquarters perspective. Some additional detail was available to me, however, once I was more directly involved on the ground and active with our reporting assets. In that case, concerning the safeguards activity at Pakistan's KANUPP reactor, it seemed unclear why the involved senior IAEA official had ignored the incident and discouraged discussion about it. Perhaps he had a political bias in favor of that country. Or, he simply he did not want to be bothered to elevate the issue within a disinterested bureaucracy. We knew certain inspectors were reluctant to report suspected anomalies at a reactor out of concern that higher-level managers did not wish to have to deal with a noncompliant situation. Moreover, each inspection situation presented its own characteristics and challenges.

Tactical issues also were in play, such as the failure of IAEA-installed and maintained surveillance equipment. At that stage of the organization's existence, the equipment was of uncertain quality and often failed, thereby depriving the inspectors of a physical record of what had occurred during their absence. A camera or inspection seal could be rendered nonfunctional, blocked or otherwise tampered with, all done in a way that assigned blame either to the equipment itself or the incompetence of the inspectors. At KANUPP, for whatever combination of reasons, failures were the norm. But the Safeguards Division was reluctant to report equipment failures, in keeping with all bureaucracies that look first to protecting their own interests in a larger organization that does not want to acknowledge its problems.

In the Pakistan case, a two- or three-person Vienna-based team was visiting the safeguarded sites on a bimonthly or quarterly schedule, but they regarded the local conditions as too demanding. Among those groups, an assignment to inspect those facilities was to be avoided if possible. In a situation where several negative factors converged, and where an inspection anomaly might exist, no one at the IAEA functional-safeguards level wanted to undertake the more intrusive inspection required to resolve the issue. Thus, the discovery of such an anomaly was not a welcomed event, and a reporting gap or disconnect developed in the safeguards-verification process. The situation created the potential for a fatal flaw in a facility of high concern, which if uncorrected could undermine the credibility of the overall program.

We had passed on our early KANUPP reporting to our State Department, with State opting to relay the information to the U.S. Mission in Vienna. At some point, someone at our Mission approached an IAEA official to explain what we suspected, and the action brought one-time results. The inspectors were shifted, and the reporting gap was closed, or should have been. The issue thereby was considered resolved. In reality, all we had managed to do was remove a one-time embarrassment.

All too obvious, that back-channel, ad-hoc arrangement had not solved the larger problem of dysfunction in the safeguards process. What we had done was compel the IAEA to fulfill its function without demanding, from a U.S.-policy standpoint, that the agency elevate its concern. The IAEA had not been compelled, objectively, to address and resolve a developing problem that should not have gone unchecked. But we—that is, both the collection and analytical sides of the CIA—realized we, on our own initiative, should take a much closer look at how the IAEA functioned. Most of our effort would focus on the safeguards area, but we also had to understand what collection opportunities might exist in the other components of the organization.

Fine-Tuning and Redirecting the Assets

If we were going to evaluate the IAEA's safeguard regime, we needed to collect sufficient information to allow our own analysts and the broader policy community to determine how well the IAEA was performing. If the agency was not functioning as chartered, if it was failing to detect and report anomalies in the nuclear programs of certain suspect nations, we should be able to report credibly on the details. At the time, I was assigned to the Station's Soviet–Eastern Europe Division, but my Chief allowed me considerable latitude to pursue proliferation targets. In part, it was because my activity on the margins of the IAEA allowed me to interact with a variety of Soviet Bloc officials. I claimed the title of Nuclear Energy Officer and ostensibly reported on the Austrian domestic nuclear program, which consisted of a single power reactor under construction. But it was enough to acquire cover for access. [NOTE 1]

Our first task was to identify all IAEA-related human sources who might be able to address the target, be they fully vetted and paid assets or simply cooperative and cleared contacts, as we called them. Then I had to place those prospective sources under either my control or shared management. That task was fairly easy. The Station had only about a half-dozen relationships that fit the category. More challenging, and valuable, was the wealth of inactive or casual contacts and validated assets who were where we needed them to be in the nuclear community and residing in the city. Most of them were not being met or, if they were being met, were not being tasked to work the nuclear target.

We also needed to understand more thoroughly the IAEA organization and how it worked; not from the SE target perspective—chasing down KGB or GRU agents—but discovering who was involved in proliferation matters. Within six months, we had a good handle on things and were planning what to do with our expanded collection of assets and contacts. We also were able to identify the gaps and could set about bringing new talent into the fold. Again, as in every Agency clandestine undertaking, the focus of new recruitment was almost exclusively on non-American, third-country nationals.

Nations of concern included the obvious would-be nuclear weapons states—North Korea, Pakistan, India, Iran and Iraq—plus some outliers picking up speed. The second-tier concerns were nations we were not sure were aspiring proliferators but definitely were on the capabilities-building side. They included South Africa, Argentina and Brazil, among others. ████████████

That lame assessment was delivered in 1980 to a disbelieving international nuclear proliferation and arms control community. The experts simply assumed the report was a U.S. whitewash ██████████████████████, which it was, at least in my opinion. Israel was not a signatory to the NPT and had no requirements to abide by any IAEA safeguards ████████ ████████████████████████████. That treaty had come into effect in 1963 and had collected 108 signatory nations, including Israel. ███████

[NOTE 2]

In our asset tasking, we looked for reporting on two different but complementary categories of protected information. First, we needed assets to collect well-sourced and detailed intelligence on evolving national nuclear capabilities; capabilities either tracked by the IAEA or unreported and undeclared to the IAEA. We tasked our assets residing in suspect countries with collecting such undeclared or suspect activity, but the efforts usually did not deliver what our analysts back home required. The fact was the IAEA employees who worked with those programs, either in Vienna or on the ground in the countries of interest, often had greater knowledge of sensitive programs than our covert collectors. Based on that reality, we needed to focus on those who could help us the most.

The laxity or indifference of IAEA people notwithstanding, we were determined to seek out and collect unreported or suspect information, both good and bad. We offered willing collectors, active in either covert or even semi-overt relationships, a secure means to communicate sensitive information to us—along with assurances we were fully capable of protecting their identities. Our well-intentioned collectors of information also knew our organization would process and disseminate the information only on a need-to-know basis. Equally important; once the analysts and policymakers received their intelligence, our protected communications channels provided them active feedback and tasking. Our officers delivered equally as much to help refine and tailor further collection. Soon, and in many cases, we produced multiple bites at the proverbial target apple, thereby narrowing and clarifying analytical and policy concerns. Our efforts accrued to the benefit of U.S. officials responsible for understanding and resolving proliferation issues by generating confidence and credibility in their work.

The Danger of Expecting Too Much from the IAEA

In a practical sense, the IAEA was not then, and is not today, up to the intelligence-collection task I have just described. It lacks a mandate to examine any activity that does not fall under a specific safeguards protocol. That includes any given bilateral agreement or a matter for which the IAEA is tasked by a separate agreement. That fact alone created a massive hole in nuclear verification. Yet the IAEA is a verification and reporting organization, with a governance structure that discourages proactive moves to investigate and challenge in areas not covered by the bilateral agreements.

To the extent the IAEA is an enforcement entity, on those rare occasions where such enforcement is directed by its Board of Governors, the strongest remedy available is a Declaration of Noncompliance. Such was the case in September 2002, when the IAEA Board declared North Korea to be in breach of its commitments after five years of failed attempts to define the nature of Pyongyang's nuclear activities. Whenever the IAEA approves a finding or declaration that a given nation is in breach of its agreements, it becomes a matter for the United Nations to resolve.

That was the situation in 1980 when I began my assignment, and it remains the case today. We had to reconcile to the fact that the IAEA was not chartered to search for or uncover undeclared activity. If an undeclared program does not involve an area covered by the safeguards program accepted by a given country, responsibility falls to some outside entity to identify the undeclared activity and press home the issue, either within the governance of the IAEA or, more publicly, by outing the suspect item.

One would think the IAEA would feel compelled to deal with a safeguards anomaly as an issue of concern. But such a case can only occur when the IAEA's leadership agrees to do so and is endorsed by the Board of Governors. The idea is such an outside-in discovery, and decloaking action would compel a safeguarded nation to declare the existence and purpose of its activity. Then, once discovered and disclosed by the IAEA, the offending country would incorporate the exposed activity into an expanded safeguards program. That is how it should have worked. Unfortunately, the IAEA's more recent history in its attempts to deal with Iran demonstrates how unrealistic the approach has proven. [NOTE 3]

Along with seeking intelligence on undeclared and suspect nuclear activities, we also collected information on the efficacy of the IAEA safeguards themselves. We wanted to know whether the inspection protocols established by given bilateral agreements actually were being followed. We pursued answers from the standpoint of the monitoring practices of the facilities involved and from the degree of transparency allowed by the countries being monitored. In short, was country "X" making verification difficult, or were the operators there cooperating with the IAEA? Also, harkening back to concerns we saw building for at least two years, what was the quality and dependability of the IAEA inspection process? We attempted to investigate that issue irrespective of the cooperation by the country being inspected or the level of transparency being achieved, We could acquire such detail only from sources directly involved in the process, either on the ground or managing personnel dispatched and charged with compiling onsite verification.

In that environment, our reporting assets did not see themselves as traitors to the organization but rather as truth-tellers attempting to compel the IAEA to work as it was chartered. We referenced that reasonable and compelling (to many) theme in recruiting and motivating each member of our clandestine reporting team.

The Osirak Strike

During the same period, dramatic nuclear events outside the IAEA's immediate control injected themselves into the mix. One of the subjects of interest in our nuclear collection efforts was the Iraqi nuclear program. At the time, Iraq had accelerated its plan to complete a world-class nuclear research center. Several IAEA member states were concerned, but to most observers the project appeared to have a long way to go before it would pose a proliferation risk. One IAEA member state did not agree and viewed the French–Iraq nuclear deal as an existential threat ██ ██ ██ ██ ██ ██ ██.

On June 7, 1981, an Israeli Air Force strike force ranged out 1,600 miles from its home base at Etzion. Eight F-16A fighter–bombers and six F-15 fighter escorts tacked down the Red Sea coast of Jordan. Using a variety of deceptions and misdirections, the planes crossed Saudi Arabia and penetrated Iraq. The F-16s delivered at least eight Mk-84, 2,000-pound penetrator bombs onto the containment structure of the larger of the two French-supplied Osirak reactors. Lasting only two minutes, the attack destroyed the facility and killed a French technician working there. Predictably, the incident triggered a firestorm of debate at UN Headquarters in New York City and at the IAEA in Vienna.

The Israeli operation, code named "Opera," had been approved after considerable debate by the Israeli Cabinet the previous October. Having failed to derail the progress of the reactor complex by other executive actions, Israeli attack-planning proceeded forthwith. When construction work neared completion at al-Tuwaitha Nuclear Center outside Baghdad, the Israeli airstrike rolled in. The attack was timed to preempt the commissioning and operation of the reactor. The timing of the attack assumed that French technicians onsite were about to introduce 72 kilograms of highly enriched uranium fuel elements into the core, an activity that would take the reactor critical.

You can find an interesting retelling of Israel's efforts to defeat the French provision of the Osirak reactor in Israel's Secret Wars: A History of Israel's Intelligence Services by Ian Black and Benny Morris. Other accounts also detail Mossad's operations in France to destroy the reactor core at the factory warehouse outside Toulon in April 1979. The covert operation came as the core component was being readied for shipment to Iraq, and that successful industrial sabotage managed to delay the program by more than a year. Also, of note is the brutal assassination program undertaken the following year in France, targeting key Iraqi scientists involved in the Osirak project.

I attended the active IAEA debate sessions that paralleled the UN Security Council debate underway in New York. On June 19, after multiple and emotional meetings, along with statements by the IAEA, Iraq and Israel, the United Nations condemned the attack with its Security Council Resolution 487, followed by a UN General Assembly resolution of condemnation in November of that year. All UN actions noted that Iraq was a party to the NPT, and that the reactor facility was under IAEA safeguards. For their part, the French perceived the attack as a direct affront to France's broader commercial and political ambitions with Iraq. The French also reasonably claimed that the design of the reactor they were in the process of delivering represented the epitome of proliferation-proof technology, only to have it leveled by Israeli duplicity.

The IAEA saw the action by a member state, namely Israel (which was then and is now still not an adherent to the NPT), as a unilateral act of aggression designed to deny another member state the ability to create a responsible nuclear research program. Not everyone saw it that way, however. Some considered the attack as a preemptive and justifiable act to deny Iraq's Saddam Hussein one critical element of nuclear weapons capability.

The companion fact was Israel's action represented an in-your-face rejection of the IAEA as a valid guarantor of a non-proliferation regime. In deciding to strike and destroy the Osirak reactor, the Israeli government essentially judged the IAEA to be incapable of preventing Iraq from using the reactor as a breeder of plutonium—an essential nuclear weapon ingredient. A related concern was Iraq's potential diversion of the reactor's 97-percent-enriched uranium fuel elements, also used in nuclear weapons—including as an ingredient in a "dirty bomb."

The fact that the Israeli government had been attempting to derail the Iraqi reactor project for years, via political approaches to France as well as outright acts of sabotage, somehow had not registered in Vienna. The Osirak attack continued to reverberate throughout the IAEA. In defense of the reactor sale, if not the IAEA itself, the French went to great lengths to explain the measures taken to protect against any illicit use of the reactor, including its design. There was general consensus within the international nuclear community that the reactor was a poor candidate for fissile materials production or diversion, with or without the benefit of the IAEA safeguards program. But the decision not to allow Iraq to initiate a nuclear research program via the pair of French reactors demonstrated that Israel was not about to risk Iraq contributing to proliferation.

Adding further fuel to the Osirak fire, with the challenge to safeguards thrown in, that same October saw the publication, in the Bulletin of Atomic Scientists, of testimony by former IAEA inspector Roger Richter before the U.S. Senate Foreign Relations Committee. Richter questioned the efficacy of the broader IAEA safeguards program in Iraq. He took the position that the more sensitive of Iraq's nuclear activities were not under safeguards. And the fact that the Osirak reactor was safeguarded was no guarantee Iraq was abiding by, or could be made to honor, the NPT based on the IAEA regime then in place. Richter's position was aggressively rebutted by U.S. experts, as well as denounced by IAEA Director General Sigvard Eklund. **[NOTE 4]**

Richter's assertions about the proliferation potential of the Osirak reactor might have been an overreach, but the other issues he raised were valid. I agreed with his point that the existence of safeguards on a selected set of facilities in a given country—in this case, Iraq—did not guarantee an undeclared and undetected covert program could not complement and access materials provided by a safeguarded facility. IAEA safeguards on one element of a national program did not ensure that other, next-door, unsafeguarded activities would not be blended into declared facilities to defeat the non-proliferation regime. I would witness the same dynamic many times in my future encounters with other suspect nations. In situations where we knew undeclared proliferation activity existed, we typically would hear the refrain, "Well, they are under IAEA safeguards, right?" The answer was, "Yes, but…" Over 40 years later, that lame approach remains the reality.

Safeguard Issues: Pakistan's KANUPP Reactor

Returning to IAEA's safeguards mission and the Station's attention to the efficacy of same, there was an established collection issue already with us when I arrived at my posting. It involved the Pakistan heavy-water power reactor and the country's broader national nuclear research program. The activity increased in importance during the summer of 1980 and would remain a U.S. policy concern, and therefore an agency collection target, for many years to come. Also in 1980, the Pakistani government was some six years down the road in attempting to proliferate by building a nuclear weapon. That decision was made in May 1974 in the immediate aftermath of the first Indian nuclear bomb detonation. The commitment to build a strategic capability had not been a hard one to make. Nor was it difficult to predict from the intelligence or policy sides of the equation.

Pakistan's effort to initiate a nuclear weapons program, coincident with a similar decision in South Korea, was abetted by the fact that Islamabad previously had committed, as early as 1960, to acquire as a national strategic priority a complete nuclear cycle and power-generation program. Several years before, the country had created the Pakistan Atomic Energy Commission for that purpose. The effort had enabled the nation to grow a small cadre of trained engineers through international cooperative programs, most substantially from the America's Atoms for Peace initiative.

America trained many future Pakistani atomic scientists in Illinois at AR-GONAUT, the Argonne Nuclear Assembly for University Training, administered by the University of Chicago. Some years before, the United States had established the facility to assist foreign engineers and researchers. Those newly minted operators returned home to staff the Atomic Energy and Nuclear Research Institute, where they in turn would instruct the next generation of Pakistani scientists. At the time, the country's nuclear leadership also began to focus on specific technologies and systems considered the core components of the overall nuclear program.

The details of Pakistan's nuclear weapons development program are well-described in Feroz Hassan Khan's "Eating Grass: The Making of the Pakistani Bomb." His account was published in 2012 as an element of Stanford University's Security Studies program. Khan's reconstruction, on pages 121-123, of the critical decision to proceed with a dedicated weapons program relates the June 15, 1974, session of the Defense Committee of the Cabinet, called some two months after the Indian test.

That meeting featured then-Prime Minister Z. A. Bhutto's comment, "The explosion has introduced a qualitative change in the situation between the two countries. Pakistan will not succumb to nuclear blackmail." And, as Khan's article notes:

> This gathering was the first formal institutional meeting to conclude that the only viable option for Pakistan was to develop a nuclear deterrent capability. From that point onward the nuclear program had officially shifted from merely acquiring a nuclear capability to decisively pursuing weapons.

As mentioned, an early PAEC priority was procurement of a heavy-water-moderated reactor, ideally one similar to or derived from the Argonne National Laboratory's then-operating Chicago Pile-5, a descendant of the first reactor at the facility built for the Manhattan Project in the 1940s. A companion priority was to construct a range of associated research facilities and fuel-manufacturing laboratories. The Pakistanis approached the U.S. government in an effort to secure those capabilities, but the United States demurred. Instead, we had offered and delivered a modest, pool-type research reactor that offered no power-generation capability and little opportunity for fuel-related activity. The deal was done under a U.S.–Pakistan bilateral nuclear cooperation agreement, concluded in 1957, that referenced U.S. assistance in both the research and power-generation sectors.

During the ensuing decade, the Pakistani nuclear community remained focused on its critical technology and hardware needs, particularly the quest for a power-generating reactor. Such a purchase ideally would be scaled for both electricity generation and plutonium production. But the domestic political turmoil, economic hardship and sustained regional instability made progress difficult. In that same period, Pakistani leadership remained fixated on India as their existential threat and regional competitor in all sectors. The rivalry and mutual distrust compelled Pakistan to compete with every aspect of India's growing power, including the ardent embrace of all things nuclear.

India had signed a host of bilateral agreements, purchased nuclear reactors and developed a broad research program. Among their acquisitions was the 40-megawatt (thermal) Canada India Utility Research Service reactor, usually referred to as CIRUS, a relatively large, heavy-water-moderated research reactor using natural uranium fuel. Obtained from Canada, the poorly safeguarded, plutonium-producing mothership eventually would generate the feedstock for India's first nuclear explosive test in 1974. CIRUS would allow India to establish a completely domestic fuel cycle for fissile-material production.

The Pakistani program had picked up momentum and direction back in 1962. At that point, the country already had defined its requirement for nuclear power-generation through third-party studies and consultancies, and it received the blessing from the IAEA to introduce such facilities. In 1965, negotiations with Canada delivered a deal for an HWM power reactor, the Canadian Deuterium-type 137-megawatt reactor. Construction of that first-generation, CANDU-type, natural-uranium-fueled reactor began in 1967 at a site near Karachi.

The Canadians provided a loan for the KANUPP, as the reactor project was called, but because of the reactor's unique proliferation potential, on that occasion Canada insisted on an extensive safeguards agreement monitored by the IAEA. After some back-and-forth on the issue (the Indian CIRUS had minimal safeguards), Pakistan agreed, and the KANUPP project went forward. By 1981, KANUPP had been generating power for a decade. As Pakistan's nuclear research capabilities matured, in company with its covert research, the KANUPP reactor's potential as an instrument of nuclear proliferation increased, IAEA safeguards notwithstanding. That particular HWM and natural-uranium-fueled reactor allowed fuel bundles to be inserted, irradiated and extracted without requiring a shutdown. And its operation could be manipulated to produce high-quality plutonium. In such a scenario, the KANUPP spent-fuel bundle, possibly undeclared for IAEA inventory purposes, could be chemically processed to separate the plutonium.

On a TDY back at Headquarters, I mulled over the situation with my colleagues, and our Intelligence Directorate analysts explained the situation so I could best organize our Station's clandestine reporting. The cold reality was our assets would have to track the IAEA's efforts to account for and monitor the movement of the fuel bundles, and IAEA inspectors had to account for the entire process. That meant from the point the fuel bundles were manufactured to where they were introduced into, irradiated in and extracted from the active reactor. Likewise, the bundles had to be tracked to where they were stored and inventoried. If Pakistan had "extra bundles" beyond those declared for accounting purposes, they needed to be detected as well. It was a challenge.

Our overriding concern was the KANUPP operators would find a way to move unreported or undeclared fuel bundles into the reactor, irradiate them there and then covertly remove them and relocate them away from the facility for use as feedstock in an undeclared reprocessing facility. At that point, we could not confirm Pakistan's leadership had decided to embark on a nuclear weapons development program. But concluding as much was a fair bet, and the plutonium route seemed the most logical path. The KANUPP reactor was the logical candidate as a ready-to-serve source for irradiated fuel capable of being diverted clandestinely. We knew Pakistan was then working very hard to acquire the capabilities needed to proceed along that fuel cycle path. **[NOTE 5]**

The IAEA safeguards instrumentation in place at KANUPP were, unfortunately, a first-generation combination of still cameras and video, and metal seals designed to detect, even post-event, unreported fuel movements and diversions, among other illicit activities. The instruments lent themselves to outright failure (camera malfunction), view blockage (intentional or not, requiring on-the-spot assessments) and failed coverage due to placement, along with routine or non-routine reactor-maintenance activities. It was the best the IAEA had to work with at the time, and those systems probably were adequate in other safeguards situations where diversion of materials was not a serious concern. In the case of KANUPP, however, it always was a struggle, even when illicit activity was not suspect.

The initial issue with KANUPP's safeguards, and the IAEA's struggle to monitor activity there properly, mainly involved instrument failures. It included failures detected at the site by the dispatched IAEA team, or the reluctance of the team to report the instrument-failure instances accurately. For example, if the onsite team found cameras blocked for extended periods of time (Reactor operators could claim platforms that had been temporarily positioned for routine maintenance, which coincidentally blocked the camera's view of critical reactor ports, were unavoidable.) they had to judge if a reportable action had occurred. In several cases, we learned of inspectors avoiding confrontations at the reactor site by simply not reporting an event that should have been documented, not to mention clarified with the operators.

Our assets within the IAEA allowed us to understand the specific nature of the events at KANUPP and the logic involved in ignoring or not completely reporting the occurrences. They also reported on post-inspection decisions made at higher IAEA levels, either to marginalize the importance of possible violations or simply bury bad news within the bureaucracy. In those instances, the issue was more of IAEA credibility than actual Pakistani-initiated events that might or might not have involved illicit activity. The problem was the inspectors' inclinations to avoid confrontations onsite, and then finesse their reporting back home in Vienna, created a situation where one would not know if, in fact, violations had occurred. Such incidents pointed a finger at possible diversions underway at KANUPP. But absent specific anomalies being reported, such indications could not be woven into the whole of the IAEA verification program.

KANUPP — The Tunnel

Beyond IAEA monitoring at the reactor itself, a possible diversion event had been detected by inspectors beginning in 1981. It occurred at an away-from-reactor location that might have been a critical element of a fuel-element diversion and movement scheme at KANUPP. The issue arose when an inspector noticed a freshly plastered-over and repainted area in the wall of the tunnel used to move fuel elements into and out of the reactor building. The existence of an auxiliary access tunnel—an area not covered by IAEA surveillance cameras—for covert fuel movement, if confirmed, would be a strong indicator that undeclared fuel was being secretly cycled into the reactor and removed as part of a well-orchestrated diversion scheme. When the inspectors asked reactor managers about the painted-over area, the explanation was not convincing: water leakage required routine wall-patching. Maybe; maybe not.

Once again, we had a problem with the discovery not being fully pursued by the inspection team, at least when it initially was detected. The inspectors and their managers in Vienna were reluctant to report it. In contrast, our clandestine reporting, in considerable detail, allowed the U.S. Mission to approach IAEA senior management informally to express concern that an activity that should have been reported might have been overlooked. At a minimum, we needed the IAEA to report the situation internally and instruct the safeguards team preparing to depart for Pakistan to examine the tunnel issue in more detail.

A related question suggested itself: How long had the recurring patch in the tunnel wall existed, and what were the implications? Had it been the situation for months or even years of reactor operations? The answer was, "who knows," mainly because safeguards teams and managers often were rotated among different inspection assignments, with the result that institutional knowledge tended to evaporate. For that reason, we never were able to determine how long the indicator had existed, nor were we ever able to determine if a concealed connection or an offshoot tunnel, which would have allowed an undetected diversion, existed.

Back home at Langley, our analysts, and their counterparts at the Department of Energy, concluded preliminarily that we had no way of assessing if a well-managed diversion program was in operation at KANUPP. Their assessment referenced numerous safeguards challenges posed by the type of the reactor itself, the quality of the safeguards program active there and, most important, Pakistani intent. We did know in 1981 that Pakistan had decided to build a nuclear device at least six years earlier, and the country also acquired a reprocessing plant, a top priority for many years. But KANUPP seemed the center stage for a covert program. It was then the only possible source of irradiated fuel that could be used to produce plutonium. Because we reasonably judged KANUPP was *the* suspect site critical to any plutonium-based weapons program, we gave the facility priority attention. **[NOTE 6]**

While we attempted to track Pakistan's nuclear developments from a third-country perspective, from the IAEA's perspective the KANUPP issue was straightforward. The Pakistani nuclear effort was capable of producing the uranium and fuel elements required for an undeclared program, and the reprocessing plant at Chashma was active and able to handle undeclared, irradiated-fuel elements from KANUPP. Beyond U.S. concerns over Pakistan's progress in rivaling the Indian program, and the geopolitical dynamic surrounding that competition, we had before us the standing issue of IAEA credibility. If KANUPP already was, or about to become, part of Pakistan's quest to build a nuclear weapon, if it occurred that the IAEA safeguards program there (as a condition of the reactor having been sold by the Canadians) had failed, and that failure had gone undetected and unreported, the IAEA would suffer a serious blow to its credibility.

Other Nuclear Targets Worthy of Attention

In the early 1980s, we had plenty of nuclear nations with undeclared but suspect ambitions to watch and report on, and we attempted to do so via a combination of overt and covert mechanisms. Among nuclear states with serious and maturing nuclear research programs underway, we judged those capable of evolving weapons programs-were Argentina, Brazil, South Africa, South Korea, North Korea, Taiwan, Iraq and Iran. Using our IAEA assets, we could work those targets within certain operational parameters to learn more about each nation's programs and intentions.

One example, Argentina, might suffice. That advanced middle-power nation had begun its nuclear research activities under the dictatorship of Juan Peron in the early 1950s. By my time, the program had delivered a substantial research community, complete with multiple research reactors and an expanding nuclear power program. The latter was anchored by the Atucha I 335-megawatt, pressurized-heavy-water reactor delivered by Siemens of Germany in 1974. The reactor, the first in all of Latin America, would be the first of many for Argentina's ambitious program. The construction of a follow-on sister plant, Atucha 2 (692 MW) had begun in 1981, with commissioning scheduled for later that decade. Also, the Canadian-supplied Embalse CANDU-type power reactor (648 MW) was scheduled to begin operation in 1983 with more of the same type of reactors in the negotiating pipeline. Sisters of the CANDUs in South Korea at Wolsung, the Argentine reactors utilized natural uranium. They were dependent on supplies of heavy water for nuclear reaction moderation and were under IAEA safeguards.

In addition, Argentina's nuclear community maintained an active program to share technology and knowhow with other middle-power nations and soon would become an exporter of nuclear technologies in its own right. The nation aspired to sell Argentine-designed and manufactured research reactors to developing nations eager to start their own programs. It aimed to establish itself as a leader among second-generation nuclear nations.

Argentina also had compiled a record of skirting international convention by interacting with a variety of suspect nations, often on a personal or professional level, or in laboratory or facility-level engagements. An early example was Argentina's sale to Israel of 90 tons of unsafeguarded uranium yellowcake in the early 1960s. ██

██

████████████████████████████████ Last, it was clear that Argentina desired to play in all aspects of the nuclear fuel cycle, including uranium enrichment. It was a path with little rationale, given the fact that the country's reactor program was centered, at that time and until today, on electric power technology that did not utilize enriched uranium fuel.

During my Station posting from 1980 to 1982, we were able to direct certain assets to collect information on the enrichment-ambition issue, given that such research could be undertaken as an undeclared activity. Our clandestine reporting describing uranium enrichment research just getting underway at the semi-remote location near Pilcaniyeu in Rio Negro Province. Supported by the research center at Bariloche, it previewed the Argentine effort. But our initial reporting lacked detail, and our Headquarters analysts, confident they knew all, reacted accordingly. Their inclination to disbelieve was conveyed to the reporting cadre at home that graded our homework in the field. Our Reports folks, in their gatekeeping role, accepted the judgment with the predictable result that Station follow-up was discouraged. The conveyed attitude was, "We know the Argentines are not doing anything of that kind, and certainly not at that location, mainly because they do not have to." We did not accept the assessment because we already had seen the movie—in my case about six years before, in Seoul. [NOTE 7]

The Argentine target was a second-tier priority, however, in company with others such as Brazil (also then embarked on its own covert program). But our primary nuclear targets continued to receive dedicated Station attention. We expanded coverage to include North Korea—to the limited extent the IAEA had access to that country—as well as the usual suspects of South Korea, Taiwan and South Africa, and we watched for any opportunity to access the Iranian and Iraqi programs. We were able, slowly but surely, to expand our reporting asset base, and we discovered new avenues to secure protected information. When I departed that unnamed city in the summer of 1982 for a new posting in East Asia, the Station's overall collection program targeted on nuclear proliferation was in good shape and getting better by the month. I handed my account off to a capable officer, and he took to the proliferation target like a duck to water.

Chapter 23. The China Connection
1981-1982

Activating 'Inactive' Assets

The Station at my unnamed city posting had its peculiarities, both within the overall Agency construct and the Station's particular priorities as instructed by the Directorate of Operations. Those tailored priorities impacted me personally as I adjusted to them and found my place. An outsider hailing from East Asia Division, my choice was to be initially assigned to the Soviet–Eastern Europe Division rather than to a smaller group working Asian targets. The close-knit SE team was populated mostly by career officers. Within the Station, joining that team was considered the place to be for the real action. As the junior officer and a non-SE new arrival, I was tasked to manage an eclectic collection of assets who, together, constituted what we called the operations support team.

In many cases, the team comprised elderly individuals who had served the Station and the DO for several decades, at varying levels of risk. But they always served with dedication and enthusiasm. They were trusted as couriers, mail drops, safe-house keepers and, infrequently, surveillance or countersurveillance operatives. In many instances, they were elderly widows who had lost their husbands to Agency activities, frequently a decade or two before, and often in broken or compromised operations in Eastern Europe. Because most if not all of those now-low-level-but-still-active support agents were natives of various Eastern European countries, they brought us their invaluable language skills.

Their skills, in turn, provided an on-call capability when needed for document translation. Plus, the multicultural understanding gave us the ability to interpret dialects of Hungarian, Czech, German, Bulgarian, Romanian and Russian describing any local situation. Just as important, the agents were dedicated anti-communists and hardcore anti-Russians, and therefore intensely loyal to the Agency and to the United States. The Agency reciprocated and treated them well, often paying what amounted to a generous monthly pension in their retirement years.

I will describe more about those mostly elderly gentlemen and ladies later. Within the larger cohort of local personalities resided a much more interesting subgroup, loosely identified as inactive assets. For one reason or another, they had been retired from active service or put on the back burner by the Station. They were individuals with whom operational contact had been formally terminated or abruptly dropped. In many instances, they had lost their entrée to targeted individuals or institutions. Nevertheless, they remained out there in the city, waiting for that call from the Station in the night; fully recruited, longstanding and ready to go.

Others in the inactive category were trusted and cooperating individuals who had agreed to work with the Agency, or with individual case officers, often based on personal friendships in a less-formal relationship. Now deactivated or inactive, the assets typically had served as discrete sources of information. Or, they had provided introductions to target Soviets or Eastern Europeans in the city's diplomatic community. In almost all cases, they remained under the radar within the Station. Within that category, most of our case officers were unaware of their existence or simply uninterested in reactivating them.

About two months into my assignment, once my daily routine with agents and my target contact and developmental tasks fell into place, I searched for and eventually discovered the depository where the file records of that eclectic collection of inactive players resided. Reading those files gave me a good feeling for the 40-year history of the Station. The documents profiled some of the more colorful officers and agents who had played on that stage. Scanning through the records, and triaging the deceased and those physically departed (from the city, in any case), I found several individuals of potential interest.

Two of the top candidates were a man-and-wife team whose Agency affiliation was textbook serendipity. The agent couple turned out to be nothing less than golden. Their information contributed substantially to our understanding of a closely held, third-party, bilateral national security relationship capable of negatively impacting the United States. It was a nascent and then-still-evolving secret partnership between Israel and the People's Republic of China. In that case, we were able to confirm and profile the military technology-transfer channel established by the former to the benefit of both China and Israel, and to the net deficit of the United States and its Allies.

Because that covert military technology relationship benefited the military capabilities of China, it seemed apparent then, and it does now, that the exchange delivered real damage to America, Israel's main supporter. The information we secured through the Station's relationship with the agent couple initially was disbelieved and discredited by Headquarters. It certainly was unwelcome there by many in positions of authority. The negative reaction to my work, and the lack of support extended by the Station itself, became a source of personal and professional frustration for me.

In fact, other intelligence successes during my brief Agency career notwithstanding, that one was a sobering experience, and it colored my attitudes toward the inner workings of certain elements of the Agency. It also opened my eyes to the greater Middle East conundrum and the objectivity compromised by the bespoke strategic partnership between America and Israel. In that regard, the year 1981 found me uninitiated in the complex American–Israeli relationship, where all actions appeared to be driven by the principle of Israeli self-interest and willful U.S. government accommodation to same.

Helmut and Marta

Given the situation I have just described, one story is worth relating in its entirety. It is of use for no other reason than the lesson it taught me, as well as others in the clandestine reporting chain; namely, do not bring home unwelcome information that complicates the policy process. Do not disrupt policy presumptions, even if you walk in the front door with the truth. In that particular case, the truth was out there, found and reported. Unfortunately, the facts when presented confronted other players in the greater scheme of things with uncomfortable realities. It became a matter of truth discovered and truth discarded.

The main actors in the story are now departed from this world and have no offspring who would be endangered by my relating the tale. Sometime in the late 1960s, Helmut—then serving in the office of his nation's Trade Commissioner in Hong Kong—approached a U.S. diplomat also serving there at the U.S. Consulate and asked to be introduced to a CIA officer. After the Station and the East Asia Division vetted his background, Helmut was accommodated some weeks later with a discreet meeting. In a dinner conversation, Helmut provided his assessment of the new world order, the situation with which America was attempting to cope as it confronted communism's march on the world. He described the extended and heavy-handed Soviet occupation of his native country.

The Russians had departed from their occupation of the city of my Station with great reluctance in 1955, but their influence remained as Mother Russia attempted to sustain its control over Eastern Europe. He volunteered to assist in the CIA fight against communism in any way reasonably possible. In essence, Helmut was a classic walk-in for the Station and the Agency. As the scion of a prominent local family, he asked nothing in return for his cooperation—the agreed main target would be China—other than to be considered one of the Station's team.

It turned out that Helmut was an established China hand within his government, including tours with the diplomatic and trade ministries. He also had a fair command of Mandarin and a good understanding of the ways of the Chinese. Over the ensuing years in Asia, he acted with considerable enthusiasm as what we called a spotter to identify and assess Chinese and other Asian target personalities. Then, back in his home city and out of government service, he established his own firm and engaged in private trade development with a focus on China and Northeast Asia.

Helmut and his wife Marta had worked with the Station on a North Korean target operating out of Pyongyang's embassy and trade mission. The North Koreans, reluctant to engage anywhere with American and other Western diplomats, self-isolated in their embassy but found the ostensibly neutral citizens and the relatively free commercial environment in the city of my posting useful to their purposes. It happened that Marta was proactive with the North Koreans, often taking the lead in pursuing relationships.

As established local businesspeople with experience in Asia, the couple was able to approach North Koreans and interact commercially with them, to the extent their stilted business practices allowed. Naturally, our Station valued such interaction. By the mid-1970s, Helmut and Marta had visited Pyongyang several times and occasionally gained the trust of selected North Korean diplomats over the years. That said, the North Koreans were distant, unpredictable and too frequently went into a shutdown mode. They typically suspended all dialog and contact outside the embassy, apparently to clean their own house.

We knew those random purges were dictated by Pyongyang. In such instances, the North Koreans would sever ties with local contacts for seemingly obtuse reasons. It had happened with Helmut and Marta a couple of years before, around 1978, resulting in a lapse of Station contact with the couple. Helmut then was consigned to the Station's inactive asset file. Nevertheless, I wanted to see if anything had changed with their contacts overall, starting with the North Koreans. I also needed to satisfy my personal curiosity by sitting with them to fill in some blank spaces in what appeared to be a fascinating life story. I activated the mutually agreed contact plan from some years back, allowed them to vet my presence at the Embassy and met them for a quiet dinner a week later in the city center.

Recontacted, I found Helmut and Marta full of life and most willing to engage with me and, by extension, the Station. Marta was nearly a generation younger than Helmut. She had escaped from Croatia as a young professional, fled to Vienna and there met and married Helmut, a confirmed bachelor. Then in his 50s, Helmut was the face of their small trading company, and Marta was the business lead and manager. Interesting, as it happened their North Korean contacts had recently reactivated themselves with an outreach to the couple, who were planning a trip to Pyongyang. All of this was good news for us, and they recommitted that evening to work covertly again with the Agency. They agreed to let me know when their trip was confirmed, and I would turn them over to our Station's North Korea referent.

That first evening, I got Helmut to open up a bit about his life story, something which revealed a great deal about his motivation. As a young man of draft age, and as the oldest son of a prominent local family with generations of affiliation to the Hapsburg Empire, he had become a junior officer in an elite unit of the German Army, a regiment to which he referred, perhaps an informal *nom de guerre* designation, as the Hoche Deutschmeister—loosely translated, the "Grand Teutonic Master." In that unit, he had fought for years on the Eastern Front against the Soviet Union's Red Army. But mid-1944 found him in Italy in combat with the Americans, as the Allies battled their way up the western side of the peninsula.

In the Monte Casino area, where some of the most brutal fighting occurred, his unit had been decimated by the U.S. Army. Most had been killed in action, and he was badly wounded and left for dead on the battlefield in the German retreat. Found unconscious by the American forces, he awoke several days later in an American field hospital, where Army surgeons put his shattered legs and arms back into place and begun the reconstruction of his battered jaw. Over the next several months, and after Germany's surrender in May 1945, Helmut remained a patient in U.S. military hospitals. Still in American care and undergoing several more surgeries, he slowly recovered alongside badly wounded American GIs. To his amazement, he found he was always treated with care and compassion by his former enemy.

Eventually discharged with a slight limp and a partially paralyzed arm, Helmut returned home in 1947 to rebuild his life. He explained that he never forgot the men who discovered him, cared for him and repaired him. He would carry that debt of gratitude for the balance of his life. As I discovered, Marta had not heard the details of that story before and, when Helmut completed his account, she was so moved she left the table for Helmut and me to sit alone.

The Israeli Connection Revealed

Some weeks later, not having heard from Helmut, I recontacted him to arrange a meeting. He was quite solemn. He invited me to his country home for an extended Saturday afternoon lunch and asked that I come alone. In his garden, he confided that he and Marta would not be going to Pyongyang after all. A recent checkup had revealed cancer. It was fast-moving and of a variety that required immediate treatment. He also told me he had not yet revealed the extent of his affliction to Marta, and he needed someone to talk to outside the family. He expected he would have less than a year to live. As it turned out, he barely had six months.

Over a meal of bratwurst and beer, Helmut explained that over the past two years he had played a central role in establishing a certain covert relationship. He was continuing to play an indirect role and had become troubled by it. He felt compelled to share the information with the U.S. government. He overviewed the activity as follows:

In mid-1979, he had been contacted by an Israeli businessman I will call Shaul. The Israeli who reached out to Helmut was reactivating a friendship that had originated in Helmut's tour of government duty in Hong Kong and China. Shaul explained he had secured the Israeli government's highest-level approval to establish a secret channel of information exchange and commerce. That channel would be keyed to Israeli military technology and with the Chinese defense and armaments industry. Certain contacts already had been made by others working for Shaul, but the Israeli business group now needed to establish the mechanics of the actual Chinese cash-for-Israeli-technology exchange.

In truth, it was an exchange initiated by the Israelis of U.S.-developed-and-owned military technology, with certain weapons often improved by an overlay of Israeli competence and deployed as operational systems in Israel. At its most basic level, the effort involved the sale of U.S.-protected defense knowhow that Tel Aviv had acquired as a consequence of the ongoing U.S.–Israel strategic relationship. At the time, as now, America faced a hostile China. Any reasonable observer could assume U.S. disapproval of any Israeli transfer of U.S.-protected-and-derived military technology.

It is fair to say, and at the time I reasonably presumed, that the transfer of sensitive U.S. military technology to China by any third party, particularly an ostensibly friendly nation, would have been to the net security deficit of the United States. In fact, in 1980, a military technology-transfer relationship between China and Israel was unthinkable from the American side, for both national security and political considerations. Had the relationship been overt, or if such a covert relationship had been proposed to U.S. government, the latter would have vetoed such a gambit out of hand. Or, so I assumed.

Helmut was asked to travel to China with Shaul to assist the Israeli side in activating such a channel, complete with an Austrian trade initiative as the cover story. Helmut agreed. Over the ensuing months, the covert Israeli–Chinese relationship fell into place. It was agreed that Helmut, based on his citizenship and the location of his company in the city of my posting, would serve as the registered agent and conduit for certain activities. It also helped that Helmut maintained deep relationships within his nation's government and knew its bureaucrats and their bureaucracy. In a sense, Helmut and his firm were a near-perfect cut-out to provide the commercial cover Shaul's organization, and the Chinese needed to conceal their protected military technology-related discussions. As needed, Helmut's locally registered firm also could facilitate the actual deals struck for selected systems, and the underlying sensitive technologies, to be sold to the Chinese.

Helmut established such a special-purpose firm, becoming the third-country facilitator for the arrangement, with Shaul and his company managing the Israeli side of the equation. On the Chinese side, the partnership involved a Chinese Ministry of Defense entity or, more correctly, a People's Liberation Army-affiliated entity. Within a few years, the organization would evolve into the Commission for Science, Technology and Industry for National Defense, or COSTIND. Various PLA-controlled front companies were involved, such as Polytechnic and Galaxy, all staffed by active-duty and retired PLA officers and civilian technicians. The latter were seconded from Chinese government-controlled engineering institutions responsible for reverse-engineering selected foreign weapons systems for domestic production. Once the underlying technology was secured, the PLA organization would serve as a funneling mechanism, allocating the acquired technology to the Chinese military research institutes best positioned to digest and extract maximum use of that technology. [NOTE 1]

Because Shaul's operation was, in effect, a government-to-government covert program—or, at a minimum, an Israeli government-authorized and coordinated activity—the mechanics of the working exchange required discrete movement to and from China on the part of the Israeli team. A key discretion was protection of the channel from knowledge by the U.S. government, then the source of much of the now-Israeli-controlled technology.

The covert movement of sensitive U.S.-origin military technology from

Israel to China was facilitated by Shaul-owned Boeing 707 passenger aircraft. Two such aircraft alternated missions, flying from Israel and staged west-to-east through several countries to deliver Israeli technologists, data and systems into the hands of the Chinese. Shaul's 707s entered Chinese airspace via a predesignated route only partially declared in advance to regional aviation authorities. The aircraft then were directed by Chinese air controllers, according to a predesignated plan, to land at a Chinese military-controlled airfield near Beijing.

The two 707s, reconditioned and serviced by Israel Aircraft Industries, were registered in Austria by Helmut and ostensibly under the lease control and management of his company. As such, the aircraft received third-country civilian designators. That is, they received country-specific tail numbers and call signs. The aircrafts' cover identities were used throughout the initial years of the secret arrangement to mask the identity of the real owners and hide the use to which they were being put.

All of the activity of course represented, at least to my knowledge, a base violation on the part of the Israelis of the conditions under which the United States had transferred the original technology or provided the individual weapons systems, complete with the technical data packages. That level of data allowed Israeli weapons firms to service the systems or, as was usually the case, engineer them for production in Israel under license.

When Helmut revealed the information, I was surprised by his unique insight into the covert program, and I recognized he had fulfilled a function that could not have been replicated by the Israelis themselves. In a sense, Helmut, as a respected and established third-country businessman, was uniquely positioned to form the company and register the aircraft as well as facilitate the initial contact on the ground in China to get the covert technology-transfer ball rolling.

Helmut explained the below-the-radar activities to me in late 1981, by which time it had been ongoing for at least two years, with several flights made and more planned. It struck me as totally believable, in that the scheme had brought Shaul, a clever and skilled opportunist, into play as the central protagonist. I knew he was well-connected in both China and Israel, sporting no less than five passports for ease of movement internationally. I had watched him and his team perform in South Korea a few years before, with a number of high-profile transactions that delivered substandard facilities from Western European countries. The ill-starred Canadian CANDU reactor deal was still being unpeeled like an onion by Canadian Parliament's graft investigation committee when I departed Seoul in the summer of 1978. Shaul was squarely in the middle of that one as well—the overall fixer and organizer of the payoffs.

Once Helmut began producing documents and detailed information to back up his assertions, there was no doubt about the magnitude of the duplicity then afoot. At least, it seemed that way to me. Over the next couple of meetings with Helmut, I collected more information, and he proved to be an excellent source. He knew several, although not all, of the weapons systems and technologies the Israelis had sold and therefore compromised to the Chinese military. They included the Israeli advanced Python 3 air-to-air missile system similar to the U.S. Sidewinder. Likewise, field artillery systems, artillery ammunition designs and tank fire-control systems. All were current-generation Israeli military technology, and most were on par or near-par with the latest versions in the U.S. military inventory.

By any yardstick, the transactions involved protected national security technology, at least in consideration of the relationship with the United States and our ongoing confrontation with China. Moreover, from the details provided by Helmut, it appeared Shaul's group, acting as the permanent liaison between the various Israeli technology and weapons providers, was settling in for a long-term stay in Beijing. Helmut had assisted in opening an office there to facilitate the expanding flow of experts, technologies and knowhow into China.

It obviously was not a one-off deal. With Shaul's group's Beijing office in place and the deal flow regularized, Helmut no longer was required to act as critical facilitator. He pronounced himself happy to be mostly out of the process. By late 1981, when he reported those events to me, his role was limited to maintaining the 707 aircraft registrations in his home country. But Helmut's locally registered firm remained a front for Shaul's covert China operation, and Helmut retained some level of knowledge, related mostly to the aircraft movements.

That said, Helmut's level of information was impressive. The details included the technologies already passed to China, the identification of the aircraft, the dates and routings of the missions flown and the identities of many of the individuals involved, including the names and passport details of the pilots. I was strongly motivated to compile and complete a report as quickly as possible for Headquarters. I did so, assuming it would be considered important information and received as such. I was to be deeply disappointed.

Unwanted Intelligence Dutifully Reported

My initial report, sent as a normal intel draft, was accompanied by a lengthy explanation about how the material was sourced. It apparently landed with a giant thud back at Langley. In separate operational channels, I chronicled my renewed relationship with Helmut and therefore assumed the report would find its proper path in the system.

Given the detail involved, I also assumed the information would be disseminated as a final intel report to the analyst community. And, given the gravity of what was being reported, I thought the policy community would welcome or at least acknowledge what it implied. It also was reasonable to expect that both the intelligence community analysts and the policymakers would be asking for more, and I tasked Helmut to collect more as aggressively as possible.

The initial feedback received at our Station was vague and confusing. It certainly was not encouraging. The report was graded as an "I," or "one," in the internal Directorate of Operations feedback process, a grade that suggested it was of mild interest at best. My initial reaction was it must have been old news to our China and Middle East teams, and therefore we had this Israeli–Chinese covert channel well-covered by other assets. My second read of the response, though, proved that was not what was being suggested. Putting it bluntly, they did not want to hear what I was conveying, and I was therefore nonplused.

I tried again, next compiling a hard copy that provided extensive detail on aircraft registrations, flight routes, call signs, personnel information (copies of pilot passports, etc.) and other details of the Israel–China arrangement. I sent it via diplomatic pouch, given its content and attachments. The reaction was the same: limited interest and no onward dissemination. It appeared that my second try had not even been shared inhouse with our Directorate of Intelligence analysts. The Station management shrugged it off. To me, however, something did not feel right.

Some weeks later, I was invited to return via TDY to Headquarters for meetings on a collection of operational developments, with the suggestion I would be able to discuss the Israel–China reporting issue. In the meantime, the message was, "don't waste your time."

Back at Headquarters, the China Reports team, with whom I maintained a passing relationship and some level of mutual trust, delicately explained my reporting did not reside in their bailiwick—as much as it could have or should have. Rather, my reporting on that delicate issue was being managed by the counterintelligence staff of the DO, where all matters relating to Israel were directed and managed. I found my way to their offices, and to the folks responsible for handling (grading or distributing or, as in this case, not distributing) my recent reporting. I was greeted coldly and dismissively.

Beyond the original report, I attempted to discuss the hard copy, or pouched, reporting, namely, the log books, flight plans, call signs and identities of the Israelis—all of which described the initial two flights into China. I referenced the collection of Shaul's commercial operatives and the pilots, plus the summaries of individual weapons systems and technologies the Israeli side was in the process of selling to the Chinese military research establishments. My effort was to no avail. The CI staff people simply were not interested in the details and did all possible to discourage any further reporting.

Prying an explanation out of CI was a real challenge, and the reasons offered for their lack of interest were lame. First, from the standpoint of the Israeli desk, the reporting was not credible because it was "farfetched" and "probably would be discounted anyway." Supporting that negative opinion was a consideration ostensibly provided by East Asia Division's China Reports team. They based their explanation on China recently allowing the Palestine Liberation Organization to open a Beijing office. The Chinese leadership had decided—so the reasoning of our crack analysts went—to take a "bold step" to enter into the warren of Middle East diplomacy. Therefore, China would never risk its budding relationship with the Arab world, including China's engagement with the Palestinians, by maintaining a covert relationship with Israel. They told me this with straight faces. The term "lame" no longer covered this, and I did not respond.

Thus, our East Asia China team had found common cause with the

Israeli-compromised CI group. My reporting did not comport with the consensus narrative and its inclination to find no fault with their Israeli brethren. They were not willing to disseminate into the broader analytical community, not to mention the policy community, such "unsubstantiated" and "single-source" reporting certain to cast aspersions on Israel. I was confounded by that logic, which I saw as a combination of *naïveté* (being generous to the DO China Reports team) in face of the clear bias of the CI staff. That staff, for whatever reasons, remained determined to ignore the reporting and discourage follow-on coverage.

As mentioned earlier, my initial reaction was the only logical explanation could be that the CI staff, the Agency writ large, the intelligence community or perhaps the entire Reagan administration at the higher policy levels, already knew of the activities. If so, perhaps they had blessed or at least acquiesced to them. But if that were the case, I could have discerned it from the various interactions with trusted colleagues at Headquarters over the next several days. Instead, reliable friends on the East Asia side who had extensive knowledge of the China target confirmed my suspicions. They admitted the Agency knew almost nothing about the Israel–China relationship. And, according to my colleagues, we had no hint of Israeli covert dealings involving the transfer of our military technology to our Cold War nemesis.

Several more senior friends at Headquarters cautioned me to, "just let it go." I soon came to accept, as my friends suggested I should, that no one in the greater Agency chain of command would protect my back. It was particularly so, given that I was a career "EA body" now assigned to a different division in the field, in a Station that was tepid at best in defending its officers. Moreover, current Station management likewise was indifferent to the thrust of my reporting. I was attempting to reveal covert activities of a protected U.S. relationship (Israel) aggressively managed within the Agency and our Directorate by CI staff. The fact that I was trying to do so with well-sourced and documented information that reflected negatively on our Israeli partners was unwelcome. **[NOTE 2]**

It was my first real experience with the CI staff and the lasting Israeli imprint of its former infamous leader, James Jesus Angleton, of whom much has been written and even more speculated. Without here addressing his obsessive support of Israel, and the depressing record of his counterspy paranoia, the extended damage the man delivered to the Agency was remarkable. It was difficult to measure the negative influence his CI staff had on the balance of the DO and the Agency writ large, but my personal appreciation was Angleton's demons endured after his forced departure.

During my time with the organization, I encountered several good and honorable men whose careers were ruined or heavily damaged by Angleton, all for no good reason. Much more damaging was his unquestioning and systemic support of Israel, even when such support conflicted with the national security priorities of the United States. Although Angleton had resigned on Christmas 1974, his deep impact persisted, and Israel's embrace of the CI staff continued to prevail, even under new leadership within the Agency. Many have suggested that Angleton was *the* most important asset, from a strategic covert action perspective, possessed by the state of Israel. I do not believe the magnitude of his betrayal of U.S. strategic interests has surfaced, and I doubt it ever will. **[NOTE 3]**

Four years later, in 1986, in a private meeting with then-Director William J. Casey, as we discussed various Israeli operations in the Middle East, he confided to me that, "Beginning with Angleton, they always get their way with us. They own us in many ways. They will be here in this office later today, and I can't fight that with my own people."

In a Headquarters corridor back in the spring of 1982, when I was attempting to defend my reporting, Angleton was long gone. But the CI staff remained atop the Israel–Agency channel, and the ghost of Angleton retained a desk in the cubicles of that staff. The painful truth was there was no way my reporting—or any other similar reporting—would be disseminated or encouraged.

The game was over and the lesson learned. During my TDY, I worked on my other projects at Headquarters and returned to my Station. A few months later, Helmut experienced a relapse of his cancer and passed away in summer 1982, shortly after I departed his city to accept a new assignment in an East Asia location. During the final months of my tour, I spent several Saturday afternoons with him and Marta, typically at their cottage on a small farm outside the city. Those extended sessions allowed me to reinforce our appreciation for his service over the years. Needless to say, I never hinted that his most recent contributions to our understanding were not well received by my Agency and by my government. He had served the United States to the best of his ability and had repaid his debt to the Americans who had dug him out of the rubble of Monte Casino, and to the Army doctors who had given him back his life.

Chapter 24. Hard Targets and Best Efforts
1981-1982

Scrapyard Treasures

Jakub was another of the Station's reactivated support agents, but a better definition of that committed young man might have been "redirected and reenergized." Jakub had fled the stifling communism of Eastern Europe for the freedom of the Western European city of my posting. He hated the communists, depreciated the Soviets and sought any reasonable assignment we could hand him. If a single word could describe Jakub, that word would be "enthusiastic."

Jakub had volunteered his services a couple of years earlier. Though vetted by polygraph, he was disappointed he had not yet been assigned a mission. I inherited him—rather, I volunteered to inherit him—after I read his file. Following our first meeting, we got down to figuring out what he *could* do for us and the cause he embraced; that is, anti-communism and the defeat of the Soviet Union. We attempted a few operations that directed him to engage and develop relationships with Third World targets milling about in the city, efforts that yielded mixed results. Of course, we ran him through some traps to test his judgment and trustworthiness. All to the good.

At some point, an item of unfinished raw intelligence crossed my desk pointing to a possible way for Jakub to wade into battle. It appeared that a group of enterprising Russian businessmen, who were well-connected to corrupt bureaucrats in the Soviet government, were enjoying a splendid business shipping specialty metal scrap into the country of my posting for recycling. Responding to demands from the Russian military establishment, the Soviet defense manufacturing sector was able to make the specialty metals and forge or cast them into components vital to their defense program. But the Soviet fabricators often were not skilled in working the raw metal, and their defense sector did not place a high priority on waste prevention, given the nature of the system. Moreover, when components were miscast or ruined in the production process, they had no ability to melt them down the damaged components and then separate the more valuable metals to be recycled and reused.

It was a typical Russian industrial policy disconnect. The same country that was series-producing the SS-20 family of ballistic missiles was somehow unable in 1981 to master the manufacture of ballpoint pens. Because their system had no real cost controls, the waste of critical materials was rampant, if not the acceptable norm. Soviet Bloc Eastern European countries typically benefited from that grossly inefficient practice when scrap materials were discarded by Russian military manufacturers. In this single case, a facility in Western Europe might benefit from such defense industry-related scrap shipments.

That intelligence collection lead was potentially significant. Among the exported specialty scrap, there conceivably could be spoiled castings or forgings from the Russian nuclear submarine program. Deep in the depths of the Cold War, the Soviet Navy's nuclear sub fleet, both attack boats and the massive, nuclear missile-armed boomers of Tom Clancy's The Hunt for Red October fame, were impressive machines of war. The attack submarine component of the force probably represented the Soviet Union's highest priority for development, series-production and deployment within their overall strategic nuclear forces program. Attempting to overmatch and outnumber the U.S. submarine fleet, the Soviets devoted an incredible effort to building the most capable nuclear-powered attack boats.

The Soviet submarine program required high-precision, high-performance cast and formed metal components to resist the enormous pressures experienced by the hulls of the deep-diving subs. In addition, the strength required for the increasingly complex nuclear reactors deployed inside those latest-generation submarine hulls drove the Soviets to explore advanced designs and materials. In the case I am describing, the scrap in which we were interested was not old or retired material but brand-new forgings and welded components that might well represent the latest combination of system designs, metals employed and assembly processes. [NOTE 1]

Working with Headquarters analysts who were attempting to connect the dots, we hypothesized a few things.

- Soviet submarine scrap components apparently were discarded into a poorly monitored recycling system and then sold through a cadre of middlemen traders. The destination of the scrap was undetermined but ostensibly limited to Mother Russia proper, for obvious security reasons.
- A covert commercial arrangement existed between a group of senior Russian bureaucrats responsible for managing the disposal of the high-value military scrap. They arranged for final destinations inside the Soviet Union and its Warsaw Pact allies.
- Some of the high-value scrap sales seemingly found their way outside the Soviet bloc, where higher prices and therefore higher profits could be attained. One such road led to a local businessman who owned a metals facility that routinely purchased and reprocessed the spoiled Soviet-origin components. That company would buy the scrap at reduced prices offered by the Russian middlemen, accept shipment at the nearby scrapyard, and then extract and resell the valuable metals in the West.

Under that slightly irregular arrangement, which apparently had been in place for many years, everyone involved profited, with the obvious exception of the Soviet state. The Russian bureaucrats who had cooked up the scheme made out like bandits, with kickback payments from the middlemen and receiving parties.

Shipments of the sensitive components were undeclared, muddled in the Russian accounting and tracking system. Somehow, the potentially valuable "scrap" managed to find its way, unaccounted for, to a location where it seemed we just might have access.

Given such a corrupted chain-of-possession, there was an outside chance that, among the specialty metal scrap crossing the border by railcar, one could identify and obtain castings and partially worked components from the Soviet nuclear submarine construction program. Secured clandestinely and subject to detailed analysis, the materials conceivably could be of significant value to the U.S. intelligence community. It was particularly true because our analysts were desperate for any and all information about the Soviet sub program. It appeared, at least to the analysts with whom I spoke, that our efforts along those lines could well benefit from the acquisition of the scrap materials.

As soon as we developed an action plan and moved ahead with it, we succeeded within a matter of weeks. A well-worn, nondescript industrial facility, tucked away in a farming area outside a small nearby town, became our target. We would send Jakub to take a closer look. He would do so by hanging out in the village to establish social contact with those working inside the plant. It was a serendipitous choice because Jakub was familiar with the village. Oddly and coincidentally, a good number of the facility's employees were fellow Czechs operating as guest laborers. They were trucked in weekly from across the border and sent home on the weekends. A few of them, on temporary hire at the facility, were from Jakub's home area back in the former Czechoslovakia.

For the record, the Scrapyard Project, as it became known, was begun due to my initiative, from beginning to end—for better or for worse. The fact was my SE Branch Chief had only mild interest in such out-of-the-box initiatives, particularly one like this, which admittedly was a longshot. But at least he was an advocate, and he supported my approach to the target.

Initially, things went well. Jakub spent long weekends in the village building a mini-database on the layout of the plant, the routine of railcar deliveries from the East, and the personalities of the facility's workers and managers. I regarded it as a multi-month process, initially building an operational picture then selectively recruiting one or more worker assets inside the plant, followed by scoping out the weekend guard force. Only then would we develop an informed operational plan for securing covert access to the facility.

We needed to be able to identify and extract selected items from the metals-reduction process. Ideally, the process would proceed during off-work hours in the facility itself, absent detection. We wanted the operation to sustain itself over a prolonged period. Our man Jakub seemed to understand our needs and goals, and by the second month his information permitted us to expand our understanding of the plant and how it functioned.

By month three, we were beginning to narrow to a selection of potential access agents, but we had not yet pitched or recruited any for the program. Likewise, the target watchman, a local villager with a heavy appetite for wurst and strong drink, was a recruitment candidate, but we agreed he would require some effort. He was important because he guarded the front gate on the weekends and was the only one inside the fence during that period. Best-laid plans.

A Surprise in the Night

One Sunday night around midnight, a special-alert message reached me at home, delivered via a third-party support agent, also known as a communications cut-out. The alert code identified Jakub as the initiator of the call. His message triggered an emergency meeting one hour later in a prearranged side street in the city center. I arrived to find a scene that was one-part horror and three parts comedy, with the comedy component wearing off quickly.

Jakub stood proudly beaming in front of a three-ton, canvas-covered truck. The truck was an obviously worse-for-wear vehicle, laboring under its load. I immediately grew concerned. The bench seat of the truck held two large men with nearly identical smiles. Jakub and his boys had delivered a "special present" just for me.

After we got past the, "What in the hell is this, and who in the hell are these guys?" phase, Jakub led me to the back of the vehicle. It seemed he and whom he called his two "fourth cousins" had had a great day at the plant. They arrived Sunday morning to engage and drink the watchman under the table by noon, after which they cased the facility. They managed to confirm that the new load in from the East was piled at the rail siding ready for the smelter. Jakub then made an executive decision that, with all the elements of his plan lining up, it was time to move into the action phase.

His two so-called relatives had borrowed a local truck, run it in the gate and parked it alongside the scrap pile. They then spent two hours picking through the scrap and tossing or manhandling the pieces they thought most interesting into the truck. Jakub assured me that the guard was deep asleep and snoring throughout the crashing of metal. According to my scrap-recovery A-Team, everything was *keine sorgen*; that is, "no worries."

The boys then drove out the gate, carefully padlocking it behind them, and headed down the road to the city. I later learned that all of this was accomplished in full view of an adjacent retirees' home. The residents apparently scrambled to line up their folding chairs on the front lawn for a ringside seat to watch the unusual Sunday activity in the scrapyard. Sometimes, you just can't make things up.

Back at our early Monday morning rendezvous, set in what had to be the quietest neighborhood in the city, I stood there with my man Jakub, his relatives and a fully loaded truck. I phoned the Station support chief and said, "I need help now. I need the back gate of the building opened, the rear delivery door ready to roll up and the Marine Guard force alerted to a 'big delivery' as soon as possible." "Big Brad," as he preferred to be called, did not skip a beat. "Okay. Check your watch. Roll through the gate in exactly 30 minutes. Out, here."

Brad had been a Special Forces medic back in Vietnam. In the thick of that fight, he had lost his hearing. I thought somehow he had been waiting for just my sort of a call in the middle of the night ever since he traded his SF kit for the Agency. Once employed by us, he had devoted years to the Agency's clandestine program in Laos, supporting Vang Pao's guerrilla operations there. Years later, he found himself in this sleepy city, angling the system to head back to Asia, where the action really was, at least for him. When our truck rolled up to the rear of the building, Brad was there to supervise. We unloaded in less than an hour and sent the boys on their way.

The following morning, after three hours of sleep, I made my way into work a bit late, around nine or so. There, I found our Station Chief standing in front of the *sanctum sanctorum* vault, the most secure inner space in the entire building. He was not happy. Our Deputy Chief, the esteemed "Three-to-five Marv," had failed to brief him about the night's events, probably because risk-adverse Marv knew almost nothing of the operation and, in any event, had been disinterested when we tried to brief him. The Chief had been caught unawares, and that was not a good thing. Now, he was not a happy camper, given that the vault, his special area, was packed with chunks of twisted scrap metal that seemingly had been beamed into the building overnight. His opening demand was, "And so where did all this shit come from?"

I explained we did not know exactly what we had. Some of it could be of potential value, because it all seemed to be of Soviet origin and military-related. One large item was an intact, if slightly damaged, weapons pod with wires protruding. Its model and serial numbers were clear. The pod obviously was newly built and had crashed somewhere on a Soviet test range. Other items were less distinct, but there was plenty to work with. Our support chief had it all photographed, inventoried, crated and shipped out to home base within two days. Out of sight, out of mind, and our Chief got his special space back. But he still was not pleased by the entire affair, and I did not blame him.

As it turned out, some of the piece parts were of value—the weapons pod, for example, was from the newest version of the Soviet attack helicopter—but most of it was not. Our experts determined that the Russians seemed to be flying a lot of new aircraft into the ground, and as they carted the aircraft pieces off the test range, the scrap quickly found its way onto a train for a ride to our scrap facility.

The bad part was the Station obviously had a blown operation on its hands. In truth, *I* had blown it. I was responsible for conceiving the approach and drafting and implementing the plan. And it was my agent—young Jakub—who had jumped the gun with his cousins and rolled a three-ton truck through the main gate of the plant, beginning a journey that would end up at the back door of our Embassy.

We had no choice but to shut down the operation. We did a damage assessment as part of the Station's post mortem. In the end, because it was a longshot to begin with, and because the initiative had attracted only limited visibility on the Headquarters side—in fact, a near-total lack of interest—the blowback on me was minimal. It helped that the facility owners apparently never noticed the midday theft of a small quantity of bent steel, so there seemed to be no repercussions at the plant. A month later, the same front-gate watchman was still sleeping the weekends away. We decided to send Jakub on a three-month vacation to another European station where he was targeted against some suspicious Czechs. We added a red flag in his file: "Warning: A highly motivated asset who remains a work in progress."

The Defecting Code Clerk Who Just 'Walked In'

In Agency or DO parlance, a walk-in literally is any foreigner who shows up at the front door of a U.S. facility overseas, typically the local Embassy, offering either to work for the U.S. government covertly or to request asylum. In certain situations, such individuals decide to do this on the fly, as in, "I find myself broke today with nowhere to go, so I'll show up at the U.S. Embassy and tell them I want to defect." In that category, individuals might have something substantial to offer but end up approaching us almost on a lark, having no idea what they want or knowing they want something (cash, shelter, emigration to America) but having nothing to offer in exchange.

Alternatively, we could receive, as an unexpected arrival, an individual who has carefully planned his approach, knows exactly what he desires to achieve— say, a new life in America for his family. Such a man knows what he needs to bring to the defection equation to make sure he gets what he wants.

The front-door screening process for such individuals is well-established and well-drilled, from the U.S. Marine guard who typically is the walk-in's first point of contact, through the State Department officer who conducts the initial interview, to the agency officer who then takes over the discussion. The last step occurs only if the initial interview determines that the foreign arrival is legitimate and can bring something of value. By its nature, it always is something of a hit-or-miss process. The individual might appear to be of value, or claim access to protected information, but then fail to reinforce his or her approach with classified documents.

The factors must be sorted out as quickly as possible and the decisions made promptly. The State visa section officer before whom the would-be defector is brought, or the Embassy duty officer making the initial assessment, almost always gets it right. The Embassy security officer, a State Department career Security Division employee, interacts with his Marine security guard component throughout the evaluation process, all in keeping with the Embassy walk-in management plan.

In rare cases, the Marine guard at the first point of encounter senses real value and immediately contacts the Station, passing along whatever identification he has been able to obtain from the walk-in. He then electronically screens the individual for physical security reasons and then moves the interviewee into a secure room. There, that person stays until traced through local and Headquarters data banks. In multiple locations where I served, I sat across a table from a walk-in a few times, usually only in cases where the individual claimed initially or was later assessed to have access to sensitive nuclear, WMD or military technology. It was particularly true in cases where we had a possible lead to denied-area target countries.

A key point here is often missed by careerists—at both State and the Agency—who dismiss or disdain the walk-in element as probable comprising posers or, worse, the so-called provocateur element. They too-often denigrate or dismiss out-of-hand those arrivals. But it is crucial that the broader diplomatic and foreign communities serving in a third country believe that the U.S. Embassy is a venue where they can present themselves for defection or an offer of cooperation and, in making such an offer, get a fair hearing.

At some point in a foreign national's career, particularly if that individual can provide something of value to the United States, the person must believe that, if he decides to approach us, he will receive an objective hearing and his identity will be protected in that risky process. If an individual considering defection to the United States has any doubt about approaching us only to be summarily turned away, he will not take that chance. In sum, he must have convinced himself we would welcome and protect him. **[NOTE 2]**

In the city of my posting in the fall of 1981, all was not quiet on the defector front. The Station found itself acting as a waypoint for the secure movement of defectors from a number of Soviet Bloc countries. As a result, the Agency was processing, as potential defectors, a combination of defense industry technicians, scientists and high-level political dissidents, with the occasional high-value intelligence officer injected into the mix. Both branch chiefs under whom I served at that location, as career SE officers, were exceptional managers in complex situations, and I came to respect them for their abilities. The fact that my first supervisor did not embrace intelligence reporting was almost beside the point in a defector-rich environment. Working around such attitudes became second nature, and we all came out well in the end.

The fact that the city was host for various UN entities, with a nonstop stream of international conferences, meant we received more than our share of walk-ins who wanted to see what might be available to them. That is, what could they obtain if they elected to cooperate by returning to their home organizations and reporting back to us covertly? A related concern, which we had to assume was an ever-present disruptive threat, involved agent-provocateur operations mounted by Soviet counterintelligence agencies, both the local KGB and GRU. Similar false-defector provocation initiatives also were in the game plan of the more active Soviet Bloc services. In such cases, the ostensible defectors, or offers of assistance by walk-ins who claimed unique access, were designed to tie up our resources and time, as well as disclose the identity of our own officers. If the Soviets were fortunate, they might have been able to place a false or double-agent into our system. The opposition was very good at such efforts.

What we had not seen in the city, at least in recent Station memory, was the crown jewel of defectors: a code clerk from a hard-target nation. That category of defector was without a doubt the most protected and highest-value acquisition a field Station could encounter.

As duty officer one fine October day, I received a cryptic call from the Marine guard on duty. The sun was not yet up, so I knew it probably was important. "Sir, I think you better get here fast." Initially worried that another three-ton truck had arrived at the building's gate with a load of scrap, but discounting the possibility once I recalled where we had stashed Jakub, I focused on the defector option. It seemed more logical than a walk-in, given it was the middle of the night and whoever was there was probably serious in his purpose. If it were a drunk or a troublemaker, the Marines would have brought in the local police.

Our defector was planted in the security containment area in the lobby, safe behind the Embassy's doors, with three Marines standing guard, weapons held safe. I found a well-dressed young man, his wife along and scared to death but well-groomed. They spoke halting English but had rehearsed their lines, with a written script to boot. If the man was the real McCoy and not an agent-provocateur, he would be the Keeper of the Keys; that is, the signals intelligence officer of one the best intelligence services in the world. He held a list of the information he was prepared to convey along with a bag of codebooks and the highest security files from the local adversary Station where he worked—or had worked until three hours before.

His request was direct. He required immediate protected asylum for himself and his wife, plus expedited relocation and resettlement to the United States. He also wanted a cash bonus to begin a new life and a contract for 10 years of work as a consultant to the Agency. The husband–wife team—and they were indeed a team, having together planned every aspect of the defection down to the last detail—were impressive and very believable. They even presented a list of the candidate small towns in America where they dreamed of being resettled. In terms of credibility, we still had to validate that the man and wife were whom they said they were.

For operational purposes, we had to assume they were legitimate defectors. As such, they were in immediate danger. Their former colleagues most probably were already on the streets of the city looking for them and would focus on the U.S. Embassy. The magnitude of the loss to that intelligence service was almost unmeasurable. We were legitimately concerned it was a recapture or shoot-on-sight situation.

In a routine that had been crafted, fine-tuned and drilled into the Station and our branch by the officer I will call Larry, we scrambled and assembled our defector-management group as quickly as possible. Within an hour of the couple's arrival at the Embassy front gate, we had moved them to a protected location. Other officers, including those fluent in the native language of the would-be defectors, rolled in to the protected location, as did extra Station security and support officers, and Station wives possessing the security clearances needed to join the mix. The female officers and wives bonded with the code clerk's wife.

In a sense, it was a once-in-a-tour opportunity, one for which our Station people lived. The reception and management of a hard-target, security service defector was the pinnacle event, and our outstanding branch chief had trained us well. The defector was repositioned, protected and debriefed sufficiently to satisfy our initial impression his was a legitimate, high-quality defection. He and his wife were covertly spirited out of the country and safe-havened in the vastness of the United States in temporary quarters within a week. Back in the city, that Eastern Bloc service from which our man had defected was devastated—at least, its local operation—and the entire intelligence staff soon was recalled home. We assumed it would take two or more years for them to rebuild their operations in-country. [NOTE 3]

Although a true operational coup for the Station, such defections were not unusual in the depth of the Cold War that was 1981. On that and several other occasions during the period, our Station got it right. Every man and woman who defected to the United States, in many cases diplomats and professionals who enjoyed elite status in their countries, served as testimony to the inherent rot of the Soviet system and foretold the system's coming collapse. We did not have to wait long.

Double-Agent Man

No recounting of my tour in that city, and our adversaries there, would be complete without a tale of double-agent doing. Shortly after my arrival, I was assigned to pick up an operation that featured a Yugoslav clandestine source who had been on the Agency payroll for several years. He was fairly young and had walked into our Embassy to volunteer his services, claiming direct access to his government's security and military activity.

Although Yugoslavia was not a member of the Warsaw Pact, and had distanced itself from Moscow under the leadership of President-for-Life Josef Tito, we nevertheless considered that nation a valid collection target. It was positioned squarely in Central Europe and was inherently unstable, given the mix of mutually antagonistic ethnic groups cobbled together to create the state after World War II. Moreover, Tito and his henchmen were wheeler-dealers, and we suspected Yugoslavia to be involved with several bad-acting nations, including Communist China, on any number of initiatives.

We met the Yugoslav asset—call him Marko the Serb—every few weeks in safe locations outside the city. When his case was turned over to me, I selected several venues in Italy for our debriefing sessions. He was incredibly punctual and always arrived bearing a good quantity of information, some of which was merely Belgrade hearsay, but some nuggets appeared to be of high interest. Marko had been vetted by the Directorate in a crosschecking process. We were certain we was whom he claimed to be. He probably enjoyed the access he asserted was his, and his lie-detector sessions showed no signs of deception. We paid him in cash and referenced no ideological motivation for his work. He just wanted to build his bankroll and eventually bail out of Yugoslavia for a new life in the West.

Yet, something about Marko was just not right. He was confident to the point of being arrogant—he seemed almost indifferent to being caught by the UBDA, the Yugoslav national security apparatus. Too often, he was quick to tell me what his "really important information is this time." We blinked hard when, during a meeting in Milan, he tried to sell us what he claimed was Tito's top-secret plan to purchase and install a new fleet of Chinese surface-to-surface missiles. He even brought a map complete with pinpoint locations of the underground silos that would house the new systems. It was beyond the believable and was not borne out by other information.

We determined that Marko was either a flat-out fabricator or an active double-agent being run by his home service against the Agency. A deeper crosscheck with other sources revealed the latter. He was, in fact, a double-agent dispatched by his own intelligence service to feed us disinformation. The information he provided was designed to emphasize that Tito was in full control in Belgrade, and his amalgamated state was a force with which the United States had to reckon.

We devised a plan to confirm our suspicions, and I set my meeting with him in Rome. That Station would support me and the security officers present, including one of our top polygraph operators. Dewey Clarridge, my former supervisor in the Western Europe Division, was now Chief of Station in Rome and was all over the mini-confrontation we had planned with Marko. We began by conducting a two-day engagement, the first with a surprise polygraph session that lasted five hours, to be followed by the normal debriefing meeting scheduled for the following day. After that first day, we congratulated him for again passing the test with flying colors—for which he had the gall to ask for a special cash bonus—and set the meeting for the following day at a separate location.

On day two we surprised him with a second polygraph, in a carefully arranged meeting with the machine and its operator that nailed him on a host of falsehoods. The encounter convinced us he had been an agent-provocateur from the day he was sent to the city to find us. We did not reveal we had him cold, only suggesting we had developed some uncertainties about his motivation. Of course, we assured him that his flow of secret information was pure gold. I explained that, in order to protect him from his own internal spy-catching service, we were electing temporarily to put him "on ice." We would suspend operations for an extended period and then recontact him. It was for his own safety.

Marko protested aggressively, far too much for such a clever man. I gave him a big hug and sent him into the night to catch the next train to Belgrade. We then proceeded to put out an Agency-wide and NATO-wide burn notice that identified our Marko in his various cover identities as a fabricator and provocateur in the employ of the Yugoslav intelligence service. We did not hear from him again, and I suspect he was retired by his home service with a mixed record.

As things turned out, the Yugoslavia that Marko served would soon be history. Tito passed away in 1990, and Yugoslavia then shattered itself into a half-dozen violently feuding pieces. As the component nations began their systematic ethnic cleansing, their long-dormant genocidal tendencies carried the day. I am sure Marko found his proper place somewhere in that horrid mix.

Chapter 25. Retrospective and Recognition
1982

Transfer to a New Assignment
and Departure from Europe

In mid-spring, an interesting opportunity presented itself that would take me back to East Asia and provide a great tour in a great city. I was asked to return to Headquarters for a meeting with Jim, the man slated to soon rotate out to what would soon become my next posting city in Asia as the incoming Station Chief there. In a no-nonsense, make-your-decision-today session, Jim laid out his plan to reorganize "his Station" and for my involvement there. He wished to move quickly to adapt its collection and reporting program to what he perceived as the revised priorities of the East Asia Division and the Agency. China loomed larger on the horizon and deserved more attention.

The Soviet intelligence presence in that Asian country seemed manageable, and the North Korean target there was worth a greater effort. It was particularly so given that the new posting he proposed would offer one of the only points of sustained access to that closed regime. Another issue deserving special effort was high technology and industrial development, including the country's nuclear program. I accepted the offer on the spot and planned for a July direct transfer to my new assignment. Going home to the East Asia Division and working on the ground in the new city was a dream assignment. That development would lead to other trajectories I could not have imagined at the time.

Recognition at Headquarters

The previous chapters dealing with my 30-month tour at the European station provide highlights of much of what occurred during that period—but not all. I have omitted certain operational activities in this narrative for a number of reasons, including source-and-method protection. Over the next two years, during my service in the Asian city, my European work was recognized when I was twice awarded one of the Agency's highest decorations for service in the field, the Intelligence Medal of Merit.

The award ceremonies occurred when I was in the Headquarters Building during TDY visits and were organized in a manner that allowed me to involve my close associates. I was particularly gratified by the presence of the man who, so very early in my career, had gained sufficient confidence in my potential to accelerate my assignment to Seoul Station. I had served there with Don Gregg, and he had become in every sense of the word my mentor. He generously found the time in his busy schedule both to attend award events and speak there. Don Gregg was then serving as the National Security Advisor to Vice President George H.W. Bush, and in 1989 he would be nominated to serve as the U.S. Ambassador to the Republic of Korea by then-President Bush.

The first IMM was presented to me by then-Deputy Director John McMahon on July 21, 1982, and references obliquely the nuclear reporting effort in Vienna. The citation reads:

> *In recognition of his especially meritorious service with the Central Intelligence Agency from May 1980 through May 1982. An extremely talented and gifted Operations Officer, his highly successful and skillful clandestine collection efforts were instrumental in providing information of considerable value to the United States Government. Mr. Lawless' exceptional initiative and extraordinary accomplishment are indeed worthy of commendation and honor. His sound judgement, outstanding dedication to duty and exemplary perseverance opened up new avenues of intelligence capabilities, justly earning the respect and admiration of superiors, colleagues and subordinates alike. Mr. Lawless' superior performance and commitment to excellence contributed significantly to the mission of the Central Intelligence Agency, reflecting great credit on himself and the Federal service.*

In a sense, the award recognized the breadth of my work in the nuclear proliferation field, from the period of the South Korean nuclear weapons program from 1974 through 1978, my attention to this broader target during my Headquarters tour from 1978 through yearend 1979, and the work accomplished in the European assignment during the 1980-1982 period. My nuclear effort in Seoul had been earlier recognized by a special commendation, and we had sought and secured recognition there for others involved in that reporting and nuclear program takedown. Yet the full impact of that effort in South Korea was not acknowledged by policymakers and Agency senior management until after I had departed that scene. The above IMM covered it all nicely.

The second IMM was presented to me by Director William J. Casey on April 26, 1984, and references special activity that is not described in my forgoing narrative concerning the European tour. That citation reads:

> *In recognition of his especially meritorious service with the Central Intelligence Agency from June 1981 through June 1982. A superbly capable Operations Officer, his professionalism, zeal and uncommon resourcefulness enabled him to provide intelligence on a major area of concern to our national policymakers. Mr. Lawless' sophisticated performance and distinguished conduct during this period reflect the highest traditions of the Operations Directorate and constitute a major achievement for the Unit-*

ed States Government. His excellent judgement and sound mastery of his craft have justly earned the respect and admiration of all those with whom he is associated. Mr. Lawless' exceptional accomplishment and selfless devotion to duty contributed significantly to the mission of the Central Intelligence Agency, reflecting great credit on himself and the Federal service.

The Agency's Directorate of Operations was, if nothing else, a merit-based institution. The DO routinely rewarded its officers with promotions in grade that, in turn, provided ample openings for greater operational responsibility. At the time I parted company with the Agency in early 1987, I had been promoted eight times in 15 years. The two Intelligence Medals of Merit were deeply appreciated, but the opportunity offered to me by the Agency to serve the nation was the source of the immense satisfaction I felt.

Chapter 18

- **NOTE 1 - See page 249**

  The best book on the entire Project Azorian operation, from both a technical and operational perspective, is <u>Project Azorian: The CIA and Raising of the K-129</u>, by Norman Polmar and Michael White, published by the Naval Institute Press in 2010. White also produced a fine documentary film "Azorian: The Raising of the K-129," released in 2009, shown in the U.K. in its original 90-minute version and in the U.S. in an unfortunately truncated 50-minute edition.

  The Polmar–White book, the related film and a more recent book by James Dean, <u>The Taking of the K-129: How The CIA Used Howard Hughes To Steal A Russian Sub In The Most Daring Covert Operation In History</u>, together provide a comprehensive account of this endeavor. The Dean book, published in 2017, draws from the heavily redacted CIA 2010 report on the Azorian operation. Notwithstanding its unfortunately hyped subtitle, this book provides a high-quality overview of the fascinating cast of personalities and varied events involved in this program.

  Providing a strong contrast to the K-129 histories mentioned above, positioned firmly in the hard-to-believe category, we have the 2005 publication of <u>Red Star Rogue: The Untold Story of a Soviet Submarine's Nuclear Strike Attempt on the U.S.</u> by Kenneth Sewell and Clint Richmond. The book basically posits that everything written and reported about the K-129 loss and recovery is either untrue or highly compromised and designed to conceal a much deeper secret. The authors suggest that the K-129, under the control of Soviet intelligence, was tasked to deliver a nuclear strike on Hawaii that would be blamed on China. The premise is that a special KGB-controlled task group joined the K-129 at the time it sailed on its patrol, with the mission of diverting the K-129 from its assigned patrol area, to close to Hawaii with the intent to deliver a nuclear missile strike that targeted the U.S. naval base at Pearl Harbor.

  The book brings a lot of detail together in an attempt to make the authors' case and raises certain aspects of the K-129's mission that are not reasonably explainable. The net of the Sewell/Richmond story is that the missile strike misfired at launch, destroyed the K-129, and the CIA recovery operation netted most of the remains. While the thesis advanced is farfetched, the book is worth the read for the simple reason that it raises a host of questions about the K-129 that have not been addressed, at least in public. I have no direct knowledge one way or the other as to the events suggested in the <u>Red Star Rogue</u> book, but the conclusion is unavoidable: the full story of K-129 has not yet been told.

- **NOTE 2 - page 252**

  The best telling of the compromise of the Azorian project by Jack Anderson and other journalists can be found in James Dean's <u>The Taking of K-129</u>, mentioned above. Anderson was determined to break the Azorian story first, and he rejected out-of-hand all attempts to dissuade him from doing so, disdaining the interests of U.S. national security. Anderson was proud of the fact that he led with the story. Ever arrogant, he claimed that he was the judge and jury as to whether the project was worthwhile, labeling it a "boondoggle" that had failed, conveniently providing himself with an excuse to violate national security. Anderson basically did not give a damn that his compromise told the Soviets exactly what they needed to know.

  Anderson's actions in March 1975 caused the project to be terminated before the recovery ship could be sent back for a second try to lift the remaining hull of the K-129. Thus, in his compromise of the operation, Anderson's move became a self-fulfilled proposition, his "scoop" ensured that the project would not succeed beyond the parts salvaged on the first run. This occurred despite Colby's success in convincing a host of other investigative reporters to sit on the story, the first among these being Seymour Hersh, who had more of the story first.

  Once Anderson broke the story, Hersh was ready with a much more detailed and accurate account, immediately followed by a host of "Project Jennifer" stories from other outlets. These untoward events had transpired only four years before Admiral Turner elected to invite Anderson into the Agency auditorium to make his pitch to a large audience. Turner's move to endorse Anderson by bringing him into the Agency building only served to encourage many of us in the Headquarters building to conclude that our Director disdained the organization, a trait he consistently demonstrated during his tenure there.

- **NOTE 3 - page 252**

  John McMahon had a 34-year career in the CIA and a range of exceptional accomplishments. He began that career as a GS-5 cable clerk and worked his way through many positions across several Directorates and programs. In January 1978, he was selected as the Deputy Director of Operations (DDO) and served until April 1982, when he was elevated to be the Deputy Director of Central Intelligence (DDCI). In the latter position, he served under Director William J. Casey and retired in March 1986 at the age of 54. His oral history interview, provided in the Agency publication "Studies in Intelligence" and posted on the Agency's library website, is titled "Unconventional and Effective: An Interview with Former DDCI John McMahon." This informal conversation is revealing from the standpoint of his many experiences, as well as his characteristic modesty.

  In addition to the event recounted in this chapter, I would have a further dealing with DDCI McMahon in 1985 when he guided me through a difficult period in my career, a complicated situation created by a Director Casey initiative. That situation and its outcome is presented in a later chapter but, at least during the 1982-1985 period of my tour in Tokyo, that saw John transition from the DDO position to DDCI, I was fortunate to meet with him on several occasions, twice as he officiated in my Intelligence Medal of Merit award ceremonies. Many of us felt that his departure in 1986 marked the end of the era when operations officers absolutely knew that senior Agency management had their backs. It was not the same when he handed over his DDCI role to Robert Gates, a career DI analyst and NSC staffer. And to many of us, nothing would ever be the same again.

Chapter 19

- NOTE 1 - page 264 [REDACTED ENTIRELY BY DOD]

Chapter 20

- NOTE 1 - page 269
  Duane Ramsdell "Dewey" Claridge was an interesting character and a man with whom I enjoyed a good working relationship. This acquaintance was mostly as a subordinate, on those occasions when our paths crossed in the building or in the field and, in later years, with the advent of William Casey as the Agency director, Dewey and I would again interact. At Headquarters before my European tour, he was my division chief, but my first field experience with him was in a planning session in 1981 during which he debriefed me on an operation, as the Rome Chief of Station, in that Station's "bubble." We met there to examine the aforementioned double-agent operation in which I was the lead case officer and for which I had been dispatched to Rome from the city in which I was posted. Against inclinations to sustain the project, Dewey's sense was to terminate and walk away from this lackluster and counterproductive endeavor. Dewey carried the day and I went back to my city a happy camper.

  In my first meetings with Dewey, I simply did not know what to make of him. I was taken aback a bit by his attire, mainly the white shoes and flashy sports coat, as well as his dramatic mannerisms. But Dewey was a focused, imaginative, and energetic man. He was an "all operations all the time" type of field manager, encouraged his officers to take risks, and backed them up when his support was needed. In later years, having become a trusted lieutenant of Director Bill Casey, Dewey ran to the edge and beyond in the Contra operation, sanctioning and managing the mining of Nicaraguan harbors in early 1984. He was eventually indicted on seven counts of perjury and making false statements to the Walsh Commission. He was pardoned

before going to trial by President George Bush on Christmas Eve 1992.

Dewey resurfaced briefly in my life-beyond-the-Agency period when I served in the Pentagon in 2002-2007. I had only occasional visibility into his private-sector intelligence-collection activity in support of the U.S. military activity in Afghanistan and Iraq, but he was still on the case. Dewey was persistent—it was hard to keep a good man down and away from the action. He passed away in April 2016.

In 2002 Dewey wrote his own Agency memoir, <u>A Spy for All Seasons: My Life in the CIA</u>, which provides some unique vignettes carefully packaged to reflect his own perspectives. A more interesting third-party profile, drawn with a critical perspective of Dewey the man and his deeds and alleged misdeeds, is provided in John Prados' more recent <u>The Ghosts of Langley: Into the CIA's Heart of Darkness</u>. In this wide-ranging critique, Prados introduces the reader to Clarridge in his "Crusaders" chapter and takes us through the Dewey-unleashed phase that carried the Agency into the dark waters of Iran–Contra.

• NOTE 2 - page 271

A fine presentation of Operation Eagle Claw is contained in the appropriately titled book <u>The Guts to Try:– The Untold Story of the Iran Hostage Rescue Mission by the On-Scene Desert Commander</u>, authored by Colonel (retired) James Kyle. This treatment of the overall operation is comprehensive, at least from the military side of the equation. Kyle spares no one from deserved criticism for the technical and operational shortcomings that combined to doom the mission. In the Epilogue that closes the book, "Anatomy of a Failed Mission," the author delivers a stinging critique of the issues at play and identifies five factors that together "broke the back" of Eagle Claw. Kyle also references the Holloway Commission, established by the DOD in late May 1980 and its investigation of the mission, a concession for an independent investigation driven in part by U.S. Congressional criticisms. Kyle offers his candid assessment of the commission's effort as being mishandled, misdirected and incomplete.

Perhaps most importantly for the purpose of this narrator's take on the role of our national leadership, Kyle absolves Jimmy Carter for most of the blame, instead pinning responsibility for the failure of the mission squarely on the shoulders of the U.S. military. He cites overall poor organization, planning and execution, overlaid by convoluted decision-making and confused command-and-control procedures. In sum, Kyle believes that the mission could have and should have succeeded, even with the aircraft failures that occurred along the way. He assigns final blame for failure to the one element he identifies as sadly missing that day at Desert One– the "guts to try."

A second accounting of the failed Eagle Claw operation, more of a critique of the various factors that combined to doom the mission, is contained in <u>The Iranian Rescue Mission: Why It Failed</u> by Paul B. Ryan. Published in 1985, it is a useful retrospective. There resides objectivity in Ryan's approach to identifying all the factors that contributed to the failure. And there were many. He also identifies President Carter's obsession with limiting casualties on the Iranian side, as I had heard firsthand at the time, and Carter's admonition to all planners that "innocent bystanders were not to be harmed" and "wanton killings" were to be avoided. Also useful is the characterization of then-Deputy Secretary of State Warren Christopher as being upset when he was told by the mission leaders that they intended to kill the Iranian guards to free the hostages. Planning and execution and mechanical failures aside, there is a lot to be learned in this text on leadership and decisiveness, or the lack of both.

A recent book, <u>Operation Eagle Claw 1980: The Disastrous Bid to End the Iran Hostage Crisis</u> by Justin Williamson, published in 2020, makes a succinct presentation of the operation. While much of the source material is summarized, the book draws heavily and objectively from over a dozen books and articles to present a balanced account. The author of this book is focused instead on a two-man Special Forces team that worked there in cooperation with the Agency team, but the net of this account does award high praise for the work done in the streets and alleys of Tehran to prepare for the arrival of the Delta Force rescue group.

More recently, referencing the 40th anniversary of the Eagle Claw operation, the CBS News network deployed a special documentary titled "Desert One" that it described as presenting "Inside the Failed 1980 Hostage Rescue in Iran." While this 90-minute production focuses on an examination of the human toll taken on the men who came together at that remote desert site, it is well done and captures the impact of this failure. The trailer can be seen at https://www.cbsnews.com/news/desert-one-inside-the-failed-1980-hostage-rescue-in-iran/.

Chapter 21

• NOTE 1 - page 284

The Iran–Iraq War raged for eight-plus years, claiming more than a million lives and consuming the wealth of both nations. After a spate of skirmishes, assassinations, executions and threats of war between the Iran of Ayatollah Khomeini and the Iraq of Saddam Hussein, serious fighting broke out in September 1980. The war lasted until mid-1988, by which time both nations had exhausted themselves and destroyed an entire generation of young men whom they had marched into battle, not to mention tens of thousands of civilians caught in the crossfire.

Although many publications are devoted to the history of that conflict, a useful reference is presented in the proceedings of a conference, "The Origins, Conduct and Impact of the Iran–Iraq War, 1980-1988" hosted by the

Woodrow Wilson International Center for Scholars in July 2004. Also recommended as providing a cogent overview of the conflict is <u>Iran at War 1500-1988</u> by Dr. Kaveh Farrokh, published in 2011.

Chapter 22

- ## NOTE 1 - page 290

Austria's single nuclear power reactor, the Zwentendorf Nuclear Power Plant, was something of a white elephant even in 1980 when I arrived to serve in this new posting. Built at a cost of nearly $2 billion during the 1972-1978 period, it was never placed into commercial operation. A national referendum in November 1978, decided by less than 1 percent of the electorate, blocked activation of that plant and canceled two companion reactors slated for construction at the same site. Because the future of this facility remained undetermined and was contested politically for several years, the reactor warranted some level of attention by the Embassy. The public's rejection of the startup of this reactor, in a nation almost wholly dependent on Soviet gas supplies, was an early signal that politics could undermine the "clean energy" promise of nuclear energy. In a sense, the Zwentendorf dilemma presented the world with the first manifestation of the "no nukes" movement capable of blocking and eventually deconstructing a completed, ready-to-generate, state-of-the-art nuclear power reactor.

- ## NOTE 2 - page 291

Entous notes that in 1969 Golda Meir and President Richard Nixon reached a firm if unwritten "understanding" that the U.S. would not insist on Israeli's participation in the NPT ███████████████████████

NOTE 3 - page 292

A case in point on the issue of forcing the IAEA to do what it is not capable of accomplishing, at least on its own, involves the never-ending saga of North Korea. The 1994 Agreed Framework agreement between the U.S. and the DPRK created a multi-layer program of incentives designed to compel the North Koreans to shut down their nuclear weapons program in return for energy guarantees that included the construction of a pair of multi-billion-dollar nuclear powerplants. As a bonus for signing the Framework, North Korea also secured (read: extorted) the provision to Pyongyang of large quantities of fuel oil to fire their thermal power plants to supply the North Korean electrical grid. This feature was to continue until the first of new nuclear reactors was commissioned, all at a cost of several hundred million dollars a year paid for by the Framework partners, including, prominently, U.S. taxpayers.

The fact was that the North Koreans were duplicitous from the outset, namely by shifting gears to undertake a clandestine and long-undetected uranium enrichment program that allowed the production of that nation's first batch of nuclear weapons. Under the Framework Agreement, the IAEA was tasked to verify critical elements of the suspect weapons program that had occurred prior to the Framework. This IAEA assignment was part of an agreed, overall effort to verify how much and what quality fissile material (plutonium) had already been produced by Pyongyang and was then available for nuclear weapons use.

After five years of failed attempts to secure the access required to complete this verification, the IAEA finally gave up trying and reported to its Board of Governors, at its annual meeting in September 2002, that its inspectors saw no way to proceed. By this time, the U.S. side was then involved in new confrontation with North Korea over its undeclared uranium enrichment-based weapons programs and little note was taken of the IAEA finding of noncompliance on Pyongyang's original commitments. The real takeaway here was, independent of the new confrontation over Pyongyang's uranium enrichment program, the famed and failed Agreed Framework could not have gone forward absent the completed verification tasks assigned to the IAEA. In this case, none of the involved parties to the Framework, to include the agreement architects resident in the Clinton Administration, gave more than a passing interest in the IAEA's inability to deliver the verification that it was tasked to accomplish.

Had IAEA been allowed to complete its sampling, it was highly likely that IAEA laboratories would have confirmed the amount and quality of the plutonium already separated by the North Koreans and not declared in the Agreed Framework. But this in-your-face failure to comply on the part of the North Koreans, and the failure to back up the IAEA's inability to make progress, allowed the Framework to proceed for several long years after it should have been suspended for noncompliance. Such was IAEA's designated role in this policy failure on the part of the U.S. Government, the latter having forced IAEA management to take on a task that those officials strongly suspected was not achievable. In this instance, the U.S. Government essentially made IAEA complicit in this policy disaster by assigning IAEA a critical task that the U.S. Government elected to not support, effectively whistling past the North Korean plutonium stockpile graveyard for years.

One does wonder if, in a situation where the uranium enrichment program had not been disclosed when it was in 2002, the U.S. and other like-minded "engagers" would have elected to prevail on the IAEA to compromise itself. IAEA should not be asked to do what it cannot reasonably do, as was the case in the North Korean Framework case. But, when the IAEA is asked or tasked, that organization should be supported fully and not treated as an afterthought or an enabler of bad policy motives. Half-declared compromises on nuclear programs and intentions always come back to bite.

• **NOTE 4 - page 295**

In a more recent situation, we saw this same dynamic evolve as the IAEA was forced to deal with the decade-long game of hide-the-nuclear-monkey provided by the Iranian nuclear program. Part of that game played out over a period, roughly 2002-2006, during which the Director General of the IAEA appeared to actively and systematically undermine the ability of his own organization to perform its mandated role. In this case of political theater, for which I had a second-row seat from my vantage point in the Pentagon policy organization, Iran stalled, misdirected, misinformed, and ultimately outmaneuvered the IAEA, thereby advancing its ability to proliferate.

The abject failure of the IAEA, overseen by a reluctant and seemingly impotent UN Security Council, during this period of aggressive Iranian expansion of its nuclear capabilities, is well-documented and now delivered history. The case study published in 2012 by the U.S. National Defense University's Center for the Study of Weapons of Mass Destruction, titled "The IAEA's Decision to Find Iran in Non-Compliance, 2002-2006" by N. Gerami and P. Goldschmidt provides a good telling of this sorry tale.

In its introduction, the NDU/CSWMD case study notes the August 2002 public outing of undeclared nuclear facilities by an Iranian exile group and tracks the harsh reality of IAEA and UN's failure to come to grips with the Iranian program. The study explains that "The IAEA had received briefings from several member states since the early 1990s that indicated possible undeclared nuclear activities in Iran. Yet IAEA inspectors needed Iranian authorities to provide physical access in order to verify the absence of undeclared nuclear material and activities."

Such cooperation with IAEA from the Iran side was not forthcoming, and a multi-year drama of failed negotiations and IAEA internal foot-dragging at the Board of Governors level ensued. Iran had learned its lessons well from IAEA's handling of the North Koreans and was emboldened to stall and prevaricate. This drawn-out process was abetted by Iran supporters at the UN Security Council level, with Russia and China as the main actors. The result: Iran was not declared to be non-compliant until March 2006 when the IAEA Board of Governors effectively forced its resistant Director General, Dr. Mohamed El Baradei, to submit a report of Iranian noncompliance to the UN Security Council. The IAEA board had forced its Director General's hand by adopting an IAEA resolution compelling him to submit the noncompliance notification.

In the NDU case study's "Epilogue" the authors overview the extent of the damage done to the IAEA's reputation and to the credibility of broader non-proliferation efforts with the comment "the handling of the Iran case by El Baradei and the IAEA Board made it politically impossible to declare other states … in noncompliance where safeguards violations had occurred." In Iran's case, suspected but undeclared nuclear facilities and activities advanced that nation's proliferation capabilities broadly while IAEA watched from the sidelines. IAEA found itself as the night watchman tied to his chair as the store was looted over a 10-year period. A neutered IAEA and a lame UN Security Council abetted those developments by repeatedly declining to declare Iran non-compliant.

• NOTE 5 - page 298

The construction of Pakistan's first dedicated weapons-grade plutonium-production reactor, Khushab-1, was initiated in 1985 and that unit came online in 1997. This initial Khushab reactor, later joined with three sister plutonium producers, generates substantial quantities of weapons-grade plutonium-239 for reprocessing at the Chashma facility. The latter creates weapons-grade plutonium metal as fissile product for onward delivery to Pakistani weapons manufacturers. None of these reactors, nor any of the associated reprocessing, fuel fabrication, fissile materials labs or weapons manufacturing facilities, are declared per se to IAEA or the international community, nor are they covered by any type of IAEA safeguards regime.

- **NOTE 6 - page 299**

In his finely detailed book referenced in the text, <u>Eating Grass</u>, Khan makes a strong case that the KANUPP reactor was never considered as a source for fissile material, including the assessment that the reactor would not have been able to generate an optimal product for reprocessing. His discussion of Pakistan's near-obsessive determination to acquire a reprocessing capability, a facility that presumably could have been mated with a heavy-water reactor to produce the irradiated fuel feedstock from which plutonium could be extracted, is interesting.

At the time, we were looking hard at the KANUPP power plant as a strong candidate for diversion, the agency and the IAEA reasonably assumed that the combination of the KANUPP reactor, and the reprocessing plant that had come on line several years before, offered Pakistan the best route to fissile material. Although we then (in 1982) did not know with certainty that Pakistan had decided in 1974 to develop a weapons capability, all the indicators suggested that this was the case and such was a reasonable assumption.

Offered the opportunity, Pakistan had opted to go the enriched uranium route with its covert centrifuge program as early as 1978, and by 1981 had a pilot plant in operation at Kahuta. By 1983, the U.S. intelligence community judged that Pakistan had an active but technically challenged enrichment program underway that could produce enough fissile material (uranium 235) by 1984 or so for one or more devices. When Pakistan suffered a setback occasioned by the massive earthquake of September 1981, China stepped in to provide Pakistan fifty kilograms of highly enriched U-235 with the bonus of a bomb design thrown into the deal. Kahuta was back on line by 1983, and the following year the master of that program, Dr. A.Q. Khan, announced that Pakistan had mastered the enriched uranium fuel cycle to produce weapons-grade fissile material.

Had this alternative enriched uranium route not become available—and for certain, the U.S. intelligence community had a very uncertain appreciation of this at the time—a reasonable assumption was that Pakistan would have traveled the plutonium path as its first priority for a weapons program. Hence KANUPP was, in any event, a highly suspect facility and a valid collection target for the Agency, not to mention a priority safeguards activity for the IAEA.

Pakistan elected to proceed aggressively down both the enriched uranium and plutonium paths to create a robust weapons capability, with a fleet of four dedicated weapons-grade plutonium-producing reactors in operation by 2014. As noted in the text, the first of these came on line in 1997 but was begun in 1987, which suggests that, at the time we were attempting to discern events at KANUPP, the Pakistani nuclear leadership had embraced the centrifuge enriched uranium route as its priority route to a weapon, but was also steadily moving toward a companion plutonium-based weapons program.

- **NOTE 7 - page 301**

  In the Argentine case, it was later confirmed that a uranium enrichment technology development program had been initiated at Pilcaniyeu about 1982 and continued for ten years, apparently with mixed results. That effort was shut down at some point but was revived in 2015, based on a requirement for enriched uranium fuel for use in Argentina's current power reactor inventory. Evidence also surfaced subsequently that researchers working with the research reactor at Basilerio Institute had confirmed their ability to develop a nuclear weapons program based on enriched uranium. Beyond the reporting mentioned in this narrative, I have limited knowledge as to how these two elements of Argentine activity came to the knowledge of the U.S. policy community. Suffice it to say, the Station's initial reporting on the enrichment activity was not given much credibility, and interest in Station reporting on these events waned. U.S. government policymakers did not benefit from this dismissive attitude, and there are lessons to be learned from this experience.

Chapter 23

- **NOTE 1 - page 307**

  The Chinese side of the Israeli engagement profiled here, a predecessor of COSTIND, involved a mishmash of PLA organizations and companies. At the time of the events here described, the PRC's Central Military Commission and the State Council were moving toward a decision to centralize all high-technology and weapons development, including the overt and covert acquisition of foreign systems and technologies. COSTIND would be formed in 1982 as a civilian ministry reporting to the State Council and working hand-in-glove to satisfy PLA research institutes' thirst for foreign military technology.

  Over the next two decades, COSTIND would continue to evolve as China's requirement for technology acquisition and theft continued to expand to satisfy the key industries that supported its military development. In 2008, COSTIND and its associated companies would be merged into a more powerful and all-encompassing organization, the Ministry of Industry and Information Technology (MIIT), later to be further elevated as the State Administration for Science, Technology and Industry for National Defense or SASTIND.

- **NOTE 2 - page 311**

  The Israel–China connection for the transfer of U.S. military technology and knowhow was replicated a few years later by a top-level U.S. Government-blessed initiative. I had no knowledge of this arrangement then, but had I had a vote then, I would have judged it to be an ill-considered action on the part of U.S. leadership. This American initiative regarding defense technology sales to China came about in 1983 when policy managers in the Reagan Administration were focused almost exclusively on the growing strategic threat of the Soviet Union. Reagan era "best and the brightest" security leaders concluded that a "China offset" to the Soviet surge in offensive capabilities might be useful.

The idea was for the U.S. to improve selected Chinese weapons systems and capabilities, thereby creating a more credible threat from China with which the Soviets would have to deal. This all would be to the net benefit of the United States, or so the calculation went. Little regard was given to the obvious fact that any improvement in Chinese military capabilities would later rebound to the detriment of the United States. Some brilliant thinking here. Three years of negotiations produced a U.S.–China agreement in April 1986. This arrangement was announced with considerable fanfare by its Pentagon and defense contractor advocates.

One highlighted program of the "Peace Pearl" deal involved the modernization of China's frontline F-8 (J-8) jet fighter by designing in and reconfiguring the aircraft with near state-of-the-art U.S. fire-control and avionics systems. This included, to the consternation of many U.S. defense experts, the AN/APG-66 (V) radar. The initial J-8 II upgrade program was valued at $550 million and the involved U.S. industry players assumed that the follow-on phases would generate multiples of this amount. Predictably, the program did not go well and there were frustrations, delays and dissatisfactions on both sides of the endeavor.

In June 1989, the Chinese leadership sent its tanks into Beijing's Tiananmen Square to literally crush the democracy demonstrators there. President George Bush had no choice but to freeze the entire military relationship, including the poster-child Peace Pearl contracts, which were then underway. A year later, both parties terminated the experiment and went their separate ways. The dissolution of this ill-conceived U.S.–China military technology cooperation agreement was probably one of the only beneficial byproducts of China's Tiananmen overreaction to the demonstrations seeking a more democratic and liberal China.

On reflection, the timing of the initial approaches made to China by the intermediaries representing the U.S. side in 1983, not that many months after I filed my first draft report from my Station at the time on the covert Israeli–China military technology link, is significant. With Israel then already working its China covert sales channel, it is logical that calculating U.S. policymakers and would-be military technology merchants had discovered a common-cause opportunity. I assume that the American advocates knew that the Israelis had beaten them to the China trough and were already feeding there, based on the sale of U.S.-origin military technology.

Two full decades later, when I accepted a senior-level policy position in the Office of the Secretary of Defense, we were still tackling the Israeli–China military technology cooperation issues. By 2000, Israeli firms had upped their game and signed a contract to equip a small fleet of Chinese Air Force airborne early warning aircraft. Those combat systems were similar in capability to our AWACS, but they featured Israeli radar systems and electronics. In that case, Israeli Aircraft Industries and Elta (electronics) were working with China to introduce Israel's Phalcon airborne early warning command and control system, installed in a Russian-built Ilyushin/Beriev A-50 (NATO code name Mainstay) aircraft. It was a straightforward commercial sale to the Chinese military blessed by the Israeli government. Israel had developed the world-class system back in the mid-1990s and was marketing it internationally by the early 2000s.

By mating a Russian military transport aircraft to Israeli-supplied systems, and integrating a Russian-cum-Chinese airframe or air platform with all-Israeli radar and processing systems, China would be getting the very best our longtime ally Israel had to sell. We had known Israel was pitching the system to other nations but simply had not imagined they would make China a priority customer. It took us two full years to compel (threaten) Israel to disengage from the program. In the end, the Israeli sale was blocked by U.S. intervention, and Israel and China reached an accommodation that left China with some, but not most, of what it wanted. China went on to build its own AWACS around indigenous (perhaps) radar systems, but the experience still compelled us to watch the China-Israeli nexus carefully. In 2002, we continued to track such adventures because we had no choice but to assume a catch-me-if-you-can situation in the U.S.–Israel–China triangle would continue to prevail in the coming years.

- **NOTE 3 - page 312**

Numerous books have been devoted to the Angleton issue, most recently The Ghost: The Secret Life of CIA Spymaster James Jesus Angleton by Jefferson Morley. I believe that a strong case could be made that Angleton was one of the single most important American personalities to be co-opted and exploited by Israel in that country's first three decades of existence. This narrative looks beyond Angleton's "mole hunt" for KGB and GRU agents in the Agency, not to mention those moles embedded in the FBI and the entire U.S. Government, to examine Angleton's parallel obsession with Israel. His was a deep and abiding relationship, professional, personal and undefinable, dedicated to supporting Israel and the Zionist cause.

As Morley details in his book on Angleton, the protagonist was an unusual individual, with many layers of mystery and deception. Morley gives broad and fair attention to Angleton's role in the survival and eventual prevalence of Israel as the U.S. ally in the region. █████████████

███

███

███

███

Although Morley treats Angleton's other "mole obsession" activities as equally damaging to American interests, I cannot take issue with his penultimate judgment that "Angleton's loyalty to Israel betrayed U.S. policy on an epic scale…" In addition to the Jefferson Morley book mentioned in the text, which was summarized in a January 1, 2018, article in The Intercept, other relevant publications include <u>Molehunt</u> by David Wise, <u>Wildness of Mirrors</u> by David Martin and <u>Cold Warrior</u> by Tom Mangold and Jeffery Goldberg.

Last, to the degree that the reader is willing to consider the depth of Angleton's possible complicity in the compromise of U.S. national security interests, let me cautiously recommend a more recent read, <u>Blood in the Water: How the US and Israel Conspired to Ambush the USS Liberty</u>, in 2019, by Joan Mellen. It provides a quasi-revisionist take on the USS *Liberty* event. She suggests a barely believable combination of motivations and manipulations that delivered the USS *Liberty* to its fate. Some of Mellen's allegations are farfetched, including the assertion that the *Liberty* was essentially set up to be attacked and destroyed for nefarious reasons by the Johnson Administration.

Notwithstanding the difficult syntax of the book, its inherent overreach, and the emotion contained therein, in this book Angleton emerges as a central player in a top-down, post-event, well-oiled cover-up of the USS *Liberty* "incident." There is more than a grain of truth here even if the book offered reviewers many opportunities to dismiss and discredit it, which has been done with great creativity and passion.

The unavoidable reality is that, in the case of the Israeli attack on the USS *Liberty*, the truth is still out there somewhere. This author is certain of one core fact: There is absolutely no doubt the attack on this ship was deliberate and premeditated; thus it is the rationale for that attack and the explanation of the cover-up engineered by the Johnson Administration, abetted by the Israeli side, which continues to defy a comprehensive explanation. A half-dozen other highly credible books by survivors of the USS *Liberty* who were under the guns of the Israelis that day, as well as research by independent authors, leave no doubt as to the intent of the attackers and the complicity of senior U.S. officials in the cover-up of the incident.

Here is the bottom line: On a bright, clear day in June 1967, off the Gaza coast, a U.S. Navy ship, flying the American flag, was bombed, strafed and torpedoed in a premediated, deliberate, coordinated and sustained attack that killed 31 U.S. servicemen and wounded an additional 171. Now, some 56 years later, we still have no acceptable explanation why such an unwarranted act was perpetuated by an ostensible ally—an act that sought to silence those men and sink their ship.

Chapter 24

- ## NOTE 1 - page 314

  As mentioned, by the early 1980s the Soviet Union was making a determined effort to outbuild, out-deploy and outgun the U.S. nuclear submarine program, in both strategic ballistic missile submarines and the companion nuclear attack submarines. At the point we were focusing on the nearby scrapyard, the Soviet Navy had no less than 48 Victor Class (Project 671) attack submarines in the water or still on the shipways, with the greatly improved Oscar II, Sierra and Akula classes due to enter service in the next few years. The Mike class would soon follow, with an incredible diving depth capability of 3,200 feet, or so it was claimed.

  The surge in operational capability and raw numbers presented an existential challenge to our Navy's undersea dominance and was a direct threat to our ballistic missile submarine fleet. A number of recent publications have defined this challenge, but the book <u>Rising Tide: The Untold Story of the Russian Submarines That Fought the Cold War</u>, by Gary Weir and Walter Boyne (2003), is an easy reference.

- ## NOTE 2 - page 319

  An Embassy code clerk typically was a career signals communication specialist who always remained within the Embassy proper or, on those rare occasions when he or she was let out of the Embassy compound, was escorted by two or more security agents. These rare individuals not only knew of details of most local operations mounted by the intelligence agency in which they were embedded, but also knew and managed the code systems and encryption devices with which that Station communicated with its home base, be it Moscow or Berlin or Prague.

- ## NOTE 3 - page 321

  In the events here described, I found the dedication and precision of my SE Branch Chief—who was not only a counterintelligence specialist but also a superb manager—impressive, probably the most so in my Agency career. I was pleased when he wrote his own book a few years back, precisely defining the challenges of counterintelligence and his approach to the craft. I have gifted that guide to a number of younger officers, one being my son-in-law, a junior FBI agent who aspires to this same counterintelligence specialty.

Chapter 25

[NO NOTES]

PART FOUR

A Return to Northeast Asia

(1982-1987)

The Path to a New Assignment

In a scene almost reminiscent of *The Godfather*, I was summoned to Headquarters in the spring of 1982 by the man who apparently had decided to become my next Station Chief. There, Jim explained how he planned to focus on two target areas in his new command, both of which required increased operational attention: China and high technology. In this next posting, I eventually would pursue the China target as a priority, and a good portion of my Station would be assigned to that task. Gaining strength and building its military and economic capacity, China was a compelling target, having become a near coequal in importance with the Russian (at that time, Soviet) threat. Jim told me his priority Station coverage also would be directed at our host country's domestic politics, in part to complement the excellent political coverage being delivered by the Embassy officers. But in Jim's assessment, much more could be done on China, and some of what already was being done there needed to be redirected.

Impressed by Jim's presentation, I accepted on the spot but noted I would have to depart my current European assignment six months short of my full three-year tour. Jim waved it aside. "Don't worry," I recall him saying. "It is already done. East Asia Division has your back, and we will take care of the paperwork next week." It was as though he was saying, "I'm gonna make the Operations Directorate an offer they can't refuse." Fine with me, and I went back to my then-current assignment to begin a months-long handover of assets and a pack-out.

On the high-technology issue, some delicate tasks existed in terms of collecting information on host-nation developments. Also, Agency attention to third-country technology, to which those in the forthcoming country of my posting had access, would be sensitive in terms of our relationship with that country. As for Japan itself, it had become a technological powerhouse in 1982, with a range and quality of progress unequaled anywhere else in the world. The only exception was the United States. But in many important areas, we were struggling to hold our own against Japanese advances. That surge on the part of Japan in key technology sectors had been building for some time, and by the early 1980s the rivalry was real and growing. The commercial and economic implications, and the policy concerns, were (slowly but surely) becoming manifest, not to mention concerns over technology with national security applications.

As U.S. policymakers awakened to Japan's challenge to American technology primacy, the imperative for the Agency was obvious: overtly or covertly collect, analyze and report on the relevant issues. Because we had long enjoyed a comfortable lead in almost all areas of technology development, and because the clandestine side of the Agency, namely, the Directorate of Operations, had almost no experience in reporting on that area, we had a new situation on our hands.

To be sure, back at Headquarters there was a wealth of analytical talent within the Directorate of Intelligence, the DO's sister directorate, devoted to tracking and reporting on technology developments, particularly those with military and weapons systems applications. There again, the traditional target of collection and analysis had been the Soviet Union and, more recently, China. In neither case was the perceived threat commercial in nature. Military systems had defined technology components, be they electronics or propulsion systems for aircraft, rocket motor and guidance systems for ballistic missiles, or armor and main-gun specifications for armored vehicles. But the ability to harness leading-edge developments in electronics and other emerging technologies to military systems and applications was just beginning to be appreciated by our industries as well as our analysts.

Within the DI, the shift to analyze Japanese high-technology activity and accomplishments more closely was relatively straightforward. It involved an in-house pivot to reassign subject matter experts, or SMEs, to follow designated Japanese activity. The operations side of the Agency was another matter entirely. There was no such established base of SMEs to pivot, and no clandestine service officers who could be assembled and assigned to the task. We would have to create that capability on the fly in my new posting. As we thought out our approach to the new target area, I experienced a *déja-vu* moment. It was Seoul in 1974 all over again. The object of our attention back then had been nuclear proliferation at a time when nobody even knew how to spell it.

My job would be to build a dedicated branch quickly in the Station, an integrated team that would establish its operational parameters and tasking. A good start existed with an officer there who had taken on some of the necessary tasks, but he was soon to depart before I arrived. I planned to start a program immediately when I arrived in August. Jim, the Station Chief, would hold my feet to the fire as that activity was, to a large degree, his own initiative. He had persuaded his seniors (and doubters) at Headquarters that it would be a worthwhile endeavor. Some were waiting for him to fail, and for me to tumble with him.

When I stepped off the plane from Washington, on August 9, 1982, I was greeted by a flashy Newsweek cover story on the local newsstands. Though I had pledged to myself never to touch that magazine again, my curiosity got the better of me. The headline read, "Japan's High-Tech Challenge," featuring a raging samurai warrior bounding through a computer screen toward the reader in full attack mode. The article chronicled the rise of Japan and forecast its dominance in supercomputers, robotics, nuclear and other fields of endeavor. It seemed I had arrived at just the right moment—or perhaps a bit late if the article was to be believed. [NOTE 1]

Before getting further into that special target, I would like to profile the situation we in the Station faced with our two established adversaries, China and the Soviet Union, as they both would play supporting roles in the months ahead. China was a true hard target, in terms of our difficulties accessing that closed system for sensitive information.

The China Target from a New Location

The entire U.S. intelligence community was confronting the task of penetrating China and responding with collection attempts from all angles, including overt monitoring and human intelligence. But agents on the ground in China were scarce, and those who did exist often had only limited access to priority collection targets. When operations were successfully mounted, however, we could derive much from clandestine reporting for the simple reason that we knew so little, and our analysts for too long had been forced to guess too much. Among the DO locations worldwide tasked to report on China, senior management looked to the Station of my new posting, reasonably pressuring us to step up our game.

The manner in which the Chinese Communist Party operated, with everything done in a highly compartmented manner, presented unique challenges for all intelligence collectors. As a result, East Asia Division often found itself unequal to the task and unable to report on selected aspects of China. The information requirements of our policymakers included the personalities and leadership structure of Beijing's inner circle of decisionmakers, as well as key relationships within the Party, and the military organization and command structure. Most critically, we were woefully deficient in our coverage of China's planning and progress with its strategic weapons programs.

I was not a China Operations career officer within East Asia Division, so initially I would not have much interaction with the Station's China team. What I did know and was able to learn concerned me, however. I saw significant efforts producing relatively little quality intelligence. From a clandestine-reporting perspective, with an informed picture of the key issues critical to policy levels in Washington, a reasonable assessment was that in 1982 the U.S. government was flying blind on China. Some might claim we knew quite a bit, insofar as our appreciation of Chinese plans and capabilities went, but our intelligence community mostly was just guessing.

Once I settled into my new assignment, and as my understanding improved about the intelligence gap we faced on just about everything China, I reflected on my recent European experience and frustration one year before; for example, on the manner in which my attempt to report from there on the evolving the Israeli–China military-technology connection essentially had been dismissed. I convinced myself my European window into that activity had been irrelevant—our China team already knew it all. Alternatively, our policy folks, at a much higher level, likewise knew it all and were giving both the Chinese and the Israelis a pass. Eventually, I would learn just how little we knew of so many important things in China.

The Soviets in Asia — Very Busy Boys

On the streets of the city in my new East Asia posting, Russians were hard to find, particularly the KGB and GRU intel types we knew were out there. For me, it was a change from the routine in my previous tour, where Soviet intel officers, particularly the Line KR or Directorate K fellows, had made a habit of engaging with Americans they suspected of being Agency operators. But the venue of my new posting was a prime area of operations for them, and the main reason they kept a low profile, at least to us in the Station, was they were busy doing other things. Their main collection activity was industrial espionage directed at Japanese companies. Russian and their Eastern Bloc compatriot intel officers sought protected research and development activity by leading Japanese corporations and research institutions. High importance was assigned to the production of components and systems for advanced commercial manufacturing, with special attention to capabilities the Soviets found impossible to generate within the homeland.

By 1982, the Soviet Union had been drawn into a full-scale military-technology competition with the United States and its allies, a contest in which Soviet antiquated production standards could not compete. Under the leadership of President Ronald Reagan, who had decided in the early months of his presidency to double down on defense expenditures, he signaled a determination to prevail in the Cold War. One element of that enhanced national security posture was development and deployment of a host of new weapons systems, most with cutting-edge technologies at their core. The Soviets were attempting to match us in system quality and capability, but they soon sensed they had joined a losing battle to America's technology leadership and underlying industrial capacity.

We knew the Soviets had scrambled to even the qualitative balance by doing everything possible to acquire sensitive technology, including proprietary commercial information, components and systems, along with complete sets of equipment. By law and an agreement among like-minded Western nations—an institution known as COCOM—they were denied access to most of those systems and technologies The Soviets detected the gaps in the regime and were quick to exploit the loopholes.

As a surging competitor of the United States, Japan was active in technologies and production processes critical to our own defense industry. As a consequence, Japan was a prime Soviet target. Unfortunately for the United States, Japan offered quality hunting with a range of targets from which the Soviets were able to cherry-pick valued information and systems. Japanese firms were eager to transact business by expanding their market share and vending to whomever with little concern for the consequences. Japanese government controls were lax at the ministerial levels assigned to monitor and control industrial development, and Japanese national security services were missing in action. Neither MITI, Japan's Ministry of International Trade and Industry, nor the National Police Agency, had a mandate to monitor, let alone checkmate, Soviet industrial spying, whether overt or covert.

By 1982, Moscow-driven tasking on technology acquisition, involving both the GRU, the Soviet military's intelligence arm, and the KGB, its civilian counterpart, had become paramount. The emphasis was second only to the ultimate reporting requirement, namely, any indication that the U.S. was planning a surprise nuclear attack on Mother Russia. From clandestine sources, we knew the GRU was receiving high marks for its technology-collection work. The Station raised the issue of technology compromise with our local security counterparts. But the Soviet surge was a huge challenge for any counterintelligence program, and in Japan there were too many points of possible leakage, too many active Soviets on the ground and too many small domestic trading companies willing to compromise themselves. As a result, there was only minimal awareness of Soviet nefarious activity and too few resources to track and counter the machinations. The problem was abetted by the fact that, beyond the normal Soviet Embassy KGB and GRU officers working under diplomatic cover, there literally were dozens of intel officers buried in the Russian trade mission and the Soviet-controlled trading companies working the byways of Japanese industry. [NOTE 2]

An important example that correlates to the time period was the so-called Toshiba scandal—a Soviet success with ramifications far beyond a simple transaction by a Japanese manufacturer. That activity was enabled by an associated domestic trading firm, and the players involved managed to pocket the equivalent of tens of millions of dollars. Although the scandal broke into the public domain in 1987, its origins were in 1982, when the acquisition of a certain type of Japanese machine tool became a top priority for the Soviet nuclear submarine program. A quick recap might be useful, particularly in the context in which we operated back then.

The Toshiba event involved Soviet success on both sides of the espionage equation. On the front end, the Soviets recruited and ran American sources who sold highly classified national defense-critical information to their KGB handlers. In doing so, the traitors allowed the Soviets to appreciate a shortcoming in a critical defense area, their nuclear submarine fleet. With the problem recognized, the Soviets were able to operationalize that information to acquire the sensitive technology needed to redress the deficiencies identified by Soviet espionage.

The Soviets penetrated U.S. defense-information systems via the Walker spy ring, centered on U.S Navy Chief Warrant Officer and communications specialist John Anthony Walker. Recruited in 1968, a KGB and GRU team ran Walker and his co-conspirators for nearly 20 years. Walker and his crew literally stole every item of classified information they could get their hands on and passed those materials on to the Soviets. They were tasked for more and came back with more. It was a case of simple greed and the excitement of the game, but in passing along U.S. communications secrets, the Walker ring rendered great damage to the security of the nation.

One of the Soviet takeaways of the conspiracy was the revelation that U.S. underwater sensor arrays and Navy submarines had become adept at detecting and identifying Soviet nuclear attack and ballistic missile submarines, sometimes at great distances, from the sounds created by their propulsion machinery. One of the components of that detection capability were the noise signals created by the propellers driving the Soviet subs through the water. The U.S. systems became so finely tuned that the machinery and propeller signatures of individual submarines were routinely identified and tracked, often throughout their patrol periods. The implications of such a technical capability greatly alarmed the Soviets, given the obvious advantage it provided to target their subs in a wartime scenario. That capability effectively checkmated the numerical advantage the Soviets were attempting to create with their massive submarine building and deployment program.

For the Soviets, the solution was straightforward: locate the highest quality state-of-the-art, computer-controlled machine tool available in the world—a sophisticated piece of machinery able to manufacture propellers and shafts to a level of quality equal to or superior to U.S. propulsion systems. Once the desired machines were identified, the Soviets planned to execute a covert plan to procure or, failing procurement, steal them to introduce the technology into their shipbuilding process. The GRU and KGB operatives did not have to look too far or too long. Japan's Toshiba Corporation built the four, five and six-axis machine tools capable of that level of precision, and the complex machines were commercially available. A Norwegian firm, Kongsberg *Våpenfabrikk*, would provide the numeric control systems that, when mated to Toshiba's machine, would automate the production process. The only catch was, because of their obvious application to military systems, both products were prohibited from being exported to Soviet Bloc nations.

The Toshiba machine tools and the companion controllers were COCOM-restricted. Understanding that important detail, if Toshiba wished to sell them to the Soviets, its management knew the company would have to deal by deception. In the event Toshiba and the Soviets found a trading company to work with, the deal was done. COCOM was avoided by misclassifying and thereby degrading the ostensible performance of the machines sold. Toshiba and the trading company got their sale, at $20 million a machine. The Soviets got their new machine tools, and the Soviet Navy got its Toshiba-tuned propellers. The U.S. Navy and the United States got the shaft, and the Walker spy ring probably got a nice bonus. **[NOTE 3]**

The Toshiba scandal became the focus of a broad investigation when it came to light in 1986, and U.S. congressional inquiries followed, with a demand for sanctions on the company and a complete review of the flawed COCOM system. It was clear the Soviets, abetted by their Warsaw Pact colleagues, had been running circles around COCOM for years, with routine procurement violations in Western Europe, the United States and Japan. **[NOTE 4]**

In the Station, we saw Japanese industry as uniquely vulnerable, but in 1982 we were only just recognizing the probing snout of the Soviet technology-acquisition bear. We knew the surge by opposition intelligence officers would only increase in the years ahead. For that reason alone, we needed to understand which advanced technologies were being developed by Japanese firms, and which of these had, or could be made to have, national security implications for the United States and the West. We also were trying to fathom the level of direction and support provided by the Japanese government ministries responsible for promoting and underwriting product-specific technologies.

'Japan, Inc.' as a Collection Target

From the vantage point of 2023, it might be difficult to discern the perception held in America in the 1980s of the magnitude of the Japanese economic threat. At the time, Japan seemed ascendant everywhere in so many fields of endeavor, an almost unstoppable force that combined hard work, focused energy and a determination to pursue technological advancement. Japan was building best-quality automobiles at competitive prices that pushed Detroit back on its heels. Its industries surged in automation and semiconductors. They innovated in process controls (Toshiba included), and invested aggressively with its profits. Rockefeller Center was in the Japanese real estate bag. Pebble Beach Golf Links was an acquisition target. U.S. firms that possessed technology or market position desired by the Japanese were being bought up, right and left. The collective advance by an island nation not yet 40 years out of its devastation from a world war was now identified as Japan, Inc. The title was well-deserved.

In the nuclear field, Japan rapidly was advancing to the status of world co-leadership. Its national program had secured U.S. acquiescence for a complete nuclear fuel cycle, including uranium enrichment and spent-fuel reprocessing. The order books of its electric power utilities permitted Japanese reactor manufacturers (again, including Toshiba) to license and build two types of pressurized-water and boiling-water reactors—with the potential to localize the entire industry.

In watching that dynamic progress play out, initially from Seoul across the Sea of Japan during the 1970s, from Western Europe during the early 1980s and then from my perch in the country beginning in 1982, I was pretty well sold on the strength and staying power of the Japanese phenomenon. The head-on challenge to America's economic dominance, including its leadership in technology and business acumen, was real and growing. A resurgent Japan did not pose a national security threat in the traditional sense, but America's failure to meet the Japanese challenge and deal effectively with it appeared destined to undermine our economic base.

For all of the above reasons, our intelligence community determined it was time to take a deeper look at where Japan was headed with its key technology programs. Our Directorate of Operations looked to East Asia Division for results. The Division, in turn, tasked the Station, and the Station turned up my new special branch to deliver the goods. I was enabled by Jim, our Chief, who understood the mission, embraced the directive and basically told me "tell me what you need." My response was I needed to build capacity quickly to catch up to where the Japanese had arrived. For that I needed a self-contained branch, I wanted my own operations officers, a reports officer who would work only on branch reporting, and case officers with some level of technical and business experience.

Within six months, we had it all, including a deputy who was second to none, a man whom I had heard about through the Headquarters grapevine and was soon to finish his tour in a nearby country. He jumped to our team full force and essentially became, in business parlance, my COO—as well as chief of staff, agent manager and report-writer supreme. Our new High Technology Branch was rounded out by a second experienced case officer, a Directorate of Intelligence analyst seconded to us for two years from Headquarters, as well as a dedicated reports officer and two, later to grow to six, outside officers. I inherited several of the last-mentioned from other Station branches who were unable to utilize their talents to maximum performance. It all was an internal staff-shifting that we welcomed and of which we made good use. [NOTE 5]

Over the next three-plus years, our HTB team focused on the Japan technology side and on selected development and commercialization efforts, such as advanced electronics, special materials (such as those utilized in the aerospace program), next-generation lasers, robotics, precision machine tools and computer-enabled machining systems. We also watched space systems, including propulsion and sensors, avionics and aerospace technologies, and telecommunications. A related priority was the manner in which the Japanese government, in a top-down fashion, supported the growth of all such activity. The key to understanding the government's central role in managing economic development was an appreciation of the master-cylinder bureaucracy that was MITI. The super ministry's role was dominant and pervasive, and it would remain so for a decade or more to come.

MITI had the ability to pick winners within the various Japanese business communities based on the technologies the bureaucrats deemed most important and the ability of those bureaucrats to direct funding in support of selected development efforts. MITI was staffed by the best and the brightest of Japan's cadre of new elite economic warriors. It provided a desired career path for the highest-level graduates of Japan's most prestigious universities: the University of Tokyo, Kyoto University and others. We worked hard to report on MITI planning, allowing that much of its activity was available via public documentation or, even if protected, was not technically classified information. Other ministries admittedly were important as well, for example, the Ministry of Foreign Affairs, involved in diplomacy and national security But for us in the HTB, it was all MITI all the time. [NOTE 6]

Our goal was to understand and be able to report how the MITI-driven system functioned in actual practice, as much as on the individual projects MITI elected to support. What amazed me, at least initially, was the manner in which the all-Japan-as-collectors system overseen by MITI not only vacuumed the world for information on competing technologies but also disseminated the information broadly and in a timely manner to all in Japan deserving to benefit.

Take, for example, the case of our NASA space program. In 1982, the agency was finalizing mission planning related to America's fleet of space shuttles. Columbia had flown the first test mission, STS-1, the previous April, and all indications suggested America was on the verge of a breakthrough in space exploration. In November 1982, the shuttle, having completed four test missions, was declared operational and ready for the business of space on a sustained basis. By the tenth mission, STS-41-B, in February 1984, the program was well off to the races and dominated all aspects of space development. Japanese engineers had attended every symposium, briefing, meeting and conference connected in any manner with the program since its inception in 1972. In each case, every aspect of those meetings was brought home to Japan, repackaged and out-briefed to companion space engineers, corporate space players, and university and space scientists. The MITI-organized information collection and dissemination program was impressive. I could not imagine anything like it in the United States, or anywhere else in the world.

Japanese Designs in Space

The ambitious efforts of the MITI industrial-management program included direct support of accelerated development of national capacity in space. MITI embraced private-sector champions capable of designing and building the rocket and satellites for the benefit of the nation. Japan was determined to play a leading role in space exploration and had made it a national priority to acquire all the elements of a successful and self-sustaining program, from rocket systems to satellites to mission-control capabilities. The programs were almost exclusively indigenous efforts, having as the lead execution organization the National Space Development Agency, or NASDA. The entity, operating under the direction of Japan's Space Activities Commission, managed the development of launch systems, satellites, and mission management and tracking systems.

The SAC, in turn, had the support of an independent government organization, the Science and Technology Agency, responsible for overall space planning as well as all space-related research conducted at national laboratories. The Institute of Space and Astronautical Science, or ISAS, a parallel organization charged with scientific efforts in space, was controlled by the Ministry of Education and had its own discrete missions and budget. As a collection target, ISAS was of equal importance to NASDA.

On the NASDA front in the area of satellite launch vehicles, Mitsubishi Heavy Industries and its partner contractors had perfected the N-1 three-stage rocket, capable of lofting a 130-kilogram satellite into geostationary orbit. In operation since its first success in 1975, when it placed Kiku (Engineering Test Satellite-One) in orbit, the system had successfully launched seven satellites by 1983, with more teeing up for a ride. NASDA had its successor, the N-II launch vehicle, in operation as well. That lifter successfully delivered three, 350-kilogram payloads since 1981 with another half-dozen lining up to be launched. The next iteration was the H-1, expected to be operational after 1985, capable of lifting a 650-kg payload to geostationary orbit. By any comparable yardstick, the 1980s saw the Japanese space program on a roll. **[NOTE 7]**

But the companion launch system program of ISAS was of even more interest to U.S. military analysts. Distinct from the NASDA effort, ISAS's scientific satellite-oriented program was centered on a family of solid-fuel rockets and involved a different collection of private-sector system suppliers. The solid-fuel propulsion factor was important in the context of Japan's growing capacity, irrespective of intent, to acquire capabilities that could be evolved to a missile program for a delivery system for a strategic weapon or conventional strike. The ISAS Mu series of launch vehicles was impressive—the Mu-3S third-generation model could boost a 300-kg satellite into a low-earth orbit, and its bigger brother, the Mu-3S II, could carry 670 kg into low-earth orbit. The Mu-3 series employed three-stages, each with solid-propellant motors, and those rockets performed with near-perfection.

We recognized that the advances demonstrated Japan's ability to master the design and series production of the type of missile system essential to create a strategic strike or counterstrike force. It also was clear that, even if such a military capability was conventional in nature, the potential to introduce a strategic alternative would be present.

Though open-source material and routine government-to-government discussions provided the United States with near full transparency on all things space in Japan, there still was a requirement to be absolutely sure we knew everything there was to know. Of particular interest was the government's out-year planning and the internal decision-making that confirmed to our analysts what we were being told by our counterparts was accurate. Japanese planning was done discretely, often by panels of experts, and the decisions arrived at in those closed groups often became policy recommendations to the highest levels of government. Moreover, budget-planning documents and briefings prepared for Japanese leadership often provided details otherwise not readily available. Understanding such details helped our policymakers sustain discussions with their Japanese government counterparts that cleared the air and made deeper bilateral cooperation possible. **[NOTE 8]**

Playing Defense on the Technology Front

As mentioned, we knew the Soviets, and more recently the Chinese, were all over the Japanese space program, seeking both overt and covert access to space-related officials, manufacturers and research institutions. The Soviet intelligence services, hunting system-design information, desired to place agents of information and influence and, through Japanese contacts, gain access to U.S. programs otherwise be denied to them. For those reasons alone, the Station attempted to track all Soviet approaches to Japanese space developments and key researchers.

None of our intelligence collection and monitoring activity was ever intended to benefit the U.S. private sector or damage Japan's economic position, and strict Agency protocols were in place to prevent it. In some situations, where a particular technology development was truly leading edge and promised to deliver an advantage for U.S. military systems, the knowledge that a Japanese capability existed spurred a direct U.S. approach. The request was an opportunity to learn more with an intent to purchase or license the technology. I recall several cases where such issues did arise—composite material being one—and in every case the U.S. side was scrupulous in its attention to detail and protocol.

In other situations where we knew or suspected the Soviets had targeted a Japanese system or technology for access, we needed to be able to provide advance warning to our Japanese counterparts. That was done in the hope they would be on guard and inclined to deny such access. In too many cases, however, we did not have the scope of contact or the knowledge of hostile activity to deny the opposition its mission. The Soviets and Chinese were able to suck volumes of sensitive information out of Japan, just as they were successful in draining the United States and other Western nations, all to the benefit of their weapons designers.

The U.S. government managed eventually to improve its counter-access game and put processes in place to mitigate technology theft and leakage to limit damage. But the Soviets and the Chinese managed to sustain and expand their collection programs over the decades. More recently, in contrast to the stumbling manner in which the Soviets, and later the Russians, attempted to apply what they gathered, the Chinese perfected their collection, distribution and exploitation programs. China's national program to steal, buy, co-opt, and otherwise secure protected technology and intellectual property for its defense industry base, as well as its government-owned firms, was relentless. It was fine-tuned over the decades and today continues to deliver to China whatever its own institutions are unable to provide. Japan was a "happy hunting ground" for technology theft in 1982, and it remains so in 2023, to the detriment of Japan and the rest of the Free World.

Chapter 27. The (Maybe) Never-Nuclear Japan 1982-1986

The Japan That Could 'Go Nuke'

One area of our high-tech responsibility involved coverage of the Japanese nuclear program. Despite our late start, the Station's clandestine source reporting soon complemented the excellent coverage delivered by our Embassy's energy counselor. Our probe of Japanese nuclear activities was designed to confirm that Japan was living up to the obligations of its bilateral agreement with the United States, mainly in the area of commercial reactor safeguards and research programs related to the nuclear fuel cycle. We also investigated any indications Japan was discreetly moving beyond its peaceful efforts into a nuclear weapons development program. The latter concern, now viewed from 2023, might seem farfetched. But it was not then, nor is it today.

For some years from my vantage in Seoul, where we were dealing with South Korea's attempt to create a nuclear weapons breakout capability, and extending through my European posting interacting with IAEA inspectors and chasing other covert nuclear programs, I kept a weather eye on Japan. I had read John Endicott's Japan's Nuclear Option: Political, Technical and Strategic Factors in 1975 during my tour in Seoul. His facts—the existing and projected nuclear programs of Japan—as well as the hypothetical paths he sketched for Japan to acquire a credible weapons capability, seemed reasonable to me. Over the years leading up to our establishment of the High Technology Branch in 1982, Japan had met or exceeded every milestone it set for itself in the nuclear field. Over the next few years, the Japanese program broadened in scope and capacity, with four paths of activity reinforcing one another. [NOTE 1]

Under a national program blessed at the Prime Minister level, Japan's Atomic Energy Commission oversaw the evolution of a master plan designed to harness and coordinate all elements of national power, defined in its 1982 "Long-Term Program on Nuclear Energy Development and Utilization." Two years later, on October 26, 1984, coinciding with Japan's official Atomic Energy Day, the AEC released an "Atomic Energy White Paper." The date celebrated 30 years since Japan formally had embraced nuclear energy, in 1954, and marked an interesting point in time given that, only nine short years earlier, American atomic weapons had vaporized two Japanese cities to end World War II.

In the early 1980s, Japan was on a nuclear sprint, and the United States needed to catch up as that well-managed program moved toward its goals. The Embassy science office was on the case, but so much was happening, and the Japanese nuclear program was so diverse and multifaceted that comprehensive reporting was a challenge. Japan's program was extremely well-coordinated, so it was appropriate that the Station should lend a hand, particularly where sensitive technology was concerned.

As suggested in the last chapter, detailed nuclear planning in Japan was the responsibility of two organizations, the Ministry of International Trade and Industry and the Science and Technology Agency. MITI's energy planning group master-planned and managed the industrial sector. Manufacturers such as Mitsubishi Heavy Industries, Hitachi and Toshiba were encouraged to incorporate the latest reactor designs from foreign vendors, ensuring domestic fabrication of light-water reactors on a turnkey basis or as complete units. A host of domestic subcontractors supported the big-three manufacturers, including world-class steel fabricators and pump, turbine generator and control system manufacturers.

The result of that national drive was that, by the late 1970s, Japan was fast approaching self-sufficiency with its nuclear sector, save for the licenses extended by U.S. and other western firms that once had enjoyed a monopoly in the nuclear business. That 1984 Atomic Energy White Paper was justified in proclaiming Japan should be recognized for its "nuclear independence." Having so arrived on the world stage, the nation was well-positioned as a candidate exporter of the nuclear systems and technology it had mastered.

On the reactor demand side, the various regionally based power utilities operated a growing fleet of the reactors, establishing order books that provided reactor suppliers with an assured market for decades to come. Japanese universities and training centers delivered a constant wave of engineering graduates to staff the power companies, manufacturers and laboratories, all working to master next-generation nuclear technologies.

Last and important, with MITI and STA oversight and funding, a collection of special-purpose entities was established to centralize key technology development. The institutions included the Japan Atomic Energy Research Institute. There, the Very High Temperature Gas-Cooled Reactor was being developed under a program initiated in 1969 and reconfirmed as a national priority by the AEC's "Long-Term Program on Nuclear Energy Development and Utilization." The activity was world-class and explored a number of areas relevant to futuristic, next-generation nuclear systems, including the use of high-temperature, high-pressure helium gas as a coolant; novel types of steel alloys; graphite core material and specialized nuclear fuel as well as control instrumentation.

Ambitions of a Fusion Future

Another nuclear area in which Japan and its JAERI team were, in the early 1980s, off to the races to establish a world leadership position was nuclear fusion. An incredibly challenging technology with the potential of taking the world beyond the fission process, the vision of controlled thermonuclear fusion was universally embraced—a reactor would not only use superabundant seawater to generate electric power but also produce its own fuel. The self-sustaining cycle would, if realized, completely alter the world's ability to access power. Japan's AEC had proposed that the nation commit to building a 400- to 800-megawatt fusion reactor by 1993, a program that would see the ongoing Engineering Test Reactor project merged with the Experimental Power Reactor effort to meet that goal.

The Japanese national commitment to commercial fusion power had deep roots, and the nation's nuclear physicists brimmed with confidence. Japan had established a Nuclear Fusion Council some years earlier, and though its long-term planning subcommittee welcomed international cooperation, there was no doubt Japan was prepared to go it alone if need be. The NFC's Taijiro Uchida, in an August 1981 interview with the American publication Fusion: At the Frontier of Science and Energy, declared it would be possible to achieve commercial fusion by 2000 if programs were accelerated. And even if they were not, it would happen in Japan by no later than 2010.

In an effort to leapfrog one phase of the process, Japan decided to move from its first-generation, small-scale JFT series experimental systems straight into the much larger and advanced JT-60. The endeavor would allow Japan to come abreast of the world-leading (at the time) Tokamak Fusion Test Reactor, slated for completion in 1982 at Princeton University. Little wonder that, amidst the bravado and commitment, the August edition of Fusion titled its cover story "Japan: Number One in Fusion?" In the minds of the Japanese researchers and government leadership, however, there was no cause for any question mark. The lead story within the publication was subtitled, "If the U.S. won't do it, we will!" In other words, Japan had made its decision: either get with the program or get out of Japan's way.

Japanese nuclear ambitions were predicated on close cooperation with the United States, but that presumption suffered a setback in May 1978. Back then, an offer by Prime Minister Takeo Fukuda to contribute $1 billion to partner with the United States to develop fusion power was rejected by President Jimmy Carter. The rejection only reinforced Japan's determination to press ahead. Two years later, the Reagan administration reversed many of Carter's energy policies, including restrained cooperation with Japan in the nuclear field, so that by 1982 all cylinders in the U.S.–Japan nuclear partnership were firing in sequence. In mid-1983, JAERI and the U.S. Department of Energy signed an agreement for the cooperative development of fusion reactor technology. Later that same year, JAERI and DOE's Oak Ridge National Laboratory began joint research programs.

In the out years, Japan's JT-60 program, consistent with other fusion research internationally, did not play out as many had hoped. Notwithstanding the disappointment, the core fact was that in the early to mid-1980s, Japan's political leadership, nuclear community, regulatory bodies and research institutes were united in their mission. All were determined to see Japan as a world leader in every aspect of nuclear energy, fusion reactors included, achieving a "first among equals" position. There was no reason, in either Japan or the United States, to suppose Japan could not meet its lofty goals.

Mastery of the Nuclear Fuel Cycle

There was one Japanese national priority, however, that gave us all on the U.S. side pause for concern: the nuclear fuel cycle. Beyond Japan's embrace of nuclear power for electricity generation and the ability to design, build and operate those plants—and outside the longer-term ambitions such as nuclear fusion and very high temperature reactor systems—the country was making a special determination. As stated in its previously mentioned 1984 Atomic Energy White Paper, "the development of an autonomous nuclear fuel cycle" was paramount for Japan. In fact, gaining such a capacity was considered an "extreme significance for energy" and an "extreme urgency."

Even now, nearly 40 years later, Japan's commitment to achieving total political independence for, and technical mastery of, all aspects of the nuclear fuel cycle remains. It has not abated since the original decision was made in the late 1950s to acquire such a capability. It remains despite the 2011 Fukushima incident and the continuing shutdown of almost every power reactor in Japan, not to mention repeated engineering failures and delays in the fuel cycle facilities. Now, as then, Japan retains plutonium metal far in excess of the requirements of any conceivable nuclear reactor program.

So it was therefore reasonable, as we refined our High Technology Branch reporting priorities in early 1983, to focus our work on the evolution of Japan's nuclear fuel cycle. We needed to be absolutely sure we had achieved visibility into every aspect of those efforts and were able to recognize Japan's capabilities as they came into place. In so doing, we reminded ourselves that we previously had undergone a showdown with the government of the Republic of Korea over those same fuel cycle issues. In that case, because we were motivated by our detection of a would-be nuclear weapons program, the U.S. government had moved aggressively to deny the Pak Chung-hee administration its planned reprocessing facility. In so doing, we essentially blocked South Korea from securing the source of plutonium that would have provided the country's military with the fissile material needed to create a weapons capability. In the case of Japan, we had a national program establishing the capability for uranium enrichment and for reprocessing, thereby allowing Japan (hypothetically) to possess two separate paths to secure fissile material.

In the parallel U.S. alliances with Japan and the ROK, in the nuclear area there was a double standard at work that had seen our government acquiesce to Japan's fuel cycle ambitions while rejecting those of the ROK. That acquiescence was a policy decision made at the highest levels to accommodate an ally's quest for energy security. One of the reasons for the decision was we held a high degree of confidence in our ability to influence the Japanese government positively, believing our security treaty would restrain any nuclear weapons ambitions.

Given those important bilateral trust and policy issues, the Agency and the Station were tasked to verify, through both overt observations and clandestine source reporting, that Japan remained on the nuclear straight and narrow. We needed to reconfirm there had been no diversions of material, no undeclared programs and no intentions for covert activity in those areas. The admonition, "no surprises," I had heard a few years back at Headquarters remained the order of the day in East Asia Division. Over those important years, we were able to confirm Japan's compliance with the terms and spirit of its commitments. Solid verification benefited the mutual security concerns of both nations ████ ████. It was good intelligence tasking for our operations officers and a worthy pursuit. I was pleased we were able to deliver high-quality reporting.

Enrichment and Reprocessing

To consolidate all fuel cycle-related work in Japan, a special entity had been chartered. The Power Reactor and Nuclear Fuel Development Corporation, or PNC as it was commonly called, was established to plan and manage those sensitive activities. During the halcyon years of the 1980s and into the 1990s, the PNC found itself lavished with government funding and staffed with the nation's best and brightest. It would earn an uneven reputation in later years, but throughout the decade when we dealt with it, the PNC was a dynamo of activity and success.

In the field of uranium enrichment, for example, the PNC aspired to refine and enrich fuel for fabrication into the assemblies that would power Japan's growing reactor fleet. The organization attempted to create a totally indigenous centrifuge program. It had begun working with enrichment in 1972, and by 1984 it was shifting from lab-scale testing of its second-generation centrifuge, the RT-2, to an expanded program. Improved devices would lead to higher-capacity, larger-scale installations in the second section of the demonstration plant by 1988. From there, assuming the PNC would be able to show the effectiveness of its homegrown technology, it would transfer the perfected centrifuge design to an entirely new entity, the Japan Nuclear Fuel Industries Company. JNFIC, initially supported by the government and by Japan's nuclear utilities—with ratepayers footing the bill based on a nationwide surcharge—would build and operate a commercial-scale facility at Rokkasho, in northern Japan's Aomori Prefecture. It was an ambitious plan, and its backers pushed on.

On the back end of the fuel cycle, the PNC had been equally aggressive over the years. It worked with hot cells and other aspects of reprocessing research, as it tuned up for the delivery of a French-built reprocessing plant. The plant, notionally declared a "pilot-scale facility," was a PNC centerpiece, and its delivery and commissioning in 1975 had drawn much attention. Located at Tōkai-mura, in Ibaraki Prefecture, the plant was based on the French version of the widely used and tried-and-true Plutonium Uranium Reduction EXtraction, or PUREX, process.

Interesting, but the functioning PNC plant in Japan was similar in size and capacity to the facility we had blocked the ROK from acquiring in 1975. The Korea Atomic Energy Research Institute had tracked the Japanese PNC purchase from a distance and determined that they needed to have that same facility. At Tōkai-mura, the technology provider was the French firm Saint Gobain Technique Novelle. After commissioning the plant, the firm and its technicians continued to assist PNC engineers throughout the 1980s. Coverage of the facility was critical to our ability to confirm full Japanese compliance in the non-proliferation sphere. If any untoward or undeclared activity were to occur in Japan, irrespective of the actor, the facility and the technology it possessed would be a lodestar. As such, it was worthy of the constant clandestine collection attention we directed at it.

Other Nuclear Activities of Interest and International Relationships

China:

Among Japan's activities in the category of developing nations, we assigned a special emphasis to the expansion of interaction with China, that is, The People's Republic of China. Japan had fought two major wars with China over the past 90 years. By 1980, the Japanese realized that Communist China, as a nation and a political system, was in place to stay. As such, Japan decided to accommodate itself to that fact for decades to come. By the time Japan elected to engage the PRC in an arm's-length nuclear relationship in the early 1980s, China was two decades into its own strategic weapons program, having detonated its first nuclear device in October 1964.

Perceiving both the United States and the Soviet Union as strategic rivals, China had undertaken a full-blown weapons development program, including requisite delivery systems. At the same time, China was pressing forward in nuclear power generation, based on Russian light-water reactor technology and uranium enrichment programs that fueled the reactors, as well as the weapons then being tested. China also was devoting scarce resources to a spectrum of nuclear research programs, including management of fuel production and reprocessing, and the domestic production of next-generation power reactors.

Consistent with its broader intent to engage positively in those areas where the Chinese were willing to interact, Japan made nuclear cooperation a touchpoint. The process of negotiating what would become the Sino–Japanese Nuclear Energy Agreement began in the margins of the Third Sino–Japanese Ministerial Meeting in Beijing in September 1983. It worked its way through six rounds of fine-tuning, was completed in July 1985 and came into effect on China's Double Ten day, October 10, 1986. Even before the nuclear discussions began, the Japan Atomic Industrial Forum had taken the lead with China in industry-to-industry contact and professional exchanges. That would continue, as JAIF worked hand-in-glove with Japan's premier business organization, Keidanren, to explore any and all potential commercial opportunities in China.

Of note, the finalized China–Japan bilateral agreement incorporated IAEA-approved language providing special safeguards for any and all transferred nuclear materials deemed "sensitive." Although Beijing then had other bilateral nuclear cooperation agreements in place—with the United States, the United Kingdom and West Germany—the Sino–Japanese agreement was the first to incorporate the new IAEA safeguards provisions.

By the time Japan made its approach to engage China under the rubric of peaceful nuclear cooperation, Beijing had established itself as an increasingly credible nuclear weapons state. Japanese national leadership was mindful of the growing threat from a traditional enemy. Japan's aggression in World War II and the damage that it had inflicted on China were constantly referenced by Beijing's leadership. When the two parties sat down to initial their bilateral nuclear cooperation agreement in 1985, China had been producing and detonating nuclear devices for two decades.

A robust nuclear weapons capability had been a national priority for Communist China from the day it seized power over the mainland in 1949. Its scientists enjoyed a kickstart from their Soviet compatriots, at least until those two nations fell out as allies in the late 1960s. By then, China no longer needed Soviet assistance, and its weapons programs surged forward. China's first test had occurred in October 1964 and involved an enriched uranium device that yielded 22 kilotons, an explosion roughly equivalent to that of the gun-type device the U.S. had deployed against Hiroshima in 1945. During the balance of the 1960s and into the t' '70s, China's nuclear teams had continued to expand their range of designs, perfecting smaller, more efficient and therefore more deliverable warheads.

By May 1966, China tested its first boosted-fission device and, a few months later, was able to demonstrate its ability to produce a nuclear warhead that could be delivered by a surface-to-surface ballistic missile. Japan was then, or soon would be, within range of a missile capable of striking anywhere in the Japanese home islands. The following year China tested its first full-yield thermonuclear weapon, which roared at 3.4 megatons. **[NOTE 2]**

The Soviet Union:

Joining the Allied effort against Japan in the final week of World War II, the U.S.S.R. was a would-be occupier of Japan. In wake of that nation's surrender in August 1945, the Soviets—as the defeated party in the 1905 Russo–Japanese War that established Japan as a world power—were a hostile force in the eyes of Japan. As the Cold War deepened in the 1970s, and gained even more momentum in the 1980s, Japan found itself on the front lines of confrontation with the Soviets in Northeast Asia. In addition to being a nuclear weapons state on the wrong side of Japan in the Cold War, the Soviet Union strived to promote its own mastery of nuclear energy in all fields, including peaceful applications in power generation and research. Thus, to Japan as an aspiring nuclear state, the Soviet

Union presented an attraction that Japan found hard to resist, particularly in advanced reactor research partnerships.

Once again eager to establish a direct relationship that would benefit the country's nuclear future, if not its industry patrons, JAIF had taken the lead with Moscow. Government-sanctioned discussions soon followed, and bilateral agreements for research on next-generation technologies fell into place, resulting in expanded exchanges of researchers and scientists. The activity was not all that different from U.S.–Soviet exchanges in the nuclear research field, but it created an opportunity for Soviet intelligence officers working the subject area to have free rein with the Japanese.

The net was that KGB and GRU operatives and their co-opted scientists routinely targeted Japanese counterparts for recruitment. The Japanese national security establishment essentially was incapable of monitoring, let alone defeating, the intrusions. By the mid-1980s, when the Station attempted to track those relationships, we found the Soviets all over the Japanese nuclear programs and researchers. Japanese advances in lasers, aeronautics, special materials, microelectronics and robotics also were fair game for aggressive recruiters and intelligence collectors. For our Station's Soviet Branch, it was not easy to counter the threat mounted by Russian, Eastern Bloc and Chinese espionage directed at Japan's rapidly evolving technology centers, particularly those hosted by nuclear- or military-related expertise.

Our Station's Liaison Branch worked with the Japanese National Police Agency and intelligence counterparts to mitigate the damage. There, the excellent relationships we enjoyed with Japanese security institutions did pay dividends, but the magnitude of the threat was difficult to surmount. All parties were conducting counterintelligence efforts against a confluence of Japan's nuclear relationships, a broad spectrum of militarily significant technologies being engaged by Soviet and Chinese operatives. All of it occurred in a permissive environment, and though I remain unsure we ever managed to get ahead of the communists' game, at least we made a dent. In the out years, after the Soviet Union collapsed and the KGB reinvented itself, and as China sharpened its capability for technology theft, Japan would find itself the once-again-and-ever target. It remains so in 2023 and will be the case as long as Japan has something of value for the opposition to collect—correction, steal.

IAEA:

Japan embraced the IAEA from the outset and became one of its lead supporters, all to the benefit of that organization and Japan's standing within the UN entity. Japan excelled in areas of technical assistance to developing nations, in multilateral cooperative research initiatives supported by IAEA and in administration of the IAEA bureaucracy. Japan also excelled in the all-important safeguards area. Japanese inspectors and engineers working on surveillance and diagnostics systems were active, eager and efficient. The result was Japan always seemed to be punching above its weight in Vienna.

There was self-interest at work. Japan closely embraced the IAEA for the simple reason that nuclear energy was to Japan both a blessing, promising as it did a high level of energy independence, and a hazard. North Korea loomed near, just across the Sea of Japan. South Korea, one could assume, already had or would someday have developed or acquired an indigenous nuclear weapons program, with an attack capability to follow. Even if Seoul's immediate nuclear ambitions had been curtailed by the United States, it was an even bet South Korea someday would drift into a more confrontational attitude toward Japan. Absent American involvement and constraint, it was a situation that could never be assumed not to turn against Japan in the long run. A parallel reasonable assumption was North Korea would develop nuclear weapons capability, both to intimidate the South and threaten U.S. bases in Japan—as well as Japan proper.

The crude and inescapable reality was South Korea and North Korea were inherently, if not congenitally, hostile to Japan. Memories were long on both sides of the narrow sea that separates them. Japan had colonized the entire peninsula and administered the populace with a heavy hand for 35 years. In both Korean states, the dislike and distrust of Japan was a widely shared emotion, which back then was still easily tapped for domestic political gain. The animosity resided deep in the belly of the general populace of both countries in the 1980s, and it presented a raw nerve to which any Korean leader, for whatever reason, could appeal at any time.

For Japan, each of the two Koreas was a near-equal concern as a potential nuclear weapons state as either China or the Soviet Union. IAEA safeguards were one of Japan's best options for containing both countries. One could assume North Korea would go its own way no matter what controls were applied, but it was reasonable that South Korea, with much more at stake, would feel compelled to stay within the safeguards regime.

There was a related consideration particular to Japan. South Korea had undertaken an ambitious nuclear power program with the promise that a score of reactors would be constructed to operate along the southeastern coast. Should there occur a Chernobyl-type malfunction or meltdown, even with one of the U.S.- or Canadian-designed reactors, there would be a strong chance of a radioactive cloud. Prevailing winds would carry that contamination directly into Japan with dire consequences. Although IAEA safeguards were modeled both to detect anomalies related to nuclear reactors and confirm the competence of reactor operators' compliance with safety procedures, there always could be a mishap. With Seoul unwilling to be second-guessed by Tokyo, let alone inspected by Japan for reactor safety, Japan had no choice but to depend on the IAEA and its operational protocols and inspections. [NOTE 3]

The concern on Japan's part for safe operations of South Korea's growing fleet of power reactors would not go away and later would be reinforced when its own reactor complex at Fukushima was overwhelmed by a tsunami and melted down. China's nuclear reactor program carried—and still carries—a similar concern for Japan. It certainly was one reason Japan wanted to cooperate aggressively with China on reactor-safety issues. But it was the South Korean reactors that remained in Japan's focus, and for good reason. Those reactors are located where they are and advertise themselves as vulnerable to a North Korean terrorist attack. The destruction of one of them, or even an attack that compromised their spent nuclear fuel ponds, would present Japan with a catastrophic prospect. The possibility remains today, with the caveat that the threat is now more recognized and more real but no more manageable. [NOTE 4]

IAEA engagement in Northeast Asia was a necessity for Japan. The agency's nuclear safeguards, intended to preempt a diversion of materials, and its nuclear reactor safety standards, made the IAEA then and now an insurance policy. In the mid-1980s, both South Korea and North Korea had acceded to the nuclear non-proliferation treaty, and each had IAEA safeguards in place at their respective facilities. Although the IAEA regime was an imperfect and vulnerable construct, the organization itself answered to the United Nations Secretariat, the General Assembly and the Security Council. In so doing, the IAEA offered some measure of assurance to Japan that the nuclear undertakings of the two Koreas were being actively monitored by a responsible third party. In future years, that assurance would not work out quite so well with North Korea. In the event Pyongyang would denounce the IAEA as an institution, reject its safeguards, leave the NPT and become a full-fledged nuclear weapons state, Japan's deepest concerns would have come to pass and remain so today.

From Japan's perspective, the IAEA was a valuable instrument worth its involvement and support. Japan's contribution to the agency likewise was useful to the United States, given that we placed great value on improving and sustaining its credibility. U.S. policymakers welcomed the fact that Japan was prepared to support the IAEA strongly and was part of a loose collection of like-minded nations that pressed for expanded nuclear export controls. From the perspective of the Station, on the clandestine collection side, our activity was narrowly focused, limited to those areas that were not well-covered by the Embassy and its interaction with Washington and Vienna.

Third Country Nuclear

Because Japan had placed itself at the forefront of peaceful nuclear activities and offered its research institutions as venues for foreign participation, we found a fair number of interesting individuals temporarily resident in Japan. Most had been dispatched by their home countries to learn from Japan or act as innocent participants in joint research projects. Some, however, did come intending to elicit sensitive information that could contribute to their nations' proliferation activities. In that regard, we targeted visitors we knew were players in sensitive programs at home, both to recruit them for Agency service or deny them any illicit fruits of their time in Japan.

From any angle, the Japanese nuclear community was a target-rich environment. Over the three-plus years I managed our High Technology Branch in

East Asia, we made maximum use of the operating space we were given and established a first-rate program of collection and reporting. I believe the U.S.–Japan security relationship became stronger for our efforts. One crucial result was providing confidence to U.S. policymakers responsible for charting bilateral technology and military cooperation in the years ahead.

Good Vibrations and Smooth Sailing

By early summer of my third year in the Asian city, it had all come together for the High Technology Branch and the Station. Working the tech targets, we focused on the nuclear- and military-related areas. We still were playing defense against the Soviets and Chinese and, ever opportunistic, we had hit full stride. My team had expanded and was working well with the balance of the Station. Our management and support staff were tight and efficient. We all enjoyed working for Jim, our Chief, mainly because he was interested in every operational area and always backed his officers to the hilt, professionally as well as personally.

Jim was a product of Chicago's South Side. He had come to an early maturity during the Depression, when he worked as a boy to support his family, and in World War II he had flown as a co-pilot in a B-17 with the Eighth Air Force in the flak-filled skies over Germany. He joined the recently hatched Agency at the time of the Korean War and was recruited by the clandestine service. He was an East Asia lifer with many tours under his belt, and he deserved to occupy the most prestigious Station Chief assignment in the Division. Some of his contemporaries among the Division's Irish mafia thought him "too sensitive" and not inclined to fight the good fight, but they were wrong. Within that closely bred group, there also resided a bit of prejudice, given Jim was an Irish Protestant. In typical fashion, Jim was indifferent to that distinction.

In my third year, Jim departed for Headquarters, where Director William J. Casey had a new position waiting for him. His replacement, another made man among the Irish mafia, was efficient, effective and distant, at least to me. That said, we got along just fine, and I anticipated a fourth and final year that would be a ride on easy street, one in which I could plan for my next tour, probably back at Headquarters, and from there explore other options for onward field assignments. At that future point, roughly in the spring of 1987, nearing 15 years in the DO with three overseas tours under my belt, I could hope for a chief's position in a small station, or perhaps deputy chief at a larger station. I had my eye on another assignment in Asia but likely would take anything they offered me. The more responsibility and the more autonomy, the better.

All such musing presupposed I would stay in the Agency. But I was having second thoughts. I always had considered the Agency and the Directorate of Operations a calling of sorts, rather than a career. My going-in position and my motivation were to serve my country in the best way possible. The Agency offered me a great opportunity to do so. They demanded a lot from me, and mostly had received it. I, in return, derived from the Agency exactly what I had sought when I signed on to the program: the satisfaction of doing a good job in a field where I could perform well and deliver. It had been a fair bargain; fairly struck and fairly delivered on both sides.

Within the DO, things were changing by the mid-1980s, but not for the good. The ground was shifting back at Headquarters, in part due to the disastrous directorship of Stansfield Turner, and part because of the lasting impact of the public raking endured during the Director William Colby years. The post-Vietnam media and Congress remained hostile to all aspects of the Agency. Pundits and historians were working hard to discredit its every activity, whether or not they even attempted to understand or appreciate anything being accomplished. What I found most distasteful was the lack of distinction between intelligence collection to support national policy decision-making and "covert action," as the Agency's antagonists presented that seemingly distasteful word. Most of us in the field woke up every morning to do our jobs and did not let it bother us too much. Still, it was clear the offensive was undermining the nation's trust and confidence in our organization.

While the Reagan administration sought to rebuild and reinvigorate the Agency, the damage had been done, and its culture was shifting perceptibly. The clandestine service resisted but was impacted nonetheless, particularly in the quality of personnel we were able to recruit into the Agency and, from that pool, select for service in the DO. I had seen some of it in my European posting, but in my current assignment the quality issue was in full view. I was distressed by the attitude of many of the first-tour officers dispatched to our Station, a couple of whom eventually were assigned to my High Technology Branch. Station-wide, maybe one in four of our new officers was a "keeper," while at least another one in four never should have been admitted to the Directorate, let alone sent to the field.

My concerns were reinforced when a senior manager from Headquarters visited us to complete an assessment of the performance of first-tour officers. When I pressed him in an informal discussion, he explained that the new wave of recruits the Agency pipeline was delivering to the Directorate was disappointing, particularly from the standpoint of motivation. When new career trainees were interviewed and asked to identify the important reasons why they joined the Agency, the responses involved pension plans, health benefits, compensation and travel overseas, with almost no mention of service to country, patriotism or any motivation that suggested they would be willing to work six days a week, all day and into the night, and take the risks that a clandestine officer should accept as the norm.

It was a different generation, with not a few exhibiting a, "What can this organization Do for Me?" attitude. For a manager, it was one thing to have to deal with a career officer who had peaked early or turned out to be a mediocre performer in his or her third tour. It was entirely another issue to have first-tour officers arrive in-country, just out of the farm training program, who were poorly motivated or incompetent, or both. In the city by 1985, we were getting them on a regular basis. Although it might seem petty or somewhat arrogant, the situation was a fact of life that had to be planned around and dealt with carefully. [NOTE 1]

Complicating our disappointment with the next generation of officers, and what I regarded as a drift in purpose back at Headquarters, was my look forward, which included the possibility of departing the Agency. I set age 40 (I was 38) as a decision point. In my assignment, I had become fascinated by advanced technology and the quantum advances technology seemed to be bringing to so many areas of business and lifestyles. I was challenged by the concept of private enterprise and entrepreneurship. I decided to wait out my tour and applied for a year at the John F. Kennedy School of Government at Harvard, where the Directorate sponsored one middle-grade officer annually. In seeking the JFK school position, I knew if I was selected to attend, I would owe the Agency three more years of service. It seemed like a plan, but all good plans founder in a storm, and a Nor'easter named Casey was brewing.

Casey at the Bat

In the spring of 1985, Director William J. Casey decided to make an extended visit to us. We learned about the impending event a couple of weeks in advance and some details through back-channel cables. We realized Casey had been extensively briefed on various Station operations, and he wanted details and was coming to talk with branch chiefs and individual officers. I did not know Bill Casey, apart from a hurried, three-day exposure back when I had been his escort officer in Seoul a decade earlier. He was then president of the U.S. Export–Import Bank, and I was the Nuclear Energy Officer, responsible for briefing him on South Korea's plans for its nuclear power program. He arrived to personally investigate the bank's growing loan portfolio in South Korea, keyed to the first Westinghouse reactors being built there. I was impressed by his knowledge of nuclear power and the specifics of the various EXIM Bank loans then pending for South Korea.

In that conversation, he warned me about middlemen vultures circling those projects and that I should be particularly cautious of both Korean and American "influence brokers" attempting to insert themselves dishonestly into them. More than I imagined then, he had been right, and I respected him for the admonition. I did not expect he would remember me from our brief encounter in Seoul, and he did not. Casey's security advance team sat with us about a week before his arrival, and we were well-prepared for his intelligence factfinding visit. [NOTE 2]

During the second day, after meetings with Japanese national security officials and a welcome dinner hosted by our intelligence counterparts, Casey sat with my deputy and me in our office for three hours to discuss our high-technology collection and reporting program. He was engaged, informed and enthusiastic about what we were doing and how we had organized ourselves. Individual targets were discussed, clandestine assets overviewed (but only in alias identities) and future plans reviewed. I found he had read his briefs well, and he not only understood our ongoing operations from a clandestine collection perspective but also was following Japanese business trends and technology.

Casey asked me to explain how it was we had "trained up" case officers with little or no commercial or high-tech background to be able to elicit and draft reporting on those complex subjects. I explained we assigned them material to read, encouraged them to become lay experts in selected areas, and guided them to help one another on tasking and reporting. For example, an officer who understood laser technology would coach another officer, or even sit with him in a debriefing session, to make sure he had gotten the information correct. I also explained how our in-branch Reports Officer functioned, mainly to ensure our draft field disseminations passed smoothly through our Station's Reports Branch with a minimum of interference and timely release to Headquarters.

As we closed the briefing, I also mentioned that, beyond the normal technical trade publications to which our officers had access, I had purchased seven subscriptions to Forbes magazine. I required each of our case officers to read that publication cover-to-cover to make them conversant in the business world in which we all had to work. Casey was pleasantly taken aback and commented, "Those are probably the only seven subscriptions to Forbes in the entire damn Agency!"

That evening, I had an extended one-on-one with Casey, hosted by our Station Chief, to discuss a special operation I had developed and managed over the past year or so. It involved a hard-target reporting source who had nothing to do with our High Technology Branch or other officers there. The asset was a unique source, and all information was protected in special operational and reporting channels, with only three of our officers knowledgeable and cleared to discuss the case. I was somewhat surprised Casey already had been briefed on the operation and arrived prepared to ask questions about the asset and the reporting being generated.

By that point in my tour, the case was occupying a third or more of my time. I expected the load would only increase during the year I had remaining. A few weeks before Casey's visit, Headquarters had set up a special reports processing team keyed exclusively to the operation. As a consequence, the tasking from the Headquarters team for my use with the asset seemed to double with every batch of draft reporting I submitted. Their appetite seemed insatiable, and I came to realize just how deficient our knowledge was of that important target. At some future point, the operation might see the light of day, and interested parties will be able to discuss the knowledge gaps the United States had in accessing that target and the degree to which we were able to close that gap with our local operation. Enough said here, but it was a fine operation, and I appreciated that Casey knew so much about it.

Casey's Special Request

When Bill Casey and his party headed home, I knew our Station writ large, and my branch's activity in particular, had given him a lot to think about. But before he departed, in a quiet aside, Casey explained to me he probably would be making a "special personal request" about a matter he considered to be unofficial, informal and outside any Agency business.

I did not think much about the conversation until a few weeks later, when I received a call from an American businessman. He had just arrived in Tokyo to stay at the Imperial Hotel, a few blocks from the Embassy. He explained he was a close friend of Bill Casey and wanted to meet me. He asked if I could sit with him and his family that evening in his room at the Imperial. That is when I met John Shaheen, a New York financier, along with his wife, two sons and his personal physician, the latter a renowned researcher at Columbia University Hospital. John was 70 at the time, like Casey an OSS veteran and a man of humble origins. John had made a career in the oil industry, accumulated a fortune and managed to lose that bounty more than once. He was the kind of man who often inclined to risk it all to take the "big chance" on the next venture. John was dying of cancer and had failed with every remediation treatment available in the United States. He was now facing the reality that he had little chance to arrest the disease.

Then John learned that a Tokyo University doctor was achieving some initial success in developing a silver-bullet treatment for his type of cancer. So, John volunteered to enter the program as a treatment subject. His cancer team in New York endorsed the effort but had cautioned him it was "a very long shot." They helped make the arrangements that brought him and his family to Tokyo. The treatments were to begin in a few days, and he wanted to enjoy Tokyo with his family before the ordeal began. I agreed to be his guide and companion and offered to help as well as I could. In any event, I was not in a position to ignore Casey's request, and John was a personable and appreciative man.

Over the weeks John remained in the city, we spent many evenings together. Our dinner conversations flowed freely, and once his family departed ahead of him to return home to New York, his personal physician and I were his only companions. John recounted his OSS days, his business career, his current situation and his pending demise. Although he had bought and managed several businesses over his lifetime, including a small fleet of radio and TV stations, his real calling was oil and, in that patch, refining. He was proud of one exceedingly ambitious project, the Come By Chance Refinery, located in a remote bay near Bear Head in Newfoundland, Canada. His project firm, Shaheen Resources, built the refinery in the 1971-1973 period on a greenfield site and operated it successfully for several years. In 1974, with great fanfare, John chartered the luxury liner Queen Elizabeth 2 to convey a large group of friends and investors on a promotional visit to view his accomplishment and celebrate his investment.

Most intensely, John reflected on his childhood. He was born and grew to manhood in a small town in Illinois not that far from my own origins. He was amazed I recognized Tampico by its name and that I knew the area. His parents had immigrated from Lebanon, found their way to that place in the Midwest and had set themselves up to run a general goods store. John was a childhood friend of the future President Ronald Reagan, three years younger but part of the gang that ran together. John's family suffered alongside the Reagans during the Great Depression. He explained that during the Depression's deepest years, his family had extended as much care to their neighbors as possible and noted that the Reagan family was one of those in great need. It was no secret that Jack Reagan had a serious problem with drinking and was consistently unemployed.

A proud and forceful woman, Ronald's mother Nelle was the family rock, taking in laundry from others and working for hardscrabble wages to keep food on the table. Of Scotch–Irish ancestry, Nelle adamantly declined charity at the Shaheen general store while seeking any work available to feed her family. John's father, determined to help the Reagans, sent his wife with milk and food to the Reagan house on a covert run when Nelle was known to be at another home doing laundry. John's mother would steal into the house—no one ever locked their door and, in fact, there were no locks on the doors in Tampico—and place food in the icebox. When John's mother discovered the icebox had no ice, she returned on a second run with a block of ice to chill the food. His mother learned always to bring along a block of ice, but she made no mention of the gesture when Nelle next visited the store to pay for her purchases, which she proudly did, always in cash.

Reflecting on his Tampico childhood, John related to me an incident that had occurred recently in, of all places, the White House. The event brought memories of that period and the friendships of that small Illinois town back to John, and to President Reagan as well. It occurred a few months after he was sworn in as 38th President, when John and several other childhood friends were invited to dine with the newly elected chief executive. Although John had been an ardent Republican and had supported the Reagan candidacy as best as he could, the dinner was about old friendships and a shared childhood. As the friends recounted pleasant memories, including a mishandled shotgun that blew a hole in the ceiling of one boy's kitchen, John said Reagan and the others laughed for hours.

When the evening grew long, the conversation turned to the Depression they all had lived through, and the suffering of their families. John leaned into the discussion to recount a particular incident he suspected none of the others knew about, in part because most people in that time kept their own counsel and did not complain. John explained that his parents' store had verged on bankruptcy for more than a year, mainly because the store accepted what was called Chicago script as payment for food. The currency was issued by a state-authorized entity and ostensibly was convertible into U.S. dollars. But the Chicago script managers were not inclined to convert the currency. The Chicago politico-bureaucrats forced those holding the script, like the Shaheen store far outside the city, to complete forms and patiently wait out the process. It was a calculated stall and resulted in delays of six months or more for those not politically connected or unwilling to pay the special commission.

In the meantime, back at the Shaheen store, food wholesalers demanded payment on delivery—in U.S. dollars—disdaining the discredited and unconvertible Chicago script the Shaheens held in bulk. John then shared with those at the table the fact that the store had been rescued by one man, Jack Reagan. A minor Democratic Party functionary and would-be political player, Ronald Reagan's father somehow had angled his party machine contacts to secure a part-time position in the currency-conversion office, thereby securing a meager but welcome flow of income for the family.

Shortly after settling into his job in the conversion office, Jack visited the Shaheen store and asked John's father for an accounting of all the script packages the store had requested for conversion, plus the stack of script still held in the safe, stuffed in a large tobacco can. John's father took the chance, handed everything over to Jack and prayed. Three weeks later, officials contacted John's parents to say that an error had apparently been made with their delayed payment. All funds due to the store, in newly printed dollars, were available for pickup. John said his mother sobbed in relief, and his father was dumbstruck. Thanks to Jack Reagan, the Shaheen general store had its money, and their store was saved.

When John told the story, there was silence at the table. President Reagan excused himself, slowly got up from the table and walked a short distance to stand in front of the fireplace. The light of flames illuminated him in an otherwise darkened part of the room. John approached the President and found him quietly crying, tears coming down his cheeks. He asked his old friend if he had said something wrong or offended him. Reagan regained his composure and responded, "John, tonight you have given me a gift that is unbelievable, something I thought impossible. You see, I have never heard anything good or positive said about my father. Tonight, among my friends from our childhood, I learned that he was not only a good man, a caring man, but was capable of doing wonderful things for others. Thank you, my old friend."

John returned to the table, rejoined his friends and took the conversation in a different direction. The President returned to the group a few minutes later, weight lifted and smiling. The evening ended well, and John realized only later that he had brought some measure of peace to a man who had tried hard to respect his father but could not bring himself to do so. Ronald Reagan was, on that night, at peace with the memory of his father.

John departed Tokyo a couple of weeks later and returned home to continue his battle with cancer. He passed away on November 1, 1985, as I was shuttling back and forth between Washington and Tokyo. His full career was chronicled in numerous obituaries and testimonials, and his relationship with Bill Casey was the subject of speculation by many Casey detractors. A passing mention of John Shaheen was made in the state inquisition otherwise known as the Special Counsel Walsh Report (Chapter 15 of that document). But in my brief relationship with John, he came across as a patriot, and a great family man to his wife, sons and sisters. I later thanked Bill Casey for the chance to become John's friend. Casey, in turn, was most appreciative that I had found time to be with John in Tokyo. It was entirely my pleasure. **[NOTE 3]**

An Unanticipated Summons

On a bright Saturday morning in October 1985, I was asked to come to the Station Chief's office, or "Up Front" as we called it. Waiting for me was our post-Jim Chief and his Deputy, and they made a stern combination for sure. The new Chief handed me a cable just arrived from Headquarters, and I could see it was a back-channel message. "You're gone from this Station. Casey has claimed you, and we don't know why or for what reason. Nobody seems to know." I read the cable twice. It instructed me to proceed posthaste, meaning fly the following day to Washington and report at 8 a.m. Monday to Casey's office. No explanation offered. Just be there. I went back to my office, talked it over with my deputy, asked Station Support to cut me travel orders and went home to pack. Thus began my next assignment and with it a whole lot of trouble.

The irony was that three days before, I had held in my hands a different back-channel cable. It was a brief note from the head of the Directorate's Personnel Assignments Division, notifying me that I had been selected to attend the JFK School the following September. It would have occurred in the fall of 1986 at the completion of my four-year tour. Although I did not realize it at the time, the nomination for a Harvard dusting had just gone out the window with the Casey summons, in good company with a lot of other careful planning.

Chapter 26

- **NOTE 1 - See page 344**

  A second coincidence contained in that issue of Newsweek, which I forced myself to digest, was a major story chronicling Ambassador Philip Habib's attempts to restore some measure of peace to the war-torn city of Beirut and the nation of Lebanon. The article, "Habib's Grueling Shuttle," awarded him high marks for undertaking the thankless task of attempting to negotiate a ceasefire and a compromise way forward for the Lebanese, the Palestinians and the Israelis. President Ronald Reagan had launched Habib on a quest that most believed was highly unlikely to deliver results. Yet Habib had thrown himself into the task, shuttling among Cairo, Rome, London, Israel and Beirut. That was the determined man I knew from my former tour in Seoul, and when I read the article, I worried that his heart could only take so much of this pounding pace.

- **NOTE 2 - page 347**

  The reference to Moscow's tasking, directed to all of its assorted intelligence agencies, diplomats, trade missions and fellow travelers worldwide, to search for any indication of the United States planning for a preemptive nuclear strike, was codenamed "Operation RyAN." By late 1981, as the Reagan team settled down to its work of winning the Cold War by overmatching the Soviet Union in virtually every category of war-making capacity, the increasingly confused and paranoid leadership of the Soviet Union convinced itself that the United States was considering nuclear strike scenarios that would erase the Soviet threat once and for all. The devolution of Soviet Politburo thinking, and the manner in which this directive descended on the KGB and GRU career officers in the field, to include Tokyo, was revealed after the collapse of the Soviet Union. An excellent recounting of this departure from reality, and the paranoia that almost sparked a world war, is related in a recent (2018) publication, <u>1983: Reagan, Andropov and the World on the Brink</u>, by Taylor Downing.

- **NOTE 3 - page 348**

  The Toshiba/Kongsberg sale was a major scandal and embarrassment for the entire Japanese establishment, most notably for MITI as the bureaucracy charged with policing such transactions. The incident has been described in great detail in a number of narratives, as well as in U.S. Congressional testimony, and has been cited repeatedly as a major failing of the entire COCOM system. Contemporary reporting provided insights into the machinations of the various Japanese firms involved in this duplicity, and the contortions by Toshiba management to achieve the sale by all means necessary. Of note, correspondent Daniel Sneider's article for The Christian Science Monitor, datelined Tokyo, July 21, 1987, and titled "Toshiba Sale: Only the Tip of Espionage Iceberg," provides particularly good flavor as the details of the scandal spilled out. A much more disciplined study of the entire incident, titled "The Toshiba–Kongsberg Incident: Shortcomings of Cocom, and Recommendations for Increased Effectiveness of Export Controls to the East Bloc," authored by Wende A. Wrubel, appeared in the American University International Law Review in 2011, Volume 4, Issue 1, Article 16. The article, apparently derived from a 1989 J.D. paper by the same author, is deep in detail with extensive citations.

• NOTE 4 - page 348

In September 1985, partly energized by the Toshiba incident, and more broadly inspired by the continuing surge in our discovery of examples of successful Soviet acquisition of sensitive U.S. technology, the CIA published a classified report, "Soviet Acquisition of Militarily Significant Western Technology: An Update." The Introduction begins with a cogent description of the ongoing situation back then.

> *In recent years, the United States Government has learned of a massive, well-organized campaign by the Soviet Union to acquire Western technology illegally and legally for its weapons and military equipment projects.*

After describing the magnitude of the Soviet effort and its success, including the observation that "the assimilation of this acquired technology is so broad that the United States and other Western nations are thus subsidizing the Soviet military buildup," the Introduction goes on to warn,

> *Western products and technology secrets are being systematically targeted by intricately organized, highly efficient collection programs specifically targeted to improve Soviet military weapons systems.*

In Japan, at the time this update report was published, the Soviet collection program had been underway, and successful, for at least five years. This report was declassified in 1999 by the CIA's Historical Review Program and is available at: https://www.cia.gov/library/readingroom/docs/CIA-RD-P84B00049R001503890021-8.pdf.

• NOTE 5 - page 350

The HTB internal reports officer component was essential in that I did not want to have our homework fact-checked, delayed or degraded by the Station's Reports Branch. All other Station branch reporting flowed into this team in a draft version, to be reformatted and repackaged for onward sending to the Headquarters reports mandarins. Once in the latter's hands. it would be further edited and repackaged for formal dissemination into the community. We accepted our Station reports officers as true professionals and welcomed their final processing of our HTB reporting, but our work at the HTB level relieved them of the responsibility of tweaking technology terminology or questioning the utility of a given line of reporting. The reports cadre were proficient on the China, Soviet, North Korean and domestic Japan political reporting, but they had no clue on semiconductors, nuclear terminology, or whatever.

In one instance where we were getting pushback on the autonomy in the reporting we enjoyed in HTB, we elected to create a bogus report that would be dispatched down the hall for a once-over by the Station reports team. The draft submission was titled "Japanese Space Agency Secret Plans for a Manned Mission to the Sun." We included some scientific background and identified several involved Japanese firms. For example, MELCO as the spacecraft builder, and the important role to be played by Toto Ceramics, responsible for the spacecraft thermal structure. Toto of course was a leading manufacturer of bathroom fixtures and had a lock on the Japanese toilet, sink and bidet market. I forgot that we had dispatched this bogus draft to our Station reports colleagues. But a few days later I found myself looking up from my desk to see a visibly upset reports chief standing before me. Our "Manned Mission to the Sun" draft was in his hand.

Terry Daly was a swell guy and maybe the best reports officer I had met, but he was not happy. "I just stopped this crap of a report from going out to Headquarters as a dissemination! My folks processed it as a serious report and expected me to release it. You have made your point, but don't try to pull this shit on me or my staff again." Then he smiled, "Besides, you failed to explain in this draft how the Japanese sun-o-nauts were going to get back after they planted their Rising Sun banner on the Sun!"

• NOTE 6 - page 350

The Soviet Union might have been the exception to this statement, but one could assume that, even if the KGB and GRU managed to acquire the same level of knowledge overtly, it was doubtful that there existed the means to process and deliver that information to those within the Soviet system who would have most benefited. On the other hand, we could also assume that Soviet intelligence collectors were active, and probably successful, in stealing a fair amount of NASA material. But here again, there would have been the issue of efficient information sharing within that compartmented system and once shared, the uneven ability of the Soviet defense industry to make anything out of it.

I am reminded that, during this tour, we had a Soviet KGB Line KR defector who had been debriefed on his own technology collection activity in Tokyo. He complained that a competitor in his Embassy, a creative GRU colleague, had received a special commendation for his success in collecting protected Japanese technology information. The GRU judged the competition on the basis of the number of pages and the weight of documents collected, e.g., 2,500 pages coming in at 43 kilos. In this success calculation, there was little regard to what was contained in the accumulated stack and forwarded to GRU Headquarters. The defector assessed that he would never be able to survive in such a volume-based system and wisely elected to leave the service and his country for good.

At the time, I reflected that I knew a few of my own Agency colleagues who would be pleased to compete on the same basis, and I worried that someone at home might be inclined to award a similar volume-based commendation. In my High Technology Branch, when we considered sending a 300-page report back to Headquarters, we always asked first, "Do you really need this monster?" The answer from the insatiable ones at home base was always "Well, yes, of course … just send it in."

- **NOTE 7 - page 352**

My reference on all things NASDA and ISAS are from my private notebooks of the period, buttressed by the publication Space in Japan 1983-1984, drafted by STA's research and Coordination Bureau, and published by Keidanren. This 30-page update report is supplemented by my collection of NASDA monthly reports and the publication Science and Technology In Japan, a comprehensive overview published quarterly by 3-T Publications, Tokyo, Japan. A supplemental document is a draft translation of a special report compiled in 1987 by the Japan Space Activities Commission's Consultative Committee on Long-Term Policy.

The SAC/CCLTP document was titled "Towards a New Era of Space Science and Technology" and was intended to compel increased budget allocations to ensure Japan's ability to claim world co-leadership in space. The report's committee of experts emphasized the melding of all elements of national capacity, including government, private sector, and academia for a maximum effort in the 21st century and beyond. The entire theme was highly aspirational and reflected Japan's growing confidence at that time in its institutions, technology and competitiveness.

- **NOTE 8 - page 352**

  After my departure in 1985, the Japanese space program continued apace, and by 1988, the nation had launched no fewer than 40 satellites. It was then moving on from NASDA's H-1 launch system to work on finalizing the design of the successor H-II. The latter MHI-designed and manufactured system would employ elements of the predecessor H-1 for its second stage, strap on the ISAS-perfected, MU series of solid-fuel boosters and employ state-of-the-art cryogenic propulsion technology. At the time, publications saw the H-II as a head-to-head competitor to the French-sponsored Ariane 44L launch system, capable of placing as much as six tons into geostationary transfer orbit. Assuming its availability four years later, in 1992, the H-II was projected to beat its French competitor to commercial operation by three full years. See here Flight International, June 18, 1998, edition, for engineering details on the H-II.

Chapter 27

- **NOTE 1 - page 354**

  John Endicott's book, Japan's Nuclear Option: Political, Technical, and Strategic Factors, published in 1975, provides a starting point for a seemingly never-ending stream of similar examinations of Japan's latent nuclear weapons capabilities. Such treatment is a testimony to the enduring potential of Japan and the concern that exists over the capabilities of its still peaceful nuclear program.

  In October 2010, 35 years after the appearance of Endicott's book, the Stimson Center, a Washington-based policy group, collected a group of Japanese political experts to produce a study titled "Japan's Nuclear Option: Security, Politics and Policy in the 21st Century." That study addressed anew Japan's nuclear weapons potential by examining the state of the U.S.–Japan alliance as an inhibiting factor, or not, as well as policy and technical considerations. The theme of the study was that, while the regional dynamic continued to evolve, generating renewed "concerns" over Japan's intentions, readers should be "reassured" that the island nation will remain a non-nuclear-weapons state, at least for the time being. Now, in 2023, some 13 years after the Stimson Center effort, we have North Korea as a declared nuclear weapons state and an aggressive nuclear-capable China, both on Japan's doorstep. With good reason, the question of "which way Japan?" still begs.

- # NOTE 2 - page 360

  By 1989, China had tested no fewer than 32 nuclear devices, including five unsuccessful tests of a neutron weapon. The very fact that China was perfecting such a weapon was ominous; this was a purposely made people-killer, the detonation of which would leave the targeted terrain and structures intact. The Chinese weaponeers would get it right on the sixth test, and that capability soon entered the expanding PRC missile delivery arsenal. An August 17, 1995, underground test of a 90-kiloton weapon optimized for delivery by China's DF-31 missile garnered considerable attention in Japan. Reacting to this notable demonstration of China's nuclear threat, the Japanese Diet formally censured China and voted to cut off all development lending to that nation.

  The following year when China suspended detonations, after 32 years of testing, at least 48 devices had been triggered in the remote desert area of Lop Nor. By any conceivable measure, China had established itself as a de facto and self-declared thermonuclear weapons state. Japan had taken notice, and its leadership continued to look to the U.S.–Japan Mutual Security Treaty, and to the U.S. "extended deterrence" commitment to protect the island nation. At the same time, Japan remained determined to "own" its own nuclear fuel cycle. There was an unspoken logic in this determination, if not a national imperative.

- # NOTE 3 - page 362

  The catastrophic event at the Soviet Union's nuclear power plant at Chernobyl, in what is now Ukraine, occurred on April 26, 1986. The reactor meltdown, and the cloud of radiation it released that contaminated hundreds of square miles, was a wakeup call for the entire world, not the least for Japan. At that time, Japan's utilities had 32 nuclear power plants in operation, including 16 each of the boiling water and pressurized water reactors types, and planned to seek approval for the construction of no fewer than 57 new plants over the next three years. Japan's reactor fleet was operating at an impressive 75.7-percent capacity, comparable to world leaders Germany (78 percent) and Sweden (80 percent), with plans to achieve even higher operating efficiencies. The announced target of the nation's Electric Power Development Coordination Council was for nuclear power to supply 34 percent of Japan's generation of electricity by the turn of the century. Japan would later expand that target to a full 50 percent in the years to follow.

  In this environment of a wholesale national commitment to nuclear power, there was no way to avoid public discussion of nuclear safety, brought to the fore by the Chernobyl incident. Soon after the incident, the Nuclear Safety Commission created a "Special Investigation Committee on the Soviet Nuclear Plant Accident" to examine the state of nuclear safety in Japan. Not surprisingly, the Committee concluded one year later that

Japanese reactor designs, operating practices and safety procedures were generally excellent and that "immediate changes…were not necessary."

Leaving aside the fact that the Chernobyl reactor involved a fatally flawed design and was poorly operated, particularly when compared with what was considered the world-class designs of the Japanese plants, the incident should still have rattled the industry much more than it did. Chernobyl and the Three Mile Incident in the United States could have been the catalyst for a complete reexamination of the vulnerability of the Japanese reactors. In 1986, the Japanese nuclear community was confident that its reactors were almost beyond risk. There was little attention then, nor would there be in the future, to the possibility of a once-in-a-generation external event fatally damaging a power reactor—namely, an earthquake-generated tsunami akin to the wave that took out the four Fukushima reactors some 20-plus years later.

• NOTE 4 - page 363

The magnitude of the risk to Japan's population posed by a nuclear accident at one of South Korea's nuclear reactor complexes cannot be understated. The threat has not abated in recent years and in fact, continues to increase, particularly with regard to the highly irradiated spent fuel assemblies that are stored outside reactor vessels in open ponds adjacent to the power reactors. Because South Korea, like Japan and other countries, has failed to solve the issue of waste fuel storage away from the reactor, many of the associated spent fuel ponds have been crammed beyond their design capacity. In South Korea, as in Japan, this is particularly true in the case of older reactors that have been discharging used fuel assemblies for thirty years or more.

An excellent presentation of this concern was compiled by South Korean nuclear safety expert Dr. Jungmin Kang in early 2019 and was then discussed in numerous venues in South Korea, Japan and the United States. Dr. Kang was recently retired from the position of Chairman of the ROK's Nuclear Safety and Security Commission, having been appointed to, and later removed from that role, by then ROK President Moon. In June 2019, Dr. Kang delivered a PowerPoint-enabled presentation hosted by the Nonproliferation Policy Education Center (NPEC) in Washington (https://npolicy. org/), in which this very issue was discussed in detail.

Dr. Kang's presentation addressed the potential for a destructive nuclear fallout over Japan in the event of a terrorist incident that would target the spent fuel ponds at one of the ROK's most overstuffed reactors (the Kori complex). His lecture, titled "If Pyongyang Attacks South Korea's Nuclear Plants, Are We Ready," emphasized the inherent vulnerability of South Korea's nuclear reactor complexes, including their spent fuel ponds.

It is highly likely that Dr. Kang was removed from his Chairmanship because he chose to center his concern on the possibility of a North Korean attack on the reactors. At the time of Dr. Kang's removal, President Moon was into his third year of attempting to accommodate the North Korean regime, and any suggestion that Pyongyang would target Seoul's reactor complexes simply did not fit with the mantra of reconciliation with the North. In any event, Dr. Kang's commonsense observations and warnings were not welcome in his home country, but his concerns have found an audience in Japan and the United States.

Beyond the concept of a North Korean attack, a similar case could be made for any event that damages or compromises these same ponds, including earthquakes or tsunami class incidents that overwhelm reactors positioned on Korea's Sea of Japan coastline. The attitude within the South Korean nuclear community is that "unlike Japan, the ROK does not have real earthquakes" and is therefore immune to this type of damage to reactor complexes. Having been awakened in Seoul by a mild earthquake in the 1970s, I beg to differ. In September 2016, a magnitude 5.8 earthquake—the strongest in Korea's recorded history—hit the southeastern city of Kyoungju, coincidentally the center of what is probably the most concentrated collection of operating nuclear power reactor complexes in the world.

Chapter 28

- **NOTE 1 - page 367**
  In the full disclosure department, my only experience with professional complaints lodged against me during my 15-year Agency career occurred during that tour when a man-and-wife tandem team filed charges against me. They claimed I had discriminated against them by requesting their reassignment from the Station to another location in the same country. In that case, I had bent over backward, and encouraged my entire branch team to do so as well, to accommodate one of the first tour pairs when that officer was assigned to my branch. The officer was a mediocre performer, less than enthusiastic about the job and more concerned with Embassy social functions and nightlife. But we all adjusted and muddled through the first year.

  The officer's partner was an abject failure in another section of the Station. Partly as a result of our success as a branch in dealing with such situations, Station management attempted to reassign this officer to us. (The branch's reputation was that we had become a re-programmer of lower-performing officers from other Station elements. As a result, we had grown in staff numbers as we incorporated these "transfers" into our operation.) I could see that managing the "tandem team" under our single roof was going to be a time sink and disruptive, so I suggested that they be transferred as a single unit to another location. It would allow them a more relaxed assignment, in a less demanding environment, and they could complete their two-year tour and go home happy. Or one hoped. The transfer was done, the couple relocated, and nearing the end of their tour, all seemed well, if not unexceptional.

I was therefore surprised when a three-member delegation of Equal Employment Opportunity officers descended on our Station from Headquarters to complete a parachute-in survey, at some point, singling me out for special attention. The EEO flying squad was a legacy of the Stansfield Turner reforms, where politically incorrect behavior was assumed to be the norm in field Stations, and gender-based discrimination routine. After interviewing all of the Station's female officers and support employees, three branch chiefs were scheduled for special interview treatment. I was one of them.

My alleged misdeed was conspiring to dispatch the tandem team, ostensibly against their will, to another location where they could redirect their energies and hopefully recover their respective reputations. I carefully explained the circumstances to the interrogators, noting Station management had actually considered just sending the twosome home short of tour but we had worked out the alternative solution. It was not good enough. Station senior management attempted to finesse the affair, but the critical report went into the record. The Station support officer told me to "shake it off" as my first EEO offense. He claimed he already had four or five to his credit. He also suggested that, given the changing times, I probably should expect to see more in my future. We all found ourselves in the "new Agency."

• NOTE 2 - page 367

One humorous aspect of the Casey visit occurred when his advance security detail sat with four of us in the Station's protected area to discuss certain "personal considerations" involved in his visit. Apart from the routine issues of diet (certain colors of M&M candy were preferred) and drink (only Dewar's would do), there was the fact that his daughter, single at the time, would be accompanying him. The advance detail asked that a separate program be organized, ideally involving the Station officers' wives, to occupy her time, with a focus on her personal interests. As our small group discussed this, the lead security officer noted, "Well, you do know that she is an aspiring thespian, so perhaps you could do something there." Station chief Jim, somewhat rough around the edges, pondered this, seemed to have some trouble, sat back and placed both hands flat on the table and pronounced, "I don't give a damn whose daughter she is, I'm not going to have my Station have any part of that crap on my watch!"

There was silence at the table. The Station support chief, my close friend from days in Seoul and elsewhere, shot me a glance, a tight smile, to communicate that we both knew what had happened. He waded in with the now-confused security team to preempt any further deterioration of the dialog. "Gentlemen, let's take that request offline for a follow-up and we will figure out a schedule for her." With that, the balance of the planning session was completed, but Jim remained visibly upset as the group broke up. The support chief dropped by my office a bit later and suggested we go together to see Jim to bring him back from the brink. We found him standing behind his desk, still fuming over his inference that he—and HIS Station—were being asked to facilitate a lesbian encounter.

My associate and I had worked out a script, which was delivered to Jim as follows, with the support chief taking the lead and I to follow: "Jim, the security guys have suggested that his daughter is an aspiring THES-BEE-AN, so we are working on it. Any ideas Rick?" Before Jim could interject, I picked it up "Yes, given that she is AN ASPIRING THES-BEE-AN. And as your support chief here suggested, doesn't that mean she wants to be a theater performer? Like an actress. Maybe we can have a group of Station wives take her to a performance at the traditional THEATER!" A sudden flash of recognition and relief passed over our Station chief. He relaxed, sat down and smiled, "Well, hell yes! Have them get organized and we will pay for everything. They can even take her to lunch at the Grill on our dime! Right after the theater!" The Grill in a nearby hotel was Jim's favorite lunch-time hangout, where he typically enjoyed massive sirloins on the grill. To our astonishment, because he was a very frugal man, Jim was offering Casey's daughter and the wives the very best he had.

The support chief and I exited stage left, mission accomplished. Jim now had it all under control, and the rest of the planning fell neatly into place. To my knowledge, no lesbian encounters occurred during that eventful visit, and both Casey and his daughter would depart Asia as two very satisfied tourists.

• NOTE 3 - page 372

The Come By Chance refinery project proved to be ill-fated, due to a variety of oil sector circumstances. The refinery fell into bankruptcy in 1976 and managed to establish a record as the single largest such filing ($500 million) in Canadian history. In retelling the tale of his Queen Elizabeth 2 charter and the voyage to the waters of Bear Head, John could not remember if his old OSS colleague had been on the cruise. But he knew for sure he had invited his dear friend Bill Casey along and that Casey was there with him, at least in spirit.

PART FIVE

Life After the CIA

(1987-2002)

Chapter 29. Casey Opts to Go 'Offline'
Fall 1985

The Cold Pitch Delivered

Although my flight back to Headquarters was uneventful, I did harbor concerns about Director Casey's summons. My biggest was that the one denied-area operation I was then managing might have blown up with an agent somehow compromised. There also was the possibility that others in the intelligence community wanted to take my operation and my asset to higher levels of risk. In such a case, I planned to resist that inclination, even though our China Operations team might want to go along with such a strategy. Whatever the catalyst for Casey's invitation, I was certain I would be surprised and probably not pleasantly so. I happened to be right.

I arrived at Dulles International Airport, located well out into the Virginia suburbs, on a Sunday afternoon and headed to my nearby hotel room, determined to get some rest before meeting with Casey the next morning. That evening, Bob Grealy, my East Asia Division Chief, called me and suggested I stop in to see him at Headquarters before meeting with Casey. He said he had "some insight" about why I had been called back with so little warning or explanation. Bob had been my third and last Chief in Seoul. We both departed end-of-tour on the same day in 1978, he for his next posting as the Chief in Hong Kong, and I for my flagpole tour at Headquarters before striking out for the previously chronicled posting in Europe.

We met in Bob's office around 7 a.m. and, to my disappointment, he did not have an explanation for Casey's actions. "Something has him worked up," he told me. "You are no longer at your current Station and you are no longer assigned to this division. Moreover, you may no longer even be in the Operations Directorate."

It was hard to grasp let alone accept what Bob was saying. He continued, "All I know is that he pulled your personnel file and told the DDO that you now worked for him directly, and that you would no longer answer to the Directorate.

"Clair is really upset," he continued. "Called me this morning to say that you were to report to him right after your meeting with Casey. He is threatened by this. Maybe he knows something I don't, but watch your back." By "Clair," Bob meant Clair George, the Agency's Deputy Director for Operations. He was essentially a god, at least in his own mind. He and his deputy, the ADDO, ruled their turf with an iron hand, brooking no interference from any other element of the Agency. DDO George was the imperial potentate of the Agency's Irish mafia, a cagey infighter who identified mostly with the Directorate's Near East Division. I barely knew the man but understood that a middle-grade case officer such as myself either ingratiated himself to him to become one of his extended gang or kept a good distance. Clair George had a deserved reputation as thin-skinned and short-tempered. Irish or not, his head of red hair signaled his combative personality.

There was no denying the fact that George was a field-tested clandestine services officer who had run successful operations all over the world. He now ran his best operations inside Headquarters, dominating the building's Seventh Floor—the Agency's executive level, where resided the office of the Director in company with all of Casey's senior managers, including the deputy directors for Operations, Intelligence, Science and Technology, and Administration.

At one point, Clair George had been a Casey favorite. The Director had promoted him from Chief of Africa Division to DDO about a year before, in the summer of 1984. George would hold that position for three-and-a-half long and difficult years, opting to retire only in December 1987, as the Iran–Contra scandal swirled around and enveloped him. But on the day I walked into Casey's office from my overseas post, that retirement and the events that attended Clair's departure were still ahead of us all. **[NOTE 1]**

I asked Bob for advice because we were all wandering in the dark at that point. He was not a Clair George fan. They had tangled over issues large and small, and he was blunt about it. "If it turns out that you are working directly with Casey and are no longer assigned to the DDO, it's your decision whether you sit down and discuss this with Clair. Either way, you definitely have made some enemies in the building over the weekend that you did not have on Friday." We shook hands. He wished me good luck and told me he would do all he could to protect me.

When I met with Casey that Monday morning, he got quickly to the point. After thanking me for attending to his close friend John Shaheen in the East Asian city, and remarking how much he had enjoyed his visit to the Station, he waded in. "I have made a decision to shake things up around here." After a, "You now work for me, and only me," speech, he fixed a stare on me and announced, "We are now going to go offline with a special operation, and I do mean completely offline." He then proceeded to sketch out his plan, an off-the-books scheme he obviously had been formulating for some time.

My initial reaction was one of disbelief. I even wondered if I understood his intent. It soon became apparent he was talking about, at least in concept, the creation of a completely detached organization he would personally control. The organization, essentially, would covertly duplicate, if not compete with, the existing Directorate of Operations, at least in certain sensitive areas. Before engaging with him on how that might be done, and asking why he had chosen me to run the organization, I wanted to understand his motivation in proposing such a radical step.

Casey laid it out as two separate frustrations that vexed him, not infrequently angering him, as he managed the Agency. His ire was aimed mostly at Operations—he simply thought it was doing a poor job in critical areas. Overall, the Directorate was performing, if not well, then adequately. But Casey had determined the Near East Division was "full of excuses and just not delivering." That seemed unnecessarily harsh. I was mindful of all the constraints that had been placed on the Agency over the previous few years, some of them coming from Congress, others from the Executive Branch and many self-imposed by an Agency bureaucracy whose priority had become to protect itself from criticism.

A parallel Casey frustration concerned his own attempts to get the Directorate to follow-up on operational leads he personally had identified among his many friends and business contacts, some dating back to his OSS days, mainly associates who still were active internationally. Others had approached him with offers of information or assistance after he became Director of Central Intelligence, and those offers were being left dead in the water by the Directorate. Bottom line; opportunities were being missed, and Casey was tired of the lame explanations offered as to why things were just too difficult to attempt.

I tried to turn the discussion away from Casey's preferred solution by explaining that so much had changed, even for me with 13-plus years under my DO belt. Such frustrations were now a fact of life. I took him through the legal morass we had to navigate before we could launch a collection operation—the second-guessing by poorly informed bureaucrats with whom we had to deal, and the impact of those hurdles on our top-down decisionmakers. Entire Stations had become risk-averse, as I had witnessed during my European tour. And it seemed the more cautious the manager or station chief, the more likely he or she was to be promoted. I did offer that the Agency had become adept at making excuses for things not getting done.

Casey agreed. He sat, shaking his head, and responded. "That is exactly why we need to go offline. So, we will do this. And we will get it done my way. And that is exactly what WE are going do!" He reminisced about his OSS days, explaining how he and others had scrambled to get things done quickly and how creative his colleagues had become in that time of war. He continued, "we are now again at war … with the Soviets, with terrorists … and it's time we started to act like it. We are the damn CIA, for Chrissake!"

I pushed him for more justification, beginning to imagine just how much trouble he was proposing that he—and now we—would be getting ourselves into with his scheme. He solemnly recounted a recent conversation with President Reagan. "Do you remember a few months back when terrorists hijacked that TWA 737 and landed at Beirut Airport?" he asked. "That went on for three days and then they killed a U.S. sailor who was a passenger. They dumped his body onto the tarmac!" I responded that I recalled the episode vividly. The flight from Athens to Rome had been hijacked by Hezbollah terrorists on our Flag Day, June 14, 1985, and diverted to Beirut. From that stop, the aircraft and passengers would endure a wild journey that lasted for two weeks and involved two stops in Algiers and two more returns to Beirut. During the aircraft's first return to Beirut, the terrorists had killed U.S. Navy Seabee diver Robert Stethem in cold blood and tossed his body onto the ground from the airliner.

Casey continued. "On the evening that the sailor was laying out there next to the plane, I sat with the President. He asked me, 'Bill, how many agents do we have in Beirut, and can't they do something about this?'" Casey paused. "He is the President, and he is my friend, and there was no way I could not tell him the truth. I said, 'Mr. President, we do not have a single agent in Beirut worthy of that name.' And he just looked at me and said nothing." Casey further explained that when he had sat with his DO leadership the following day, they gave him a dozen reasons why they had no assets in Beirut. But, he asserted, "We are the CIA, and this is absolutely unacceptable! But I know I will probably get the same answer if I ask the same question next week or next year."

Casey concluded he had no choice but to create a separate operation that would break with established norms to give him the capabilities he was convinced we needed to fight the terrorist wars of the present and future. I could see it had become a personal conviction, if not an obsession.

I told him I did not think I was the person to undertake the mission he was demanding, in large part because I had no background in the Middle East. Apart from mixing with Arabs and Iranians during my European tour, and having spent some time with a Kurd who had educated me on the history of his people, I was a complete novice in the otherworldly milieu of the area known as the Levant. I could think of a dozen other officers with more experience than I in the region.

Casey waved off my defense, saying he had thought about others and had rejected them as too conventional or too cautious. He also alluded to the probability that any such officer home-based with the Middle East Division would remain loyal to that division and mindset, and not him. If that was his implication, he probably was right.

As he saw it, the new offline organization would be deployed to make good use of his business relationships, and none of the officers he had spoken to knew how to talk with such people, gain their confidence and make them feel as if the Agency was really working with them. He was convinced several of his contacts were in a position to do "special things," based on business access and longstanding foreign relationships. He also thought those men would be willing and able to influence their foreign contacts to do things they would never do in a traditional Agency clandestine relationship. His bottom line: "Let's see what my friends can do, and then we will push them hard to do it, for their country."

I again tried to beg off, gave ground and then hit upon a solution. I asked to speak with John McMahon, Casey's Deputy, to talk through the idea and work out some details. We needed to determine how it might be best done—if it was to be done. Casey agreed and gave me three days to run the traps and come back to him. He wanted a plan, and he wanted his operation up and running within a month, or sooner. He had a lot of contacts and many ideas for action to pass along to us. I left the meeting not surprised so much as depressed. I walked down the corridor to search out McMahon, the Deputy Director of Central Intelligence, whom I thought was going to save me from this fate. But I thought wrong.

McMahon's Take: You Have No Choice

It almost seemed that John was waiting for me to walk into his office. I considered him a friend, or at least a trusted colleague, based on a couple of shared experiences I previously have described in these pages. He began with, "Okay, I was expecting you. Sit down and tell me everything Casey had to say." He knew of Casey's obsession and that Casey had a plan to go outside the Directorate, even outside normal Agency boundaries, to "buck the system." He understood that Casey's goal was to create an action-oriented, "damn the torpedoes" capability, one that harkened back to his OSS days of derring-do, smash and bang.

After I confirmed John's suspicions, and he stopped shaking his head as if to say, "I just knew it," I offered that I would simply refuse to take on Casey's directive, telling him it could not be done, probably should not be done. John rejected the idea. "You see, if you do that, he will just find somebody else to do it. And they will agree to do it for whatever combination of reasons. And that person and I will not be having this conversation. Casey is determined, and he will not be diverted from this course. You don't know him well enough." I listened but did not like where things were heading. I missed East Asia already.

"You and I are right now talking 'containment and redirection,' and you can do it." John obviously had thought things through. "You can give him what he wants, maybe 50-60 percent, and he will be satisfied with that. The fact is, Casey IS absolutely right. The Agency and the Directorate are risk-averse, scared of lawyers and the Congress, with too many career-first people. But you and I are not going to change that." His theme was, Casey was going to do it, and somebody had to take it on. I was that somebody. John and I had to figure out what we had to do.

I still did not agree to go along. I told John of my plans to finish my last year at my assigned Station then attend the JFK School the following year, plus a half-dozen reasons why I should not accept the responsibility. John rejected them all. "You are in the game now, and I want you to stay with this. If you don't, there will be somebody else, and I won't trust their judgment. Casey will get himself and everybody in this building into deep trouble." John finished with, "So, let's see what we can do to manage for damage control." We talked further for a time, and a plan of sorts emerged. I would take it on and build a small team of officers we trusted. John liked the approach, because it could be framed and monitored for compliance.

I needed a second-in-command, a master organizer who could design and manage the financial and logistics aspects. I had a candidate, the officer who had been second-in-command at my former Station's support division. John knew the man well, and I knew the two had worked together on the Agency's U-2 program, both at the aircraft's birthplace in Area 51, and later when the system was deployed overseas. John remembered the man's work in Taiwan, when the Agency flew its all-black spy planes over China with Taiwanese pilots. He picked up the phone, found the individual in the Headquarters building, and told him he had a new job. He would be working with me on a special project, and his fate had been decided. My new Number One tracked me down in the building a few hours later, armed with a hundred questions but ready to go. I was fortunate to have someone with me whom John trusted to keep all of our logistics and finances on the straight and narrow.

A Plan Emerges

The following day, we met with John to talk details. I had sketched out how I thought things might be organized, but I needed a sanity check. My new deputy had put together a draft plan of finance for an operation consisting of a handful of officers, with more to be added over a period of several months, supported by a couple of logistics types. We also needed to recruit employees who would be sworn to secrecy but not made privy to the actual operational details. I had a couple in mind.

We all were determined to get it right on the legal side. We had a series of meetings with Agency General Counsel Stanley Sporkin, who turned out to be quite an addition to our Casey containment team. John had asked Stan to get together with us, ideally on a close-hold basis, so I could explain our situation and gain his insights and direction. Stan was a man with deep experience in the byways of government and the legal constraints Congress placed on the Agency. During a brainstorming session lasting over an hour, and forewarned by John, Stan had a pile of materials on his desk, and it was obvious his staff had done some research.

Stan sketched out what he believed was our best approach: essentially creating an operation that remained within the Agency, compliant with most regulations but deeply protected as what was termed a Proscribed and Limited, or P and L, activity. We agreed it was important that our operation would be subject to oversight by the Agency's Office of Inspector General. That latter feature was critical. We assumed, first, no matter what course the operation took, sooner or later it would come under scrutiny by either the Executive Branch or Congress. The scrutiny might depend on its success, but it was more likely attention would be drawn to our operation by failure. As a second consideration, we were mindful that the DO senior management, in particular the DDO himself and his Near East Division, deeply resented the Casey initiative. We assumed those folks, in full-blown, "protect the turf" mode, would do all they could to undermine and discredit the operation.

In our discussion with Stan Sporkin, we determined we needed to get the bureaucratic wiring right, to maximize the Agency's visibility into our planned operation. Working with appropriate internal Agency managers, we were able to come up with an approach fully aligned with its legal authorities and accepted practices, and meeting both the spirit and letter of the law. It was not to be an offline operation, as the Director might have imagined, nor any Air America endeavor of a bygone era. **[NOTE 2]**

We had our coordinating relationship at hand when Casey appointed Jim, our former Station Chief, to head the Operations Directorate's Domestic Contact Division. To Casey's disappointment, that division was not performing well, and he had drafted Jim to reorganize and reboot it. The process had begun just a few weeks earlier, and John McMahon had accepted my suggestion to create a reporting relationship with Jim. John thought it wise and waved us away with a, "Go see Jim, and tell him I approve." Jim was responsive and enthusiastic, and he promised to play his part. He noted his direct report supervisor, DDO Clair George, would be unhappy that Jim had accepted the role. He would require top cover from Casey and McMahon, and he asked that I ensure it, which I did. Throughout the 18 months I would manage Casey's special project, Jim was with us every step of the way.

Ambassador Peter Dailey Stands Up

To accomplish our objectives and to have a reasonable chance to meet the goals assigned to us by Director Casey, we needed to create appropriate access mechanisms. We also needed the advice and guidance of those who had moved into the new space in which we would be compelled to operate. We looked to find a suitable senior advisor who was both trusted by Casey and willing to assist us. We therefore were fortunate that Ambassador Peter Dailey walked in the door and offered his services after we had met with General Counsel Sporkin. Peter had joined the Agency at Casey's request after completing a two-year posting as Ambassador to the Republic of Ireland. A successful entrepreneur in advertising and public relations, Peter served as the Agency's Counselor to the Director from mid-1985 and worked with Casey to interact with the White House and Congress. Because Peter enjoyed a close relationship with President Reagan, with a personality that reflected calm and confidence, he managed to smooth some of Casey's rough edges. One of his assignments was to find ways to compromise with other senior administration officials, as well as Casey's critics in Congress, thereby mitigating tensions that had developed as a consequence of Casey's style.

Peter sat with us to outline his concept. By mutual agreement, we leveraged our recent experience in selected high-technology areas, notably telecommunications, plus our work in Asia. Peter offered to provide the business acumen we lacked, as well as his reputation, supplemented by his Rolodex. Peter was a true believer in Casey's approach and an advocate for such an offline operation. He had spent six months at Casey's elbow observing the daily process within the Agency.

Peter's professional assessment of the Agency at large, and the Operations

Directorate in particular, was highly critical but prescriptive. He saw a growing bureaucracy increasingly satisfied with itself, its initiative flattened by layers of unnecessary process and an inherent avoidance of risk-taking. The more rocks he turned over, the more he understood Casey's frustration. But like Casey, he had few solutions. [NOTE 3]

Over the months, Peter Daily and I worked closely together to get our operation up and functioning, We discussed what he perceived as the deterioration of the Agency. As a patriotic American who had signed on with Casey to contribute, he wanted to understand how the devolution had occurred, at least in the nearly 14 years I had experienced it firsthand. When asked what was the secret of *his* success, he responded with his three rules of management: "Hire great people. Give those trusted lieutenants goals and the authority and the discretion to reach those goals. And stay the hell out of town!" Peter had determined that the Agency was performing far below its potential. It had too many employees and needed a house-cleaning and wholesale change in mindset. I admired his dedication, respected his opinion and welcomed his assistance to our small undertaking. Peter stayed the course with Casey and did not stop trying.

When we again sat down with Casey, I asked the parties involved in vetting our proposal to join the group, more for their endorsement of our preferred structure than anything else. John McMahon voiced his approval by saying he thought our plan gave us plenty of room to run with the "Casey special operation." Jim expressed his belief that he could manage the Directorate side of the issue, that is, the politics of keeping DDO George off our back. Peter Daily explained how he would support the creation and operation of the new entity. We had Stan Sporkin's stamp of approval as well, and with my deputy we had a project manager with demonstrated mastery of the logistics and funding issues. I asked for a small office down the hall from Casey and McMahon, with space for two support officers to maintain our operational files. We got that as well.

All that activity took place within 10 days of my initial Monday-morning meeting with Casey. We were off to the races. In truth, those of us around Casey had organized a program that stood apart from the Operations Directorate but was far from offline. If anything, we were only slightly to the side of the normal Agency structure and well within the parameters of what was considered legal and appropriate.

Now underway, I made a two-week run back to my former Asian posting to transfer operational control of my responsibilities there and pack-out for relocation to Virginia. It was not a pleasant parting. I could not explain to Station management why I had been called back, nor describe in even general terms what I would be doing. For one thing, I was not sure myself. I did assume, in my new capacity, that I probably would be back at the same location shortly. My High Technology Branch deputy stepped up to take over management, and the team there did not miss a step in the transition. With my agents and asset relationships transferred, I was able to sever all relationships with the Station and make a clean break. I would miss that city and the opportunity it had provided, but my focus now was on what I had accepted. One way or another, I had been dragooned for special service by Casey. I had the uneasy feeling the recruitment by the OSS veteran had sealed my Agency career, and not for the good.

Initial Operations

By the time I returned to Headquarters, my new deputy had our operation established in its new offices, and our Seventh-Floor location was staffed and functioning. A former career-trainee classmate had come forward, a woman for whom I had the utmost respect, and asked to manage that office, essentially serving as my personal link with Casey. She was an exceptional writer and master organizer, and she managed to get on well with almost everyone. She had been warned, however, that if she elected to work with me, her career in the DO would be over. She told the dissuaders she really had not planned to be a Chief of Station in Europe, anyway, so she let the chips fall where they may. I was doubly pleased she had rejected out-of-hand hints by the DO that she made a bad choice by joining our team.

Within the building, our operation had been registered within the Directorate and assigned its funny names, or pseudonyms. Stan Sporkin's team had double-blessed our legal standing, and we had gained our independent Agency budget authority. We then set ourselves in a location some distance from Headquarters and began our work. Some of the candidate contacts were directed to us by Peter Dailey. On contacts for possible exploitation, we started with a short list that included Casey nominees, plus some nonperforming leads we had inherited from DO divisions. We added some of our own, mostly by activating relationships developed over the years in Asia and Europe. In the first category of the Casey relationships, we found them to be a very diverse group, men running in ages from 50 to 80. The older generation had plenty of time for us and welcomed our attention, but most were well past their operational primes, with their best foreign contacts either dead or dying.

Yet some of them provided great leads to younger fellows, basically sons and daughters of the men of Casey's OSS generation. It was a time-consuming effort to deal with the "Casey's gang," but in the end it proved useful because of the introductions they could make and the endorsements of trust they extended on our behalf. Such introductions provided entrée to individuals who otherwise would have not responded to an approach from an Agency officer. As a consequence of the Casey contact screening, we budgeted three days a week in New York City, at least at the outset, and tapering off as we separated the wheat from the chaff.

In the area of screening existing or defunct relationships within DO divisions, we found most desks cooperative, understanding they were dealing with a Casey-directed operation. We pulled the case files, looked for value that had gone unnoticed or ignored, and set up a recontact program when someone suggested potential value. East Asia Division, with Bob Greely at the helm, was most cooperative, as was Europe Division.

As expected, the Near East Division shut us down by ignoring our requests for meetings. When we began to make progress with a certain case we had independently developed, and that effort crossed lines with an ongoing program being mounted by the NE folks, we usually opted to back off to avoid open conflict. In some situations, however, the opportunity was too compelling, and the potential to be gained too high, for us to walk away. In such cases, however, the sparks did fly.

In the category of self-developed contacts evolving into operations, we were able to make use of existing or former relationships, often prominent business leaders in Asia or Europe. In Asia, when we arrived in a given country, we always met with the local Station, usually at the Chief level in a secure location. My inclination always was to brief the local sheriff on our plan of contact to the degree possible and bring him into our loop, gaining his support. In most cases, it went well, mainly because we never asked or tasked our foreign contact to undertake actions in their home country. Our target was always a third country, such as Libya, Iran or Russia, where Agency operations were constrained, and where we knew foreign firms enjoyed high-level relationships and access.

My only problem in those friendly Station encounters came when senior officers, aware I had direct contact with Casey, pushed me to obtain onward assignments for them. On other occasions, they asked me to communicate with Directorate leadership over private concerns they did not wish to convey in their own back-channel communications. I avoided such situations whenever possible, and I soon discovered that any attempt to service those requests led to trouble, with the burn too often falling on me.

Lebanon and Beyond

Casey had fixated on the Lebanon issue, and rightly so, given the ceaseless political disruption in that country and the ever-present potential offered by Beirut as a launch point for terrorist operations throughout the world. Lebanon deserved to be a high-priority Agency and Directorate target, and recent events in Beirut had driven Casey to determine he had to have a parallel offline operation to offset what he saw as poor performance by the standing team. He directed our small group to focus on securing access there, and we attempted to deliver.

Our Beirut Embassy had been destroyed two years earlier, in April 1983, wiping out the Station and a visiting Agency team, killing one of our most senior and respected Middle East officers, Robert Ames. Six months later, in October, the U.S. Marine barracks in Beirut was destroyed by a truck bomb, killing 241 and prompting a withdrawal of our ground-force presence there. Those incidents, and a dozen others, highlighted by the more recent hijacking of TWA 847 and the murder of our Navy's Robert Stethem, combined to tag Beirut with the well-deserved descriptor, "terrorist cesspool." **[NOTE 1]**

Beyond Beirut the city, Lebanon at large was an equally hopeless situation, a nation on the ropes, with Iranian-backed Hezbollah gaining ground through assassinations, intimidation, bribery and manipulation. The nonstop feuding among Lebanon's competing ethnic communities and their squabbling political groups signaled nothing was going to get better there, and the worst was still to come. Events proved the assessment correct, and the downward spiral continues, even now, nearly 40 years later. I was in no way familiar with the situation, and my group wanted to avoid being there. But we had no choice and stepped out to do whatever we could to close with the enemy. Besides, Casey demanded it.

One companion issue Casey mentioned to me every time we sat down involved the fate of our former Beirut Chief of Station, William F. Buckley, who had been kidnapped off the street in Beirut 18 months before, on March 16, 1984. We knew Hezbollah had grabbed him on his way to the Embassy, or at least that he was in Hezbollah hands shortly after his kidnapping, and the group subjected him to extended torture and interrogation. About the time I began working with Casey in October, we received reports that Buckley had been executed by those Iranian-funded terrorists. Others suggested he had died due to sustained mistreatment by the various groups holding him. At the time, there was no way to verify his death or even confirm he remained in Lebanon—Iran being a possible destination. We did know, from videos released in Athens over a period of several months, that Buckley had been tortured and forced to sign a lengthy "confession" of his Agency activities in Lebanon.

In October 1985, when the terrorist group Islamic Jihad announced it had executed Buckley, we also received reports he died the previous June, but his fate could not be confirmed. Casey was obsessed with Buckley, in part because he had approved the dispatch of a former Agency paramilitary officer (a 20-year veteran of the Directorate's Special Activities Division), who had volunteered for the Beirut assignment. Ted Shackley, a mentor of Buckley from their days together in Vietnam, had endorsed the high-risk assignment and, after the kidnapping, stepped in to take personal responsibility for attempting to arrange his recovery.

Casey asked me to confirm, quietly and beyond the assurances he received from his DO leadership, that every possible avenue for Buckley's recovery, or at least word of his fate, was being explored. After my own inquiries at the case-officer levels in the Near East and European divisions, I was able to reassure him that every station in the world had made Buckley a priority tasking. The problem was Lebanon remained a dark hole operationally, dominated by rumor and leaked information calculated to mislead and confuse. [NOTE 2]

One vignette on the sad life that hung in the balance occurred about a year later, in late 1986, when I again sat in Casey's office, that time with our Deputy Director of Operations and his NE Division chief. It was a typical faceoff, where Casey was being asked to arbitrate between NE and my team, the former alleging an ostensible transgression on my unit's part, wherein we had "crossed lines and entered NE turf." At the conclusion of the gathering, with tempers still hot, Casey went back to the subject of Buckley and asked, "Do we know anything new about Buckley?" The response was, "Well, now we are 99-percent sure he is dead." Casey's eyes remained focused on the surface of the conference table. When he pushed for details, the response was, "We have it first hand, from the mouth of Saddam Hussein to General (Vernon) Walters, that Buckley was killed last fall. And if anybody would know what's really going on in the Middle East, it would be Saddam."

With that, Casey looked up from the table, glanced at each of us in turn, shook his head and said, "Not good enough for me." I gained increased respect for Casey that day. And though I was well aware of the efforts and the pain felt by our DO leadership concerning Buckley, it seemed Casey took it to a different level. If Buckley was dead, Casey would need it to be 100-percent confirmed, whatever that meant. And he wanted the body back for the man's family to bury. It was also an Irish–Catholic longing to bring a warrior home. The Buckley disappearance would remain an open wound for years to come, and Casey later would make a personal request to me to do all possible to resolve Buckley's fate. It was a demand he repeated to me privately on the day he was struck down by a stroke that would claim his life.

The Libyan Connection

Our small team probed everywhere to find a new channel of agent operations that would permit discrete communication, intelligence collection and possible covert action in the Middle East. One location where we initiated operational contacts was a Western European city, in part because it was a wide-open metropolis with a variety of characters who either were established there or using the venue for fly-in meetings and business dealings. The city was connected to the balance of Europe, the nations of the Soviet Bloc, both North Africa (the Arab Maghreb states) and the Middle East. An extensive Lebanese expat community existed there as well, with Maronite Christians, and Shia and Sunni Muslims living and working side-by-side, as they had for generations back home. There was a free flow of business, information and contacts, plus it hosted an active travel pattern back and forth with Beirut. We needed to take advantage of that mix.

The entrée into Libya, and later into Lebanon, coincidentally came about when we met with one of our Asian business contacts to debrief him on his company's Libyan activity. I had known the man for over 20 years, and I watched his corporate empire expand from a humble, one-building factory to a multinational business empire. After several meetings and some arm-twisting, he agreed to cooperate with the Agency by introducing one of the consultants he knew who had high-level contacts in Libya. The man, whom I will call Thali, had established himself as an entrepreneur throughout North and Central Africa. In one country, he partnered with its government to own and operate a small airline that shuttled passengers and air cargo among various destinations on the continent. Most of his activity was purely commercial, but we suspected some smuggling might be thrown into the mix. With Libyan dictator Muammar Gaddafi and his inner circle, who knew what the airline had been up to, or what it would be asked to do?

Thali's airline was a bit ramshackled in terms of aircraft and operations. In one of our meetings, he arrived sporting an unusual belt barely visible beneath his suit jacket. When I asked about it, he said it was a "quiet memorial" to one of his airline's former pilots who recently died. The pilot had crafted the belt and gifted it to Thali a year or so before, when he and his best friend, also a career pilot, suddenly resigned from Thali's mini-airline and headed to Florida. It was the pilot's habit to crochet in flight, needles moving as the plane plowed on for hours through the African airspace. It later turned out that Thali's two best pilots had defected from his airline to join an operation flying missions in Central America. For the partners, it was a return to the fold where they had long served as contract soldiers of fortune for air operations. Both died in the wreckage of their Fairchild C-123K Provider cargo plane when it crashed in the Nicaraguan jungle on October 5, 1986. **[NOTE 3]**

The crash had been part of an operation supplying the Contras, a rebel group fighting the Sandinista Junta of National Reconstruction, a Marxist cabal that had taken over the Nicaraguan government in 1979. Soon thereafter, the supply operation became very public. The aircraft, the dead crew, the documents they carried—not to mention the tons of AK-47s and ammunition remaining—all were topped off by the public confession of the plane's "kicker," one Eugene Hasenfus. He tied the operation back to the Agency and to the highest levels of our government. The latter included Marine Lieutenant Colonel Oliver North, assigned to the staff of the National Security Council. The two pilots, it turned out, had flown under periodic contracts for the Agency for two decades in remote operations all over the world. But somehow, by some odd coincidence, prior to their terminal employment in Central America they had found themselves working for a shady secondhand airline in Africa. And one of them had knitted a belt for their employer and our newfound acquaintance, Thali.

In coopting Thali, we really were not interested in his airline. At first glance, he seemed to offer access to the Gaddafi inner circle, and he appeared knowledgeable of the close cadre of personalities who sat with the Libyan leader. We found it useful that Thali enjoyed access to the "people of the tent"—tribal loyalists trusted by the paranoid dictator to move outside Libya and operate internationally. Once he agreed to cooperate, Thali identified personalities near Gaddafi as well as selected members of the Libyan leader's security and intelligence organizations. But it also soon became clear that Thali himself was not part of the Libyan regime's inner circle. The question then begged, what else could the man do for us? **[NOTE 4]**

There were a number of intelligence-collection priorities related to Libya, including indications of Gaddafi interest in nuclear and chemical warfare capabilities. But the one on which we were asked to focus involved the aftermath of the airstrike mounted against Gaddafi earlier that year by the U.S. military. On April 15, 1986, in retaliation for a Libyan-inspired terror bombing in Germany, President Reagan authorized Operation El Dorado Canyon, a combined air attack on targets in and near Tripoli. Air Force F-111 Aardvark fighter–bombers, flying from bases in the United Kingdom, and U.S. Navy A-6 Intruders and F/A-18 Hornets, flying off the decks of aircraft carriers USS *America* and USS *Coral Sea* positioned in the Mediterranean Sea, delivered a clear message. The attacks missed killing Colonel Gaddafi but ravaged Libyan air defenses and destroyed much of his air force, army facilities and commando bases.

Our Air Force strike group involved two variants of the swing-wing aircraft: the latest version F-111F and its companion the EF-111—the latter an electronic-countermeasures aircraft dispatched to protect the strike element by jamming the Libyan radar systems. The 24 U.K.-based F-111Fs and their companion EF-111As were accompanied by no less than 28 tankers needed to supply the mission to Libya and return, a combined fleet of some 57 aircraft. The U.S. Navy Intruders hit their targets with iron bombs, and the Hornets disabled air defenses in their first combat deployment with HARM and Shrike radar-killing missiles.

In the attack, one U.S. plane had been lost, an F-111, tail number 389, call sign "Karma 52." Its pilot and weapons-system operator, respectively, Captain Fernando Ribas-Dominicci and Captain Paul F. Flores, were killed in action. The

United States wanted the remains of its two airmen returned for proper intern-ment. When third-party diplomatic approaches failed, President Reagan asked Director Casey to make a special effort to accomplish this, even though we es-sentially had been in an undeclared war with Libya less than a year before. Other Agency sources confirmed the death of the men and that the remains of Captain Ribas-Dominicci had been recovered and were being held by the regime. We needed to see what was possible by establishing a direct dialog with Gaddafi's trusted comrades.

A secondary but still important goal was to recover as much of the F-111's avionics as possible. We knew from other sources that Gaddafi had harvested the wreckage of the downed aircraft, and his military was busy inventorying its parts. We were concerned because the EF-111F version carried, among other classified systems, the just-deployed AN/AVQ-26 Pave Tack electro-optic tar-geting pod. We knew the Soviets, seeking to secure maximum advantage from their fraternal relationship with Gaddafi, had been involved in the recovery of the aircraft. While Soviet support probably was designed to compensate for the disastrously ineffective performance of their air defense systems sold to Libya, there was a new opportunity to ingratiate themselves to the Libyans. The Soviets knew the Pave Tack was among the wreckage and wanted access to the system. They also wanted the entire aircraft, and we knew they were negotiating to buy it or swap it for new missiles. It seemed likely the Libyans would be willing to deal with their Soviet friends, if they had not already done so. **[NOTE 5]**

To pursue both objectives—the recovery of the aircrew remains and certain aircraft systems—we had little option but to open a direct channel for discussion. We did it in fairly short order, using a connection to Gaddafi's chief of securi-ty (and brother-in-law) Abdullah al-Senussi, who agreed to a meeting in Malta, provided certain security considerations were observed. On our side, we needed to present a negotiator who held credibility external to the Agency, a known in-ternational personality who would be placing himself at risk while at the same time demonstrating he enjoyed the imprimatur of senior U.S. leadership. The man we selected—whom I may not name—was a public entertainment figure, a known friend of President Reagan and a man who enjoyed the confidence of Director Casey. He considered the task to be an act of patriotism and, after we briefed him on the issues and the risks involved, pronounced himself ready to travel.

The meeting came off fairly well, with the Libyans arriving willing to talk. They knew in advance what we wanted. They confirmed they had recovered and were holding the remains of the pilot but also explained that they had failed to recover the remains of Captain Flores. They also claimed they had successfully recovered the wreckage of the aircraft, plus the "black boxes" and systems. The head Libyan also said that, although the Soviets were pressing them hard to turn over the EF-111F systems, they had thus far refused. It seemed unlikely the Lib-yans had denied the Soviets the opportunity to exploit our systems, but we also assessed that Gaddafi was cagey enough to perceive value in withholding them, probably to maximize his leverage with both us and the Soviets.

On the negative side, the Libyans did not admit to any ill deeds, let alone the recent bombing in Germany. And they remained coy about any cooperation. They were adamant that Libya and Gaddafi were stridently opposed to radical Islamists and were at crossed swords with the Iranians and Hezbollah. They suggested they would be eager to cooperate with the Agency in those selected areas of mutual concern. At that point, other Operations Directorate elements stepped in to continue the contacts, and our group was transitioned out of the picture. Better put, having initiated the contact and opening that channel of communication, my group was displaced by those claiming expertise in the region. The transitioning did not go well, but I assumed it was because Gaddafi could not bring himself to forgo some of his revolutionary practices and methods.

The Casey Collection of Close Friends and Associates

We continued during 1986 to meet and debrief a collection of Casey's longtime friends and acquaintances. The 1950s and 1960s had been the time of their lives for them, a generation then in its prime. The immediate post-war era of increasing prosperity, and a time when everything seemed to be in play, had made America predominant on the world stage. Deals were there for the taking everywhere. Insurance executives, oil barons, chemical industry captains, commodity and metals traders plus prominent public figures all answered Casey's phone calls and gave us an open door for sit-down sessions.

Those meetings with business leaders served to address a Casey frustration with Agency officers responsible for interacting with the American business community, all done on an overt-contact and declared-as-Agency basis with cooperative U.S. citizens. More often than not, our case officers returned from meetings with Casey associates to report, "No disseminatable intelligence was collected. Recommend no further contact." When Casey questioned his friends, he often discovered, to his embarrassment, "That Agency guy (or gal) didn't understand a damn thing I was talking about!"

I understood what was happening, however. Because Domestic Contact Division officers were graded on their ability to generate reporting, a productive meeting would have them come away with a document in hand, a ready-made report to submit. Any meeting that involved hand-holding an elderly businessman, who first wanted to reminisce about a big deal he had done 20 years previously before moving into a discussion that might produce a report, was not perceived as a good use of an Agency officer's time. Also, in most cases, the assigned officer indeed had no idea what the hell the businessman was talking about, had no context for the discussion and tended to do little or no research before attending a first meeting. It wasn't that case officers were lazy. Rather, they preferred to meet with mid-level businessmen who would hand them a document, such as a blueprint for a new airport in a foreign nation of interest, instead of having to draft a report developed from a conversation. The latter effort might have produced a document of interest to the analysts on the other end of the intelligence equation, but too much effort was required.

In Casey's mind, a reasonable third priority for my group, as other operations would allow, was, "Sit with these folks, build a relationship, and elicit anything they can offer, and do so over months, not a damn one-shot meeting for an hour!" Easier said than done. Those people were still quite busy in their careers. Most tended to lose interest when it appeared what they wanted to talk about, for example a new pipeline in Iraq, did not resonate with their Agency contact. In the area of intelligence collection, Casey's instincts were right. There was valuable information in the heads of the contacts, but mining it efficiently was tough.

One way to address the issue was to take Casey's master list of 70 or so "high-quality contacts" and distill it into maybe a dozen individuals who seemed to have valuable contacts or quality information, or both. The approach worked well for over a year, and we were able to develop trusted relationships, typically at dinner or a Saturday morning brunch in a contact's home. From those discussions, quite often information did flow, and new contacts surfaced. Almost all resided in foreign countries and enjoyed mutual trust with our Casey contacts based on longstanding personal relationships.

For example, the Agency became interested in the plans for a rumored new pipeline in Iraq. We needed to know who in Iraq, or in Israel or Syria, was involved in the politics of the project, and we wanted to confirm the details of its financing and construction. The bottom line was those businesspeople, Casey's friends, often knew things well before contracts were signed and the dirt was turned to build them. Knowing the plans, and the personalities acting behind the scenes to promote or benefit from the dealings, was often useful. Such advance or early information had value, from both an intelligence collection and dissemination perspective as well as from the field-operations angle. Understanding which foreign players were doing what, and for whom, presented information other officers forward-deployed in individual country stations could exploit. We did our best in a short-lived effort.

Taro the 'Street Boy of Los Angeles'

One man, Kay Sugahara, caught and held my interest based on his life story. An orphaned Nisei boy building roads in Los Angeles, he became in a few short years an OSS officer in Indochina, running operations against the Japanese Army during World War II. He shifted after the war to become a combination intel guy and entrepreneur, working the streets of Tokyo from the day the U.S. military occupied the city. Kay had befriended the political leadership of Japan while that country was pulling itself up out of the ashes. He built a shipping company from scratch that would become, by the 1980s, the largest fleet of refrigerated vessels in the world. Kay was in his 80s when we met, and I discovered he was in touch on a regular basis with the then-current leadership of Japan, corresponding with them and calling them from his New York office.

Kay was writing his own autobiography and had relationships to share, as he had told Director Casey. I met with him regularly and listened to his stories, relaying his oral "update reports" and memos back to the boss at Langley. My mid-level servicing effort generally kept them both happy. It was a pleasure for me to deal with Kay, and I learned quite a bit about the inner workings of the Japanese political system. Although little of real substance came out of our meetings, Casey wanted to stay in contact with his friend and was able to show him respect with our attention. For those of us who interacted with him, including my righthand deputy, it was an enjoyable experience. As we were able, we shared time and learning in our engagements with a spirited and deeply patriotic American.

Texas Oil and a Man of the World

Another notable contact was an oilman extraordinaire, Texas-born and bred, then in his early 60s and operating in full form. A fascinating personality in his own right, he was a man who did things his way and didn't give a damn what anyone thought about it. He had approached Casey through a mutual friend and asked for a one-on-one dialog on Iraq, based on his business there and the personal relationship he had forged over several years with Saddam Hussein. Casey handed off the matter to me, and I agreed to meet the man at Washington's National Airport, where he was flying in to pick us up in his Learjet 45 business aircraft. My deputy was with me and, after introductions and some small talk, we launched down the runway with our oilman at the controls, the jet turning its nose toward Texas and the private airfield at his ranch.

It turned out that the individual, a dirt-poor farm boy born in Beaumont, and a crop-duster pilot from age 15, had attended Texas A&M for a year. After Pearl Harbor, he found his calling in the U.S. Army Air Corps. In the war, he had flown B-25 Mitchell attack bombers in the Fifth Air Force in the South Pacific. A decorated veteran, he had returned to Texas A&M to earn his engineering degree and then worked his way through the oil industry in a bottom-up success story.

The man was never subtle. He wanted a relationship with the Reagan White House inner circle, Casey being his desired point of entry. He sought to be the administration's designated intermediary with Saddam and wanted to open a new oilfield in Iraq. His ambition was not a stretch politically because, at that point in the history of the modern Middle East, America was dealing positively with Saddam and Iraq. In mid-1986, that country was in the sixth year of its head-to-head conflict with Iran, a slog of a war that had taken hundreds of thousands of lives. Provoked by Iran's Ayatollah Ruhollah Khomeini but initiated by Saddam with an invasion of his Shiite neighbor, the war had exhausted both countries and reached a stalemate. But it remained an all-out conflict, in which both sides were determined to prevail. The formal U.S. position toward Saddam and his regime was one of calculated ambiguity. We sought to offset the established dominance of Iraq by the Soviet Union by supporting Iraq's position with intelligence and non-lethal materiel and economic aid.

Our oilman wished to bring the United States into a deeper relationship with Iraq at a time when many believed Saddam and his country were on their back foot militarily. Iran had gained a temporary advantage, pressing its human-wave offensives into Iraq proper. We took what the oilman had to offer to our foreign policy folks at the State Department and left it to the National Security Council staff at the White House to decide on any next steps. To my knowledge, we were not able to work with him on his Iraq initiative. That said, we considered him a reliable contact, a patriotic American, and we vouched for his credibility and trustworthiness to others within Reagan's inner circle. Casey was pleased we had vetted the approach, and we stayed close to our oilman in the ensuing months, in part because of the high-quality contacts to whom he led us. **[NOTE 6]**

To Bomb or Not to Bomb

A final example of our ability to exploit the higher-level business relationships Director Casey envisioned was our involvement with an Asian business leader. I explained to our newfound friend the concerns of the U.S. government and confirmed that his company was building a facility based on a design from a European firm. I asked for his assistance in understanding exactly what equipment was being installed in the soon-to-be-completed complex. He offered to bring his construction supervisor to be debriefed by our Agency team, but I explained we would need more. We wanted the blueprints of the plant, equipment lists and the identity of all suppliers, along with names of the involved technicians.

He agreed and sent along a package of detailed information within a couple of weeks. But he did have one request: If the United States planned to bomb the place into oblivion, could we please give him advance notice so he could move his construction people down the road a bit. I said we would do what we could, but I could not make any promises. It had been his decision to seek the contract to construct the facility, and he certainly knew the risks of doing business in that country. He obviously was making good money there and stood a good chance of getting additional contracts. I suggested that he weigh all of it and make his own business decisions, but the lives of several dozen of his own men were on the line. Our analysts were quite pleased with the blueprints and the data dump, and they passed along the project contract and engineering details as finished intelligence to those who might need it.

Whatever planning for what we called a "kinetic action" was then underway, or was not yet underway, it certainly benefited from the information we were able to place into their laps. To this day, I have no idea what the new Libyan owners intended to do with their fine chemical plant, but I suspected the worst. I have no idea if we or another friendly power elected to take no chances. Our mission was to obtain the detailed information, and we did exactly that.

And the Contras? No Way, José!

Occasionally, Director Casey would forget he and I had established certain parameters, including avoidance of any activities that strained the rules by which we had agreed; parameters that had the blessings of Deputy Director McMahon and Agency General Counsel Sporkin. As a meeting closed one day in the fall of 1986, Casey asked me to stay behind for another "special tasking." He explained he had just put received a call from former President Richard Nixon, then visiting New York. Casey noted, "Nixon just told me to get someone to New York tonight. He's having dinner with Madame Chiang Kai-shek, and there will be an extra seat at her table." I asked what the subject might be, if he knew. He replied, "Nixon said, 'She's good for at least a million for the Contras,' so come on up and collect the check over dinner."

I cautioned the Director that though it was indeed good news, I knew next to nothing about the Contra operation. I did not believe it would be wise for me or my group to be involved in such a solicitation. He pressed me a bit, noting I would get along with her just great because I knew Taiwan well, adding, "you two can talk China all night." We discussed it a bit more, and Casey came around to agree that my sitting down to dinner with Madame Chiang probably was not a good idea. He asked whom I thought should make the run. I mentioned another officer I suspected was connected, at least tangentially, with the Contra effort. He agreed and picked up the phone to summon the officer for the run to New York, the dinner and, hopefully, the check. I went back to my small office down the hall, sat with my office manager there and shared the Casey discussion. Cautioning that, like a lot of interactions with Casey, it was not for the record. I remarked, "I think we just dodged a big one!" At that point, I had no idea just how *big* that "Contra thing" was, or would soon become.

Dancing with Amal, and the Ollie North Show

Back on the European scene, we soon discerned that our man Thali had other attributes, not the least of which involved contacts in the Middle East within the Shia community. Operating in Europe, we attempted to establish a direct relationship with the main Shia-affiliated political organization, Amal. Our goal was to secure (optimally) a clandestine reporting asset within that important group or, at a minimum, a trusted contact from whom we could collect information on our main target: Hezbollah. We pressed Thali to make introductions.

Beyond intelligence on Hezbollah, an organization we assumed was a common enemy of both Amal and the United States, we knew the Iranians were working through the terrorist group to establish ever-deeper roots in Beirut. A companion goal was to open a direct channel of discussion with Amal leadership. If established, we could turn it over to our policymakers—once that portion of the U.S. foreign affairs team figured out what it wanted to do in Lebanon. The goal was to probe Amal for any opportunity for cooperation, covert or overt, that would permit them to work with the United States to counter the growing influence of Hezbollah.

Also, when possible, we would seek help to detect that organization's planning for terror operations. There also was the matter of the Western hostages then being held by Hezbollah-managed affiliates and criminal gangs, and our mandate to pinpoint their locations for rescue operations. Thali worked the tasking well, in part because he believed only the United States could save his Shia community, and Lebanon itself, from an eventual takeover by Iran and its proxy Hezbollah.

At the point we realized we were in a position to establish such a direct contact, we took the decision back to Casey and our Directorate leadership for a sanity check. The involved Operations division opposed it for several reasons, some of which seemed reasonable and others farfetched. But Casey thought differently. He was determined to carry forward and sought White House approval to do so.

I accompanied Casey for a two-on-one meeting with Admiral John Poindexter, the President's National Security Advisor. In that session, Casey asked me to lay out the progress we had made and suggest what might be possible in mounting an operation to cooperate with Amal covertly. The policy requirement was to reduce the influence of Hezbollah by any means and checkmate its ability to run terror operations in Lebanon, the Middle East and, as it was expanding its reach, internationally. After some discussion, Poindexter called one of his assistants into the room and asked, "What is our policy regarding Lebanon, and what is our involvement there?" The answer was a shrug, followed by, "Really, after the bombing of the Marine barracks, we haven't had one."

After some silence, Poindexter noted the Marine barracks bombing had occurred several months before. He assumed that someone, somewhere in the U.S. government, did have a policy on Lebanon, and such policy would state it would be in the U.S. national interest to counter Hezbollah. It was obvious something had to be done to confront the terror group directly, or even indirectly, via a proxy such as Amal. He asked us to proceed carefully.

Casey agreed to keep Poindexter advised. A brief discussion of no consequence then took place, but we declined to share operational details and personal identities with the good Admiral or his NSC aide, Marine Lieutenant Colonel Oliver North. I received my mandate to press forward with the Amal dialog. But, in those few minutes in Poindexter's office, I had just landed myself a seat in front of Iran–Contra Independent Prosecutor Lawrence Walsh a year or so later, courtesy of the indomitable but not-so-helpful Ollie North.

In the coming weeks, we managed to meet in our favorite European city with a senior Amal official who was dispatched to parley with us by Amal leader Nabih Berri, who also held the position of Speaker in the Lebanese Parliament. The initial meeting was mostly pro forma, each side demonstrating their respective bona fides and mandates to discuss what was possible in the struggle against Hezbollah. Above all, Amal wanted guns and equipment—lots of rifles and ammunition, squad-level communications devices and of course money. The Amal representative explained that, thanks to Iran, their organization was massively outgunned by Hezbollah, and Amal's traditional Big Brother and protector, Syria, had long kept Amal on a "starvation diet" as a means of exercising political control over the Shia community in Lebanon.

In that initial dialog with Amal, we sought clarity on the fate of former station chief Bill Buckley; his return if he was still alive or, at the bare minimum, return of his remains if he was deceased. Other Western hostages were being held, and others soon would be added to the mix. We knew Hezbollah planners were being encouraged by the Iranians—not that any encouragement was needed—to mount new operations against the United States and other Western countries. In our discussions, we found Amal to be evasive, if not disingenuous, probably because they had no firm answers to provide. But we did manage to get into some detail regarding how Hezbollah and its Iranian sponsors managed a collection of factions and gangs in shattered Lebanon, and how the Iranian proxy force sanctioned the dirty work of hostage-taking, hostage-holding and targeted assassinations.

Our protected dialog with Amal leadership made only incremental progress and faced resistance within Headquarters from the usual cadre of second-guessing, turf-conscious players. Amal's credibility was not helped by the squabbling undercurrent we detected within the organization. Notwithstanding the negatives, what we had gained was a direct channel to Amal, and through Amal to the Shiite population being pressed into a corner by Hezbollah and squeezed by Syria. The latter's enforcement was delivered by Syrian military intelligence operatives who had set themselves up to manage Syria's interests in Beirut.

My personal involvement in the operation ended soon thereafter, when I transitioned our project to new management. At that point, I had begun my Agency out-processing that would permit my planned January 1987 departure. The relationships were destined to outlive my Agency career in the coming years, to good and bad effects. I felt, however, we had responded well to Casey's demand that we "get something, anything, going in Lebanon!"

The above-abbreviated profiles of relationships and activities undertaken by our small team of Casey special-project operatives represent a taste of what we were able to generate over the 15 or so months I headed that effort. Other activities at some point might be declassified and brought to light, but in initiating and sustaining the operation, it was an interesting ride. Recalling one of Casey's objectives to "shake up the sleepy establishment of the Directorate," I believe he managed to do that, in spades.

Chapter 31. Agency Departure and Afterward
Late 1986-Mid-1988

Conflicts at the Flagpole

As 1986 wore on, we hit our stride with project activity in Europe and in our American executive-contacts program. I also found myself in various cities in the Far East, where we pursued Agency relationships and undertook sensitive discussions Casey wished to keep at the level of one-on-one exchanges with our chiefs of station. We added a couple of veteran case officers to our program team, men with whom I had worked in the past. I trusted them to maintain the relationships we had established with the senior business executives. Approaching year-end, with my decision to leave the Agency firmed up, I wanted to be sure there would be a small group inherited by my replacement, assuming Casey wanted to continue our special project after my departure.

I knew, however, that any carry-forward after I was no longer a part of the special activity equation was problematic. It was particularly so, given the active opposition we faced from the established senior players in the Directorate of Operations. But we had to try. A political storm was gathering on the Seventh Floor at Langley, and we were never far from the center of it. Although we had taken every reasonable precaution to keep within the letter of the law, based on arrangements we had made with Deputy Director McMahon and General Counsel Sporkin, our authority to operate was constantly being challenged and undercut by the establishment leadership—who remained threatened by our existence and by Casey's unwavering support.

As the chief of the reorganized Domestic Contacts Division, Jim had done his best to insulate us from attacks by the other Operations divisions. But it was a thankless, rearguard action. Jim was disliked and disrespected by the other, senior-level Directorate managers, many of whom had become jealous of his close relationship with Casey. But Jim was a fighter, and he did his best to protect us in his typical mediator-cum-cheerleader role.

Long-simmering tensions came to a head around October 1986, when a series of events related to our attempts to work the Lebanon problem ignited a bonfire. In a leadup, I had experienced a nasty run-in with a senior Near East Division manager, who confronted me the day after Casey and I had met with National Security Advisor John Poindexter and his aide. Hearing of our meeting, he had reached out to invite me to his office for a "friendly conversation" that became confrontational.

"Who the hell do you think you are, trying to take the Ollie North relationship away from me?" he demanded. I told him I didn't know Ollie North, did not seek to become his friend and frankly did not see any value in doing so. The manager became even more irate and basically accused me of lying. It was evident that the man, like others from his division, thought I was an opportunist attempting to elevate myself and my program to denigrate and displace them. I abruptly walked out of the room, realizing I had made the right decision to part with the Agency. And that guy was all-Agency. He would be a feature for a long time to come, and my enemy for sure.

A few days later, I was asked to meet with another senior manager from the same division, regarding my activity in Europe and the Middle East target there. Not prepared for the attack, I walked into another buzzsaw. I was asked to explain why I was now in sustained contact with Thali, and why I was tasking him to do things for the Agency. I attempted to explain how we had gained access to him and secured a level of control over him. I described how we were directing Thali to collect intelligence related to Lebanon and Libya, and the information he seemed able to provide was useful. I then was informed I was "disrupting operations that had been underway for several months," that is, covert efforts the division had mounted to gain access to Thali. The efforts obviously were well-planned and expensive in terms of case-officer time. Their comments confirmed that someone at Headquarters determined Thali was of significant intelligence value.

I did not understand the issue. We already had established access and enjoyed a measure of direct control, not to mention control over Thali's third-party employer. That employer had agreed to continue paying the bill to keep Thali under our influence and willing to do our bidding, at least up to a point. What possibly could be the problem? Perhaps the division responsible had failed to achieve our level of success in securing a good measure of control over the asset, to the point where we were directing his collection to the Agency's benefit.

The manager's answer astounded me. He said they were working to recruit the boyfriend of Thali's maid, with the intention of then recruiting *her*. Once the maid was recruited, she would be directed to install a listening device in the home, to be monitored by a surveillance team set up in a nearby apartment. But the "operation" had a timeline I had disrupted. My reply was straight-faced. "Why don't you just tell us what you want to know, and we will ask him directly." It was not what the manager wanted to hear. It was a perfect example of the kind of ass-backward, indirect and complicated approach to many targets of priority interest that drove Casey crazy.

I was told my actions were "disruptive" and would be reported and placed in the record. At that point I was asked to leave the office. Beyond what we already were asking of our friend Thali in that certain European city, I never was told what else the intricately planned operation to install the device in the man's apartment hoped to accomplish. This was not about "results." It was all about "the process" and the ownership of operational turf, pure and simple. The bureaucrats had taken over the Agency, and the inmates were now running the asylum.

Recognizing that the long knives were out, I asked Jim to arrange a meeting with the Agency's Inspector General to allow me to request an investigation of our entire operation. I wanted to preempt others from doing so. And I wanted some degree of control over how the investigation was mounted and what records would be made available. I realized at that point we needed an accurate description of how our project had come about and the structure we had put in place to comply with the regulations governing such activity. We would open all our protected files, allow interviews galore and take polygraph tests as required.

I also took time to explain to Casey why I thought it all needed to be done—to protect our group, and to protect him. He just shook his head in disbelief. The investigation began posthaste and was completed within a few weeks. We received a clean bill of health, for the record. Those who learned of the IG activity and hoped we would be damaged by it were disappointed. Sad, however, that the entire relationship had devolved to such a state, but it probably was unavoidable, given the resentment Casey's initiative had engendered.

A Rant and a Reflection

My penultimate experience in the theater of hostile contact inside the building occurred a week or so later. I was summoned by Clair George, the DDO himself, for a one-on-one chat in his office. He informed me he was tired of hearing from Director Casey what my group was doing or what it ostensibly had accomplished. He did not believe half of what was being claimed, either by me or by Casey. Further, by agreeing to work with Casey in an offline operation, I had embarrassed the Operations Directorate and destroyed my Agency career. By accepting Casey's offer and doing his bidding, I obviously had chosen to advance myself and become a traitor to my fellow clandestine service officers. He said he would personally see to it that I never served overseas in a significant position again. He declared, in a finger-pointing threat, that I would never be posted as either a deputy chief of station in a large post or as chief in a small one, at least as long as he served in his position. I explained I had done what I thought was right, and I had cleared everything with a man I respected, Deputy Director of Central Intelligence John McMahon. I apologized for any embarrassment my actions had caused the Directorate or the DDO personally.

George was having none of it. He began ranting, demanding that I get out of his office. As I walked down the eerily quiet hallway on the Seventh Floor, he suddenly emerged from his office, stood in the hallway and elevated his diatribe by several decibels.

"I will see your ass stamping license plates in Leavenworth if I can! You are DONE in this Agency, done in the DO. You are finished. DO YOU HEAR ME? YOU ARE FUCKING FINISHED!"

As he continued his rant, and as I continued to walk away, attempting to ignore the ruckus, other Seventh Floor employees poked their heads out of doorways to watch and hear the DDO's unhinged performance. Mostly clerks and secretaries, but also a few senior folks, all seemingly enjoying the one-way exchange.

Jim, who happened to be standing in his outer office and heard the uproar, stepped into the hallway as I was passing by. With George still yelling at the top of his voice, Jim motioned me out of the hallway and into his suite.

"What the hell was that all about?" Jim asked me. "I think I can still hear Clair screaming down there!" I explained what had happened, and he understood. It had been building for months, and George had other dragons at his door, including the Contra debacle. That imbroglio later would sweep him up, see him indicted by a grand jury and, later, convicted for lying to Congress. Jim offered to speak with Casey and then go to George to smooth things over. I asked him to not do so. I simply did not care anymore.

Leadership Changes and Challenges

During that period of expanded and increasingly hostile challenges by the established Operations Directorate leadership, we experienced an important transition in the Agency's front office. Robert Gates replaced John McMahon as Deputy Director in the spring when John retired after 35 years of service and moved into a second career in the private sector. John had been more than a friend. In the special Casey program in which we found ourselves, he was our ultimate bureaucratic protector and quiet advocate. He knew what we were doing, trusted us to stay within the lines, and did not concern himself with the details.

Bob Gates was an entirely different critter. He was a career analyst from the Directorate of Intelligence, the "other side" of the Agency house, and he proved to be no fan of Operations. He had no history with our side and really did not understand the mentality of the clandestine service. He seemed uninterested in trying to figure out the DDO position, and those in the Directorate reciprocated by holding him at a distance. We found Gates to be both risk-averse and knowledge-averse. That is, he was a determined non-operator who did not want to know about things that might get him or the Agency into trouble. I did not blame him, given that his immediate superior, Director William J. Casey, was something of a wild man and unpredictable, save for his predilection to accept any risk worthy of the name. Compared to the McMahon–Casey complementary partnership, the Gates–Casey arrangement was an odd combination that did not work well.

More simply put, during our eight-month period of interaction—despite Clair George's rant, I would remain at the Agency that much longer—it appeared Bob Gates was leery of Casey and afraid of Casey's inclinations. To be fair, Gates was much more than a career analyst who had climbed to the top of the Agency. He was an experienced policy infighter with lots of time clocked at the National Security Council and around the White House. He knew the ropes there and was confident in his ability to navigate interagency conflicts and personalities. He picked his issues carefully, avoiding those where he did not hold leverage and risked losing a policy battle.

After Gates took over from McMahon in early summer 1986, I discerned that Bob wanted nothing to do with our ostensibly "offline" operation. On those occasions when I would meet with Casey in his office, Bob would excuse himself and make a pronounced exit from the room, often slipping between the sliding doors and closing them behind him, as Casey and I began a conversation. In those months when Bob Gates and I overlapped in his new position, I can recall only one time when he sat in on a meeting with Casey in which I was present. As I remember, he did not utter a word.

Gates's inclination to avoid any contact with or involvement in our project presented no issues from my side. But the signaling was clear; he knew nothing and would not be there if we needed him in a Seventh Floor bar fight. The positive aspect was Bob did not seem to have a lot of trust in the judgment of the Operations Directorate's senior leadership. It also seemed he probably was more concerned with what some of them were up to, at the behest of Casey, than he was with us. It was the time of the helter-skelter, Iran–Contra activity, the mining of the harbor in Nicaragua, and the various dealings concocted among Casey, Ollie North and the DO's Dewey Clarridge, enabled by Contra-contaminated case officers. The cast was supported by a host of outside contractors and facilitators, individuals who either had thrown themselves into the true offline pot that was the Contras or been invited in by Casey and company. The fact that our operation had nothing to do with any of that mess probably did not even occur to Gates. But he also did not want to take any chances we *were* somehow involved. It was a reasonable defensive posture for a career political operative.

Attesting to the degree of intentional distancing to which Gates retreated, we have his characterization of our operation, and his understanding of how we organized ourselves, in his own words. I found one of the most misunderstood references to our project's brief existence in Gates's book, From the Shadows: The Ultimate Insider's Story of Five Presidents and How They Won the Cold War. An expansive autobiographical tome, it was published by Simon & Schuster in 1996, some 10 years after I parted company with Mr. Gates at the Agency. In his chapter, "Reagan's Sword: Casey at CIA," under the appropriately titled section, "Casey and the DO: Frustration and Trouble," Gates recounted his and others' attempts to respond to Casey's demands that more be done to address opportunities in the private sector. **[NOTE 1]**

Continuing in that vein, Gates observed Casey elected to bypass the DO structure by reaching down to find an individual case officer whom he (Casey) liked and trusted, and "gave him the task of making these contacts." Beyond an accurate depiction of Casey's growing frustration with the DO, Gates conveyed his ignorance of the real chain of events that had delivered me to Casey's world. Gates goes off on a tangent to note that, "the officer's improbable pseudonym was Lawless." Gates confided that he, Deputy Director McMahon and Acting

DDO John Stein were "extremely uneasy about Casey running this man (pseudonym Lawless) without checks or supervision." Gates noted that McMahon "finally succeeded in corralling this operation—mostly—and bringing Lawless and some of Casey's other independent operators back into the bureaucratic tent under a new Assistant DDO."

Gates, therefore, misunderstood that my Agency and DO pseudonym was "Lawless," which was a bit of a joke in and of itself. When the Gates book was published, several Agency friends called or emailed to ask if my covert name or alias identity was Lawless, could I please tell them what my real name was? We DO officers all had career-duration "pseudos." But neither the project nor my Agency pseudo was "Lawless," as much as our Operations Directorate nemesis gang might have wished was the case.

I could imagine how Gates had been left with this assumption, with Casey telling Gates, as they huddled in Casey's office, "I have Lawless coming into see me now, you want to sit in?" Gates would then remember that he had urgent business elsewhere and exit stage left before I even stepped into the room. For Gates, the mere mention of the "Lawless operation" by Casey was his cue to depart the scene of the potential crime and avoid any contamination of his position by a controversial operational discussion. Beyond that simple misunderstanding, it was clear in his account Gates had no idea I had gone to McMahon the same day Casey broached the project with me. He had no appreciation that we quickly had worked out a solution, with the support of General Counsel Sporkin, and our activity was fully integrated into the Agency system. **[NOTE 2]**

Beyond that fundamental misunderstanding, which is excusable given Gates's late arrival on the scene and his determination to remain uninformed, the balance of that portion of his book is painfully accurate. Gates notes such activities (as ours) reflected Casey's "unhappiness and frustration with the Directorate of Operations," and by as early as late 1981, as he quotes from a Casey memo, "neither the DCI (himself) nor the DDCI (McMahon) know what is being done." The Casey memo he quotes was drafted four years before the Director called me back from Japan. As Gates continued, "It was easy to see that he was fed up with the DO. It was just too cautious, too bureaucratic, too slow, too timid, and too unimaginative. Too much a closed shop. Not at all like the OSS."

Having described the frustration on Casey's part, Gates proceeded in his next paragraph to set the reader straight (my caustic characterization). He explained that,

> The kind of imaginative rule-bending, "beat-the-bureaucracy," freelancing and risk-taking that could be tolerated and even encouraged in wartime, in the OSS, was unacceptable in the fourth decade of the Cold War. Such an approach was an anachronism. Casey was not oblivious to this. He was too smart for that. But his instincts and impulses, the imperviousness of the DO bureaucracy—and his commitment to the war against the Soviets—all inclined [Casey] to the old way of operating, to the approach he had learned in the OSS and from Donovan.

Gates's commentary managed to have it three ways. First, he blessed the wisdom of Casey but defined him as anachronistic, basically a throwback incapable of understanding the realities of the new world order of things. Gates did highlight the ineptitude of the DO, employing Casey's words to do so, but then came around to acknowledge that America and the Agency had found themselves "at war against the Soviets."

Gates completed his circle of logic by suggesting Casey's chosen path; that is, an OSS-inspired, take-off-the-gloves approach to operations should be trodden only if we really were in a war. Excuse me, but we *were* then in a war. We had a Cold War standoff assured by nuclear weapons deployed under a strategy involving mutually assured destruction, and a hot war where we faced off conventionally against Soviet aggression in Afghanistan, among other locations.

Casey plainly thought we were in an international conflict with the Soviet Union and the war required a degree of risk-taking the Agency and the DO were incapable of delivering to the front lines. Many of us at the case-officer level agreed with Casey. Gates was comfortable in his own policy-wonk, assessment-generating and bureaucratic-maneuvering world. His career-informed frame of reference had little to do with clandestine operations and Agency people in the field.

Moreover, Gates did not trust the DO, did not like the leading personalities of its leadership and was not intimidated by them. He sought to take the DO down a notch or three. Gates came from a place that regarded the Operations Directorate as the component of the Agency that had dominated the institution since its inception. He worked diligently to foster the ascension of his home base, the Intelligence Directorate, to the highest possible level of influence, with the goal of setting a new balance between the two. Ideally, he would be able to end permanently the dominance of the Operations Directorate over the Agency writ large.

We on the Operations side would take little comfort in the internal clash that played out in 1987 and beyond. Disagreements among Agency leadership, when combined with Casey's penchant for maneuvering around protocols, gave Gates and his allies running room. Casey's sudden departure from the scene as 1986 rolled into 1987 allowed Gates and others to leverage the resulting instability to the benefit of the DI side. The result would be a steady wearing-down of Operations, the ascension of its rival and the elevation of those, such as John Brennan, who posed as "operators" but were anything but, at least in the sense of clandestine service. The process would continue over many years and culminate where it is, in 2023, with the Operations Directorate reorganized out of existence. Mission accomplished. There now are no real operators in the Agency, because real operations are no longer allowed to exist.

What Gates did not understand, at least at the time, and others did appreciate all too well, was Casey was using our small group to accomplish two complementary objectives. First, Casey wanted to demonstrate he was correct in his insistence that our Operations Directorate had left unattended and untapped a resource of real potential, namely, American and foreign business leaders who traveled widely and routinely dealt at levels above normal intelligence-collection activity. Second, and perhaps more confrontational, Casey wanted to hang what operational successes our small group had in the face of the DO leadership. He had come reluctantly but firmly to the conclusion that the Directorate's leadership mainly comprised careerists who had made a habit of explaining why they could not get things done. Casey wanted to embarrass them by forcing them to adopt a more aggressive approach.

The in-your-face posturing on Casey's part did succeed in showing up and angering senior Operations managers. Those men heretofore had been immune from having to prove why a given task was beyond their reach, and they dodged Casey's demands for improved performance for five long years. But Casey's approach also made those same people our declared enemy, a tough collection of operators determined to exact revenge by discrediting and degrading our small project team. We knew the score and understood that anyone associated with us soon would pay the price, and we accepted it as part of the bargain.

Eve of Departure

I previously agreed when I took the job from Casey, more than a year before in the fall of 1985, that I would serve through 1986 and planned to resign early the following year. A few weeks before that departure, I submitted my resignation paperwork with an effective date in mid-January. Casey and I discussed my resignation in early December when I reviewed with him the plans for my handover of the unit to another officer. In that case, though there was some uncertainty, I proposed a temporary solution. One of my more experienced case officers would succeed me. Then, an officer acceptable to and nominated by the Near East Division, one of their own, would step up to take the position in the new year. I knew Operations was determined to assert control over my project. Their goal would be to merge it into their structure and then disband it as soon as they could concoct an explanation that would pass muster with Casey. I told Casey I expected the leadership of the Operations Directorate would have its way with us, and our offline unit would functionally cease to exist by mid-1987.

Casey explained he planned to resign as well. His target was summer 1987, and he noted he already had discussed the plan with President Reagan. Casey thought he could be of more value to the country if he claimed a leading role in the upcoming presidential campaign, which he assumed would see Vice President George H.W. Bush as the Republican nominee. He asked me again to remain with him and continue managing the active program for an additional six months or so. The Casey pitch was, "Let's continue to shake things up here for a while and then depart at the same time." I respectfully declined, and he didn't force the issue.

That same evening, at home, about nine o'clock, I had a knock on the door. Peter Dailey, the Director's Counselor and close friend, stood on my porch. We sat down for a chat. He said he had my personnel file on his desk and discussed my planned resignation with Casey. Peter asked me to consider staying on, at least for another year or two. He said he could smooth things over with Operations and bring me back into that fold. He promised that my career could continue as before, and he would make sure I received the JFK School appointment the following September. He also explained that, even as Casey departed, he planned to stay on for another year in his Counselor to the Director position until at least January 1989; that is, until the Reagan administration transitioned into that of George Bush.

I thanked Peter for his gesture and explained I had made my decision some time ago. I was now 40 and needed to move on in life. If I did not do so, I probably would stay with the Agency until I died there in the saddle or they threw me out at 80. I loved the CIA and the DO, but it no longer loved me. I offered that, in my opinion, the people now running the Agency and the DO as well were plowing it into the ground. I was not bothered by the threats of retaliation because those men would be gone within a few years, but I just wanted to be done with it all. My 15 years had been a fairly struck bargain: I wanted to serve my country. I had been offered a wonderful opportunity to do so by the Agency, and I had delivered to the best of my ability. Peter asked me to reconsider and speak with him and Casey together after the new year, before my resignation became effective. It was the polite thing to do, and I agreed. But things did not turn out that way—as they seldom do.

A few days later, I trekked to the Old Executive Office Building, next door to the White House, to meet with my patron, Don Gregg, then serving as Vice President Bush's National Security Advisor. Don had been my first station chief and my strong advocate throughout my career. He had come "across the river" to Headquarters to attend all three awards ceremonies in which I was honored. We had stayed in touch, but he was surprised to learn via the Agency old-boy grapevine that I had turned in my resignation paperwork. He was both perplexed and upset, and he asked, "How can you do this when you have a great future career with the Agency in front of you?" I explained my reasons as best I could. But it was clear that Don took my decision personally as almost a betrayal of his confidence and support over the 15 years I had known him. The breach did not heal over the years ahead. I should have anticipated such from a man who expected a lot from me.

That same sense of denial mixed with betrayal came from others with whom I worked along the way, including Jim, another former chief, who had served as my protector at Headquarters. And Bob, my Chief in Seoul, now East Asia Division Chief at Headquarters, expressed similar disappointment. Still others with whom I had worked as peers or as junior officers exhibited the same attitude in those final weeks, to the point where I tried to say clear of the main building. I failed then to realize that, in many of their eyes, I had abandoned a ship on which

I had signed on to serve, if not for life then certainly for a full career. The attitude was, you simply do not leave once you have been inducted into the club of the Agency's clandestine service. That was particularly so for anyone anointed as an East Asia hand.

The Last Day — A Tragedy

In mid-December, I returned to Langley to say farewell to my small team there and thank them for their support in difficult circumstances. I also met with my East Asia Division colleagues, as well as Jim and his team. Needless to say, I avoided the Directorate's front office. I did not expect them to be lighting candles for me there. My final appointment was with Director Casey, and he had set aside 20 minutes or so for us to discuss a number of pending issues.

Prior to stepping into that meeting, I stopped at the small office occupied by his security detail, men with whom I had become friendly over the last year or so. A senior Office of Security manager pulled me aside and cautioned, "I see you are on the Director's schedule today. He's not in very good shape." He explained that earlier in the morning, when Casey was getting into the car at his home, he had lost his balance, slipped and, "well, he sort of fell." Another offered that "He said he is okay, and he seems okay now, but we are not sure." I asked if they had called the Agency doctor, and they said they were considering doing so when I walked in. They asked me to make my own assessment and come back and see them after my meeting. I suggested that they not wait for me and they might want to call the doctor now. As I headed to see Casey, they were on the phone to the medical office.

In our meeting, Casey looked pale, distant and unfocused, but he snapped to a more-alert state when we talked specifics. He looked tired, and I asked if he had had a bad night or bad news. He insisted he was fine. We checked off our list of items, and strangely he mentioned Bill Buckley again, a topic he had not raised with me for weeks. We agreed to meet in a month or so, once I figured out what I was going to do with the balance of my life. He mentioned the upcoming presidential campaign and his friend, Judge Bill Clark, and asked me to see him about a matter. After we said our good-byes and shook hands, I returned to the security officers' room. They told me the doctors were on their way up, were "next in" with the Director and not to worry. I assumed that, indeed, things would be just fine. I walked down to the main lobby, turned in my badge, walked to the visitors' parking lot and drove away. I had no intention of coming back.

As I learned later, on that day about an hour or so after my farewell meeting with Bill Casey, he suffered a major stroke. The event displaced him from his office, and he began a decline that would cast him into a coma and claim his life several weeks later. In weeks prior to his stroke, he had been hammered and drained by the Iran–Contra scandal. Congressional committees with bones in their teeth had compelled him to testify almost nonstop. The political target was the Reagan presidency, the administration, the White House staff and the

Agency. But the growing inquisition had Bill Casey in its gunsights, and they knew he was vulnerable, both to the truth of his actions and weakness of his body.

The Robert Gates book devotes a good deal of space to the events of that sad period, roughly November 1986 through February 1987. In those accounts, Gates comes off exceptionally well, and for good reason. He was regularly at Casey's side as Acting DCI and friend. He guided Casey and his family through the period of the Director's physical and mental deterioration and helped facilitate Casey's resignation with honor and dignity.

In the coming weeks and months, Washington would be consumed by Iran–Contra, with that clown show sucking all of the oxygen out of the public-policy room. Congress was outraged that its own duplicity on Central America had been more than matched by the White House and Casey, both determined to do whatever possible to checkmate the Soviets, the Cubans and their Sandinista handmaidens in Nicaragua. Gates would be nominated to fill the Casey position in late January 1987 and then denied that post when he was compelled to withdraw his nomination in early March. He had little choice. He faced a barrage of accusations from a Democratic-controlled Congress. Pulling back his nomination saved the Reagan team no little embarrassment. The political class had scented blood in the water, and the media thrashed about to deliver the bodies, hoping to ferret out as many links as possible to the Agency. Gates had become a prime target of speculation, and his decision to step back and accept a lower profile was a calculated but selfless move.

Watching it all play out as a born-again civilian, I assumed my time at the Agency had passed, and I would be free to find a new career in the private sector. I set up my own company, worked with some friends to create a technology consultancy and tried my best to ignore the headlines and the ranting media. Bill Casey passed away quietly, and I thought that with his death and my having cut my connections with the Agency, it would all be behind me. But as the Eagles sing in their classic, "Hotel California," paraphrasing, you can check out any time you want, but you can never leave. How true.

A Second Tragedy

Although I had fully disengaged from my team, former (retired) colleagues and friends occasionally contacted me for updates on events that impacted the associates I left behind. My small organization continued to function for several months and, as I had anticipated, with Casey gone and Gates in change, the Operations Directorate leadership carefully but decisively brought the project back into the fold. For the remaining few months it functioned, it would serve under the Directorate's Near East Division, as well it should have. My replacement as project chief was an up-and-coming younger officer, an established Arabist who obviously was destined for Agency and Directorate stardom.

On December 21, 1988, nearly two years after I had left the Central

Intelligence Agency, in the dark skies over Lockerbie, Scotland, a Pan American Airlines 747 passenger aircraft was blown out of the sky. All 243 passengers on board, 16 crew members and 11 residents of the town below died that snowy night. The aircraft, *Clipper Maid of the Seas*, had departed London's Heathrow Airport about 38 minutes before and was homebound for Detroit, with a stop planned in New York City. Matt Gannon was 34 years old when he died.
[NOTE 3]

Chapter 32. Chief Inspector Walsh
and a Korean Diplomat
1987

The Walsh Cadre Calls

A few months after my departure from the Agency, I received a summons from Iran–Contra Special Counsel Lawrence Walsh and his merry crew of investigators. History records that Walsh set up shop in December 1986 when, at the request of U.S. Attorney General Edwin Meese, the United States Court of Appeals for the District of Columbia Circuit appointed him as an Independent Counsel. Walsh was charged to investigate a range of activities associated with the still-unfolding Iran–Contra scandal, including:

> the sale of arms to Iran, any intermediaries and financing involved with such sales and transfers ... any diversion of funds from such activity to the benefit of insurgents (meaning The Contras) ... and any coordination that offered support to any insurgents engaged in armed conflict with the government of Nicaragua since 1984.

It was a broad hunting license for a deep and wide dive into all aspects of the second Reagan term.

Walsh's seemingly interminable prosecutorial endeavor lasted over six years. By the time he formally turned in the results of his enterprise, titled "Final Report of the Independent Counsel for Iran/Contra Matters," on August 4, 1993, he had explored every street and alley where he might secure a conviction of involved members of the Reagan administration. The Walsh gunsights were set on the White House and the Agency. In the former, the goal was to implicate President Reagan and his inner circle. In the Agency area, the targets were Director Casey and the leadership of the Directorate of Operations. Because of my proximity to Casey and the interactions on the Seventh Floor, I assumed I would be called as the investigation picked up momentum in the spring of 1987. That assumption proved correct. In fairly short order, I received my summons to sit down with the Walsh group.

My first session did not go well for either party. When I presented myself, I found an Agency legal counsel waiting for me. He was a nice guy but someone who clearly was in the dark about why I might be there and what I knew or did not know. In the meeting room, I found several of Walsh's lawyers impatient to get the interview rolling, with Department of Justice- or FBI-delegated assistants transcribing away as we talked. Incredibly, the Walsh team began by reading a letter or a dictate from Acting Director Robert Gates, directing that all Agency employees were to provide full cooperation with the investigation. The implication was that failure to cooperate fully with Walsh and his team would be grounds for dismissal. I asked how the letter applied to me. I was told, "We know that you are still an Agency employee and that you have just shifted from one cover to another." I rejected the assertion and explained I had resigned from the Agency, fully and completely. I had no connection, officially or informally; no involvement with the Agency since February 1987 and none currently.

The response was, "We don't believe you, and you must respect the Gates instruction." I tried to explain I would not be bound by the Gates letter, but I had no problem providing an affidavit attesting I was not an active Agency employee. The lead lawyer countered with something like, "We have your file, we have read it and we know that you are still active. You must acknowledge this fact." I refused and explained I was there to discuss anything they wished and would be bound by what I told them, as I had absolutely nothing to conceal.

After an intermission, during which they apparently checked with Headquarters to confirm my status, we resumed, and the subject turned, as I knew it would, to Casey. It was clear from the first exchange they were determined to nail the late William J. Casey to the wall.

Although he had slipped from Walsh's grip with his coma and death, Director Casey remained the big target. Lesser candidates for indictment were other senior Agency officers, including now-Acting Director Gates, the DDO Clair George and the flamboyant-as-ever senior operations officer, Duane R. "Dewey" Clarridge. Other senior officers who had become enmeshed in the entire Iran–Contra mess also were being stalked in hopes they would turn on their colleagues or superiors with damning testimony. On the White House side, everyone up to and including President Reagan was targeted, as well as Vice President George H.W. Bush and his National Security Advisor, my close friend and former patron, Don Gregg. In November 1992, as the presidential election approached, Walsh indicted several of those men for alleged crimes and misdemeanors related to Iran–Contra. But when I sat for my interview in early 1987, the reckoning remained five years in the future, and I had no idea then how Walsh and company might attempt to implicate me.

The interview referenced Casey's datebook, the log kept by his front office of his appointments and meetings. Most of my private sessions were noted, but many were not, probably because they came about when Casey spotted an opening in his schedule and summoned me down the hall. Somehow, he was very good at finding me during those infrequent times when I was in the building and not in my office or traveling overseas. Each meeting with Casey that was identified caused the Walsh prosecutors to ask what was discussed. I explained that in most cases I simply could not remember. But I did note, to their disappointment, that none of the meetings had any relevance to Iran or Iran–Contra.

As the Committee investigators pressed the issue, I emphasized I had stayed away from those activities, and Casey had respected my operational distance. It was a mutually agreed, if informal, compartmentation of sorts. I took pains to emphasize I typically did not keep a record of what was discussed, unless it involved a decision to take an action, and I assumed Casey did not as well. Finally, I reiterated that because I was no longer an employee of the Agency, and had no access to classified records, I was not in a position to access compartmented files to reconstruct a given meeting, even if demanded.

The Walsh team declined to accept my explanation and departed for individual meetings in his office. On those occasions when I did recall the subjects covered in a given session with Casey, I shared them with the interrogators, avoiding any details about individual assets or ongoing operations. Things became heated when we moved into a discussion of Lebanon and my group's interaction with the Amal organization, focusing on the interaction with Amal we had developed. I described a meeting at the NSC staff offices with Admiral Poindexter and our exchange on the pros and cons of opening a channel for intelligence and possible cooperation with Amal and the Lebanese Shiite community. The Walsh people clearly were going somewhere specific with their line of questioning. They seemed to think they were about to connect that meeting, and the Amal initiative, with Iran and the funding transfer to the Contra operation in Nicaragua.

I then was read a text the Walsh investigators described as a recovered NSC staff PROF, or machine-generated memo, prepared by Lieutenant Colonel Oliver North. The short memo ostensibly described a discussion among Casey, Poindexter, North and me. The suggestion was that I was not telling the full truth in my description of the meeting. I asked them to read it again and, when they did, I told them it was "mostly garbage." The PROF obviously had been crafted to show North as being in the center of the conversation when, in fact, he had not been called into Poindexter's office until the last 10 minutes of the meeting. I said he was either guessing or recounting something Poindexter told him after the fact. I was adamant that the PROF account was inaccurate, and if they intended to use other North-generated PROF versions of NSC meetings, they should either divide by five or find someone who was willing to validate what was presented as fact. I would be willing to state that the account presented to me was incorrect and that it exaggerated and misconstrued the meeting. As far as I was concerned, the memo was irrelevant.

A long silence followed. I noticed the transcribers had stopped typing some minutes back. I wondered if they were thinking what I was suggesting: If the PROF was incorrect, and I was willing to attest to it, what did that mean for North's other self-promoting PROFs? The Walsh team apparently had expected I would confirm North's version of the meeting. Or, perhaps they were on to North and wanted me to say he intentionally misrepresented what Poindexter had decided. In any event, the memo did not accurately convey what Casey said, nor what we had agreed to do going forward with the Amal channel. I refused to assign intent and reiterated the PROF read to me by the Walsh investigators, for whatever combinations of reasons, was not an accurate record of the meeting.

I had been there from beginning to end, and the PROF account was inaccurate.

I also emphasized that was my only interaction with North. I had no reason to believe he was uniformly inaccurate or not well-meaning with his PROFs. Mine was a one-off encounter, and I successfully avoided all future invitations from Director Casey to interact with North. Also—although I did not mention it to the Walsh people—back in the summer and fall of 1986, I had other issues inside Headquarters that involved senior Directorate leadership. Several of those more senior officers considered themselves to be North's friends. Facing a no-win situation with North, and having zero aspirations to become his friend, I took care to not disrupt those relationships.

As the discussion with the Walsh team progressed, I sensed growing frustration in the room. The refrain from across the table became, "But you spent all this time alone with Casey, and you were not a party to the Iran arms deal nor involved the Contra operation? Very difficult to believe!" After attempts to reconstruct several meetings I had with Casey, some of which might have been useful to the group, and others not so, the session came to an end. I was asked to make myself available for a repeat performance. [NOTE 1]

Chuck Yeager and the Sound Barrier

There was another appointment in the Casey datebook stirring the curiosity of the Walsh group that day. It involved a long, one-on-one, late-afternoon session, apparently followed by a Casey dinner engagement. To the Walsh sleuths, it looked suspicious. I was asked to explain the Casey meeting, and fortunately I did recall it. We had had a brief exchange on the subject of Vietnam-era MIA reporting. I attempted to assuage Casey's concerns that his DO team was failing him. Casey had determined, some time before, that Operations was not doing enough to address the possibility that U.S. military pilots lost over Vietnam and Laos during the war had not returned home in 1973. There always had been a suspicion that when Henry Kissinger negotiated the Paris Peace Accords, allowing the United States to abandon South Vietnam to its fate, neither he nor President Nixon had placed a high priority on the return of our captured pilots.

As I sat with Casey in his office a decade after the North Vietnamese had prevailed, that possibility remained an emotional issue for many. Patriotic Americans focused on the issue of men left behind included Texas businessman H. Ross Perot. The billionaire was deeply patriotic and repeatedly had lobbied the Director for more certainty on the issue. I met with him in the company of Casey to discuss his admirable passion.

After I explained to Casey how East Asia Division was managing that politically sensitive intelligence-collection requirement, he pronounced himself only partially satisfied. True to his character, Casey told me to go back to all possible sources for a second run. But then he shifted gears and asked me to stay a bit and help him develop some remarks he had committed to make that same evening.

It was an OSS reunion dinner of sorts. A lady who had been in the French Resistance in World War II was being honored, and Casey was expected to speak. He uncharacteristically admitted, "I don't think I have anything interesting to say."

I glanced at his bookcase, at volumes I had cataloged in my mind during previous sessions that lingered. I reached out to retrieve a copy of Yeager: An Autobiography. I asked if he knew who Chuck Yeager was and what he had done. Casey knew but could not make a connection with the dinner event. I explained that Yeager was one of America's true heroes, a combat pilot who served for 30 years in three wars and had retired as a Brigadier General. His career anointed him as one of the greatest jet-age test pilots in our history. On October 14, 1947, he had flown the Bell X-1 at Mach 1.1 to become the first man to break the sound barrier.

Before all that, Yeager had been a young Army Air Forces pilot who had been shot down on his eighth mission over France in March 1944. Our fighter aircraft back then were clearing the skies of the Luftwaffe in the runup to the Allied invasion of Normandy. Having parachuted from his burning P-51 Mustang, Yeager found himself on the ground in hostile territory. Hunted by the Germans, he was a candidate for imprisonment as a POW or worse. Yeager was rescued by the Marquis—the French resistance—and after some weeks with them was smuggled out of France on an escape route that carried him over the mountains of Spain to freedom.

Once back in the United Kingdom at his fighter base, Yeager and a colleague took issue with a regulation that prohibited any pilot who had been shot down over occupied France and then assisted by the Resistance from flying again over hostile territory. After several appeals, he was reinstated to fly combat missions, and he quickly made up for lost time. Over Germany in the coming months, again flying a P-51, Yeager became an 11-victory ace, with five kills in a single day. He would also be among the first to defeat the German ME-202 jet fighter in air combat.

Casey understood completely and earmarked the book where Yeager described how the Marquis had rescued him, took him under their wing, and organized his return to his unit. Because of the courage of the Marquis, Chuck Yeager, in company with many other U.S. flyers shot down over France, would live to fly and fight again. Chuck Yeager, the man who broke the sound barrier, was alive and able to accomplish this feat because his life was saved by the Resistance. Yeager had his opportunity to be Yeager of Bell X-1 legend because of the efforts of the people Casey was to honor that evening. The Director was pleased, and he said he would spell that out, holding Yeager's book as his prop. **[NOTE 2]**

From Bad to Worse with Walsh

In my next round with team Walsh, things went south even before the session began. It happened that I had been contacted a few days before by a third party, a person whom I trusted, who related a disturbing story. Apparently, one of the lead members of the Walsh investigation group had relocated to Washington from New York City, in company with his girlfriend. The woman found employment with a major data-processing firm in Northern Virginia and had boasted to her co-workers that she had spent the early morning hours in her boyfriend's apartment reading through several volumes of my Agency personnel file; that is, my classified, encrypted, identity-based employment records.

She could cite Stations where I had worked, the cover positions I had occupied, and the performance evaluations made by my managers over the years. Amazing, but she also knew of the Casey-directed operation and somehow was able to name a company I had started after my resignation from the Agency. Before the Walsh session began, I sat with an attorney in an anteroom and asked if a certain Walsh lead counsel was hosting the meeting that day, the same man who had managed my previous encounter. His arrogance and presumptuousness riled me in that initial session, but I maintained my composure. This next time I would not. I was told he was indeed in the next room waiting to begin my second interview.

I explained to the lawyer if that individual was in the room when I walked in, I would begin my discussion with an accusation of personal misconduct on his part. I planned to describe the compromise of classified information—information contained in my personnel file—and demand, on the record, that he be removed from any further involvement with Agency interviews. A few minutes later when I was shown into the room, my New York hotshot lawyer friend was not present. The discussion was dry and perfunctory and mercifully brief. I walked out, never to be recalled. When the Walsh report was issued six years later, at a cost to U.S. taxpayers of tens of millions of dollars, I was not included in the tome.

Walsh did get his indictments and some convictions, albeit somewhat desperately in the weeks before the November 1992 election, which saw Bill Clinton defeat a seemingly disinterested George H.W. Bush. Thankfully, President Bush, in the waning days of his administration, saw through the hypocrisy of the Walsh show and pardoned all of the convicted and indicted parties, including Clair George and Defense Secretary Caspar Weinberger, on Christmas Eve 1992. I could imagine Casey, who no doubt was at the heart of the Iran–Contra scheme, was still out there thumbing his nose at the entire affair when Walsh finally got around to delivering his final report in the summer of 1993.

Disappointments and Disrespect but No Regrets

In those months after my departure from the Agency, I was disappointed to learn that my parting was being intentionally misrepresented by several officers. Some of them were men whom I had respected and with whom I had worked positively and professionally over many years. In one case, the new Chief of Station in a key Asian post met with a group of officers I previously had supervised. In that session, he had gone out of his way to place a cloud over my decision to leave the

Agency. His words reached me within days of his uttering them, to wit, "Let's just say that Lawless's departure was a mutual decision for reasons that I cannot go into."

The below-the-belt hit came from a man whom I had gone out of my way to defend and even advocate for his current position. The entire leadership of the Directorate had been determined to block his advance in large part because his personality grated. I had explained to Casey that the man should be given a chance, and though he had developed a well-deserved reputation as an arrogant self-promoter, he was a good manager who got things done. It helped that I could explain the candidate was an odd-man-out Boston Irishman caught up in a feud that pitted the New York and Boston mini-mafias against one another. Our Station Chief-to-be had managed to alienate both sides, and it took Casey's intervention to instruct the Directorate to award him the choice assignment. The shame of it was, I had no need to defend myself with my former colleagues as they saw through most of the haze. Still, it rankled. His reputation suffered from his attempt to denigrate me, but he was characteristically oblivious.

The same level of calculated disdain and disrespect emanated from Langley as well. My adversaries attempted to even the score by damaging my reputation, in company with that of a man for whom I had worked. Bill Casey had made a lot of senior career officers unhappy with his often-stinging criticism and his demands that more be done with the resources at hand. Casey also managed to pull many of those same people into the Iran–Contra tar pit he had helped create. In departing the scene and dying when he did, Casey left many of them in the Walsh investigation net to struggle for several years. And as they struggled, their resentment of everything related to Casey grew. Many of them would remain in leadership positions for years to come, as the Walsh team slogged forward. My name, when it was remembered and recalled, drew their ire and criticism.

Finally, John McMahon, former General Counsel Sporkin, the East Asia Division chiefs whom I had served directly—those who knew the real chain of events and decisions behind the creation of our special project team—were now long gone, and no one remained in the building to set the record straight. The post-Casey team, under Acting Director Gates, was absorbed with self-preservation and a restructuring that allowed the new leadership to punish and undermine Operations. Agency leadership had no time to defend the actions or reputation of Bill Casey, let alone any of us who had been directly associated with the man, either as a volunteer or as an officer drafted into his action. Even if the Gates team tried to defend their immediate predecessors, it would have been a difficult road to travel in the charged political atmosphere of Washington in the third year of Reagan's second term. But such was the fate of any Agency officer who could be portrayed as having been cast out, or cast overboard, from the floundering ship that was the CIA in 1987.

On to Better Things

That spring, adjusting to life outside government service for the first time in 15 years, I established my own consulting firm, in company with partners well-versed in Asia business ventures. We elected to specialize in telecommunications, more specifically, in mobile systems being newly deployed in Asia. Two complementary developments encouraged that focus: the availability of a new generation of digital cellular technology that increased the efficiency of the systems on offer, and the pending deregulation of national telecom systems in selected Asian nations. The latter promised to break the monopoly enjoyed by state-owned companies with awards of cellular operating licenses to private sector firms. U.S. firms could partner there, as they had the expertise required to build and operate the best cellular systems in the world. A third coincidental development was the deregulation of the U.S. domestic telecom sector by a judicial order that broke up American Telephone & Telegraph, otherwise known as Ma Bell. That judgment created seven well-funded and experienced regional operating companies, all eager to spread their wings overseas.

Our firm established its head office in Washington and quickly installed satellite offices in Seoul and Tokyo. Initially, we operated there with local partners on a shoestring budget. As our work progressed, and we added U.S. clients, we were able to grow our commercial footprint by adding Taipei and Beijing. Our work took us into projects throughout Asia, and we enjoyed early success with joint ventures in South Korea, Japan and Taiwan. In the following years, we expanded our telecom-related programs to pursue market-entry opportunities for our U.S. telecom customers in China and Southeast Asia as well.

During that entire period, I made it an absolute rule I would not contact or interact with any active Agency officer, overseas or in the United States. Nor would I approach any U.S. Embassy contacts to request assistance. I had seen retired Agency people, busy with their second-career commercial assignments, reach out to former colleagues in overseas stations to seek assistance on one task or another. I thought it highly inappropriate, and I judged that such initiatives always placed the officer being approached in a difficult position.

A Korean Diplomat Held Hostage

Despite my proper caution, in the summer of 1987, I became deeply involved in an event that pulled me back into the morass of Middle East intrigue and Beirut duplicity. It happened during a visit to Seoul on our telecommunications project there. I was approached by a retired Korean businessman with whom I had bonded back in the mid-1970s. Mr. Chung had retired several years before as the chairman of a major shipbuilding company and had enjoyed stature among the business and government elite of the nation. He and I had bonded on shipbuilding—one of my core tasks in the Embassy's Commercial Section—and he had more or less taken me under his wing to educate me about the corporate and technical workings of tanker sales, construction and operations. He was my mentor in that area, and he also helped me understand the vagaries of Korean politics, clans and the business conglomerates, known internationally as *chae-bols*.

I had not seen Mr. Chung in many years, and I found him in failing health but a man with a mission. He sought to free a Korean diplomat who had been kidnapped and held hostage in Beirut for over a year. He knew of my career employment and had heard that, in recent years, I had gained experience in the Middle East, including Lebanon. He asked if I would meet with a senior Korean Ministry of Foreign Affairs official to discuss the situation the Republic of Korea faced with its kidnapped diplomat. I agreed but did not commit to undertake any effort on behalf of Second Secretary Do Chae-sung, late of the South Korean Embassy in Beirut.

A few days later, we sat down with a small MOFA team over dinner, with the vice minister as our host. He explained that Second Secretary Do had been kidnapped in West Beirut in late January 1986, possibly as a result of mistaken identity, by a terror group or kidnapping gang operating in Lebanon. He allowed it was possible the kidnappers thought they had captured a Japanese diplomat, because the group then was targeting the Japanese for ransom and might have misidentified Mr. Do.

The kidnappers, a pro-Libyan criminal group calling itself the Revolution-ary Commando Cell, claimed to be aligned with the Libyan government. Al-though that link was unproven, the gang did appear to enjoy support from various Islamic terror and political organizations in Lebanon, including Hezbollah. The RCC also had tactical support from the Syrian occupation forces that had entered Lebanon in February 1987, and they had some level of contact with the dominant local Shiite political and militia, Amal. The RCC initially held Mr. Do with at least two other prisoners, but they later separated him and held him in isolation, attempting to arrange a ransom payment in the amount of $10 million. During that same period, some 20-plus foreign nationals were being held prisoners in Lebanon, mostly by pro-Iranian Shiite groups or gangs, including eight U.S. citizens and several Europeans. The release of selected foreign prisoners recently had been facilitated by Amal, under the leadership of Nabih Berri, who then was also the Minister of Justice of the legitimate government of Lebanon.

The senior MOFA officials explained that the ROK government recently had been approached by an intermediary, offering to facilitate the release of Mr. Do from captivity in Beirut. Mr. Do was characterized as being "near death and partly insane," based on the duration of his captivity, the conditions in which he was being held (in isolation and in a "dark hole in the ground") and the fact he was not receiving any medical attention. According to the MOFA officials, the intermediaries had provided some unspecified proof Mr. Do was still alive and confirmation he indeed was slowly dying, had become disoriented and was tending toward insanity. The intermediaries asked for several million dollars and promised that Mr. Do could be released within a "few months" if payment was provided upfront. The MOFA officials said they did not trust the middlemen but did believe, from other reliable sources, that Mr. Do was in danger of dying.

The MOFA officials asserted that the immediate safe recovery of Mr. Do was important for several reasons, and the Presidential Blue House now considered it a "life and death issue." Also, then-ROK President Chun Doo-hwan had become personally involved in the Do issue, or the Do *sakon,* as it was called in Korean. Chun told the MOFA to do whatever was necessary to safely recover diplomat Do, supplying a no-later-than goal of year-end 1987.

President Chun viewed the Do issue as reflecting negatively on the ROK government, the reputation of the MOFA as a ministry and on his own administration. I also suspected Chun wanted to do everything possible to remove any distractions from the pending Seoul Olympics of 1988. The capture of the Olympic Games was one of Chun's proudest achievements, and it would not do to have diplomat Do still held hostage in Beirut when the Games began.

Businessman Chung, present in the meeting with MOFA officials, provided a broader political context. He explained that President Chun was nearing the end of his five-year term of office and was determined to show his success in the final months of his administration. Chun did not want the Do issue to "transfer as an unresolved problem" to his successor. A politically worst-case scenario would see Chun hand over the presidency to his hand-picked successor in February 1988 with diplomat Do still a hostage. An even-worse-case scenario was the possibility that Do would be declared dead on the eve of the opening of the Olympics in July. Fortunately for diplomat Do, his safe recovery had become a political priority for Chun rather than remaining a missing diplomat who could be expended or ignored.

I agreed to discuss the issue with trusted friends in Europe to see if there was any possibility to recover Mr. Do. I promised to get back to the MOFA officials on my next trip to Seoul, scheduled a month later. I met soon thereafter with a close friend in Geneva, here identified only as Vartan, a Swiss businessman with longstanding relationships in Beirut. Although a Christian, Vartan enjoyed lifelong relationships with Shiite, Sunni, Christian Orthodox and other religious groups in Lebanon, either directly as childhood friends or through Christian military officers. Vartan was respected as an honest businessman and family man who was reliable and trustworthy.

Through that channel, I soon was able to confirm that diplomat Do was alive but had been held in a hole and was in a poor physical and mental state, as earlier reported. It appeared his captors had tired of holding him and either would let him die or sell him off to another bandit group. Mr. Do's captors were prepared to exchange him for a cash payment but had no way of making it happen. We determined that such could be accomplished in a sequenced exchange that would deliver him into safe, third-party hands in Beirut, namely, the leader of Amal, Nabih Berri. Vartan knew and trusted Mr. Berri and told me he thought it would be possible to accomplish the release safely if all parties moved quickly.

An Agreement to Free Diplomat Do

On my next business trip to Seoul, I relayed the information to the MOFA officials. Within days, they approved a plan to exchange an amount of funds for Mr. Do, using Vartan as their trusted representative. The meeting took place in late September 1987. The ROK side then agreed that, of the amount of funds to be transferred in exchange for Second Secretary Do, one-half would be transferred to Vartan for onward passage to Beirut and to Amal only when it was demonstrated that Do was alive and available for exchange. The balance of funds would be made for onward transfer from Geneva to Amal in Beirut when it was confirmed Mr. Do was safely in third-party hands (Amal leader Berri) and available for safe passage out of Beirut.

In the Seoul meeting, the MOFA officials again emphasized the importance of securing Mr. Do's release before the scheduled ROK Presidential election in December 1987. I told them Do probably could be brought safely back to Seoul within 30-60 days if the ROK government really wanted to make it happen. But if the Chun administration only was posturing in undertaking the attempt to rescue their diplomat, to enable Chun to claim he tried but failed, I was not interested in helping them. The MOFA officials assured me that was not the case, that President Chun wanted their colleague returned to Seoul and to his family.

In addition to the release of Mr. Do, I placed two additional conditions on the exchange. First, we would require a status report on the other hostages being held in Beirut with proof of their health condition. We wanted to confirm they likewise were still alive by means of video or photo evidence. A second condition was the return of the remains of U.S. diplomat William Buckley. While serving as the CIA Chief of Station in Beirut, Bill Buckley had been kidnapped by Hezbollah affiliates in March 1984, and in October 1985 Islamic Jihad announced it had executed him. The MOFA officials accepted my conditions. The recovery of Buckley's remains was important for me and my former Agency colleagues, and I had an obligation to honor the late William Casey's request in the balance.

Back in Washington, violating my own rule of no contact with the Agency, I approached a former associate who then was serving in a senior position on the National Security Council staff. Explaining the Do situation, and my own goals in working his release, I asked if there were any objections to my undertaking the effort. There were none, save the normal, "keep us informed" request. I considered it an acquiescence, if not approval, by senior levels of the U.S. government for the recovery of diplomat Do.

On October 20, 1987, Amal provided a photo of Second Secretary Do holding an American news magazine I had provided him and marked. I was satisfied Mr. Do was alive as of that week's edition and that Amal had been able to establish a direct dialog with his kidnappers. The Amal side, acting in the name of Interior Minister Berri, stated to Vartan in Switzerland that Amal had reached agreement with the kidnappers, and diplomat Do would be transferred within a matter of days. I provided the information to the MOFA officials, then in Switzerland, including the photo. They checked with Seoul and asked that the exchange proceed as previously agreed.

A few days later a courier moved from Switzerland to Beirut carrying the first half of the payment, the funds provided in Switzerland by MOFA officials. On arrival at Beirut International Airport, the courier was seized by a group of Syrian intelligence officers, under the command of Colonel Ghazi Kanaan, then running Syrian operations in Beirut but soon to become Syria's Interior Affairs Minister. The group appropriated half of the initial payment and allowed the balance to go forward to Amal. At the same time, a terrorist gang associated with Hezbollah, based on information provided by the Syrians, attempted to intercept and steal the balance of the initial payment. In searching for the courier and the remaining funds, the gang raided several homes and exchanged gunfire with Amal militia attempting to protect the funds from being stolen. In one apartment raid, the shootout produced several dead and wounded on each side.

On about October 26th, Amal acted in good faith to complete its part of the agreement. It was based in large part on Vartan's assurances that all aspects of the deal would be realized so long as diplomat Do was safely returned. Amal took possession of Do and found him to be physically and mentally exhausted, totally disoriented and incoherent to the degree that he was barely able to speak. They fed him, bathed him, provided him with basic medical attention and clothing, all to prepare him for onward movement, just as we had agreed. Because other militia groups, including Hezbollah and the Syrians, were aggressively searching for Do with the intent of kidnapping him anew, Amal relocated him to the personal residence of Justice Minister (and Amal leader) Berri. The latter opted to buy time while arrangements were made to remove Do from Lebanon. During that time, several phone calls were made from Mr. Berri's apartment with Do speaking, as best he could, with the MOFA officials in Geneva awaiting his exit from Beirut. The MOFA officials pronounced themselves satisfied they were speaking with their colleague, and they asked that the transfer proceed.

South Korean Betrayal at the Critical Point

At a critical juncture, with the MOFA officials obligated to make the second half of the payment, they informed me, with no hint of embarrassment, that a "serious problem" had developed in Seoul. It seemed that the transfer of the second half of the payment would be "delayed until the problem was resolved." I explained that, with their stall, the MOFA officials and the ROK government essentially were breaking the agreement and delaying the movement of their diplomat to safety. In so doing, they were irresponsibly placing Mr. Do and those who were protecting him at risk of death or kidnapping. To me, it was an incredible breach of our agreement, if not an outright betrayal on the part of the ROK government. I struggled to explain the turn of events to others who then faced the situation firsthand.

The MOFA officials offered no explanation, refusing to take any responsibility but still insisting that Mr. Do be brought safely out of Beirut as soon as possible. In making this "please trust us" request, they explained they could arrange for the second funds transfer but could do so only when Do was out of Lebanon and safe in their hands. On the second night, as the Berri family dressed Do in a new suit for his onward movement toward home, word spread in Beirut that a second payment was due to be paid for Do. Our diplomat had become a hunted property, as Amal leadership had predicted he would if the transition did not run smoothly.

The next day passed with no resolution. The MOFA officials in Geneva explained to me that a "bureaucratic fight" had developed in Seoul. It was vaguely explained as an inter-ministerial turf war at the level of the Presidential Blue House. Apparently, when the MOFA briefed President Chun and his senior staff on the status of Mr. Do, the Korean CIA demanded that the operation be placed under their control. Our MOFA associates blamed the KCIA Director for interference, and the Blue House staff and President Chun for indecisiveness and delay, and then declared the entire matter out of their hands.

At that point, I elected to reach out to the one man whom I thought might be able to intervene directly in the Blue House struggle—my friend Kim Chung-yul, the retired ROK Air Force general, former Minister of Defense and former Ambassador to the United States. He was now Prime Minister of Korea, recently installed by Chun as a compromise premier. Kim's sudden elevation from retirement to the position of Prime Minister had been an attempt to leverage his status as a respected military leader to bolster the lagging credibility of Chun's government. That administration had been challenged by charges of family corruption, including illicit dealings on the part of Chun's wife and brother.

To my relief, Prime Minister Kim took my phone call and listened as I explained the situation that was unfolding. I asked for his personal intervention. Kim knew nothing of the entire matter, which I suspected, given he was not part of the Blue House inner circle. It did not surprise me. Chun and his core group tended to the conspiracy side of political endeavor and action. The attempt to bring Do home was clearly a political stunt, as the squabble over who was in control, not to mention who would get the credit, demonstrated.

Prime Minister Kim promised to inject himself into the issue immediately and attempt to help, but he made no promises about the outcome. A few hours later, he called me back. He explained that this was a fight among Angaebu (the KCIA), the Wheymubu (the Foreign Ministry) and an unnamed third party close to President Chun who wanted to become more involved. Kim had no ability to intervene and was sorry he could not. It was all politics. With great reluctance, I accepted his explanation because he was an honorable man, someone attempting to do the right thing amid a gang of self-dealing politicians and opportunists. As the end of Chun's term approached, the Chun loyalists and camp followers were about to lose their places at the administration's trough. In such an environment, I deeply appreciated Kim's efforts and told him so.

In Geneva, I explained to Vartan that I was unable to resolve the problem and saw no way forward with the feuding Koreans. Vartan then took his own action. He knew Second Secretary Do's life was in danger and that Mr. Berri personally, as well as his family, had been placed in a serious predicament by the inaction and betrayal by the South Korean government. Vartan used his personal funds to pay the balance then due to Amal and rushed the second payment by courier to Beirut. The following day, October 28, 1987, the transaction completed, but the MOFA officials still refused to accept any responsibility. Fortunately, diplomat Do was safely moved by Amal from Beirut to Amman, Jordan. There he was met by the MOFA individuals we had pre-positioned to complete Do's return to his countrymen.

Second Secretary Do then was escorted to a U.S. military facility in Europe for medical attention and debriefing. Once those necessities were completed, he was flown immediately back to Seoul in a specially chartered Korean Air Lines jet. On his arrival at Kimpo Airport, he was met with great fanfare by President Chun and the MOFA leadership. As the KAL 747 rolled to a stop to discharge its celebrity passenger, Chun stood tall and claimed full credit for "rescuing" his diplomat and returning him home to Seoul and his family. With no hint of shame, the ROK Foreign Ministry feted its diplomatic team to the South Korean media as having dramatically recovered their man.

In the coming months, Chun would have his election, the Presidency would be transferred and the Seoul Olympics would turn out to be a grand success for South Korea. Pyongyang, furious at the International Olympic Committee's refusal to permit, essentially, a shared hosting of the 1988 Summer Games, boycotted, and the Communist regime plotted and mounted terrorist attacks designed to disrupt the event in Seoul. And, as diplomat Do regained his health and his sanity with his family, life moved on. [NOTE 3]

Salt Poured into the Wound

The extended aftermath of Do's safe return was ugly. The Ministry of Foreign Affairs officials involved in organizing the original request refused further discussion with me. They also rebuffed attempts by Vartan's representatives, who were dispatched to Seoul to discuss the issue with them. The MOFA officials declared from a distance they had done all possible to complete the exchange, but the entire matter had been taken out of their hands by Chun's Blue House. By blaming the KCIA and President Chun's senior staff for the broken agreement, our trusted MOFA senior bureaucrats washed their hands of the entire event. The Koreans have an expression for this; *check-im chong-kak*, which means, literally, "responsibility transferred," but more figuratively translates to "your problem, not mine." Yet these were the clowns I had promised Vartan and others they could trust. [NOTE 4]

At no point did the MOFA ever make a serious attempt to resolve the issue.

The Chun government conveniently transitioned into the Roh Moo-hyun government, with prosecutors warming up for investigations of massive corruption by the departed regime. The Roh administration could reference the Do affair as a Chun problem, and its attitude became, "We have now turned away from the entire incident. If other people decided to save Mr. Do's life by completing the agreement, those people did so at their own risk."

Based on such logic, the MOFA and the Roh government owed nothing to anyone. Even for one long-experienced in Korean duplicity, I found their stance difficult to understand. In breaking the agreement at the most dangerous stage of the rescue, the MOFA officials understood full well they were placing their diplomat's life in danger. But their actions made it clear they did not give a damn about the man's life.

Beginning in November 1987, and proceeding for several years thereafter, the government rejected all attempts by Vartan to recover the funds he expended to secure the safe return of Mr. Do. Each new administration in Seoul blamed the Chun administration's "internal ROK government rivalries and politics" and duplicity. When I pressed officials in later years on that fundamental betrayal, one suggested if I could convince Vartan to come to Seoul, perhaps the Blue House would consider giving him "some kind of a medal." I explained Vartan would not lower himself to such a gesture. He had saved Do's life and would live with the disrespect for his actions shown by the highest levels of the South Korean government.

The manner in which the Do rescue played out, including the actions of the Syrian military group, and the roaming militia of the warring Shiite and Sunni factions, denied us any chance of completing the other two conditions included in the Do operation. Regarding my request for the remains of Agency Officer William Buckley, Amal licked its wounds and took its own hit on the funds stolen by the Syrians. They informed me they felt no responsibility to recover Buckley's remains. Here again, in addition to my having, inadvertently, misled Vartan about the trustworthiness of the South Koreans, I missed the opportunity to deliver on my personal pledge to the late Director Bill Casey. Agency officer Buckley would not be coming home.

Nor was there any attempt to account for, let alone videotape, the remaining Western hostages. The combination of the Syrian seizure of a good portion of the initial funds, and the ROK government's delay and betrayal on the second payment, served to ensure there would be no returns save for diplomat Do. For me, it made several bitter pills to swallow. Not the least of them was the ending of respect for a country I had served in for almost six years. It was a learning experience, and I was satisfied that I, in company with my friend Vartan, had delivered as promised on our part of the arrangement. No thanks to his own country and his own service, Korean diplomat Second Secretary Do Chae-sung was out of his Beirut hole and home safe and sound with his family. **[NOTE 5]**

The Final Weeks of the 1988 Presidential Election

In early October 1988, with Ronald Reagan preparing to move quietly into retirement, George H.W. Bush was pressing his campaign to become the 41st President of the United States. At that point, with the nominating conventions in the rearview mirror, the election campaign almost had run its course. The Democrats, somewhat desperate after having nominated the hapless pairing of Massachusetts Governor Dukakis and New York Congresswoman Geraldine Ferraro, were struggling with the certainty of defeat. Beyond the frustration of the Democratic machine itself, the national mainstream media, in both print and broadcast manifestations, was trending desperate if not irrational, in a panic to pull a comeback victory for their candidate. The liberal amalgam not only despised President Reagan, but they also despised Vice President Bush, a man they universally considered too well-bred and, worst of all, a Republican career politician tainted by the Reagan mantle. The mainstream media could barely hide its disdain for Bush, and they sought every opportunity to disparage him.

At the 11th hour in the campaign, an opportunity to slam Vice President Bush presented itself. The accusation was made, and then aggressively promoted, that Bush and his campaign organization, ostensibly desperate to cinch the election by any means, had been secretly negotiating for some months to pull off a major political *coup de main*. The ploy would be to stage the release, ideally on the eve of the election, of several or all foreign hostages then being held in Lebanon by various terrorist groups. The accusation was ready-made red meat for the media and the Democrats, as they sought to cast Bush in a conspiratorial mode. The implication was Bush, or the Reagan legacy team, was willing to subordinate U.S. foreign policy objectives and principles, if not ethical conduct, to the whims of his election campaign. **[NOTE 1]**

The public catalyst for that exercise in accusation by the American media was a well-staged and well-advertised (and therefore well-attended) interview on October 4th in Paris with one Seyyed Abolhassan Banisadr, former President of the Ayatollah state of Iran. The interview had been previewed by a little-noted news article in an obscure Beirut newspaper. It had the foul odor of a media-placement operation, delivered to satisfy a range of possible benefactors, any one of whom might benefit from a Bush defeat.

In his Paris interview, Banisadr alleged that the Vice President, with an active hand in all things Middle East, had orchestrated a covert program that would see the hostages conveyed to Bush, or to the U.S. government, in a manner that would allow him to claim credit in the days before the election. Banisadr asserted that the operation was consistent with his black hand in all major activities over recent years in the Iran–Iraq dynamic. The surge of activity ostensibly included the negotiated ceasefire and eventual truce that ended the bloody war a few months before, in August 1988.

By the time he sat down for the interview, the former Iranian president had been roundly discredited for his frequent flights of fancy, abject paranoia and various chemical addictions. His attraction for the American media was his claim that he possessed detailed information on the Bush hostage plan. According to his reckoning, the instrument of Bush's covert action was one Richard Lawless, a "known CIA operative with connections to Bush and his family." The totally fabricated tale was a feast for the famished news outlets, ever hungry for a juicy story in the doldrums of the election. **[NOTE 2]**

Banisadr apparently provided reporters with a wealth of details on the ongoing but secret hostage-negotiations process. His exchanges with reporters played out over a week or so, driven by a run of furious publishing activity endorsed by claims of "fact-checking." The carnival of speculation was abetted by hyperactive editorial attention from the home offices of numerous publications, mostly New York City-based and U.S. broadcast channels. The frenzy was encouraged by the members of the liberal press, which managed to convince themselves they were all working a real story. But it soon became obvious that left-leaning media types all saw in it the potential to do real damage to the Bush campaign, if not erode his then-considerable lead.

The Bangkok Ambush

When the fiasco began, I was operating in the isolated backwaters of Laos, in and out of Vientiane. There, I was laboring away and swatting mosquitos in my capacity as a private-sector business owner specializing in telecommunications. Sensing a commercial opportunity for our American client, we were attempting to assess the possibility of deploying a cellular-phone system under a licensing arrangement the Laotian communist-in-name-only government appeared to be willing to award to a foreign-led consortium. We were working as part of a joint venture that would have paired an established U.S. Baby Bell cellular system operator, interested in bringing its technology and experience to Laos, with a Korean conglomerate that had good contacts in the isolated country. Our technical-assessment team had crossed into Laos by air the previous week from Bangkok, about the time Banisadr was sitting down with his newfound U.S. media friends in Paris.

The entrance of our telecom survey team into Laos had seen us risk our lives in a beat-up Russian Antonov An-24 turboprop airliner operated by Lao Aviation. The duct-taped, Kiev-built aircraft was flown by a disheveled Ukrainian pilot who appeared to be vodka-fueled. He exhibited a demeanor that strongly suggested he did not really want to be anywhere in Asia, let alone Laos. But he did know his airplane. When he planted it on the runway outside Vientiane in a hammer-down landing, I could see him at a 10-foot distance in the cockpit—there was no door—throw both hands into the air as if to say, "Damn, we made it again!" I quipped to one of our telecom team that the NATO reporting name for the aircraft was "CRASH." When I later explained its NATO ID was really "COKE," he replied that, given the erratic behavior of our pilot, the latter designation probably was even more appropriate.

During our week in Laos, we subsisted in a down-at-the-heels hotel built by the East Germans in the early 1960s and endured a week of meetings with various senior government officials. Those fellows were good communists all, each of them attempting to cajole us into renting their "personal homes" at exorbitant rates for the office we considered establishing there. By the time of our departure, we pretty much had concluded that Laos badly needed a modern telecommunications system, but we were about 20 years too soon with our cellular approach. Vowing never again to fly with our Ukrainian pilot, we crossed from Laos into Thailand on a small barge that chugged across the mighty Mekong River, which divides the two countries. We did not realize that, at the time of our crossing, a cadre of reporters was already assembling at the Bangkok hotel where our team was scheduled to overnight before flying out of Thailand.

When we arrived at the hotel, the Thai National Police were waiting for us at the gate and guided us away from the main entrance. They hustled us through the basement to a set of rooms in an isolated wing, but we were not told the nature of their concern. We were reassured by the management and the police that we would be protected until the "news people problem" was sorted out. We were cautioned, however, that a score of local and foreign journalists was camped out in the lobby, refusing to leave. The pack demanded to meet with us, and, according to rumor, more were on the way to Bangkok from Singapore and Hong Kong. I could only assume it had something to do with our run into Laos.

It was coincidental bad timing for us because, during that same week, a self-declared "covert American operative" on a "special mission" in search of U.S. MIAs from the Vietnam conflict had caused a minor Thai–Laos border incident. That Rambo-like character, probably well-meaning, had been detained while scattering leaflets with 10-dollar bills attached along the banks of, and in the waters of, the Mekong. Chucking leaflets off the barge apparently was his idea of clandestine information-gathering and, to be sure, his effort had gathered plenty of local attention. There could be no other explanation for the manner in which we had been rushed into our rooms, with guards placed in the corridor. The Thai military police managing our hotel sequestration were unable to offer us otherwise, as the mystery deepened.

After a few phone calls, plus a note smuggled into our room by a hotel service employee, we began to fill in the picture. The Banisadr interview apparently triggered a worldwide manhunt for me that had been underway for a week. Someone tipped off the media people that I was in Laos but headed back to Bangkok. Our Laotian excursion encouraged the newshounds to conclude I was obviously the right man, a covert operator with secret missions underway all over the world. Under that assumption, I had become a target for media capture in a confrontation in Bangkok.

It was hard to put it all together from the hotel room. But one decent American reporter, dispatched from his office in Hong Kong to track me down, was kind enough to scribble that smuggled message to me. The note was attached to a huge fruit basket that made its way into my room on day two. In essence, it said:

> *First of all, I apologize for being a part of this press circus. I don't really want to be here. My boss in New York told me to find you, interview and photograph you. You are the STORY OF THE WEEK. These guys are obsessed with the claims coming out of Paris. I think it's pure crap, but here I am in Bangkok in the hotel lobby. So, can we talk? I want to go home.*

I did not talk to anyone from the media, but the motley reporting crew hanging out in the lobby would not go away. Several of them had checked into the hotel, and most became permanent residents at the main bar, providing a revenue surge that impressed the management. Our entire telecom survey team was smuggled out of the hotel on night three in an ambulance van, processed as VIPs at the airport and flown out to Hong Kong. We left the posse of reporters wandering around the lobby, angry that they failed to get a story. The Thai authorities did not understand what was going on and really didn't seem to care. They just were glad to see us leave Bangkok and the country.

The Frenzy Feeds on Itself

A couple of days later, back in my Washington office, the media madness reached new levels. Each of the three mainstream TV networks featured elements of the story on their evening news broadcasts, adding new details and weaving in fragments of my intelligence career as they were ferreted out. Producers were overlaying that line with photos and passport cutouts. In Paris, Banisadr was holding court daily, reveling in the attention being shown him by the American reporters. He appeared delighted to spin new tales to satisfy the throng and speculate on who had done what to organize the secret discussions. Back in Washington, reporters fouled up the building lobby and banged on our outer office door. We kept it barred and weathered the storm, but we were clearly under siege.

The Sunday Washington Post, on October 9, 1988, caught the mood with a story by London Sunday Times correspondent Mark Hosenball, aptly headlined, "If It's October … Then It's Time for an Iranian Conspiracy Theory." The story took readers through the Reagan–Casey 1980 election rumors promoted by the original "October Surprise" allegation then brought it all into the current election cycle by observing that the story had moved from the left-liberal media to grab mainstream attention. It noted Banisadr's involvement in that earlier nonevent (when he had then been the Iranian President) and characterized his current behavior as "Charlie Chaplinesque." Hosenball's article also referenced the Iranian's recent speculation-packed interview in Playboy magazine where Banisadr revisited and embellished the 1980 era story for his interviewer, none other than the 1960s radical Abby Hoffman. The Washington Post article then focused on the present assertions with,

> Last week Banisadr upped the ante, claiming that Bush had sent a new emissary, Richard Lawless, to Paris recently to try to spring American hostages in Lebanon. The White House denied the charge. As did Lawless.

Companion wire service stories picked up on Banisadr's claim that I had been meeting secretly with none other than current Iranian leader Ali Akbar Hashemi Rafsanjani since February on the hostage issue, the meetings undertaken on behalf of Vice President Bush. Apparently, I recently had arranged for the release of a dual U.S.–Indian citizen held by Hezbollah, now in U.S. hands for a debriefing session. At the same time the Bush team was reacting to the coverage blitz, in an effort to throw cold water on the disorganized rumors, they managed to confirm to the media that, "Lawless ... a Washington, D.C., businessman ... and former CIA official," was indeed around and doing something nefarious.

Secretary of State George Shultz, in a news conference at the United Nations, contributed unhelpfully by confirming there were private individuals "out there operating" who were falsely claiming to represent the U.S. government and trying to set up hostage deals with Iran. Shultz went on an unscripted rant to attack the "freelancers" who were trying to involve themselves, declaring that the unnamed (by Shultz) would-be players should "just butt out." The Secretary's offhand comments helped fan the media flames. Thank you, George.

One item from a U.S. wire service penetrated my shield, based on an introduction by a mutual friend. He offered that, "if what Banisadr says about you is only partly true, you should get the Nobel Peace Prize." When I pressed him, he explained that Banisadr was now promoting an expanded history of my work in the Middle East over the last few years, first as a special Agency operator who worked for Casey, and more recently as an independent operative who reported directly to Vice President Bush, tasked to "handle the Middle East."

My accomplishments, per Banisadr's account, included the negotiated settlement of the Iran–Iraq war, or at least the standstill arrangement holding those two bloodied nations from one another's throats. Hearing this, I was of course incredulous. My new friend pushed me with a, "So, did you do any of this shit?" I insisted I had done nothing of the kind, had no ongoing relationship with the Agency and certainly had no relationship with Vice President Bush. The fellow simply said, "Well, nobody is prepared to believe that. This is too big a story."

When I discovered that Banisadr and his cohorts had expanded on the original story to increase my reputation as a high-level bargainer, I appreciated better the extent of the bum's rush I was being given. Quoting Banisadr, the media explained that for the past year I actually had been negotiating on behalf of Bush in Switzerland with representatives of Rafsanjani. Our claimed objective was to reach a detailed agreement that, per another Washington Post article, provided for, "the end of the Iran–Iraq war, a new regional 'good neighbor' role for Iran, a halt to Iran-sponsored terrorism and the freeing of American hostages by September." The article revealed there were unspecified U.S. demands, or quid pro quos, for intervening to force an end to war, as well as Banisadr's explanation that the whole deal had been blocked by Mullah-in-chief Khomeini. Per Banisadr, Khomeini was concerned that Rafsanjani's "peacemaking" would stir up Iranian zealots opposed to dealing with the "Great Satan that was the United States," thereby undermining the regime.

After a few days on the defensive in Washington, I gave in to the forces arrayed against me. I released my own statement for the record, which said, in part,

> *I have never in my entire career had any direct or indirect contact with any Iranian government officials or Iranian nationals claiming to represent the Iranian government or any Iranian-related interests.* I also noted that, *I deny that I have any active relationship with anyone on the staff of Vice President Bush or the Bush campaign organization which relates in any way to this or any similar issue.*

Deeming it to be a fairly comprehensive denial, the New York Times went back to Banisadr and pressed him. His response was dismissive. "Well, it was probably him." **[NOTE 3]**

Everything came to a head a few days before the election. Holes already had begun to appear, and some expressed doubt, but momentum remained. The Big Three network evening news producers, writers and presenters were beginning to conclude, albeit with reluctance, that the tales being spun about me by Banisadr were getting too wild to sell. Perhaps he was a cokehead, delusional or being used by others to foment trouble for Bush. (I suspected all three.) But the story would not die an easy death. White House spokesman Marlin Fitzwater, with obvious good intentions, and looking to distance candidate Bush from the story, offered on-the-record as well as off-camera comments. Among those were, "Yes, there is this guy out there named Richard Lawless, doing some things, but he has no relationship with our White House or Vice President Bush." **[NOTE 4]**

More informally conveyed by Marlin or his staff, but nevertheless reportable, was, "This guy is former CIA, but we really don't know what he is up to out there." Marlin did not do me any favors, and his comments did not contribute to a reduction in the attention. Obviously, in the minds of the "let's get Bush" crowd, such clarifications only meant Bush was disowning his operative. To them, it was just the old "plausible denial" routine on his part. The story seemed to have legs, and the media appeared determined to keep it alive.

Peter Jennings Steps In

Then, anchorman Peter Jennings of the ABC Evening News approached me through a friend and asked for a direct dialog. I agreed. In our calls, he offered to take a professional approach that would be factually based and insisted he wanted to "get it right," irrespective of what his producers wanted him to do. He had his team distill Banisadr's claims down to a series of dates and events over the last three months when, Banisadr insisted, I had met with Iranian and Lebanese terrorist group representatives in Paris. I agreed and sent my team to a local hotel café with all of my travel records, including airline tickets and hotel receipts, plus my passport with its entry and exit stamps. The two groups spent time comparing notes, reconstructing my every move. The approach worked—but only up to a point.

When Peter and I spoke later that same day, he brought it all home. "Richard, I absolutely believe you, and I think this whole show is garbage. I would like to put it to rest. But we have a problem." I had my records spread out on my desk in front of me; the worksheets his people and mine had created. I responded with a bit of anger. "Look, Peter, we have given you everything, including a receipt from a damn Chinese restaurant in Seoul. Every day is covered, every flight. So, the idea that I was meeting secretly with the damn Iranians is a total crock!"

Peter was patient. "But not every day has been accounted for. The most important day, a Saturday in early August, is missing. This is the day that Banisadr places you in Room 401 of the Hotel Royal Monceau in Paris with the Iranians, negotiating the hostage deal that was scheduled to come off in a week or so. Richard, where were you then? It is simply not there. There is no record of your location on that day. No hotel. No airline tickets. Nothing." I looked at the worksheet and reluctantly admitted that he was right. I agreed to call him back. That Saturday was a total blank spot.

It took me an hour to figure it out. By chance, when I slammed my desk drawer out of frustration, a red paper ticket floated up and landed on the floor. "ONE BEER," read the ticket. Then it hit me. I had stopped in Chicago, making a slight detour on my Tokyo to New York run. I had rented a car at O'Hare airport and drove home to Peoria. I spent the night there to celebrate my mother's birthday. By chance, I had arrived in my hometown on a special day. I attended with my father and brother the annual Bartonville Village Volunteer Fire Department Fish Fry. I spent that Saturday evening with my family, eating channel catfish and quaffing cups of Pabst Blue Ribbon fresh from the local brewery. I shut down the evening with my dad, my brother and a half-dozen high school friends. The following morning, I drove to Chicago and flew on to New York, heading to London or wherever. But for sure, that Saturday night I was in the beer tent in Bartonville. I called Peter and reported my revelation.

He was delighted. "You were at a fish fry in Bartonville, Illinois, with a hundred other locals? Look, I just need one respected member of that community, not one of the beer drinkers, to confirm you were there in that tent that night, and it's all over. Banisadr is still insisting that you were five thousand miles away, sitting in that hotel room with a bunch of Iranians. Get me in direct contact with that person."

My mind raced. "I have my witness. He is both the mayor of Bartonville and the chief of police. He sat at the front of the main tent at the fish fry all night selling beer tickets. He has known me since I was eight years old. His name is Archie Yeley, but you can call him Doc." Peter responded with some enthusiasm. "Give me his phone number, I am calling him right now."

A few minutes later Peter called me back. "Richard, we still have a problem. I talked to your 'Doc' in his Bartonville City Hall office. He said you were there all night at that annual fish fry, and he sold you and your dad and your brother Bob a whole bunch of beer tickets. He also said you all drank beer until two in the morning and that he closed the place down. Then he sat down and had a few beers with you guys." I was pleased, "Yes, Peter, so there you have it!"

Peter seemed frustrated, and continued, "So, then I asked him if anybody put him up to this answer, meaning was he covering for you. And do you know what he said? He said, 'I'm a loyal American and I only take my orders from my Commander-in-Chief. And … that's the President of the United States of America. And whatever he tells me to do, I do it!'" Peter continued, "So, you tell me, what the hell do I do with that? Archie 'Doc" Yeley is the Bartonville Chief of Police, knows you and only takes his orders from the President of the United States of America. What's this about? Are you gaming me here?"

I racked my brain for a response. "Peter, Doc is a Korean War vet, I think he was with the Wolfhounds there (the 27th Infantry Regiment). You probably jammed him up. He knows who I am and what I was, CIA and all that. He probably thought you were playing him. Think about it!"

Peter came right back with, "Okay, you know I am a Canadian, I come from a small town just like you, maybe 500 people. Everybody knows everybody. So, I get it. Doc thinks he is protecting you, and he is telling me that he 'only takes his orders from his Commander-in-Chief.' He even said something about 1600 Pennsylvania Avenue! So, what do we do now? I have two hours before I go on national news tonight, and I have my script prepared. I want to brand this as a nonstory, and I believe you. But now I have Police Chief Yeley's admission that he is really working for President Reagan. What do you suggest we do?"

I thought about it and said, "Okay, I will call my father. He is probably sitting in the backyard about five blocks away from Archie. I will tell him to drive down the hill, sit with Doc, and tell him to knock off all the 'I work for the President' crap. He will answer every question you ask him, no bullshit. So, call Doc back in 20 minutes. Talk to my father if you have to. Agreed?"

About 30 anxious minutes later, I received Peter's call. He simply said, "Well, we had a great discussion. It's done and over, and thank you." I never spoke again to Peter, but he had done his job. I called Doc Yeley a few days later, thanked him for being a friend and for being a loyal American. His only reply was, "Well, we took care of it, kid, didn't we." It was a statement, not a question.

Doc might well have believed Banisadr for all I knew. WE had indeed taken care of it, whatever he thought "it" might involve.

Hometown Attention

After Jennings set things straight, and the Paris troublemaker went back into seclusion, media coverage at the national level quickly abated. But there remained some repercussions. The local daily, The Peoria Journal Star, had picked up the original Banisadr story and replayed it with the overlay of local flavor. Interest in the village of Bartonville remained high, at least among those of the anti-Bush crowd, who were inclined to believe anything. A neighbor spotted my father burning papers in his backyard (my father was a bit obsessed with his "burn barrel" and sought to employ it daily). The neighbor called the local paper to report the "suspicious activity." He claimed I actually was working a covert operations out of my parents' home, having sleuthed out that I was still registered at my parents' address to vote in Illinois.

When the reporters showed up at my father's front door and headed for the backyard to check the burn barrel, Dad went for his 12-gauge Remington shotgun. A warning shot or two might be needed and, after all, they were trespassers. My more balanced mother called the Bartonville Police dispatcher. Doc Yeley rolled up a few minutes later in his cruiser, confronted the local press and sent them away. He then walked down the street to have a conversation with the informant and suggested he mind his own business. My father, then still serving as the Chairman of Peoria County Sherriff's Merit Commission, thought it was all great sport and got a lot of mileage out of the entire incident with his buddies. His attitude was, "Well, my son is finally getting the recognition he deserves." Like many others, my father was firmly convinced I was still working with the Agency. It was beyond his imagination that I would have left a job that allowed me to serve our country, just as it was Doc Yeley's assumption that he was doing his patriotic duty to protect me and my mission, whatever it was, from prying journalists. They were great people, and hometowns are always the best.

October Aftermath: Setting the Record Straight

The November election produced a Bush victory, and the much-anticipated October Surprise hostage release had not happened. But the media attention, my ostensible connection to dubious activities involving volatile Middle East personalities, to say nothing of nutty Banisadr himself, had harmed me. In the case of our main client, the major American telecom operator with an ambitious plan to expand internationally, a decision was made to stand down on new projects, at least with my firm. I had partners and employees to pay, and we had opened offices in Japan, South Korea and Taiwan. We needed to maintain our business momentum and, like many startup firms, we scrambled to cover our costs. In almost every case, our clients were solid, and they satisfied themselves it was all

441

bunk. They reconfirmed their places in our fold. But reputational damage had been done.

I was determined to set the public record straight. We needed to satisfy existing clients the October Surprise tales had been bogus and to place on the record for use with future clients that my reputation had been contaminated with false information and innuendo. The effort required me to seek retractions from specific media firms that had propagated false stories, wherever there was a statement that could be publicly accessed. I was fortunate to find an exceptional legal man to represent me in the endeavor. Tom Green was widely acknowledged for his aggressiveness—he had been judged by his peers to be the "Meanest Lawyer in Washington" for several years' running. Tom accepted my case with conviction and delivered results. On the media front, we went after a public television network that had falsely asserted I had done a number of bad deeds on behalf of now-President Bush. They agreed to issue a correction for the record. It was an admission to which I could refer potential clients, if so needed, although no such need developed.

On the Agency side, I had a more delicate problem. Back in 1972, when I "onboarded" as a career trainee, I had signed a secrecy agreement. I was not allowed to acknowledge employment and career as a clandestine services officer during the 15-year active duty period. After I departed the Agency in 1987, Marlin Fitzwater's initiative from the White House podium declaring me to be a "former CIA officer" had placed me in the position that my public CV was no longer sustainable.

Marlin, from the office of the President, essentially had blown my cover. I had to agree with Marlin, which technically was a violation of my Agency secrecy agreement, and admit for whom I had worked.

Tom Green took this on by insisting that we address it frontally by going to the Agency to reference Fitzwater's statement and ask that my requirement to maintain my cover be removed. We drafted a proposed statement by the Agency that acknowledged my career and areas of focus. It took Tom and me some time to resolve the matter, but we managed to do so. The result was a statement, on Agency letterhead I was allowed to use publicly, that confirmed my career employment and identified my areas of activity, specifically nuclear proliferation and East Asian security affairs.

As it turned out, with my Agency career established as public knowledge, I had no reason to use the statement. But its mere existence provided me peace of mind, by tangibly reaffirming I had devoted 15 years of my life in service to my country as a clandestine services officer in an organization I deeply respected.

Chapter 29

• **NOTE 1 - See page 385**

Clair George had an exemplary career with the Agency and was an Operations Directorate standout. He had come into the Agency after military tours in the Far East, with assignments in Korea and Japan, and had worked as a case officer in the Middle East, Africa and Europe. He had been Chief of Station in Beirut and had volunteered to serve in that position in Athens when the incumbent Agency Station Chief was assassinated by terrorists in 1976.

He also had the distinction of being the highest-ranking Agency official to stand trial as a consequence of the Iran–Contra scandal. Indicted in September 1991 on nine counts, he walked away in a mistrial. But special counsel Lawrence Walsh persisted and George was reindicted and convicted of two charges. President George H.W. Bush stepped in before Clair George could be sentenced and granted him and five others "full and unconditional" pardons on Christmas Eve 1992. George was loyal to the Agency and was caught up in a scandal not of his making but of which he became a virtual prisoner. Clair Elroy George passed away in August 2011 at age 81.

• **NOTE 2 - page 390**

Stanley Sporkin, hand-picked by his old friend Director William Casey to serve as the Agency's General Counsel, made his reputation as a "take-no-prisoners" enforcement chief at the U.S. Securities and Exchange Commission. He was a relentless prosecutor of corporate crime, including illegal payoffs and political contributions that skirted the law. His aggressive approach during the early and mid-1970s encouraged the U.S. Congress to enact the Foreign Corrupt Practices Act in 1977, a law that has become the international gold standard for corporate dealings over the years.

After his stint as the Agency's General Counsel, Stan served with great distinction as a Federal District Judge in the District of Colombia for 15 years, retiring in 1986. Stan passed away in April 2020 at age 88. My experience with him at the Agency was episodic but he never failed to start every conversation with an admonition, "we are going to have to do the right thing here, letter of the law, but let's see what we do." My understanding during the period we worked with Casey and our project was that Stan was the go-to man within the Agency to shape, redirect and contain Director Casey's inclinations to undertake operations that risked violating the law or the intent of Congress. In some cases, Iran–Contra for one, he was obviously not successful in dissuading the Director from wandering from the straight and narrow.

• **NOTE 3 - page 391**

Peter Dailey was the son of immigrant parents from County Wicklow, Ireland. He was a standout athlete at UCLA, ran for touchdowns in the Rose Bowl of the 1955 season and was inducted to that university's Hall of Fame in 1989. After service in the U.S. Navy, Peter founded his own advertising firm, which merged with the world's then-largest such firm, Interpublic Group, eventually leading that company. Peter was a close friend and confidant of President Reagan. He was the lead media strategist in Reagan's successful 1980 presidential campaign. He and Reagan confidant Judge William Clark played the key role to bring in William Casey as the overall campaign manager after Reagan's early primary defeat in New Hampshire. Peter was appointed as our Ambassador to Ireland and served there from 1982-1984.

Peter joined the Agency as Casey's counselor and remained in that role until well after Casey's departure in early 1987. Peter was later appointed by President Reagan, and reaffirmed in that appointment by President George H.W. Bush, as a member of the U.S. Arms Control and Disarmament Agency's General Advisory Committee, where he served until 1994. Peter H. Dailey passed away in March 2018 at age 87. It was a pleasure to serve with Peter and those of us working on our special project immensely enjoyed the many hours that our small group spent with him.

Peter was also responsible for introducing me to a man who would become a close friend, the aforementioned former National Security Advisor Judge William Clark. Peter and Bill had been friends for many years, and in company with Bill Casey, would form the core of a mini-Irish mafia that associated themselves with and protected President Reagan throughout and beyond his presidency. In this group, I would include former Ambassador John Gavin, who, like Clark and Daily hailed from southern California and came together to support Ronald Reagan when he first ran for governor of California.

Each of these Reagan loyalists found his own place in their relationships with First Lady Nancy Reagan, often acting as a screen or calming influence within the family inner circle. Bill Casey was a late arrival on the Reagan team scene and was one of the relationships that required management by Reagan's trusted inner circle. As Bill Clark explained to me, "Casey was smart enough to figure all this out and he accepted direction well. Bill had staying power as a man who was deeply trusted by the President. In any event, the President was reluctant to fire anyone who had served him well. Casey fell into this protected category, but Casey really needed all the help we could give him."

Chapter 30

- ## NOTE 1 - page 394
  An excellent account of the career of Robert Ames, and a penetrating description of the cross-currents and jumbled policy process of the U.S. Government during this period, can be found in Kai Birds' 2014 book The Good Spy: The Life and Death of Robert Ames. It is a work of truth and a wonderful study of the man and his profession, not to mention the commitment Bob Ames brought to his profession.

- ## NOTE 2 - page 395
  The remains of Beirut station chief William Buckley would not be recovered for another six years, until Christmas week 1991, when a United Nations Observation Group officer was directed to the burial site. We later came to believe that Buckley had either died or been killed in that June-October 1985 period. His sixteen months of torture and interrogation, with a variety of inquisitors having their turns with him, pumped him for all manner of information and left him a physically and mentally destroyed man.

- ## NOTE 3 - page 396
  The shootdown of the Agency-sponsored C-123 aircraft by a Sandinista soldier's shoulder-fired missile helped ignite the Iran–Contra scandal. The aircraft was operated by Corporate Air Services, which in turn was related to Southern Air Transport. The October 1986 ill-fated mission involved the resupply of anti-Sandinista Contra forces with weapons and equipment, in a para-cargo run that had become almost a routine undertaking. Veteran contract pilots had died that day, including William Cooper and Wallace Blain Sawyer, in company with their radioman, Nicaraguan Freddy Vilches, when their crippled aircraft slammed into the jungle. But the airplane's "kicker," one Eugene Hasenfus, a former U.S. Marine from Wisconsin, managed to bail out through the open cargo door as the aircraft went down. He was captured by Sandinista forces and was persuaded to sing like a songbird for his capturers. International media attention to the crash and Hasenfus' testimony was immediate and intense.

- ## NOTE 4 - page 397
  One of the first issues we had to sort out on this man was exactly who he was. It occurred that one of Gaddafi's most trusted lieutenants had a name identical to that of our new friend Thali and shared with our friend the same birth year and month. Our fellow intelligence organizations had been tracking this Libyan, actually both men, under the assumption that the two individuals were one and the same. For several years, they had mapped "his" movements and relationships all over the Maghreb and Western Europe. In

several cases, it appeared that this individual had the ability to be in two locations at the same time, hundreds of miles apart. No matter, the file that had been built managed to assume our Thali was a strong player for Gaddafi on the international scene, an intelligence operative with several false identities, and even a possible terrorism enabler. Not true.

As I paged through the file, knowing Thali to the limited degree I did, it became clear that we had been tracking two individuals who did not even know of the other's existence, let alone share any responsibilities. It took me some time to get other collectors on the same wavelength, to then work backward to separate the two files, one man to each, so that we could begin to accurately track their respective lives, travels and contacts. The result was that our Thali turned out to be a much less menacing persona, and our work with him proceeded apace.

- ## NOTE 5 - page 398

Two books of note relate the strike on Libya, Raid on Qaddafi: The Untold Story of History's Longest Fighter Mission by the Pilot Who Directed It, by Robert E. Venkus (1992) and El Dorado Canyon, Reagan's Undeclared War with Qaddafi, by Joseph Stank (2002). Also, a very readable summary of the action by Tom Demerly appeared more recently in The Aviationist on April 15, 2020, titled "On This Day in 1986, Operation El Dorado Canyon, the F-111's Shining Moment." Other relevant articles include Walter J. Boyle's "El Dorado Canyon" which appeared in the 12 July 2008 edition of Air Force Magazine and Judy G. Endicott's "Raid on Libya: Operation El Dorado Canyon."

In his article in The Aviationist, Demerly addresses one of the most enduring misunderstandings related to the event. Delivered history suggested that the complicated route that the U.S. Air Force component of strike force was forced to fly, a path that took the aircraft from the U.K., down the Atlantic Ocean and around Spain to enter and transit the Mediterranean, before delivering the attack on the Libyan targets, was a product of a French-led political disruption intended to blunt the strike. U.S. mission planners had to deal with and plan around a refusal by France, Spain and Italy to allow the U.S. to overfly those nations en route to their Libyan targets. Demerly suggests that rather than opposing the U.S. strike on Gaddafi, French President Mitterrand had instead supported the strike but demanded, as his price for approving any overflight of France, that the U.S. undertake and lead a more comprehensive military action that would result in Gaddafi's overthrow.

I am not sure that such an explanation closes the case or absolves the French from causing this operation to be much more difficult than it otherwise needed to be. But France's decision to deny the U.S. overflight rights no doubt damaged the relationship between the U.S. and France for some time, as well it should have.

- **NOTE 6 - page 402**

  In future years, with the circumstances involving Saddam Hussein and Iraq dramatically altered by that nation's invasion of Kuwait, and Saddam's determination to wage war on Saudi Arabia, most nations in the Middle East, and half the world, our Texas oilman caught grief from the U.S. Government. In October 2007, after a lengthy and hard-fought court battle, he pleaded guilty to conspiring to make illegal payments related to the United Nation's Oil for Food program. Although dozens of oil companies fell into this category of business legerdemain, many believed that he had been singled out in an effort to make an example of a prominent U.S. oilman. But he was a survivor and rallied to rebuild a multi-billion-dollar oil operation.

Chapter 31

- **NOTE 1 - page 410**

  That comment in the Gates book was a reference to the new position crafted by Casey for his righthand man, former station chief Jim. Jim's installation at Headquarters by Casey had been done in an earlier attempt to light a fire under the DO bureaucracy, most of whom considered the business community to inhabit a level akin to that occupied by the untouchables of India. In his own way, Jim worked within the established Agency structure in an effort to deliver a better intelligence product from the business community. In so doing, Jim reaped the scorn of the Operations Directorate's senior management, who watched him carefully and undercut him when they could. When Casey determined that Jim could not get the full job done operating within the confines of the bureaucracy, he had reached out to my East Asia station to pull me in to create the offline activity he deemed to be unavoidable.

- **NOTE 2 - page 411**

  Some 20 years later, Bob Gates and I would have an opportunity to correct his misunderstanding that my name was an Agency pseudonym. The venue was Gates's new office in the Pentagon. I was then serving as the acting Assistant Secretary of Defense for Asian and Pacific Security Affairs in the Office of the Secretary of Defense. I had offered to rejoin government in the wake of 9/11 and was invited to join the DOD policy team by Secretary Donald Rumsfeld in mid-2002. I left the private sector with some reluctance, but I was eager to serve again and the DOD's OSD Asia policy shop seemed to be an ideal match. My original understanding with Secretary Rumsfeld, whom I respected immensely, was that I would stay three years. He had later asked that I remain throughout his tenure there, and I had agreed. He had given me great latitude to do my job, and my Asia policy team was working with vigor and success to update our alliance relationships in Asia. The Rumsfeld resignation in 2006 had delivered Bob Gates to the Pentagon as the new Secretary.

I had a decision to make, either remain with Gates, assuming he wanted me to stay, or resign and return to the private sector.

On his second day on the job, Gates asked to meet with me in his office. In our one-on-one session, he requested that I consider remaining for at least another year, and I agreed. But I admitted that I was burning out fast and would plan to leave sometime before the end of the Bush 43 term, probably in 2008. He was satisfied and when we stood to part company, he smiled and offered something along the lines of "Looks like I got it a bit wrong in my book. I really did think that the Casey offline operation was named "Lawless" or something like that." I said it was all okay, that I didn't expect him to remember everything. I had assumed that Casey had not done much to clarify the issue back in 1986.

I had a great year and then some with Gates in the Pentagon. He gave me and my Asia policy team plenty of room to run, his full confidence, and we reciprocated that trust. I think we did him well in Asia and allowed him to focus on other, more-vexing issues, namely Afghanistan, Iraq, NATO and terrorism. After my resignation from the Pentagon in August 2007, having devoted five years in that capacity, I agreed to continue to serve informally as his special advisor for alliance management, which I did for the next two years.

• NOTE 3 - page 417

A thorough investigation of the events surrounding the terror bombing of Pan Am Flight 103 led to the conclusion that the government of Libya had mounted the operation. A case was built around this suspicion, arrests were made, followed by the indictment and conviction of two Libyan operatives for the crime. The case was hardly open and shut, and doubts attended this course of prosecution from the outset. It remains unclear to this day as to the identity of the true sponsors; that is, the initiators, of this act.

I have no doubt that Matt Gannon's presence on that flight, in company with the two State Department officers, was a coincidence. This event came five years after the kidnapping in Beirut of William F. Buckley, the Agency's Chief of Station there. These losses were on top of the loss of our entire American Embassy in the bombing of 1983 to include the Agency Station, not to mention the destruction of the U.S. Marine Barracks later. Beirut was a hell-hole then, remained so throughout the interim period and is more so today. For further information on the career of Matt Gannon, the reader is directed to the Agency's "honoring heroes" site and the entry for Matt Gannon. His career is profiled as are his activities in the Middle East on the eve of his return to home on the Pan Am flight.

My personal conviction, both at the time of the Pan Am bombing and more certainly today, is that the Libyans, however tangentially involved, were not the ultimate source or sponsoring initiators of the bombing. All indications point to Iran, and many of my fellow Agency officers, including those most directly involved in the region in the days and weeks after the bombing, agree wholeheartedly with this conclusion. Most are convinced that this was a retaliatory action conceived, directed and undertaken by the Iranian government, utilizing proxy actors in Europe to complete the deed. The latter were most probably the Popular Force for the Liberation of Palestine–General Command, a terrorist group for hire that was then active in Western Europe.

Tehran needed no special incentive to strike at the United States. Six months earlier, in an accidental engagement in the Persian Gulf, the U.S. Navy had shot down an Iran Air Airbus 600, killing 290 passengers and crew. As a result, Tehran's leadership had vowed revenge and were willing to pay handsomely to secure it. The final and complete story of Pan Am 103 is yet to be told in a convincing narrative, but it would not surprise me to learn that the act was the result of a cash transaction, with Tehran the source. In any event, one hopes the final reckoning will be soon and just.

Among the books that have been written about the Lockerbie event, Their Darkest Day: The Tragedy of Pan Am 103 and Its Legacy of Hope by Matthew Cox and Tom Foster might be useful. Compiled in 1992, the story remained unavoidably incomplete in explaining the intricacies of the Christmas Eve 1988 disaster. Nevertheless, it relates well the destruction of lives and the sad aftermath that descended in a rain of fire and debris on the village of Lockerbie.

Chapter 32

• NOTE 1 - page 421

Although a good number of books have recounted the Iran–Contra Affair and the investigations and inquires that sad series of events occasioned, one of the best might be Theodore Draper's A Very Thin Line: The Iran–Contra Affairs, which appeared in 1991. Notwithstanding the fact that many additive details have surfaced over the ensuing 32 years, the Draper account captured the personalities and events quite well, including the bungled planning and execution that characterized almost every element of the amateurs-at-work production and the incompetence with which the entire Walsh operation was mounted.

• NOTE 2 - page 422

Chuck Yeager celebrated his 97th birthday on February 23, 2020, and maintained his own Twitter account until his passing on December 7, 2020. The obituaries published in The New York Times on December 8th, in The Washington Post on December 9th and in Aviation Week & Space Technology on December 18th, taken together provide an excellent testimony to the life of this man. In the 1983 movie, *The Right Stuff*, he is portrayed by Sam Shepard.

Yeager even managed a cameo appearance as the bartender at the test pilots' hangout, "Pancho's Happy Bottom Riding Club." He was the winner of the Collier Trophy for aviation excellence and was awarded the Presidential Medal of Freedom in 1985. By any accounting, his life seemed to defy the old maxim "There are old fighter pilots, and there are bold fighter pilots, but there are no old, bold fighter pilots!" Chuck Yeager obviously did not get that memo. Yeager's Bell X-1, which he named the "Glamorous Glennis" after his wife, is displayed proudly in the Smithsonian's National Air and Space Museum in Washington. In addition to Yeager's autobiography mentioned in the text, a more recent book by Dan Hampton, Chasing the Demon: A Secret History of the Quest for the Sound Barrier and the Band of American Aces Who Conquered It, appeared in 2018 and does justice to the courage of Yeager and these men.

• **NOTE 3 - page 431**

As noted in the text, while the diplomat Do hostage incident was playing out in Beirut, Geneva and Seoul, at the same time South Korea was rushing to complete preparations for the forthcoming 1988 Summer Olympics. Further in the north of the peninsula, North Korea was equally busy, advancing its schemes to undermine the Games. In Pyongyang in September 1987, Kim Jong-il, son of North Korea's founder and the Great Leader's successor-in-waiting, personally approved a dedicated act of terrorism. In November, two North Korean agents, posing as Japanese citizens, traveled from Pyongyang, transited through Moscow, Budapest, Vienna, and Belgrade to meet their North Korean intelligence handlers in Baghdad. The man and woman agent team there boarded KAL flight 858 with some special luggage.

After planting explosives in an overhead bin, the agents disembarked in Abu Dhabi and calmly boarded another flight to head home to North Korea. Hours later, on November 29th, the KAL 707 aircraft, freshly adorned with its "Seoul Olympics 1988" livery, exploded in a ball of fire and tumbled into the Andaman Sea. All 115 passengers and crew aboard the aircraft were killed, allowing the proud son of the Great Leader to report "mission accomplished" to his father.

• **NOTE 4 - page 431**

Some 10 years after the safe return of diplomat Do, in the fall of 1997, I happened to be in Seoul on business and was approached by a Korean journalist. Song Moon-hong, a respected investigative reporter, was attempting to compile a 10th-anniversary retrospective account of Do's return from Beirut. But he was having a problem getting information from the diplomats and government officials he had approached, all of whom were known to have been involved, but most declined to discuss details. I assisted him in redrafting the story, essentially collaborating with him to tell it as it happened.

The article appeared as the cover article in the January 1998 edition of the monthly Shin Dong-a Journal and included an addendum interview with me. The journal, a product of Korea's largest daily vernacular news daily, enjoyed broad circulation among the country's professional elite. Song's story, "Excavating A Hidden History," provided a highly accurate version of the Do return and managed to blend in some of the shadier elements of the Chun regime. In the latter area, the author noted that, although Chun and his family had been found to have amassed hundreds of millions of dollars in corrupt payoffs during his term, the then President of South Korea had been unwilling to inject a relatively small amount of his illicitly acquired funds to complete the Do rescue.

Diplomat Do, long fully recovered, was advancing in his diplomatic career, and was then posted again in the Middle East, serving as Consul General in Jeddah. When contacted by the journalist Song, Do declined to comment and noted only that he knew nothing about his return from captivity. That was hardly a mystery, given he had occupied a squalid hole in the ground for almost two years before he was dragged out of that pit and spirited out of Beirut to return home safely. Nor did Do know his Ministry of Foreign Affairs had welched on the agreement that brought him home to Seoul, or that his country was prepared to allow him to die in Beirut in the bargain.

• NOTE 5 - page 432

The remains of Agency officer William Francis Buckley finally were recovered in December 1991, four years after my failed attempt to do so in conjunction with the diplomat Do rescue and return. CIA officer Buckley was buried with full military honors in Arlington National Cemetery. He is honored by the 51st star in an assembly of 150, all recognizing those Agency officers who gave their lives in the line of duty and are memorialized on the CIA's Memorial Wall at Langley. His Agency awards and military honors include, among others, the Intelligence Star, the Distinguished Intelligence Cross, the Silver Star, the Bronze Star and the Combat Infantryman's Badge. As a former Special Forces officer, the last-named honor might have been the most important of those made to him. But his Agency career on the paramilitary front earned him no less respect from the colleagues who served with him. Casey had asked him to go to Beirut, and he went. It's what soldiers do.

Chapter 33

- ## NOTE 1 - page 433

In many ways, this October 1988 allegation leveled against the George Bush team was a repeat of an earlier October Surprise conspiracy theory, one that had been advanced in the wake of the election victory of Ronald Reagan some eight years earlier. The political charge made at that time suggested that Reagan campaign operatives, in the months before the 1980 election, had opened a secret channel of communication with the Iranian regime to discuss the U.S. hostages then being held in Tehran by that government. Those U.S. diplomats had been imprisoned as a consequence of the assault on the U.S. Embassy over a year before.

The first October Surprise theory was that a Reagan team, led by campaign manager Bill Casey and then-candidate National Security Advisor Richard Allen, had sought and received a commitment that any release of the U.S. Embassy hostages would be delayed until after the November 1980 presidential election. Presumably, such a delay would deprive President Carter of any political benefit he might otherwise have received prior to election day had Carter secured the release of the hostages. In the event, the American hostages were released by the Iranian government and headed home as President Reagan was being sworn into office, ending 444 days in captivity.

Although the allegation there had been a secret agreement that benefited the Reagan team had surfaced in the weeks immediately after the election, the real momentum for a disciplined political attack occurred at the time the Iran–Contra affair broke into the open almost six years later, in late 1986. The Iranians, and certain middlemen involved in the arms shipments that accompanied the Reagan administration's back-channel dealings with Tehran, were more than happy to pour gasoline on the political fire. Wild stories were concocted and propagated by an eager anti-Reagan–Bush media, and the assertions picked up a life force of their own. Attempts were made to contaminate then-Vice President Bush, including allegations that his National Security Advisor, my Agency mentor Donald Gregg, had been involved in 1980 nefarious activity that led to a hostage release delay until President Reagan took office.

Not unlike the vampire that will not die, the original October Surprise allegation, dating to the 1980 Presidential election and alleging the Reagan team conspired with the Iranians to delay the release of the U.S. hostages in Tehran, was recently resurrected by a media determined to breathe new life into the shop-worn story. On March 18, 2023, the New York Times excitedly reported, in a story headlined, "A Four-Decade Secret: One Man's Story of Sabotaging Carter's Re-election," new revelations on the part of Texas politician and long-time Democratic political fixer Ben Barnes. The Barnes out-of-the-closet claim is that he, in the company of former Texas Governor and U.S. Treasury Secretary John Connally, traveled in the weeks before the 1980 election to meet with leaders in several Middle Eastern countries to carry a none-to-subtle message: Don't release the hostages before the election.

The balance of the Times tale was that, although it was a "private trip" on Connally's part, he was carrying a special message to ingratiate himself with the Reagan team, thereby allowing Connally to claim an important role in that candidate's administration. If one swallows the Barnes tale that such a message was sent, the reader must then assume the various, unidentified Arab leaders conveyed the same message to Tehran and the Ayatollahs. And as a result of the message, the Iranians snapped to and did the dirty deed, thereby denying Carter a come-from-behind election victory.

Picking up on the Times story a few days later, and calling it a "blockbuster," online news aggregator The Intercept offered its own take. In an item titled, "A Short History of Everyone Who Confirmed Reagan's October Surprise Before the New York Times," The Intercept placed Barnes and his yarn in the company of such stalwart October Surprise conspiracy advocates as former Iranian President Abolhassan Banisadr, former Palestine Liberation Organization leader Yasser Arafat, former French military officer and master spy Alexandre de Marenches (who recanted), the Russian government and former Israeli Prime Minister Yitzhak Shamir—whose defining comment was, "I know in America, they know it."

Strong stuff that, from still-obsessed media that continue to grub for ways to denigrate the Reagan presidency. As they say in Texas, "All hat, no cattle."

• NOTE 2 - page 434

Speaking of Banisadr, he would claim firsthand knowledge of the Reagan team hostage "deal" and add that he wanted to share his take on the event. In 1991, fully 11 years after the broadly discredited claim made against the Reagan team, books were still being written asserting that there had been a covert arrangement that guaranteed Reagan's victory over Carter. The claim has remained "delivered wisdom" among the political left and remained an unproven allegation that was in favor over the years. It still had momentum in late 1988, when the media crowd self-activated in a frenzy to claim that a second or repeat October Surprise was in the works.

• NOTE 3 - page 438

Interesting that one book often cited as the ground truth on the original 1980 tale of skullduggery, October Surprise, authored by Barbara Honegger in 1989, attempted to drag me into the mix. On the positive side of responsible journalism, Steve Emerson, writing for The New Republic in 1989, dove into the details of the original 1980 allegations and concluded that, "The (1980) conspiracy as currently postulated is a total fabrication." An investigation mounted by a U.S. Senate committee in 1992 issued a report that came to the same conclusion.

• NOTE 4 - page 438

The quote comes from a lengthy October 7th article by Norman Kempster of the Los Angeles Times, datelined the United Nations in New York and headlined, "Shultz Tells Private Hostage Negotiators to 'Butt Out.'" The story identified me as the man nominated for the go-between role by Banisadr and solicited a comment on me from Iranian Foreign Minister Velayati, then attending to business at the United Nations in New York. Velayati had the presence of mind to make a declaratory statement on Lawless that was anything but convincing; to whit, "We do not have such a man in our country." My reaction was, thanks a million Velayati; that comment really cleared things up.

PART SIX

The Nukes Still Out There

(2002-2022)

Bush 43 Takes on the North Korean Nuclear Problem

In August 2002, I rejoined the U.S. government just in time to participate in the latest iteration of the 50-year nuclear dance with North Korea, and I soon became deeply involved in the renewed nuclear discussions that began in autumn of that year. My arrival at the Pentagon, serving as Deputy Under Secretary of Defense for Asian and Pacific Affairs, was more about 9/11 and wanting to serve my country again than it was about my expertise on North Korea. That said, I had little doubt my mandate would include a new engagement with the ever-hostile entity. In the Asia–Pacific office, we were responsible for crafting and managing defense and national security policy for the entire region, with an obvious focus on our Alliance relationships with Japan, Australia and South Korea, among others. I had agreed to serve two years as a political appointee in President George W. Bush's administration and had severed all business commitments to give my work at the Pentagon in the East Asia region my full attention.

In accepting the position, I assumed most of my time would be devoted to reassessments of our core alliances, to be followed by a restructuring of several of them. Defense Secretary Donald Rumsfeld recently had committed, based on discussions with his peers at the National Security Council and with President Bush, to undertake a global review of America's strategic posture and our international security commitments. Japan and South Korea ranked high on the list of assessments, as did our relationships with Australia and Singapore. Indeed, over the next five years, we made fundamental changes in the way the Japanese and Korean alliances were organized in an attempt to bring both security partnerships forward to confront new realities. The management of the two relationships, plus a half-dozen other bilateral engagements, consumed most of our energy. We had ongoing issues with Singapore, Australia, India and Pakistan, plus the growing confrontation with China as an emerging peer competitor, with its expanding political, economic and military power. But North Korea, as was its wont, managed to elbow its way into my life and our collective undertakings, some days taking up all of our time. **[NOTE 1]**

Trouble was brewing on the North Korean nuclear front in late summer 2002. U.S. intelligence assessments concluded that the Pyongyang regime, in violation of commitments it had accepted in 1994 under the Agreed Framework, might have undertaken a covert program to enrich uranium through the use of centrifuge technology. If substantiated, the violation would have scuttled the entire Framework, under which the North Koreans were directly and substantially benefiting in their energy sector, in return for giving up their plutonium-based nuclear weapons efforts. At that point, by the terms of the Framework, North Korea had been receiving fuel oil shipments from the U.S. side valued at hundreds of millions of dollars a year, and the non-North Korean adherents to the agreement, the U.S. included, were preparing to ship the final components of the deal to North Korea—a $2 billion, two-reactor nuclear powerplant.

In October, a State Department-led interagency delegation visited Pyongyang to confer with North Korean officials on the status of Pyongyang's cooperation in the nuclear field and the progress of the Agreed Framework. The leader was State's Asia Director James Kelly, my counterpart, and the group included my Japan–Korea Branch Chief, as well as a Joint Chiefs of Staff member. I had arrived at the Pentagon only days before departure and did not have all my required security clearances. Therefore, I was not in a position to travel officially. In all later interactions on the North Korea front, I would lead the Secretary of Defense's policy team. All told, it was a strong assembly. We did not expect, however, that the visit would become the catalyst that triggered a years-long diplomatic confrontation with the Kim family's Hermit Kingdom.

As mentioned, the U.S. policy community's main concern centered on indications of Pyongyang's undeclared activity on the materials-procurement front, something that suggested the North Koreans might be planning, or possibly already had begun, a covert uranium-enrichment program. Such an undeclared program would provide a second path to a nuclear device, independent of the previously detected plutonium route at the Yongbyon research facility. A centrifuge operation, even if only in a research phase, would be a blatant violation of the Agreed Framework, not to mention a breach of the North's earlier bilateral agreement with South Korea. Under that 1992 North–South treaty, both nations had committed to not produce fissile material, via either the uranium enrichment mode or the reprocessing approach to yield high-purity plutonium.

To the surprise of the Kelly delegation, during a discussion on North Korea's nuclear activities, a senior official essentially confirmed that Pyongyang had a uranium enrichment program in place, with the blunt admonition it really was no one's business but North Korea's. The statement later was characterized as, "Yes, we are doing that, so what?" Other interpretations were less clear, but the important point was the North Koreans made absolutely no attempt to deny it. The delegation took it as an in-your-face confirmation of what had been only a strong suspicion going into the visit, and the group reported the development to the U.S. policy community upon their return home.

Back in Washington, some controversy later attended the account of the exchange. The accommodationist crowd was eager to sustain the quasi-sacred Agreed Framework at any cost, suggesting that the North Korean official might have been misheard. Or, perhaps, the U.S. side had mistaken his remarks as a confirmation, when in fact all he was suggesting was North Korea had the right to do whatever it wished, including enrichment. But we elected to assume the worst, and the intelligence community was tasked to undertake a much deeper dive. Working backward from the recent indicators, the analysts assembled a retrospective, all-source assessment that spanned the 2000-2002 period. Although the picture was incomplete, the conclusion was North Korea had been acquiring what it needed for a nascent, centrifuge-based, uranium enrichment program for several years. Given the beaver-like diligence we had seen in the past, it was possible North Korea could well have had a pilot facility in place and operating when Kelly's team sat down in Pyongyang. In fact, they had done so.

In the coming months, we substantiated the initial conclusion that a program existed, but a definitive assessment eluded our analysts. Whatever the extent of that activity, International Atomic Energy Agency investigators had failed to detect such a program for the simple reason that it was an undeclared activity at an unknown location and therefore not even part of the IAEA's agreed mandate in that country. Then the proverbial canary in the proliferation coal mine sang, and the region was reawakened to the reborn threat.

A Flawed Framework with the IAEA Caught in the Middle

Beyond the concern over a possible undeclared uranium enrichment program, representing a baldfaced violation of the Agreed Framework, there remained the issue of North Korean non-compliance with a specific safeguards program, a companion component within the Framework, which the IAEA had been tasked to deliver. The safeguards effort essentially was a catch-up scramble on the part of the agency designed to resolve important uncertainties in the prior history of the plutonium program at Pyongyang's Yongbyon facility—formal name Yongbyon Nuclear Science and Weapons Research Center. The North Koreans ostensibly had abandoned that effort as a condition of the Framework but had committed to work with the IAEA to complete a full accounting of what already had occurred at the facility.

Up to the point that the plutonium reprocessing plant was shuttered as a consequence of the Framework, the core issue was the quantity of plutonium the North Koreans actually had separated. How much bombmaking material did they accumulate at the time the Agreement was signed? They claimed only minimal amounts of fissile material for research purposes, but our negotiators had no option but to seek confirmation.

The matter was resolved in 1994 when the North Koreans agreed to cooperate with the IAEA to verify their accounting. That commitment tied directly to milestones in the balance of the overall deal. And so began a diligent, multi-year attempt by IAEA inspectors to validate the North Korean plutonium holdings— or, rather, their claimed non-holdings of fissile material. Year after year, the IAEA struggled but failed in its task when the operators at Yongbyon refused access to a key nuclear waste storage facility. Had the IAEA inspected the structure and successfully sampled the waste material enclosed therein, they could have determined what quantities, and to what extent, the North Koreans had operated their research reactor and reprocessing plant to generate plutonium, and to what purity. The higher the quality of the refined plutonium, the better the explosive material; thus the less material required for a nuclear weapon.

Depending on how much credit one gave North Korea for the device-design part of the overall equation, one could judge the number of weapons that could be derived from a given quantity of reprocessed plutonium. By refusing access to Yongbyon, the North Koreans could keep to the side whatever weapons-grade material they already possessed when they entered the Agreed Framework, essentially sidestepping commitments they made. They knew exactly what they were doing, and we did as well, even if many of us were inclined to ignore reality.

The standing requirement for the IAEA to complete an accurate accounting was a key enabler for other provisions of the Framework, including shipment of nuclear reactor components to a facility at Shinpo, along the northeast coast. The repeated failure of IAEA inspectors to complete the verification task resurfaced in summer 2002 to threaten the overall program. It was probable the North Koreans expected the Bush administration to ignore the issue of Framework noncompliance, but the situation no longer could be finessed at IAEA headquarters. When IAEA management sent the annual report to its Board of Directors in mid-September, the agency called out the North Koreans. The IAEA Board had little choice but to report the development to the United Nations Security Council, which it did.

Years later, a senior IAEA Safeguards Directorate official and I reminisced about the agency's relationship with the United States at the time the Agreed Framework was concluded. He explained the situation in which IAEA leadership found itself and lamented that the U.S. negotiators brought the Framework to the IAEA in Vienna basically as a done deal. They essentially dictated the IAEA's tasks regarding verification of North Korean claims on the plutonium side. IAEA management initially resisted the assignment, because they knew it would be extremely difficult to accomplish, given the attitude of the North Koreans. The IAEA had been dealing with Pyongyang for many years, with mixed success. In the end, the agency reluctantly accepted a no-win assignment so the United States could conclude the Framework. It turned out to be a thankless task, as expected, and when the end came years later, the IAEA finally was forced to report it had failed.

By 2002, it had taken eight full years of failed IAEA efforts to confirm, in unambiguous terms, that North Korea was not then, nor had it ever been, in compliance with that fundamental aspect of the Agreed Framework. Equally important, at the time the Kelly delegation returned from Pyongyang, and we sat down to discuss our options, the United States and its associated nations were closing in on the delivery of major components for two large-scale nuclear power reactors under construction at Shinpo. It was a multi-billion-dollar project, paid for in its entirety by the United States, South Korea and Japan. The three nations had joined together in a determined effort to support the compromise reached under the Agreed Framework.

The twin-reactor concession was in response to the North Korean claim that they had undertaken their plutonium-based reactor and reprocessing programs at their nuclear research center at Yongbyon as a matter of national economic survival. Pyongyang was energy resource-poor and it was, therefore, a state imperative for the country to seek a supply of electrical energy derived from peaceful nuclear power reactors. Fair enough. But linking that rationale to plans for larger, natural-uranium-fueled, graphite-moderated, plutonium-producing reactors at Yongbyon was absurd. Those reactors would be inherently inefficient and incapable of generating any reasonable level of electrical power. Again, the larger-scale, plutonium-producing reactor and reprocessing angle was a ruse designed to secure ever more fissile material that Pyongyang could then weaponize.

For better or worse, U.S. negotiators accepted at face value that line of reasoning, mainly to secure an agreement that promised to shut down the nuclear weapons program assumed underway at Yongbyon. The commitment to supply the two commercial-scale, light-water reactors as part of the Agreed Framework involved the presumption—and the implied commitment—that North Korea would be able to satisfy its power generation demands by the replacement reactors. By accepting the shutdown of the existing research reactor at Yongbyon, and foregoing the new graphite-moderated reactors there, the North Koreans were accepting that their reprocessing days were behind them. The companion assumption was the acquisition of fissile material derived from indigenous reactors was then removed from the North Korean program, thereby closing the door on their plutonium-based weapons effort. Dream on.

The IAEA safeguards failure at Yongbyon yielded a low profile on the political front. But the failure did trigger, automatically by the terms of the Agreed Framework, suspension of the shipment of the power reactor vessels and other components from the Japanese and other manufacturers. The administration of President Bill Clinton conceivably could have allowed the shipment of the heavy components by issuing a waiver, as had been done in the past, but it is doubtful either the Japanese or the South Korean governments would have concurred. It would have been particularly true in the wake of the IAEA report of its failed verification on the plutonium waste front. If the North Koreans, confronted by their IAEA standoff, were expecting such a waiver, they were disappointed. It was particularly so when the uranium enrichment issue surfaced in the same timeframe.

Approaching the Six-Party Talks

The combination of revelations set the stage for discussions among the three nations that together supported the Agreed Framework with economic assistance, fuel oil shipments and the provision of the two nuclear powerplants—that is, the United States, Japan and South Korea. In the September-December period, we met several times, bilaterally and trilaterally, to create a common position. The immediate issue was the likelihood that Pyongyang had been in violation of the Framework for many years with its covert uranium program, but we also faced the reality of the failed IAEA safeguards and the impact on the Shinpo project.

There was a strong consensus that North Korea needed to be confronted directly on both the uranium enrichment and plutonium retention aspects of the problem. The three parties agreed there was no option but to suspend the fuel oil shipments and freeze the Shinpo project. While the provision of the new nuclear power reactors was the obvious jewel in the Agreed Framework crown, the supply of free fuel oil was a daily necessity for the North Korean regime. We assumed its disruption would have a more immediate impact, or at least get the North Koreans to sit down and find a solution to the impasse. In any event, Pyongyang cried foul, demanded the Shinpo project proceed and the fuel oil shipments, as well as other assistance, continue.

By December 2002, the three-nation consultations produced a unified approach, in parallel with discussions we initiated with the Chinese government and later with the Russians. In Beijing, as we pushed our Chinese colleagues to address the issue, we found them mildly interested in becoming involved but claiming to be totally uninformed about what had happened in the Agreed Framework or subsequent to that accord. But the meetings did suggest a possible way forward.

Beijing offered to host what became known as the Six-Party Talks and in doing so had two complementary goals. First, by placing itself in the middle of the renewed engagement with North Korea, in what essentially was a crisis situation, Beijing saw an opportunity to regain a level of influence and relevance in its testy relationship with Pyongyang. Over the years, the two communist regimes had become estranged, and the gulf between them deepened with the advent of the leadership transition in the North when the second generation of the Kim dynasty took over. The two no longer enjoyed a "lips and teeth" pairing, if ever they had, but we were unsure how hostile the relationship had become or how much we could expect the Chinese to add to a solution.

Equally attractive to Beijing was the chance to host and act as the moderator among the five other nations most critical to the stability of Northeast Asia. A related consideration was the PRC's Ministry of Foreign Affairs, which was routinely disrespected as an organization by both the Chinese Communist Party and other government senior bureaucrats as mere functionaries (the "interpreters"). They perceived an opening to secure improved status in the overall system. It seemed later that, in taking on the mission, the ministry officials had no idea how difficult it would be to play the moderator role.

In the case of the Russians, they awoke to the Six-Party opportunity eager to reinsert themselves into the "politics of the Korean vortex." With no solutions of their own, they viewed the talks as an opening to reclaim a level of influence that had waned since the demise of the Soviet Union.

After a procedural warmup meeting in Beijing to confirm the structure, our Beijing hosts stocked up on the immense quantities of cognac required for their guests from Pyongyang, and the formal Six-Party Talks began.

It is interesting to note, now in 2023, the manner in which some commentators continue to misremember and misstate how events in 2002 and 2003 came together to produce the policy crisis we faced when the talks commenced. That line of thought and complaint, advanced by some East Asia experts and North Korean watchers, can be paraphrased as the following:

> *The Bush Administration approach, from 2002 forward, overturned the hallowed Agreed Framework. In so doing, Bush 43 machinations disrupted all the progress that had been made to that date and upended all future possibilities for a denuclearized Korean Peninsula.*

Such a take on the entire chain of events and the facts then on the ground is, politely stated, pure hogwash. **[NOTE 2]**

The realities of the day, and the convergence of a host of negative factors—including Pyongyang's noncompliance with plutonium verification and our discovery of the covert uranium enrichment program—assured the breakdown of the Agreed Framework. A confrontation was only a matter of time, and the Bush administration either had to ignore all of the warning lights and give Pyongyang a pass, or acknowledge we had a significant problem that had to be frontally addressed. The assertion that the Bush team had other options was then, and remains today, absurd. I suspect at least four of the other nations sitting at the table in Beijing to face the North Koreans would agree. In joining the Six-Party talks, neither China nor Russia, Pyongyang's long-suffering comrades, would deny we had reached a nuclear impasse.

Indeed, had the North allowed the IAEA access to the waste storage facilities at Yongbyon, it is probable the inspectors would have discovered, certainly within three years of the Agreed Framework coming into force, that North Korea had reprocessed and separated sufficient fissile material for three to five devices. A three-party (U.S.–IAEA–North Korea) confrontation on the going-in violation would have occurred, and a compromise would have been possible. Such would have required Pyongyang to declare and consign the fissile material for safeguarding, and the IAEA to sequester or otherwise neuter that stock of weapons-grade material. North Korea also would have had to forgo fabrication of declared and safeguarded fissile material into nuclear weapons. But the Agreed Framework could have survived.

Similarly, at the time of the 2002 confrontation that resulted in the Six-Party Talks, the North Koreans could have come clean on their activities and sought compromises, allowing the Framework to continue. But as tensions built throughout 2003 in the talks in Beijing, it grew more difficult for them to hide their achievements. Instead, the Kim regime had its delegates assert that Pyongyang had every intention of continuing on its current path by building more and better weapons while developing the means to deliver them.

Compromise beyond deception was never in the cards, not in 1994 with the Agreed Framework, and certainly not in September 2005 when we concluded a preliminary understanding among the six parties on further steps to "denuclearize the Korean Peninsula." Within a few months, Pyongyang denounced the entire process. Its delegation made additional claims to create new confrontations, all of which led to the ouster of IAEA inspectors and a formal renunciation of the non-proliferation treaty. The Democratic People's Republic of Korea became the first and only nation to leave the agreement. In doing so, it rejected any constraints on nuclear weapons activity, thereby doubling down on its rogue nuclear state stature.

In their minds, the North Korean leadership had arrived as a nuclear power. Others, including the United States, declined to admit all involved parties likewise had arrived at that critical inflection point. It was a Rodney Dangerfield-like, "We don't get no respect!" reaction to others depreciating their claimed capability. Better yet, irritated by their progressive South Korean compatriots, mumbling that the North Koreans had no "real nuclear device capability" until they actually detonated one, the North proceeded to detonate device after device, and shoot missile after missile, to drive home their claim.

During the Six-Party talks, it also was interesting to watch the reaction of the representatives of other nations when the North Koreans boasted they not only had every right to possess a nuclear weapons capability but also to demonstrate that capability and acquire and deploy the systems required to deliver weapons to a desired location. Hard swallows all around, with some suggesting, including our Chinese hosts, that perhaps we really had not heard correctly what the North Koreans stated in a formal plenary session. No. We all heard what the folks from Pyongyang wanted us to hear and take home. **[NOTE 3]**

Nuclear North Korea in 2023

We now find ourselves at a well-primed point of nuclear combustion, and we are compelled to continue to find ways to adjust to the new reality, which a highly successful nuclear proliferation program has delivered. There remain, I believe, solutions out there, perhaps some at either end of the conventional option spectrum. In this regard, I hope my experiences inform the discussion and decision process, and perhaps contribute to future endeavors to address and resolve a persistently vexing but vital issue.

CHAPTER 34 Notes

- **NOTE 1 - See page 456**

   As mentioned in the Introduction, the U.S. intelligence community, with the CIA in the lead, failed systemically in appreciating the scope, pace and capabilities of the North Korean nuclear program for over 30 years. That failure was both one of collection, including the abysmal record of clandestine reporting as well as analysis. Torrey Froscher, a former Agency nuclear analyst, attempted to explain elements of the failure in the December 2019 Studies in Intelligence (Volume 63, Number 4). His article, titled "North Korea's Nuclear Program: The Early Days, 1984-2002," divides the failure over that 18-year period into three phases, taking readers through the Agreed Framework and depositing us at the eve of the Six-Party Talks.

   The article interestingly begins with a quote from my Seoul Station Chief Don Gregg, the former National Security Advisor to Vice President George H.W. Bush. Gregg, who later would serve as U.S. Ambassador to South Korea, is quoted as pronouncing North Korea to be, "the longest-running intelligence failure in the history of American espionage." I believe the Froscher essay, while provocative and insightful, does not do justice to the magnitude of the intelligence misread. I do not agree with some of the explanations made in the article that might serve to excuse rather than explain the disconnections among the IC analysts, and between the analysts and the denial crew on the policy side. That said, the essay is a valuable assessment of how intelligence ineptitude helped ensure failure in the diplomatic policy-development process.

   Working that same theme, Dr. Henry Sokolski, director of the Nuclear Policy Education Center, a Washington-based, public policy entity focused on the challenge of nuclear proliferation, offered NPEC's own assessment of our intelligence process on North Korea. His paper, titled "Improving the Role of Intelligence in Counterproliferation Policymaking: Report of the "Speaking Truth to Nonproliferation Project, 2018," appeared in the March 2019 edition of the CIA's Studies in Intelligence (Volume 63 Number 1). The Sokolski article summarizes the mentioned NPEC report and referenced case studies that NPEC judged to identify, "when and how intelligence shaped nonproliferation policy actions and, if not, why."

   I participated in the NPEC "Speaking Truth…" project and therein described in some detail the Agency's successful detection and takedown of the South Korean nuclear program. That case study was not included in the NPEC Project's final report, lost on the cutting room floor in company with others involving certain proliferating nations. The omission might have occurred because NPEC judged my and other case studies to be too sensitive. It also is possible that the deleted case studies were considered less consequential, but I doubt it. This particular experience notwithstanding, Dr. Sokolski and NPEC do fine service to their mission of educating the public and those in U.S. government service on the fundamentals of proliferation policy. As of this writing (January 2023), I serve as a member of NPEC's board of advisors. I am pleased to participate in the organization's mission of educating a broad spectrum of government employees, congressional staff members and others influential in the policy process on the technologies and politics of nuclear proliferation.

• NOTE 2 - page 462

A few years ago, I responded to an opinion piece in the Wall Street Journal in a case where the fallacious "blame Bush 43" argument was unabashedly deployed. I noted that, while the Agreed Framework was fatally flawed from a verification point of view, it would have had a fair chance of success if only the North Koreans had abided by their commitments. All parties could have built on the Clinton-era initiative, and North Korea would have prospered, its economy fueled by a more open engagement with the United States and the other regional players. Its future energy needs would have been secured by the massive nuclear reactor complex at Shinpo provided by other nations that had been eager to engage and would have been sustained in future years at no cost to Pyongyang. But the North Koreans, ever the gamesmen, wanted it both ways—engagement for immediate economic benefit and a nuclear power program on a gratis basis, all while sustaining a covert nuclear weapons program through the uranium enrichment ploy.

• NOTE 3 - page 463

In this narrative I have elected to avoid any further accounting of these Six-Party Talks or discuss the intelligence assessments that informed the process. Nor have I described the policy deliberations within the U.S. government that provided guidance to those of us sitting in Beijing at the table with the North Koreans. Unmentioned as well are the competing agendas of the four other parties at the table, and the tribulations we suffered at the hands of our progressive South Korean compatriots. There is much to offer and a good deal of truth-telling to be done, but that exercise must wait for another day.

EPILOGUE: The Hunt Must Continue

Many of us, some long in the service and others young into the game, are still out there hunting nukes. It must be so. The men and women who have signed on to address this threat—the intelligence officers, the clandestine collectors, the technical analysts and those who advise policymakers—cannot relax and cannot relent. We do not have the luxury of downplaying any possibility of a nuclear-tipped missile or a crude device threatening our homeland, or the homeland of others who look to American intelligence as their first line of defense. Just as partner nations feel the existential danger of nuclear-equipped regional rivals, nations such as America, which have the capability to deter a national nuclear program, still must imagine and deal with the threat of non-nation–state nuclear terrorism.

We therefore find ourselves confronted for the foreseeable future with the proliferation threats residing in two equally nasty categories. In one, we face national programs designed to provide a potentially hostile nation with a permanent strategic weapons capability, most with the means to get themselves where they want to be. At the opposite end of the nuclear spectrum exist single actors or terrorist teams capable of assembling all elements of a use-once crude device. We should assume that the possession of such a WMD capability will encourage its use, and the owner would be prepared to pull that trigger tomorrow for whatever combination of reasons. In either case, the threat is real, it is tangible, and it is not the stuff of *Black Sunday* fiction or super-agent movies any longer.

Nation–State Proliferation Overt and Covert

Nation–state proliferation involves the conscious act of exploring every path to an indigenous nuclear weapons capability and systematically building a comprehensive program to achieve the coveted "nuclear weapons state" status. We have active players today, and more undoubtedly will surface in near future. As in the instances of Taiwan, South Korea, South Africa, Libya, Syria, and others I have mentioned where covert programs were detected and defeated, at least for now, there have been marked successes. In those cases, intelligence has played a critical role in detecting, defining and defeating such programs. Once alert to hidden or semi-overt activities, dedicated efforts were made to penetrate all elements of the planning and development process of the target proliferators. The actions typically led to political confrontations and ad hoc partnerships among like-threatened nations that eventually defeated such efforts.

Some of the takedowns had a higher profile—as was the case in Libya and South Africa, where political events permitted a once-clandestine program to be exposed and disabled. Other compelled terminations were low profile, at least to the degree that important components of a given bilateral relationship were not damaged in the process. South Korea and Taiwan are good examples. But in those situations, we were fortunate to have the intelligence we needed and the leverage to act decisively on our assessment.

In instances of covert programs that failed of their own accord, and were less well-covered as they struggled to gain momentum, after-the-event intelligence collection and evaluation allowed us postmortem assessments of what had transpired. It was useful to assess how far the efforts had progressed, the technology paths being pursued, and the political or other factors that caused the programs to collapse or be collapsed. An excellent and still-relevant example was the nuclear weapons program of Saddam Hussein's Iraq as it existed in the years prior to the First Persian Gulf War of August 1990-February 1991.

In the wake of that war, international inspectors discovered a covert nuclear weapons development effort in progress since 1982, virtually a decade before. That program remained undetected by IAEA and therefore unchallenged by the international community, and it was discovered and terminated only as a consequence of Iraq's defeat in the war. Three quotes, lifted from a three-part report from the "Deadly Arsenals" publication of the Carnegie Endowment for International Peace, suffice to describe the magnitude of the wholesale intelligence "miss" in Iraq.

- "Iraq's efforts to produce weapons-grade uranium used virtually every feasible uranium-enrichment process, including electromagnetic isotope separation, the use of gas centrifuges, chemical enrichment, gaseous diffusion and laser isotope separation."
- "Iraq's EMIS program went undetected because it did not rely on state-of-the-art imported equipment whose acquisition might have given the effort away. Indeed the EMIS program might have remained hidden from IAEA inspection teams but for the fact that it was revealed by an Iraqi nuclear engineer after the war." (Recall here that after the termination of the war, Saddam still was in charge in Iraq, and the multi-billion-dollar clandestine effort was his personal priority.)
- "Iraqi scientists also organized secret attempts to produce and separate small quantities of plutonium in IAEA-safeguarded facilities at the Tuwaitha nuclear research center." (While that second path to fissile material via the plutonium route was in its infancy, the Iraqis still were hard at work when the war ended their efforts.)

Beyond the obvious embarrassment of that grand failure within the U.S. and international intelligence communities, not to mention enabling of the failure provided by IAEA inspections, which were hoodwinked at every turn, there were more long-term implications created by the 10-year lapse in detection. When the second Gulf War loomed in spring 2003, the U.S. analytical community was asked to assess the possibility that Hussain's Iraq had managed, over the elapsed period, to reconstitute his strategic-weapons program. Saddam continually bragged that he had done so, the implication being Iraq possessed nuclear and / or chemical weapons systems he would not hesitate to use on any perceived foe. Intelligence again was woefully incomplete, signals were mixed and disinformation flowed.

Our intelligence community, having been badly burned, if not professionally scarred, by its failures in the First Gulf War, on that second occasion opted to err on the side of more aggressive assessments. The rest is history. But the assertion that the Bush administration pushed its intelligence community into a corner by demanding it determine that "Iraq is in possession of weapons of mass destruction" is only one part of the story. The insistence by the Bush team that our community so declare Iraq, resisted by some as "unsubstantiated," found our weapons analysts incompletely informed by the very people they depended on: America's intelligence collectors. For good reason, our analysts were inclined to assume the worst. The earlier intelligence failure in 1990, overlain by an absence of quality intelligence in 2003, and reinforced by a Saddam claiming he possessed such a WMD capability, delivered the "slam dunk" assessment that turned out to be dead wrong, or mostly so.

From my East Asia perch in the Pentagon in that spring of 2003, I watched from a distance as that drama played out. Unlike many of my Pentagon policy colleagues, I had experienced the tug and pull of the analytical process in situations where they were compelled to make judgments based on poor information. Those same analysts also had to contend with pressure from the policy side to downplay or water-down assessments that could erode the standing of favored or protected policy positions. The star-crossed Agreed Framework was one such example, but I had experienced several others. In almost every case, the analysts opted to take the safest course: "unable to confirm such activity at this time." It was a cop-out, but no one ever wants to "get out over the tips of one's skis" in offering an intelligence judgment one is not prepared to defend. And no one wants to disappoint a policy official married to a decision, even one that could be found wanting.

My point is that, in the case of the Iraqi WMD finding in 2003 that helped pave the way to our second war with Iraq, previous intelligence failures were the handmaidens of misjudgments. They should be recognized as such. Once made, admissions of failure should be prescriptive and help us avoid repeating such failures. Nuclear proliferation portends a catastrophic event if we get the assessment wrong. We need to get it right at the point of collection, so that our analysts have the best chance to reach informed conclusions. With all assessments passed to our policymakers, we will ensure our nation is equipped to reach the best possible decisions, and do so in a timely manner.

Ongoing Intelligence Challenges

While I have discussed in detail North Korea as an established nuclear weapons state, and likewise other second-tier nuclear weapons states, such as Pakistan, India and ███████████, the fact that each now has its own established programs and weapons systems in place should not deter us from actively collecting against them. Where such systems already exist, improvements in numbers, and the quality of devices, mobility, and location must be tracked and actively monitored. Our national technical means, as the process is commonly described, will provide much of this, but nothing comes close to a human clandestine reporting asset with direct or even indirect access to the intricacies of the threat. An asset who can be tasked to report in detail and does so over time is worth his or her weight in gold, and great skill and patience is required to secure such.

In the case of each nuclear nation in which we seek protected information, we need to define that nation's capabilities precisely. That means warheads and delivery and control systems in place for use by the command authority that manages and releases those weapons. We must understand the planning that attends the weapons. If at all possible, we need to confirm the scenarios for their first or retaliatory use, as well as the intent of decisionmakers who have in their hands the release codes. All of this is particularly true where national leadership has delegated weapons-use authorities to lower levels of the military, such as the tactical nuclear weapons deployed by Pakistan and others. That aspect was poorly understood by the United States in the Cold War, and we continue to struggle with it today. Witness the Cuban Missile Crisis of October 1962, where Soviet commanders on the ground in Cuba had the authority to use tactical nuclear systems—which the United States was not even aware were already in Cuba. Local authority for use had even been delegated to weapons positioned to strike our base at Guantanamo.

Beyond the self-declared and de facto nuclear weapons states, we have a category of nations racing to complete programs that will yield full-blown systems of warheads mated to missile and other delivery systems. These would-be nuclear players might not be there yet, but they are doing everything required to reach their goal quickly and comprehensively. *The* case in point is Iran. The world has been focused, with good reason, on the ability of Iran to create a nuclear weapons design and manufacturing program based on fissile material production from its centrifuge program.

Beyond the fissile material itself, Iran has induced, or indigenously developed, the various weapons components required to create and sustain such an approach at an industrial level. Through several decades of national-level dedication, successful espionage and technical theft, as well as selected commercial transactions, the Iranians now have all they need to possess such a strategic capability. That program will be capable of delivering weapons-quality warheads to Iran's leadership within a few short years, notwithstanding the hopes of many

American and European accommodators who bemoan such an assessment. Collective "denial" has allowed the United States, Western Europe, Russia and China to finesse that reality, and their head-in-the-sand posture has helped to deliver Iran to where it is today.

My own assessment, having had no access to any level of classified information on Iran for 30 or more years, is Iranian nuclear capability might have been out of the proverbial barn and running for some time. Simple prudence suggests we at least consider the worst-case scenario. It is possible Tehran has possessed two to four tactical nuclear devices purchased on the Central Asian black market at the time of the extended collapse of the Soviet Union, during the 1990-1995 period.

My own suspicion is that the Iranians, having held these devices for perhaps 25 or more years, retain little confidence in their ability to work as designed. The value of any former Soviet weapon would lie with the fissile material contained in the device's core. This would suggest the high-explosives testing activity we have discovered in Iran over recent years might have had as its purpose, at least in part, confirming to the Iranians that they have the ability to detonate the devices. Thus, to my mind, we could be facing an Iran that already possesses a nuclear weapons capability, albeit only on a one-off or three-off basis. I am sure that such a "far out" assessment would be rejected out of hand by most analysts. In the gray world of nuclear proliferation, however, there have been stranger developments, and nothing is impossible.

My concern with the Iranians was reinforced in private conversations with retired General Alexander Lebed, former Russian national security advisor to President Boris Yeltsin. Sitting with me over dinner in Tokyo in the early 1990s, Lebed discussed the subject of "loose or missing nukes," which he recently had surfaced, only to be roundly criticized in the Russian and Western media. His point to me was not so much what he knew to be true about the disposition of various types of "suitcase" and small tactical weapons, but rather what neither he nor any Russian nuclear manager did know. That is, how many tactical nuclear weapons existed at the time of the breakup of the Soviet Union, how many existed in Russia when Lebed asked for an accounting, and what devices, if any, had been inherited by the new nations that had been the Soviet Union. If any could not be accounted for, where might they have gone and with whom? His real issue was that the new Russia did not possess an accurate inventory of what existed and where each device was. Although General Lebed was not necessarily suggesting that any device was "missing," he thought the possibility important enough to insist on an accounting.

Lebed explained that, in raising this question at the highest levels—as would seem to be his prerogative—he had received no cooperation from the military officers who should have been willing to address the matter. Because he had long been a thorn in the side of the Russian military leadership, mainly for his criticism of the war in Chechnya, the leadership was not inclined to admit there was a problem, let alone work with him to sort it out. He was not given a chance to resolve the dilemma.

Russia's current president, Vladimir Putin reportedly regarded Lebed as a threat to his KGB clique and removed him from the Moscow scene, arranging to have Lebed elected as governor of Krasnoyarsk Krai region in 1998. Lebed was killed in the crash of his Mi-8 helicopter in April 2002, two years after Putin rose officially to the presidency. At that time, at age 52, Lebed still was regarded as an uncompromised and uncompromising direct rival to Putin based on his gruff personality, war-hero status and popularity. The Mi-8 crash was considered highly suspicious, and many assume an act of sabotage claimed the life of one of Putin's potential challengers.

Iran will continue to be a major proliferation challenge, and intelligence collection, be it overt or covert, satellite or human assets on the ground in Iran, will do much to determine what options we have to mitigate the threat. The Joint Comprehensive Plan of Action of July 14, 2015, was a political band-aid slapped on a festering wound that no longer would ever heal. To my mind, it was a political charade organized by President Barack Obama and Secretary of State John Kerry to allow a posture that the Iranians would discard after they had milked it for all it was worth. In many unpleasant ways, the JCPOA that remains, at least as a life raft for the Europeans to cling to in the hope the Biden Administration will climb back aboard, reminds one of the flawed and inherently doomed Agreed Framework involving North Korea.

Whatever political cover the current JCPOA arrangement, or another "understanding" along the way, might provide to the Iranians, an aggressive intelligence program will be vital to track their progress. And whatever access the IAEA is allowed, however well-meaning its intentions or thorough its inspections, the agency will not be up to the task at hand. As I have emphasized, the IAEA should not be expected to do what it is not capable of doing, and that is particularly so in special challenges posed by Iran. Unless there is a regime change in Tehran, it will be similar to our North Korea experience: the Ayatollahs and the country's Islamic Revolutionary Guard Corps—Iran's ruthless military—will slog forward and will not be denied their strategic-weapons capability.

Collection Targets in Waiting

Something else I have suggested elsewhere: We should expect more candidate proliferator nations to emerge—Turkey, Saudi Arabia, Egypt, Japan, and South Korea come to mind. But other credible players loom in the distance. In such instances, the United States might not have the leverage required to dissuade a given nation from pursuing its weapons capability goal, even if we decide that dissuasion is in our national interest and worth the effort required.

In the case of Japan, we might not be inclined to discourage that nation, possibly because our leadership has decided it no longer wishes to carry the burden of defending Japan's strategic interests, that is, its existence. In such a case, we should expect Japan to go its own way as quickly and efficiently as possible. It might also happen that Japan's decision to make such a dramatic departure from its post-World War II "nuclear allergy" would not be sanctioned by the United States. Rather, our decision could be based on Japan's perception that the U.S. nuclear deterrent is no longer credible, our protestations to the contrary notwithstanding. Irrespective of Japan's near- and middle-term course, once again, quality intelligence will continue to inform U.S. policymakers as to that nation's intent and its capabilities in this critical area.

Other nations of current- and middle-term interest as potential proliferators include South Korea, for all the reasons mentioned; the Ottoman-resurgent Turkey under President Recep Tayyip Erdoğan; and perhaps even Saudi Arabia, responding to the reality of a nuclear Iran. Other nations possessing critical nuclear technologies, which could be sold or bartered to potential proliferators, also need to be independently monitored. The cooperation that now exists, either on a bilateral basis or through multilateral arrangements such as the Nuclear Suppliers Group, or both, is incredibly important. The current collection of nuclear-have states include most of the Western European nations, Canada, Argentina and Brazil, Russia and China, among others.

But formal channels of cooperation are inadequate for a number of reasons, including the obvious fact that not each nation is capable of monitoring or controlling its own private sector or its research laboratories. Soviet missile designs have found their way to North Korea from a reborn Ukraine and Belarus. Russian researchers also followed the money to bring advanced laser technology and who knows what else to China. China's claimed inability to control its own firms and their exports, despite the fact that it is one of the most authoritarian states on the planet, is the example that proves the point. The United States and other nations have confronted the Chinese to demand their state-owned or private-sector firms be blocked from supplying sanctioned materials. The usual response is feigned surprise and promises to do better, but "better" never materializes. Yet, this is a task that cannot be delegated to a nation incapable or unwilling to constrain its own proliferation vendors.

Terrorist Bombs and Vulnerable Reactors

In 2023, and forever in the future, there is no magic involved in the design or construction of a nuclear device. The information now is out there in abundance, and any engineer or mechanical designer can access basic descriptions of the mechanics of a device, at least to point they have confidence that some sort of an explosion involving fissile material can be made to occur.

Intent is more important than capability. Even a poorly designed or ill-performing device, when properly delivered to the point of the attack, can create a high-impact terrorism act. The combination of explosive destruction can lead to contamination on a semi-permanent scale at a high-value target. Think London, Tokyo, New York's Wall Street or our Capitol Building in Washington. Other nuclear-related targets, several with much lower public profiles but with a potential for substantial disruption and economic impact, also exist and offer terrorist actors softer targets.

Commercial nuclear powerplants, with reactors designed to defeat mechanical defects and prevent meltdown, are highly vulnerable to terrorist attacks. Many of them, in America, Europe, Japan and other nations, are lightly protected and would have little chance of defeating a moderately well-organized assault by even a small group bent on disabling or destroying such a target. Equally important, most nuclear powerplants have spent-fuel ponds adjacent to the reactor buildings that are stuffed to the maximum with highly radioactive nuclear fuel elements discharged from active reactors over the years. Some fuel assemblies are "hot" in the sense they are recently removed from the active reactors, while others have cooled for years, awaiting onward movement to permanent and secure storage facilities. The result is a continuing buildup of targets of opportunity that, if attacked and the waste scattered, would create chaos for the facility, the community, the nation and every locale downwind from the breach. And although the threat of this category of nuclear terrorism is well recognized, the only way it can be prevented is not at the point and time of the attack. Rather, such groups must be detected, tracked, penetrated, preempted and destroyed before they can get anywhere near a nuclear powerplant. That is a task only intelligence operators can execute effectively.

A Gauntlet Thrown at the Next Generation

We, therefore, have a pair of proliferation threats. There are national programs designed to provide a potentially hostile nation with a strategic capability. And, at the opposite end of the spectrum, there are small actors determined to do bad with crude nuclear devices or attacks on our vulnerable nuclear infrastructure. Neither threat will lessen in a world more fractured than at any time in recent history, and certainly more diversely hostile than at any time since the advent of nuclear weapons. Nevertheless, many of us are still out there, hunting nukes, and more will be called to this endeavor. We need to find the bad actors, define them, and neutralize them with alacrity. Let us all hope we are up to the task before us.

APPRECIATIONS

In relating these personal experiences, I believe it important to acknowledge the successes of clandestine collection within the broader U.S. intelligence effort, particularly in the face of a growing narrative that attempts to define covert operations as uniform failures. It is critical that we understand the contribution that such successful actions have made towards the U.S.'s ability to shape and execute foreign policy.

In the same vein, it is also worthwhile to examine firsthand intelligence failures, missed opportunities and misfires that occurred along the way. Taken together, the hope is that these experiences provide a balanced perspective as to what good intelligence can accomplish if properly organized and managed. As in any endeavor involving calculations of risk and reward, limitations exist as to what can be accomplished, no matter how determined the effort is. Finally, a program of successful intelligence collection does not presuppose success, but rather only the increased chance of success.

I should add that none of the events described here identify specific individuals beyond those already publicly identified. None of this narrative in any way compromises intelligence sources and methods. In several cases, I have gone to extreme lengths to avoid compromising any sources. Further, in every case where operations were successful and continue to have relevance today or involve individuals who could in any way be impacted by an open discussion, all references to such are avoided.

Four decades on, many of the central players involved in these happenings have passed from this life, including almost all the players in South Korea as well as most of the individuals encountered during the ensuing years in other locations. With elements of these tales already told or partially told, it is a good time to set the record straight. I sincerely hope that my telling of these events contributes to a better understanding of the intelligence process, the inherent unpredictability of events and the search for truth.

A no less important goal is to properly characterize the motivation of Americans who choose to serve their nation, irrespective of how any American elects to manifest that service. Of course, with all of these experiences told first hand, there is room for omission or mistake, not to mention memory lapses with so many years now having passed. I accept full responsibility for any such errors and omissions. I welcome commentary that identifies such matters or clarifies aspects of actions that were not understood when they occurred or remain so today.

All in all, it was a rewarding experience, and I am thankful that my country allowed me to serve the greatest nation on the face of the earth as best as I was able. I must also extend my appreciation to those leaders who afforded me the opportunity to be on the field where the action was; those who trusted me to perform my service, be it the U.S. Army, the Central Intelligence Agency or the Pentagon.

APPENDIX

The following collection of documents further informs certain events described in this book, specifically, the declassified U.S. government cables and memoranda referenced in the text related to the nuclear weapons programs of the Republic of Korea, that is, selected declassified documents. The collections were assembled by the National Security Archive at The George Washington University, in Washington. You can find them at https://nsarchive.gwu.edu (see QR code below). The National Security Archive, founded in 1985, is a 501, non-governmental, non-profit research and archival institution located on the university campus. Most of the material was assembled under the NSA's Nuclear Vault Program, with each posting presented in the format of either a Briefing Book, which assembles a collection of related materials, or as individual declassified documents.

I encourage interested readers to sample and study the collection.

1. NSA Briefing Book Number 690, November 20, 2019

The First Nukes on the Korean Peninsula
Excerpt: *"Stationed nuclear weapons, some of which were huge, in South Korea while senior Defense Department officials pointed to ... surface ships, and elsewhere. A key deployment site was South Korea, a major ally in East Asia..."*

2. NSA Briefing Book Number 582, March 22, 2017

Stopping Korea from Going Nuclear, Part I
Excerpt:
> *"Washington, D.C., March 2017. President Park Chung-hee reportedly instructed South Korean scientists to build nuclear bombs by 1977 ... Today's posting, the first of two on U.S. policy toward South Korea's atomic weapons program in the mid-1970s..."*

3. **NSA Briefing Book Number 584, April 12, 2017**

   Stopping Korea from Going Nuclear, Part II
   Excerpt:
   > *"Washington, D.C., April ... had to use a combination of approaches to keep South Korea's Park dictatorship from going forward ... the allies had delivered a 'knockout blow' against the South Korean nuclear plans."*

4. **NSA Briefing Book Number 668, April 1, 2018**

   Kissinger State Department Insisted that South Koreans Break Contract with French for Reprocessing Plant
   Excerpt:
   > *"Washington, D.C., April 10, 2019 — South Korea's bid to acquire a nuclear weapons capability..."*

5. **NSA Briefing Book Number 431**

   Studies in Intelligence: New Articles from The CIA's In-House Journal
   Excerpt:
   > *"United States and Canada Related Links, Reading the North Korea Tea Leaves, April 11, 2013 ... Carter's plan to withdraw U.S. ground forces from South Korea. A description of the evolution of ... Carter's plan to withdraw U.S. ground forces from South Korea."*

6. **Related NSA Document**

   U.S. Embassy to Canada Telegram 1421 to State Department, "Purchase of Canadian CANDU Reactor,"18 April 1975, Confidential Excerpt:
   > *"to be attached to the sale of a nuclear reactor to South Korea and arrangements to finance the transaction. Kissinger State Department Insisted that South Koreans Break Contract with French for Reprocessing..."*

7. Related NSA Document

State Department Telegram 135500 to U. S. Embassy South Korea, "ROK [Republic of Korea] Nuclear Fuel Regional Reprocessing Plans," 10 June 1975, Secret Excerpt:

"a 'more open discussion about reprocessing with the South Koreans as well as talks with the French about ... increase[ing] their nuclear weapons potential.' Despite the South Korean argument that their proposed reactor and ... with the French about U.S. 'special concerns' over Korea"

8. Related NSA Document

State Department Telegram 195214 to U.S. Embassy South Korea, "ROK Nuclear Fuel Reprocessing Plans," 16 August 1975, Secret Excerpt: *"The ambassador was to convey 'serious concern' about South Korea's plans to develop a reprocessing facility ... Kissinger State Department insisted that South Koreans break contract with French for Reprocessing..."*

9. Related NSA Document

State Department Telegram 226011 to U.S. Embassy South Korea, "ROK Nuclear Fuel Reprocessing Plans," 22 September 1975, Secret, excised copy Excerpt:

"adverse responses from various quarters of the South Korean government to U.S. statements of concern ... As [in] previously declassified documents, the South Koreans gave an 'unequivocally negative' response to ... State Department Telegram 226011 to U.S. Embassy South Korea, 'ROK Nuclear Fuel Reprocessing Plans,' 22 September"

10. Related NSA Document

U.S. Embassy Japan Telegram 17749 to State Department, "Bilateral Approach to GOJ on Regional Reprocessing," 13 December 1975, Secret, Part 1 Only, Part 2 Missing from State Department microfilm Excerpt:

"Kissinger State Department insisted that South Koreans break contract with French for reprocessing"

11. **Related NSA Document**

    U.S. Embassy South Korea Telegram 0026 to Department of State, "ROK Nuclear Reprocessing," 5 January 1976, Secret, excised copy

    Excerpt:

    > *"the Canadian reactor [should] be used to leverage the South Korean government to cancel its plans for the French ... reprocessing plant"*

12. **NSA Briefing Book Number 570**

    The Vela Incident: South Atlantic Mystery Flash in September 1979 Raised Questions about Nuclear Test

    Excerpt:

    > *"flash detected by a U.S. Vela satellite over the South Atlantic on the night of 22 September 1979 was likely a..."*

INDEX

A

Afghanistan, 330, 412, 448
Agreed Framework, U.S.–North Korea, 20-21, 456-463, 468, 471
Ames, Robert, 394
Anderson, Jack, 349, 352
Angleton, James Jesus, 311
Argentina, 21, 168, 290, 300-301, 472
ARGONAUT, 296
Australia, 103, 456

B

Baker, Howard, Jr., 199
ballistic missiles, 94, 136, 139, 189, 313, 344, 360
ballistic missile submarines, 109, 348
ballistic missile technology, 20
    ISAS Mu, 352
    Nike Hercules, 47, 50, 136-139, 140, 189, 193
    surface-to-air missiles, 50, 137
    surface-to-surface missiles, 133, 137-138, 193, 322, 360
    weapons delivery systems, 136-139
Bangkok, 434-436
Banisadr, Seyyed Abolhassan, 433-434, 435, 436-438, 439-440, 441
Barrett, Mark, 204
Beamer, Robert, 42, 44-46, 47, 60
Beirut, 386-387, 394-395, 396, 403, 405, 425-427, 428-429, 430-431, 432, 433
Belgium, 168
Berri, Nabih, 404, 426, 427, 428-429, 430-431
Bhutto, Z.A., 296
Bonifas, Arthur, 204, 243
Brazil, 21,168, 290, 300, 301, 472
Brown, George, 198
Brzezinski, Zbigniew, 196
Buckley, William F. "Bill," 394-395, 405, 415, 428, 432
Bush, George H.W., 86, 325, 413, 414, 419, 423, 433-434, 437-438, 441-442
Bush, George W., 456
    Bush administration, 459, 462, 468

C

Canada, 34, 155, 158-165, 168, 182-184, 262, 286, 297, 369, 472
    Atomic Energy of Canada Limited, 158-161, 164-165

D

E

F

G

H

Habib, Philip C., 82-83, 84-85, 86-89, 90, 99, 111-112, 152, 171, 173, 174, 177, 178, 180, 198
Hahm Pyong-choon, 177
Hasenfus, Eugene, 397
Helfrich, Jerry, Dr., 122, 125
Helms, Richard, 66-67
Helmut and Marta (covert asset aliases), 304-305, 306-309, 312
    Shaul (covert asset alias), 306-309
High Technology Branch, 350, 354, 357, 363, 365, 366, 368, 391
Hitachi, 355
Hitt, A.B., 44-45
Hong Kong, 304, 306, 384, 435-436
Hosenball, Mark, 436-437
Hunt for Red October, The, 314
Hussein, Saddam, 294, 395, 401-402, 467-468

I

India, 21, 121, 160, 169, 286, 287, 288, 290, 297, 300, 437, 456, 469
    Smiling Buddha nuclear test, 125, 160, 169, 259, 286, 295, 296
Indochina, 400
Ingersoll, Robert, 177
intelligence failures, 20, 21, 468
intelligence officers, 67, 319, 320, 348, 466
International Atomic Energy Agency, 25, 110, 116, 120, 150, 151, 158, 159, 161-162, 168, 172, 177, 187, 253, 257-260, 276, 277-278, 279, 282, 286, 287-289, 290-291, 292, 293-295, 297-298, 299-300, 301, 354, 360, 361-363, 458-460, 461-463, 467, 471
    Board of Governors, 258, 292
    Safeguards Division, 258, 288, 289
Iran, 20, 21, 268, 269, 271, 272-273, 274-277, 283, 290, 292, 300, 301, 385, 387, 393, 394-395, 399, 401, 403-405, 410, 415, 416, 418-421, 424, 426, 433, 434, 436-438, 439-440, 469-471
    Desert One, 270, 272
    Operation Eagle Claw, 269-271
    hostage crisis, 269-271, 272
Iran–Contra, 268, 385, 396, 403, 409, 410, 415-416, 418-421
Iraq, 283-284, 286, 293-295, 300, 301, 400, 401-402, 434, 437-438, 467-468
    Osirak strike, 293-395
Israel, 291, 293-294, 301, 303, 306-308, 309-312, 345, 400
Italy, 28, 305, 321

J

K

M

MacEachen, Allan, 163, 183
MacElvoy, Hugh "Mac," 128-130, 135, 141, 143, 148, 254-255
Mansfield, Mike, 198
MARKHAM, 65-66
Marko the Serb, 321-323
McMahon, John, 250, 251, 252, 255, 325, 387, 388-389, 390, 391, 403, 406, 408, 409-411, 424
Meese, Edwin, 418
Mitsubishi Heavy Industries, 351, 355
Mr. Chang (covert asset alias), 131-133, 134, 148
Mr. Chung (covert asset alias), 425-427
Mr. Johnson (covert asset alias), 61-62
Mr. Nam (covert asset alias), 186, 187-188, 189
Muslims, 396
    Shiite, 396, 401, 403-405, 420, 426, 427, 432
    Sunni, 396, 427, 432

N

Nam Duck-woo, 175, 176
NATO, 52, 65, 137, 280, 284-285, 322, 435
New York Times, 198, 249
Newsweek, 272-273, 344
    David Gates, 272
Nixon, Richard M., 40, 57, 108, 179, 403, 421
    Nixon administration, 117
North Korea, 19-20, 21, 22-25, 34-36, 37-39, 40, 41-42, 47-50, 51, 53, 55, 57-60, 65-66, 86, 94, 99, 101, 105, 107-108, 109-110, 114-115, 124, 132-133, 136, 137, 139, 143-147, 193, 194, 197, 201, 202-203, 204-205, 206, 210, 216, 217, 264, 286, 287, 290, 292, 300, 301, 304-305, 324, 362-363, 456-457, 458-460, 461-463, 469, 471, 472
    Korean Workers Party, 19, 38
    Shinpo facility, 459, 460, 461
    Wonsan harbor incident, 35-36, 37
    Yongbyon facility, 457, 458-460
North, Oliver, 397, 404, 420
Northeast Asia, 19, 22-24, 69, 94, 200, 304, 360, 363, 461
nuclear accidents
    Chernobyl, 362
    Fukushima, 357, 362
    Tokai–Mura, 169, 358, 359

nuclear deterrence, 23, 52, 55, 144, 147, 197, 296, 472

nuclear non-proliferation, 19, 20, 21, 24, 25, 123, 125, 152-153, 168, 200, 257, 264, 287, 288, 294-295, 359, 363

nuclear proliferation, 21, 169, 192, 217, 249, 257-260, 264, 286, 291, 297, 301, 325, 344, 442, 463

    strategic weapons, 22, 98, 107, 116, 118, 123, 124, 126, 128, 133, 136, 138-139, 140, 147, 148-149, 150, 153, 156, 157, 162, 167, 169, 175, 179-180, 182, 184, 185-186, 187-188, 190, 191, 192, 193, 195, 197, 200, 201, 345, 359, 466,

    strategic weapons states, 21, 468, 471

nuclear reactors

    Atucha I, 300

    CANDU, 121, 158-159, 160, 161-162, 163-164, 165, 183-184, 297, 300, 308

    Chicago Pile-5, 296

    CIRUS, 297

    control rods, 23-24

    fissile material, 120, 121-122, 161, 162, 166, 182, 193, 198, 287, 294, 297, 357, 457, 458, 460, 462, 467, 469-470, 472

    heavy-water-moderated, 158, 296-297

    KANUPP 1, 259

    Kori 1, 117, 118, 120, 122, 158, 162, 256-257, 379

    Kori 2, 158, 172-173, 178, 180, 184, 379

    NRX, 159-160, 161-162, 188

    nuclear fuel cycle, 116, 118-119, 120-121, 122-123, 125, 149, 151, 154, 156, 158, 159, 162, 166, 167, 168, 169, 170, 171, 174, 175-176, 180, 185, 186, 187-188, 189, 193, 278, 297, 298, 301, 349, 354, 357, 358

    plutonium, 118-119, 120-122, 123, 135, 142, 143, 151, 159, 160, 161-162, 166, 177, 178, 182, 198, 294, 296-298, 299, 357, 457, 458-460, 461, 462, 467

    pressurized-heavy-water, 158, 300

    pressurized-water, 117, 120, 158, 167, 349

    PUREX, 358

    reactor core, 23-24, 55, 135, 166, 293-294, 355

    reprocessing, 119, 120, 122, 123, 150, 151-152, 154, 157, 158, 159, 161, 162, 163, 167-168, 169-170, 172-173, 174, 175-176, 177, 178-179, 180, 182-183, 184, 187-188, 189, 193, 194, 297, 299-300, 349, 357, 358, 359, 457, 458-460

    research reactors, 20, 110, 118, 121, 122, 123, 155, 159-161, 188, 257, 258, 275, 296, 297, 300, 459, 460

    Taiwan Research Reactor, 160

    TRIGA, 118

    uranium, 118, 120-121, 122, 158-159, 160-161, 162, 167, 193, 293, 294, 297, 300, 301, 349, 357, 358, 359-360, 456-457, 458, 460, 461, 462, 467

    Very High Temperature Gas-Cooled Reactor, 355, 357

nuclear weapons
   covert weapons, 20, 115, 123, 166, 170, 185, 186, 187, 189, 202, 286
   Manhattan Project, 120, 121, 287, 296
nuclear arsenal
nuclear strike, 23, 52, 65
nuclear weapons development, 21, 130, 133, 153-154, 180, 184, 296, 298, 354, 467
   thermonuclear weapon, 360
   uranium enrichment, 119, 120, 193, 301, 349, 357, 358, 359, 457-458, 460, 461, 462, 467
Nyárádi, Miklós, 61

O

Oak Ridge National Laboratory, 356
Office of Strategic Services (OSS), 267
Oh Won-chol, 185-186, 187, 188-189, 194
Organization for Economic Co-operation and Development (OECD), 201
OXCART project, 250

P

Pak Chung-hee, 37, 38, 47, 49, 50-51, 86-88, 97-98, 99, 100, 104-106, 107, 113-116, 119-120, 126-127, 130, 131, 135, 136, 139-141, 143-144, 152-153, 156-157, 162-163, 164, 166, 169, 171, 175-176, 177, 178-179, 180-182, 183, 184, 185-186, 187, 188-190, 191, 192-195, 196, 200, 201, 202-203, 204-205, 206, 208-211, 213, 214, 215-216
12-12 incident, 215-216
   assassination, 49, 200, 215
   Hanahwae-Ho, 208
   Pak government, 22, 99, 101, 110, 111, 114-115, 117-119, 123, 132, 143, 145, 148-149, 161, 163, 166, 170, 177, 185, 199, 202, 213, 357
   Presidential Security Service, 88, 114, 202, 209-210
   Yulgok Plan, 135-136, 137-138, 139-140, 147, 187
Pak Jon-gyu, (Pistol Pak), 209
Pakistan, 21, 151, 160, 168, 169, 259, 260, 286, 288, 289, 290, 295-298, 299-300, 456, 469
   Islamabad, 295
   Pakistan Atomic Energy Commission, (PAEC), 295, 296
   U.S.–Pakistan bilateral nuclear cooperation agreement, 296
Pao, Vang, 317
Park Tong-chin, 196
Park Tong-sun (aka Tongsun Park), 255-257
Paul (Seoul Operations Branch chief), 81-82

Poindexter, John, 404, 406, 420

Princeton University, 356

Project Azorian, 248-249, 252

Putin, Vladimir, 471

Pyongyang, 19-20, 22-23, 36, 37, 38-39, 41, 53, 55, 59, 108, 110, 132, 146-147, 193, 206, 292, 304-305, 306, 363, 431, 456-457, 458-460, 461-463

R

Rafsanjani, Ali Akbar Hashemi, 437-438

Reagan, Ronald, 271, 281, 346, 370-371, 386, 390, 397, 398, 401, 413, 415, 418, 419, 424, 433, 436, 440

    Operation El Dorado Canyon, 397

    Reagan administration, 25, 311, 356, 366, 402, 414, 416, 418

Rhee, Syngman, 49, 54, 97, 143-147

    Rhee government, 97, 143

Ribas-Dominicci, Fernando, 397-398

Richter, Roger, 295

Roh Moo-hyun, 432

    Roh administration, 432

Roh Tae-woo, 211

Romania, 21, 302

Rumsfeld, Donald, 456

Russia, 20, 109, 121, 144, 280-281, 287, 304, 314, 343, 347, 359, 361, 393, 434, 462, 470-471, 472

    Russian (language), 63, 65, 279, 302

    Russians, 110, 137, 278, 280-281, 282, 284-285, 288, 304, 313-315, 317, 346, 353, 461-462

S

Saint-Gobain Techniques Novelle, 151, 168, 169-170, 177, 182, 184, 189

Sandia National Laboratory, 125, 142

Scowcroft, Brent, 159, 172

al-Senussi, Abdullah, 398

Seoul, 22-23, 27, 34, 37, 38, 39, 40, 41-43, 44, 49, 58, 60, 69, 82-83, 87, 89, 94, 96, 100, 101, 104, 113-114, 118, 129, 130, 131, 135, 144, 145, 148, 157, 158, 160, 161-162, 163, 170, 177, 178, 180-181, 183, 184, 185, 187-188, 189, 193, 194, 195, 196, 197, 198, 199, 200-201, 202, 203, 205, 206, 209, 210, 215, 216, 301, 362, 425, 427, 428, 429-431, 432, 439

    Canadian Embassy, 161, 163

    Japanese Embassy, 203

    Philippine Embassy, 102

    U.S. Embassy, 81, 82, 84-85, 87, 89, 90, 91-92, 93, 96, 111, 125, 140-141, 150-

Korea Atomic Energy Research Institute (KAERI), 117-119, 120, 122, 123, 159, 16, 161, 166-167, 169, 171, 174, 175-177, 182, 184, 186, 188, 189-190, 193
Korea Electric Power Company (KEPCO), 117, 118, 121, 122, 158, 159, 164-165, 186
Korean Central Intelligence Agency (KCIA), 41-42, 43, 47, 49, 50-51, 60, 97, 104, 115, 150, 176, 209-210, 214, 215-216
Korean Military Academy (KMA), 97-98
Korean National Police (KNP), 42, 47, 49, 51, 60
Ministry of Energy, 118
Ministry of Finance, 118
Ministry of Foreign Affairs (MOFA), 161, 350, 426-427, 428-429, 430-431, 432
Ministry of National Defense, 101, 113, 114, 118, 126, 146, 147, 150, 210
Ministry of Science and Technology (MOST), 117, 118, 119, 123, 160, 161, 166, 169, 174, 176, 182, 184
National Assembly, 197
Navy patrol ship *Cheonan*, 39
Navy patrol ship *Tang Po*, 38
Nuclear Energy Commission (NEC), 117, 119, 121
Okpo, 186
Pohang, 186
Pohang Steel, 99, 102
ROK Air Force, 145, 430
South Koreans, 94, 95, 119, 122, 135, 147, 163, 168, 170
Taeduk Science City, 122
Southeast Asia, 27, 31, 33, 67, 425
South China Sea, 31
Soviet Union, 50, 52, 53, 61, 65, 94, 107, 108-109, 110, 124, 125, 137, 139, 144, 146, 197, 217, 248-249, 257-258, 260, 264, 277, 278-279, 280-281, 282, 284-285, 286, 290, 302, 304, 305, 313-315, 317, 319, 321, 324, 343-345, 346-348, 352-353, 359, 360-361, 362, 365, 386, 398, 411-412, 416, 462, 469, 470, 472
Eastern Bloc, 278, 281, 321, 346, 361
GRU, 258, 264, 278-279, 290, 319, 346-348, 361
KGB, 258, 264, 278-279, 280-281, 282, 290, 319, 346-348, 361, 471
Line KR, 278-279, 280, 282, 346
Soviet Bloc, 63, 319, 396
Warsaw Pact, 53, 264, 279, 314, 321, 348
Sporkin, Stanley, 389, 390-391, 392, 403, 406, 411, 424
Spy-vs.-Spy, 283
Stanford University, 296
Stiles, John, 163
Strategic Integrated Operational Plan (SIOP), 197
strategic nuclear deterrence, 23

W

Walker, John Anthony, 347-348

Walsh, Lawrence, 404, 418-421, 422-423, 424

Washington, 22, 49, 61, 62, 82, 86, 91, 94, 98, 99, 111, 123, 124, 136, 145, 150, 152, 154, 155, 156, 159, 161, 163, 171-173, 175, 177, 178, 180-181, 182, 183, 185, 187, 189, 193, 194, 195, 196, 198, 199, 204-205, 207, 255, 257, 261, 271, 272, 286, 344, 345, 363, 371, 372, 401, 416, 423, 424, 425, 428, 436-438, 442, 457, 473

    Canadian Embassy in, 183

    ROK Ambassador to, 188

    White House, 52, 162, 196, 271, 272, 370, 390, 401-402, 404, 409, 414, 415, 416, 418, 419, 437, 438, 442

Washington Post, 198, 436, 438

Weinberger, Caspar, 423

West Germany, 280, 286, 360

Westinghouse, 158

Y

Yeager, Chuck, 421-422

Yeley, Archie, 440-441

Yi Pyong-hui, 174, 176

Yoon Suk-yeol, 23

Young, Andrew, 253

Yugoslavia, 267, 321-323

    Belgrade, 321, 322

    Josef Tito, 267, 321

    UBDA, 322

Yuk Young-su, Madame, 203, 209

Yuri (Russian counterpart), 280-282

Made in the USA
Columbia, SC
08 November 2024

24b53649-a4db-46de-ab42-683dd3711f5fR03